Structuring Sense

'Hagit Borer's two volumes are a truly impressive achievement. She develops an original and careful theoretical framework, with far-reaching implications, as she describes. And she applies it in what have traditionally, and plausibly, been the two major domains of language: nominals and predication (event structure). The application is deeply informed and scrupulously executed, as well as remarkably comprehensive, covering a wide range of typologically different languages, and with much new material. No less valuable is her careful critical review of the rich literature on these topics, drawing from it where appropriate, identifying problems and developing alternatives within the general framework she has developed. These are sure to become basic sources for further inquiry into the fundamental issues she explores with such insight and understanding.'

Noam Chomsky

'Syntacticians like Borer define the big research questions for the rest of us. Two provocative and inspiring books.'

Angelika Kratzer

Hagit Borer's three-volume work proposes a constructionist approach, driven by Universal Grammar, to the interfaces between morphology, syntax and semantics and in doing so presents a fundamental reformulation of how language and grammar are structured in human minds and brains. Volume III will be published in 2006.

PUBLISHED

Volume I: In Name Only
Volume II: The Normal Course of Events

IN PREPARATION

Volume III: Taking Form (working title)

The Normal Course of Events

HAGIT BORER

OXFORD
UNIVERSITY PRESS

Great Clarendon Street, Oxford OX2 6DP
Oxford University Press is a department of the University of Oxford.
It furthers the University's objective of excellence in research, scholarship,
and education by publishing worldwide in

Oxford New York

Auckland Cape Town Dar es Salaam Hong Kong Karachi
Kuala Lumpur Madrid Melbourne Mexico City Nairobi
New Delhi Shanghai Taipei Toronto

With offices in

Argentina Austria Brazil Chile Czech Republic France Greece
Guatemala Hungary Italy Japan South Korea Poland Portugal
Singapore Switzerland Thailand Turkey Ukraine Vietnam

Published in the United States
by Oxford University Press Inc., New York

© Hagit Borer 2005

The moral rights of the author have been asserted
Database right Oxford University Press (maker)

First published 2005

All rights reserved. No part of this publication may be reproduced,
stored in a retrieval system, or transmitted, in any form or by any means,
without the prior permission in writing of Oxford University Press,
or as expressly permitted by law, or under terms agreed with the appropriate
reprographics rights organization. Enquiries concerning reproduction
outside the scope of the above should be sent to the Rights Department,
Oxford University Press, at the address above

You must not circulate this book in any other binding or cover
and you must impose the same condition on any acquirer

British Library Cataloguing in Publication Data

Data available

Library of Congress Cataloging in Publication Data

Data available

ISBN 0–19–926391–4 (hbk.)
ISBN 0–19–926392–2 (pbk.)

Typeset by Peter Kahrel Ltd.
Printed in Great Britain
on acid-free paper by
Biddles Ltd., www.biddles.co.uk

To Mata, Monjek, and Benek Taffet
In memory of your lives

T'was [$_A$ brillig], and *the* [$_{NP}$ [$_A$ slithy] tove*s*]
Did [$_V$ gyre] and [$_V$ gimble] *in the* [$_N$ wabe]:
All [$_A$ mimsy] *were the* [$_N$ borogove*s*],
And *the* [$_{NP}$ [$_{A/N}$ mome] rath*s*] [$_V$ *out*grabe]

Jabberwocky
Lewis Carroll, *Through the Looking Glass*
(annotated)

Acknowledgements

It is in the nature of any true knowledge that it can only be gained on the basis of already existing knowledge. To the extent that I have gained any knowledge, it is a pleasure to acknowledge the intellectual debt that this work owes to the knowledge previously gained by Gennaro Chierchia, Noam Chomsky, Hana Filip, Henk Verkuyl, Paul Kiparsky, Angelika Kratzer, Manfred Krifka, Beth Levin, Pino Longobardi, Terry Parsons, Malka Rappaport, Betsy Ritter, and Carol Tenny. I have not always agreed with their conclusions, but their work is the foundation upon which this book is based.

The ideas which have come to be this book were first born in January 1993, while I was a visitor at the OTS at the University of Utrecht. They reached maturity while I was a Belle van Zuylen Visiting Chair at the University of Utrecht in the fall of 2000. I would like to recognize with gratitude the linguistics community at the University of Utrecht for serving as such a wonderful audience to this work at its infancy and as it was reaching culmination (no pun intended), and for providing me with such a hospitable working environment. Special thanks go to Martin Everaert and to Eric Reuland for making it possible, to Peter Ackema and Maaike Schoorlemmer for more helpful suggestions than I can possibly acknowledge, and most of all, to Denis Delfitto for pointing out the right direction to me on some truly significant semantic issues.

As this project was progressing through childhood and adolescence, my colleagues as well as students and visitors, both at the University of Massachusetts at Amherst and at the University of Southern California, saw it through with numerous helpful suggestions. I thank, especially, Christine Bartels, Laura Benua, Angelika Kratzer, Barbara Partee, and Peggy Speas at UMass, and Jim Higginbotham, Audrey Li, Roumi Pancheva, Barry Schein, and Philippe Schlenker, at USC. Very special thanks go to David Nicolas for a close early reading of my fledgling attempts at semantics, and to Nathan Klinedinst, who made extensive suggestions for improvements on matters ranging from content to style.

During the years, as this work was going through its growing pains, it has been presented and taught in many places where audiences were extremely generous with their responses and suggestions. Special thanks go to David Adger, Richard Breheny, and Bill McClure for a particularly active feedback during my summer class in Girona in 1994, as well as to my graduate classes at UMass in Spring of 1996 and at USC in the spring of 2001. I benefited greatly from comments made by Artemis Alexiadou, Maya Arad, Lisa Cheng, Edit Doron, David Embick, Nomi Erteschik-Shir, Abdelkader Fassi Fehri, Hana Filip, Rafaella Folli, Irene Heim, Norbert Hornstein, Angeliek van Hout, Idan Landau, Agnieszka Lazorczyk, Beth Levin, Gillian Ramchand, Malka Rappaport, Tova Rapoport, Tanya Reinhart, Henk van Riemsdijk, Gemma Rigau, Ur Shlonsky, Michele Sigler, Tal Siloni, Peter Svenonius, Donca Steriade, and many many others, to be sure, who I can no longer recall, during many presentations and conversations, who took the time to understand what I am trying to do, and who did their best to be helpful.

Last, but not least, special thanks go to my co-settlers of Catan, Bernhard Rohrbacher and Tim Stowell, for their love, friendship, and support. It was fun, wasn't it?

HB

Los Angeles
March 2003

Contents

Acknowledgements vii
Contents to Volume I xii
Abbreviations xv
A Note on Transcription xvi

Part I Setting Course

1 Exo-Skeletal Explanations—A Recap 3
   1.1 How Grammatical are Words? 3
   1.2 Functional Structure and the Architecture of Heads 11
      1.2.1 General considerations 11
      1.2.2 Licensing functional structure: abstract head features and f-morphs 14
      1.2.3 Functional heads as open values 15
      1.2.4 What's in a head? 19
   1.3 A Note on Inflection 22
   1.4 A Note on Idioms 25

2 Why Events? 30
   2.1 Variable-behaviour Verbs 30
      2.1.1 The paradigm 30
      2.1.2 Evidence for syntactic representation for variable-behaviour verbs 36
   2.2 But Why Aktionsart? 47
   2.3 UTAH? 55
   2.4 Severing the Internal Argument from its Verb 59

Part II The Projection of Arguments

3 Structuring Telicity 69
   3.1 Preliminaries 69
   3.2 Structuring Quantity 73
      3.2.1 Quantity objects 73
      3.2.2 The architecture of event structures 79
   3.3 Prepositional Licensing 87
      3.3.1 Cascade structures 87
      3.3.2 The conative alternation and the *spray–load* alternation 91

Contents

4 (A)structuring Atelicity ... 97
  4.1 Where Are We? ... 97
  4.2 Atelic Transitives and Partitive Case ... 99
  4.3 Impersonal Null Subjects and the Unaccusative–Unergative Paradigm ... 112

5 Interpreting Telicity ... 121
  5.1 Introduction ... 121
  5.2 Against Lexical Encoding ... 127
  5.3 To Quantity or to Quantize? ... 143
  5.4 Scalar Representations and Telicity ... 149

6 Direct Range Assignment: The Slavic Paradigm ... 155
  6.1 From the Head to the Specifier: Quantity prefixes and DP interpretation ... 155
  6.2 Against Atelic Agreement ... 160
  6.3 Licensing DP-internal Structure ... 173

7 Direct Range Assignment: Telicity without Verkuyl's Generalization ... 182
  7.1 Slavic Intransitive Perfectives ... 182
  7.2 Does the Perfective Mark Quantity? ... 190
  7.3 Telicity Without Verkuyl's Generalization—English ... 200
    7.3.1 Range assignment to $[_{Asp_Q} \langle e \rangle_\#]$ through an adverb of quantification ... 200
    7.3.2 Particles and prepositions as range assigners ... 203
    7.3.3 An open issue: predicate modifiers or range assigners? ... 209

8 How Fine-Grained? ... 214
  8.1 Preliminaries ... 214
    8.1.1 Event structure or argument structure? ... 215
    8.1.2 Against decomposition—resultatives and others ... 220
  8.2 What Gets Modified? ... 232
    8.2.1 Preliminaries ... 232
    8.2.2 Referring to quantity, referring to non-quantity ... 232
    8.2.3 Anti-telicity effects 1: Hebrew reflexive datives ... 234
    8.2.4 Anti-telicity effects 2: nominalizer -*ing* ... 239
  8.3 A Somewhat Speculative Note on the Conceptual Status of Some Predicate Modifiers ... 245

Part III Locatives and Event Structure

9 The Existential Road: Unergatives and Transitives — 255
- 9.1 Introduction: Post-verbal Nominatives — 255
- 9.2 Projecting the Event Argument — 261
- 9.3 Assigning Range to $\langle e \rangle_E$—The Locative Paradigm — 272
  - 9.3.1 Post-verbal nominatives in unergative structures — 272
  - 9.3.2 Locatives and unergative constructions — 275
- 9.4 Why Locatives? — 285
  - 9.4.1 The distribution of locatives and existentials — 285
  - 9.4.2 Existentially binding the event?
       Existentially binding the DP? — 289
- 9.5 Why a Weak Subject? — 298
  - 9.5.1 A brief note on incorporation — 301
- 9.6 Transitive Expletives? In Hebrew?? — 303
- 9.7 Conclusion — 305

10 Slavification and Unaccusatives — 306
- 10.1 Re-Examining the Paradigm — 306
- 10.2 And Returning to Erupting Riots — 319
- 10.3 Achievements? — 326
- 10.4 Summary — 338

11 Forward Oh! — 343
- 11.1 Inter-Language and Intra-Language Variation — 343
- 11.2 Some Final Notes on the Nature of Listemes — 346
  - 11.2.1 Introductory comments — 346
  - 11.2.2 More on phonological indices — 347
  - 11.2.3 A last note on idioms — 354

References — 356
Index — 374

Contents to Volume I

Acknowledgements	vi
Abbreviations	xiv
A Note on Transcription	xv

Part I Exo-Skeletal Explanations

1 Structuring Sense: Introductory Comments	3
1.1 How Grammatical are Words?	3
1.2 Some Preliminary Notes on Functional Structure	14
1.2.1 A note on the syntax–semantics interface	14
1.2.2 Projecting functional structure	17
1.2.3 Specifiers, complements	22
2 Nuts and Bolts	30
2.1 The Architecture of the Grammar	30
2.1.1 Licensing functional structure: abstract head features and f-morphs	30
2.1.2 Functional heads as open values: adverbs of quantification	34
2.1.3 Range assignment through specifier–head agreement and definiteness marking	38
2.1.3.1 A brief summary	42
2.1.4 What's in a Head?	43
2.1.5 Ordering within the L-D	48
2.2 A Note on Inflection	51
2.3 An Overview	58

Part II Determining Structures

3 The Proper Way	63
3.1 The Distribution of Determiners	63
3.2 Proper Names	70
3.2.1 Proper or common?	70
3.2.2 Some more on proper names with determiners	82

4	Some Stuff: On the Mass–Count Distinction	86
	4.1 Plurals as Classifiers	86
	4.1.1 Classifying Chinese	86
	4.1.2 A little more on the mass–count distinction in Chinese	97
	4.2 On the Flexibility of the Mass–Count Distinction	101
	4.3 A Classifier Phrase for English	109
	4.4 Creating Individuals	120
	4.5 Noun Stems in Compounds, or How Seriously Lexicalists Take the Lexicon	132
5	Things that Count: Null D	136
	5.1 The Works	136
	5.2 The Interpretation of Indefinites	144
6	Things that Count: Null # and Others	160
	6.1 Null # and the Interpretation of Definite Articles	160
	6.2 Heads vs. Specifiers	169
	6.3 Proper Names, Supplemental	174
	6.4 Chinese Individuals—Some Final Thoughts	178
	6.5 Concluding Part II	188

Part III Another Language, Another System

7	*One* is the Loneliest Number	193
	7.1 Introduction	193
	7.1.1 On some differences between 'one' and other quantifiers	193
	7.1.2 (Ac)counting (for) Hebrew singulars	201
	7.2 The Hebrew Definite Article Revisited	211
	7.2.1 Construct state and the licensing of cardinals in definite descriptions	211
	7.2.2 Quantifiers in specifiers	221
	7.2.3 The structure of Hebrew singulars—final touches	223
	7.3 A bit More on Quantifiers as Specifiers in Hebrew, and a Speculative Note	225

8	Cheese and Olives, Bottles and Cups: Notes on Measure Phrases and Container Phrases	238
	8.1 An Overview of the Hebrew Determiner System	238
	8.2 Hebrew 'Massifiers'	242
	8.2.1 Grocerese nominals	242
	8.2.2 Structure for Grocerese nominals	247
	8.2.3 Container phrases	251
9	Some Concluding Notes on Language Variation	261

References   267
Index   285

Abbreviations

A	Agent (subject of transitive predicate)	M	masculine
ABS	absolutive case	NEUT	neuter
ACC	accusative case	NEG	negative
ADESS	adessive case	NOM	nominative case
Adj.	adjective	NO.EXT	negative existential
AGR	agreement	NPI	negative polarity item
APASS	antipassive	OM	object marker
ART	article	#P	Quantity Phrase
ASP	aspect	PASS	passive
Asp_Q	quantity-Aspect	PART	partitive operator
AUX	auxiliary	PL	plural
CL	classifier	PP	past participle
D	determiner	PRT	partitive case
DEF	definite	PST	past tense
DEM	demonstrative	REFL	reflexive
dim	diminutive	s-o-q	subject-of-quantity
DP	determiner phrase	SG	singular
ECM	Exceptional Case Marking	TOP	topic
EP	Event Phrase	Unacc	unaccusative
EPP	Extended Projection Principle	Unerg	unergative
ERG	ergative case	UTAH	Universal Theta-Assignment Hypothesis
EXT	existential	XS	exo-skeletal
F	feminine		
FUT	future		
FP	functional projection		
F^sP	shell functional projection		
GEN	genitive case		
IMP	imperative		
Imperf.	Imperfective		
IND	indicative		
INDEF	indefinite		
INESS	inessive case		
INF	infinitive		
INSTR	instrumental case		
INTRANS	intransitive		
LOC	locative case		

A Note on Transcription

The Hebrew transcription used in this work represents a compromise between the pronunciation of Modern Hebrew and an attempt to render the examples, at least up to a point, morpho-phonologically transparent. Specifically, in Modern Hebrew pronunciation, spirantized *k* is pronounced as /x/, otherwise occurring in the language, spirantized *b* is pronounced as /v/ otherwise occurring in the language, and the pronunciation /k/ is associated with two distinct segments, one which spirantizes, and one which does not. Further, although contemporary phonological processes still distinguish between the historical glottal stop (') and the historical pharyngeal fricative (ʿ), both are pronounced as glottal stops in Modern Hebrew. Wishing to help the reader to discern relatedness between morpho-phonologically related forms, the following transcription conventions are adopted:

Historical glottal stop (א)	'
Historical pharyngeal fricative (ע)	ʿ
Spirantized *b* (ב)	b̲
v (consonantal ו)	v
x (ח)	x
Spirantizable *k* (when unspirantized: כ)	k
Spirantized *k* (כ)	k̲
non-spirantizable *k* (ק)	q
Spirantized *p* (פ)	p̲

Part I
Setting Course

1

Exo-Skeletal Explanations—
A Recap

1.1 How Grammatical are Words?

Consider briefly the conclusions that we reached in Volume I in our discussion of the nominal system. We concluded that nouns are, on the whole, listemes which are unspecified with respect to many of their relevant grammatical properties. The distinction between proper names and common nouns, the distinction between mass nouns and count nouns; between generic expressions and existential expressions; between weak and strong interpretations for indefinites—all these turn out to revolve not around lexical properties of particular items, but rather, around the grammatical properties of the functional structure in which they are embedded. The listemes themselves only 'determine' that functional structure insofar as some denote concepts which are 'odd' in certain grammatical contexts, in the sense that such grammatical contexts return an interpretation that conflicts with world knowledge. Thus *Kim* is 'odd' as a common noun, and *rabbit* is 'odd' as a mass noun. Given an appropriate context, however, much of this oddity can be overridden. This, I suggest, is exactly what we expect from concepts, as opposed to grammatical properties. Information provided by the grammatical (i.e. functional) system cannot be thus overridden. The quantity properties of *three*, *every*, and *a lot of* cannot be contextualized, nor can a noun with plural inflection ever be interpreted as (undivided) mass, no matter how salient the context. While an expression such as *a round square* can be assigned interpretation by rendering the meanings of *round* and *square* fuzzy and impressionistic, no such fuzziness is available to rescue *one cats*, *much cats*, or, for that matter, *one pants* or *much scissors*.

Within the nominal domain, the assumption that, say, *cats* is the same 'lexical' item regardless of whether or not it receives a generic or an existential interpretation is rarely controversial, as is the assumption that an explanation for the

---

The content of Chapter 1, Sections 1.1–3 is largely (although not exclusively) a summary of the more detailed discussion in Chapters 1 and 2 of Volume I. The reader is referred to the relevant chapters for a more thorough justification of various claims.

distinct properties of generic *cats* and existential *cats* should be sought within the domain of structure, be it semantic or syntactic, and not by appealing to lexical mapping rules. However, when we turn to the verbal domain, we find an altogether different tradition. Presented with triplets such as *break*.TRANS, *break*.INTRANS, *break*.MIDDLE, the most common strategy has been to assume that each is associated with a distinct lexical entity, which is in turn associated with a distinct argument structure or thematic grid. Although the entries are clearly related by means of more or less formal mapping rules, giving rise to some measure of generality (see, in particular, Williams 1981; Bresnan and Kanerva 1989; Bresnan and Moshi 1990; Grimshaw 1990; Levin and Rappaport Hovav 1986; Levin and Rappaport Hovav 1992*a*, *b*, 1995; Rappaport Hovav and Levin 1989; Reinhart 1996, 2000; and much related work), the important fact here is that these mapping operations are crucially assumed to apply to information in lexical entries, resulting in a unique syntactic projection for each of the instantiations of *break*, for instance. If a similar logic were to be applied to the nominal domain, and assuming our conclusion that, for example, weak indefinites have a null D, but strong indefinites have a filled D (cf. Volume I, Chapter 5, Section 5.1), it would entail the existence of a lexical operation on the entry for *cat*, for instance, converting it from a weak indefinite to a strong indefinite (or the other way around). On a par with the assumption that modified lexical verbal entries give rise to the projection of distinct syntactic structure for their arguments, a similar rationale applied to the nominal domain would dictate that the 'weak' entry for *cat* be specified to project in the context of a null D (and an overt determiner in #), and the 'strong' entry would require the projection of an overt determiner in D. To the best of my knowledge, this type of logic has not been pursued within the nominal domain. Rather, it is typically taken for granted that the entry in question is uniform, and that the burden of distinguishing between the strong and the weak readings is assumed by whatever structure, be it syntactic or semantic, is associated with the determiner, a functional element.

The characterization of words and structures and the division of grammatical labour between them has always been a major component of the generative linguistic agenda. From the mid-1960s onwards, in some generative traditions, an increasingly central role was played by the lexicon, construed as the reservoir of lexical entries. A lexical entry consists not only of the arbitrary pairing of sound and meaning, but also of a variety of formal diacritics, which translate into a set of instructions for the syntax. Within such an approach, the entry for a listeme such as *kick* contains crucially the information that it is a verb with a particular syntactic insertion frame, however derived. Starting with Grimshaw (1979) and Pesetsky (1982), a rich tradition developed of attempting to derive syntactic insertion frames as well as syntactic category from facets of lexical semantics. Nor is the agenda thus described model-specific. Although the Government–Binding model and its descendants on the one hand, and, for example, Lexical-Functional Grammar or Head-driven Phrase Structure Grammar in their various incarnations, on the other, may differ as to the relevant level of representation onto which such lexico-semantic distinctions are initially mapped, these approaches do share an important assumption. All assume that a well-defined entry point into the formal component of the grammar (however characterized) exists, and that it consists of the deterministic output of lexical properties in conjunction with certain combinatorial principles (and see Chapter 1 in Volume I for elaboration). Rappaport Hovav and Levin (1998) refer to such approaches as 'projectionist'. We note that they are fundamentally *endocentric*, in that they construct the properties of larger units from the properties of some central lexical entry, which is itself presumably to be projected as a syntactic head. In Volume I, I referred to such approaches as *endo-skeletal*. Schematically, endo-skeletal approaches subscribe to some articulation of the scheme in (1), where L_K is some choice of a listeme, P is its lexical semantics, possibly as translated into some Predicate–Argument Structure, C refers to a combinatorial system with some well-defined formal properties, and R_K is a well-defined formal representation.

(1) $P(L_K) + C \rightarrow R_K$

We already noted in Chapter 1 of Volume I that the formula in (1) is a type of checking system. Concretely, assuming R_K to be a phrase marker, it *agrees* with the properties of the terminals embedded within it. As a simple illustration of this point, consider *kick* again, and assume its relevant properties, however arrived at, to be the existence of two thematic roles—call them *agent* and *patient*—alongside some linking conventions which force agents to be external, in some well-defined sense, and patients to be internal, in some well-defined sense. The resulting syntactic structure, assuming it to be something like (2a), agrees with the relevant properties of *kick*, in allowing its lexically specified properties to be checked against the appropriate projection of arguments in specific syntactic positions (or, in minimalist terms, the agent merges in a position where it checks the relevant properties of *kick*). In contrast, (2b–c) are ungrammatical, not because there is anything wrong with the phrase marker as such, but because the properties of *kick* fail to agree with the emerging structure.

(2) a. [$_{VP}$ *agent*   [$_{V'}$ kick *patient*]]
     b. [$_{VP}$ *patient* [$_{V'}$ kick *agent*]]
     c. [$_{VP}$ [$_{V'}$ kick [$_{PP}$ P *agent*] [$_{PP}$ P *patient*]]]

The endo-skeletal approach contrasts with the approach I referred to as exo-skeletal—or the *XS*-approach—in which the structure is independent of the properties of specific listemes. Specifically, suppose that the conventional treatment of nouns is correct, and should be extended to verbs as well. Under such a treatment the differences between, for example, *break*.TRANS, *break*.INTRANS, and *break*.MIDDLE are no longer to be determined by lexical properties, but rather by the functional structure in which *break* is embedded. The distinctions between transitive, intransitive, and middle *break* are to be attributed to properties of the associated structures, rather than to properties of distinct (related) lexical entries. Put differently, just as the presence of a null D with *cat* yielded a weak indefinite, but an overt determiner in D gave rise to a strong indefinite, so *break*, in the context of a structure licensing two arguments, would be transitive, but in the context of a structure licensing only one argument, would be either a middle or an intransitive, depending on the structure projected. In turn, as in the case of the nominal system, we would expect it to be possible for world knowledge associated with the meaning of some concepts to render some argument structure combinations infelicitous. We note that in traditional systems, which appeal to lexical specification to determine argument structure, world knowledge is crucially appealed to as well, typically under the label 'selectional restrictions'. Consider, for instance, the verbs *eat* and *drink*. In the argument-structure models that I am aware of (the one proposed here being no exception), *eat* and *drink* are treated in a virtually identical fashion. They are assumed to assign the same semantic roles, in systems that utilize such roles, or to select the same grammatical functions, within systems that describe verbs in that fashion. They are further assumed to be embedded in the same set of syntactic structures, whether derived from their lexical specification, or independent of it. Yet, of course, *eat* and *drink* are not synonyms, and it is precisely this that results in the distinct oddity of (3a–b).[1]

---

[1] An interesting exception to the syntactic identity of *eat* and *drink* is presented by the ambiguity of (ia), vs. the non-ambiguity of (ib):

(i) a. Kim drank.
    b. Pat ate.

While both (ia) and (ib) have a reading on which the understood object of the verb is some appropriate substance for drinking or eating, respectively (e.g. water, juice, bread, lunch), (ia) also has a reading whereby the understood object of *drink* is alcoholic, and the predicate is understood as a property of *Kim* rather than an event (i.e. Kim was an alcoholic). However, to the best of my knowledge, there is no way of capturing this distinction between *eat* and *drink* within any existing theory of semantic roles, short of assuming that the verb *drink* is ambiguous between a reading of consuming a beverage, and a reading of habitual consumption of alcohol. Note in this context that *Kim smokes* has the same reading as (ia). Thanks to R. Kayne (pers. comm.) for pointing out these examples to me.

(3) a. Kim drank (up) the steak.
    b. Pat ate (up) the water.

The oddity of (3a–b) derives from our world knowledge that drinking is a mode of consumption associated with liquids, and that steaks are solids; that eating is a mode of consumption associated with solids, but water is liquid. In turn, the oddity of (3a–b) can be overridden in a manner typical of restrictions born of world knowledge rather than grammar, thereby giving rise to a 'coercion' effect. Such overriding can be accomplished either by modifying our presuppositions regarding the objects consumed (e.g. a liquefied steak can be drunk; frozen water can be eaten), or by modifying our presuppositions about the consumption mode. Such modifications are clearly in evidence with so-called metaphoric uses of *drink* and *eat*, as in (4a–b):

(4) a. She drank him with her eyes.
    b. She ate him with her eyes.

In both (4a) and (3b), the context conjures up the manner of consumption aspect of *eat* and *drink*, but not the nourishment-taking aspect. For example, *drink* in (4a) really means something like 'absorb', while *eat* in (4b) means a possibly more aggressive form of viewing. All these properties could, in principle, be listed as part of the lexical entries of *drink* and *eat*. We note, however, that, at least in the case of *eat* and *drink*, they never give rise to structural differences of any discernible sort, and as such appear to be the sort of distinctions which the grammar does not care to make. Under the plausible assumption that distinctions that are not grammaticalized do not belong in the grammar but are properties of the conceptual system and its interaction with world knowledge, some appeal to the conceptual, extra-grammatical system is necessary in any framework, even those within the endo-skeletal family of models. Our claim here is that such an appeal to an extra-grammatical conceptual system, together with the grammar of functional projections, suffices to characterize the distribution of verbs, just as it suffices to characterize the distribution of nouns.[2]

The notorious flexibility illustrated here and in Volume I for listemes is by and large restricted to the domain of so-called 'open-class items'—that is, to

---

[2] Within Chomsky's (1965) *Aspects* model, the lexical entry for *drink* includes the specification that *drink* requires a +liquid theme, while *eat* requires a +solid theme. From a formal perspective, however, +liquid theme and +solid theme are distinct formal objects, and all generalizations ranging over them need to be justified. No such justification is required, of course, if the specification ±liquid is relegated to the conceptual component. In effect, then, we are saying here that 'selectional restrictions', in the sense of *Aspects*, belong with the conceptual system, and not with the grammar. This is not to say that concepts do not have formal properties, but rather to claim that formal properties of concepts, should they turn out to exist, need not correspond to formal grammatical properties.

substantive, as opposed to grammatical formatives. No such flexibility is attested for closed-class items: for grammatical formatives (henceforth, functional vocabulary). Quantifiers, cardinals, past-tense markers, and the various species of derivational affixation are rarely susceptible. *The* is *the*; *every* is *every*; *-able* makes an adjective; past-tense markers are compatible only with verbs. This rigidity of grammatical formatives carries over to phrases in which such grammatical formatives are included, as we already noted. Thus *three cats* cannot be made mass or singular; *every cat* cannot be made plural or mass; *permissible* cannot be made a verb; *walked* cannot be made a noun or a present tense verb. If this is a valid distinction, then the dividing line here is not between vocabulary items and syntactic structure, but between substantive vocabulary, on the one hand, and functional vocabulary (including derivational affixation) and syntactic structure, on the other.[3]

The proposed dividing line, I believe, is a crucial one, and distinguishes between what is grammatically real—structures and formal properties of functional items—and what may be very real, but not grammatically so—properties of substantive vocabulary. The latter, I propose, are creatures born of perception and conceptualization, representing an intricate web of layers upon layers of a complex perceptual structure and emerging world knowledge, concepts which come to represent it, the reflection upon these concepts, and so on. Their properties, however characterized, are fundamentally not grammatical. That they can be so easily overridden by the grammar emerges from the fact that the grammar only cares about its own. It does not override grammatical properties. As for the conceptual properties of words, we must ask whether they have grammatical reality at all.

If we conclude that they do not, a very specific picture emerges of the interface between the grammatical, computational system and the cognitive module responsible for the emergence of substantive listemes. Contrary to common assumptions, there is, in fact, no direct interface, as such, between the conceptual system and the grammar, in that properties of concepts do not feed directly into the determination of any grammatical properties. A substantive listeme is a unit of the conceptual system, however organized and conceived, and has no grammatical properties.[4] Its use will return a meaning based fundamentally

---

[3] And see n. 4 in Chapter 1, Volume I, for some important notes on the boundary which separates functional vocabulary from substantive listemes.

[4] By the absence of grammatical properties, I am referring not only to the absence of category or of argument structure specification, but also to the absence of overt grammatical marking of any sort, be it syntactic, morphological, or inflectional. Thus while *form* is plausibly a listeme, *the form, formation*, or *formed* are not. While *form* has no grammatical properties—in the relevant sense—this is of course not the case for *the form, formation*, and *formed*, each of which encodes the existence of some grammatical structure which is non-coercible and constrained by strict computational principles.

on its conceptual value. A grammatical structure will return an interpretation as well, based on combinatorial, computational principles of interpretation assignment, as linked with the structural and the formal-semantic properties of functional vocabulary and syntactic structure. In a cognitive place which is neither the grammar nor the conceptual system—call it the 'making sense' component—these two outputs will be compared. Here the overall felicity of any linguistic behaviour would emerge as a direct function of the extent to which these two outputs match each other. It is in the nature of things that the two outputs will not always match, or at least, not in a straightforward way. In the event of a mismatch, the grammar will always prevail. The interpretation put forth by the conceptual component can and will stretch, as much as possible within the confines of the concept under consideration, so as to match the rigid, absolute interpretational constraints circumscribed by the grammar. The more the conceptual system stretches, the more the utterance will appear 'odd' or metaphoric, and at times, the oddity may be so extreme that it becomes difficult to distinguish from a straightforward case of ungrammaticality, where by 'ungrammaticality' I would like to refer exclusively to the effect created by the violation of formal computational principles.[5]

Within an XS-model, then, the particular final meaning associated with any phrase is a combination of, on the one hand, its syntactic structure and the interpretation returned for that structure by the formal semantic component, and, on the other hand, by whatever value is assigned by the conceptual system and world knowledge to the particular listemes embedded within that structure. These listemes, I suggest, function as modifiers of that structure. The picture that emerges is thus as in (5a) (and compare with (5b), a particular instantiation of the more general scheme discussed in (1)):

(5) a. Structure → predicate–argument structure/event structure; (category) → event interpretation → meaning assignment to structure.
 b. (Lexical-semantics of a verb) → predicate–argument structure; (category) → structure

In the next chapters I will elaborate on the scheme in (5a). I will propose a specific structure, where by structure I mean functional structure, which will in turn be translated, semantically, into a predicate–argument structure, and, more specifically, into an event structure. Before I proceed, however, some

---

[5] And see Chapter 1 in Volume I, as well as Borer (2003*a*), for some phonological considerations and for some discussion of vocabulary choice inter-linguistically. Likewise, for a discussion of category assignment to category neutral listemes.

methodological clarifications are in order. Much of the discussion in Volume I addressed the division of labour between properties of listemes and the syntax. In what follows, I will continue to bring forth arguments that support a rich syntactic functional component, and a correspondingly impoverished lexical component. In turn, I will also propose a very specific syntactic functional structure for event structure, and will proceed to justify it as well. However, the validity of postulating an impoverished lexicon, in the sense employed here, is quite independent of the validity of any specific functional structure I will propose. In other words, it may very well turn out that the lexicon is every bit as impoverished as I suggest, but that the syntactic structure required in the presence of such an impoverished lexicon is different from that proposed below. Such differences could arise in several domains. For instance, it may turn out that it is wrong to assume that the relevant computational burden is carried by functional categories rather than by 'lexical' categories, where by functional categories we mean nodes headed by items from the functional lexicon, and where by 'lexical' categories we mean nodes such as NP, VP, AP, etc., headed by N, V, A, etc. It may further turn out that the burden of computation is carried by functional structure, but that the particular view of functional structure presented in this work is wrong. Finally, it may turn out that the functional structure implicated, which is based here on aktionsart and event structure, is neither aktionsart nor linked to event structure.[6]

Most of these issues are fundamentally empirical in nature: it is up to the present study to justify the view of functional structure presented here, and the specific representations proposed for event structure. For any XS-type approach these remain possible but not necessary executions. Chapter 2 is devoted to a justification of the use of event structure and aktionsart as the functional building blocks of syntax. In Chapters 3–10 the syntax and the interpretation of the proposed event structure are spelled out in greater detail, providing additional evidence both for an event-based approach and for its specific execution. As always, the ultimate explanatory success of the analyses presented here would remain the strongest argument in their favour.

---

[6] Thus Marantz (1997, 1999, 2000), within a constructionist approach (often labelled 'neo-constructionism'), proposes structures that are quite distinct from those proposed in this work, and which are not based on event structure. As already noted in Volume I (cf. Chapter 1, n. 12), Marantz's (1999, 2000) proposal also differs from ours in assuming that the important structural building blocks are not functional labels, as such, but rather, n and v (at times known as little n and little v). To some extent, the debate here is notational rather than contentful, as one could of course define any functional projection dominating VP as v, or alternatively, define v as F° with the relevant set of features. For some possible considerations, see Volume I, Chapter 1, Section 1.2.2.

1.2 Functional Structure and the Architecture of Heads

1.2.1 *General considerations*

Crucially, the attempt to account for the properties of syntactic structures in this work proceeds from the generalizations in (6):

(6) a. All aspects of the computation emerge from properties of structure, rather than properties of (substantive) listemes.
   b. The burden of the computation is shouldered by the properties of functional items, where by functional items we refer both to functional vocabulary (including all grammatical formatives and affixation) and to functional structure.

Some of the specific formal properties of functional structure assumed in this work and their motivation are considered in great detail in Chapters 1 (Section 1.2) and 2 of Volume I. To summarize some of the points made there, I point out that the grammar as it now stands gives us no way to determine the specific internal architecture or the relative order of functional nodes, as notions such as head, complement, and specifier, developed to describe lexical syntactic projections and argument structure, do not carry over in a straightforward way to the functional domain. On the other hand, the existence of functional structure, the fixed hierarchical ordering of at least some functional projections with respect to each other, and the placement of some constituents in functional specifiers, can be shown to be an empirical fact. Suppose we assume, then, that like other arbitrary elements in the grammar, the properties of functional structures are innate and universal. If this is the case then the internal architecture for functional projections as well as the order of functional nodes are a syntactic given, and are not reducible to semantic selection. They are, in a sense, 'pure' syntactic structures, which cannot be otherwise derived. In turn, and assuming that the hierarchical structure of functional projections is a given, and that notions such as specifier and complement are purely syntactic without any selectional or lexical content, the most parsimonious approach must postulate a fixed, universal inventory of functional nodes with a fixed, universal order of projection, a constant of all human grammars.[7] Specifically, I will assume that phrase structure is constrained in the following ways:

(7) a. All phrasal projections have an X^{max} and an X^{min} (but in line with Chomsky 1995b these are derived notions, rather than primitives, and the same node may be both X^{max} and X^{min}).

---

[7] And see Borer and Rohrbacher (2003) for some learnability considerations in this context.

b. Every phrasal projection has at most one specifier and at most one complement (specifically, there is a unique maximal daughter of X^{max} which enters specifier–head relations with X^{min}).

If, indeed, listemes are devoid of any syntactic properties, it follows that arguments must be interpreted in conjunction with structural configurations, and I will assume that this is achieved through a merger of such arguments as specifiers of functional projections which are related to event structure. An obvious query now concerns the internal architecture of lexical projections. As already observed by Ouhalla (1991), within current approaches to syntactic architecture, lexical projections, by the end of the derivation, are radically emptied of much of their overt material anyway. It is typically assumed that the head raises to some superordinate functional head, while the direct arguments, in search of case, merge a copy in some functional specifier. There remains little overt evidence, then, to attest to the presumed 'base' position of direct arguments, or to suggest that they ever were within the lexical domain.

Nonetheless, the lexical projection is not entirely phonologically empty. First, the head does not always move, overtly or covertly. For instance, I argued explicitly in Chapter 4 of Volume I that in English, N does not move for mass and singular interpretation, and that movement of N for proper names is covert (cf. Chapter 3 in Volume I). Plausibly, the lexical domain will also continue to include elements which do not move to a functional specifier—such as clausal complements and PP complements—but which, in turn, display hierarchical relations with each other, thereby attesting to the existence of some architecture within the lexical projection. I return to this matter in greater detail in Chapter 3, Section 3.3, (and see also Chapter 2, Section 2.1.5, in Volume I). Focusing for the time being on the head and on direct arguments, suppose we define a lexical domain (L-Domain, or L-D), as the domain that emerges from the merger of some listeme from the conceptual array, where the 'conceptual array' is a selection of unordered listemes. The subsequent merger of functional heads with the L-Domain gives rise to the schematic structure in (8) (and assuming head-movement, specifically, for listeme-3).

Consider now in greater detail the properties of schematic structures such as (8). By assumption the order of F-1 and F-2, as well as at least the category label of F-1, are givens of UG (see Volume I, Chapter 1, Section 1.2.2, for a discussion of the category label of F-2). The specific merger of listeme-1 and listeme-2 as [Spec,F-1] or [Spec,F-2] will result in a particular interpretation (e.g. 'subject', in some well-defined sense; 'object', in some well-defined sense, etc.). Finally, listeme-3, by virtue of having merged a copy in some head, becomes, perforce, the head of L-D. If L-D is categorized as a V by some appropriate functional

(8)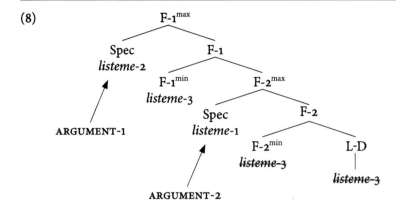

structure (such as Tense), listeme-3 becomes a verb. If L-D is categorized as N, it becomes a noun, etc. We note that merger at F^{min} is not required to determine the head status of listeme-3. Even if it remains in L-D, it will be verbalized (under Tense), quite simply because L-D will be categorized as V by Tense, and is in need of a head, and there are no other candidates for that function. We may thus assume that the choice of a head for L-D in a structure such as (8) may be arbitrary, but has consequences. If listeme-3 is chosen as a head, any other listeme remaining in L-D must project a non-minimal phrase, or linear ordering would fail and the derivation would crash.

As an illustration, consider a conceptual array consisting of *boat*, *sink*, *dog* and F-1 being T. The structure in (8) will correctly generate all the utterances in (9):[8]

(9) a. (the) *dog boat*(ed) (three) *sink*(s).
 b. (the three) *sink*(s) *boat*(ed) (some) *dog*(s).
 c. (The) *sink*(s) *dog*(ged) (the) *boat*.
 d. (The) *boat*(s) *dog*(ged) (the) *sink*.
 e. (The three) *dog*(s) *sank* (the) *boat*.
 f. (The) *boat sank* (the) *dog*(s).

The scheme in (8) is, of course, in need of much further elaboration concerning both general and particular aspects of the execution. Some of these issues involve the specific choices for F and L, and the relationship between them, and the manner in which the relationship between any particular F and its specifier determines the interpretation of that specifier. Some of these matters were already addressed in Volume I. Thus, a specific choice for functional structure within the nominal domain was motivated (including, specifically, DP, #P, and

---

[8] And see n. 17 in Chapter 1 of Volume I for some crucial notes on the execution of these derivations.

CL^{max}), and the role of elements which merge as specifiers of these projections was elaborated on. Before we turn to the workings of this scheme within the domain of events, a review of some crucial additional structural assumptions is in order.

1.2.2 *Licensing functional structure: abstract head features and f-morphs*

Suppose we consider in greater detail the diagram in (8). I assumed that the conceptual array consists of listemes. The general reservoir of such listemes constitutes the *encyclopedia*, a list of all arbitrary pairings of sound and meaning, where by sound we mean a phonological index, and by meaning we refer to the appropriate package of conceptual properties associated with such an index. Alongside the encyclopedia, and distinct from it, the grammar has a functional lexicon, including, in essence, grammatical formatives. These, I assume, come primarily in two varieties: independent grammatical functional formatives (f-morphs), for example *the* and *will*, and (phonologically abstract) head features such as ⟨*pst*⟩, for past tense. Consider now a preliminary proposal for the emergence of syntactic structure. Specifically, suppose the abstract head feature ⟨*pst*⟩ merges with the L-Domain, to give rise to the structure in (10):

(10)　[⟨*pst*⟩ [$_{L-D}$ listeme-1 listeme-2]]

Assuming free copy and merger (and abstracting away from the possibly covert nature of verb movement in English), in principle any of the listemes in the conceptual array may merge within the L-D, and any listeme in the L-D may merge a copy in T, but under standard assumptions, only one may do so. That element will thus become an X^{min}, and hence by necessity the head of L-D. In turn, L-D will become a VP in the context [⟨*pst*⟩ [$_{L-D}$　]], in effect making its head in T as well as the copy of that head in L-D a V. It only remains to be hoped that some post-derivational phonological storage area will be capable of dispensing, for the resulting V.⟨*pst*⟩ structure, a well-formed phonological representation. If it does not, the derivation would not converge and ungrammaticality would result.

Consider now the derivation of future tense in English. A derivation in which a listeme merges a copy in T would not converge. This might be either because there is no abstract head feature ⟨*fut*⟩ in English, or more plausibly, because the combination V.⟨*fut*⟩ fails to give rise to an appropriate phonological representation. On the other hand, a well-formed derivation with a future interpretation could still result just in case the f-morph *will* merges with L-D. Here, too, L-D will become a VP and some listeme within it will become the relevant head.

The two modes of licensing functional structure—the one associated with the English past tense and the other with the English future—are, I believe, the two major strategies universally available. One involves the projection of an abstract head feature, which requires movement of a head to be instantiated. The output of this head movement gives rise to an [L.⟨*feature*⟩] complex, the input to the phonology, which will (or will not) dispense a phonological representation of it. The other strategy involves the licensing of functional structure through an independent f-morph. In this latter case, head movement is not needed, and, at least in the case of English *will*, is in fact blocked. As is obvious, these two strategies do not characterize an inter-grammatical situation, but, rather, an intra-grammatical one, putting forth a view of language variation which is firmly associated with the morpho-phonological properties of grammatical formatives, rather than with syntactic structures or the semantics of grammatical formatives as such.

Viewing matters in general terms, the emerging picture could be schematized by the diagram in (11).

(11)

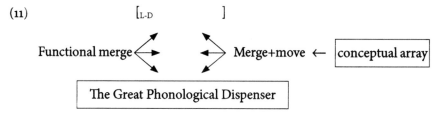

1.2.3 Functional heads as open values

Consider now the following paradigm (and see also Volume I, Chapter 2, Section 2.1.2 and Chapter 5, Section 5.1 for fuller discussion).

(12) a. During the summer, water in the pond mostly evaporates.
b. Hummingbirds always die young.

(13) a. Water in the pond is mostly lost through evaporation.
b. Hummingbirds always drink from our birdfeeder.

Of particular importance is the well-known fact that the adverbs of quantification in (12)–(13) may range either over the interpretation of the event (a reading most salient in (13)) or over the interpretation of the subject alone (a reading most salient in (12); see Lewis 1975; Heim 1982; Doetjes 1997 for some relevant discussion). Crucially, the readings are mutually exclusive. Setting aside the specific reasons for the preferred readings in (12)–(13), we note that even if it were plausible that all hummingbirds in the world drink from our birdfeeder, under that reading it would not necessarily imply that they are constantly doing so. Likewise, (13a) cannot mean that most water is mostly lost. Finally, we note that under the nominal reading, the DP under consideration can include no other quantifier. Examples (14a–b), under the relevant reading, are ungrammatical (the adverb of quantification can only range over the event):

(14) a. Most/all hummingbirds always die.
    b. Most/all water in the pond mostly evaporates.

It thus emerges that adverbs of quantification, when associated with a nominal expression, are in complementary distribution with DP-internal quantifiers. In the discussion of this paradigm in Chapter 2 in Volume I, I concluded that such complementary distribution emerges from the fact that the adverb of quantification binds, in some syntactically well-defined sense, some functional structure within the DP, while in the event readings the adverb of quantification binds, in some equally well-defined syntactic sense, some functional structure which is related to the event. Focusing on the nominal cases, it is precisely because the adverb binds some otherwise unspecified value within the nominal, that a DP-internal quantifier may not do so. A DP-internal quantifier and an adverb of quantification are thus in structural competition, not because of their specific projection site, but because both function as operators, binding the same variable. But if this is the case then functional heads are best viewed as operator–variable pairs, rather than as singleton terminals.

A concrete formulation of this proposal would be to view functional heads as open values with a category label, which are in turn assigned range by a variety of means. The specific open value here, heading, as we have argued in Volume I, a Quantity Phrase (#P) is $\langle e \rangle_{\#}$. The emerging representation, and abstracting away from the DP projection, is as in (15):

(15) $[_{\#P} \langle e \rangle_{\#} [_{NP} \quad]]$

In (15) $\langle e \rangle$ is an open value and the subscript # marks its categorial membership. $\langle e \rangle_{\#}$ may be assigned range, in English, either by an f-morph (*most, all, three*, etc.) that merges with it (cf. (16a)) or by an adverb of quantification (cf. 16b)). Although in English, range assignment to $\langle e \rangle_{\#}$ through an abstract head feature is not instantiated, in Hebrew it may be assigned range by the dual abstract head feature, with the resulting representation in (16c) (see Volume I, Chapter 7, Section 7.1.2. for discussion) (superscripting indicates range assignment):

(16) a. $[_{\#P} \text{most}^3 \langle e^3 \rangle_{\#}]$ $[_{NP} \quad]]$
    b. ADV⁴ $[_{\#P} \langle e^4 \rangle_{\#}]$ $[_{NP} \quad]]$
    c. $[_{\#P} \text{~~yom.~~} \langle \mathit{dual}^2 \rangle \langle e^2 \rangle_{\#}$ $[_{NP} \text{~~yom~~}]] \rightarrow$ yomayim
                                                  day   'two days'

Suppose we refer to range assignment by an f-morph or a head feature as direct range assignment, and to range assignment by an adverb of quantification, or a discourse operator, as indirect range assignment. The intuition here is that range assignment by a member of the functional lexicon of the given language, dedicated to the assignment of range to a specific open value, and projecting as a head (in a sense to be elaborated on shortly), is more 'direct'. As it turns out, indirect range assignment is instantiated in one more important domain—that of specifier–head agreement. As a brief illustration, consider definiteness in English (and see Chapter 6 in Volume I for extensive discussion).

The marking of definiteness in English is, at first sight, a simple matter. We may assume that D is headed by an open value, call it $\langle e \rangle_d$, where the assignment of range to $\langle e \rangle_d$ translates to the assignment of a referential index to objects. In turn, the f-morphs *the, this, that*, etc. assign range to $\langle e \rangle_d$ (and see Chapter 3 in Volume I for much discussion of the semantic content of such assignment). The emerging structure is as in (17). As *the* is a (free) f-morph, N-movement to D is neither expected nor attested.

(17) [$_{DP}$ the.$\langle e \rangle_d$ [(AP) [$_{NP}$ cat]]]

As it turns out, however, (17) is not the only way of assigning range to $\langle e \rangle_d$ in English. Specifically, consider the contrast in (18):

(18) a. the dog's ear
      b. a dog's ear

As is well known, (18a) is a definite description, but (18b) is not. Furthermore, as is equally well known, a definite article is barred in (19) (and see Volume I, Chapter 2, Section 2.1.3, for a discussion of (18b)):

(19) a. *The dog's the ear.
      b. *The [the dog's ear].

Intuitively, it is clear that definiteness, for the nominal in (18a), is mediated through the definiteness of the possessor DP *the dog*, presumably in [Spec, DP]. Suppose, then, that just like in the case of adverbs of quantification, specifier–head relations can give rise to *indirect* range assignment. Because the possessor is in [Spec, DP], and because it is itself marked as definite through its own DP-functional structure, it will assign range to $\langle e \rangle_d$, providing it is in specifier–head agreement with it. The resulting configuration, for definites, is as in (20):

(20) [$_{DP}$ [$_{DP}$ the dog's]^3 $\langle e^3 \rangle_d$ ... [$_{NP}$ ear]]

To summarize the salient aspects of the system proposed here:

a. Functional structures are headed by categorically labelled open values which must be assigned range by the appropriate functional operator.
b. The functional lexicon of each language makes available an array of range assigners for specified open values. Such range assigners come primarily in two varieties; f-morphs, independent morphemes, which are linked with a phonological index, and abstract head features. The latter require the support of some head (L, possibly F), a fact that typically translates to obligatory head movement in such contexts.
c. The derivation converges just in case the phonology dispenses a representation for the combination of head.⟨*head feature*⟩.
d. Two modes of indirect range assignment are possible (i.e. range assignment) by elements which are not necessarily specified, in the functional lexicon, as range assigners for a particular open value, and which are not heads). One involves range assignment by an adverb of quantification or a discourse operator. The second involves specifier–head agreement.

Before I turn to some additional formal ramifications of the view of functional heads as open values, one important note is in order. I have ruled out the double marking of any open functional value by more than one range assigner as a case of vacuous quantification (e.g. in the discussion of the complementarity between adverbs of quantification and other range assigners to $\langle e \rangle_\#$), thereby making a strong prediction concerning the absence of double marking in natural language. Some ramifications of this prediction are discussed in detail in Chapter 6. The system does not, however, predict a one-to-one correspondence between a functional range assigner and an open value, just as operators, in general, are not assumed to bind at most one variable. It is perfectly possible for a specific grammatical formative, be it a head feature or an f-morph, to bind more than one open value, should the range of its semantic properties allow it. The assumption that such a configuration is licit in the grammar, and is mediated through head movement, was already extensively used in Volume I. To illustrate, I assumed that strong quantifiers may assign range to both $\langle e \rangle_\#$ and $\langle e \rangle_d$, and that such double range assignment is accomplished through the movement of the relevant quantifier from its initial merger site (e.g. in #) and the merger of a copy in D. For *every*, for instance, the relevant emerging structure is (essentially) as in (21):

(21) [$_{DP}$ every.$\langle e \rangle_d$ [$_{\#P}$ ~~every~~.$\langle e \rangle_\#$ [dog]]]

In effect, then, functional elements which assign range to more than one open value are thus semantically 'portmanteau' elements, a point already discussed extensively in Chapter 4 of Volume I.

1.2.4 *What's in a head?*

The notion of 'head', as it emerges from the previous discussion, deviates architecturally from what is typically assumed by canonical phrase-structural accounts, which—with their fundamentally bottom-up approach to categorical properties—do not distinguish between the lowest phrasal label and the terminal it dominates. In X′-theory (and its predecessors), entries, lexical or functional, are typically inserted under X°, as in (22a). In Bare Phrase Structural accounts, the identity between the lowest label instantiation and the terminal is even more strongly stated, in that it is the terminal itself which projects, iteratively, up the tree, as in (22b).

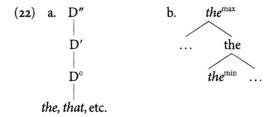

(22) a. D″ │ D′ │ D° │ *the, that*, etc.   b. *the*^{max} … *the* *the*^{min} …

In (22a–b), the question of how the appropriate value is associated with the relevant syntactic projection (i.e. how range is assigned) does not arise. In (22a), it is typically assumed that some percolation mechanism is responsible for the association of the properties of the maximal projection with those of the terminal. In (22b), the maximal projection is but an expansion of the terminal, and the statement of the relationship is even more direct. In turn, neither system allows, in a natural fashion, for the statement of the relations which we called indirect range assignment, in which the relevant properties of the maximal projection—and its head—do not emerge from within the projection itself and are not mediated by the categorial and semantic properties of the terminal. Rather, they emerge from the availability of an outside operator, associated with a presumably null functional head. Within Bare Phrase Structure the problem is particularly acute, since if phrases project from terminals, in the absence of an (overt) terminal, we would have to assume the existence of an abstract, phonologically null entry with some well-defined properties, which agrees, by some mechanism to be specified, with some material which is outside the main projection line—indeed, outside the maximal projection altogether—as in the case of adverbs of quantification. Note further that the direct projection of lexical terminals as in (22b) does not in fact circumvent the need to specify a syntactic category for *the*, or the fact that, for example, both *the* and *that* have a determiner distribution cannot be stated. Rather, we must assume that *the* or *that* are specified as having the categorial value D, and that it is their sharing of it that accounts for their similar distribution.

Suppose, however, that we structurally separate the category label from the terminal, or in terms of the system proposed here, separate the open value from the range assignment. Specifically, let us assume that (functional) category labels are just labelled open values, and that the functional terminals associated with them are best viewed as operators which assign range to them. On that view, what *the* and *that* have in common is that both can assign range to the same open value, that associated with the category label D, and projecting as $\langle e \rangle_d$. In and of themselves, however, they are **not** D. Indeed, they have no syntactic category whatsoever. Of course, $\langle e \rangle_d$ can project without a projection-internal range assigner, in which case range could still be assigned, indirectly, by an adverb of quantification or a discourse operator, or through specifier-head agreement. In such a case there will not be a terminal associated with the head, but DP would still have a head—$\langle e \rangle_d$, which is interpreted through indirect range assignment. Supposing this to be on the right track, an (overt) categorial head emerges as a pair, in which one member provides the category label and the open value, while the other, optional one, provides the range assigned to that value. We can thus assume the structure in (23), where $\langle e \rangle_F$ is some functional open value of the type F, where $R(F)$ is a range assigner to $\langle e \rangle_F$, and where co-superscripting notates range assignment:

(23)

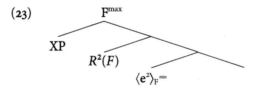

A detailed formal justification for the structure in (23) is not undertaken here, as phrasal architecture is by and large orthogonal to the main focus of this study (but see Borer, forthcoming, for much additional discussion). Some aspects of the structure in (23) nevertheless need to be pointed out. First, it does not involve (a base-generated) adjunction of $R^2(F)$ to $\langle e^2 \rangle_F^{min}$, and as such it does not entail a violation of the Extension Condition of Chomsky (1995a) and subsequent work. Secondly, it allows for a natural statement of head movement without a resulting violation of the Extension Condition, and also in conformity with the Uniformity Condition of Chomsky (1995b). Specifically, note that we may assume the existence of movement which affects solely $R(F)$ (but not $\langle e \rangle_F$). $R(F)$ may in turn merge with some higher open value, assigning range to it, without resulting in the inheritance of categorial properties, as $R(F)$, in and of itself, does not have a category. Further, as $R(F)$ is part of a head pair by definition, it is not maximal in either one of its instantiations, and the Uniformity

Condition is adhered to. The emerging structure would be as in (24), and would involve grammatical formatives which can assign range to more than one open value, *every*, for instance, as in (21), without assuming adjunction.

(24)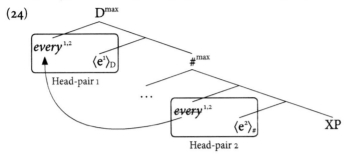

To the extent that a range assigner can thus move and merge a copy with a higher categorial open value, and to the extent that we are correct in assuming that such grammatical formatives are range assigners and not, in and of themselves, associated with a category label, the typical complications associated with head movement, in which a subordinate labelled X^{min} adjoins to a higher labelled Y^{min}, do not emerge (and see Volume I, Chapter 2, Section 2.1.4, as well as Borer, forthcoming for some comments on head adjunction).

Finally, the configuration in (25) is fundamentally ambiguous, in that $R^2(F)$ may be either a specifier or a member of a head-pair.

Recall now that it was specifically denied that there is an inherent semantics for specifiers (as opposed to non-specifiers) in the functional domain, making the structural ambiguity of (25) immaterial, especially as we just concluded that open values may be assigned range, indirectly, through specifier–head agreement. As $R^2(F)$ is by definition both minimal and maximal, if it is a specifier, no particular problem emerges.[9]

(25)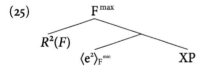

---

[9] I suggested in Volume I, Chapter 2, Section 2.2, (and see below for a summary) that head features are not morphemic. Assuming that morphemes do project, this means that head features, as such, are not nodes in the structures. Rather, a head feature is a semantic specification that is instantiated in the context of an appropriate lexical head. Thus in (i), ⟨*pst*⟩ is instantiated on *kick*, in a position which enables it to assign range to ⟨e⟩$_T$. The emerging structure does not involve the branching of ⟨*pst*⟩.*kick*, and the head pair consists of ⟨*pst*⟩.*kick* and ⟨e⟩$_T$. Interestingly, if it is assumed that inflection is base-generated on a stem, as in Chomsky (1991, 1995a, and subsequent work), the non-branching nature of ⟨*pst*⟩.*kick* in (i) follows directly.

(i)

1.3 A Note on Inflection

The model presented thus far puts forth a particular view of the relationship between, for example, a verb and past-tense inflection in English. We proposed that such a relation consists of the instantiation, on a V-head, of an abstract head feature, which is itself neither morphemic nor is it associated with a general fixed phonological representation. As such, this proposal is incompatible with much current research which postulates an isomorphism between inflection and syntactic structure, assuming, specifically, that inflected words are built, morpho-phonologically, through the movement of heads and their attachment to inflectional morphemes heading functional structure.

The approach is also incompatible with many morphological non-syntactic analyses of inflection as morphemic and compositional, and as such, constituting a unified module with derivational morphology (cf. Williams 1981; Lieber 1980, and much subsequent work). In contrast, it is fully compatible with the view of inflection within the family of approaches called *Word and Paradigm* (see, especially, Matthews 1972; Anderson 1982, 1992; Beard 1981, 1995). In Chapter 2, Section 2.2 (Volume I) I review some reasons to reject a hierarchical representation for (most of) inflection. When put together with a hierarchical view of (at least some of) derivational morphology, as proposed in Borer (2003*a*, forthcoming), a picture emerges in which, rather contrary to tradition, (much of) inflectional marking is non-syntactic and non-hierarchical, while (much of) derivation is hierarchical, and at least at times, syntactic (the reader is referred to Stump 1998 for an excellent review of the relevant considerations with respect to inflection).

As the multiplicity of reservations in the above paragraph indicates, the division that emerges correlates only partially with the classical division between inflection and derivation. And indeed, I believe the distinction to be largely useless, morphologically. While there is a notion of inflection which is syntactically coherent, and is based on syntactic function, that notion does not translate usefully to any morpho-phonological generalizations. At the bottom of the confusion, I believe, is the conflation of syntactic function with morpho-phonological form. When viewed functionally, inflection is perfectly coherent. Morpho-phonologically, however, it turns out to consist of two distinct operations. One is morphologically compositional and hierarchical (English V + *ing*, for progressive, being an example), the other is neither morphological nor hierarchical (English V.⟨*pst*⟩ being an illustration, with ⟨*pst*⟩ as a non-morphemic head feature and the combination as a non-branching syntactic node).

To recapitulate some of the conclusions proposed in Volume I, Chapter 2, Section 2.2, I note that to the extent that inflected forms are syntactically regular, this is so because, for example, the appropriateness of marking a particular noun as accusative is determined by a particular syntactic context, and has, presumably, syntactic conditioning of a well-defined, regular sort. Further, with the exception of whatever interpretation is imposed on an accusative noun by virtue of being in some particular syntactic position (i.e. that position which is responsible for the appropriateness of accusative case), typically no other meaning is added to the noun. The interpretation of inflected forms is thus compositional, in the same sense that the interpretation of syntactic structures is compositional.

As it turns out, the compositional meaning of inflected forms as well as their syntactic conditioning is often translated into a rather different claim, according to which inflectional *morphology* is syntactic and regular, and as such, constitutes a word-formation module which is distinct from derivational morphology, which is lexical and irregular. According to this logic, the best way to capture the regularity of inflection is to assume that inflected morpho-phonological units, as such, are compositional in the same sense that syntactic phrases are compositional, and are put together by syntactic composition principles. It is precisely here that serious problems emerge, due to the conflation of function and form. While the function of inflection is clearly regular and syntactic, no such claim can be made about its form. In fact, morpho-phonologically, inflectional form is notoriously erratic, involving listed relations between stems and marking, accidental gaps, and stem changes which do not yield easily to a characterization in terms of compositional morphology (and see, in this very context Halle 1973; Anderson 1982, 1992; Beard 1981, 1995, and many others).

In fact, when viewed exclusively from a morpho-phonological perspective, much of inflection is considerably more idiosyncratic than so-called derivational marking. If regularity in the morphological domain is measured against the predictability of form from function and function from form, we note that neither derivation nor inflection exhibit a predictability of form from function. If, for example, PAST or PLURAL are functions, in the relevant sense, and if NOM is a function, in that same sense, their form is not predictable from their function. However, in the derivational domain, function is pretty much predictable from form. Thus a verb, when combined with -(*a*)*tion*, is a noun, a complex form ending in *-ize* a verb, etc. Not so within the domain of (much of) inflection, where the function is not predictable from the form, either.

Following the detailed discussion in Volume I, Chapter 2, Section 2.2, I will assume that the best way to view (most of) inflection is not as morphemic in nature, but rather as *amorphous*, in the sense of Anderson (1992). Within such a view, phonological representations are paradigmatic, and inflection is a process of mapping from a set of non-morphemic representations, such as V.⟨*pst*⟩

to a complex phonological entry, which contains a full list of potentially unpredictable forms. Within such a view, we note, regular forms, for example, *walk* → *walked*~past~ and *walk* → *walked*~participle~ need not be listed. Rather, a phonological realization convention would spell out *walk.⟨pst⟩* as *walked* and *walk*.PARTICIPLE as *walked* as well. The application of such a phonological realization convention would be triggered when a specific phonological index comes without a paradigm (and see Beard 1995 and Anderson 1982, 1992 for more specific executions and some relevant theoretical considerations, as well as Stump 1998 for a review).

More crucially from the perspective of the present study, I believe that pending significant additional insight into the nature of inflection, the course of action is to radically separate form and function within the domain of inflection. The reader may recall that I suggested that abstract head features must be realized on stems (L-heads, but possibly at times f-morphs as well). Seeking to integrate that particular view with a view of non-morphemic inflection, I will assume that while more than one head feature can be realized on a single L-head, those features are neither ordered nor hierarchically organized. Specifically, for a representation such as (26a), the input to the phonological component is as in (26b):

(26) a. [$_{F-1}$ L-head.⟨*f3*⟩.⟨*f2*⟩.⟨*f1*⟩ ⟨e$_{F1}$⟩ [$_{F-2}$ ~~L-head~~.⟨*f3*⟩.⟨*f2*⟩ ⟨e$_{F2}$⟩ [$_{F-3}$ ~~L-head~~.⟨*f3*⟩ ⟨e$_{F3}$⟩ [$_{L-D}$ ~~L-head~~]]]].
b. L-head.⟨*f3*⟩.⟨*f2*⟩.⟨*f1*⟩ (with{⟨*f3*⟩.⟨*f2*⟩.⟨*f1*⟩} as an unordered set).

The structure in (26b), in turn, serves as the basis for the choice between members of the paradigm given by the relevant phonological entry. While some phonological sub-regularities associated with the realization of some feature combinations are of course expected and attested, the forms remain, crucially, morphological simpletons, and there is no expectation for either linear or hierarchical correlations between the syntactic structure and the placement of inflectional marking.[10]

This said, it is clear that some markings which are functionally inflectional are extremely regular. Thus, for instance, *-ing* in its function as the progressive attaches to virtually all English verbs, and never triggers any stem allomorphy or meaning change. It thus stands to reason that *-ing*, unlike, for instance, past tense in English, is not an abstract head feature, but rather a *bound* f-morph, differing from an f-morph such as *the* in forcing the movement of some L-head

---

[10] And see Volume I, Chapter 2, n. 20, for a comparison between the system of inflectional morphology advanced in this work and Distributed Morphology.

to support it. As such -*ing* patterns with (much of) derivational morphology (and is, in fact, at times classified as such), where affixes do give rise to a hierarchical combination with their host stem, and where, at least at times, movement of an L-stem is required. This issue is however set aside for the remainder of this book. The reader is referred to Borer (forthcoming) for a detailed discussion.

1.4 A Note on Idioms

The vocabulary of the system we are putting forth here consists of, on the one hand, listemes (where by listemes we refer to a pairing of a conceptual feature bundle with a phonological index), and on the other, of members of the functional lexicon, including abstract head features, free f-morphs as well as, possibly, bound f-morphs. Its formal vocabulary consists of category labels associated with open values (e.g. $\langle e \rangle_d$) which are in need of range assignment.[11] Combinatorial principles in the syntactic domain consist of (some version of) Bare Phrase Structure, together with merge and move. We set aside here the possibility that a parallel set of combinatorial principles are responsible for the formation of hierarchical structure within derivational morphology.

Before proceeding, a comment is in order on the nature of units which do not lend themselves to such a perfectly combinatorial account. Thus consider the utterances in (27):

(27)   a.   trousers (cf. shirts)
        b.   cross (that) bridge when (we) come to (it) (cf. cross that bridge when we come to it, literally)
        c.   depend on (cf. sit on)
        d.   kick the bucket (cf. kick the bucket, literally)

The constituents in (27) have very clear, characterizable formal properties which parallel exactly those associated with counterpart non-fixed expressions, for example those given in parentheses in (27). *Trousers* is plural, and must trigger plural agreement, where relevant. *On* in *depend on* is a preposition, its complement must be a DP, and the resulting PP acts on a par with other PPs syntactically. *Kick*, in its idiomatic instantiation in (27d), has categorial selection properties akin to those of its non-idiomatic instantiation, as is true for *cross* in (27b), and *bucket* in (27d) must be a DP and must be in a case position, as is true for *bridge* in (27b).

---

[11] See Borer (forthcoming) for some discussion of 'pure' categorizers, such as -*ation* (N), -*al* (A), etc. within an XS model.

Nevertheless, something extra must be said about the constituents in (27), addressing the fact that they have, as wholes, interpretations which are listed, in some relatively well-understood sense. Their interpretations are not derived compositionally from the meaning of their parts. The fact that the meanings of these expressions are listed requires an obvious extension of the notion of *listeme*, as presented thus far. Specifically, we must allow for the linking of conceptual packaging, so to speak, not just with a phonological index, but, more specifically, with structured phonological material. We note, in this context, that the information *must* be structured. Thus it would not do to list the meaning TROUSERS with a phonological index that would spell out as /trauzerz/, as such a realization would fail to capture the fact that *trousers* is plural. Rather, it would appear, the best way to capture the properties of *trousers* would be as in (28), where, by convention, square brackets indicate a relation which is internal to the 'extended projection' line:

(28) TROUSERS ⇔ $[\pi_3+\langle e\rangle_{div}]$

In (28), TROUSERS stands for the relevant conceptual meaning. π_3 stands for the phonological index /trauzer/, and $\langle e\rangle_{div}$ stands for a piece of functional structure which must be assigned range, specifically, as I argued in Chapter 4 in Volume I, by so-called plural inflection.

Consider in greater detail the predictions of the representation in (28). Note, first, that there is no information here that *trousers* is N, although, of course, it always is. This follows directly from the fact that $\langle e\rangle_{div}$ is a nominalizer. In conjunction with the listeme *trouser*, the structure in (29) results, in which *trouser* is properly nominalized:

(29) $[_{DIV} \langle e\rangle_{div} [_{L\text{-}D}$ trouser$]] \Rightarrow [_{DIV} \langle e\rangle_{div} [_N$ trouser$]]$

As it turns out, the representation in (29) is incomplete. I argued that $\langle e\rangle_{div}$ in English can be assigned range both by so-called plural marking and by singular-producing f-morphs (*a, every, each*). Only the former is licit, however, for the idiom in (27a). A more accurate representation, then, would be as in (30), where α stands for non-singular $\langle div\rangle$ range assignment (and note in this context that we can now dispense with the categorial label DIV for the open value $\langle e^\alpha\rangle$ in (30), as it is fully predictable from the fact that α, by assumption non-singular $\langle div\rangle$, assigns range to $\langle e\rangle_{div}$):

(30) TROUSERS ⇔ $[\pi_3+\langle e^\alpha\rangle]$

The only means for assigning range to $\langle e^\alpha\rangle$ in English is through the abstract head feature $\langle div^\alpha\rangle$, which must be realized on an L-head. The emerging structure would thus be as in (31):

(31) [$_{DIV}$ trouser.⟨div^a⟩⟨e^a⟩ [$_N$ ~~trouser~~]] → /trauzerz/

The representation for *trousers* further allows, indeed presupposes, the existence of the phonological index *trouser*, and indeed, such an index clearly does exist independently of *trousers*, appearing both in compounds (*trouser leg*) and in isolation, for instance, as a verb.[12]

Consider now (27b). Following a similar logic, the best representation for the complex expression here should likewise consist of a combination of otherwise existing building blocks, i.e. open values and listemes. Focusing on the combination of *cross* and *bridge*, a plausible representation would be as in (32):

(32) MEANING ⇔ [π_2+ ⟨e⟩$_{Asp}$]+π_4(+adjunct)

In (32), MEANING is whatever the relevant idiom means. The sound component of our complex expression here consists of two phonological indices, specifically those associated with *cross*(π_2) and *bridge*(π_4), and of a piece of functional structure, the open value ⟨e⟩$_{Asp}$, which by assumption is the functional node responsible for the licensing of a direct argument, and which is in turn a verbalizer (and see Chapters 3–8 for much additional elaboration). Note now that at least for the first part of the idiom (adjunct excluded) very little needs to be said beyond what is otherwise provided by the grammar to derive *cross the road* or similar expressions. I will argue in Chapter 3 that range is assigned to ⟨e⟩$_{Asp}$ in English through agreement with a (quantity) DP in its specifier, and that the specifier in question acts as a nominalizer, in the relevant sense. It thus emerges that the only well-formed output for (32) is as in (33) (we are abstracting away from the fact that verb movement would further raise the verb to a position above [Spec,Asp]):[13]

(33) [$_{Asp}$ $\pi_{4(bridge)}$ [$_{Asp}$ ⟨e⟩ [$_{L-D}$ $\pi_{2(cross)}$]] ⇒ [$_{Asp}$ [$_{DP}$ $\pi_{4(bridge)}$] [$_{Asp}$ ⟨e⟩ [$_V$ $\pi_{2(cross)}$]]]]

One more thing needs to be said about (33), to exclude the emergence of a mass-noun interpretation for *bridge*. I argued in Chapter 4 in Volume I that the mass–count distinction is represented through the presence of the open value ⟨e⟩$_{div}$ in count, but not in mass nouns. Thus a complete representation for the idiom in (27b) should be as in (34):

(34) MEANING ⇔ [π_2+ ⟨e⟩$_{Asp}$]+ [π_4+ ⟨e⟩$_{div}$)] (+ adjunct)

---

[12] The Oxford Dictionary lists the verb *trouser* as meaning, colloquially, to pocket. Native speakers consulted find the expression 'to trouser the untrousered' whimsical, but entirely comprehensible.

[13] By assumption, (33) consists of the full conceptual array for a given phase, thereby forcing π_4 to merge in [Spec,Asp]. We set aside the possibility, if indeed instantiated, of idioms which represent a partial conceptual array for a given phase, and the manner in which the representation of idioms can be fine-tuned so as to ensure that the correct phonological index is associated with a specific syntactic position, in such cases.

Note that nothing more needs to be said here about the DP in [Spec,Asp], as its quantity and definiteness properties are largely free, allowing plural, singular, definite, indefinite, quantified, etc. (and see Williams 1994 for a related discussion).[14] Although, as in the case of *trousers*, $\langle e \rangle_{div}$ must project (hence excluding mass noun complement), unlike the case of *trousers*, there is no specification here of what range must be assigned to it, thereby suggesting that at least two degrees of specification are allowed for idiomatic expressions. In one of these cases, it suffices to specify a particular open value (with its categorial label); in the second, an open value is specified alongside a narrower set of possible range assigners, with some relevant property α.

When the idiomatic expression in (27d) is considered, we note that the representation in (34) does not suffice. Specifically, *the bucket* is fixed here, allowing no other range assigners to $\langle e \rangle_d$ (**this bucket*; **that bucket*), no plural marking (**the buckets*), and no quantifiers (**a bucket*; **every bucket*; **the one bucket*). Not only must *bucket* be specified as associated with whatever functional open values would make it singular and definite, it must also specify the specific f-morph which assigns range (under the assumption that, e.g., *this* assigns singular and definite range, but is nevertheless excluded for *kick the bucket*). The resulting representation must thus include the phonological index for *the* (say π_7). I argued in Volume I (Chapter 6) that the definite article always assigns range to both $\langle e \rangle_d$ and $\langle e \rangle_\#$ and furthermore that for singular structures (but not for plurals), *the* assigns range to $\langle e \rangle_{div}$ as well. The most parsimonious representation for the idiom in (27d) is thus as in (35). Note specifically that as *the* always assigns range to $\langle e \rangle_\#$ and $\langle e \rangle_d$, specifying *the* as a range assigner to $\langle e \rangle_{div}$ suffices to derive the fact that *the bucket* must be singular and definite:

(35)   MEANING $\Leftrightarrow [\pi_5 + \langle e \rangle_{Asp}] + [\pi_6 + \langle e^{\pi_7} \rangle_{div}]$

where π_5 is the phonological index for *kick*, π_6 the phonological index for *bucket* and π_7 for *the*, and where the superscript π_7 for $\langle e \rangle_{div}$ indicates that it must be assigned ranged by *the*.

---

[14] The account here is guilty of some oversimplification. (i), note, is well formed, although *bridges* is not a quantity DP, and as we shall argue, not licensed in [Spec,Asp] but rather in (the Case-marked) position [Spec,F*P]. The reader is referred to Chapters 4 and 6 for an extensive discussion of the licensing of non-quantity DPs as direct objects. However, once that discussion is considered, it should be obvious that the necessary modification for (33), to account for the presence of non-quantity DPs, is relatively straightforward:

(i) Experts cross bridges when they come to them.

I am setting aside here the fuller representation of this idiom which must include the representation for the adjunct. We note that one additional mechanism that must be available for idioms is some type of indexation, accounting for the obligatory co-reference of *bridge* and the pronoun in the adjunct, as well as the obligatory co-reference of *one* with the subject in reflexive idioms such as *crane one's neck*.

Degree of specification in idioms, then, allows a gradation:[15]

(36) a. $[\pi_i + \langle e \rangle_X]$ (e.g. $\langle e \rangle_{div}$ for *bridge*, with range assigned to $\langle e \rangle_{div}$ by any available assigner).
b. $[\pi_j + \langle e^\alpha \rangle]$ (where e.g. α is non-singular $\langle div \rangle$ for *trousers*, causing $\langle e \rangle$ to be $\langle e \rangle_{div}$).
c. $[\pi_k + \langle e^{\pi_3} \rangle_{div}]$ (e.g. where π_3 is *the*, for *bucket*, forcing the projection of $\langle e \rangle_\#$ and $\langle e \rangle_d$).

It now emerges that our last idiom, (27c), is in many respects like (36c). Assuming, specifically, that prepositions are f-morphs (see Baker 2003 for a detailed discussion), we may represent *depend on* as in (37), where π_9 is the phonological index of *depend*, and $\langle e^{on} \rangle$ corresponds to an open value that must be assigned range by the f-morph *on*:

(37) MEANING $\Leftrightarrow \pi_9 + [\langle e^{on} \rangle$

One difference between the representations considered thus far and (37) is worth noting. While all representations considered thus far included a listeme together with an open value which categorized it, this is not the case in (37), where, by assumption, the emerging PP is not in the extended projection line of *depend*, and thus cannot verbalize it. Thus while the idiomatic representations in (36) all give rise to a representation which is perforce already categorized, this is not the case for (37), where *depend* must be categorized by whatever other mechanisms are available in the grammar, be they syntactic or morphological. I will return to this point, and to idioms, in Chapter 11 where I will suggest that such categorizing, for *depend*, emerges from the prefix *de-*.

To conclude this brief discussion of idioms, we note that idiosyncratic selection, such that it does exist in the grammar and is associated with particular listemes, is integrated here into a system which consists of phonological indices and functional structure, but no categorially marked listemes. While representations such as those in (36)–(37) do go beyond the pure sound–meaning pair, they nevertheless are restricted to the formal vocabulary introduced here, and do not involve a formal extension of the grammar.

---

[15] We note that although for e.g. *trousers* the representations in (36b–c) appear identical, this need not be the case. Thus the representation in (36b) would allow, in principle, more than one range assigner to $\langle e \rangle$, if the language has more than one range assigner associated with the same (relevant) semantic value, (e.g., *the* and *this* for $\langle e \rangle_d$). Thus the representation would allow in principle for the possibility of a language which has more than one means of assigning non-singular value to $\langle e \rangle_{div}$ to have both instantiated in cases of *pluralia tantum*.

If abstract head features do not have an independent phonological index, as suggested in Chapter 1, Section 1.3, we predict that type (36c) would never be instantiated with abstract head features. That is, an idiom could not be specified as being associated with an idiosyncratic plurality marker distinct from that typically associated with non-idiomatic plural instantiations of the same word, e.g. *childs* instead of *children*. This prediction seems eminently plausible, but its ramifications will not be pursued here any further.

2

Why Events?

2.1 Variable-behaviour Verbs[1]

2.1.1 *The paradigm*

The fundamental premise of the remainder of this work is that argument structure is licensed by functional syntactic structure, and specifically, functional structure that is interpreted as event structure. This syntactic structure, in turn, affects aspects of the basic meaning of its L-head, where by L-head we mean a (category-neutral) listeme, part of the conceptual array. The functional structure may further have the effect of 'verbalizing' the L-domain (if not already verbalized by categorial morphology), where by the L-domain we mean the maximal category the L-head projects.[2] The L-head, or, more accurately, the listeme, in turn functions as a modifier of the structure, giving rise to appropriateness or oddity, as the case may be, and as already discussed extensively. To the extent that argument structure is altogether severed from the properties of the L-head that is to become the verb, we expect massive polysemy. Such polysemy was already illustrated within the nominal domain. We now turn our attention to at least one well-known case of polysemy within the verbal domain. In the remainder of this chapter, we will illustrate this polysemy within the domain of

---

[1] Earlier versions of this section, as well as some sections of Chapter 3, appeared in Borer (1994, 1998*a*). The text which follows here differs from these versions in important ways, notably in setting aside the mapping hypothesis account proposed in Borer (1994), and in developing a more formal account of aspect within the more general approach to functional structure proposed and motivated in Volume I.

The argument in this section is based fundamentally on the status of polysemy within the verbal domain. An examination of polysemy within the intransitive domain and otherwise has led van Hout (1992) to conclusions which are rather similar to our own concerning the division of labour between the syntax and the lexicon. Van Hout (1996) and subsequent work, however, weakens the conclusions of van Hout (1992), in assuming that verbs *are* lexically specified as ±telic. I return to aspects of these distinct systems throughout the ensuing discussion.

[2] Or, alternatively, adjectivizing the L-domain. We already noted (see Volume I, Chapter 1, Section 1.2, and see also Chapter 1, Section 1.1), that L-domains are category neutral only insofar as they are headed by a category-neutral listeme, and that as a result, categorizing by functional structure is only 'visible' for what appear like productive Ø-alternation (or conversion) cases. As there are no productive Ø-alternations/conversions involving adjectives in English, it would appear that for reasons that may or may not be English-specific, adjectives, as L-heads, are never 'pure' category-less listemes. Rather, all adjectives are already 'like' *verbalize* and not like *form*, and the L-Ds they project are always categorized vacuously by the functional structure. See n. 25 for some additional brief comments.

verb structures, arguing not only that it occurs, but that its best characterization is through the projection of functional structure which is interpreted as event structure.

The starting point of our discussion is the paradigm of so-called 'variable-behaviour verbs', which went unnoticed for many years, but has received massive attention in the past decade. The reader should note that 'variable-behaviour verb' here is a technical term, referring specifically to intransitive verbs that show a variable unaccusative–unergative behaviour. While many other verbs show polysemy, and are hence variable-behaviour verbs, our discussion here focuses on this specific subset, as contrasts associated with their variable behaviour can be easily illustrated.

If one considers the analysis of the unaccusative–unergative distinction as it comes to us within the GB tradition, starting, say, with Burzio (1981, 1986) and continuing with much subsequent work, the picture is more or less as in (1). Setting aside verbs that occur with indirect complementation or with clausal complements, there are essentially three types of verb that take direct arguments, and which we will refer to as *transitive, unaccusative,* and *unergative*.[3] As there are only two types of direct argument, this picture covers all logical possibilities:[4]

(1) *Transitive*   *Unaccusative*   *Unergative*
     [$_{VP}$ *External* [$_{V'}$ V *Internal*]]   [$_{VP}$ ∅ [$_{V'}$ V *Internal*]]   [$_{VP}$ *External* [$_{V'}$ V ∅]]

The empirical consequences of the paradigm in (1) have been considered to provide considerable evidence for endo-skeletal (or projectionist) approaches. The systematic syntactic patterning of arguments of unaccusative verbs with direct objects, vs. the systematic syntactic patterning of arguments of unergative verbs with subjects of transitives appears to lend considerable credence to the view that information concerning the syntactic projection of arguments is, indeed, specified in the lexical entry of the verb. In turn, to the extent that

---

[3] Terminology, as well as original classification, from Perlmutter (1978). However, as Perlmutter did not associate the classification with lexical entries of verbs and properties listed therein, and was, in fact, quite aware of the problems for such a lexical encoding presented by variable-behaviour verbs, the following critique does not apply to his research.

[4] We are concerned here solely with verbs that take direct nominal arguments. A notational clarification is therefore in order: the term *unaccusative* has been used ambiguously in the literature to refer to two distinct verbal types, both sharing the absence of an external argument: intransitive verbs, whose sole argument displays some syntactic diagnostics typically associated with direct objects; and verbs which do not project a direct nominal argument altogether (i.e. raising-to-subject verbs, weather verbs). In this study, the term *unaccusative* is restricted to the first type, and the second type is not discussed any further. Note that aspectual properties correlated with the unaccusative–unergative distinction have been stated with respect to those intransitives which take direct nominal arguments, and that the 'raising' type is typically stative, rather than eventive, a fact that is rather easy to correlate with the absence of an internal direct argument, in line with the discussion to follow.

the class of unaccusative and unergative verbs is overwhelmingly the same in different languages, lexical information concerning the syntactic projection of arguments would appear to derive from the verb's lexical semantics.

However, as has been observed in numerous studies, the unaccusative–unergative alternation is not nearly as stable and lexical-entry dependent as it is occasionally presented to be. Thus, consider the following well-known examples:

(2) a. Jan heeft gesprongen. (Dutch)
 Jan has jumped

 b. Jan is in de sloot gesprongen.
 Jan is in the ditch jumped
 'Jan jumped into the ditch.'

(3) a. Gianni ha corso. (Italian)
 Gianni has run

 b. Gianni e corso a casa.
 Gianni is run to home

(4) a. *Ne hanno corso/i due.
 of-them have run two

 b. Ne sono corsi due a casa.
 of-them are run.AGR two to home (Hoekstra and Mulder 1990)

(5) a. ha.xadašot hericu 'et dan le.misrado. (Hebrew)
 the.news made.run OM Dan to.office.his
 'The news made Dan run to his office.'

 b. #ha.xadašot hericu 'et dan be.misrado.
 the.news made.run OM Dan in.office-his
 'The news made Dan run in his office.'

 c. ha.boss heric 'et dan be.misrado/l.-misrado.
 the.boss made-run OM Dan in.office-his/to.office his
 'The boss made Dan run in his office/to his office.'

(6) In het tweede bedrijf werd er door de nieuwe acteur
 in the second act was there by the new actor
 op het juiste ogenblik gevallen. (Dutch; Perlmutter 1978)
 on cue fallen

(7) a. ha.praxim nablu le-rani/li. (Hebrew)
 the.flowers wilted to-Rani
 'Rani's/my flowers wilted.'

b. ha.praxim₁ na*b*lu lahem₁.
      the.flowers wilted to.them
      'The flowers were wilting (implies self-directed motion).'

(8) a. ha.qir hitporer le-rina/la.
       the.wall crumbled to.Rina
       'Rina's/her wall crumbled.'
    b. ha.kir₁ hitporer lo₁ (le-'ito).
       the.wall crumbled to.it (slowly)
       'The wall was crumbling slowly.'

The paradigms in (2)–(4) illustrates that verbs typically classified as unergative, such as *springen* 'jump' in Dutch and *correre* 'run' in Italian, which typically take an unergative auxiliary (*hebben* and *avere* respectively) and which do not allow *ne*-cliticization (Italian), exhibit the full range of unaccusative characteristics, selecting *zijn* and *essere* and allowing *ne* cliticization, if a PP specifying a terminal point of the motion is added. Example (5) illustrates that in Hebrew, the verb *rac* 'run', under causativization (*heric* 'make run') results in an obligatory *agent* interpretation without a PP terminal, but allows a non-agentive *causer* reading in the presence of a PP terminal. If indeed, as is often argued (see Hale and Keyser 1993; Reinhart 1996), causatives associated with unaccusatives allow a non-agentive causer reading, but not causatives which are associated unergatives, this would suggest that *rac* 'ran' is an unaccusative in the context of 'to his office' but unergative in the context of 'in his office'.

Although it is sometimes assumed that the presence of an overt result phrase or a terminal PP is crucial for the emergence of variable behaviour (cf. Hoekstra and Mulder 1990), this appears to be the case, if at all, only for manner of motion verbs with meanings such as 'jump', 'run', etc. When other intransitives are considered, both unergative and unaccusative diagnostics can emerge in the absence of any additional structure. Sentence (6) illustrates that the Dutch impersonal passive, argued to be restricted to unergative verbs, can occur with the verb *vallen* 'fall', typically classified as unaccusative, provided that self-directed motion is ascribed to the argument (*fall on purpose*). Examples (7) and (8) illustrate that in Hebrew the argument of verbs such as *na*b*al* 'wilt' and *hitporer* 'crumble' (among many others) can be either internal, allowing a possessor dative, or external, allowing a reflexive dative.⁵

---

⁵ The following is a description of the distribution of possessor dative and reflexive dative, as argued for in Borer and Grodzinsky (1986). I return to these diagnostics in Section 2.2.1.2. Note that the descriptions in (i) and (ii) do not range over the same type of linguistic domains. While the distribution of possessor datives is a species of binding (or movement, as Landau 1997 argues), the distribution of reflexive

It has been further observed (already by Perlmutter 1978, but see especially Van Valin 1990) that the unaccusative–unergative diagnostics associated with variable-behaviour verbs are linked to clear interpretational correlations. Specifically, syntactic unaccusative diagnostics are associated with telic and non-agentive characteristics. Syntactic unergative diagnostics, on the other hand, are typically associated with atelicity and with agentive interpretation.[6] As an illustration, (7a), where *nabal* is associated with a possessor dative, and is hence an unaccusative, clearly means that the flowers have died, rendering (9a) anomalous. On the other hand, (7b), associated with a reflexive dative, and hence unergative, implies that the flowers were engaged in a wilting activity, and no termination is implied, making (9b) perfectly felicitous:

(9) a. ??ha.praxim nablu le-rani me-axat 'ad šaloš ve-'az   yarad gešem
      the.flowers wilted to.Rani from 1pm to 3pm and then fell   rain

     ve-hem hiťošešu.
     and-they recovered

   b. ha.praxim$_2$ nablu lahem$_2$ me-axat 'ad šaloš ve-'az   yarad gešem
      the.flowers wilted to.them from 1pm to 3pm and then fell   rain

     ve-hem hiťošešu.
     and-they recovered

datives is linked to argument structure, or to event structure, as I shall argue, and not to a position, as such (and see Chapter 8, Section 8.2.3, for the analysis of reflexive datives):

(i)   Possessor dative binds the determiner of the possessed NP (D-structure)
(ii) Reflexive dative is coindexed with an external argument.

[6] Within the area of aktionsart and *aspect*, terminological proliferation as well as terminological confusion is rampant. In what follows, I will use terminology in the following way:

(i) a. Telic: a semantic, aktionsart, term. Vendler's *accomplishments* and *achievements*; Bach's (1986) *eventives*, as distinct from either *states* or *activities*; Kiparsky's (1998) *boundedness*.
    b. Atelic: not *telic*; Vendler's *activities* and *states*.
    c. *Accomplishment, achievement, activity*, and *state* are used following Vendler's original classification.
    d. Perfective: a morphological term. The grammatical marking on verbs in, for example, Slavic languages, typically referred to by traditional grammarians as *perfective*, and at times argued to correlate with telicity (see Chapters 6 and 7 for much discussion).
    e. Imperfective: a morphological term. Not perfective—that is, the bare (unmarked) stem in Slavic languages (primary imperfective); the imperfective-marked stem in Slavic languages (secondary imperfective), at times argued to correlate with atelicity, at other times argued to correlate with progressive (see Chapter 6 for discussion).
    f. Perfect: a morphosyntactic-semantic term, referring to the morphological realization of bound grammatical aspect. In English, marked with the morpheme -*en* (*eaten, danced*). Not implicated in aktionsart.
    g. Progressive: a morphosyntactic-semantic term, referring to [*be* V+*ing*] forms within the verbal domain in English. I will argue that it is not implicated in aktionsart and is an instance of outer (grammatical) aspect in the sense of Verkuyl (1972) (see Chapter 8, Section 8.2.4, for some discussion).

The systematic correlation between telicity/atelicity and unaccusative–unergative diagnostics has led Dowty (1991) to stating the following correlations (henceforth Dowty's correlations):

(10) *Dowty's correlations*
 Agentive, Atelic: definitely unergative
 Non-Agentive, Telic: definitely unaccusative

If indeed the distinction between unaccusative intransitive verbs and unergative intransitive verbs is not stable and fixed, and one and the same verb may appear in both classes, and if indeed Dowty's correlations are robust, then one is tempted to argue, as has Van Valin (1990), that the unaccusative–unergative distinction is altogether *not* a syntactic one, but rather, an aspectual–semantic one. It is not a property of a particular lexical entry, but rather, a property of the entire predicate, of which the meaning of the verb is just one part. An (intransitive) predicate may be either agentive–atelic or non-agentive–telic, and if properties such as auxiliary selection and *ne*-cliticization are dependent on aspectual distinctions, there remains no motivation for assuming that arguments of unaccusatives and unergatives merge in different syntactic positions, or are distinct syntactically at any level. Further, within such an approach, it seems, the need for a PP which defines a terminal point in (2)–(4) receives a natural account: the predicate, rather than the verb itself, is telic in the presence of such a PP and hence we expect 'unaccusative' diagnostics. In the absence of such a terminal point, atelicity results, and 'unergative' diagnostics are attested.

What is at stake here, note, is the relationship between syntactic structure and interpretation. Suppose Dowty is correct, and it is truly the case that the unaccusative–unergative distinction has systematic semantic content. Several options are open to us: we could argue that the unergative/unaccusative distinction has independent semantic and syntactic formal properties. In other words, that unaccusative verbs select an internal argument, and, quite independently, predicates headed by unaccusative verbs receive a telic interpretation. This is clearly the worst theory. To the extent that Dowty's correlations are true and universal, stating them in terms of independent properties of the syntax and the semantics of unaccusatives and unergatives makes them arbitrary and unexplained. If these properties are indeed entirely independent, why should telicity correlate systematically with an internal, rather than external argument?

On the other hand, it could be the case that the unaccusative–unergative distinction has primarily semantic properties, and that diagnostics erstwhile considered syntactic are, in fact, semantic in nature, in that they do not indicate, specifically, a different (underlying) position for the sole direct argument. If that is indeed the case, then all intransitives could project as in (11), making the need for movement to subject position, in the case of unaccusatives, unnecessary. From the perspective of the syntactic computation, note, abandoning such movement is actually economical. In turn, auxiliary selection, for example, could be accommodated by specifying that certain auxiliaries are sensitive to the relevant semantic distinction (e.g. via selection—it could be proposed, for instance, that *zijn* selects, or checks the properties of, a telic predicate). This is in essence the solution adopted by Van Valin (1990) (and see also Dowty 1979, where this position is explicitly defended).

(11) [$_S$ Kim ... [$_{VP}$ arrived/laughed]]

Crucially, the issue here is empirical. If, as Van Valin contends, the unaccusative–unergative syntactic diagnostics can be reanalaysed in terms of the compositional semantics of predicates, then the syntactic diagnostics of the unaccusative–unergative distinction should systematically correlate with the telic/atelic distinction. For instance, auxiliary selection should always be reducible to (a)telicity, *ne*-cliticization should only co-occur with telic predicates, impersonal passive should always co-occur with atelic predicates, the reflexive dative in Hebrew should always co-occur with atelicity, while possessor datives should only co-occur with telic predicates, etc. If, on the other hand, it turns out that some properties of the syntactic diagnostics of the unergative/unaccusative distinction cannot be reduced to the telic/atelic distinction, and that they require unaccusatives to have a syntactically projected internal argument, and unergatives to have a syntactically projected external argument, then it would follow that the distinction cannot be fully reducible to the compositional semantics of predicates, but rather, is syntactically reflected.

Finally, should it turn out that the unaccusative–unergative distinction is associated both with a semantic distinction and with a distinction of syntactic argument projection, a parsimonious theory would attempt to derive one of them from the other. There are two logical possibilities of course. One could attempt to derive the distinct syntax from the distinct semantics. As we will see, this is the route pursued by Levin and Rappaport Hovav (1989), and Levin and Rappaport Hovav (1992*a*, *b*). On the other hand, one may try to derive the distinct semantics from the distinct syntax. This will be the direction pursued in this study.

First, however, we must convince ourselves that the unaccusative–unergative distinction is indeed associated with a syntactic distinction that is not reducible to its semantic properties.

2.1.2 *Evidence for syntactic representation for variable-behaviour verbs*

An argument for syntactic representation of the unaccusative–unergative distinction, postulating an internal argument for the former but not for the latter, is presented by Levin and Rappaport Hovav (1989) based on the distribution of partitive *ne* cliticization in Italian. Note, as our starting point, that the distribution of *ne* (in intransitive) constitutes a subset of telic environments. Specifically, partitive *ne* cliticization is possible, in telic intransitives, from a post-verbal subject, but not from a pre-verbal subject, as illustrated by (12):

(12) a. Ne   arrivanno [molti ne].
of-them arrive   many

b. *[molti ne] *ne* arrivanno.

Following primarily Belletti and Rizzi (1981), Levin and Rappaport Hovav (1989) assume that the pre-verbal–post-verbal asymmetry here is reducible to proper government. While the post-verbal trace of *ne* is properly governed by the verb, this is not the case for the pre-verbal trace, leading to ungrammaticality. In turn, as is well known, post-verbal subjects of unergative verbs do not allow *ne* cliticization, as illustrated by (13), presumably because the post-verbal subject of unergatives is outside the VP, and is not governed by the verb:

(13) *ne   telephonano [molti ne]
of-them telephone   many

This explanation, Levin and Rappaport Hovav point out, is only available if the post-verbal [molti ne] occupies different structural positions in unergative and unaccusative constructions, thereby suggesting a syntactic distinction between the two, with an 'external' argument for unergatives, and a syntactic 'internal' argument for unaccusatives.

We note, as an aside, that to the extent that *ne*-cliticization is possible in atelic transitive structures, from the direct object, as (14) illustrates, a semantic explanation for the distribution of *ne*-cliticization would have to take into account at least some syntax, and could not be based purely on the semantics of (a)telicity.

(14) a. Kim *ne* ha spinti [molti ne] (per molte ore).
Kim *ne* has pushed many   (for many hours)

b. Kim *ne* ha guidate [molte ne] (per molte ore).
Kim *ne* has driven many   (for many hours)

The properties of *ne*-cliticization in transitives aside, however, the argument advanced in Levin and Rappaport Hovav (1989) is weakened by the fact that partitive *ne*-cliticization is only possible from (weak) indefinites, which are independently restricted pre-verbally in Italian. Further, as Van Valin (1990) points out, an explanation for the post-verbal restriction may be available in terms of the focus–topic distinction, with post-verbal position favoured independently of government. If the post-verbal restriction is otherwise explained, and given that *ne* is, to begin with, only possible, for intransitives, in telic contexts, then it may very well turn out (as conceded, in fact, in Levin and Rappaport Hovav 1992*b*) that there is no conclusive argument from *ne* cliticization for the syntactic projection of an internal argument in unaccusatives and its availability may receive an exclusively semantic explanation.[7]

Everaert (1992) gives another argument for the syntactic representation of the unaccusative–unergative distinction. He observes the following auxiliary selection in light-verb idiomatic constructions in Dutch:

(15) a. Het vliegtuig *is* geland.
       the plane   is landed

   b. De voorstelling *is* begonnen.
      the performance is begun

(16) a. Het vliegtuig *heeft* een landing gemaakt.
       the plane   has   a   landing made

   b. De voorstelling *heeft* een aanvang genomen.
      the performance has   a   beginning taken

For any aspectual calculus, Everaert notes, (15a) and (16a) on the one hand, and (15b) and (16b) on the other, are synonymous. Both are telic in the relevant sense, and the NPs 'landing' and 'beginning' are clearly not arguments, but rather part of a complex predicate. In fact, an aspectual calculus of the type proposed in Dowty (1979) and adopted by Van Valin (1990) would decompose a verb such as *geland* 'landed' into BECOME+CUL(mination), thereby making it particularly difficult to distinguish from *een landing gemaakt* 'make landing', with a virtually identical semantic representation. Yet, in (15a–b) the auxiliary *zijn* is selected, whereas in (16a–b) the auxiliary *hebben* is selected. It appears, then, that auxiliary selection here is sensitive not to telicity, or agentivity, but rather to the presence of a syntactic NP object, even devoid as it is of any actual argumenthood or semantic role that could serve to distinguish it from (15a–b). A purely semantic approach would be hard pressed to account for these facts without supplementing the semantic restriction on auxiliary selection with a syntactic insertion frame, barring *zijn* in the presence of an NP complement,

---

[7] And see Chapter 7 at n. 13, as well as Chapter 9, Section 9.3.2, for the suggestion that the *ne*-cliticization test, as such, is orthogonal to the unaccusative–unergative distinction.
 We note that auxiliary selection for intransitives, typically used in distinguishing unaccusatives from unergatives, is in actuality inconclusive under any account. It appears that the only unfailingly robust generalization concerning auxiliary selection within the event domain is that intransitive atelic (nonstative) predicates always select *avere*/*hebben*. However, adjectives, both unaccusative and unergative, select *essere*/*zijn*, as do reflexives, making the selection of *essere*/*zijn* uninformative with respect to determination of event type. For a compelling argument that reflexives are *not* unaccusatives (contra Marantz 1984 and much subsequent work), see Reinhart and Siloni (2003). See also n. 23 for some relevant comments.

regardless of its semantics. We note, however, that to the extent that a semantic account would have to be sensitive to syntactic transitivity anyway in order to account for *ne*-cliticization in atelic transitives, the argument advanced in Everaert may not be conclusive either. Rather, it appears, what is necessary is a syntactic test which is not attested in a subset of telic contexts, but rather, is clearly and demonstrably oblivious to (a)telicity.

Consider, in view of this, another argument for the syntactic projection of the unaccusative–unergative distinction, from the distribution of possessor datives in Hebrew. Borer and Grodzinsky (1986) argue that possessor datives in Hebrew exhibit, in essence, binding-like characteristics with respect to the determiner of the possessed DP.[8] Assuming the possessor dative to be in a position c-commanding all (traditional) VP-internal material (and not the 'external' argument), it is hardly surprising to find that it can exhibit possession relations with any complement DP, either a direct object or a DP-complement of a selected preposition, as illustrated by (17). It can further exhibit possession relations with DPs within PP adjuncts, as (18) illustrate, or subjects of small clauses. In fact, the only systematically excluded possession relation is with an 'external' argument, as illustrated by (17a) and (18b) (indices in curly brackets notate possible possession relations).[9]

---

[8] See Landau (1997) for an account of the distribution of possessor datives in terms of possessor raising. Note that as raising environments and binding environments are almost identical, and both share the exclusion of external arguments and the inclusion of c-commanded adjuncts or complement PPs, Landau's account makes the same predictions with respect to the matter at hand as does a binding account. Landau further notes that experiencers do not allow possessor datives, a fact which he reduces to the high projection site of experiencers, a result likewise compatible with a binding approach.

E. Doron (pers. comm.) notes that the restriction against possessor datives with external arguments disappears in cases of inalienable possession expressed with possessive datives, giving rise to the contrast in (i)–(ii):

(i) ha.šen   mitnadnedet li.
    the.tooth swings   to.me
    'My tooth is loose.'

(ii) *ha.ʿec   mitnadned li.
     the.tree swings   to.me
     'My tree swings.'

Inalienable possession examples are thus systematically avoided here and in all subsequent diagnostic uses of possessive datives. Given the purely diagnostic role of the possessive dative phenomena in this work, no attempt is made to account for the different behaviour of inalienable possession and other forms of possessive datives.

[9] In (17a–b) a coincidental possession of 'boys' or 'girl' by 'Rani' is possible, resulting in the interpretation 'Rani's son' and 'Rani's daughter', respectively. However, this co-reference between the external argument and the possessive dative cannot satisfy the condition on the occurrence of a possessor dative, as in such cases the fence or the piano as well must be possessed by Rani, resulting in the possibility of (17a–b) meaning 'Rani$_i$'s sons cut his$_i$ fence', 'Rani$_i$'s daughter played his$_i$ piano', but not 'Rani's sons cut the fence' or 'Rani's daughter played the piano'.

(17) a. ha₁.yeladim xat̲ku le-rani₍*₁,₂₎ 'et ha₂.gader?
the.boys cut to-Rani ACC the.fence
'*Rani's boys (=Rani's sons) cut the fence'
'The boys cut Rani's fence.'

b. ha.yalda₁ nigna le-rani₍*₁,₂₎ ba-psanter₂.
the.girl played to-Rani in-the.piano
'*Rani's girl (=Rani's daughter) played the piano.'
'The girl played Rani's piano.'

(18) a. ha₁.yeladim zarku (le-rina₍*₁,₂,₃,₄₎ 'et ha₂.kadur le-tox ha₃.gina
the.boys threw to-Rina ACC the.ball into the.garden

'al-yad ha₄.mitbax.
next-to the.kitchen

'*Rina's sons threw the ball into the garden (while) next to the kitchen.'
'The boys threw Rina's ball into the garden, (while) next to the kitchen.'
'The boys threw the ball into Rina's garden, (while) next to the kitchen.'
'The boys threw the ball into the garden, (while) next to Rina's kitchen.'

b. ha₁.xatulim yilelu le-rina₍*₁,₂,₃₎ mi-taxat la₃-xalon bi-zman
the.cats whined to-Rina under to.the.window during

ha₂.šena.
the.nap

'*Rina's cats whined under the window during naptime.'
'The cats whined under the window during Rina's nap.'
'The cats whined under Rina's window during naptime.'

Unlike *ne*-cliticization, then, possessor datives, in transitive or intransitive domains, are not restricted to a subset of telic contexts. In (17a), the possessor dative occurs as part of a transitive accomplishment, exhibiting a possession relation with the direct object. However, in (17b), an atelic structure with a complement PP, a possessor dative is possible with respect to the object of P, *psanter* 'piano'. This, note, is an environment which in Italian and Dutch would require the auxiliaries *avere* or *hebben*, respectively, and which would not allow *ne*-cliticization (for a post-verbal subject). Finally, in (18b), again an atelic structure, possession by a possessor dative is possible into an array of PP adjuncts. Here, again, Italian and Dutch would select unergative auxiliaries and *ne*-cliticization would be blocked (again, for post-verbal subjects).

Consider now the relationship between possessor datives and subjects of intransitive verbs. (18b) already illustrates that subjects of unergative intransitives (with activity/process interpretation) cannot be 'possessed' by dative possessors. However, this is not the case with subjects of unaccusative intransitives (with telic interpretation), where the relationship is possible with the subject post- or pre-verbal (see Borer and Grodzinsky 1986 for discussion of binding in the latter case):

(19) a. ha₂.mitriya nap̱la le-rani₍₂₎.
 the.umbrella fell to-Rani
 'Rani's umbrella fell.'

 b. nap̱la le-rani₍₂₎ ha₂.mitriya.
 fell to-Rani the.umbrella
 'Rani's umbrella fell.'

 c. ha₂.mitriya nap̱la le-rani₍₂,₃,₄₎ al ha₃.šḇil le-yad ha₄.mitbax.
 the.umbrella fell to-Rani on the path next-to the.kitchen
 'Rani's umbrella fell on the path, next to the kitchen.'
 'The umbrella fell on Rani's path, next to the kitchen.?'
 'The umbrella fell on the path, next to Rani's kitchen.'

As is evident from (17)–(19), a possessor dative can express a possession relation with an unaccusative subject, as well as with any DP in a complement position or within a PP adjunct. On the other hand, it cannot express a possession relation with an unergative or transitive subject. It is hard to see how this state of affairs can be reduced to an aspectual distinction, with or without syntactic transitivity taken into account, given the fact that possessor datives are clearly blind to aspectual distinctions in the domain of both transitives and intransitives. Thus (17b) and (18) clearly involve an activity, while (17a) and (18a) are telic, but the range of possible possessor–dative relationships is the same, without any effect on the resulting event interpretation. The configuration that allows possession by the possessor dative is thus purely structural, arguing for a distinct syntactic positioning of the unaccusative subject and the unergative subject. While the former must be internal to the c-command domain of the possessor dative, on a par with complements and PP adjuncts, the latter must be external to that c-command domain, on a par with subjects of transitive sentences. It is thus evident that at some level of representation the subject of (7a), involving an accomplishment, is projected lower than the subject of (7b), involving an activity, resulting in the licensing of a possessor dative in the former but not in the latter.[10]

---

[10] Sentence (7b), recall, has a reflexive dative. As already noted in n. 5, the reflexive dative (in contrast with the possessor dative) does interact with event structure, and is, in effect, compatible only with atelic predicates (whether stative or eventive). It could not, however, be equated with the English progressive (presumably, a case of outer aspect in the sense of Verkuyl 1972 and subsequent literature), as I will show

It therefore follows that the unaccusative–unergative distinction is hierarchically represented in the syntax, in that the former involves an argument occupying the same syntactic position as a direct object, while the latter involves an argument occupying the same syntactic position as a subject of a transitive. The assumption that all diagnostics of the unaccusative–unergative distinction can be reduced to semantic properties of predicates, or that they can be stated on structures in which the subjects of unaccusatives and unergatives occupy the same position, must then be rejected. Rather, we must consider the other logical parsimonious options—either deriving the distinct syntax of the arguments from the semantically distinct event interpretations, or alternatively, deriving the semantically distinct event interpretations from the distinct syntax of the arguments.[11]

Levin and Rappaport Hovav (1992b), who address this issue within a fundamentally endo-skeletal approach, write, in comparing their own approach to a constructionist one:[12]

> Verbs that show variable behaviour of this kind are always associated with more than one meaning; each meaning turns out to be correlated with the predicted syntactic properties, including membership in the unaccusative or unergative class. The question, however, is whether the change in meaning displayed by a particular variable-behaviour verb is to be attributed to its appearance in a particular construction, as the constructional approach would claim, or to the existence of some lexical rule which gives rise to multiple semantic classifications of verbs, which then license the appearance of these verbs in more than one construction, as the lexical approach would have to claim. [...] The constructional approach predicts that ... verbs are free to appear in a range of constructions (and hence meanings) constrained only by the compatibility of the 'core' meaning of the verb with the semantics of the construction. [...] The lexical approach, in contrast, does not make this prediction ... [in turn there is a] need for lexical rules which specify multiple class membership. In addition, the multiple classification of verbs is manifested in a variety of constructions, suggesting that verbs are classified once and for all for class membership.   (Levin and Rappaport Hovav 1992b: 12, 13)

---

directly in Chapter 8, Section 8.2.3. Most specifically, unlike the English progressive, which is by and large oblivious to its surroundings (unergative, unaccusative, some statives, passive), reflexive datives cannot co-occur with passives and unaccusatives.

[11] In both Dowty (1991) and Krifka (1989, 1992, 1998), the semantic similarities between objects of telic transitives and subjects of telic intransitives are captured by appealing to the notion theme, presumably projected either as a direct object or as a subject of intransitives. The distribution of possessor dative in Hebrew is clearly a problem for these accounts, and to any account that seeks to de-link the properties of the direct argument in telic constructions from a fixed (internal) syntactic position.

To the extent that it can be demonstrated that subjects of telic unaccusatives and objects of telic transitives *are* in the same position, on the other hand, this is fully compatible with the claim which we will otherwise advance, according to which the relevant property of the so-called quantized (or quantity) argument is not its thematic role, but its syntactic position.

[12] In subsequent work, Rappaport Hovav and Levin refer to the 'lexical' approach as the projectionist approach (1998).

Levin and Rappaport Hovav, in a manner consistent with their theoretical approach, then proceed to suggest multiple (but related) entries for variable-behaviour verbs. Within an endo-skeletal approach, their type of solution is indeed the only available one. If the syntax of argument structure projects deterministically from specifications associated with lexical entries, different argument structure projections must reflect different lexical specifications, and hence, distinct, albeit related, entries. However, the desirability of postulating two distinct lexical entries for variable-behaviour verbs, with the sole lexical-semantic distinction involving telicity, is questionable, especially if we concur with Mittwoch (1991) that all 'accomplishment verbs' in English are in actuality ambiguous between an accomplishment reading and an activity reading.[13] Quite plainly, if the value ±telic is allowed to be associated with lexical entries as such, then whenever a verb, intransitive or transitive, may occur in both a telic and an atelic context, it would have to have two lexical entries. Not only would such an account require numerous intransitive and transitive verbs to have a double entry, it would also require two lexical entries for well-known pairs such as those in (20)–(21).

(20) a. I sprayed the wall with the paint (in two hours).
     b. I sprayed the paint on the wall (in two hours).

(21) a. I ate the cake (in ten minutes).
     b. I ate at the cake (*in ten minutes).

As is well known, in (20a) an accomplishment interpretation is associated with *spray the wall* (and *spray with the paint* remains an atelic process), whereas the accomplishment interpretation is associated with *spray the paint* in (20b) (and *spray on the wall* remains an atelic process). Example (21a) is largely interpreted as an accomplishment, while (21b) may only be interpreted as an activity. If two distinct lexical entries are associated with Hebrew 'wilt', one telic (and unaccusative) and the other atelic (and unergative), then two distinct entries

---

[13] For these reasons and some others, Levin and Rappaport Hovav (1995) abandon the claim that variable-behaviour verbs represent aspectual distinctions, and argue instead that variable-behaviour verbs in the intended sense are a class of intransitives derived through (lexical) detransitivization (following suggestions in Chierchia 1989 and Reinhart 1991). Depending on the presence or absence of an external causer interpretation, an unergative or an unaccusative entry results. This latter solution, in turn, leaves open the question of whether or not Dowty's correlations are correct or not. If indeed they are, then within the Levin and Rappaport Hovav system, the correlation between telicity and the presence of an external cause must be otherwise explained. In Section 2.2 as well as in Chapters 3, 4, and 6, I return to additional detailed justification of the event-structure, aktionsart, approach to argument structure, assuming, for the time being, the correctness of Dowty's correlations. For a detailed criticism of the 'external causer' account see Reinhart (2000), who assumes that all unaccusatives, not just those which show variable behaviour, are derived from transitives through existential binding of the external argument, and that all have an 'unergative' correlate which is in actuality a lexical reflexive involving binding of the internal argument. For an additional brief comment, see n. 23.

must be likewise associated with *spray*, one being telic with respect to a theme, but atelic with respect to a location, and the other telic with respect to a location and atelic with respect to a theme (with an additional entry, note, to mark the fact that (20a–b) need not be telic at all). Likewise, two entries for *eat*, one associated with an atelic process (and selecting an optional PP) and one with an accomplishment (and selecting an obligatory direct object).

An even trickier complication is presented by the contrast between (22a) and (22b):

(22) a. Kim built the houses (in three months).
     b. Kim built houses (*in three months).

As is well known, (22a), with a definite object, may have a single event, accomplishment reading. (22b), with a bare-plural object, can only be interpreted as an activity under a single event reading. (Alternatively, it can be interpreted iteratively, a reading we largely set aside for the remainder of this work.) If (a)telicity distinctions trigger distinct lexicalizations, then it follows that *build* would have to have two distinct lexical entries: an atelic process entry which only allows determinerless NPs as internal direct arguments, and an accomplishment reading, which bars determinerless NPs as internal direct arguments. To quote Dowty (1991) on the undesirability of moves of this nature, specifically for the unaccusative–unergative distinction as proposed by Levin and Rappaport Hovav (1992*a*, *b*):

Hypothesizing that a large semantically coherent group of verbs have duplicate categorization in unaccusative and unergative syntactic classes (and with corresponding different semantics in the two frames) would be missing the point, I argue ... I would argue that the correct analysis is ... semantic ... instead of or in addition to the syntactic type. (Dowty 1991: 608).

We note, following Dowty, that postulating two distinct entries, mediated or not through lexical rules, in order to capture the meaning differences in (20)–(22), appears equally undesirable.

The debate here, focusing as it does on intransitive verbs, concerns two issues which are at least partially independent of each other. One is whether the sole argument of intransitive verbs may project in different positions, correlating with interpretational differences. The second is whether argument structure projects deterministically from lexical entries or not. Levin and Rappaport Hovav (1992*a*, *b*, as well as 1995) (and see also Reinhart 1991, 1996, 2000) answer both questions in the positive: the projection of arguments is determined by lexical information, and the sole argument of intransitives does project in different positions depending on lexically specified or lexically derived factors (such as role features and lexical mapping operations, as in Reinhart's system, aspectual value, as in Levin and Rappaport Hovav 1992a, b, or a variety of linking rules connecting roles with positions, as in Levin and Rappaport Hovav 1995). The Van Valin–Dowty approach, on the other hand, gives a negative answer to both. While syntactic structures associated with different aktionsart values may vary (e.g. [$_{VP}$ run PP$_{dir}$] is telic while [$_{VP}$ run] is atelic), projection of the argument of intransitives does not vary—it always projects as (the external) subject. Furthermore, argument structure does not project deterministically from lexical entries depending on the lexico-semantic properties of a specific entry or the role assignment associated with it. The double positive and double negative responses, however, are not the only logical possibilities. If one subscribes to the view that argument structure projects deterministically from lexical entries, it indeed must follow that different syntactic configurations which are associated with a single verb must reflect the existence of multiple (possibly related) lexical entries. However, one could subscribe to the view that the sole argument of intransitives projects in different positions as correlating with interpretational factors, while still maintaining that arguments do not project deterministically from lexical entries. From the perspective of a constructionist or XS-approach, if distinct syntactic structures are indeed associated with different aktionsart values, and if aktionsart values are computed on the basis of the syntactic structure rather than the lexical entries of the verbs involved, there is no reason in principle to exclude the possibility that these different syntactic structures include not only the presence of a directional PP, but also a distinct syntactic position for the sole argument of intransitives.

We have seen that there are rather compelling empirical reasons to assume that the syntactic positions of unaccusative and unergative arguments are distinct. We must then reject this aspect of the Van Valin–Dowty approach. If we further assume that these syntactic distinctions correlate with semantic ones, we are left with two logical choices:

(23) a. If argument structure projects from the lexicon, the distinct syntax of unaccusatives and unergatives means that there are two entries for variable-behaviour verbs, together with lexical mapping rules which modify argument structure configurations.
      b. If we wish to reject the systematic existence of two distinct entries for variable-behaviour verbs, then it follows that at least the syntax of variable-behaviour verbs, and by extension, the syntax of argument structure, cannot project from the lexicon.

We saw that the first option is the one pursued by Levin and Rappaport Hovav, and by Reinhart (1996, 2000). In this work, however, I will take seriously the objections raised by Dowty (1991), and assume that (23b) is the correct option. Variable-behaviour verbs in all their manifestations are a single item. The structure within which they are embedded and the interpretation of that structure are not derived from properties of the lexicon, but rather are in line with general properties of functional structure and its mapping onto the interpretational component. Aspectuality, in the sense of Dowty's correlations, is not a property of verbs, or any argument takers, but rather of specific, universal, syntactic structures. In turn, the particular interpretation of arguments as, say, 'agentive' or 'non-agentive' will become an entailment from the aktionsart of the entire event. Very schematically, because an event such as a window's breaking is telic, the argument in *the window broke* is 'non-agentive', and likewise, because an event such as a *laughing* is atelic, the argument in *Kim laughed* is 'agentive'. From this perspective, all direct arguments bear a relationship with the event, rather than the verb, and the verb itself is a modifier of that event, rather than a determinant of its interpretation.[14]

The reader may object now that another possibility must be considered, according to which the syntax of arguments does project from the lexicon, but, in accordance with Baker 1985 and 1988, and adopting the assumption that there are no grammatical function changing rules, variable-behaviour verbs project a specific syntax (say that of unaccusatives), which in turn is syntactically modified to give rise to the syntax of the alternative frame. We return to this possibility and to a review of other current approaches to argument structure projection in Section 2.3, where we argue that the behaviour of intransitives is incompatible with any version of UTAH. Before we do so, however, we turn to another important issue—a prima facie justification of the use of aktionsart as the building block for the syntax of arguments.

---

[14] Although clearly some aspects of the event, as a whole, do not figure in the determination of argument interpretation or placement. Thus, for instance, a negated accomplishment such as *Kim didn't build a house (in two months)* still has the syntax of an accomplishment, and an 'agentive' subject of such a negated accomplishment remains interpreted as an 'agent', although, clearly, nothing has been accomplished, and the 'agent' has not exercised its 'agenthood' in any relevant sense (and compare with the ungrammaticality of **Kim didn't build houses in two months*). A clear illustration of this fact is the oddity associated with inanimate 'agents' in cases such as *the wind tried to break the window*, which does not disappear under negation, with *the wind didn't try to break the window* equally odd. Similar generalizations hold for the English progressive, which negates culmination when associated with telic predicates, but which does not appear to change the restrictions on argument structure associated with these predicates. And most striking of all, note that *for x-time*, usually taken to be a test for atelicity, when adjoined to an atelic predicate turns it into a telic, bound predicate (e.g. it is *quantized* in the sense of Krifka 1989, 1992). This distinction, in essence, is in line with the distinction postulated by Verkuyl (1972) between inner aspect and outer aspect. In what follows I will assume that both negation and the English progressive are instantiations of outer aspect, as are time duration adverbs such as *for-x-time*, all functioning as operators on existing event structure configurations, rather than as determinants of them. For some additional comments on the progressive as outer aspect, see Chapter 8, Section 8.2.4.

2.2 But Why Aktionsart?

Van Valin's account, as well as Dowty's correlations, range over the domain of aktionsart, claiming it to be the relevant domain for the characterization of event structure and argument structure. A particularly strong claim in this respect has been made by Tenny (1987, 1992, and subsequent work), who explicitly proposes to replace the existing inventory of thematic roles, based on characterizing the mode of interaction of an argument with an event, with aspectual roles, linked to the way in which particular arguments interact with the determination of aktionsart. However, the relevance of aktionsart in determining argument structure in general, and in determining the unaccusative–unergative distinction in particular, must be independently justified.

The justification, note, must address two issues. First, we must argue that aktionsart is syntactically represented, and is not just an interpretational effect. Secondly, we must show that to the extent that aktionsart is syntactically represented, its syntactic structure is implicated in the interpretation of arguments.

That aktionsart and argument structure are indeed related has been often pointed out, and there is little doubt that characteristics of the object contribute to determining event type (cf. Verkuyl 1972 and subsequent work; Dowty 1979, 1991; Tenny 1987, 1994; Krifka 1992, 1998, among many others). Rosen (1999), in reviewing previous results on the interaction between the direct object and the overall event type, cites the following:

(24) a. Addition of direct object gives rise to telicity:
  i. Bill ran for five minutes/*in five minutes.
  ii. Bill ran the mile *for five minutes/in five minutes.[15]
 b. Cognate objects give rise to telicity:
  i. Terry sang for an hour/*in an hour.
  ii. Terry sang a ballad ?for an hour/in an hour.
 c. X's *way* constructions give rise to telicity:
  i. Marcia sang for an hour/*in an hour.
  ii. Marcia sang her way to the Met in 10 years/*for ten years.
 d. Fake reflexives give rise to telicity:
  i. Terry swam for an hour/*in an hour.
  ii. Terry swam herself to sleep in an hour/*for an hour.

---

[15] Judgements from Rosen (1999). Native speakers report that (24a) is possible with an atelic construal in certain contexts, e.g. if 'the mile' is understood as a particular stretch, rather than defining the length of the running.

e. The conative alternation (cf. (21)) gives rise to atelicity:
   i. I ate the cake for ten minutes/in ten minutes.
   ii. I ate at the cake for ten minutes/*in ten minutes.
f. Antipassive gives rise to atelicity:
   i. Junna-p Anna kunip-p-a-a.
   Junna-ERG$_2$ Anna.ABS$_1$ kiss-IND-(TRANS)-3SG$_2$/3SG$_1$
   'Junna kissed Anna.'
   ii. Junna (Anna-mik) kunis-si-vu-q.
   Junna.ABS$_2$ (Anna-INTRANS) kiss-APASS-(intrans)-3SG.A$_2$
   'Junna kisses/is kissing Anna.'
   (Inuit; Bittner and Hale 1996)
g. The addition of an (ECM) object, in resultative constructions, triggers telicity:
   i. Terry ran for an hour/*in an hour.
   ii. Terry ran us ragged in an hour/*for an hour.
h. Verb particles with 'objects' trigger telicity:
   i. Terry thought for an hour/*in an hour.
   ii. Terry thought an answer up in an hour/*for an hour.

Clearly, as has been often observed, the examples in (24a–h) demonstrate that whether or not an object is present largely affects the resulting aktionsart. As Rosen further points out, internal properties of the object DP are implicated as well. Thus mass nouns and bare plurals block a telic interpretation (as already illustrated by (22)), and partitive vs. accusative case marking on the object in Finnish reflects the overall (a)telicity of the resulting predicate (see Chapter 4 for extensive discussion):

(25) a. Anne rakensi taloa.
    Anne built house-PRT
    'Anne was building a/the house.'
  b. Anne rakensi talon.
    Anne built house-ACC
    'Anne built a/the house.'

There is no doubt, then, that aktionsart is syntactically represented, and shows sensitivity to syntactic structure. There is further no doubt that there is massive interaction between aktionsart, and more specifically telicity, and the existence and the structure of the direct 'internal' argument. We note in this context that the relevant relation cannot be captured in terms of thematic relations between the verb and its arguments, as telicity is induced in at least (24d) and (24g) (and possibly in other cases as well) by a direct argument which cannot be viewed as a thematic object of the verb.

The question, then, is not whether aktionsart is syntactically represented, and whether or not it shows sensitivity to the placement of arguments. Rather, we must ask whether the relevant semantic roles associated with arguments are indeed exclusively those that are implicated in event structure, or, alternatively, whether the aktionsart system exists alongside a more traditional thematic system. This question, note, is actually independent of the question posed in Section 2.1, about the source of event structure and aktionsart roles. It is thus possible for roles to be event-oriented, but nevertheless still projected from lexical entries which are in turn provided with aktionsart value, and indeed, systems which project event arguments partially or wholly from lexical entries have been proposed (e.g. by Tenny 1987, 1994; van Hout 1992, 1996; van Voorst 1993). It has been pointed out frequently, however, that it is precisely within the domain of aktionsart and event structure that one finds the greatest variability between verbal insertion frames (in the sense of variable behaviour already discussed). It is thus not particularly surprising that it is precisely within approaches to argument structure that subscribe to event roles, rather than thematic roles, that syntactic approaches to argument projection are most influential.

In turn, as syntactic structure for aktionsart and some statement of its interaction with, at least, some arguments is clearly necessary, the null hypothesis would be that this is the only structure that is relevant for the projection and the interpretation of arguments. Suppose, then, that we adopt the essence of the proposal made by Tenny (1987 1994), according to which the syntactically relevant argumental roles are those that are aspectually relevant. We will, however, depart from Tenny's system in assuming that these argumental roles do not emerge as a result of mapping from lexical entries to specific syntactic positions with specific properties, but rather, that they are 'created', so to speak, in the relevant positions. From this perspective, note, the role that would be assigned to *the shoes* in *Jenny polished (up) her shoes (in five minutes)* is one and the same as the role that would be assigned to *shoes* in *Jenny ran her shoes rugged (in five minutes)*, both contributing to the emergence of telicity in the same sense and receiving their interpretation in the same syntactic position. We note as an aside that to the extent that this execution is valid, it is entirely incompatible with Exceptional Case Marking accounts for constructions such as those in (24d) and (24g) (i.e. accounts that postulate exceptional government across a phrasal boundary for such structures), but is fully compatible with any account which posits a uniform position for all accusative-marked DPs.[16] In the remainder

---

[16] In turn, to the extent that ECM subjects also participate in an additional event, if there is one, which

of this volume I will develop a system which can account for role assignment to DPs within such an aspectual structure. I will argue that only direct arguments interact with event structure. Although event structure can be syntactically affected by constituents other than direct arguments, these constituents will not be DPs. The privileged relationship of direct arguments with event structure will follow directly from their positioning as specifiers of functional nodes that are dedicated to the computation of event structure. Indirect arguments, in turn, are interpreted through the mediation of prepositions, and are aspectually inert.[17] Before I turn to the development of such a system, however, a number of possible objections must be contended with.[18]

In objecting to the linkage of argument roles and event structure, and in reference specifically to Dowty's correlations, Reinhart (1991, 1996, 2000) challenges the claim that unaccusative verbs are always telic. Specifically, Reinhart (1996) points to the meaning contrast between (26)–(27), on the one hand, and (28), on the other, citing a test from Kamp (1979) and Partee (1984). The test appealed to involves the interpretation of coordinated verbs. Two telic verbs, when coordinated, give rise to a sequential interpretation. For this reason, the truth conditions of (26a) and (26b) are quite distinct, as are the truth conditions of (27a) and (27b). On the other hand, the coordination of atelic verbs does allow a sim-

---

is embedded under the relevant telic event, such a relationship could be encoded via raising, control, or any of the other usual methods. For some discussion of resultative constructions, see Chapter 8, Section 8.1.2.

[17] We note as an aside that insofar as indirect arguments are not interpreted through the event structure, it is at least possible, in principle, that some (functional) structure which is not part of the event computation system is responsible for their interpretation, beyond the specific proposals made in this work. We leave this matter aside, however, noting that if indeed this is the case, it would suggest the existence of two distinct syntactic representations, utilizing distinct primitives and category types, and generating two distinct outputs which then need to be integrated, a possibility which is quite intriguing and quite possibly on the right track.

[18] The brief discussion in the text is by no means an attempt to review all syntactic approaches to the projection of arguments, or to aspectual distinctions. Van Hout (1992) independently proposes a 'syntactic' account rather akin to that presented in Borer (1994) and motivated largely by similar considerations. Aspects of her work are addressed in subsequent chapters. Travis (1994, 1997, 2000), McClure (1995), Ramchand (1997), Davis and Demirdash (1995, 2000), Schmitt (1996), and Ritter and Rosen (1998, 2000), who all assume a syntactic approach to aktionsart, nevertheless adopt mixed systems, where traditional roles (thematic or others) assigned lexically co-exist alongside aspectual roles, at times partially listed and checked, so to speak, against particular syntactic configurations, and at times assigned by the structure. Finally, we acknowledge here the seminal work of Hale and Keyser (1993). Although their system is fundamentally lexical in assuming that the relevant architecture characterizes argument structure internal to specific entries, they nevertheless postulate principles of argument interpretation which are architectural, and not head-based, and are independent of any properties of the verb itself. In that it derives the interpretation of arguments from structure, and not the other way around, their work continues to be extremely influential within the domain of syntactic approaches to event structure and argument structure. For work that directly continues the Hale and Keyser tradition, see Erteschik-Shir and Rapoport (1995, 2001). The reader is referred to Rosen (1999) for an excellent review of syntactic approaches to events.

ultaneous interpretation, hence the synonymous readings of (28a) and (28b) (although a sequential reading is also possible):

(26) a. The vase broke and fell.
　　 b. The vase fell and broke.

(27) a. The apple dropped and reddened.
　　 b. The apple reddened and dropped.

(28) a. Kim ran and sang.
　　 b. Kim sang and ran.

　Now, Reinhart suggests, consider the unaccusative verbs *twist* and *spin*. By traditional tests, they are indeed unaccusative: they are related to a transitive entry with a possible inanimate causer, they (could) express a change of state, they allow resultative constructions, etc. If indeed unaccusative verbs are telic, we expect the truth conditions for (29a) and (29b) to differ. However, this is not the case. *Spin* and *twist* certainly allow a simultaneous reading, and as such (29a) and (29b) can be interpreted as truth-conditionally equivalent:

(29) a. The yarn twisted and spinned.
　　 b. The yarn spinned and twisted.　(Reinhart 1996)

　It follows, Reinhart concludes, that unaccusativity and telicity simply do not go hand in hand, and hence that Dowty's correlations are wrong.

　Some aspects of Reinhart's argument are independently problematic, as it turns out. Others, we will show, are orthogonal to the claims made here. Note first that the coordinated events in (26) and (27) are not just interpreted as sequential, but as having a causal relation, the first having caused the second. The truth conditions of (26a), (27a) and (26b), (27b) do not just differ in terms of which event took place first, but also in terms of which event caused the other. Suppose we consider, then, two verbs that do not easily permit such a causal connection. Specifically, suppose we take the verb *redden*, classified by Reinhart as telic due to the contrast in (27a–b), and coordinate it with a semantically equivalent verb such as *yellow*. In an utterance such as (30), neither *reddening* nor *yellowing* caused the other, and the simultaneous *reddening* and *yellowing* of a ripening fruit (at its opposing extremities, say) is certainly plausible. The contrasts in (26a–b) and (27a–b) are not replicated with (30a–b). Although a sequential reading is available, so is a simultaneous one, and the truth conditions of (30a) and (30b) could be identical:

(30) a. The apple yellowed and reddened.
　　 b. The apple reddened and yellowed.

One could conclude, based on the truth conditional equivalence of (30a–b), that the telicity test used by Reinhart is simply not a valid one. However, considered from a slightly different perspective, it turns out that the coordination test for telicity *is* a valid one. While (30a–b) can be truth-conditionally equivalent, it is also the case that on this simultaneous reading, *yellow* and *redden* are interpreted as activities, and not as accomplishments (or achievements). Specifically, note that a simultaneous reading of (30a–b) means that the apple underwent some yellowing and reddening, but not that the apple simultaneously became both yellow and red. Further, when an activity reading is truly unavailable (e.g. in some achievements), a sequential reading is forced, regardless of causality, as (31) illustrates:

(31) a. The guest understood the solution and left.
  b. The guest left and understood the solution.

On the other hand, if the tests are valid, then it appears that neither *yellow* nor *redden* are unambiguously telic or atelic, but rather, they are variable-behaviour verbs in the sense discussed already. This, of course, is true of *twist* and *spin* as well; both have a telic and a non-telic interpretation. What now of verbs such as *drop* and *burn*, which seem to imply an end point rather strongly? Well, it turns out that if a sufficiently plausible context is conjured, *burn* and *drop*, and even *fall* and *break apart*, can be coordinated with a simultaneous interpretation and atelic process reading resulting:

(32) a. We watched [the asteroid drop/fall (through the atmosphere) and burn/break apart for several minutes].
  b. We watched [the asteroid burn/break apart and drop/fall (through the atmosphere) for several minutes].
  (cf. We watched [the guest understand the problem and leave (*for several minutes)] vs. we watched [the guest leave and understand the problem (*for several minutes)] with a sequential interpretation only)

If we suppose the asteroid in question to have been ejected out of the atmosphere at some point subsequent to the event in (32) (some mass having been lost, naturally), thereby continuing its free fall through space indefinitely, then the utterances in (32) are well-formed, without a culmination, insofar as the asteroid neither fell apart completely, nor did it burn up completely. What can we conclude from this? Simultaneity does appear to correlate with an atelic process interpretation (although lack of simultaneity clearly does not necessarily correlate with a telic reading), and telicity does appear to correlate with a sequential reading. However, the classifications that emerge here for most verbs are rather vague. It seems that too many verbs typically considered telic can be construed as simultaneous with another telic verb, with a resulting atelic process interpretation, confirming Mittwoch's (1991) claim that all accomplishment verbs in English can have an atelic process interpretation.

But this state of affairs is hardly a problem for the system proposed here if telicity, or lack thereof, is not a property of verbs, but rather a property of syntactic structures. The source of atelicity in (30a–b) is not the verbs *yellow* and *redden*, but rather the syntactic structure within which they are embedded. Specifically, the claim put forth here is that the sole direct argument of (intransitive) clauses with an activity interpretation will display behaviours associated with external arguments, while the sole direct argument of (intransitive) clauses with an accomplishment/achievement interpretation will display syntactic behaviours associated with internal arguments. It therefore follows that when a verb such as (intransitive) *redden* is coordinated with another verb and a simultaneous reading emerges, the syntactic behaviour will be that of unergatives. On the other hand, when *redden* is coordinated with another verb and a sequential reading emerges, the syntactic behaviour could be that of unaccusatives.[19]

In turn, we predict that if we force a predicate to be telic, a sequential reading will emerge, but not so if we force it to be atelic. Using the distribution of datives in Hebrew, we can see that this prediction is borne out. Specifically, recall that possessor datives require the possessed to be in the (traditional) VP, and that reflexive datives require an external argument. Suppose, now, that we coordinate two intransitive variable-behaviour verbs, in our intended sense, in the context of a possessor dative. The only grammatical reading requires an internal argument, forcing an unaccusative structure, and hence by assumption telicity as well. We therefore predict that a simultaneous reading would disappear in the context of possessor datives. The converse should hold in the presence of a reflexive dative, where the obligatoriness of an external argument would force an atelic process reading. Here, simultaneity is expected to be possible. The facts in (33)–(35) confirm these predictions.

(33)   ha.mete'or nisra<u>p</u> ve-napal/napa<u>l</u> ve-nisra<u>p</u>.   (Ambiguous)
        the.meteor burned and fell/fell   and burned
        'The meteor burned and fell/fell and burned.'

(34) a. ha.mete'or napa<u>l</u> le-ran ve-nisra<u>p</u>.
          the.meteor fell   to-Ran and-burned

---

[19] There is no argument here against endo-skeletal approaches to this issue, and more specifically, there is no argument here against the approach proposed in Levin and Rappaport Hovav (1992a, b) to which Reinhart (1996) specifically objects. As the verbs used by Reinhart are all variable-behaviour verbs, an endo-skeletal account postulating two entries, one telic/unaccusative and the other atelic/unergative, could handle the facts just as well.

b. ha.mete'or napal ve-nisrap le-ran.
the.meteor fell and-burned to-Ran
'Ran's meteor fell and (then) burned.'
(e.g. in a physics class, with students writing programs simulating meteoric trajectories)

(35) a. ha.mete'or$_i$ nisrap ve-napallo$_i$.
the.meteor burned and-fell to.it

b. ha.mete'or$_i$ napal lo$_i$ ve-nisrap.
the.meteor burned to.it and-fell
'The fell and burned.' (simultaneity is possible but not forced)

Reinhart's facts, then, prove wrong the claim that verbs such as *spin*, or for that matter, *burn* and *redden*, are telic, but are entirely neutral concerning the claim that telic events are associated with unaccusative syntax, while atelic events are associated with unergative syntax. The facts in (33)–(35), while still compatible with an endo-skeletal approach, actually support Dowty's correlations, and any account that correlates (a)telicity with the projection of arguments.[20]

Despite the massive polysemy within the domain of intransitive verbs, as is well known, not all intransitive verbs are possible as both unaccusatives and unergatives. Two notable exceptions are agentive verbs of manner of motion (in the sense of Levin 1993) when they occur without a terminal complement, and achievement verbs, in the sense of Vendler (1967), indicating, it is sometimes proposed, an instantaneous culminating change. The failure of such polysemy exactly in these cases, I will argue, is not accidental. In the former, it follows from the fact that agentive manner of motion verbs are originator modifiers, in a sense to be made more precise in Chapter 8, Section 8.3. In the latter, I will suggest, the verbs in question are idioms, in the technical sense discussed in Chapter 1, Section 1.4, i.e. incorporating a functional range assigner which forces the projection of a particular structure (i.e. the equivalent, within the

---

[20] To the extent that verbs such as *nisrap* 'burn' or *napal* 'fall' behave as unaccusatives in (34), but as unergatives in (35), Levin and Rappaport Hovav (1995) would have to argue that in the first occurrence, an external cause is implied, but not so in the second occurrence. No such interpretational differences are in evidence, however, casting serious doubt on their classification. For Reinhart (2000), on the other hand, the 'unergative' variants of *nisrap* 'burn' and *napal* 'fall' would involve a reflexive interpretation, i.e. the meteor burned itself and caused itself to fall. We note that at least under the most common interpretation of the term reflexive as applied to intransitives (e.g. in *Mary washed*, or *Kim rolled down the hill*), no reflexive interpretation seems to be implicated here. We believe that both distinctions involve over-determination, representations too fine-grained, usurping roles that in actuality belong with world knowledge. The relevant contrast, I will suggest, is that which holds between notions such as originator (of a non-stative event) and subject-of-quantity on the one hand, and other possibly finer conceptual distinctions (e.g. those which distinguish *eat* from *drink*) but which have no grammatical correlates (and see Chapter 1, Section 1.1, for discussion).

verbal domain, of *trousers*). I return to the discussion of achievements and their interpretation in Chapter 10, Sections 10.2–3.

2.3 UTAH?

It is worthwhile starting this section by delineating the ways in which the approach to be proposed here is distinct from, and akin to, some of the dominant approaches to argument structure, taking as our starting point the Universal Theta-Assignment Hypothesis (UTAH), proposed by Baker (1988).

Quite contrary to much work that is informed by endo-skeletal considerations, the system proposed by Baker bars modifications of lexical entries so as to give rise to a different argument structure configuration, and thus a particular lexical entry (an 'item') must always project in the same way, giving rise to a unique representation. In turn, all appearance of argument structure modification is mediated through the existence of syntactic structures (often headed by syntactically projected morphology), or through incorporation. Clearly, to the extent that the system presented here derives argument structure variations associated with the same verbal listeme syntactically, rather than lexically, it is very much a continuation of Baker's research agenda. We further share with the UTAH agenda the assumption that particular syntactic positions are inherently linked with particular argumental interpretations.

On the other hand, however, UTAH is a fundamentally endo-skeletal approach, and argument structure is very much viewed as a property of lexical items, which in turn determines D-structure or some other fragment of the representation. Within that system, then, there are lexical entries with a given configuration of semantic roles, together with fixed, possibly universal linking conventions. Once projected, the 'fixed' structure may be embedded within an architecture that would add, appear to eliminate, or appear to modify the assignment site of a role. Crucially, role addition is the result of adding an argument taker (with no change to the argument structure of the item itself), and role elimination is only apparent, emerging actually from incorporation, role-assignment to an affix, existential binding of an argument, etc. UTAH is fundamentally committed to viewing the constant relations between the structure and the interpretation of arguments as mediated through the head selecting those arguments. Hence, relations between items must stay fixed, which means that if a verb stem assigns a theme role in a particular position, the verb stem-theme relation will be realized in that same position throughout the derivation. The system proposed here, on the other hand, does not require mediation by a lexical item to fix the interpretation of a particular role (nor does it use notions such as theme and patient). For this reason, we may keep fixed the relationship between structure and argumental interpretation, but allow different instantiations of a particular stem to be associated with different argument structure interpretations. As an illustration, for proponents of UTAH, all instantiations of *drop* must have the same syntactico-thematic configuration. Consider, in this view, some of the possible instantiations of *drop* in (36):[21]

(36) drop.TRANS; drop.UNACC; drop.UNERG; [$_A$ dropped]; [$_A$ droppable]; [$_N$ drop]

The verb stem *drop* must be assumed, within a UTAH approach, to be associated with the same thematic and syntactic configuration in all these instantiations. Further, as thematic roles cannot be eliminated, by hypothesis, it follows that all verbs which alternate between transitive and intransitive variants must start as intransitive, and have the external argument added through a separate, abstract, CAUSE-type head, which may or may not be realized morpho-phonologically. In turn, because *drop*.INTRANS is (typically assumed to be) an unaccusative verb, its argument (presumably a *theme*) projects internally, and must do so for all instantiations of *drop*. Yet, as is well known, adjectival passives are unergative, syntactically, rather than unaccusative, rendering the derivation of [$_A$ dropped] a serious problem for UTAH (as is often in fact conceded by advocates of that approach; see Baker 2003 for some discussion). Similar considerations apply to *droppable*, which has unergative properties, rather than unaccusative, as would be expected under a UTAH-type approach. No less problematic is the fact that both *dropped* and *droppable* are derived from transitive *drop*, but none shows any evidence for the sort of implicit external argument present in verbal passives, presenting yet another problem for UTAH. Finally, the nominal *drop* does not allow any of the arguments of the verb stem, thereby raising not only the problem of a missing external argument, but also a missing internal argument.

The paradigm of variable-behaviour verbs, in the technical sense used here, presents a particularly tricky problem. Within the UTAH approach, strict linking regulations dictate the relations between particular syntactic positions and

---

[21] A full review of the UTAH system is clearly outside the scope of this work. It might be worth pointing out, however, that UTAH as formulated in Baker 1988 is inherently vague, in providing no proper definition for the notion 'item'. Most crucially, from analyses presented in the body of the work, it appears that by 'item' Baker means stem, i.e. *drink* in [$_A$ drinkable] and in [$_V$ drink] are the same item. It could be argued, however, that 'items' are words, in which case [$_A$ drinkable] and [$_V$ drink] are distinct items, and one does not expect UTAH to apply to them. The empirical predictions here, note, are vastly different, and specifically, the preservation of the insight of UTAH, under the latter instantiation, would require one to argue that *drinkable* is distinct from *drink*, but not so, e.g. *make-drink*, in synthetic languages which realize this form as a single morpho-phonological word. See Borer (1998*b*) for a fuller review. See also Baker (2003) for some follow up discussion.

thematic interpretations. Specifically, to the extent that unaccusatives have an internal argument, that internal argument is interpreted as a theme, and to the extent that unergatives have an external argument, that external argument cannot be interpreted as a theme, but rather, must be interpreted as an agent or as a causer.[22] Assuming that variable-behaviour verbs project from one specific entry, and that syntactic operations bring about their second 'instantiation', we note that there are no syntactic mapping operations which could possibly bring about the change in the role assigned to the single argument.[23]

Within the system to be presented here, these problems do not arise, as the projection of arguments is entirely independent of any lexical information. The encyclopedic information associated with the listeme *drop* does not include any syntactic information whatsoever about argument structure, nor is the merger of *drop* linked in any sense with a fixed set of roles. Rather, *drop* could be, in principle, embedded under any of the schematic syntactic structures in (37), where it is the distinct syntax of the functional structure associated with the arguments which determines their interpretation, rather than any information associated with *drop*:

(37) a. [$_{FP_1}$ [SUBJECT-OF-CHANGE] $\langle e \rangle_{F_1}$ [$_{VP}$ [$_V$ drop]]]

 b. [$_{FP_2}$ [SUBJECT-OF-PROCESS] $\langle e \rangle_{F_2}$ [$_{VP}$ [$_V$ drop]]]

 c. [$_{FP_2}$ [SUBJECT-OF-PROCESS] $\langle e \rangle_{F_2}$ [$_{FP_1}$ [SUBJECT-OF-CHANGE] $\langle e \rangle_{F_1}$ [$_{VP}$ [$_V$ drop]]]]

 d. [$_{DP}$ $\langle e \rangle_d$ [$_{NP}$ [$_N$ drop]]]]

(38)   [$_{FP_3}$ [SUBJECT-OF-STATE] $\langle e \rangle_{F_3}$ [$_{AP}$ [$_A$ drop(-aff)]]]

The syntax of roles such as subject-of-change, subject-of-process, and subject-of-state—assuming these roles, subject to further elaboration, to be roughly the correct approximation of instantiated event roles—is distinct, although each of these structures is universally fixed as associated with a given argumental interpretation. If the listeme *drop* is embedded within the structure in (37a),

---

[22] Or possibly as an instrument, goal, or experiencer, but this is orthogonal to our discussion.

[23] Note that a syntactic, rather than lexical, realization of Reinhart's (2000) system would encounter serious problems. The external role cannot be eliminated, in principle, but only assigned to an affix. Assignment to an affix, for unaccusatives, would predict properties akin to those of implicit arguments in passives, contra to fact. As for reflexivization, the prediction would be that syntactic reflexivization involving absorption of the internal argument would leave a trace in the object position, but there is no evidence for the existence of such a trace in unergatives. If, on the other hand, reflexivization involves absorption of the external argument (cf. Marantz 1984; Kayne 1993, among others), we predict unergatives to pattern with unaccusatives, projecting an internal rather than an external argument, again contrary to the facts. For a recent discussion of this and other related issues, see Reinhart and Siloni (2003) and Siloni (2001).

it will be 'unaccusative'. If it is embedded within the structure in (37b), it will be 'unergative'. If embedded within the structure in (37c) it will be 'transitive', and if embedded within the structure in (37d), *drop* will project an N, with no arguments. Finally, the structure in (38), a combination of functional and morphological structure, will yield an adjective.[24,25]

In turn, note, argument structure modification, if assumed to be accomplished through the type of structural schemata in (37)–(38), no longer must be mediated through morphology, which within UTAH system is the basis of adding arguments (e.g. causative morphology), absorbing or existentially binding arguments (such as passive morphology), etc. We note that a category-neutral, morphologically unmarked stem can, in principle, be embedded within the structures in (37) (but probably not (38), see n. 25). To the extent that a language marks phonologically the differences between the syntactic contexts in (37), such marking must be functional, the type of marking we have analysed as the spell-out of head features, or alternatively, through the merger of f-morphs (see Chapter 1, Section 1.2.2, for discussion). In turn, the L-domain in (37) is categorized solely by the functional structure, which is also implicated in the assignment of roles to the DPs.

But if (syntactically projected) morphology is no longer allowed to be implicated in the modification of lexically-specified argument structure, through selecting head-assigned arguments or absorbing them, claims regarding the syntax/morphology isomorphism, extremely popular in the wake of UTAH, are likewise weakened. Note that within the UTAH approach, a morpheme such as *-en*, whether adjectival or verbal, must project syntactically, as it (appears to) modify the argument structure of the verb it is attached to (and likewise, of course, for *-able*). However, if the relationship between argument structure and L-heads is severed, then regardless of whether or not some morphology does project syntactically, it no longer needs to project overtly or covertly solely to resolve problems in the mapping from lexical entries to argument structure representations. To illustrate, the motivation for projecting an abstract verb,

---

[24] The structure in (38), but not (37a–d), requires the intervention of categorizing adjectival morphology (*-able, -en*). As we noted earlier (cf. n. 2), in English, and perhaps universally, morphological structure is needed to turn a stem into an adjective. For this reason, in (38) there must be morphological structure, within the L-domain, which will 'adjectivize' the L-head, rendering any dominating functional structure which is incompatible with the existence of such an adjective ill formed. This is not the case with (underived) verbs or with (underived) nouns, which may involve stems 'verbalized' or 'nominalized', respectively, directly by the functional structure, requiring no additional morphology, at least in English. See Borer (2003a, forthcoming) for some further discussion.

[25] This view, note, is compatible with at least some interpretations of the pre-cursor of UTAH, the Universal Alignment Hypothesis (cf. Perlmutter and Postal 1984), which subscribes to the existence of structural-interpretational correlations, but which does not link them inherently to information in the lexical entries of argument takers.

roughly with the meaning CAUSE, so as to assign an external role to *drop*, has evaporated, as has the need for such abstract verbs to actually exist.

2.4 Severing the *Internal* Argument from its Verb

Kratzer (1994, 1996), in a detailed study of the properties of so-called external arguments and their relationship with the verb, concludes (correctly in our opinion) that it is wrong to assume that verbs assign external arguments. Rather, she proposes, external arguments are assigned by a functional projection which dominates the VP, VoiceP.[26] In turn, severing the external argument from the verb gives rise to a system that Kratzer (1999) refers to as semi-Davidsonian, based as it is on the fundamental insight of Davidson (1967, 1980) on the nature of the event argument. Specifically, she proposes that the syntax of 'external' arguments maps directly onto a Neo-Davidsonian representation, introducing an independent predicate of the event argument. In turn, the internal argument remains associated with the verb, at least syntactically. It therefore follows that the lexical entry for *feed* is as in (40a), where *feed* is a two-place predicate (external argument having been severed). The 'external' argument, on the other hand, is introduced syntactically by VoiceP. The resulting representation (translating somewhat to Neo-Davidsonian notation, and ignoring the mapping of *the dog* to a *theme* role) is as in (40b):

(39) Jane fed the dog

(40) a. (feed (theme) (e))
 b. ∃e [Agent (Jane, e) & (feed (the dog) (e))]

Suppose we endorse fully the claim that severing the 'external' argument from the verb is a syntactic realization of a Neo-Davidsonian association, as Kratzer claims. Taking this conclusion one step further, however, note that in this work, we seek to sever not only the external argument from the verb, but also the internal argument. By the logic followed in Kratzer, the result is a syntactic structure which not only represents a Neo-Davidsonian-type association of the 'external' argument, but also a Neo-Davidsonian-type association of the 'internal' argument, or in other words, a full Neo-Davidsonian representation, much in line with Parsons (1990), although I will depart from Parsons' assumption that the relevant roles are thematic ones. Specifically, with respect to (39) on its telic interpretation, I will suggest a full Neo-Davidsonian representation,

---

[26] The reader is referred to Chapter 8, Section 8.1.1, for some comparison between Kratzer's VoiceP (active and passive) and the assumptions made in this work concerning the assignment of 'external' arguments.

based on the fact that neither internal nor external arguments are assigned by the verb, as represented in (41). 'Quantity' here refers to a telic predicate, and the role labels 'originator' and 'subject-of-quantity' (roughly, subject-of-structured-change) are computed on the basis of the relevant functional structure (see Chapter 3 for elaboration):

(41) $\exists$e [quantity (e) & originator (Jane, e) & subject-of-quantity (the dog, e) & feed (e)]

In view of the claim that all 'direct' arguments are assigned by functional event structure, it is worthwhile to consider the arguments for severing the external argument from the verb and assessing the extent to which similar arguments can be made to support severing the internal argument from the verb. As it turns out, the main argument in favour of disassociating the verb from the external argument comes from the major simplification that would emerge in the statement of grammatical rules. A prime example discussed by Kratzer (op. cit.) is that of the adjectival passive. Kratzer points out that a well-known asymmetry between verbal passives and adjectival passives involves the fact that the former retains properties of the external argument (e.g. implicit argument control as well as the barring of *self* anaphors as *by*-phrases), but no such properties are associated with adjectival passives, where the external argument of the original verb seems truly gone. We noted earlier that the behaviour of adjectival passives, with their external argument apparently gone, presents a prima facie problem for proponents of UTAH. To the extent that adjectival passives are predicted by UTAH to be derived syntactically, rather than lexically, disappearance of the external argument is extremely problematic. Not so, Kratzer points out, in a theory that does not assume that verbs have external arguments. Within such a theory, the disappearance of the external argument follows directly from the fact that the relevant functional structure which licenses the 'external' argument of the original verb (VoiceP for Kratzer) does not project in adjectival passives, or, as we will suggest here, from the fact that 'external' arguments, *originators*, are entailments from some event structure, rather than roles assigned by such structure, and are clearly dispensable in the absence of that structure.

But a similar rationale has already been shown to be applicable with respect to internal arguments. We already noted that in de-verbal nominals such as *drop*, for instance, no arguments are projected whatsoever. Within a theory that severs both external and internal arguments from the verb, nothing needs to be said about [$_N$ drop] beyond the fact that it is embedded under a functional structure that licenses neither 'external' nor 'internal' arguments—that is, nominalizing functional structure. Within a theory that assumes that both external and internal arguments are assigned by the lexical item, the disappearance of both arguments in nominal *drop* (as well as in derived result nominals such as *the examinations*) must be explained. While a theory that severs the external, but not the internal, argument from the verb need not explain its disappearance, it still must contend with the disappearance of the internal argument.[27]

Note further that any theory that assumes internal, but not external, lexical assignment, when combined with UTAH or similar restrictions on lexical argument structure modification, is faced with serious problems in accounting for the properties of variable-behaviour verbs. The issue here, to recall, is not the 'loss' or the change in the nature of an external argument, but rather involves an internal argument. While it is cost-free within such an approach to state the presence of an external argument for the unergative variant, the presence of an internal argument in the unaccusative variant, but not in the unergative variant, poses precisely the same problems as it does for full lexical projection accounts.

Finally, we note that Kratzer's own account of adjectival passives (op. cit.) avoids running into a mapping problem of this sort only at the cost of descriptive adequacy. Specifically, as is well known, adjectival passives do not just involve the loss of the 'external' argument of their source verb, they also involve the 'externalization' of the internal argument of that source verb (cf. Levin and Rappaport Hovav 1986). Specifically, adjectival passives behave like unergative verbs, and not like unaccusative verbs. To illustrate, consider the following paradigms which show that diagnostics of unaccusativity apply to verbal passives, but not to adjectival passives:

(42) a. *Verbal passive*
Takie studenty nikogda ne prinjaty v universitet. (Russian)
such students never NEG accepted in university
(M.NOM.PL) (PL)
'Such students are never accepted in the university.'

b. *Verbal passive*
Takix studentov nikogda ne prinjato v universitet.
(M.GEN.PL) (NEUT.SG)

(43) a. *Adjectival passive*
Takie manery nikogda ne prinjaty v xorosix klubax. (Russian)
such manners never NEG acceptable in good clubs
(F.NOM.PL) (PL)

---

[27] This is a problem faced not only by Kratzer's model, but also by Harley 1995, Marantz 1997, and various similar approaches, which postulate the lexical projection of 'internal' but not 'external' arguments. See Borer (2003a, forthcoming) for an extensive discussion in the context of derived nominals.

b. *Adjectival passive*
     *Takix maner nikogda ne prinjato v xorosix klubax.
     (F.GEN.PL)   (NEUT.SG)
     (Russian; Pesetsky 1982)

(44) a. *Verbal passive, possessor dative*
     ha.ʿuga hunxa   li   ʿal šulxan.   (Hebrew)
     the.cake placed(V.PASS) to.me on table
     'My cake was placed on a table.'

  b. *Verbal passive, possessor dative*
     ha.xeder qušat   li   be-praxim.
     the.room decorated(V.PASS) to.me with-flowers
     'My room was decorated with flowers.'

(45) a. *Verbal passive, reflexive dative*
     *ha.ʿuga₂ hunxa   la₂   ʿal šulxan.   (Hebrew)
     the.cake placed(V.PASS) to.it on table

  b. *Verbal passive, reflexive dative*
     *ha.xeder₂ qušat   lo₂   be-praxim.
     the.room decorated(V.PASS) to.it with.flowers

(46) a. *Adjectival passive, possessor dative*
     *ha.ʿuga hayta munaxat   li   ʿal šulxan.   (Hebrew)
     the.cake was   placed(A.PASS) to.me on table

  b. *Adjectival passive, possessor dative*
     *ha.xeder haya mequšat   li   be-praxim.
     the.room was decorated(A.PASS) to.me with-flowers

(47) a. *Adjectival passive, reflexive dative*
     ha.ʿuga₂ hayta munaxat   la₂   ʿal šulxan.   (Hebrew)
     the.cake was   placed(A.PASS) to.it on table
     'The cake was lying on the table.'

  b. *Adjectival passive, reflexive dative*
     ha.xeder₂ haya mequšat   lo₂   be-praxim.
     the.room was decorated(A.PASS) to.it in-flowers
     'The room was decorated with flowers.'

Genitive of negation, in Russian, marks unaccusative subjects and subjects of verbal passive, but not unergative subjects. As Pesetsky (1982) points out, it may not be associated with adjectival passives. Hebrew reflexive dative, associated with external arguments, may not be associated with subjects of verbal passives or subjects of unaccusatives. They are licit in conjunction with unergative subjects, as well as with subjects of adjectival passives. Possessor datives, on the other hand, are barred with adjectival passives, although licit with both subjects of unaccusatives and subjects of verbal passives. Similar facts are reported for Italian *ne*-cliticization by Belletti and Rizzi (1981), barred in adjectival passives, although licit with unaccusatives and with verbal passives. Within the Kratzer model, there is simply no way to 'externalize' the internal argument, which is projected from the lexical entry of the verb. Kratzer's structures indeed do not involve externalization, projecting the argument of adjectival passives in [Spec,VP], the very same position in which the internal argument is projected in both actives and passives. As a result, the unergative behaviour of adjectival passives remains unexplained. No such problems are faced by a model that severs both external and internal arguments from the verb.[28,29]

---

[28] The assumption that the argument of adjectival passives projects internally (specifically, in [Spec, P/AP], as do arguments of verbal passives) is supplemented in Kratzer (1994, 1996) by the assumption that adjectives are either raising or control structures, roughly as in (i):

(i) a. *Stage-level adjectives*
     [$_{COP}$· Ø   [$_{AP}$ [$_{VP}$ *internal* V]]]

   b. *Individual-level adjectives*
     [$_{COP}$· *external* [$_{AP}$ [$_{VP}$ *internal*/PRO V]]]

The structures in (ia–b) predict that while subjects of stage-level adjectives should exhibit unaccusative diagnostics, subjects of individual-level adjectives should exhibit both unaccusative and unergative diagnostics. We note in this context that to the extent that the genitive-of-negation in Russian and possessor datives in Hebrew are unaccusative diagnostics, both structures in (ia–b) make the wrong predictions. Reflexive datives in Hebrew, on the other hand, are altogether incompatible with individual level predicates, but do occur with stage level adjectives, including adjectival passives (see Section 8.2.3 for some additional comments). To the extent that they are possible with stage-level adjectives, the structure in (ia) fails to predict this.

[29] Kratzer gives two more arguments for severing the external argument from the verb. As both involve an asymmetry between internal and external arguments, both could be construed as arguments against severing the internal argument from the verb. The first argument concerns the well-known paradigm discussed in Marantz (1984), which shows that the semi-idiomatized expressions involving the verb and its direct object exist, while idioms involving the subject are considerably rarer. The second argument involves the impossibility of realizing the so-called external argument in derived nominals, derived by Kratzer from the absence of an event argument (and hence a VoiceP) in derived nominals. For extensive argumentation that so-called external arguments *are* realized in derived nominals, see Rozwadowska (2000), as well as Borer (1999b, 2003a, forthcoming). As for the observations made by Marantz (1984) concerning semi-idiomatized expressions, Kratzer opts to state them (with respect to the verb *kill*) as follows:

Assuming ... that *kill* has its traditional denotation ... its denotation would be a function *f* with the following properties: if its argument is an animate being *a*, F yields a function that assigns truth to any individual *b* if *b* kills *a*. If its argument is a time interval *a*, *f* yields a function that assigns truth to any individual *b* if *b* wastes *a*. If its argument is a conversation or discussion *a*, *f* delivers ... a function that assigns truth to any individual *b* if *b* dampens *a*. And so on. (Kratzer, op. cit., 10–11)

By assumption, Kratzer suggests, there could be no such relations between the verb and the 'external' argument, thereby suggesting an asymmetry between external and internal arguments. However, the assumption is by no means a correct one. Consider the pairs in (i) and (ii) as an illustration:

The remainder of this volume is devoted to articulating the syntactic, semantic, and morphological ramifications of severing both direct arguments from the verb. In Chapter 3, I discuss the projection of functional event structure, arguing specifically for an Event Phrase (EP) and for an Aspectual Quantity Phrase ($Asp_Q P$). In the context of both of these nodes, argument role labels may emerge, those of *originator* and *subject-of-quantity*, respectively. In both cases, however, it is not the structure itself that assigns a role. Rather, the role is assigned as an entailment from the event structure. The appearance of an obligatory argument, especially in the case of unaccusatives and telic transitives, I will argue, does not arise from assignment relations, but rather, from the need to assign range to aspectual structure, which must occur under well-defined syntactic conditions, specifically, under specifier–head relations. As such, the existence of well-defined formal syntactic conditions on the emergence of a telic interpretation will provide a strong argument for the syntactic representation of event structure. Crucially, I will assume that while 'telicity' is structurally represented, 'atelicity' is that which emerges in the absence of telicity, thereby ascribing to the telic-atelic distinction the same type of structural variation that was already motivated for the distinction between quantity and non-quantity nominals. These matters are discussed in Chapter 4.

In Chapter 5, I turn to an elaboration of the notion of *quantity*, as proposed in this work both for nominals and for events. The notion will be argued to be the same one in both cases, differing in some important ways from e.g. Krifka's (1992, 1998) notion of quantization. In that context, I will further argue for the syntactic, rather than lexical, representation of event argument roles, for the view of telicity as the 'structuring' of atelicity, and for the emergence of argu-

---

(i) a. The wall touched the fence.
  b. Jane touched Amy.
(ii) a. Sincerity frightened the boy.
  b. Amy frightened the boy.

While (ib) is ambiguous, the choice of subject in (ia), an 'external' argument, excludes an eventive (non-stative) reading and forces a stative reading. Likewise, while (iib) is ambiguous, the choice of subject in (iia) excludes a causative reading, and forces a psychological predicate reading. Within the approach advocated here, neither suggests selection by the verb, but simply the existence of a set of selectional restrictions which are imposed by world knowledge, and which favour a particular syntactic computation. To the extent that semi-idiomatized expressions clearly do exist with respect to 'external' as well as 'internal' arguments, they show that there is no case here for the proposed asymmetry.

It might be interesting to note that even with respect to the paradigm of the verb *kill*, while (iiia) is ambiguous, (iiib) forces an 'idiomatic' reading, as we know that *attitudes*, fortunately, cannot literally kill:

(iii) a. You are killing me.
  b. Your attitude is killing me.

ment interpretation as an entailment from event structure, rather than as a direct assignment relationship.

In Chapter 6 I turn to cases where range assignment in event structure is marked morphologically, specifically, through the Slavic perfective system. I will argue that the perfective system *is* fundamentally the marking of aktionsart (although this does not hold for the imperfective system), and that just as within languages such as English or Hebrew quantity marking of the argument translates into quantity marking of an aspectual head, so in Slavic languages, quantity marking on the head (i.e. a quantity head feature) translates into quantity marking on the argument. One of the most important predictions of the system presented here is that in well-defined structural environments, telicity could exist without an 'internal' argument. That this is indeed the case will be argued in detail in Chapter 7.

Chapter 8 explores the level of graininess desirable for the system as a whole, as well as some additional residual issues touching specifically on the implications the system has for resultative constructions and for manner of motion-verbs. It ends with some broad reflections on the nature of the interaction between the conceptual system and the grammatical system.

In Part III (Chapters 9–10) I turn to the licensing of event arguments, arguing specifically that the event argument, projected as part of the EP node, must be existentially bound, and that such existential binding is responsible for the emergence of effects otherwise attributed to Chomsky's (1981) Extended Projection Principle. The chapter will involve a close examination of locative clitics in Hebrew and their existential function, which in conjunction with the binding of the event argument give rise to a wide range of word orders and interpretations otherwise absent in the language.

Finally, Chapter 11 concludes this study with a discussion of some open issues and possible future research agendas, focusing largely on some unresolved properties of listemes.

Part II
The Projection of Arguments

3

Structuring Telicity

3.1 Preliminaries

To recapitulate, lexical entries do not contain information about the projection of arguments, nor are there any specified links between the lexical semantics of individual lexical items and syntactic positions. Argument interpretation is (at least up to a point) independent of the meaning of listemes. It follows that there is no level of representation that is the deterministic realization of information projected from the lexicon (i.e. D-structure, if such a level indeed exists, is not GF-θ). In turn, the assignment of roles to arguments is accomplished primarily by the syntax of those arguments, which, we assumed, is based on event structure. Specifically, argument structure is computed (in LF) on the basis of the syntactic configuration. L-heads such as verbs and nouns are, in essence, modifiers of structures, with their syntactic properties determined by the hierarchical syntactic and morphological structure dominating them.

A very clear prediction emerges in a system that computes argument roles and event interpretation exclusively on the basis of their syntax, not based on properties of listemes. As already pointed out by Levin and Rappaport Hovav (1992*b*), such a system 'predicts that ... verbs are free to appear in a range of constructions (and hence meanings) constrained only by the compatibility of the "core" meaning of the verb with the semantics of the construction.' (op cit.). We have already suggested explicitly that the existence of variable-behaviour verbs, in the technical sense intended in Chapter 2, is an illustration of precisely such freedom. A rather striking further illustration, already noted in Chapter 1 of Volume I, is the paradigm in (1), from Clark and Clark (1979):

(1) a. The fire stations sirened throughout the raid.
    b. The factory sirened midday and everyone stopped for lunch.
    c. The police sirened the Porsche to a stop.
    d. The police car sirened up to the accident.
    e. The police car sirened the daylights out of me.

What is striking about the paradigm in (1) is that while there is a shared meaning between all occurrences of the denominal verb *siren* (i.e. the emission of a sirening noise), this shared meaning does not correlate with any commonality in argument structure projection. The situation is quite the contrary. Each of the sentences in (1a–e) takes on the event interpretation imposed on it by the syntax of the arguments, with the verb *siren* interpreted as a modifier of that event. Sentence (1a), note, is the only one of these in which the event is restricted to the emission of a siren noise. Sentence (1b) involves an event of signalling by means of emitting a siren noise, (1c) involves an event of bringing on a result, or forcing, by means of emitting a siren noise, (1c) involves an event of locomotion (probably hurried) while emitting a siren noise, and finally, (1e) is a psychological predicate, describing an event of scaring by means of emitting a siren noise. If we wished to trace the projection of the arguments in (1) to lexical information, we would have to state that the verb *siren* has five lexical entries, each with a somewhat different meaning, and each with a different argument structure specification, provided by at least four lexical mapping operations, determining its five distinct syntactic projection environments. If, however, we adopt a syntactic approach to the projection of arguments, we still need to specify five different syntactic constructions or templates, each with its own meaning, but there need only be a single item, *siren*, meaning, indeed, the emission of a siren noise, together with whatever world knowledge and connotations are associated specifically with sirens (e.g. loud noise, used by police cars and ambulances in particular situations, etc.). However, there will be no argument structure information provided. The particular event in which *siren* is embedded will be determined by the syntax it finds itself in, and not by *siren* itself.

Two important questions must be addressed now. One concerns the actual syntax of arguments, which must be such that the range of interpretations associated with *siren*, for example, can be derived. The second concerns the obvious fact that most verbs in English cannot actually be embedded within all the contexts in (1). How, then, can we prevent any event structure based exclusively on the syntax of arguments from overgenerating wildly? In the following sections I turn to the syntax of arguments. Issues of overgeneration, and specifically, the exclusion of some verbs in some insertion frames with some argument structure combinations will be treated throughout the following five chapters, at points where such discussion is relevant.[1]

Recall now that listemes merge directly from the conceptual array, and that their syntactic as well as their grammatically relevant interpretational properties are derived from the properties of functional structure. Assuming now a

---

[1] The reader is referred, specifically, to Chapter 8, Section 8.3, where the exclusion of manner intransitive verbs in telic contexts is discussed and to Chapter 10, Sections 10.2–3, where the exclusion of so-called achievements in atelic contexts is analysed. See Chapter 11, Section 11.2, for a brief discussion of issues that are relevant to the number of arguments.

conceptual array consisting of, for instance, *chase, skunk*, and *cat*, together with the (aritrary) choice of *chase* as the L-head of the L-domain, the construction of structure above the L-domain headed by *chase* must now proceed in accordance with the following guidelines (the reader is referred to Volume I, Chapter 1, Section 1.2, as well as to the summary in Chapter 1, Sections 1.2.2, and 1.2.3, where the selection of an appropriate head and appropriate label for L-D is considered and where the premises in (2a–b) are originally introduced).[2]

(2) a. A listeme inserted from the conceptual array may merge with some functional head to give rise to a specifier of a functional projection associated with both interpretational properties and categorial properties.
   b. A listeme may merge within the (original) L-domain if a semantically appropriate preposition or inherent case marker merges with it, and the resulting PP merges within the L-domain.

Consider first (2a), according to which either one of the non-head listemes in the conceptual array, or indeed, both, could merge as some specific functional, possibly case-assigning specifier with a well-defined set of properties, such as [Spec,AgrO] or its structural equivalent. Such a merger, we assume, would instantaneously categorize the merged element as an L-head of a nominal projection, as determined by the inherent categorial properties of the relevant functional head. Specifically, as only nominal projections may receive case, if the relevant specifier position is a potential case position, it will categorize its L-head as a nominal. If only DPs (but not NPs, #Ps, etc.) may receive case, the relevant nominal projection would further become a DP. It will further be assigned case, if such case is available in that position. After DP categorization, relevant entries in the functional lexicon, including both categorical labels and functional items, should become available for merger in the manner already described in detail, giving rise to the construction of a full nominal functional structure in the relevant specifier position.[3]

A scheme of the possible resulting argumental configurations for the relevant conceptual array is in (3) (verb movement ignored).

---

[2] Listemes may also merge as (non-projecting) bare stems, and subsequently must undergo incorporation onto a host (cf. Chomsky 1995b). I set this possibility aside here, only noting that incorporation, together with the resulting lack of referentiality for the incorporated stem, is clearly very easy to accommodate within the system presented here. See Volume I, Chapter 2, Section 2.1.4 for some brief comments, as well as Borer (forthcoming) for some discussion.

[3] I am abstracting away here from some general questions concerning the construction of a phrasal projection in a phrasal specifier within a system which adheres to Bare Phrase Structure and to the Extension Condition of Chomsky (1995a). This issue, note, is not specific to the proposals made here; it applies to any Minimalist execution.

(3) a. [$_{FP_1}$ [$_D$ cat-NOM]   [$_{FP_2}$ [$_D$ skunk-ACC] [$_{VP}$ chase]]]
    b. [$_{FP_1}$ [$_D$ skunk-NOM] [$_{FP_2}$ [$_D$ cat-ACC]   [$_{VP}$ chase]]]

Suppose now that accusative case is available, optionally, for the specifier of a functional projection which I will label Asp$_Q^{max}$ (Q for quantity), the merger of which, like that of all functional labels, is optional as well. Suppose further that Asp$_Q^{max}$ is the syntactic projection responsible for telic interpretation.[4] We return shortly to the notion *quantity* and to its relevance here. Tackling the syntactic structure first, suppose the architecture of Asp$_Q^{max}$ is as in (4), with the DP (or its copy) in the specifier position interpreted as subject-of-quantity (henceforth s-o-q), roughly subject-of-structured change, and Asp$_Q$ and its c-command domain of interpreted as a quantity predicate:

(4)

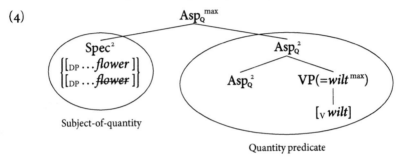

The relation between s-o-q and quantity in (4) is instantiated in a specifier–head configuration, as notated by the superscript 2, assigned to both subject and predicate, a point to which we will return shortly. We may assume for the time being that the configuration [[$_{Spec, Asp}$ DP^2][Asp$_Q^2$]], when otherwise well-formed, gives rise to a telic interpretation.[5] Neither the aspectual head nor its DP specifier suffices to give rise to telicity. But when [[$_{Spec, Asp}$ DP^2][Asp$_Q^2$] is well formed, a telic interpretation does emerge, which consists of a quantity predicate, and a s-o-q interpretation assigned to the DP in [Spec, Asp$_Q$].

---

[4] Asp$_Q^{max}$, with Q standing for 'quantity', is a re-labelling, as well as a re-conceptualization of the nodes labelled in Borer (1994, 1998a) as Asp$_{EM}^{max}$ and Asp$_E^{max}$, respectively. The reason for this re-conceptualization will become clear enough as we proceed. Structurally, Asp$_Q$ is the equivalent of Chomsky's AgrO, and its existence can be motivated by the same structural considerations. See Runner (1995) for such arguments. I assume no functional projections specifically and exclusively dedicated to agreement (and see also Iatridou 1990 and Chomsky 1995a on this point). See van Hout (1992, 1996) and Schmitt (1996) for the formally similar claim that AgrO checks both accusative case and telicity. I believe, however, that both van Hout and Schmitt err in correlating structural objective case with telicity so strongly. See Chapter 4, Section 4.2, for discussion.

[5] I am setting aside for the remainder of this chapter cases in which telicity is licensed without a subject of quantity altogether. These cases will be discussed at some length in Chapter 7. The cases discussed in the text all investigate the conditions that hold whenever there is indeed a DP-object, interpreted as subject of quantity, involved in the derivation of a telic interpretation.

3.2 Structuring Quantity

3.2.1 *Quantity objects*

It has been suggested by Verkuyl (1972, 1989, 1995) that the presence of an argument with some specific properties (for Verkuyl, 'specified quantity of A', [+SQA]) is essential for the emergence of a telic interpretation, an assumption that has proven very influential in subsequent treatments of aktionsart (see Platzack 1979; Tenny 1987; Dowty 1991; Krifka 1992, 1998, among many others). Wishing to abstract away, for the moment, from the debate concerning the relevant properties of the argument in question (and the accuracy of the generalization in general), suppose we put together the broad description in (5), referring to it without prejudice as Verkuyl's generalization:[6]

(5) *Verkuyl's Generalization*
Telic interpretation can only emerge in the context of a direct argument with property α.

To illustrate, the examples in (6) have direct arguments generally assumed to have property α, and give rise to a possible telic interpretation, but not so for the examples in (7), in which the direct arguments presumably do not have property α:

(6) a. Kim ate some apples.
  b. Pat drank too much beer.
  c. Robin read two books.
  d. Marcia built a house.

(7) a. Kim ate apples.
  b. Pat drank beer.

Although the nature of property α is generally sought within the domain of quantification, its precise characterization is not agreed upon, and we will argue that it corresponds to the notion of 'quantity' already developed in Chapter 4 of Volume I in the context of DP structure. Note that the structure in (4) captures Verkuyl's generalization in postulating an obligatory direct argument, which, in turn, may or may not have property α.

Elaborating more on the nature of the structure in (4) and the role played by the DP in [Spec, Asp$_Q$], suppose we adopt the prevailing view that the

---

[6] That Verkuyl's generalization should be derived from configurational specifier–head agreement relations is proposed in Benua and Borer (1996); Borer (1995, 1998a), as well as in Schmitt (1996). In Ch. 6, Sect. 6.1 I return to cases in which specifier–head agreement works the other way around, and the properties of the head are copied onto the specifier.

telicity–atelicity distinction is to be viewed as parallel to the semantic distinction attested within the nominal domain between quantity and non-quantity expressions. Recall that in discussing the mass–count distinction I concluded that neither bare mass nouns nor bare plurals are quantities (alternatively, they are homogeneous) in a very specific structural sense, i.e. in that they do not project a Quantity Phrase (#P), thus deriving the fact that quantity is not part of their interpretation. Now following Link (1983, 1987), Bach (1986), Krifka (1989, 1992), and much subsequent literature, let us assume that a similar distinction should be applied in the domain of events, where telic events are quantities, in the sense that they involve quantification over event divisions, while atelic events are homogeneous, in the sense already discussed in the context of DP structure. Some of the relevant structures for quantity DPs and homogeneous DPs are given in (8)–(9). The definitions for homogeneous and quantity are in (10). (See Volume I, Chapter 4, Section 4.4, for discussion of those definitions in the context of DP structure; see Chapter 5, Sections 5.2–3, for a more detailed discussion of these definition within the domain of event structure.)

(8) *Non-quantity (homogeneous) structures*
   a. Determinerless mass   [$_{DP}$ ⟨e⟩$_d$]   [$_{NP}$ salt]]
   b. Determinerless plural   [$_{DP}$ ⟨e⟩$_d$]   [$_{CL}$ dogs [$_{NP}$ ~~dog~~]]]

(9) *Quantity (non-homogeneous) structures*
   a. Quantity (indefinite) mass   [$_{DP}$ ⟨e⟩$_d$] [$_{\#P}$ Q ⟨e⟩$_\#$]   [$_{NP}$ salt]]]
   b. Quantity (indefinite) plurals   [$_{DP}$ ⟨e⟩$_d$] [$_{\#P}$ Q ⟨e⟩$_\#$] [$_{CL}$ dogs [$_{NP}$ ~~dog~~]]]]
   c. Quantity (indefinite) singular   [$_{DP}$ ⟨e⟩$_d$] [$_{\#P}$ a ⟨e⟩$_\#$]   [$_{NP}$ dog]]]
   d. Definite mass   [$_{DP}$ the ⟨e⟩$_d$] [$_{\#P}$ ~~the~~ ⟨e⟩$_\#$]   [$_{NP}$ salt]]]
   e. Definite plurals   [$_{DP}$ the ⟨e⟩$_d$] [$_{\#P}$ ~~the~~ ⟨e⟩$_\#$] [$_{CL}$ dogs [$_{NP}$ ~~dog~~]]]]
   f. Definite singular   [$_{DP}$ the ⟨e⟩$_d$] [$_{\#P}$ ~~the~~ ⟨e⟩$_\#$] [$_{CL}$ ~~the~~ [$_{NP}$ dog]]]]

(10) a. P is *homogeneous* iff P is *cumulative* and *divisive*.
      i. P is *divisive* iff $\forall x\ [P(x) \to \exists y\ (P(y) \land y < x)] \land \forall x,y\ [P(x) \land P(y) \land y < x \to P(x-y)]$
      ii. P is *cumulative* iff $\forall x\ [P(x) \land P(y) \to P(x \cup y)]$
   b. P is *quantity* iff P is not homogeneous.

Suppose we assume now that on a par with the nominal domain where quantity is realized as syntactic structure (#P), in the aspectual domain quantity is likewise syntactically realized in the form of a functional head dominating an open value in need of range assignment. Specifically, suppose we adapt the essence of Krifka's (1992) analysis to our structures. Krifka assumes that all verbs are inherently atelic, in the sense that they do not specify a culmination point, but only a path. In turn, a quantized theme functions as an operator in his system, giving rise to telicity, in essence measuring out the event (to use the terminology of Tenny 1987, 1994), and thereby giving rise to culmination. Note, now, that within the approach defended here, the basic 'atelicity' of verbs follows from the fact that items within the conceptual array have no grammatical properties. If verbal stems, just like nominal stems, are unstructured stuff, then in the absence of syntactic 'structuring' they will remain so. We suggested that both bare mass interpretation and bare plural interpretation for nouns was indicative of the absence of such structure. For mass, this involved the absence of both a classifier phrase and a quantity phrase, leaving the nominal 'stuff' undivided and non-quantity, and hence mass. For bare plurals, there was division through the projection of CL^{max}, but that division left an output that was neither uniform nor 'quantitied', in the absence of a quantity phrase. In a parallel fashion, we may assume that in the absence of any quantity structure, verbal stems are not quantities, and hence are, within the verbal domain, the equivalent of non-quality, homogeneous nominals, that is, they are atelic. It also follows, as we will argue in Chapter 4, that just as bare mass nouns and bare plurals involved less structure, so homogeneous events, or atelic events, will require less structure (and see Tenny 1994 for a similar conclusion).

The verb stem, inherently without quantity (or any other interpretational properties which are relevant for event structure and argument role assignment), is now to be embedded within a quantity phrase, which will potentially assign quantity to the event, i.e. make it telic (and see Chapter 5 for more discussion of the quantity–telicity connection). However, such a quantity phrase, labelled Asp_Q^{max} in the verbal domain, is headed by a $\langle e \rangle_\#$ open value in need of range assignment. English does not provide dedicated range assigners to $[_{Asp_Q}\langle e \rangle_\#]$, which is to say, there is neither a head feature nor an f-morph which can assign range to $[_{Asp_Q}\langle e \rangle_\#]$, and which would functionally be the equivalent, within the verbal domain, of independent morphemes such as *three, some,* and *every*.[7] But range assignment to $[_{Asp_Q}\langle e \rangle_\#]$ is available, if we assume it to be mediat-

---

[7] Note that it is possible that the head feature exists in English, but that there is no well-formed phonological realization for V.⟨quantity⟩. That execution is clearly to be favoured if we opt for a system in which all grammars share an identical reservoir of abstract head features, but in some languages no phonological well-formed output exists for their realization. For a brief discussion of this point, see Chapter 11, Section 11.1.

Arguably, some particles as well as directional prepositions in English do actually assign range directly to $[_{Asp_Q}\langle e \rangle_\#]$, which gives rise to a telic interpretation:

(i) a. Jake ran to the store.
 b. The army took over.
 c. Robin swam away.

I return to direct range assignment to $[_{Asp_Q}\langle e \rangle_\#]$ by adjuncts and particles in Chapter 7, Section 7.3.

ed through specifier–head agreement between the DP in the specifier of Asp_Q^{max} and its head, Asp_Q°.[8] Thus, if the DP in [Spec, Asp_Q] is a quantity, which is to say, has one of the structures in (9) but not one of the structures in (8), $[_{Asp_Q}\langle e\rangle_\#]$ will be assigned range and telicity will emerge. In essence, then, we derive Verkuyl's generalization from the possibility of assigning range to $[_{Asp_Q}\langle e\rangle_\#]$ through specifier–head agreement, together with the absence of a direct range assigner to $[_{Asp_Q}\langle e\rangle_\#]$ in English (or, for that matter, in Hebrew, Italian, Spanish, and numerous other languages which largely obey Verkuyl's generalization, but see n. 7). The sense in which the DP argument assigns quantity to the event is thus similar to the sense in which a particular determiner assigns quantity to mass or to mass divisions. To use previous terminology, the quantity DP in [Spec, Asp_Q] selects a reticule, a webbing network with a fixed number of divisions, which it superimposes on the event, thereby giving rise to a quantity event (and see Volume I, Chapter 4, Section 4.4, for the relevant discussion in nominals).[9]

Elaborating on the structure in (4), an s-o-q interpretation is assigned to the DP in [Spec, Asp_Q] just in case that DP is quantity, precisely because when the DP is quantity, the quantity property can be copied onto $[_{Asp_Q}\langle e\rangle_\#]$, thereby giving rise to a well-formed quantity predicate. The fuller structure is in (11a), where Q-i stands for the particular Q value of the quantity DP, assigned, in turn,

---

[8] See Volume I, Chapter 2, Section 2.1.3, as well as the brief summary in Chapter 1, Section 1.2.3 of this volume for a discussion of range assignment through specifier–head agreement. For a detailed discussion of range assignment through specifier–head agreement in the nominal domain, see especially Volume I, Chapter 6, Section 6.2, and Chapter 7, Sections 7.2.2 and 7.3.

[9] A similar notion of quantity events, specifically in reference to accomplishments, has recently been suggested by Rothstein (2000b). Rothstein proposes that accomplishments involve the superimposition, on ACTIVITY events, of an incremental BECOME event, which in turn give rise to a set of (sub-)culminations. Again along lines quite similar to those proposed here, Rothstein further assumes that the relationship between ACTIVITY and BECOME is at least in some sense a modificational one: '... the function of the incremental BECOME event is to "keep track" of the progress of the activity. This requires imposing a developmental structure, or ordered part structure, on the activity (this includes assigning it a culmination), and we do this by relating it to the developmental structure of the BECOME event via an incremental relation.'

The accounts do, however, differ in two important ways. First, Rothstein continues to assume that accomplishments consist of two events, specifically those of ACTIVITY and BECOME, in the relevant sense. Secondly, she continues to assume that BECOME itself can be decomposed into a development event and a culmination event, and that 'since the culmination event is part of the BECOME event, it must share an argument with it; thus the argument of the culmination event is the argument of the BECOME event'. In contrast, I assume that the relationship between activity and quantity is not that of being sub-events of a larger event, but rather, in some sense, a relation of event modification. When a (non-stative) event is associated with Asp_Q, it becomes a structured event, i.e. quantity. There is no motivation here, I believe, for postulating two events rather than a single one (and see Chapter 8, Section 8.1, as well as Chapter 10, Section 10.3, for some more discussion of this point). Secondly, in the account outlined here, the emergence of a culmination event or an argument of the culmination event in the sense used by Rothstein remains an epiphenomenon which (may) emerge from the existence of quantity predicates, but which does not, in and of itself, define what quantity predicates, or telicity, are all about. I suggested, and will proceed to illustrate in Chapters 5 and 6, that a quantity interpretation is possible without a culmination event (in the sense used by Rothstein) as well as with a culmination that is not predicated of an argument.

to $[_{Asp_Q}\langle e \rangle_\#]$. The relevant (fragment) of the Neo-Davidsonian interpretation is in (11b):

(11) a.

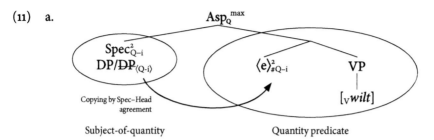

b. Wilt(e) & subject-of-quantity (*the flower*, e).

Telic predicates, our quantity predicates, are typically assumed to require culmination, and we note that if indeed such a culmination exists, homogeneity directly fails and the predicate is quantity. However, at least logically, homogeneity may fail without culmination, for instance if the event specifies a starting point, rather than an end point. Thus culmination is sufficient, but not necessary, to give rise to quantity predicates. The notion of quantity used here, as motivated within the nominal domain (see Volume I, Chapter 4, Section 4.4), is not identical to that of quantization suggested by Krifka (1992, 1998). Specifically, and contra Krifka, I proposed that the failure of divisiveness, as defined in (10ai) is sufficient to give rise to non-homogeneity. Applied within the domain of events, and in reference to the emergence of telicity, this means that for quantity to hold for a predicate P, there may in fact be a subpart of P which is itself P. In other words, it need not be the case, as argued by Krifka, that every proper part of a telic event is itself not a telic event of the same type.

But if some subparts of an event E, where E is 'telic' (i.e. quantity), may themselves be 'telic' events of the same type, it follows that there may in principle be more than one (sub-)culmination, so to speak, or differently put, it need not be the case that no sub-event of P can culminate, as would be the case for Krifka's quantized predicates. We therefore submit that subject-of-quantity (when present) may indeed be interpreted in conjunction with some culmination, but that the culmination need not coincide with the end of the event as a whole. Further, quantity may exist even in the absence of any culmination, intermediate or final to the event (e.g. when a starting point is specified). It therefore follows that telicity as well as the presence of a subject-of-quantity are not dependent on a well-defined end to the event (its telos, in the terminology of Higginbotham 2000a).[10] It is precisely in this sense that subject-of-quantity is interpreted as a

---

[10] Note that it also follows that the 'final' sub-event of E, along the time axis, need not itself culminate. See Chapter 5 for much discussion. This prediction points to another potential difference between the view of telicity proposed here and that advanced in Rothstein (2000b), although it is harder to pinpoint

subject of (quantifiable) change (rather than e.g. subject-of-result or subject-of-target-state). I return to this matter in great detail in Chapter 5, where the notion of telicity put forth here is compared in detail with the notions proposed in Krifka (op. cit.), Kiparsky (1998), and Kennedy and Levin (2000).

Quantity events, which most typically *are* associated with a culmination point that signals the end of the event, are otherwise instantiated in the grammar in count derived nominals, argued by Mourelatos (1978) to correspond to the culmination point of a telic event:[11]

(12) a. There were three eruptions by Vesuvius.
 b. There was a capsizing of the boat by Mary.
 c. There were three late arrivals of a train.
 d. For hours there was (*a) pushing of the cart by John.
 e. For hours there was (*a) painting of the Nativity by Jones.
 f. There was at least one pushing of the cart to New York by John.

In addition, the distribution of subjects-of-quantity, precisely insofar as they may be interpreted as the subjects of some (potentially intermediate) culmination point, generally correlates with the distribution of subjects of adjectival passives, exemplified in (13):[12,13]

---

due to the different assumptions made by the two accounts. Thus it is unclear, in Rothstein's account, what would be the fate of intermediate culminations. It could be, for instance, that to the extent that ACTIVITY and BECOME are separate events, the former may continue past the latter, thereby giving rise to an intermediate culmination. On the other hand, if independent conditions force the ACTIVITY event and the BECOME event to co-terminate although neither causally nor temporally ordered by Rothstein's account, intermediate culminations become impossible to handle.

[11] The grammaticality of (12a–c) presents a problem for Grimshaw (1990), who claims that Complex Event Nominals cannot occur with indefinite determiners or a plural marker. In fact, we believe that Grimshaw's claim is true, unsurprisingly, for atelic Complex Event Nominals, but not for telic ones, precisely because telic Complex Event nominals are quantity, while atelic nominals are akin to *mass* in the sense discussed here. For a detailed study of event structure in nominals, see Borer (forthcoming).

[12] But note the grammaticality of *the pushed car*, contrary to prediction. Intuitively, however, *the pushed car* is most saliently interpreted not as the car which is in the process of being pushed, but the car which has been pushed some distance already, opening up the possibility that a sub-culmination, of sorts, has been defined by the implied change of location.

[13] Levin and Rappaport Hovav (1986) note that although the goal argument does passivize in double object constructions (*Kim was given a car*), it cannot be modified by an adjectival passive (**the given woman*). However, it is the goal argument which induces telicity, as is clear from the judgements in (i):

(i) a. I gave Mary juice in two minutes.
 b. I gave babies the/much milk (*in two minutes).

In turn, the 'goal' argument in (i) has a delimiting function (in the sense of Tenny 1987, 1994). I return to the issue of delimitation, specifically through PPs, in Chapter 7, Section 7.3, where it is proposed that such delimitation is achieved not through a direct argument of the event, but through adjunct adverbs functioning as range assigners to aspectual structure. To be consistent with that approach, one would have to claim that the 'goal' argument in (i) is not a direct argument of the event, but rather, must include a hidden preposition of sorts. These comments notwithstanding, double object constructions remain largely outside the scope of this study.

(13) a. the wilted flower
 b. the moved car
 c. the reddened apple
 d. the twisted yarn
 e. the fallen tree
 f. the arrived train

In the remainder of this chapter, I will focus primarily on the syntactic properties of the structure in (4) and other aspectual structures implicated in the projection of arguments. The interaction of these syntactic structures with semantic considerations is addressed in Chapter 5.

3.2.2 The architecture of event structures

In Chapter 4 I turn to derivations in which the DP direct object is homogeneous, in the sense of (10), having one of the structures in (8), and to the resulting event structure. But let us first review the syntax of derivations in which the DP is quantity. Consider again the derivation of variable-behaviour verbs, or, more specifically, the derivations of unergative and unaccusative structures. Two optionalities are associated, by assumption, with Asp_Q^{max}. Like any functional category, it may or may not merge in a particular derivation (with interpretational consequences). In turn, when Asp_Q does merge, its specifier may or may not be associated with (accusative) case. Consider now the three possible resulting derivations when only one argument is projected, assuming that argument to be a quantity DP:[14]

(14) a. Asp_Q projected, no accusative case assigned

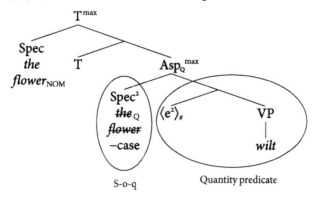

---

[14] Here, as well as in the remainder of this chapter, verb movement is only represented if relevant to the resulting structure, specifically, if the language has a head feature which results in forcing the verb to move to Asp_Q or to some other event-related functional head. For completeness sake, I assume that

b. Asp_Q projected, accusative case assigned

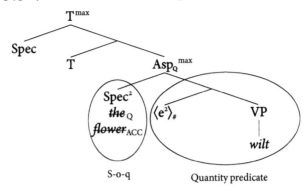

c. Asp_Q not projected (accusative case clearly unavailable)

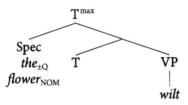

In (14a), Asp_Q is projected, and hence must be assigned range. The argument moving and merging with it, if quantity, assigns range to [_{Asp_Q}⟨e⟩_#], resulting in the formation of a telic, quantity predicate, the specifier of which (the quantity DP) is interpreted as s-o-q. However, as case is not available in this position by assumption, the s-o-q DP must move to receive nominative case, presumably in [Spec,TP]. This, I assume, is an unaccusative derivation, the syntactic context that is responsible for the generation of syntactic unaccusativity effects. The interpretation, in turn, is that of quantity, or in other words, telic.

The derivation in (14b), on the other hand, is ruled out by a familiar reason, being clearly in violation of Burzio's generalization. Although Burzio's generalization was originally stated in terms of θ-role assignment, and therefore not transferable directly to the system proposed here, more recent attempts to reduce it to structural conditions are directly applicable to the structure in (14b).

English verbs do undergo overt short verb movement (cf. Pesetsky 1989; Johnson 1991), and specifically, that they move higher than Asp_Q. Movement of the object to Asp_Q is overt as well. See Runner (1995) for extensive discussion. The presumed landing site of the verb in English is neither considered nor represented in any of the diagrams here. For structure above TP, see directly below.

Regardless of how that generalization is explained, be it by the obligatoriness of nominative case, as in Borer (1986), or through effects of the Agree operation of Chomsky (2000), the structure in (14b) would be ruled out, as required. We note at this point that to the extent that (14b) is ruled out, for example by some statement on the obligatoriness of nominative case in tensed contexts, accusative case for Asp_Q is not really optional for any given derivation. Rather, it is assigned if and only if nominative is assigned to a distinct chain. Thus not only is accusative assigned only in the presence of a nominative, but if nominative is otherwise assigned to a distinct chain, and Asp_Q is projected, it must assign accusative case, as in that case there must be a DP in [Spec, Asp_Q] to assign range to $[_{Asp_Q}\langle e\rangle_\#]$, which is in need of case. This outcome is rather straightforwardly derivable, we note, and hence it need not be independently stipulated that Asp_Q is an optional case assigner. We leave the specific implementation of this result aside, however, as it is largely peripheral to our main concerns here.[15]

Finally, consider (14c). Here, Asp_Q does not merge and there is no Asp_Q^{max}, and so a DP in need of case must merge with T, to become [Spec, TP] and receive nominative case. The aspectual properties of Asp_Q are thus not part of this derivation, and a telic interpretation is an impossibility. However, in the absence of lexically assigned semantic roles, and, for that matter, in the absence of event structure, we must ask how the sole argument in (14c) receives its interpretation.

Viewed differently, it is clear that something is missing in the syntactic representations of event structures proposed thus far. Harking back to the nominal arena, I argued that distinctions between homogeneous or non-homogeneous DPs were encoded internal to the DP domain, and the properties of the predicate, below D, determined what would ultimately be predicated of the referent of that entire DP. In turn, the predication relations between, for instance, #P and the referent of the entire DP were encoded through the assignment of range to $\langle e\rangle_d$. If we assume, in a similar fashion, that Asp_Q indicates the existence of a predicate of an event, it follows that Asp_Q, or, more specifically, the property of quantity, is a property of the event argument, and hence must be somehow associated with it. But in the representations given thus far, no such relationship between quantity and the event argument is represented.

---

[15] Although in English nominative-case assignment is only available, presumably, in [Spec, TP], this may not be the case universally. Assuming nominative case realized in positions lower than [Spec, TP] to be licensed in some functional specifier through the I-Subject system proposed in Borer (1986), or alternatively, through the Agree operation of Chomsky (2000), we expect it to be possible, in principle, for the s-o-q in (14a) to receive nominative case in [Spec, Asp_Q] without moving to [Spec, TP]. In Chapter 10, Section 10.1, such cases will be considered briefly.

Adopting a fundamentally Davidsonian approach (cf. Davidson 1967, 1980; Parsons 1990), and assuming that event structure does correspond to syntactic functional structure, we must postulate an event node, which will in turn host the event argument, and will be predicated of Asp_Q, or similar event structures. Suppose we call this node EP, for Event Phrase. Just like $\langle e \rangle_d$, where range assignment amounted to establishing a mapping from predicates to reference, so range assignment to the head of EP, $\langle e \rangle_E$, is responsible for establishing a mapping from predicates to events. When the predicate under consideration is Asp_Q, the event is interpreted as a quantity event. What, however, transpires when Asp_Q is not projected? How is the event interpreted? As atelic, for sure, but does the grammar make additional distinctions here, specifically, as involving the distinction between stative events, and activity events?

A number of logical possibilities present themselves here, which I will review, but I will not attempt to choose between them. It could be the case, in a minimally specified theory, that there is no grammatically valid distinction between stative and eventive atelic predicates. Such a claim has been made (most recently by Reinhart 2000, based on Bennet and Partee 1972). Its immediate attraction lies in the fact that both eventive atelic predicates and stative predicates are homogeneous, a fact that would follow directly from the absence of Asp_Q. Some drawbacks to such a classification include the fact that adjectival predicates occur in statives, but not in eventive atelic predicates, and the fact that at least some statives allow their direct object, when a bare NP, to receive a generic interpretation, a possibility never attested within the eventive domain (see Smith 1999 for a careful review of the relevant issues here, and for the conclusion that activity predicates are distinct from statives).

A second possibility then is to maintain the distinction between eventive atelic predicates and states and to claim that statives have some event structure which may preempt the verbalization (e.g. by T), otherwise forced within the non-stative domain. That very same structure, in turn, could also license generic direct objects. On the other hand, no such special event structure is available for atelic eventives. Atelic eventive, then, would be the default interpretation in the absence of either quantity structure or stative structure.

Finally, it is possible that EPs come in more than one flavour, which is to say, event arguments come in more than one flavour. Eventives would thus involve one type of EP, essentially denoting a process, while statives would involve another type of EP, denoting a state. In the presence of an eventive EP, a well-formed Asp_Q would give rise to a quantity event, a type of process. In the absence of a well-formed Asp_Q, an atelic eventive, and activity, would emerge, precisely a non-quantity process.

From the perspective of the overall agenda proposed in this work, the second option, which postulates some functional structure for states (thereby potentially preempting VP categorization) but assigns no special stative or eventive structure to EP itself is conceptually the most attractive. However, it is also clear that the substantiation of such a proposal must rely on a full articulation of the structure of stative predicates, a task beyond the scope of this work. Assuming such a task to be in principle possible, but setting it aside here, I will for the remainder of this work assume that EP, as such, is interpreted as a non-quantity process, activity, unless otherwise specified. Some consequences and predictions, specifically of the claim that activities are not grammatical objects, as such, but quantity and state are, are pursued in Chapter 8.[16]

We must now ask what, if anything, assigns range to $\langle e \rangle_E$. Suppose we assume, for the time being—though subject to extensive discussion and revision in Part III (Chapters 9, 10)—that any element in [Spec, EP] may somehow assign range to $\langle e \rangle_E$.[17] Suppose we further assume that any event participant in [Spec, EP] which is not otherwise assigned interpretation is interpreted as the originator of the process denoted by EP (henceforth *originator*, following terminology introduced by van Voorst 1988), where by 'otherwise' we mean either as subject-of-quantity, or through the mediation of a preposition (and see below, Section 3.3, for discussion). In fact, borrowing an insight of Davis and Demirdash (1995), we may assume that such an argument is interpreted as the originator of the process by entailment, rather than by direct assignment. As such, the projection of EP does not imply the existence of an originator, regardless of whether EP is telic or atelic.[18] The structures in (14), then (apart from (14b), which is independently ungrammatical), must be augmented as follows:[19, 20]

---

[16] The reader is referred to Arad (1998, 1999) for an interesting discussion of (stative) psychological predicates within a (neo-) constructionist model, where it is suggested, largely on the basis of polysemy, that it is structure rather than lexical specification of verbs which creates stative psychological predicates.

[17] In fact, we will argue that assigning range to $\langle e \rangle_E$ amounts to binding it existentially, and that an element in [Spec, EP] may so do if it has, itself, existential force. See Chapter 9 (especially Section 9.2) for a detailed discussion.

[18] Note that Dowty's correlations, as stated in Chapter 2, require agentive intransitives to be atelic, but do not suggest that all intransitive atelics have agentive subjects. In Chapter 9 we return to the licensing of EPs without an originator and to the interpretation DPs which are neither in [Spec, EP] nor in [Spec, Asp_Q]. The atelicity of agentive intransitives is discussed in Chapter 8, Section 8.3.

[19] Travis (1994, 1997, 2000) likewise argues for the existence of an EP node, responsible for the licensing of the event argument in the Davidsonian sense. We return to her notion of EP, as well as to an extensive discussion of the nature of EP and range assignment to $\langle e \rangle_E$, in Chapter 9.

[20] The representations in (15), as well as representations in the remainder of this chapter, do not conform to the Chain Condition in that structural nominative case is not associated with the highest member of the chain. In turn, if there are indeed grammatical objects such as *Chains*, the chain consisting of *the flower* and its copy meets a looser condition, requiring a unique case.

(15) a. Unaccusatives

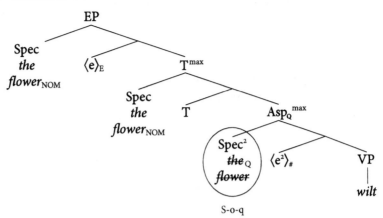

b. Unergatives:

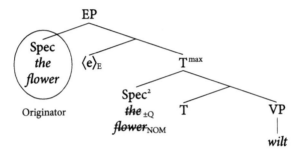

The corresponding Neo-Davidsonian representations are in (16) (but see Chapter 8, Section 8.1, for more discussion on whether there is a need for the specification *activity* in (16b), given the assumption that non-quantity, non-state events are activity by default):

(16) a. ∃e [quantity (e) & subject-of-quantity (the flower, e) & wilt (e)].
 b. ∃e [activity (e) & originator (the flower, e) & wilt (e)].

Note that regardless of the final landing site of the flower in [Spec, EP], as unaccusative diagnostics require a well-formed Asp_Q, we do not expect (15b) to display such diagnostics.[21]

---

[21] It is worth emphasizing at this point that EP, by assumption, even when interpreted as a non-quantity and non-state (i.e. as activity, as in (15b) and (16b)), *does not* in and of itself correspond to activity, or atelicity, but rather, is a node responsible for mapping between event predicates and the event argument. If those predicates include a statement about quantity or *state*, the event argument will be predicated of them. Otherwise, a homogeneous, non-stative interpretation will emerge (i.e. activity), rather

Consider now the representation of quantity transitives, such as *Anna read the book (in two hours)*:

(17) a.

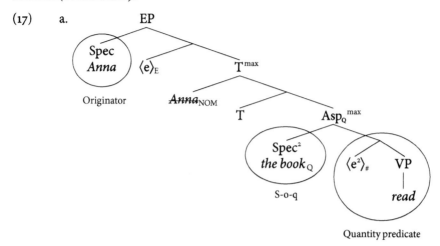

b. ∃e [quantity (e) & originator (Anna, e) & subject-of-quantity (the book, e) & read (e)].

If the only mode of argumental licensing considered is that in (2a) which applies to all direct arguments, then to become arguments, both *Anna* and *book* must merge as functional specifiers, as in (17). Further, unless we assume some additional mechanisms of structural case assignment, Asp_Q must project to assign accusative case to one of these arguments. Once Asp_Q is projected and a listeme merges to become its specifier, if that listeme is expanded as a quantity DP, it will assign range to $[_{Asp_Q}\langle e\rangle_\#]$, with the consequent quantity predicate formation. The other argument, if the conceptual array indeed does contain two, will result from the merger of a listeme (no higher than) [Spec, TP], where it is expanded and receives case. By the assumptions made thus far, it will proceed to move to [Spec, EP], to license EP by assigning range to $\langle e\rangle_E$. The argument in [Spec, Asp_Q] is interpreted as a subject-of-quantity. The argument licensing EP is now interpreted as originator and c-commands the s-o-q 'internal' argument, as required.[22] Note that if either argument in (17) may merge as a specifier of

---

on a par with the emergence of a (bare) mass or plural reading within the DP domain in the absence of any quantity structure. In Chapters 4 and 6 I will argue explicitly that (non-stative) atelicity, as such, is not structurally represented, and hence never gives rise to agreement effects of the type required within the quantity domain.

[22] The terms 'internal' and 'external', originally introduced in Williams 1981 to describe the linking of particular arguments in lexical entries with syntactic positions, are used here purely descriptively, to refer to arguments which are assigned their role lower in the structure (in [Spec, Asp_Q] or [Spec, F*P], see below) or higher in the structure (e.g. in [Spec, EP]), respectively. No lexical or semantic linking regularities are implied by the terms, as such.

either functional head, this system actually dispenses with a particular aspect of the Minimalist Program's checking mechanism, which is designed to ensure that the argument with the 'right' thematic role moves to the 'right' specifier. In Chomsky (1992 and subsequent literature), the need to ensure that internal arguments move to [Spec,AgrO] and external arguments to [Spec,AgrS] (or equivalent case-assigning nodes) presents considerable complications. As in our system arguments do not have a role until they merge in the specifier that assigns role to them, no such complications arise, and domain extensions of the type represented by the Equidistance Principle are rendered unnecessary. In turn, of course, we make the prediction that the grammar would generate freely expressions such as *the book read Anna*, alongside expressions such as *Anna read the book*. The grammar, however, would generate *the book read Anna* only with the interpretation whereby *the book* is the reader and *Anna* is being read, which is indeed the only interpretation that the sentence has, the very reason for its oddity. That oddity, however, clearly should be attributed to conflicts with world knowledge and not to grammatical principles, and just like other world-knowledge-triggered oddities, it can be overridden by (a sufficiently creative) context.

One point is worth noting with respect to quantity interpretations, as in (15a), (16a), and (17). Contra much literature (McCawley 1968; Dowty 1979; Parsons 1990; Pustejovsky 1995; Higginbotham 2000b, among others, and see also Hale and Keyser 1993), I do not assume that the reading event in (17), for example, is semantically decomposed into a process (or an activity) sub-event and a result/state sub-event (alternatively, a culmination or a telos). Rather, the presence of Asp_Q and a quantity predicate is indicative of the existence of a non-stative event with some internal quantifiable divisions. Should such event divisions have an argument, this argument will be interpreted as the subject of 'structured' (and hence possibly, but not necessarily, incremental) change (i.e. subject-of-quantity). Should one of the event divisions culminate, the subject-of-quantity would be interpreted in conjunction with such a culmination. However, such a culmination need not give rise to whatever resulting state holds at the end of the event, nor does it have to coincide with the end of the event, time-wise, or play any role in either the syntactic representation or in the Neo-Davidsonian representation. In this respect, whatever resulting state follows the end point of the event, from the perspective of the time axis, is truly a resultant state in the sense in Parsons (1990), which does not distinguish between whatever state prevails after telic or atelic events. I return to this issue in greater detail in Chapter 5, Sections 5.2–3, as well as in Chapter 8, Section 8.1.

3.3 Prepositional Licensing

3.3.1 *Cascade structures*

In addition to being assigned interpretation through their merger as event-structure related functional specifiers, arguments could also be assigned interpretation through attachment within the L-domain, a point already discussed in Volume I, Chapter 1 (Section 1.2) and summarized in Chapter 1, Section 1.2.1, in this volume. Such direct attachment within the L-D, I suggested, is possible when a listeme merges with a P. The merger with P would categorize the listeme as an L-head of a DP. In turn, the preposition assigns both inherent case and an appropriate interpretation to the DP thus constructed. The resulting PP will then merge with the (copy of the) L-head of L-D. I have assumed throughout this work that both direct object movement and (short) verb movement are overt in English. As a consequence, the only (non-sentential) phrases that can remain in the VP, by spellout, are non-direct arguments—that is, PPs or possibly modifiers and other predicates of some sort. It follows that when such a PP merges with the copy of the L-head, linear considerations regulating the order of the copy of the L-head and the merged PP are irrelevant (cf. Chomsky 1995*b*), and we thereby sidestep, at least within the verbalized L-domain, any questions concerning the head parameter (although issues may still remain, as to the linearization of head and PP complements, in the domain of nominals, and specifically for singular and bare Ns which, by assumption, remain in the N-domain; see Volume I, Chapter 4 for the relevant structures).[23]

---

[23] Of course, a P head may also merge with a PP, not just a DP, therefore giving rise to the possibility that P categorizes its sister as a P. However, as prepositions are members of the functional lexicon, a PP can only project from a functional head, not from a substantive listeme. Thus, if a merged P categorizes its sister as a PP, an additional preposition would need to merge with the relevant structure to license the emerging PP, and so on, ad infinitum. In turn, any merger of a (non-functional) listeme directly with P within such a structure would immediately give rise to its categorization as N.

Given the provisions for the projection of *idioms*, in the technical sense defined in Chapter 1, Section 1.4, our description of the grammar of PPs can be extended to the properties of both particles and semantically bleached prepositions, idiosyncratically associated with specific verbs, as in e.g. (ia–b) listed as in (ii) (see also Chapter 7, Sections 7.3.2, and Chapter 10, Sections 2–3 for additional discussion of idioms).

(i) a. I looked the reference up.
    b. We decided on a dishwasher.

(ii)   Listeme$_\alpha$ [$_P$ β]
       where α is a phonological index and β is a particular value for P.

A separate host of questions which we set aside here, but which do not seem to present, at least prima facie, any particular formal difficulty, involve predicate modifiers and non-selected adjuncts which may remain internal to the L-domain. For some discussion of the interaction of such modifiers and adjuncts in the context of event structure, see Chapter 7, Section 7.3, as well as Chapter 8, Section 8.3. We fur-

Consider now cases in which more than one listeme is stranded within the L-domain. As the architecture of L-Ds is not governed by argument structure considerations, principles of argument ordering (the thematic hierarchy, linking rules, mapping rules, etc.) are not available here, and hence, to the extent that more than one listeme is licensed internal to the VP, the grammar, as such, does not give us any means of ordering them with respect to one another. However, the order of PPs within the VP *is* notoriously free, even when they are non-adjuncts, in ways which are never attested for direct arguments, as illustrated by (18):[24]

(18) a. I talked with Kim about Pat.
      b. I talked about Pat with Kim.

If indeed PPs are the means by which unstructured listemes are licensed within the L-domain, such freedom in word order is exactly what we expect.

On the other hand, as is well known, although both (18a) and (18b) are possible, the resulting structure is not flat. Rather, as argued extensively by Pesetsky (1995), precedence relations are translated here directly to architectural ones, pretty much along the lines predicted by the Linear Correspondence Axiom of Kayne (1994), with a correlation between left to right ordering and c-command relations. These effects are illustrated here in English as well as in Hebrew:

(19) a. Sue spoke **to** these people$_i$ **about** each other$_i$'s friends **in** Bill's house.
      b. John spoke to Mary **about** these people$_i$ **in** each other$_i$'s houses **on** Tuesday.
      c. Sue gave books **to** these people$_i$ **on** each other$_i$'s birthdays.
          (Pesetsky 1995: 172, ex. (451))

(20) a. Sue spoke **with** every boy **about** his mother this morning.
      b. ?Sue spoke **about** every boy **with** his mother this morning.

ther remain silent on the question of clausal complements, even when they complement eventive verbs (such as *say, scream, whisper, decide*). A prima facie desirable result, from our perspective, would place such complements (or a silent copy thereof) in [Spec,Asp$_Q$], when telicity is induced (plausibly with e.g. *decide*), but leave them in the VP without need for case licensing, if no telicity is induced. In either case, one would have to elaborate on the linearity conditions that would order such clauses following PPs, and not preceding them. Prosodic considerations, typically invoked for such a purpose quite independently, would be likewise available within the approach put forth here.

[24] As is well known, *to*-marked 'goals' are not as free as other PPs:

(i) I spoke to Kim about Pat.
     ??I spoke about Pat to Kim. (Neutral intonation)

For this and other reasons, it is tempting to assume that the role of goal is likewise assigned in a functional specifier, and is thus a role associated with event structure, accounting, among other things, for dative alternations, an intuition that is further supported by the delimiting role of goals. We return briefly to the properties of delimiters in Chapter 7, Section 7.3. See also n. 13 for some more brief comments.

c. *Sue spoke **with** his mother **about** every boy this morning.
d. *Sue spoke **about** his mother **with** every boy this morning.

(21) a. soxaxti ʕim kol yeled ʕal 'ima šelo ha.boqer.
talked.1SG with every boy about mother his this.morning
b. soxaxti ʕal kol yeled ʕim 'ima šelo ha.boqer.
talked.1SG about every boy with mother his this.morning
c. *soxaxti ʕal 'ima šelo ʕim kol yeled ha.boqer.
talked.1SG about mother his with every boy this.morning
d. *soxaxti ʕim 'ima šelo ʕal kol yeled ha.boqer.
talked.1SG with mother his about every boy this.morning

In turn, the architecturally constrained, but argumentally free, configuration illustrated by (19)–(21) is precisely what we expect if phrasal architecture within the L-domain is constructed by means of principles that are architectural in nature, and which are blind to argument structure. Consider an L-domain with two or more unmoved listemes, with the conceptual array in (22a) (verb and possible direct arguments omitted). Note first that the merger of two listemes, as in (22b), is in itself ungrammatical, as there is no way to assign either a head or a category to the emerging structure. Nor can it be rescued by the attachment of a preposition, as there would still be no way to determine the head for the complement, even if categorized as a DP by the merged P (cf. for (22bii)). Suppose, however, that one of the listemes merges with P, to give rise to (22c). The second listeme can now merge with the structure in ((22c) as either a specifier (cf. (22d), or a head (22e)). While (22d) is straightforwardly well formed, (22e) is not, as there is no way to assign a category either to the listeme head, or to the category it projects. Structure (24d) is thus the only possibility here. The application of merge with any additional listemes follows similar logic. The resulting structure is precisely a cascade (in the sense of Pesetsky 1995), as illustrated by (23) (and the reader is referred to Pesetsky, op. cit. for detailed argumentation for the structure in (23)):[25]

---

[25] In fact, the structure in (22e) could be assigned category, e.g. DP, if it merged with a P, which would categorize it as a DP (or alternatively, with some categorizing morphology), with the structure in (i) or some equivalent thereof emerging:

(i) about

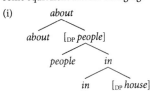

Structure (i) is, of course, a licit structure with a licit interpretation. The question, however, is whether it could emerge as a result of two unordered listemes in the L-domain that is to become the VP, given

(22) a. Conceptual array: people, friend, house.

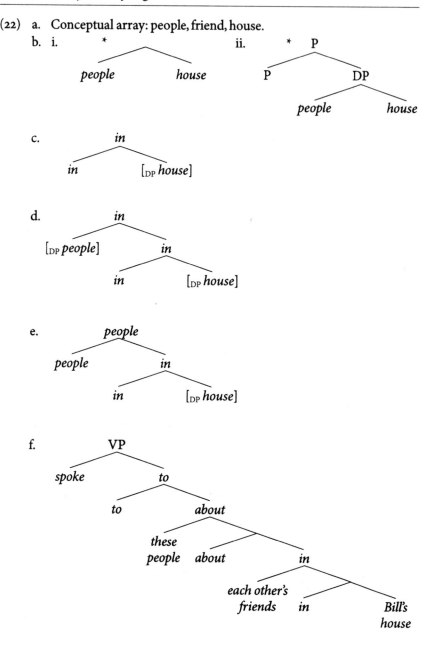

the conceptual array in (22a). Note, specifically, that in (i), the PP *in (Bill's) house* is within the L-domain of the N-head *people* (and would be within the L-domain of some L-head under any categorization of the structure in (i)) and hence in a distinct phase from the conceptual array within the L-domain of the verb. There are, then, overriding theoretical reasons to seek the exclusion of the derivation in (i) as a pos-

3.3.2 *The conative alternation and the* spray–load *alternation*

Consider now from this perspective the conative alternation, as illustrated by examples such as (23)–(24):[26]

(23) a. I ate the cake in five minutes/for five minutes.
 b. I ate at the cake *in five minutes/for five minutes.

(24) a. hikiti 'et ha.šaken   tok xaci šaʕa/bemešek xaci šaʕa. (Hebrew)
  beat.1SG OM the.neighbour in half an hour/for half an hour
  'I beat (up) the neighbour in half an hour/for half an hour.'
 b. hikiti ba-top   *tok xaci šaʕa/bemešek xaci šaʕa.
  beat.1SG in-the.drum *in half an hour/for half an hour
  'I beat the drum in half an hour/for half an hour.'   (Atelic reading)
 c. #hikiti ba-šaken.
  beat.1SG in-the.neighbour
  'I beat the neighbour.' (Atelic reading)
 d. #hikiti 'et ha.top.
  beat.1SG ACC the.drum
  'I beat up the drum.'

We now have a natural, straightforward explanation for the conative alternation, which does not require a dual representation for English *eat* and Hebrew *hika* 'beat', nor for the many other verbs that display similar behaviour. The interpretation of a listeme as an argument, we noted, could result from one of two operations—it may merge as [Spec, Asp$_Q$], licensing telicity (if expanded as quantity in the relevant formal sense), in the manner discussed in Section 3.1.2. Otherwise, it may merge with a P, which in turn merges directly with the (copy) of the V-head, thus being categorized, assigned inherent case, and interpreted through an appropriate preposition—in the case of the conative alternation, *at* in English, and *be-* (literally 'in') in Hebrew. While it will continue to be interpreted as the 'affected' argument, which is to say, the substance being eaten in (23), or the entity being beaten in (24), when merger as [Spec, Asp$_Q$] takes place, a telic interpretation will emerge, but not so when the argument is licensed through a prepositional merger, quite simply because the relevant

---

sible output from the conceptual array in (22a). In turn, the question here is a general one, and is likely to emerge within any execution of the Bare-Phrase Structure system, if combined with assumptions about initial arrays and phased application. Thus within standard executions of the MP, it is likewise not clear what could block the derivation in (i) for a numeration containing e.g. *about (the), people, in, (Bill's), house*, alongside a derivation that would give rise to the intended reading, in which both *about people* and *in (Bill's) house* are modifiers of the verb, and not of a nominal head.

[26] I return in Chapter 4 to the atelic reading of transitive sentences such as (24a) and (25a).

argument is not in [Spec, Asp$_Q$], and as a result, [$_{Asp_Q}\langle e\rangle_\#$], if projected at all, cannot be assigned range, making an Asp$_Q$ node ill-formed and a telic interpretation unavailable.[27]

A similar account is available for the well-known *spray–load* alternation, illustrated in (25):

(25) a. Kim stuffed the pillow with the feathers (in two hours).
　　 b. Kim stuffed the feathers into the pillow (in two hours).
　　 c. Pat loaded the wagon with the hay (in two hours).
　　 d. Pat loaded the hay on the wagon (in two hours).

In accordance with the assumptions made so far, consider the conceptual arrays in (26) (V-head, arbitrarily selected, in parentheses):

(26) $\left\{\begin{array}{l}\text{(spray), paint, wall, Kim}\\\text{(load), wagon, hay, Kim}\\\text{(stuff), feather(s), pillow, Kim}\end{array}\right\}$

Only two structural case positions are (universally) available and hence only two of the arguments in (26) could be structurally licensed, thereby becoming direct arguments. Suppose the structure associated with the two direct arguments is that of regular telic transitives, in essence, as in (17), with both assigned interpretation in the context of event structure, one as a subject-of-quantity, the other as originator. The remaining third argument, with no possibility of being structurally licensed, can only be interpreted through the attachment of an appropriate preposition. Notice now that in principle, both location and subject matter (or theme), the two roles typically associated with *spraying*, *loading*, and *stuffing*, could serve as subjects-of-quantity. In fact, in the system presented here, roles such as location and subject matter (or theme) do not have any formal status within the event structure and if anything, could only be properties of complements of some particular prepositions. It follows, then, in the contexts

---

[27] This may be an appropriate place to point out that affectedness, as a syntactically active phenomenon, does not fully correlate with telicity. We note, first, that any attempt to define 'affectedness' in a common-sense fashion would have a hard time distinguishing between the sense in which a cake is impacted by being 'eaten at', or a drum by being 'beaten at', and the sense in which a book is impacted by being read, a ball by being kicked, or the neighbour by being beaten. Yet, *read a book*, *kick a ball*, or Hebrew *hika 'et ha.šaxen* 'beat the neighbour' may be telic but *eat at a cake*, and Hebrew *hika ba-tof* 'beat at the drum' may not be. At least one established test for affectedness, middle formation, typically taken to be possible only for affected objects, (cf. Roberts 1987) excludes creation verbs which are telic, but allows activity transitives, which are atelic, showing that telicity is neither necessary nor sufficient to define affectedness:

(i) a. *Pictures of loved ones paint easily.
　　b. *Houses in the countryside build easily.
　　c. This car drives easily.

For additional criticism of the notion 'affectedness' in conjunction with telicity, see Jackendoff (1996).

of the conceptual arrays in (26), that (at least) two outputs are possible. There is one in which an understood location is the subject-of-quantity, and any structured change is measured with respect to that location. The understood subject matter is licensed through the attachment of an appropriate preposition and PP attachment to the L-head. This gives rise to (25a), typically assumed to imply, most saliently, the filling of the entire pillow in two hours, but not necessarily the exhaustion of the feathers (cf. structure (27a)). In the second derivation, on the other hand, it is the understood subject matter that is the subject-of-quantity, and structured change is measured with respect to the subject matter *feathers*, leaving the location indifferent to the event structure, to be realized through the attachment of an appropriate preposition and PP attachment to the L-head (cf. structure (27b)). In this case, we derive the (most salient) reading in which the feathers have been exhausted in two hours, but the pillow not necessarily full. In both cases, a quantity reading, to the extent that it involves a measurable change, gives rise to such a measurable change reading with respect to that quantity DP which induces the quantity property, but not with respect to the argument which has remained in the L-domain licensed through merger with P. While it remains true, then, that quantity direct objects (tend to) induce a telic interpretation, but not (typically) indirect objects, we note that within the approach postulated here, we need not assume that these effects are restricted to themes (contra Dowty 1991 and Krifka 1989, 1992), nor do we need to resort to a double listing for the verb, with either location or subject matter (or, location or theme) as the direct argument. In the presence of the array (26), the existence of the structures in (27a–b) with the representations in (28) follows directly (*or-tor* = originator of process).

(27) a.

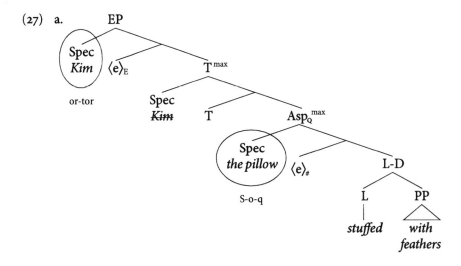

94   *The Projection of Arguments*

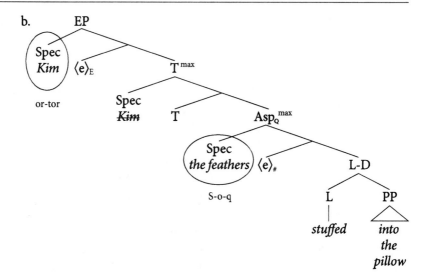

(28) a. ∃e [quantity (e) & originator (Kim, e) & subject-of-quantity (the pillow, e) & WITH (the feathers, e) & stuff (e)].
  b. ∃e [quantity (e) & originator (Kim, e) & subject-of-quantity (the feathers, e) & INTO (the pillow, e) & stuff (e)].

Of course, given a conceptual array including *Kim, feathers,* and *pillow,* and assuming the free merger of prepositions, the system outlined here also predicts the possibility of all the sentences in (30) (setting aside the trivially grammatical readings of (29c–d) with a dyadic argument structure and an adjunctive reading for the PP, for instance, *I stuffed the pillow while I was on the feathers*):[28]

---

[28] In addition, we predict, with an atelic reading, the following, in which both 'internal arguments' are licensed through a PP, and none as a direct argument:

(i) a. I sprayed with the paint on the wall.
   b. *I loaded at/with the hay on the wagon.
   c. *I stuffed with the feathers into the pillow.

We note that while (ia) is grammatical, (ib–c) are not. Intuitively, it appears, the ungrammaticality of (ib–c) derives from a requirement that the structures associated with *load* and *stuff* be transitive, although the specific role of the direct argument seems rather immaterial. For some brief comments on the possibly idiomatic nature of obligatory transitivity, see Chapter 11, Section 11.2.

Another unresolved issue here concerns the well-known absence of *spray–load* effects with cases such as those in (ii)–(iii). Within the approach proposed here, the impossibility of (iib) and (iiib) must be attributed to the conceptual infelicity of introducing divisions within a *filling* event by anything other than a container, and by the conceptual infelicity of introducing divisions within a *pouring* event by anything other than a liquid. Granting that any true explanation must delve deeper into the nature of concepts than is attempted here, we leave this matter aside:

(29) a. I stuffed the feathers with the pillow.
b. I stuffed the pillow into the feathers.
c. I stuffed the feathers on/about/under/in/at the pillows.
d. I stuffed the pillow on/about/under/over/at the feathers.

I believe, however, that this is in fact a positive result. While none of the sentences in (29) involves a particularly common event in the world as we know it, sufficiently generous assumptions about the nature of pillows and feathers in some worlds would certainly allow (29a–b) without any radical modification of the meaning of *stuff*. A coherent interpretation of (29c–d), on the other hand, arises according to the degree of modification we are willing to make to the world as we know it. The main point here is that rather than give rise to ungrammaticality, they give rise to oddity, which may be reconciled if we are willing to reconcile ourselves to giving up on at least some of the archetypal properties associated with concepts such as *stuff*, *feathers*, and *pillows*.[29]

Note now that the domain from which roles such as subject-of-quantity and originator come is entirely distinct from the domain including roles such as locative, affected subject matter, and so forth. While locative, affected-subject-matter, etc. are specifically linked to the function of prepositions, subject-of-quantity and originator are linked to event structure. Thus while notions such as location, affected-subject-matter, etc. may have some grammatical reality, that grammatical reality is not realizable within the domain of direct event arguments. Likewise, subject-of-quantity and originator can only be licit in the context of event structure, and may never be realized in the context of prepositions. It is precisely because of this that no preposition can assign a subject-of-quantity interpretation, and no preposition can assign an originator interpretation.[30]

(ii) a. Kim filled the glass with water.
b. *Kim filled the water into the glass.

(iii) a. Robin poured water into the sink.
b. *Robin poured the sink with water.

[29] To illustrate, *stuff under/over/on* are clearly acceptable, if we imagine a shelving space constrained from all directions, and *stuffing* interpreted essentially as an action modifier synonymous with *placing within a restricted space*. With prepositions such as *at* and *about*, such a reading is possible insofar as they allow a location reading which is compatible with the modificational reading of *stuff*.

[30] It therefore follows that the preposition *by*, in *by*-phrases as they occur in passives, cannot, by itself, be the assigner of an originator role in utterances such as those in (ib), and that to the extent that an originator interpretation is associated with verbal passive constructions, it reflects the fact that aspectually there are no structural differences between active and passive sentences. It is thus precisely the non-availability of an originator role outside the event domain which rules out (ic).

(i) a. Kim broke the window.
b. The window was broken by Kim.
c. *The window broke by Kim.

In Chapter 4 we turn to the structure of atelic events, focusing especially on the structure of atelic transitives. Chapter 5 focuses on the semantic interpretation of telicity and quantity within the domain of events. Some extensions and ramifications are pursued in Chapters 6–8.

In terms of the proposal made in this work, it means that to the extent that in (ib) Kim is perceived as an originator, such an interpretation must be assigned within the direct domain of the event (e.g. to a null pronominal) and *by*-phrases must be interpreted as doubling phrases, along the lines suggested in Jaeggli (1986*a*) and Baker, Johnson, and Roberts (1989). I return to a more detailed discussion of the licensing of *originator* interpretation in Chapter 9.

4

(A)structuring Atelicity

4.1 Where Are We?

A number of questions emerge immediately in considering the derivations outlined in Chapter 3 (cf. (15) and (17)). These questions are summarized in (1):

(1) a. What of transitive structures which do not have a subject-of-quantity direct object? How are their objects assigned case, and how do the arguments receive distinct interpretation? This question applies, in principle, both to quantity direct objects, as in (2a–b), as well to non-quantity direct objects, as in (2c).
b. Verkuyl's generalization was derived from the absence of direct range assignment to $[_{Asp_Q}\langle e\rangle_{\#}]$ in languages such as English. Such absence forced range assignment to $[_{Asp_Q}\langle e\rangle_{\#}]$ to be indirect (i.e. through specifier–head relations), thereby necessitating a quantity DP in [Spec, Asp$_Q$]. But when the UG picture is considered, it should at least be possible to assign range to $[_{Asp_Q}\langle e\rangle_{\#}]$ directly. Are such cases of direct range assignment to $[_{Asp_Q}\langle e\rangle_{\#}]$ attested? Note that we predict that if and when they are, telicity could emerge in exception to Verkuyl's generalization.
c. What of post-verbal subjects in transitive sentences? As they are by assumption not in [Spec,EP], how is $\langle e\rangle_E$ assigned range, and how is the post-verbal subject interpreted? Quite independently, what does range assignment to $\langle e\rangle_E$ consist of, and why is it necessary?

(2) a. Kim pushed the cart.
b. Pat pulled the wagon.
c. Robin built houses.

An additional question can be formulated on the basis of the analysis of quantity as telicity proposed in Chapter 3. As is well known, two of Vendler's (1967) verb classes correspond to telic events—accomplishments and achievements, distinguished primarily based on instantaneity.[1] Smith (1991), in turn,

---

[1] Dowty (1979) proposes that the accomplishment–achievement distinction further involves the presence of an agent in the former, but not in the latter (see also Van Valin 1991). We note, however,

proposes that instantaneous events may or may not be telic (e.g. *jump, cough*, etc. are instantaneous, but not telic). What is the status of the distinction between achievements and accomplishments within the quantity approach to telicity? Are achievements a unified class? Can the telic structures proposed thus far differentiate between achievements and accomplishments? Alternatively, is the distinction even grammatically valid? Its grammatical validity has been questioned—by Parsons (1990) and Verkuyl (1989), for instance.

In the remainder of this chapter, I focus on the question in (1a). After discussing in greater detail the interpretation of quantity structures in Chapter 5, I return, in Chapters 6 and 7, to question (1b), discussing direct range assignment to $[_{Asp_Q}\langle e\rangle_\#]$ and quantity interpretation without a quantity direct object. In Chapter 8, some issues of graininess in the emerging system are considered, together with the status of residual issues, such as resultatives and manner-of-motion intransitive verbs. In Part VI, I return to range assignment to $\langle e\rangle_E$, discussing in that context the rationale for such range assignment, as well as its properties in a broad array of constructions, including those with post-verbal subjects in unergative (Chapter 9) and unaccusative (Chapter 10) structures. The system emerging here and some of its ramifications pursued, especially, in Chapters 7 and 10, will lead us to the conclusion that while there is indeed something special about so-called achievements which distinguishes them from so-called accomplishments, that distinction does not consist of classifying achievements as a distinct event type. Rather, both achievements and accomplishments have quantity structures, as realized through the projection and the assignment of range to $[_{Asp_Q}\langle e\rangle_\#]$. Achievements, I will suggest, are not in and of themselves a uniform class, but, rather, idioms, in which $[_{Asp_Q}\langle e\rangle_\#]$ must merge (and Asp_Q project), and where at least sometimes, $[_{Asp_Q}\langle e\rangle_\#]$ must be assigned a specific range by a specific direct range assigner. Telicity, perforce, emerges.

Finally, Chapter 11 concludes this book with some additional discussion of the syntax as proposed within an XS-model and its interaction with both linguistic variation and other cognitive modules.

---

that, at first sight at least, some classical achievements have an agentive interpretation (e.g. (ia–b)), while intransitive telic events as (iia–b) are not instantaneous (and hence not achievements), but do not have an agent, either (for some recent criticism of the claim that accomplishments require a causer, see Kennedy and Levin 2000; for more discussion of the accomplishment–achievement divide, see Chapter 10, Sections 10.2–3):

(i) a. Pat reached the summit.
    b. Kim won the race.
(ii) a. The apple reddened (in two weeks).
    b. The wall fell apart (in two hours).

4.2 Atelic Transitives and Partitive Case

Turning first to the question of atelic, eventive (non-stative) transitives, their existence is, of course, well documented, as is the fact that case is clearly available to direct objects, regardless of telicity. Interestingly, however, in languages that display finer morphological distinctions than English, direct objects in atelic contexts are not assigned accusative case. For instance, as is well known, accusative case in Finnish, within the eventive domain, is reserved to direct objects in telic predicates. In atelic eventive predicates, direct objects receive partitive case. This contrast is illustrated in (3)–(4) (examples from Vainikka and Maling 1993 and de Hoop 1992).[2]

---

[2] Kiparsky (1998, 2001) notes a number of cases in which accusative case occurs in atelic contexts, specifically with stative verbs such as *omistaa* 'own' and *nähdä* 'see', illustrated by (i):

(i)   Omist-i-n   karhu-nb.
        own.PST.1SG bear.ACC

To the extent that the accusative–partitive alternation in Finnish is indicative of event structure, then, this may indicate that statives are not a unified structural class, that more than one structure is projected in statives, and that in at least one of these structures, the case assigned to direct arguments is homophonous with the case assigned in eventive telic constructions (in this context, Kiparsky notes that Estonian, which otherwise has a case-assignment system identical to that of Finnish, nevertheless assigns partitive in cases such as those in (i)). As statives are largely outside the scope of this work, we will not attempt to pursue this distinction any further, noting only that in English as well, statives such as *own* and *see* do not behave like e.g. psychological statives, in barring a generic reading for a bare plural in their object position, possible (indeed forced) in the case of psychological statives:

(ii) a. I like cats (true of all typical cats that I like them).
     b. Tenured professors own homes (not true of all typical homes that tenured professors own them).

Ultimately, it might be that the correct theory of event structure will involve a property that some telic predicates and some statives have in common, and which is marked by means of accusative case. We set this aside, however, for the remainder of this work.

Within the eventive domain, accusative case always entails a telic predicate. The converse, we note, is not the case, in that at least in some cases, 'inner telicity' survives in the presence of partitive case. These cases, as claimed by Kiparsky (2001), involve negation, illustrated in (iii), and generics, illustrated in (iv):

(iii)   E-n   saa karhu-a/#karhu-n.
         not.1SG get bear.PRT/#bear.ACC
(iv)   Puutarhuri istutt-i   paljon tätä   ruusu-a.
         gardener   plant.PST.3SG much this.PRT rose.PRT
         'The gardener planted this (kind of) rose a lot.'

I will assume that (iii) and (iv) are cases of outer aspect, in the sense of Verkuyl (1972) and that at least on some level the assignment of partitive case is computed on the basis of full sentential aspect, rather than that associated with the V-headed functional complex alone.

An interesting case is presented by the partitive case associated with intransitive presentational bare NP subjects, as illustrated in (v):

(v) a.   Lapsi.a   on nyt   synty-nyt.
         child.PL-PRT now be.3SG born-PP
         'Children have been born.'

(3) a. Anne rakensi taloa.
Anne built house.PRT
'Anne was building a/the house.'

b. Han luki kirjaa.
he read book.PRT
'He was reading a/the book.'

c. Tiina heitti keihasta.
Tiina threw javelin.PRT
'Tiina threw the javelin.'

d. Kirjoitin juuri naita kutsukortteja perjantaina, kun soitit.
I.wrote just these.PRT invitations.PRT on.Friday when you.called
'I was just writing these invitations on Friday when you called.'

(4) a. Han luki kirjan.
he read book.ACC
'He read a/the book.'

b. Anne rakensi talon.
Anne built house.ACC
'Anne built a/the house.'

c. Tiina heitti keihaan metsaan.
Tiina threw javelin.ACC into-the.forest

d. Kirjoitin nama kutsukortit perjantaina.
I.wrote these.ACC invitations.ACC on.Friday
'I wrote (and finished) these invitations on Friday when you called.'

Note that the differing aktionsart value associated with the members of the pairs in (3)–(4) must emerge from the grammatical marking of the direct object, rather than from an inherent specification of (a)telicity associated with the verb. In the terminology already used here, then, *read*, *build*, and *throw* are variable-

b. Tää.llä virta-a joki.a.
here.ADESS flow.3SG river.PL
'There flows a river here.'

c. Tehtaa.ssa työskentele-e nais-i-a.
factory.INESS work.3SG women.PL.PRT
'There are women working in this factory.'

Kiparsky (1998, 2001) assumes that cases such as those in (v) are unbound (atelic, in effect), due to the unbound nature of the relevant NP argument. As such, the possibility of partitive case is unproblematic here. This said, in Chapter 10 I discuss extensively cases of telicity with (post-verbal, nominative) bare NP (non-quantity) subjects in presentational cases, suggesting that in such cases telicity could be licensed through the presence of a locative, overt or covert. This raises the possibility that such telicity may be available for at least some cases of presentationals, in spite of the fact that the argument is partitive. This discussion remains largely speculative here and I set it aside for the rest of this work.

behaviour verbs. Although their variability cannot be described by appealing to the unaccusative–unergative dimension, as these are transitive contexts, they do differ in their telicity value, and that difference correlates here, as in the unaccusative–unergative case, with a grammatical distinction.[3]

Within a theory which assumes both structural case and inherent case, and which further associates particular case values with particular structural configurations (e.g. accusative case in [Spec,AgrO] or [Spec,Asp$_Q$], nominative case in [Spec,TP] or [Spec,AgrS], or, alternatively, nominative case through I-Subject coindexation or *Agree*), the distinction between the assignment of partitive case and accusative case must correspond to some formal difference. Further, if accusative case is structural, we cannot suggest that verbs such as *read*, *build*, and *throw*, among many others in Finnish, optionally assign accusative or partitive. As accusative case is structural, its assignment cannot be associated with lexical specification, typically linked with a particular interpretation and with inherent case. Rather, we must assume, at the very least, that accusative case is a type of inflectional marking, subject to licensing through either structural checking or assignment in the context of specific architecture, and realized phonologically on the DP or the N. How, then, can the difference between accusative and partitive be characterized in a way that would further capture the telicity distinctions associated with each of these case realizations?

One option which is immediately available, and which has been often suggested in the literature on partitive case, is to assume that partitive case, but not accusative case, is inherent and is assigned by a lexical head, specifically the verb, in a direct complementation context (i.e. under government). One of the better known executions of this idea is in Belletti (1988), where it is suggested that inherent partitive case is available (abstractly) in unaccusative contexts such as those in (5), and one of its properties is that it imposes an indefinite restriction on its recipient:

(5) a. There arrived three children (yesterday).
　　b. There is *the/a cat-PRT in the garden.

Belletti's account is not concerned with aktionsart, or with the assignment of partitive case in transitive contexts, but rather with deriving indefinite effects

---

[3] Care must be taken here in determining what, precisely, the domain of quantity and homogeneity is. Take an example such as (3c), with the Finnish verb *heitti* 'throw' and with a partitive-marked object, indicating homogeneity. Note that while the thrown item, the javelin, undergoes a homogeneous motion, the originator, the thrower, is not part of that homogeneity, as it indicates a starting point to the motion. In turn, as we already noted, the existence of an originator, or its absence, is neutral with respect to the quantity interpretation of non-stative events (although it does mark the absence of a stative interpretation). If we assume that the domain of event, as relevant to the determination of telicity, is below both EP and TP, however, then the event in (3c) is homogeneous as desired.

for subjects in post-verbal positions, a property which (5a) and (5b) have in common (and note that if partitive case blocks telicity, the assumption that *children* is partitive in the telic (5a) would be at least prima facie problematic; see n. 2 for a brief comment, as well as Chapters 9 and 10 for discussion of telicity in presentational *there* insertion cases). Can her account be extended, however, to the telicity/case correlations displayed in (3)–(4)?

At least at first glance, such an extension might appear attractive. We argued that a quantity direct object in [Spec, Asp$_Q$] is essential to induce telicity. In turn, direct objects in [Spec, Asp$_Q$] receive accusative case. Why not argue, then, that the cases in (3) are precisely cases where the direct object does not move to [Spec, Asp$_Q$]? If that were so, neither accusative case nor telicity could emerge, and the argument could only be licensed by attaching directly to the L-D in the company of an appropriate preposition, or, in a clear extension, an appropriate (abstract) inherent case marker. And in fact, de Hoop (1992) and van Hout (1992, 1996, 2001) have proposed analyses that are compatible with this general direction (and see also Ramchand 1997). De Hoop, working within a traditional approach to argument projection, argues that partitive case is associated with weak NPs while accusative case is associated with strong NPs. In turn, it is precisely the class of strong NPs that trigger telicity, she claims, in the sense of satisfying Verkuyl's generalization. Weak NPs, on the other hand, fail to trigger telicity and are assigned partitive case.[4] Van Hout (1992, 1996), working within a framework very akin to our own but endorsing the weak–partitive and strong–accusative correlations, explicitly proposes that the licensing of telicity is linked with 'strong object case' in the sense of de Hoop (1992), and that such assignment involves movement to [Spec, AgrO], the structural equivalent of our [Spec, Asp$_Q$] position, and furthermore, a node in which a telicity feature is checked. Ramchand (1997), in a variation of this approach, proposes that strong case is available in [Spec, VP], while weak case (genitive, in Scottish Gaelic) involves verbal complements.[5] Finally, although van Hout (1996, 2001)

---

[4] Although de Hoop does not assume that partitive case is inherent, but rather, a structural weak case, assigned to weak NPs, sensitive to non-thematic considerations.

[5] Some care needs to be taken to distinguish between what we call here partitive case, based, largely on descriptions in Kiparsky (1998, 2001), and the fact that some perceived complements may be attached, internal to the VP, by means of prepositional licensing of some sort. The relevant distinction, in a language such as English, would emerge when attempting to compare the atelic reading of real transitives, as in (i), with the atelic reading of so-called conative sentences, as in (iib) or the genitive complement in (iic):

(i)   a.   Kim pushed the cart.
        b.   We read the bible in church last Sunday.
        c.   I read books.

(ii)   a.   I ate the cake.
        b.   I ate at the cake.
        c.   I ate of the cake.

is not explicit about her proposed mechanism of weak case assignment, within the model she suggests, it is not possible for weak case to be structural, as there are no structural case-assigning specifiers available other than [Spec,AgrO], an accusative-case assigner.[6] For van Hout, then, there remain two logical possibilities. Weak, or partitive, case may be assigned inherently, as proposed, in essence, by Belletti. Alternatively, van Hout's discussion (as well as de Hoop's) is compatible with the possibility that weak NPs, functioning as event modifiers, are predicates of sorts, which do not need licensing by case assignment at all (and see van Geenhoven 1998 for an explicit proposal along these lines). Either way, weak NPs and partitive case are assumed to be available in situ, a claim further supported in de Hoop by the fact that object shift applies, in Dutch and German, to strong NPs, but not to weak NPs. The de Hoop–van Hout approach, then, can be summarized as in (6):

(6) a. Strong DP ⇔ movement to [Spec,AgrO]
 b. Weak DP ⇔ in-situ case (no movement); alternatively, semantic incorporation
 c. Telicity → strong DP [7]

The existence of linguistic devices that give rise to (iib–c) is beyond dispute, as is the fact that telicity cannot emerge in such contexts. We note, however, that in these cases there is little reason to believe that a weak interpretation is imposed on the relevant *at*/*of* object. It may very well turn out that the genitive marking, discussed in Ramchand (1997), and associated with atelic reading, is an instantiation of the conative alternation or of the partitive complement in (iic). The question under consideration here, however, is the status of the direct objects in (ia–c), and whether or not there is evidence to distinguish their syntactic positioning as well as their interpretation as weak or strong from that of their counterparts in telic structures. Both claims are made by van Hout (op. cit.). The latter claim is made by de Hoop (op. cit.). For some more relevant contrasts, see Chapter 5, Section 5.2.

[6] Although, presumably, the notion of structural case could be modified so as to allow it both in functional specifiers and in government configuration. Such a move, unfortunately, would do away with both a unified description for structural vs. inherent case and with a unified account for ECM constructions, see below for some discussion.

[7] Van Hout's (1996, 2001) system retains a degree of lexical specification greater than that proposed in this work. Specifically, she assumes that verbs may be associated with event types (i.e. *kill, murder, open*, etc. are inherently telic). Furthermore, within van Hout's system, AgrOP checks, rather than 'creates', telicity. The telicity feature in AgrO is always checked by the verb, although the telicity marking on the verb need not be inherent to the lexical listing of that verb. Rather, the verb may 'inherit' telicity from a telic predicate (i.e. a predicate rendered telic through the intervention of particles, delimiting PPs, or resultatives), or through the presence in the structure of an incremental Theme argument. The projection of AgrOP, in turn, triggers the merger of a DP in its specifier, thereby giving rise to Verkuyl's generalization. This approach commits van Hout to the claim that accusative case is necessary, but not sufficient, to trigger telicity. Within her system, for instance, a stative verb, e.g. a psych verb, would still project in the context of an AgrO node and be associated with accusative case, but telicity will not be induced because the verb is associated with a stative inherent feature. In the model presented here, on the other hand, the structure of psych predicates and statives, by definition, will not involve the projection of Asp_Q, and hence whatever case is available to objects of psych predicates, and whatever its morphological realization, it would represent a distinct structure from that associated with accusative case in telic transitives. We note that in Finnish, stative transitive predicates verbs are typically associated with partitive case (but see n. 2 for some comments on accusative case in stative contexts).

Regardless of the prima facie attraction of such an approach to the difference between accusative case and partitive case, I will argue that empirical evidence overwhelmingly shows it to be the wrong analysis. Following Maling and Vainikka (1993) and Vainikka (1993), I will show that partitive case is structural and is insensitive to the distinction between strong and weak NPs. Furthermore, telicity itself is insensitive to the distinction between strong and weak NPs, contra de Hoop (1992), van Hout (1992, 1996), and Borer (1994). The correct distinction is not the weak–strong one, but rather the quantity–homogeneity one, as outlined earlier. Homogeneous DPs are certainly weak (semantically as well as syntactically, if by weak we mean, as discussed in Chapter 5 in Volume I, an absence of DP-internal range assignment to $\langle e \rangle_d$, and hence a variable in D). Nevertheless, their distribution and their properties do not correlate with the distribution and the properties of quantity weak NPs or partitive case. Finally, I will appeal to Vikner (1995) in rejecting the analysis of object shift in Dutch and German as movement for case, thereby seriously weakening the claim that object shift of strong, but not weak DPs is relevant to the location of partitive case assignment or to event structure in general.

Let us turn first to the putative correlation between partitive and accusative case and the weak–strong distinction. Note now that in the absence of an overt article in Finnish, the direct objects in (3)–(4) are, in principle, ambiguous between a definite and an indefinite reading. A definite reading is certainly pragmatically less plausible in some atelic contexts (e.g. if a house only comes to existence at the end of the building event, an event of *building the house* is pragmatically less plausible, although certainly not impossible to construe), while an indefinite reading is equally pragmatically odd in telic contexts, especially in the past tense (thus if I finished reading a book, it acquires a rather particular reference, but although describing the event with *I finished a book*, where *a book* is a non-specific indefinite, might be pragmatically odd, it is, again, certainly not impossible). When such pragmatic factors are set aside, however, it turns out that native speakers of Finnish find definite (and hence strong) readings of the objects in (3) fully acceptable. Yet a definite NP, by the de Hoop–van Hout system, must receive accusative case, and must, in the context of these particular verbs, trigger telicity under van Hout's approach. Likewise, indefinite readings are available for the objects in (4), predicted erroneously, within the de Hoop–van Hout system, to receive partitive case and induce atelicity (and see Kiparsky 1998, where the de Hoop system is directly criticized).

Even more damning are the following examples, from Maling and Vainikka (1993):

(7) Presidentti ampui kaikkia lintuja.
president shot all.PRT birds.PRT (also most.PRT)
'The president was shooting at all the birds.'

While the definite–indefinite interpretation of article-less DPs may be subject to some vagueness, this is clearly not the case in (7), where partitive case is attached to a strong quantifier. In addition to being a clear counter-example to the strong NP/accusative generalization, it also serves as a counter-example to van Hout's execution of de Hoop's system, according to which all strong NPs map onto [Spec,AgrO] to receive accusative case, thereby displaying object shift diagnostics and triggering telicity. To the extent that there is any validity, then, to the Mapping Hypothesis of Diesing (1992), it is clear that telicity could not be derived from it (again, contra Borer 1994 and van Hout 1992, 1996). We further note that as the strong quantifier in (7) is capable of taking wide scope, its occurrence as a partitive in an atelic sentence, as in (7), constitutes a serious problem for all attempts to derive atelicity or the distribution of partitive case from the assumption that partitively-marked nominals, or for that matter, any direct objects in atelic structures, are predicates which incorporate semantically onto the verb, giving rise to a semantically intransitive complex predicate. It is worthwhile noting at this point that Belletti's original attempt to derive the indefiniteness restriction from the properties of partitive case as otherwise attested in Finnish, for example, would likewise have to be abandoned at this point (and see Ramchand 1997, for a similar conclusion).[8]

We conclude, then, that the [weak NP ⇔ partitive], [strong NP ⇔ accusative] generalization is simply empirically incorrect, and that therefore the distribution of partitive case cannot be accounted for by assuming that weak DPs stay in the VP, while strong ones move to a functional specifier triggering telicity

---

[8] As pointed out by Kiparsky (1998), partitive case does impose a definiteness restriction when it is assigned to subjects of intransitive verbs. One could thus argue that these serve as the relevant comparison set for Belletti's data. However, two important differences remain even within the domain of intransitive subjects between cases of partitive case in Finnish, and the class of cases studied by Belletti (1988). First, and most importantly, partitive subjects in Finnish do not trigger subject–verb agreement, and rather, the verb is inflected as a default third-person singular, in contrast with the post-verbal unaccusative subjects studied by Belletti (1988), which display full agreement. Secondly, as Kiparsky (1998) points out, only a subset of indefinites are possible in such contexts, namely, determinerless ones (bare plurals and bare mass nouns), making this class characterizable as homogeneous (or unbound, in the terminology of Kiparsky, op. cit.), rather than weak, or indefinite. Of course, as the homogeneity–quantity distinction is, to begin with, the one relevant for aspectual differences, rather than the weak–strong distinction, this is not surprising. The class of post-verbal (indefinite) subjects studied by Belletti, on the other hand, appears to be best characterized by the obligatoriness of existential binding, and hence correlates precisely with the strong–weak distinction, and not with the homogeneity–quantity distinction, suggesting that a partitive case account for post-verbal unaccusatives is altogether implausible. For a detailed discussion of weak post-verbal subjects, see Chapter 9.

and receiving accusative case. Nevertheless, one could suggest the weakening of (6) to (8):

(8) a. Strong DP ← movement to [Spec,AgrO].
 b. Weak DP → in-situ case.
 c. Telicity → filled [Spec,AgrO].

In essence, (8) involves an optional movement for strong DPs to [Spec,AgrO]. If such movement takes place, it results in accusative case and in telicity. If, on the other hand, the strong DP stays in the VP, it is assigned weak, possibly inherent case, and no telicity emerges. As it turns out, however, such a weakening to (8) does not do much to solve our problems. First, as Maling and Vainikka (1993) and Vainikka (1993) show, partitive case cannot possibly be an inherent case, as it is found in ECM contexts such as those in (9):

(9) Anne pitaa   [Helsinkilaisia   kummallisina].
 Anne considers Helsinki.folks.PRT strange

In (9), partitive is assigned to the subject of the small clause [Helsinki.folks strange]. The sentence is, of course, atelic, and as such, does not serve as a counter-example to the claim that partitive case in Finnish correlates with atelicity. However, as *Helsinkilaisia* 'Helsinki folks' can hardly be an argument of *pitaa* 'consider', by common assumptions it would not be possible for it to be assigned inherent case by 'consider'. On the other hand, if partitive case is structural, this casts much prima facie doubt on the assumption that it stays in the VP. If we assume that it does, note, we must presuppose not only two distinct structural case assignment mechanisms, one under government and one under specifier–head agreement, but also two distinct configurations of ECM, one involving raising to [Spec,AgrO], the other involving direct structural case assignment in situ. Yet evidence for raising to [Spec,AgrO] (see, particularly, Postal 1974, as adapted by Runner 1995 and others) does not vary along telicity lines.

Recall now that indirect evidence for the in-situ status of partitive case is argued to come from the fact that weak NPs in Dutch and in German do not undergo object shift, but strong NPs do. The line of argumentation is as follows:

(10) a. [−shift ⇔ weak NP] ⇔ [weak NP ⇔ weak case]
 b. [+shift ⇔ strong NP] ⇔ [strong NP ⇔ strong case]
 c. Weak case ⇔ VP-internal (no-shift)
 d. Strong case ⇔ VP-external (shift)

However, as argued very convincingly by Vikner (1995), object shift in both

Dutch and German is not a case of A-movement, and hence cannot be conflated with movement to receive case. That weak NPs do not undergo object shift while strong NPs do is beyond dispute. However, there is no particular reason to think that case movement triggers this shift, or that it reflects different case assignment configurations. If indeed Vikner is correct, these are cases of A'-movement of an already case-marked DP from its case position, and are, at least in principle, neutral with respect to the kind of case assigned (thus PPs exhibit similar movement possibilities). Nor do the predicted shifted/unshifted correlations emerge in Finnish, where, as Kiparsky (1998) shows, both partitives and accusatives undergo object shift, contrary to expectation under the approach in (10)

And finally and most crucially, the implicational relations between telicity and strong NPs (the latter is necessary for the former) is quite simply incorrect. Thus consider the following examples, all constructed so as to avoid any possible construal of the weak NP as a specific indefinite:[9]

(11) a. You have to publish two books (in one year) to get tenure.
b. She always eats an apple (in two minutes) before she leaves.
c. She will build a house in the Berkshires next year (in three months).

Sentences (11a–c) are all very telic indeed, and yet the direct objects are all weak NPs. On the other hand, the telic interpretation of (11a–c) is a very small mystery if we consider the relevant distinction to be that which separates quantity nominal expressions from homogeneous ones. *Two books, an apple*, and *a house* are all quantities. Their ability to trigger a telic reading is thus fully anticipated.

The picture that emerges, then, is that there is no correlation between weak NPs and telicity, or between weak NPs and partitive case. There is indeed a correlation between partitive case and atelicity. But such a correlation cannot be reduced to inherent case vs. structural case, weak NPs vs. strong NPs, weak case vs. strong case, or the mapping hypothesis. Rather, the relations between partitive case and atelicity must find another explanation, which will be formally strong enough to express the aktionsart correlations, on the one hand, and general enough to allow for the free variation attested with respect to particular verbs as illustrated by (3)–(4), on the other. Finally, it must capture the fundamentally structural, rather than inherent, nature of partitive case. Note that, descriptively, the interaction between partitive case and event structure could be stated as in (12):

---

[9] Special thanks go to an anonymous one-time visitor to my class in Girona in summer 1994 for bringing the example in (11a) to my attention.

(12) DPs marked as partitive, even when quantities, cannot assign range to $[_{Asp_Q}\langle e \rangle_\#]$, nor do they allow any another DP to do so.[10]

It follows from (12) that in the presence of a DP marked as partitive, Asp_Q^{max} may not be well-formed, or at the very least, it follows that it cannot be headed by $\langle e \rangle_\#$. It therefore follows that telicity cannot be induced. Suppose, now, that a functional structure could be projected which is not headed by $\langle e \rangle_\#$, or by any other functional open value. Such a functional structure is but a shell of a structure, being devoid of a semantically contentful head. Could such a structure ever be licensed? I will assume that such a projection is, indeed, possible, but under very well-defined circumstances: it is possible iff it is phonologically licensed. Specifically, and modifying slightly Speas (1994), I will assume the licensing principle in (13):[11]

(13) X^{max} must be licensed at PF or at LF

Quite crudely put, (13) means that projections in general, and functional projections in particular, are only licensed if they actually do something. Such 'doing something' may consist of dominating a (semantically) open value in need of range; this would be a case of LF licensing. Alternatively, XP could be licensed by being the realization site of some phonological features such as case. In other words, a functional projection, say FP, could be licensed either by dominating an open value in need of range (and selecting from the functional array an appropriate range assigner), by assigning case, or of course by both. Thus Asp_Q^{max} may have both semantic and case assigning properties, as is the case in transitive telic derivations. On the other hand, it may have only semantic properties, as is the case for Asp_Q in unaccusative derivations. Finally, if semantical-

---

[10] Interestingly, accusative case and partitive case do co-occur in Finnish (see, especially Pereltsvaig 2000). Crucially, however, the generalization in (12) still holds: whenever a partitive-marked DP occurs, $[_{Asp_Q} \langle e \rangle_\#]$ may not be assigned range, and telicity cannot emerge. Thus although in the following case (from Pereltsvaig 2000) the adverb is accusative, the event is atelic:

(i) Maria luki kirjaa kioko illan
Maria.NOM read book.PRT whole evening.ACC

As Pereltsvaig notes, it is the partitive complement in (i) which is understood as the 'direct object', and never the accusative-marked one, which is typically interpreted as an adverb. In other words, the configuration in which the object is marked as accusative (and triggers quantity interpretation) and the adverb is marked as partitive never arise. In turn, the availability of an additional mechanism which may assign accusative (and at times nominative) to adverbs is independently motivated, and gives rise to two accusatives in Russian, in Arabic, and elsewhere. We set aside here the nature of the mechanism which allows for such additional case marking for adverbs, such that it is necessary, satisfied that it is clearly not accomplished in [Spec, Asp_Q], and hence does not bear on the complementarity of partitive and accusative for elements interpreted as 'direct objects'.

[11] Speas (1994) targets specifically functional projections as subject to phonological or semantic licensing. Note, however, that as L-Ds always contain substantive elements (or their copies), their LF licensing is trivially met, making the restriction of the licensing condition to functional structure unnecessary.

ly vacuous, it must be phonologically licensed by assigning case (and note here that for a functional head to be in the movement path of the verb does not satisfy phonological licensing. See Speas 1994 for the relevant discussion). In turn, it is not surprising that languages with a fine-grained case marking system should opt to signal morphologically the difference between a semantically contentful functional projection (=Asp$_Q$), and a semantically vacuous one. Finnish, we suggest, is such a language, in which DPs in the specifier of a contentful functional projection (=Asp$_Q$) are marked as accusative, while DPs in the specifier of a shell FP, corresponding structurally to Asp$_Q$, are marked as partitive. Crucially, then, the structure of atelic transitives does not involve an atelic objective node, nor does the grammar provide us with atelic structure as such. Atelic interpretation remains that which is available in the absence of a dedicated structure, namely, Asp$_Q$. The shell FP (henceforth F^{s}P) that we suppose here, and which assigns partitive case, is devoid of any semantic properties, and quite possibly is the correlate, within the verbal domain, of structural *of* insertion (see n. 10 for some additional comments). That partitive case is found both in (certain) eventive structures and in stative structures is, in turn, a direct result of the fact that for different reasons, neither projects a (semantically contentful) Asp$_Q$.

Returning, then, to cases of atelic transitives such as those in (2), I propose that they have the structure in (14a–b).

(14)

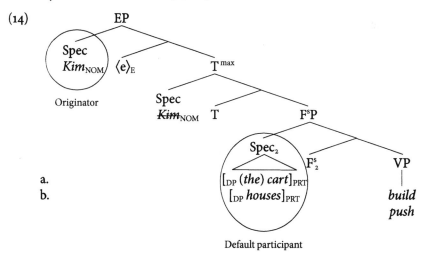

a.
b.

(15) $\exists$e [activity (e) & originator (Kim, e), & participant (the cart, e) & push (e)]

From the perspective of derivational considerations, note that the causal relationship in the structure in (14) could go either way. Within a checking-type model, it could be assumed that partitive case is base-generated on the relevant N. As partitive case must be checked in [Spec, F^{s}P] (where F^{s}P stands for a shell functional projection otherwise headed by Asp$_Q$), any derivation which selects to merge [$_{Asp_Q}\langle e \rangle_\#$] with VP will not converge, as Asp$_Q$ cannot check partitive case. In this way, the base-generation of partitive case on N would block a telic derivation. The base-generation of partitive case on N, however, does not represent the only execution consistent with our structural assumptions. Suppose, instead, that partitive case represents a (semantically vacuous, and therefore phonologically contentful) value associated with F^s which is realized through specifier–head relationship with a DP in [Spec, F^{s}P]. Such a relationship would represent precisely a structural shell of the specifier–head agreement in the case of quantity assignment to [$_{Asp_Q}\langle e \rangle_\#$], where it is semantically contentful, but where it need not be phonologically realized. Under such an execution, it is the merger of F^s that would rule out any derivation in which an overt N did not merge with F^s to become its specifier. Thus it would be the merger of F^s that would both block a telic derivation as well as force a transitive derivation, with a direct object marked as partitive.

Turning to the interpretation of arguments such as *the cart* or *houses* in (14), I suggest that they are assigned a default participant interpretation, to be calculated on the basis of other, fully specified components of the event.[12] Specifically, if event representations with a default participant, such as (14b), are viewed as an algebraic formula with one variable, it becomes rather trivial to calculate the value of the participant as the participant in an event which is otherwise an activity, which is predicated of *push* and which has a specific originator (i.e. *Kim*). Of course, *the cart* or *houses* in (14) could be interpreted as affected, or as undergoing some change. This, however, does not suffice to give rise to a quantity interpretation, as quantity requires quantifiable event divisions, in turn licensed through the projection of Asp$_Q$, the assignment of appropriate range to [$_{Asp_Q}\langle e \rangle_\#$], and to predication of the event argument of quantity, all impossible for structures such as those in (14).

Note that if, from such an algebraic perspective, each event representation is a single formula, we derive, as indeed expected, the impossibility of a resolution for more than one default participant value within one event. Such a prediction is, indeed, not only directly derivable from the need to calculate the value of participants, but also from the very obvious fact that in the presence of more than one default argument, proper c-command relations could not be estab-

---

[12] The existence of a default argumental interpretation, as associated with L-heads which do not project argument structure in and of themselves, was first suggested in Borer (1994), and has recently been proposed for external arguments within derived nominals by Marantz (1997).

lished, and all explanatory hope would be lost. To see that this is true, consider specifically the initial array in (16a). Suppose now that F^{s}P projects, rather than Asp$_Q$, and that there is no EP node to license an originator interpretation, or alternatively, that EP does not give rise to an originator interpretation, an option which is discussed in Chapter 9, Section 9.2):

(16) a. Horse, pull, farmer
 b. ([$_{EP}$) [$_{TP}$ horse.NOM [$_{FsP}$ farmer.PRT [$_{VP}$ pull]]
 c. ([$_{EP}$) [$_{TP}$ farmer.NOM [$_{FsP}$ horse.PRT [$_{VP}$ pull]]

While (16b) and (16c) would give rise to a fixed word order and fixed c-command relations, there is, in actuality, no way within the system under development here to prevent the structure in (16b) from having the interpretation 'the farmer pulled the horse', or the structure in (16c) from having the interpretation 'the horse pulled the farmer'. Even if by default we can conclude that the event must have a puller and a pulled, deriving the fact that the puller c-commands the pulled and not the other way around is not possible if both arguments receive a default interpretation.

In addition to stressing the need for an EP node for atelic transitive structures which, in turn, must be associated in this particular derivation with an originator interpretation, this conclusion also serves to reiterate the question already posed in (1c). Subjects of atelic predicates are not always in a sentence initial position, and often occur post-verbally, and hence are by definition not in [Spec,EP], but in all likelihood, in [Spec,TP]. We now note that if they occur post-verbally in conjunction with the projection of an F^{s}P, that is, a transitive sentence with a non-quantity activity interpretation, we cannot assume that they are interpreted by default, as the argument in [Spec,F^{s}P] is already interpreted by default. To illustrate from Hebrew, as in (17a), if one were to assume that the pre-verbal PP constituent, *ba-rexob ha-raši* 'in the main road' is in [Spec,EP], thereby assigning range to ⟨e⟩$_E$, it would follow that *šloša susim* 'three horses' cannot be assigned an *originator* role, and hence must be assigned a default participant role. However, as the event is clearly not a quantity, *ha.'ikar*, 'the farmer', must be assigned a default role as well. As a result, under a derivation such as that in (17b) the sentence would be uninterpretable. As it is grammatical, an alternative derivation must be available:

(17) a. ba-rexob ha.raši mašku šloša susim 'et ha.'ikar
 in the main road, pulled three horses OM the.farmer

 be-mešek šaloš ša^{c}ot.
 for three hours

b. *[$_{EP}$ ba-rexo<u>b</u> ha-raši ma<u>š</u>ku [$_{TP}$ šloša susim [$_{FsP}$ 'et ha.'ikar [$_{VP}$ ~~mašku~~]].
    in the main road pulled   three horses   OM the.farmer
                                            default   default

Similar logic applies to transitive expletive constructions, in which the expletive is at least plausible in [Spec,EP], and, if atelic, both arguments appear to receive a default interpretation. More, then, must be said on the interpretation of originators and on the licensing of EP, a matter to which I return in detail in Chapter 9.

4.3 Impersonal Null Subjects and the Unaccusative–Unergative Paradigm

An interesting confirmation of the relationship between syntactic event structure and the projection of arguments is provided by the behaviour of impersonal constructions, exemplified here in Italian, Spanish, and Hebrew, based on Jaeggli (1986*b*), Cinque (1988), and Borer (1998*a*), respectively:

(18) a. da<u>p</u>ku/do<u>p</u>kim   ba-delet.   (Hebrew;
       knock.PST.3PL.M/knock.PRES.3PL.M on-the.door   Borer 1998*a*)
       'Someone knocked/knocks on the door.'

     b. hi<u>p</u>cicu/ma<u>p</u>cicim 'et le<u>b</u>anon ha.boqer.
       bomb.PST.3PL.M   OM Lebanon this.morning
       'Lebanon was/is (being) bombed this morning.'

     c. šamʕu 'otam corxim ha.boqer.
       heard them scream this morning
       'Someone heard them screaming this morning.'

(19) a. Llaman a la porta.   (Spanish; Jaeggli 1986*b*)
       call.PL at the door
       'Someone is calling at the door.'

     b. Aseguran que van a venir a arreglar la heladera manana
       assure.PL that go.PL to come to fix   the refrigerator tomorrow
       de manana.
       morning
       'I am assured that someone will come to fix the refrigerator tomorrow morning.'

(20) a. Prima, hanno telefonato: mi pareva tua sorella.   (Italian;
       earlier have.PL telephoned me seems your sister   Cinque 1988)
       'There was a phone call earlier. I think it was your sister.'
   b. Lo hanno cercato: era un signore anziano.
       him have.PL searched was a man old
       'Somebody was looking for him. It was an old man.'
   c. Hanno comprato i giudici. Pare sia stato l'avvocato.
       have.PL bought the judge seems was the lawyer
       'The judge was bought. Apparently by the lawyer.'

The null subjects in (18)–(20) are clearly interpreted as indefinite and non-specific. Further, the meaning of the sentences in (18)–(20) clearly resembles that of passive constructions. Suppose, then, that the understood subject in (18)–(20) is an indefinite *pro*. Note, strikingly, that in Hebrew, Italian, and Spanish, this *pro* is plural, insofar as it triggers plural agreement, raising immediately the possibility that it has the internal structure of a bare plural, making it a non-quantitied structure, akin to that of bare plurals (and see (8b) of Chapter 3, repeated here as (21)):

(21)   Determinerless plural [$_{DP}$ ⟨e⟩$_d$ [$_{CL}$ dogs [$_{NP}$ ~~dog~~]]]

Even more suggestive, in this respect, is the fact that such null subjects, triggering plural agreement, may have a generic reading as well, as illustrated by the Italian and Hebrew examples in (22)–(23):[13]

(22) a. Li,   odiano   gli sranieri.   (Cinque 1988)
       there, hate.PL.M   strangers
       'They hate strangers there.'
   b. Qui, lavorano anche di sabato.
       'Here, they work even on Saturday.'
   c. In questo ufficio, sonon molto gentili col pubblico.
       'In this office, they are very kind to the public.'

(23) a. be-šabuʿot 'oklim gbina.   (Borer 1998a)
       in-Pentecost eat.PL.M cheese
       'One eats cheese in Pentecost.'

---

[13] A variant that is singular is discussed both by Jaeggli (1986) and by Cinque (1988). Crucially, however, the singular variant only co-occurs with *si*, suggesting that unlike the 'bare plural' *pro* discussed here, the singular variant must be morphologically licensed. For a review of some important differences between indefinite *pro* and *si*-constructions see references.

b. be-yemey ha.beynayim he'eminu še-ha.ʿolam šatu'ax.
   in the middle ages believe.PL.M that-the.world flat
   'In the Middle Ages it was believed (universally) that the world is flat.'

c. mixuc la-ʿir šomʿim ciporim.
   outside the.city hear.PL.M birds
   'One hears birds outside the city.'

The null subjects in such constructions are clearly distinct from (definite) personal pronouns. It could not be argued, for instance, that these are just instances of pro-drop applied to a third-person personal pronoun, meaning 'they', as they are licit in contexts which do not allow a definite personal pronoun. Specifically, Modern Hebrew does not allow null subjects with a definite pronoun interpretation in present tense, and in future and past, null subjects with a definite pronoun interpretation (in main clauses) are excluded for third person contexts. The (indefinite) plural *pro*, on the other hand, is licit with both generic and existential readings in present tense as well as in future and past. Thus contrasting with the grammaticality of (18) and (23), we have the cases in (24)–(25), ungrammatical without an overt pronoun:

(24) a. *(hem) 'oklim gbina.
        *(they.DEF) eat.PRES.3PL.M cheese

   b. *(hem) qor'im sparim.
        *(they.DEF) read.PRES.3PL.M books

(25) a. *(hem) 'aklu gbina.
        *(they.DEF) ate.3PL.M cheese

   b. *(hem) yiqre'u saprim.
        *(they.DEF) read.FUT.3PL.M books

As the licensing conditions for null definite pronouns and null indefinite/generic 'bare plural' pronouns are clearly different, we must assume that they are, indeed, distinct elements. With respect to the structure proposed in Volume I for nominals, and adapting slightly the analysis of Ritter (1995), suppose that definite pronouns, null or overt, always assign range to $\langle e \rangle_{\#}$. In turn, if they move to D, they assign range to $\langle e \rangle_d$ as well, giving rise to a discourse anaphor interpretation, much along the lines of the definite article *the* (typically, first- and second-person pronouns; optionally for third-person pronouns). If they do not move to D, $\langle e \rangle_d$ cannot be assigned range internal to the DP, and a variable reading emerges (typically third-person pronouns). On the other hand, if we are correct in assuming that the null indefinite *pro* in (18)–(20) is akin to a bare plural, then it occurs in a structure which involve the projection of CL^{max} (therefore being a divided nominal), but in which $\langle e \rangle_\#$ does not merge, giving rise to a non-quantity DP. Crucially, in Volume I, Chapter 5, I argued that an existential operator only assigns range to $\langle e \rangle_d$, and never to $\langle e \rangle_\#$, thereby accounting for the possible co-occurrence of existential closure and weak determiners. On the other hand, a generic operator assigns range to both $\langle e \rangle_d$ and $\langle e \rangle_\#$, excluding the occurrence of any other determiners. The range of relevant structures, when applied to the null indefinite pronominals under consideration, are in (26):[14]

(26) a. Non-Quantity (homogeneous) null plural pronouns, existential reading:.

   $\exists^i$ [$_{DP} \langle e^i \rangle_d$]   [$_{CL}$ *pro* $\langle div \rangle \langle e \rangle_{DIV}$ [$_{NP}$ *pro*]]]

b. Quantity (non-homogeneous), variable null plural pronoun.

   $\exists^i$ [$_{DP} \langle e^i \rangle_d$]   [$_{\#P}$ *pro* $\langle \# \rangle \langle e \rangle_\#$ [$_{CL}$ *pro* $\langle div \rangle \langle e \rangle_{DIV}$ [$_{NP}$ *pro*]]]]

c. Quantity (non-homogeneous), discourse anaphor null plural pronoun:.

   [$_{DP}$ *pro* $\langle def \rangle \langle e \rangle_d$ [$_{\#P}$ *pro* $\langle \# \rangle \langle e \rangle_\#$ [$_{CL}$ *pro* $\langle div \rangle \langle e \rangle_{DIV}$ [$_{NP}$ *pro*]]]]

d. Quantity (non-homogeneous), generic null plural pronoun:.

   GEN$_i$ [$_{DP} \langle e_{GEN} \rangle_d$]   [$_{\#P} \langle e_{GEN} \rangle_\#$]   [$_{CL}$ *pro* $\langle div \rangle \langle e \rangle_{DIV}$ [$_{NP}$ *pro*]]]]

Consider now, in view of the structures in (26), the behaviour of null subjects in Hebrew embedded clauses. As is well documented, Hebrew does allow null third-person definite pronouns in embedded contexts, but only in future and past, and only when they are co-referential with a matrix argument, as (27) illustrates:

(27) a. hem$_2$ 'amru še-pro$_{2/*3}$ 'aklu   gbina.
        they said that   ate.3PL.M cheese
        'They$_2$ said that they$_2$ ate cheese.'

   b. hem$_2$ hexlitu še-pro$_{2/*3}$ yiqre'u   sparim.
      they decided that   read.FUT.2PL.M books
      'They$_1$ decided that they$_1$ will read books.'

---

[14] Considerations of space prohibit us from a fuller exploration of the structure of pronouns in this work. We note, however, that with respect to the structures in (26), and null pronouns in general, a mechanism must be available which copies some relevant values from agreement features onto some functional heads. Specifically, onto $\langle div \rangle$, so as to allow it to assign range to $\langle e \rangle_{DIV}$ (in all 'count' cases) and to $\langle def \rangle$ and $\langle \# \rangle$, when $\langle e \rangle_\#$ and $\langle e \rangle_d$ merge and must be assigned range internal to the DP. I assume that traditional identification mechanisms, involving some copying of agreement features under specifier-head configurations, or the I-Subject mechanism (alternatively, Chomsky's 2000 *Agree*) will take care of these tasks, leaving aside further discussion of this point. For some additional discussion of the relevant facts in Hebrew, see Borer (1986, 1989, 1998a). For the essence of the treatment of pronouns here, as well as an insightful discussion of the relationship between DP, #P (NumP), and the interpretation of null and overt pronouns, see Ritter (1995).

When the embedded sentence is in present tense, a null subject in the embedded clause is altogether ungrammatical, regardless of its co-reference with a matrix argument:

(28) a. *hem₂ 'amru še-pro₂ 'oklim   gbina.
        they said that   eat.PRES.3PL.M cheese
        '*They₁ said that they₁ eat cheese.'

   b. *hem₂ hexlitu še-pro₂ qor'im   sparim.
        they decided that   read.PRES.3PL.M books
        '*They₁ decided that they₁ read books.'

Interestingly, however, when a null existential plural subject does occur in an embedded context, be it present or past/future, it cannot be interpreted as co-referential with the matrix subject, even if that subject is itself a null plural *pro* interpreted as an existential:

(29) 'omrim/'amru   še-mapcicim   'et lebanon.
     say.PL.M/said.PL.M that-bomb.PL.M OM Lebanon
     'It is said (by x) that Lebanon is being bombed (by y/*x).'

On the other hand, a null plural *pro* can serve as an antecedent for another null subject (provided that it is not itself a null plural *pro* with an existential interpretation):

(30) a. pro hexlitu   (PRO) le-hapcic 'et lebanon.
        decided.3PL.M   to bomb OM Lebanon
        'It was decided (by x) to bomb Lebanon.'

   b. hexlitu   še-pro yapcicu   'et lebanon.
      decided.3PL.M that   bomb.FUT.3PL.M OM Lebanon

If we assume that our plural *pro* is indeed akin to a bare plural expression in projecting without a #P, as in (26a), and if we further assume that ⟨e⟩_d in such representations is subject to existential closure, these facts could be easily explained. As existential reading is by definition a reading available in the absence of any discourse antecedent, to the extent that the structure in (26a) is subject to existential closure, we expect it to bar any co-reference with any antecedent, including a pronoun which is itself subject to existential closure. On the other hand, no such conditions hold concerning the ability of existentially closed expressions to serve as antecedents. Once introduced into the discourse, their ability to antecede a pronoun is fully anticipated.

Needless to say, when a generic reading is assigned to the relevant null pronoun, it may be co-referential with another generic expression, again a fact that is hardly surprising, as two generic expressions can certainly co-refer, even if no binding relations are established between them:

(31) a. kše-pro₂ maxlitim (PRO₂) le-hikašel, qaše le-hacliax.
when decide.PRES.3PL.M to-fail hard to-succeed
'When one decides to fail, it is hard to succeed.'

b. im pro₃ ma'aminim še pro₃ yekolim, 'az pro₃
if believe.PRES.3PL.M that capable.PRES.3PL.M then
maclixim.
succeed.PRES.3PL.m
'If one believes that one is capable, then one succeeds.'

One important difference between null existential *pro* and overt bare (existentially interpreted) plurals does exist, as directly illustrated by the grammaticality of the initial paradigm, (18)–(20). Bare plurals with an existential reading, in Hebrew, Spanish, and Italian, are ungrammatical precisely in the context in which they are grammatical for existential *pro*. To illustrate from Hebrew, note the ungrammaticality of the examples in (32), regardless of the position of the subject, when compared with (18):[15]

(32) a. *škenim dapku ba-delet.
neighbours knocked.PL in-the.door

b. *dapku škenim ba-delet.
knocked.PL neighbours in-the.door

c. *dapku ba-delet škenim.
knocked.PL in-the.door neighbours

Suppose we assume, as is common, that (32a,c) are ungrammatical because the bare plural subject is outside the scope of existential closure. At least in Hebrew, (32b) is ungrammatical as part of a general restriction on the occurrence of V1 clauses (and see Part III for an extensive discussion of paradigms such as those in (32)). But for null existential *pro*, at least one of these positions must be available, or we would predict, erroneously, that they could never occur. What could be the reason for such a contrast? We note that as null existential *pro* displays full subject–verb agreement, and occurs freely in tensed clauses, it is not plausible to assume that it is somehow allowed in a position which restricts overt bare plurals because it is excused from case assignment, for example. We

---

[15] The ungrammaticality of (32a,c), when contrasted with the grammaticality of (18) translates directly to a similar contrast in Spanish and Italian, where existentially interpreted bare plurals are impossible pre-verbally. The ungrammaticality of (32b), on the other hand, is more language specific, in that post-verbal subjects in V1 contexts are more highly restricted in Hebrew than they appear to be in Spanish or Italian.

118   *The Projection of Arguments*

therefore must conclude that unlike bare plurals, null existential *pro* may be existentially bound outside the domain of the verb. Differently put, we must assume that null existential *pro* is existentially closed internal to the DP, thereby making its distribution freer than that of DPs which need to be existentially bound from without. The structure of existential null *pro*, in an extension from (26a), must be as in (33):[16]

(33)   [$_{DP}$ ∃$_i$⟨e$_i$⟩$_d$ [$_{CL}$ *pro* ⟨e⟩$_{DIV}$ [$_{NP}$ ~~*pro*~~]]]

Armed with these conclusions concerning the properties of null plural pronouns, consider a well-known fact about their distribution. As argued by Jaeggli (1986b) for Spanish, and by Cinque (1988) for Italian, and as is the case for Hebrew as well, it turns out that null pronouns with a bare plural interpretation do not occur in unaccusative contexts with an existential interpretation. Thus (34)–(36) are ungrammatical (or, we submit, have a very coerced reading):[17,18]

(34) a. *naplu/noplim   ba-xacer   ha.boqer.   (Hebrew;
         fell.3PL.m/fall.PRES.3PL.M in-the.yard this.morning   Borer 1998a)
         'Someone fell/is falling in the yard this morning.'

     b. *kap'u/kop'im   ba-šeleg.
         froze.PL.m/freeze.PL.M   in-the.snow
         'Someone froze/is freezing in the snow.'

(35) a. *Llegan   cansados despues de un viaje tan largo.   (Spanish;
         arrive.PL tired   after   of a trip so long   Jaeggli 1986b))
         'Someone arrives tired after such a long trip.'

---

[16] In yet another departure from the distribution of bare (existentially bound) plurals, plural indefinite *pro* cannot occur, in Hebrew, in object position. This restriction, however, is clearly subsumed under the general restriction against null pronouns in non-subject position, and is hence of no direct relevance to our discussion here.

[17] Likewise, they are barred as subjects of passives, as pointed out by Jaeggli (1986b) and Cinque (op. cit.). For a detailed discussion, see Borer (1998a).

[18] Pesetsky (1995) suggests that the relevant null pronoun construction (with an existential reading) must be agentive, thereby accounting for its exclusion in unaccusatives and passives. Note, however, that (18c) clearly disconfirms this suggestion, in having an existential reading together with an experiencer subject. Similar examples are in (i):

(i) a. hirgišu   še-hu niknas.
         feel.PST.3PL.M   that-he entered
         'Somebody noticed/felt that he entered.'

     b. garu   'ecli   ba-dira   kše-hayiti   be-xopeš.
         lived.PST.3PL.M *chez*-me in-the.apartment when-was.1SG   in-vacation
         'Somebody lived in my apartment when I was on vacation.'

It is nevertheless the case that null plural pronouns, with either existential or generic reading, must be interpreted as animate, a fact that does tend to be conflated with agentivity, all the more so for an element which is independently barred as a subject of unaccusatives or passives. Animacy, in turn, also characterizes so-called big PRO.

b. *Mueren en defensa de la democracia.
   die.PL in defence of the democracy
   'Someone dies in defence of democracy.'

(36) *Sono venuti a vedere: era una signora anziana.
   are come.PL to see: it was an elderly woman
   'Someone came to see. It was an old woman.' (the 'comer')
   (Italian; Cinque 1988)

Examples (34)–(36) contrast with (37)–(38), in which bare-plural *pro* has a generic interpretation, and is grammatical in unaccusative contexts:

(37) a. [Kše-kop̱cim me-ha.gag] nop̱lim le-mata.
      [when-jump.PL.M from-the roof] fall.M.PL down
      'For all x, when x jumps from the roof, x falls down.'
      (Hebrew; Borer 1998a)

   b. [Be-antartiqa] qop'im ba-šeleg 'im mitxolelet seᶜara.
      [in Antarctica] freeze.PL.M in-the.snow if happens storm
      'In Antarctica, one freezes in the snow if there is a storm.'

(38) a. Qui, sono educati in un'atmosfera protestante molto rigida.
      here are.PL educated in an atmosphere protestant very rigid
      'Here, one is educated in a very strict Protestant atmosphere.'

   b. Qui, vanno a scuola gia a quattro anni.
      here go.PL to school when four years
      'Here, one goes to school at age four.'
      (Cinque 1988)

(39) c. Ai Tropici, muoiono giovani.
      in.the Tropics die.PL young.PL
      'In the tropics, one dies young.'

   d. In Inghiliterra, arrivono presto per incontrare la regina.
      in England arrive.PL early to meet the queen
      'In England, one arrives early to meet the queen.'
      (A. Vecchiato, pers. comm.)

Consider now how such a contrast can be accounted for within the system presented here. Recall that (non-generic) bare plurals and mass nouns are non-quantity structures. Recall that by definition, unaccusatives are structures in which Asp$_Q$ is projected, [$_{\text{Asp}_Q}\langle e \rangle_{\#}$] is assigned range by a quantity DP in [Spec, Asp$_Q$], and that DP, in turn, is interpreted as subject-of-quantity. If, however, the structure under consideration is such that the conceptual array includes at most one argument, and if, by assumption, that argument is non-quantity, an unaccusative structure could never emerge. No such restriction applies to unergative structures, where the relevant argument could move directly to [Spec, EP] (having merged, presumably, in [Spec, TP]), giving rise to a non-quantity, activity reading without any difficulty. Recall now that we crucially assumed that existential closure does not consist of assigning range to $\langle e \rangle_\#$, but only of assigning range, indeed binding, $\langle e \rangle_d$. It is precisely that fact which allowed the co-occurrence of existential closure and weak determiners. On the other hand, generics, we suggested, assigned range to both $\langle e \rangle_d$ and $\langle e \rangle_\#$, making their occurrence with other determiners, weak or strong, impossible. It therefore follows that *pro* with an existential reading is not a quantity structure (cf. 26a) and cannot license unaccusative structures. However, it could co-exist with unergative structures. On the other hand, *pro* with a generic interpretation could occur in both unaccusative and unergative structures. Both predictions are born out empirically, as demonstrated earlier, thereby providing independent evidence for the DP structure proposed here, for the view of syntactic quantity suggested, and for the building blocks of event structure. The relevant (intransitive) configurations are in (40)–(41):

(40) *Existential pro*
  a. *[$_{EP}$ *pro-ex* [$_{TP}$ ~~*pro-ex*~~ [$_{Asp_Q}$ ~~*pro-ex*~~ $\langle e \rangle_\#$ [$_{VP}$ ...
      ([$_{Asp_Q}$ $\langle e \rangle_\#$ not assigned range)
  b. *[$_{EP}$ *pro-ex* [$_{TP}$ ~~*pro-ex*~~ [$_{F^sP}$ ~~*pro-ex*~~ $\langle e \rangle_\#$ [$_{VP}$ ...
      (F^sP is not phonologically licensed—partitive case cannot be assigned due to Burzio's generalization)
  c. [$_{EP}$ *pro-ex* [$_{TP}$ ~~*pro-ex*~~   [$_{VP}$ ...
      (licit, unergative, atelic derivation)

(41) *Generic pro*
  a. [$_{EP}$ *pro-gen* [$_{TP}$ ~~*pro-gen*~~ [$_{Asp_Q}$ ~~*pro-gen*~~ $\langle e \rangle_\#$ [$_{VP}$ ...
      (licit, unaccusative derivation)
  b. *[$_{EP}$ *pro-gen* [$_{TP}$ ~~*pro-gen*~~ [$_{F^sP}$ ~~*pro-gen*~~ $\langle e \rangle_\#$ [$_{VP}$ ...
      (F^sP is not phonologically licensed—partitive case cannot be assigned due to Burzio's generalization)
  c. [$_{EP}$ *pro-gen* [$_{TP}$ ~~*pro-gen*~~   [$_{VP}$ ...
      (licit, unergative, atelic derivation)

5

Interpreting Telicity

5.1 Introduction

The account given for the projection of arguments in the previous chapters rests very heavily on the existence of a particular syntactic configuration, which leads to an event structure and an argumental interpretation of a specific sort. Most prominently, it involved postulating a structure which is sufficient (but as we will see, not necessary) to give rise to a telic interpretation, and which results in the assignment of an event participant role to the direct object. More specifically, the account rests on the following premises:

A. The semantics of (at least some aspects of) event structure is read off the syntax of functional structures with specific range assigned to the functional heads.
B. At least for a well-defined subset of telic interpretations, such range assignment is met in a particular syntactic configuration, specifically, that of specifier–head agreement, with the structure in (1):
(1) $[_{Asp_Q} DP^{\alpha}_{\#} [_{Asp_Q} \langle e^{\alpha} \rangle_{\#}]]$ (with α the specific quantity value of $[_{DP} \langle e \rangle_{\#}]$)

It is precisely this syntactic configuration which gives content to the often-discussed homomorphism between the quantificational properties of events and the quantificational properties of nominals. Within the syntactic domain, this homomorphism derives from the fact that both nominals and events may (or may not) be syntactically specified as quantity, where by quantity we mean the existence of quantifiable divisions, ranging semantically over a similar class of predicates within the nominal domain and the event domain, and from the fact that specifier–head agreement may copy the quantity value of a nominal onto the head that it is attached to, thereby giving rise to quantifiable event divisions.

C. As the crucial property here is quantity, syntactically represented and semantically interpreted in accordance with that syntactic structure, no role whatsoever is played by the lexical semantics of items involved, which is to say, neither the lexical semantics of the verb nor of a direct argument which meets Verkuyl's generalization does or can play a formal role in the determination of telicity. Furthermore, to the extent that we deny the existence of lexical specification concerning argument structure, and in following Tenny's (1987, 1992, 1994) attempt to reduce all argument roles to those of event participants, we must reject any account of telicity which crucially relies on the assignment of some particular role to some particular argument, such as theme, regardless of whether it is assigned by the verb or through any other means.

It is worthwhile noting that to the extent that there is indeed a clear direct mapping between the properties of overt determiners associated with the direct object (in an English-type language) and event interpretation, and to the extent that it can be shown that the relationship between direct objects and event interpretation obeys well-defined syntactic conditions, the system we are developing here constitutes a strong argument for a view of the syntax–semantics interface according to which the syntax constructs formulas that the semantic component then interprets. While it may still be the case that distinct syntactic structures could be assigned an identical interpretation, if the picture here is on the right track, it seriously challenges a semantic picture which allows a single syntactic structure to be manipulated by the semantics so as to give rise to distinct interpretations (e.g. through typeshifting).

These conclusions notwithstanding, the account offered for telicity thus far remains incomplete with respect to some crucial interpretational issues. Specifically, we must address lexical specification and thematic role assignment, typically claimed to play a crucial role in the determination of telicity, as clearly within the account proposed here they could not assume this task. Further, the interpretational consequences of replacing Krifka's (1989, 1992) quantization with quantity, in the relevant sense, must be discussed in detail. I turn to this task directly, in Sections 5.2 and 5.3, where I argue against the lexico-semantic encoding of any properties which give rise to telic structures, and where I elaborate further on the notion of quantity, contrasting it with Krifka's quantization and Kiparsky's (1998) boundedness.

Quantity, when associated with Asp_Q, has a role akin to that attributed to #P within the nominal domain. It selects, with respect to a particular event, a specific quantity reticule, providing quantification to divisions of that event. Syntactically, quantity interpretation emerges from the projection of a specific open value, $[_{Asp_Q}\langle e\rangle_\#]$, which must be assigned range. The structure in (1), as well as Verkuyl's generalization, crucially emerges as a result of the fact that (in the languages considered thus far) there is no regular paradigm in the functional lexicon, be it in the form of a phonologically realizable head feature or an independent f-morph, that merges with $[_{Asp_Q}\langle e\rangle_\#]$ and assigns range directly to it. The only systematic way to assign range to $[_{Asp_Q}\langle e\rangle_\#]$ is thus indirectly, through specifier–head agreement, requiring the existence of a quantity DP.

Surely, however, the absence of such functional range assignment, through either an f-morph or a head feature, is a language-specific, or even construction-specific fact. Further, recall that, at least in the nominal domain, range can be assigned through an adverb of quantification. Thus, in principle, we expect the occurrence, in some languages, of overt functional marking on the verb, reflecting the existence of a head feature that can assign range directly to $[_{Asp_Q}\langle e\rangle_\#]$, and/or an independent f-morph likewise assigning range directly to $[_{Asp_Q}\langle e\rangle_\#]$. Alternatively, an adverb of some sort could assign range to $[_{Asp_Q}\langle e\rangle_\#]$. In turn, should it turn out to be possible for such range assignment to occur, we expect the occurrence of a quantity DP to no longer be crucial for the emergence of telicity, contra Verkuyl's generalization. Schematically, such structures would be as in (2a–b):

(2) Telicity (through direct range assignment):
    a. $[_{Asp_Q}(DP_{\pm\#}) V.\langle\alpha\rangle \quad \langle e^\alpha\rangle_\# [_{VP} \text{V}]]$
    b. $[_{Asp_Q}(DP_{\pm\#}) [f\text{-}morph]^\alpha \; \langle e^\alpha\rangle_\# [_{VP} V]]$
    c. $[adverb^\alpha \; [_{Asp_Q}(DP_{\pm\#}) \quad\quad \langle e^\alpha\rangle_\# [_{VP} V] \; adverb^\alpha]]$

([f-morph]$^\alpha$ = free functional morpheme with an α range; $\langle\alpha\rangle$ = a head feature with the relevant range)

Note that if indeed telicity is possible without a quantity DP, it indicates that the emergence of a subject-of-quantity interpretation is the (optional) effect of telicity, rather than its cause. In turn, recall that the originator interpretation, associated with [Spec,EP], was assumed to be an effect of the structure, rather than a cause, a point to which I return at some length in Chapter 9. If subject-of-quantity is likewise not obligatory in telic configurations, the asymmetry between originators and subjects-of-quantity disappears, and all direct event arguments turn out to be entailments from event structure, rather than assignment relations between particular nodes and referential expressions. Verkuyl's generalization, and the argumental interpretations associated with it, valid as they are for a broad range of telic constructions, turn out to reflect one specific mechanism of range assignment to $[_{Asp_Q}\langle e\rangle_\#]$—namely, that associated with quantity specifiers—on the one hand, and the absence (in the typically discussed languages) of direct range assigners for $[_{Asp_Q}\langle e\rangle_\#]$, on the other.

Even more crucially, consider the following possibility. In a language such as English, there are neither aspectual f-morphs nor (realizable) head features which can assign range to $[_{Asp_Q}\langle e\rangle_\#]$, and hence $[_{Asp_Q}\langle e\rangle_\#]$ must be assigned range through a quantity DP in [Spec,Asp$_Q$]. Specifier–head agreement, however, is at least prima facie a symmetric relation. It is thus fully predicted by the system proposed here that alongside the structure in (1), we would find the structure in (3) (where the arrow indicates indirect range assignment):

(3) $[_{Asp_Q} ([_{DP} \langle e^\alpha \rangle_\#) [_{Asp_Q} \langle \alpha \rangle \langle e^\alpha \rangle_\#]]$

In (3), $[_{Asp_Q}\langle e \rangle_\#]$ is assigned range directly through one of the mechanisms in (2a–c). In turn, through specifier–head agreement, the value of $[_{Asp_Q}\langle e \rangle_\#]$ is transmitted to $[_{DP} \langle e \rangle_\#]$, turning it into a quantity DP, in the absence of an independent range assigner to $\langle e \rangle_\#$ within the DP. Thus in structures such as (2a–c), we expect no DP at all, or alternatively, a DP with the range assigned to $[_{DP} \langle e \rangle_\#]$ inherited from the quantity properties of Asp_Q. Elaborating, as the assignment of range to $[_{Asp_Q}\langle e \rangle_\#]$ in (2a–c) is clearly not dependent on the DP, we do not expect Verkuyl's generalization to hold, and whether or not there is a DP in [Spec, Asp_Q] becomes orthogonal to the presence of telic interpretation. If, however, a DP does project in [Spec, Asp_Q], and if it does contain an open value for $\langle e \rangle_\#$, we predict that through specifier–head agreement, it would be the value assigned to Asp_Q, through an independent f-morph or a head feature, that would assign value to $[_{DP} \langle e \rangle_\#]$. To the extent that there is a specifier for Asp_Q, then, we do expect it to exhibit the same sort of agreement phenomena as we saw in languages that must obey Verkuyl's generalization to assign range to Asp_Q. In these cases, however, it would be the value of the head that would be copied onto the specifier, rather than the other way around.

Are there actually structures such as those in (2)–(3), involving, specifically, direct range assignment to Asp_Q, without a direct argument, without a DP in [Spec, Asp_Q]? Note that if there are, not only do they serve as evidence that Verkuyl's generalization does not hold universally, but further, they pose a serious problem for accounts that crucially derive telicity from the existence of a DP argument with particular properties. For instance, if cases such as (2)–(3) do occur, the existence of a (quantity) *incremental theme* could not be argued to be a necessary semantic (or syntactic) condition for telicity, contra Dowty (1991) and Krifka (1992).[1]

Turning to atelicity, we concurred with Tenny (1994) that atelicity is associated with the absence of the relevant event structure—that is, quantity.[2] Specif-

---

[1] And see also Schmitt (1996). Although she does analyse cases in which properties of heads are copied onto specifiers in telic contexts as cases of specifier–head agreement, she nevertheless continues to subscribe to the view that a direct object is necessary to derive telicity. We note that within such an approach, Verkuyl's generalization cannot be derived from the need of Asp_Q, or the predicate in general, to be assigned quantificational properties, but must be a primitive.

[2] Although, contrary to Tenny (1987, 1994), the structure under consideration is not lexical in nature, thereby preempting objections articulated in Filip (1996).

ically, atelicity emerges whenever the structure in (1) is missing. The structure in (1) might be missing in a variety of contexts, at least three of which were mentioned. First, the event might be stative. Secondly, the structure might be missing when a sole direct argument is otherwise licensed, as in the case of unergatives, for instance, or conatives. Third, the structure might be missing if a shell FP (F^{s}P) is projected, assigning partitive case to its DP specifier. In all these cases atelicity emerges, but it is clear that atelics are not a uniform class, in that the term ranges, as a description, at least over atelic intransitive eventives (unergative structures), atelic transitive eventives (partitive constructions), and statives. It follows that while there may be well-formedness conditions associated with telicity (quantity DP, etc.), there should not be any which are associated with atelicity. Rather, we expect to find distinct well-formedness conditions associated with various structures which, by virtue of lacking the structure in (1), are atelic, but which are otherwise distinct. Thus, for instance, we suggested that F^{s}P may only project if phonologically licensed, and that the conative alternation involves an originator, together with an argument licensed in the L-domain through the merger of a preposition. Although both of these configurations are atelic, the well-formedness considerations are distinct and unrelated to atelicity, as such. Likewise, if it is correct to assume that stative events include a specialized structure, they may be subject to well-formedness conditions of their own, which, in turn, would not apply to other atelic configurations. In this respect, the account of atelicity offered here differs from the account given in Krifka (1992) and from its extension in Filip (1996), both of which crucially assume that atelicity does involve a specific set of properties.

I already argued in Chapter 4 that atelicity is the absence of quantity structure, and not a dedicated structure in and of itself. In Chapters 6 and 7 I return to the investigation of atelicity, as well as to the study of telicity that is associated with direct range assignment to Asp$_Q$. Specifically, I will be concerned with empirical evidence for the following claims:

A. Atelicity is lack of telicity. There is no atelic structure as such. Telicity, on the other hand, is quantity structure, consisting of a reticule which is superimposed, so to speak, on unstructured events, thereby associating them with quantified divisions (and see Rothstein 2000b, for a similar conceptualization of the properties of accomplishments).

B. Verkuyl's generalization captures the essential property of indirect range assignment to $[_{Asp_Q}\langle e \rangle_{\#}]$, one of three possible modes of assigning range to $[_{Asp_Q}\langle e \rangle_{\#}]$. In the presence of direct range assignment, Asp$_Q$ could be well-formed without a (quantity) DP specifier, and hence in violation of Verkuyl's generalization.

We will see that structures in which range is assigned directly to $[_{\text{Asp}_Q}\langle e \rangle_\#]$ do exist, as expected, thereby lending support to the specifier–head agreement mechanism suggested as an account for Verkuyl's generalization. They further constitute strong support for the syntactic representation of telicity and event structure proposed here.

I suggested that both inter-language and intra-language variation could and should be traced back to the mode in which open functional values are assigned range, alongside the specific range of values associated with any given functional marker (numerals were counters in English, but both counters and dividers in Hungarian, etc. See Volume I, Chapter 4) Likewise, within the verbal domain, I suggest, variation is to be traced back to range assignment modes and specific values associated with specific range assigners. The English functional lexicon, for example, does not list a head feature (alternatively, does not provide a phonological realization for a head feature), or an f-morph which can assign range directly to $[_{\text{Asp}_Q}\langle e \rangle_\#]$. On the other hand, it does include f-morphs which assign range to $[_{\text{DP}} \langle e \rangle_\#]$. As a result, range assignment to $[_{\text{Asp}_Q}\langle e \rangle_\#]$ can be, and typically is, accomplished through specifier–head agreement. On the other hand, Slavic languages do have head features that can assign range directly to $[_{\text{Asp}_Q}\langle e \rangle_\#]$, but a limited inventory of f-morphs and head features that can assign range directly to $\langle e \rangle_d$ (specifically, no definite or indefinite determiners). As a result, range assignment to the value $\langle e \rangle_d$ of the DP in [Spec, Asp$_Q$], and, by extension, at least sometimes to $[_{\text{DP}} \langle e \rangle_\#]$, can be accomplished through specifier–head agreement.[3]

As in the case of the nominal system, it will turn out that language-internally, more than one mode of range assignment may be available for the same open value. While English predominantly assigns range indirectly to $[_{\text{Asp}_Q}\langle e \rangle_\#]$, we will see that in some constructions direct assignment is available, making the projection of a quantity DP unnecessary. I return to this issue in Chapter 7. Likewise, Hebrew, in which range to $[_{\text{Asp}_Q}\langle e \rangle_\#]$ is typically assigned indirectly, and range to $[_{\text{DP}} \langle e \rangle_\#]$ directly, exhibits constructions in which range is assigned directly to $[_{\text{Asp}_Q}\langle e \rangle_\#]$, and indirectly to $[_{\text{DP}} \langle e \rangle_\#]$. I return to this last issue in Part III, where direct range assignment to event functional nodes in Hebrew is studied in great detail.

---

[3] Bulgarian and, at times, Serbo-Croatian, have been argued to have definite determiners of a type which is not attested in other Slavic languages such as Polish, Czech, and Russian. In turn, these determiners are often analysed as adjectival in nature. If they are indeed adjectival, they should be compatible, in principle, with range assignment to $[_{\text{DP}} \langle e \rangle_\#]$ through specifier–head agreement with Asp$_Q$, with the adjectival structure within such DPs functioning as a modifier of the range assigner to $[_{\text{DP}} \langle e \rangle_\#]$. For some relevant discussion of the potential modificational function of some adjectives and determiners, see Volume I, Chapters 6 and 7.

5.2 Against Lexical Encoding

Consider again paradigms such as those in (4):

(4) a. Kim built houses. (conceptual array: *Kim, build, house*)
 b. Robin pushed the cart. (conceptual array: *Robin, push, cart*)

Recall now that the merger of Asp$_Q$ is altogether optional. If Asp$_Q$ does not merge with VP, telicity will never emerge, nor will any argument receive accusative case. If a shell F merges with VP, on the other hand, only an atelic transitive derivation can emerge, as a shell F is only licensed if its specifier is associated with (partitive) case. And finally, if neither Asp$_Q$ nor F merge with VP, the conceptual array associated with (4a–b), for example, could only result in a converging derivation if one of the arguments is licensed VP-internally, through an adjoined preposition or through incorporation (and see Borer, forthcoming, for discussion of incorporation within the L-domain).

Suppose now that Asp$_Q$, with its [$_{Asp_Q}\langle e \rangle_\#$] open range, does merge with VP, and that the conceptual array is as in (4a). Suppose, further, that no quantity head merges with *houses*. As a result, *houses* comes to have the DP structure associated with bare plurals, repeated here as (5):

(5) [$_{DP} \langle e \rangle_d$ [$_{CL^{max}}$ house.$\langle div \rangle \langle e \rangle_{DIV}$ [$_{NP}$ ~~house~~]]]

That derivation, clearly, will not converge. Although [$_{DP}$ houses] will presumably receive accusative case, as [$_{DP} \langle e \rangle_\#$] does not project, [$_{Asp_Q}\langle e \rangle_\#$] cannot be assigned range and the derivation will collapse. The representation of this ungrammatical derivation is in (6) (where [–Q] refers to a non-quantity structure, specifically here, a non-quantity DP).

However, such an account appears unavailable for the impossibility of a telic derivation for sentences such as those in (4b). Note specifically that the relevant

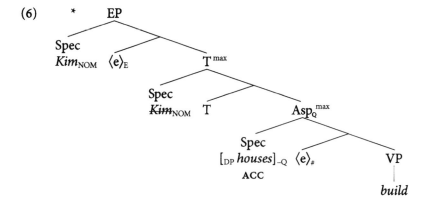

argument, *the cart*, is in fact a quantity, and hence could and should give rise to telicity. Of course, an atelic derivation is available, but we predict for (4b), in contrast with (4a), an ambiguity. In other words, (4b) should behave just like those cases in Finnish in which a verb-argument combination receives a telic interpretation in the context of accusative case, but an atelic one in the context of partitive.

Standard judgements, however, are rather clear in the case of (4b). A telic interpretation, in the absence of an independently specified delimiting point (e.g. *push the cart to New York*) is very difficult, if not impossible, to get. But are we actually dealing here with properties of the verb *push*? Should we resolve the issue by assuming that *push*, for instance, is [–ADD TO], in the sense of Verkuyl (1972, 1993) and that as such, it blocks a telic reading even in the presence of a quantity DP? The sentences in (7) suggest that this would be a hasty move indeed, unjustified by the telic interpretation clearly available here for the verbs *push* and *pull*:

(7) a. Kim pushed the button/the lever.
    b. Kim pulled the rope/the lever.

To make matters worse, it turns out that (7a–b) themselves are actually ambiguous. Suppose I push a button to and fro on the surface of a flat table, without a well-defined end point in mind. This, clearly, would be akin to pushing a cart, and a sentence describing it would have an atelic reading. If, on the other hand, a button is pushed (realistically or figuratively) such that it produces a clear result (a bell ringing, someone going nuts, etc.) the event is a telic one. A very similar point, concerning the inability of lexical items as such to determine (a)telicity is made by Schein (2002), who discusses examples such as (8):

(8) Johnny Reb heaved the cannon towards the Union battery (in ten seconds/for ten seconds).

As Schein notes (and see also the discussion in Jackendoff 1996), if the action denoted here involves heaving the cannon in a straight trajectory towards the enemy lines, due north for example, an atelic reading is natural, and a telic one anomalous. If, on the other hand, the heaving under consideration involves rotating the cannon initially pointing, for example, northeast, toward the enemy lines directly to the north, then a telic reading is fully natural. The illustration here, note, does not concern the properties of either the direct argument or the verb, but rather those of the directional preposition *towards*, but nevertheless, it is clear that the same point is valid for the examples in (7). The trajectory of pushing or heaving, together with the function of such pushing or heaving and the presumed nature of the object pushed, when combined with a bit of common sense and world knowledge, will in all likelihood give rise to the correct interpretation. From the point of view of the grammar, however, it is clear that the meanings associated with the concepts *push* and *button*, or for that matter, *heave* and *towards*, are in and of themselves neither sufficient nor necessary to induce telicity (or lack thereof), and that the information associated with trajectory and function is neither grammatically nor lexically marked. Rather, it is clearly based on world knowledge (e.g. pushing buttons and pulling ropes is consistent with a well-established telic event; pushing carts is not). We must conclude, then, that it is precisely the grammatical event structure associated with specific utterances, as realized in Finnish through the accusative/partitive distinction, which is responsible for the ambiguity of (7a–b), rather than the lexical properties of the verb, the noun, and/or their combination. In other words, given an event structure, common sense and world knowledge are called upon to render the meaning of the individual concepts involved compatible with it. The emergence of a felicitous reading is then directly dependent on the degree to which the interpretation returned by the structure can be reconciled with those concepts. Thus a telic structure associated with pushing a button will give rise to an interpretation of a bell sound, while the absence of such a structure will give rise to a non-directed motion.

Similar effects can be observed with verbs which are typically assumed to involve no change of state at all, that is, verbs most saliently associated with a stative interpretation. Thus consider (9), where the presence of adverbs such as *twice* forces an eventive reading, as argued by Mourelatos (1978) and Bach (1981):

(9) a. Kim loved Robin twice last summer.
    b. The wall touched the fence (#twice today).
    c. Kim touched the fence (twice today).

Specifically, because *twice* and similar adverbials in effect force the projection of Asp_Q, a quantity structure, *love* and *touch* in (9a–b) are 'coerced' and forced to be conceptually compatible with an eventive, rather than stative, interpretation. In turn, the conceptual component returns a much more felicitous output for an eventive event predicated of *love* or *touch* as associated with human subjects, than for an eventive event predicated of *touch*, as associated with an inanimate subject. In all these cases, there is little sense in claiming that the anomaly or felicity emerges from the properties of *love* or *touch* (and see Chapter 7, Section 7.3.1, for a more detailed discussion of range assignment to $[_{Asp_Q}\langle e \rangle_{\#}]$ in such cases, as well as argumentation that they are not instances of outer aspect, in the sense of Verkuyl 1972 and subsequent work; similar cases of 'coercion' in Finnish will be discussed shortly).

In claiming that the relevant domain for aktionsart distinctions is not the lexical specifications of verbal listemes (together with their lexically selected arguments), this work deviates from much literature on aktionsart, including (but not restricted to) Verkuyl (1972, 1989, 1993), Tenny (1987, 1992, 1994), Dowty (1991), Krifka (1989, 1992), Filip (1992, 1993, 1996, 2000), Levin and Rappaport Hovav (1989, 1992a, b, but not 1995), van Hout (1996), Schmitt (1996), Ramchand (1997), and Kiparsky (1998), in which a variety of lexical properties are attributed to verbs.

Similarly, we must reject claims that the lexical semantics of the noun which conforms to Verkuyl's generalization, or the specific role-assignment relations it has with the verb, is crucial to the emergence of telicity. While the lexical properties of the relevant verbs proposed to be relevant are typically associated with graduality or scalar implicature (see, most recently, Hay, Kennedy, and Levin 1999), the nouns which meet Verkuyl's generalization, in addition to requiring a theme role, are typically argued to be associated with a property which allows the natural partitioning of the event into gradual subparts, a property not unlike that argued by Tenny (1987) to give rise to measuring out the event, or alternatively, to its delimitation. In Krifka's (1998) terms, the homomorphism between events and objects, defined in (10), must hold:[4]

(10) a. *Uniqueness of objects*
   There can be no two distinct objects which bear relation R to the same event.

  b. *Uniqueness of events*
   There can be no two distinct events which bear R to the same object.

  c. *Mapping to objects*
   If an event bears R to an object, any subpart of the event bears R to some subpart of the object.

  d. *Mapping to events*
   If an event bears R to an object, any subpart of the object bears R to some subpart of the event.

---

[4] From Krifka (1998):

(i) θ shows uniqueness of events, UE(θ) iff
$\forall x, y \in U_P \forall e \in U_E [\theta(x, e) \wedge y \leq_P x \rightarrow \exists! e' [e' \leq_E e \wedge \theta(y.e')]]$

(ii) θ shows uniqueness of objects, UO(θ) iff
$\forall x \in U_P \forall e, e' \in U_E [\theta(x, e) \wedge e' \leq_E e \rightarrow \exists! y [y \leq_P x \wedge \theta(y.e')]]$

(iii) θ shows mapping to events, ME(θ) iff
$\forall x, y \in U_P \forall e \in U_E [\theta(x, e) \wedge y \leq_P x \rightarrow \exists e' [e' \leq_E e \wedge \theta(y.e')]]$

(iv) θ shows mapping to objects, MO(θ), iff:
$\forall x \in U_P \forall e, e' \in U_E [\theta(x, e) \wedge e' \leq_E e \rightarrow \exists y [y \leq_P x \wedge \theta(y.e')]]$

The event–object mapping in (10) is intended to capture both the mapping of events onto quantized objects (e.g. reading three books), and the mapping of events onto properties of an object which is the theme of the relevant verb, and which, by virtue of its ontological properties, is capable of partitioning the event in the relevant way. Consider, as an illustrative example, the reading of a (single) book that involves, presumably, a unique event of reading a unique book. In turn, it consists of a series of sub-events, each of these sub-events defined on the basis of divisions introduced naturally by the object 'book'. Each such sub-event may be a reading of a chapter, a reading of a page, or even a reading of a single word. None of these subparts of the book are, in turn, a book, nor are any of the sub-events (e.g. the reading of Chapter 5) the same as the whole event, namely reading a book. In turn, the incremental theme must be quantized, in the sense of (11). Thus no subpart of a book is a book, making *a book* quantized, but there are subparts of books that are books, and thereby *books* is not quantized. Rather, *books* is cumulative, as books added to books are *books* (see definition in (12)). Following a similar line of reasoning, a reading of books when added to a reading of books yields an event of reading books, and the event denoted by *read books* certainly could have subparts which are likewise readings of books. But not so for an event of reading a book added to another such event, which instead gives rise to two events, each consisting of reading one book. Similarly, no part of a reading of a book is, in itself, a reading of a book (with a culminating interpretation). Thus, in the presence of a cumulative theme, at least (10c, d) do not hold (and arguably, neither do (10a, b)). The relationship between telicity and quantization is regulated by (13) (all definitions from Krifka 1998):

(11) $\forall X \subseteq U_P[\text{QUA}_P(X) \leftrightarrow \forall x,y[X(x) \wedge X(y) \rightarrow \neg y <_P x]]$
(X is quantized iff for all x,y with the property X, y is not a proper part of x)

(12) $\forall X \subseteq U_P[\text{CUM}_P(X) \leftrightarrow \exists x,y[X(x) \wedge X(y) \wedge \neg x = y] \wedge \forall x,y[X(x) \wedge X(y) \rightarrow X(x \oplus y)]]$
(X is cumulative iff there exist y, x with the property X (and x distinct from y) such that X is a property of the sum $x+y$)

(13) a. Telicity is the property of an event predicate X that applies to event e such that all parts of e that fall under X are initial and final parts of e.
 b. If a quantized predicate X applies to some event e then it does not apply to any proper part of e. Hence the only e' such that $X(e')$ and $e' \leq e$ is e itself.

We note first two obvious problems with the use of the term 'theme' here as the relevant notion of the object, evoking lexical properties of a selecting verb as the relevant notion of the object. First, direct objects may induce telicity even when they are clearly not arguments of the verb, as in resultatives, for instance:

(14) a. We sang the baby asleep.
 b. We ran our shoes threadbare.

According to traditional views, *the baby* and *our shoes* in (14) are not arguments of the verb. Within an approach that depends on the thematic relations between the verb and the object, then, some sort of typeshifting would be required to convert the direct object into a derived theme of some sort, as well as to postulate, in a manner that would need to be particular to each event, what the resulting relations would be between the verb and its theme (and see Rothstein 2000b for a similar objection). I return to a discussion of this point and to resultatives in general in Chapter 8, Section 8.1. Similar problems for any constrained theory of thematic role assignment are presented by the *way* construction (and see Chapter 2, Section 2.3, for some discussion):

(15) We danced our way to the ball.

Secondly, under plausible theories of thematic role assignment, the thematic relations which hold for verbs such as *spray* and *load* are constant across their different instantiations. For example, *spray* is as in (16a), with the sprayed constantly a *theme*, and the target of spraying constantly a location. And yet in (16c) it is clearly not the *theme* which is the 'measured' object, telicity-wise, but rather the location:

(16) a. Spray: (*agent*), *theme*, *location*.
 b. Kim sprayed the paint on the wall.
      theme   *location*
 c. Kim sprayed the wall with the paint.
      location   *theme*

Of course, an operation involving either lexical mapping or typeshifting of some sort could be defined so as to reassign the role of theme to *the wall* in (16c). Such an operation, however, would render any account of telicity which crucially makes reference to theme circular in obvious ways.

Setting aside the obvious problems for the notion of incremental theme presented by (14)–(16), let us return to the ambiguity of (7). Note now that the object *the button* (or, for that matter, *the cart*), is a theme of *push* on both telic and atelic readings, and that it is likewise quantity, or quantized in both. Finally, the relations between *the button* and *push* (or *the cart* and *push*) satisfy (10a–b) for both telic and atelic readings (and excluding iterative pushing of the same button or the same cart). As for (10c–d), it is hard to see how the properties of *the button* as a participant in either a telic or an atelic event could be reconciled with such statements, especially as it is hard to see how *a button* as such measures out an event, or undergoes incremental change in any sense, as depending on the trajectory of the pushing. Now it could be suggested that the telic event and the atelic event pick up on distinct properties of the button, which may or may not be true. It may also be proposed that there are two lexical entries for *button* (as well as for *rope, book, mountain*, and the many other nominals which are comfortable, with the very same verbs, in both telic and atelic contexts). However, it is precisely at this point that the account becomes circular. Because telic events, by anybody's definition, are incremental, and because they are specifically characterizable as having sub-events which are distinct from the event itself (and note here that this is true of quantization in Krifka's definition as well as of quantity according to the definition given here) any attempt to construe a button as part of the telic event would require imagining sensible subevents to the pushing, consisting, presumably, of measurable partial, rather than complete pushing, as defined by a well-established culmination (e.g. the ringing of the bell). It would therefore also require conceptualizing buttons as things that can be in a state of being partially pushed (but, note, the very same button, incrementality here defined only as a point along a path, rather than subparts of the object). An atelic event does not have quantifiable sub-events that are distinct from the whole, and hence no such conceptualization is necessary. However, what is at stake here is not properties of *button* or its relations with *push*, but rather, properties of the event. To assume that the properties of buttons are somehow implicated in bringing them about not only requires multiple lexical entries for *button*, but is clearly putting the picture on its head. We note that our objection here is not to the characterization of telic events as gradual, or as consisting of sub-events, or even as consisting, at least at times, of mapping onto subparts of the object. Rather, we object to this characterization being described as emerging from the lexical semantics, or indeed, the ontological properties of either the verb denotation, or denotation of the noun that heads the direct object.[5]

The objection raised here joins a number of other objections to the conceptualization of telic events as consisting of the mapping of subparts of events to subparts of objects and vice versa. Thus an event of building a house may

---

[5] In fact, this point is basically conceded in Krifka (1998), who notes that the reason for the failure of telicity for *push the cart* is that 'if the pushing of the cart goes on in an event *e*, then it typically goes on during parts of *e* as well' (p. 212). Granting that this is indeed the case, however, one wonders what, beyond whatever structure would force such homogeneity, is the role played by the lexical semantics of the verb, the lexical semantics of the object, or the thematic relations between them.

consist of much activity that does not map onto house parts (hiring an architect, reviewing blueprints, buying lumber, etc.). An event of reading an article, even if it does culminate, may include a re-reading of various sections, or indeed, reading the article twice, assuming that the first reading did not yield satisfactory comprehension, thereby violating both quantization and the homomorphism between sub-events and parts of the object. To echo another well-discussed objection (cf. Tenny 1987; Dowty 1991; Verkuyl 1993; Kratzer 1994; Schein 2002, among others), we note that for the propositions in (17), with a telic interpretation, the object cannot provide a natural end point for measuring out the event, in the intended sense:

(17) a. Her face reddened.
b. Her mood brightened.
c. We cooked the eggs.
d. We filled the room with smoke.
e. We wrote a sequence of numbers.

Suppose we consider as an illustration of the problem here (17d), based on the discussion in Schein (2002). Suppose we define 'full of smoke' for my living room as a milligram of smoke per cubic yard of air. We can then measure the event, by mapping filling of smoke to cubic yards of air in the room, to the point that the room is full. Suppose, however, we continue to pump smoke into the room subsequent to that point, stopping when there are two milligrams of smoke per cubic yard. This is clearly not a new event, nor has the filling become an event of 'overfilling' the room with smoke. Nor can we assume that the definition of 'full' is relativized here, or a clear circularity would emerge, so that full is precisely when the event was over, and hence only a posteriori can the relevant room parts be defined with respect to the filling event. The problem, we note, is a particularly acute one because *smoke*, the substance being filled into the room, is a mass noun, and hence we cannot assume that it is itself the relevant object in (10), and that subparts of the event map onto subparts of *smoke*.[6]

Suppose we turn now to analyses that make crucial appeal to some gradual property (of events) associated with the lexical properties of the verb, and see how they fare with respect to the ambiguity of (7)–(8). Specifically, consider some aspects of the analyses proposed by Verkuyl (1972, 1989, 1993) and

---

[6] As such, *fill the room with smoke* is not amenable to the solution which Krifka (1998) proposes for the telicity of both (ia) and (ib), which involves the scoping out of the italicized DP from within the domain of the *in three minutes* phrase, thereby acquiring an interpretation associated with a given, but unspecified amount (I return to these issues in Section 5.3):

(i) a. We wrote *a sequence of numbers* in three minutes.
b. We ate *some apples* in three minutes.

Kiparsky (1998). Kiparsky, studying partitive case and taking as his starting point the assumption that the distribution of partitive and accusative case is indicative of the property ±*bounded* of verbal predicates, suggests an account of aspect in which it follows compositionally from the lexical properties of the head verb and its object, largely following Verkuyl (1989) and Krifka (1989, 1992). Within the eventive domain, the ±bounded distinction is in effect equivalent to ±telic.[7] We already discussed briefly the notion ±bounded in the context of DP structure and interpretation. Specifically, the lexical properties under consideration are formulated in terms of the properties *divisive*, *cumulative*, and *diverse*, as in (18) (and see Chapter 4, Section 4.4 in Volume I, and, in this volume, Chapter 3, Section 3.2, for some discussion):[8]

(18) a. P is *divisive* iff $\forall x \, [P(x) \land \neg atom(x) \rightarrow \exists y [y \subset x \land P(y)]]$
(P is divisive if and only if for all x with property P, where x is non-atomic, there is a y, proper subset of x, with the property P)

b. P is *cumulative* iff $\forall x \, [P(x) \land \neg sup(x, P) \rightarrow \exists (y)[x \subset y \land P(y)]$
(P is cumulative if and only if for all x with property P, where x is not the maximal element with property P, there is a y, proper superset of x with the property P)

c. P is *diverse* iff $\forall x \forall y [P(x) \land P(y) \land x \neq y \rightarrow \neg x \subset y \land \neg y \subset x]$
(P is diverse if and only if for all x with the property P and all y with the property P, and x distinct from y, x is not a proper subset of y and y is not a proper subset of x)

(19) A predicate P is *unbounded* (−B) iff it is divisive and cumulative and not diverse

By extension, then, a predicate P is bounded (+B) if it is not unbounded, which may be the case, for example, if it is divisive but not cumulative, cumulative but not divisive, diverse but neither divisive nor cumulative, etc. (see Volume I, Chapter 4, Section 4.4, for some discussion). Finally, the properties ±B may be properties of lexical items as well as properties of phrases (e.g. DPs).

---

[7] As Kiparsky (op. cit.) notes, unboundedness, as marked by partitive case, is a notion akin but not identical to that of atelicity. Most crucially, while all (transitive) telic predicates are accusative, and all partitive-marked predicates are atelic, it is not the case that all atelic predicates are partitive, but rather, some statives are marked with accusative case, a matter already touched upon in n. 2 in Chapter 4. I noted there that within the domain of eventives, the correlation is a perfect one, and that the distribution of accusative case in Finnish suggests that some generalization concerning the uniform behaviour of some telic eventives and a specific subset of statives is yet to be uncovered. We continue to set this matter aside for the remainder of this work, assuming that a careful investigation of the structure of stative predicates will reveal a workable solution.

[8] The reader is referred to Kiparsky (op. cit.) for the specific justification of the inclusion of the restrictions non-atomic and non-maximal (*supremum*) in the definitions in (18).

–B predicates, by this definition, are *bombs, food, run, throw at*, etc. +B predicates, on the other hand, are *few bombs, drop, read something in a short time*, etc. The statements in (20) regulate the relations between the meaning of the VP-predicate and its subparts, and determine the distribution of partitive case.

(20) a. A VP predicate is unbounded if it has either an unbounded head or an unbounded argument.
b. The object of an unbounded VP is obligatorily partitive.

Examples of the workings of this system are in (21)–(22):

(21) a. They touched (−B) the bombs (+B) for an hour (#in an hour)
→ partitive
b. They dropped (+B) bombs (−B) for an hour (#in an hour)
→ partitive

(22) a. They dropped (+B) the bombs (+B) in an hour (#for an hour)
→ accusative
b. They dropped (+B) many bombs (+B) in an hour (#for an hour)
→ accusative

Note now that Kiparsky tacitly assumes a fundamental asymmetry between the properties of verbs and the properties of arguments. While for verbs the ±B feature appears to be linked with the lexical entry of a single stem, this is clearly not the case for arguments, where the ±B feature is associated with the phrasal level (NP or DP), and not with the lexical entry of a particular noun. A similar asymmetry is found in Verkuyl (1972, 1989, 1993), where properties that are relevant for telicity are marked on the lexical verb within the verbal domain (as the feature [+ADD TO]) but on the determiner, rather than the lexical noun, within the nominal system (as the feature [+SQA]). To the extent that the ±B feature or the feature [+SQA] on determiners correspond semantically to quantity functional structure within nominals (cf. (8)–(9), Chapter 3, and related discussion in Volume I, Chapters 4–6), I certainly concur with the conclusion that it is a property of nominal *phrases* (be they NPs or DPs), and not of lexical head nouns, as such. The remaining question, then, is whether or not the assignment of the ±B feature or the [+ADD TO] feature to verbs, as a component of their lexical semantics, actually derives the properties of the aspectual system in an insightful manner.

Consider from this perspective again the ambiguities in (7), which are prima facie problematic for any unambiguous semantic classification of the verb *push* as either +B or −B, or as [+ADD TO] or [−ADD TO]. If *push* is classified as −B or [−ADD TO], we predict the ungrammaticality of any telic configuration involving *push*. If, on the other hand, *push* is +B or [+ADD TO], we predict (7a) to be telic, as it clearly involves a +B/[+SQA] object. Within both the Verkuyl system and the Kiparsky system, then, verbs such as *push* must be classified as ±B, [±ADD TO], or alternatively, remain unspecified. And indeed, Verkuyl (op. cit.) does assume such ambiguity, while Kiparsky (1998) specifically postulates a large class of verbs that are unspecified for the property B (see Chapter 4, (3)–(4), for illustration).[9]

If, however, a verb such as *push* (as well as verbs of creation and destruction, verbs 'whose progress is mapped out into the parts of the objects,' and assorted other verbs, including *beat, shoot, name, investigate*, and others) can be freely assigned either a +B or a −B classification, or alternatively, [+ADD TO] or [−ADD TO], the telicity or lack thereof of (7a–b) could not emerge from the lexical semantics of the verb, and must have another source (or alternatively, we must subscribe to the rather incoherent notion that *push* has distinct lexical semantics in its two different realizations). For Verkuyl (1993) to classify such verbs as [±ADD TO], or for Kiparsky to classify them as unspecified for boundedness, amounts to conceding that at least with respect to these verbs, the lexical semantics of the verb plays no role whatsoever in determining telicity. But to make matters worse, telicity could not possibly emerge either from the determiner system or from the properties of the head N, as the NPs in (7a–b) are uniformly +B/[+SQA]. What, then, is the source of the telicity/atelicity (or alternatively, bounded/unbounded reading) in such examples, or the equivalent ones in Finnish?

Interestingly, in Finnish, although the interpretation of such predicates is clearly underdetermined by the semantics of their parts, morphologically and syntactically, they are entirely regular. As Kiparsky observes, 'once their boundedness is fixed they are treated in exactly the same way as . . . aspectually unambiguous verbs' (p. 286), in that the emerging morphological and syntactic properties associated with accusatively marked and partitively marked predicates become entirely indistinguishable from the properties of predicates which are headed by verbs that are, by assumption, lexically marked as +B or −B.

Kiparsky (1996) takes this latter fact, along with the fact that aspectual interpretation is accomplished at the VP level, and not at the level of any one lexical entry, to be evidence for the existence of a purely formal, morphosyntactic component of the aspectual system.[10] Specifically, he assumes that partitive

---

[9] Although Verkuyl (1993) specifically suggests that the verb *push* is [±ADD TO], for other transitive verbs which do not easily give rise to a telic interpretation, he assumes the presence of a hidden preposition.

[10] Although the discussion in Kiparsky (1998) is consistent with this conclusion, the point is not explicitly made, although Kiparsky (1998) does assume that the purely formal properties of partitive case and imperfective morphology in Slavic have the ability to coerce predicates, see below.

and (Slavic) imperfective morphology is −B, while accusative (in Finnish) and (Slavic) perfective morphology is +B. The distribution of ±B morphology, in turn, is keyed to the semantic properties of boundedness of the VP verbal head and nominal object, if these are informative enough—that is, when the verb is unambiguously +B or −B. When the verb is unspecified, however, it appears that it is the morphology on the object or the verb (and whatever syntactic structure it reflects) that ends up forcing the VP to be interpreted as +B or −B, respectively. Furthermore, Kiparsky (1998) observes, (morphological) aspect as well as partitive case can coerce shifts in the lexical meaning of verbs. Thus verbs which are, by assumption, lexically marked as +B can occur with partitive case or imperfective morphology, in Slavic, giving rise to unboundedness (as in the Russian examples in (23)), while −B verbs can occur with accusative case or perfective morphology, giving rise to boundedness (as in the Finnish examples in (24)).[11]

(23) a. On da-va-l (Imp.) mne den'gi, a ja ne vzja-l. (Perf.)
   he give-PST-3SG.M me money, but I not take.PST.-3SG.M
   'He tried to give me money, but I refused.'
   (Leinonen 1984, as cited in Kiparsky, op. cit.)

   b. Ja vas obman-yva-l (Imp.), no mog li obman-u-t.
   I you deceive-PST-3SG.M but could-PST-3SG.M Q deceive-INF
   'I tried to deceive you, but could I deceive you?'

(24) a. Hiero-i-n si-tä.
   rub-PST-1SG it-PRT
   'I rubbed it.'

   b. Hiero-i-n sen pehmeä-ksi.
   rub-PST-1SG it-ACC soft-SG
   'I kneaded it soft.'

   c. Ravist-i-n mato-n.
   shake-PST-1SG carpet-ACC
   'I shook (out) the carpet.'

   d. iti makas-i lapse-nsa kuoliaa-ksi.
   mother lie-PST-3SG child-ACC dead-SG
   'The mother lay her child dead.' (killed him by lying on him)

---

[11] Note that at least some of the pairs in (24) involve resultatives, and hence could be argued to be independently telic. This point, however, is orthogonal to the discussion here. If the existence of resultative structures changes event structure, it implies that the properties of the verbs, as such, cannot determine telicity, and that telicity is syntactically structured, precisely the point we seek to make here.

e. Jussi maalas-i talo-n.
   Jussi paint-PST-3SG house-ACC
   'Jussi painted the (whole) house.'

f. Jussi maalas-i talo-a.
   Jussi paint-PST-3SG house-PRT
   'Jussi was painting the house.'

g. Rakast-i-n tei-tä.
   love-PST-1SG you-PL-PRT
   'I loved you.'

j. Rakast-i-n te-i-dä-t rappio-lle.
   love-PST-1SG you-PL-ACC ruin-ADESS
   'I loved you to ruin.'

In every single case in which the morphosyntax and the (assumed) lexical semantics of the verb are at odds, as well as in all cases in which the semantics of the verb is assumed to be underdetermined, it is the morphosyntax which prevails. For all such cases, one wonders what role, if any, the lexical semantics of the verb plays in the determination of aspect, given that grammatically, if not conceptually, it can be cancelled. The assignment of the ±B feature to verbs thus appears redundant in a very large number of cases. Rather, it appears, the majority of verbs can occur in both partitive and accusative contexts, and 'coercion' is what emerges whenever the semantic interpretation of a syntactic (or morphosyntactic) structure leads to a clash with the conceptual, encyclopedic meaning of the listeme embedded within that syntactic frame.

There remain, then, those relatively few verb-types in which the perceived lexical semantics of the verb and the morphosyntactic marking are never at odds, and where only one morphosyntactic marking, either imperfective or perfective, either partitive or accusative, is possible (the reader should recall, however, that the only Finnish verbs under consideration here are transitive, as we are specifically focusing on the partitive–accusative division, which is irrelevant for intransitive predicates). All transitive constructions which do not allow accusative case (and a bounded/telic interpretation), or allow it under an extremely coerced interpretation only, turn out to be stative (and see (9) for the relevant comparison with 'coerced' statives in English). Under the assumption already advanced here that at least the relevant stative events do not project an Asp_Q, the absence of both accusative case and a telic/bounded interpretation for statives follows (but see n. 7 for some relevant discussion). A more interesting challenge is presented by eventive transitive constructions which do not allow partitive case (and an unbounded/atelic interpretation), and which all turn out to be achievements, in the sense of Vendler (1967)—that is, punctual or instantaneous telic events. I return to the discussion of achievements in Chapter 10, Sections 10.2–3. The absence of partitive case in achievements, in turn, patterns with the absence of variable behaviour for intransitive achievements, already touched upon in Chapter 2, Section 2.2. The picture here is a general one. Intransitive agentive verbs of manner of motion (in the sense of Levin 1993) reject telic structure; some achievement verbs, so-called, resist atelic structure. These two cases aside, however, the picture presented by Kiparsky (op. cit.) does not support a lexical account. In fact, it directly undermines it, in showing conclusively that a substantial formal, morphosyntactic component is involved, and that it systematically can override conflicting lexical information and assign formal interpretation in the face of undetermined lexical information.

Why, then, is it so difficult to get a telic reading for (4b)? I suggest that here, as elsewhere, what is responsible is world knowledge. The motion pattern associated with the concepts *cart* and *wagon* (i.e. parallel to a surface) is very salient, especially in view of their transportation function, making the relevant world knowledge very hard to override. To the extent that situations in which this knowledge is overridden can be constructed, they must involve abstracting away from the motion/transportation meaning associated with the concepts *cart* and *wagon*, and from their extremely salient locomotion mode. I leave it to the reader to imagine such scenarios. While not easy to construct, they are nonetheless possible.

Crucially, however, our predictions here go beyond the properties of *push* and *pull*. In fact, we predict directly that all (non-stative) transitive verbs should be ambiguous between a telic reading and an atelic reading, and that any anomalies which emerge are attributable to conflicts with world knowledge, rather than to grammatical factors. We already saw that classical cases of atelic transitives are, in fact, potentially ambiguous between an atelic and a telic reading. Can it further be shown that classic telic cases are too?

Although it has been rather standard in the literature to assume that transitive verbs such as *read, write, climb, eat, destroy*, etc. are telic, increasing grass-root pressure has led to revision of this claim. As it turns out many, if not most, native speakers of English find those verbs fully acceptable in the context of the adjuncts in (25):[12]

(25) a. We read the bible in Church today for two hours.
 b. Pat climbed the mountain in two hours/for two hours.

---

[12] I am particularly grateful to my class in Girona in summer of 1994 for insisting on the judgements in (25), which have been pivotal in the emergence of the present model, designed precisely to capture them. For a recent objection to the notion of 'incremental theme', based on ambiguities such as those in (25), see Rothstein (2000b).

c. Kim wrote (and re-wrote) this letter in a week/for a week.
d. For how long do you intend to eat this chicken?
e. Jan destroyed her relationship with her parents for decades.

It would be useful to compare the (at times) relative possibility of the atelic readings of (25a–e) with the complete impossibility of using an atelic modifier in at least some verb-particle constructions which are unambiguously telic, and the impossibility of modifying clearly atelic expressions with telic modifiers:

(26) a. I wrote this letter up in a week/*for a week.
     b. I ate the cake up in two minutes/*for two minutes.
     c. I broke my office down in three days/*for three days.

(27)   I ate at the cake for an hour/*in an hour

(28)   Hebrew
     a. mašakti   'et ha.xebel tok   šaloš daqot/bemešek šaloš daqot.
        pulled.1SG OM the.rope inside three minutes/for three minutes
     b. mašakti   ba-xebel   *tok šaloš daqot/bemešek šaloš daqot.
        pulled.1SG in-the.rope *inside   three minutes/for three minutes
     c. hikiti   'et ha.šaken   tok   šaloš šaʿot/be-mešek šaloš šaʿot.
        beat.1SG OM the.neighbour inside three minutes/for three minutes
     d. hikiti   ba-top   *tok šaloš šaʿot/be-mešek šaloš šaʿot.
        beat.1SG in-the.drum *inside three minutes/for three minutes
     e. qarati   'et ha.seper tok   šaloš šaʿot/be-mešek šaloš šaʿot.
        read.1SG OM the.book inside three minutes/for three minutes
     f. qarati   ba-sefer   *tok šaloš šaʿot/be-mešek šaloš šaʿot.
        read.1SG in-the.book *inside three minutes/for three minutes

We conclude, then, that as in the case of the unaccusative–unergative alternation, massive ambiguity appears to be associated with different dyadic arrays (that is, arrays which select two participants), allowing them to occur in (at least) two distinct structures: a telic, accusative one, and an atelic, partitive one.[13]

Before turning to a comparison of the specific definitions of quantity and quantization, one potential objection must be dealt with. One could propose, at this point, that the conclusion reached here, according to which lexical specifications of telicity are unhelpful, may lead to an entirely different conclusion from the one adopted here. Thus instead of arguing in favour of syntactic

---

[13] I will return in Chapter 6, Section 6.2, to Krifka's analysis of Finnish partitive case, in the context of a discussion of the properties of the Slavic (im)perfective system.

structures which determine event structure, and for the structural ambiguity of (7a–b), one could argue that (7a–b) are simply vague, and are interpreted in accordance with world knowledge, indeed, but not in conjunction with specific syntactic structures. Such a position is taken in Schein (2002), who suggests that telicity, such that it is attested as part of the grammar, is induced by time measure expressions such as *in x time*, and specifically, by the scoping out of the direct object, or some other constituent, from within the domain of the *in x time* phrase. Thus the grammar will assign a telic interpretation to (29a), just in case *the fish* scopes outside the domain of *in two minutes*, but as there is no *in x time* phrase in (29b), it will remain vague, with culmination, or lack thereof, determined outside the domain of grammar, by world knowledge alone:

(29) a. Bernhard fed the fish in two minutes.
 b. Bernhard fed the fish.

However, any analysis of telicity as induced by the relevant time-measure phrase faces serious difficulty in accounting for the distribution of partitive and accusative case in Finnish, which is independent of the presence of such measure phrases. Thus, in considering the examples of partitive and accusative case in Finnish (cf. (3)–(4) in Chapter 4, as well as (24)), we note that a telic or an atelic reading emerges irrespective of the presence of time-measure phrases, solely through the presence of case, clearly reflecting the existence of a structure which is interpreted unambiguously as telic or atelic, without any such time-measure phrases.[14]

I return shortly to the scoping out analysis, assumed also in Krifka (1998) and to some problems with it. With respect to the role of *in x time*, I suggest that it is fundamentally different from that which is played either by adverbs such as *once* or *twice*, or by delimiting expressions such as *to the store* or *down*. Most importantly, while *once* and *to the store* give rise to a telic reading by themselves, *in x-time* expressions do not, as attested by the contrasts in (31):[15]

---

[14] Barry Schein (pers. comm.) proposes that these difficulties could be solved if partitive case in Finnish is treated on a par with the English progressive. Note, however, that as partitive case occurs with statives, such a reduction is at least prima facie not easy to accomplish. Further, even if the partitive is analysed as a progressive, one still needs to account for the fact that accusative case is not possible with an atelic interpretation, for presumably non-progressive cases, such as *we read the bible in church*. Finally, as Kiparsky (1998) notes, there is a progressive construction in Finnish, which requires an auxiliary and has a distribution distinct from that of partitive case.

[15] And note in this respect that the expression *for x-time*, usually treated as a diagnostic of atelicity, returns a bound, quantity reading, and thus must be viewed as an operator on atelic predicates which turns them into telic ones. Not so for *in x-time*, which, we argue, is a modifier of quantity, and not an operator. See Chapter 7, Section 7.3.3, for some discussion of this point, as well as some additional discussion of the dividing line between predicate modifiers and range assigners.

(30) a. Kim ran *once in two months*.
    b. Kim ran *to the store in two hours*.
    b. *Kim ran *in two months*.
    c. Kim loved Robin *twice in three months*.
    d. #Kim loved Robin *in three months*.

Rather, I will assume that *in x-time* is a predicate modifier, specifically modifying quantity, and hence requiring the projection of Asp_Q. Note, in this respect, that *in x-time* has the effect of equating the time of culmination with the actual end of the event itself. As I will suggest below, however, quantity readings do emerge in the presence of intermediate culminations, which can be followed by a non-culminating sub-event. In fact, it may very well turn out that the prevailing theoretical focus on the diagnostic value of *in x-time* expressions as a test for telicity has resulted in explanations for telicity which focus on end point culminations, thereby obscuring the theoretical significance of intermediate culminations.[16]

5.3 To Quantity or to Quantize?

In Volume I, Chapter 4, Section 4.4, it was noted already that Krifka's (1992, 1998) definition of quantization gives rise to a number of problems. First, of the class of DPs which induce telicity in accordance with Verkuyl's generalization, those in (31) (among others) are (arguably) quantized in the relevant sense. Those in (32) (among others) are not:

(31) a. three books (and likewise all cardinals)
    b. the book
    c. every book
    d. a book

(32) a. some books
    b. more than three books
    c. at least three books
    d. unas   manzanas
       INDEF.PL apples
    e. several books
    f. many books

---

[16] If, indeed, telic events do not require an end point, or a *telos*, the term 'telicity' is clearly a misnomer. This fact notwithstanding, I will continue to use it, with the clear understanding that what is denoted by the term is the existence of a quantity predicate (or its absence, in the case of atelicity), rather than the existence (or absence) of a *telos*.

I further noted that the notion of boundedness as suggested by Kiparsky (1998) potentially resolves some of these problems, in allowing a bounded reading in the presence of either cumulativity or divisive reference, but not both. However, we saw that while this would appropriately classify *at least three books* as bounded (cumulative, but not divisive), it would continue to classify, incorrectly, *some books*, *several books* and *unas manzanas* as unbounded (both cumulative and divisive, and see Volume I, Chapter 4, Section 4.4, for a detailed discussion of this point).

Krifka (1998), in attempting to address these problems, proposes that quantifiers such as those in (32) scope outside the domain of the time-measure phrase *in x-time*, thereby giving rise to an interpretation of a fixed amount (and see Schein 2002, for a similar assumption reached from a different perspective). There are, however, a number of problems with this proposal. First, we note that Krifka (1998), in assuming the scoping out of phrases such as *some books*, appeals to de Hoop's (1992) correlation between a weak interpretation and scoping out, in turn correlated with telicity. I reviewed this claim in Chapter 4, Section 4.2, concluding that weak DP interpretation cannot possibly be correlated with telicity. It was further noted that to the extent that weak DPs, such as weak *some* DPs, do give rise to telicity, if one assumes that they scope out of the domain of time-measure phrases, it must be assumed that there are at least three distinct positions for *some*: weak *some*, which does not give rise to telicity, does not scope above time-measure phrases, and does not exhibit object-shift; weak *some* (identical reading) which does scope above time-measure phrases, and does give rise to telicity, but which nevertheless does not object-shift, and finally, strong *some*, which scopes above time-measure phrases, giving rise to a strong interpretation, and to telicity, and which does object-shift.

Consider now the following paradigm, based on Carlson (1977a, b):

(33) a. *Bill ate apples and Bill didn't eat apples.
  b. Bill ate sóme apples and Bill didn't eat sóme apples.

The paradigm in (33), Carlson argues, follows from the fact that *sóme apples* does not have the properties of *apples*, however similar their interpretation might be in certain contexts. Specifically, as *sóme apples* may scope outside the domain of negation, no contradiction emerges in (33b). However, *apples* cannot scope outside the domain of negation, and as a result, (33a) asserts a contradiction.

As it turns out, English marks phonologically the distinction between strong and weak *some*, through the presence in the former of primary stress, absent in the latter. In view of this, consider (34)–(35):

(34) *Bill ate *sm* apples and Bill didn't eat *sm* apples.

(35) a. Bill ate *sm* apples in half an hour.
b. *Bill ate *sm* apples in half an hour and Bill didn't eat *sm* apples in half an hour.
c. Bill ate *sóme* apples in half an hour and Bill didn't eat *sóme* apples in half an hour.

Note specifically that *sm apples* can induce telicity, but cannot scope outside the domain of negation, leaving us with the inevitable conclusion that if, indeed, scoping out is required for telicity to emerge then *sm* scopes to some position above the time-measure phrase, but below negation, with no discernible effects on its interpretation beyond telicity. We note further that *sm apples* can receive a variable, distributive reading and induce telicity at the same time, thus in (36) *sm articles* is clearly within the scope of *every professor*. Note further that (36) is ambiguous between a reading in which *sm* distributes over (*in*) *a month* (i.e. for each professor, there are a number of articles such that each of them has been written in one month), and a reading in which *sm* does not distribute over (*in*) *a month*, but rather, for each professor there is a number of articles bigger than one such that they have been written in the same month. Both readings are telic. If indeed telicity requires *sm books* to scope outside the domain of *in a month*, this ambiguity would need an explanation which is not scope related:[17]

(36) Every professor wrote *sm* articles in a month.

Given these complications, it would appear that a solution to the problems presented by the non-quantized DPs in (32) should be sought elsewhere. As it turns out, Krifka's notion of quantization faces yet another problem. Consider cases such as those in (37):

(37) a. Kim ran to the store.
b. The ship sank (to the bottom of the ocean).
c. Pat walked home.

We note that while (37a–c) are telic, they are not quantized. In fact, they are neither quantized nor cumulative. Specifically, there are proper subparts of an event of Pat having walked home which are events of Pat having walked home, including all subparts of the walking event that terminate at home, regardless of their starting point. Faced with this difficulty, Krifka (1998) separates the notion of telicity from the notion of quantization, stating that while the latter implies

---

[17] And see Zucchi and White (2001) for some of these objections as well as others.

the former, the former does not imply the latter, an unfortunate conclusion, as it leads one to wonder what the explanatory role of quantization might be.

Consider, however, the notion of *homogeneity* I proposed in Volume I, Chapter 4, Section 4.4, to resolve the problems associated with the paradigm in (32). I proposed, largely following Kiparsky (1996), that homogeneity be defined on the basis of cumulativity and divisiveness, the latter slightly modified from Krifka (1992), and requiring, specifically, every interval of P to be P. As such it is distinct from the definition of *divisive* formulated by Kiparsky (1998), (see (18a), which requires some part of P to be P.[18]

(38) P is divisive iff $\forall x\,[P(x) \to \exists y\,(P(y) \land y < x)] \land \forall x,y\,[P(x) \land P(y) \land y < x \to P(x-y)]$

A prima facie impediment to the definition of atelicity (or unboundedness, or homogeneity) in terms of divisiveness as in (38) would be the fact that bare plurals, if analysed as sets of singulars, are not divisive in the intended sense. I suggested, however, that 'plural' inflection, so called, does not mark the existence of a set of singulars, but rather, an infinite number of possible division configurations of mass, with any possible number of cells, including none and one. In turn, it is the task of the quantity function, projected as the head of the nominal quantity phrase, #P, to select from among the many reticules made available through the dividing function that function which matches its properties. Thus *three* would select a reticule which has three cells, thereby giving rise to three individuals, for instance, three books. Further, I assumed that *some* or *several* would likewise select a reticule, that which corresponds, roughly, to the set of 'any (smallish) number (distinct from one)' (and see Volume I, Chapter 4, Section 4.3, for discussion of the principled exclusion of numeral *one* in this context).

Consider now again the application of the notion divisive as formulated in (38) to DPs specifically. *Books* is now divisive, as required, as there are no parts of *books* which are not *books*, *a book* no longer being part of *books*. On the other hand, all plural selecting quantifiers, including cumulative ones, such as *some NP, many NP, several NP, more than three NP, at least three NP*, etc. are indeed sets of singulars and hence non-divisive, in the required sense, as they all have individuals associated with them, as created by the reticule-selecting function of *three, several, many, some*, etc. In turn, as they are not divisive, they may give rise to a telic interpretation, if we assume, along the lines of the rationale established in Kiparsky (1996, 1998), that a bound or telic interpretation is to be

---

[18] The reader is alerted to the fact that the definition of 'divisive' in (38) is altered slightly from that proposed by Krifka (1992), in order to bypass at least some questions concerning the minimal parts problem; see Volume I, Chapter 4, Section 4.4 for some comments.

defined in terms of the failure of homogeneity, or unboundedness. A similar rationale applies to all the cases in (32). As I noted in Volume I, Chapter 4, in a language such as English (or for that matter, any language which has determiners in the functional lexicon capable of assigning range to [$_{DP}$ ⟨e⟩$_{\#}$]), the strict correlation between the presence of an overt determiner and the emergence of a non-homogeneous reading provides independent evidence not only for the presence of the specific execution proposed here, but also for a system in which realized syntactic structures largely underlie semantic interpretation.

Assuming that cumulativity is part of the picture here, note that the notions non-divisive and quantized are distinct in the following way. While Krifka's quantization is only met if no proper part of an x that is P has the property P, non-divisive reference may be met even if there are proper subparts of x with the property P, provided that there is at least one such subpart which when subtracted from x gives rise to a proper part of x which does not have the property P.

Suppose, then, that we replace the notion quantization as proposed by Krifka with a weaker notion, labelled quantity, as defined in (39).

(39) a. Quantity: P is a quantity iff P is not homogeneous.
 b. P is homogeneous iff P is cumulative and divisive.

(40) a. P is cumulative iff $\forall x [P(x) \land P(y) \rightarrow P(x \cup y)]$.
 b. P is divisive iff $\forall x [P(x) \rightarrow \exists y (P(y) \land y < x)] \land \forall x,y [P(x) \land P(y) \land y < x \rightarrow P(x-y)]$.

We may now dispense with the need to define telicity distinctly from quantity, and rather reduce the former to the latter. The cases which proved problematic for Krifka (1992, 1998) are now tractable. In these cases, predicates as well as DPs that were non-quantized turn out to be quantities, and hence to give rise to telicity, as required. To illustrate, *run to the store*, *more than three books*, and *some books* are all quantities, as none of them are homogeneous. Further, consider again our event of continuing to fill a room with smoke past some conventional, agreed-upon point counting as full, as discussed in Section 5.2. In this case, there clearly is a sub-event of the filling which is likewise a filling of the room with smoke—that is, if the filling commenced at point 1 and ends at point 100, the event transpiring from point 2 to point 100 is a filling of the room with smoke, but its subtraction from the 1–100 event would give rise to a proper part which is not, itself, a filling of the room with smoke, quite regardless of the fact that the filling event may continue past the point of *full*. The predicate, then, is non-homogeneous, or quantity, and is telic as predicted. Finally, the fact that an event falling under *build a house* (under a non-activity interpretation) may involve actions which cannot be measured by the progression of the house, or the fact that an event falling under *read a book* (under a non-activity interpretation) may consist of re-readings of some of its portions, is quite simply irrelevant. As both events must include sub-events which do not fall under *build a house* and *read a book*, respectively, and which can be obtained by subtracting sub-events that do from the main event, both predicates are quantities, and hence telic.

We note, finally, that Kiparsky's (1998) boundedness does not face problems in at least some of these cases, notably *run to the store* and the like, in which both cumulativity and quantization fail. This is because telicity, or boundedness, emerges if either cumulativity or divisiveness, in Kiparsky's sense, fails. While the predicates in (37) are divisive, by Kiparsky's definition, they are not cumulative, and hence a bounded reading is predicted, as necessary. A more tricky issue for boundedness is presented by *fill the room with smoke*, with the filling event progressing beyond the full point, or *eat more than three apples*. Thus both are divisive by Kiparsky (1998) (as both include some sub-interval which is *fill the room with smoke* or *eat more than three apples*) and both are cumulative, as both, when non-maximal, include a superset event which is *eat more than three apples* or *fill the room with smoke*. It thus emerges not only that both cumulativity and divisiveness are required to properly define quantity (and telicity), but that the notion of divisiveness must be essentially like that originally proposed in Krifka (1992) (and used in Kiparsky 1996), and not its modification in Kiparsky (1998).

The weakening of the condition on telicity is not without consequences. Note that such a notion of telicity is incompatible with the complete mapping of sub-events to sub-parts of the object, and the converse, argued for by Krifka. On the other hand, we also noted that the complete mapping between sub-events and subparts of the object is not without its own problems. More importantly, if the mapping (10c–d) is abandoned, we no longer predict that a telic event must culminate when the object is exhausted, so to speak. Therefore, this notion of telicity does not predict co-finality, or for that matter, co-initiality. Rather, it suffices that there be some sub-part of an event with the property P which is not itself P. We note that any reference either to the final point of the event or its initial point is sufficient to establish a sub-interval within P which is not P, specifically any interval which excludes either the initial or final point, and hence any specification of an initial or final point will immediately give rise to telicity. If, however, some intermediate point within the event should turn out to be sufficiently well differentiated from the rest of the event, in involving, specifically, the (sub-)culmination of some sub-event, we predict the emergence of a telic reading without co-finality.

Consider, in this view, the paradigm in (41):

(41) a. Kim ate more than enough meat.
   b. Robin read at least three books.
   c. We filled the room with smoke.

We do not actually know how much meat Kim ate, or how many books Robin read. What we do know, however, is the point at which the predicates in (41) become non-homogeneous. As soon as Kim ate enough meat, regardless of whether or not she proceeded to eat, the event became non-homogeneous, and hence telic. As soon as the room became full of smoke, according to whatever definition of 'full of smoke' is in effect, and regardless of whether or not the filling proceeded, the event became telic. It is, in fact, entirely consistent with a situation where the sub-event that follows the eating of more than enough meat, for instance, is not itself a culminating one (in the aktionsart sense), in that the final amount of meat eaten remains immaterial for the truth conditions, just as how far John ran is immaterial for the truth conditions of *John ran*. Co-finality, then, becomes a special case of telicity. We submit that it has become such a dominant criterion in the discussion of aktionsart due to the prevalence of the *in x-time* test for telicity, which, while certainly testing telicity, is also testing telicity of a very particular kind, namely that which arises at the very end of the event. In Chapter 7, Sections 7.1–2, I touch briefly upon cases which are quantity, by the definition in (39), but where quantity is induced by an initial state, and no final point is specified or entailed. The existence of such cases, together with the successful application of telic diagnostics to them, will provide further support for the modified approach to telicity advocated here.

5.4 Scalar Representations and Telicity

In recent articles, Hay, Kennedy, and Levin (1999) and Kennedy and Levin (2000) advanced a proposal linking telicity to scalar representations. More specifically, they propose the following:

(42) The scalar structure of the degree of change determines the telicity of the predicate, *since the terminal point of the entire event corresponds to the sum of the degree to which the affected argument possesses the measured property at the beginning of the event plus the degree of change* δ [emphasis mine, HB]:
   a. If δ is *quantized* (has a maximal value) an end point for the event can be identified, and the predicate should be telic.
   b. If δ is not *quantized* (does not have a maximal value), an end point of the event cannot be identified (based on the semantics of the predicate), and the predicate should be atelic.

Before I turn to the evidence in favour of the view of telicity in (42), note that defining telicity in terms of the scalar structure of the predicate is fully compatible, indeed, is a specific articulation of the view elaborated here, according to which telicity emerges as a result of the predicate being quantity, where quantity is understood in terms of quantified divisions.[19] And yet, as formulated, the conditions in (42) present a bit of a puzzle. Specifically, we note that a degree of change can be fully identified and measured even if it is not maximal. With respect to the italicized portion of (42), then, it is not clear why the measurability of change, as expressed through the measured property at the beginning of the event, plus the degree of change, must coincide with the terminal point of the entire event. In fact, it does not follow from the scalar structure of degree-of-change predicates, nor is it necessary to give rise to measurable change, and represents an independent stipulation within the view in (42), which, we submit, is unnecessary. To consider some examples already discussed, formulating previous observations in terms of degree of change, we note that for examples such as *eat more than three apples*, or *fill the room with smoke*, a degree of change is measurable, although it need not coincide with the terminal point of the entire event. Specifically, if we view the eating of apples as having a scalar structure, determined in this case by the quantity properties of the direct object, as already argued, we note that it is perfectly easy to measure the degree-of-change in the 'affected object', the apples, precisely to the point at which three apples were eaten, but not beyond that, illustrating clearly that the coincidence of measurability and the terminal point of the event is but a special case of telic interpretation. Likewise, the degree to which the room is full of smoke is measurable at the point at which it can be defined as *full of smoke*, although filling may proceed past that point, and the final amount of smoke in the room beyond whatever it takes to qualify as *full*, may not be measurable. The replacement in (42) of *quantized*, with its implication of maximal point, with quantity as defined here requiring rather than a maximal point, quite simply a well-defined point with respect to which a degree-of-change could be measured, is thus both conceptually and empirically warranted.

Adopting, then, the perspective that degree-of-change, as defined on the basis of quantified event divisions, is the essence of telicity, but disagreeing with the assumption that the point of measurement is the event terminus, suppose we omit the italicized portion of (42), and reformulate (42a–b) as in (43).

(43) a. If δ is quantity (has quantified divisions) a measuring point for the degree of change can be identified, and the predicate should be telic.

---

[19] Although scalar structures may turn out to be a special case of quantity predicates. We leave this issue aside.

b. If δ is not quantity (does not have quantified divisions), a measuring point for the degree of change cannot be identified and the predicate should be atelic.

Having adopted a slightly modified version of this important insight into the nature of quantity predicates, consider now the way in which the account presented here differs from the perspective proposed by Hay et al. (op. cit.) and Kennedy and Levin (op. cit.). Crucially, for Hay et al. and Kennedy and Levin, the existence of a degree of change derives primarily (although not exclusively) from the lexical semantics of the verb. As such, their perspective is an articulation and a modification of notions such as *path*, or [+ADD TO], which have been proposed as a lexical semantic characterization of verbs which may give rise to a telic interpretation. Studying in great detail the properties of de-adjectival verbs, and following the work of Hay (1998) and Kennedy and McNally (1999), they propose that quantized degree of change (de-adjectival) verbs inherit from the source adjective both their scalar properties and the existence of a well-defined terminal point (the property of being a closed scale). To illustrate, while gradable adjectives such as *straight*, *empty*, and *dry* have a maximal value (and are hence *closed-scale* adjectives), this is not the case for *long*, *wide*, *short*, and so on, which are *open-scale* adjectives, in that there is no maximal value for length or for width (and see references for the relevant tests). Thus the verb *straighten*, derived from the gradable, closed-scale adjective *straight*, gives rise to telic predicates, while the verb *lengthen*, derived from the gradable, open-scale adjective *long*, gives rise to an atelic predicate, as illustrated by the following contrasts:

(44) a. They are straightening the rope ≠> they have straightened the rope (telic).
b. They are lengthening the rope ⇒ they have lengthened the rope (atelic).

Consider now this picture from the perspective of an XS-approach. I have argued consistently that telicity, as such, could not come from the lexical semantics of particular listemes, regardless of whether or not they are categorized as verbs, adjectives, or otherwise, but rather, that it emerges from a particular grammatical structure which creates a quantity predicate. The quantity predicate, in turn, is licensed through the assignment of range to a functional head $[_{Asp_Q}\langle e \rangle_\#]$, which is accomplished through formal grammatical means that are entirely oblivious to the specific meaning of (substantive) listemes embedded within the structure. At the very best, such listemes could be viewed as modifiers of particular structures, giving rise to conceptual felicity, or lack thereof, as depending on the degree of conflict between the meaning of such concepts, extra grammatically determined, and the interpretation returned by the computational system. It is thus clear that any view that attributes the telicity of (44a), for instance, to the lexical semantics of *straight* cannot be adopted here. It would thus appear, at least at first sight, that the existence of effects such as those in (44), and the extent to which they do correlate with the perceived interpretation of the source adjectives, serves as a counter-example to the account developed here, and to the XS-approach in general.

But what appears problematic at first sight, upon closer investigation turns out to be an asset. Kennedy and Levin (2000), in pursuing the implications of their view, do note that context plays an overwhelming role in actually determining the telicity, or lack thereof, of predicates with de-adjectival verbs. Thus alongside (44a–b), they acknowledge the existence of (45a–b):

(45) a. The tailor is lengthening my pants ⇏ the tailor has lengthened my pants.
   b. They straightened the rope, but not completely.

To these cases in which the lexical semantics of the source adjective seems to under-determine the emerging value of the predicate, we may add the following:

(46) a. The workers straightened the fence on Monday and on Tuesday (one event).[20]
   b. The workers straightened the fence for several hours.
   c. I emptied the pool for several hours this morning, but it is still not completely empty.
   d. The apple reddened for several days and then it dropped before it was actually red.
   e. We allowed the apple to ripen for several weeks, but we actually picked it before it was completely ripe.

In commenting on this, Kennedy and Levin note that when degree-of-change is explicitly provided by linguistic material, rather than by the lexical semantics of the verb or adjective in question, telicity cannot be cancelled:

(47) a. *They straightened the rope completely, but the rope isn't completely straight.

---

[20] See Verkuyl (1989) for the relevant test, distinguishing a possible single event reading for atelic events vs. an obligatory two-event reading for the minimally contrasting case in (i):
(i) The prospectors found gold on Sunday and on Monday.
For a detailed discussion of obligatory telicity, as in (i), see Chapter 10.

b. *They widened the road 5 metres, but the road didn't increase in width by 5 metres.

Unfortunately, the conclusion they reach on the basis of this is that 'telicity is not strictly determined by the linguistic representation', a conclusion which in fact is inconsistent with the fact that telicity in (47) cannot be cancelled. The conclusion, I believe, should be that telicity *is* determined strictly by linguistic representation, but that the meaning of listemes is not a linguistic representation. Consider how such an account could be executed. Telic, quantity predicates would project an $[_{Asp_Q}\langle e \rangle_\#]$, thereby imposing a scalar structure, with measurable degree of change, on the event under consideration. In turn, no such quantity structure is available for atelic predicates, in which some progression may still be implied, but in the absence of a quantity structure, without well-defined points for measuring it. Within the XS model, the actual listemes embedded within these respective structures, recall, are fundamentally modifiers, rather than determinants of the structure. They do, however, have meaning, as determined by their salient contextual and conceptual properties. Thus our concept of *straight* does have an absolute maximal value, (in turn coercible, as with all other concepts), while our concept of *crooked* does not, *dry* has conceptually a maximal value, while *wet* does not.[21] A case of embedding a form such as *straighten* (already verbalized, we note, but still devoid of any argument selecting properties) in the context of non-quantity structure is thus a clear case in which the conceptual system returns a measurable meaning, but the grammar returns an unmeasurable one. Likewise, *lengthen* embedded in a quantity context, even without any additional measurement information provided, is a case of the conceptual system returning an unmeasurable meaning, while the grammar returns a measurable one. Both of these cases are neither more nor less complex (and are in actuality considerably less extreme, in terms of their effect) than other cases of grammatical-conceptual conflict such as *three bloods* and *much dog*, which are extremely odd without a context, and much improved when a supporting one is provided (and see Volume I, Chapter 4, Section 4.2, for an extensive discussion).

When viewed from this perspective, the uncancellability of telicity in (47) emerges directly from the fact that in these cases the *grammar*, rather than the lexical semantics of any particular listeme, has forced the projection of telic structure. Assuming, rather straightforwardly, that the syntactic/functional constituent DegP, presumably dominating *completely*, as well as *five metres*, is a

---

[21] And we note here the clear divergence of the conceptual system from physical reality, where a notion such as 'dry' is just as relative as the notion 'wet', and where absolute dryness is a virtually impossible condition to meet on the surface of this particular planet.

modifier of Asp_Q—that is, a modifier of quantity—its presence forces the projection of quantity in (47a–b), with the impossibility of cancelling telicity as a consequence.

I therefore conclude that while Hay et al. (op. cit.) and Kennedy and Levin (op. cit.) have uncovered an important property of telicity here, they are mistaken in assuming that this property emerges from the lexical semantics of listemes, as well as in concluding, as is inevitable from their perspective, that telicity is not strictly grammatical. Quite contrary to their conclusion, I believe, telicity *is* strictly represented by the grammar. It is the meaning of listemes which is not thus represented.

6

Direct Range Assignment: The Slavic Paradigm

6.1 From the Head to the Specifier: Quantity prefixes and DP interpretation

The existence of markers which typically occur on the verb and which function as range assigners for a DP is well documented, argued to occur in languages as typologically distinct as Walpiri (Hale 1989), Haisla (Bach 1995), Chichewa (Dalrymple, Mchombo, and Peters 1994), and West Greenlandic (Bittner 1995), as well as in Slavic languages (Filip 1992, 1993). An illustration is given in (1). Note that in (1), the affix *puta* 'part' assigns range to the object DP, *ngapa* 'water', itself occurring without any marking.[1]

(1) a. Ngapa O-ju puta-nga-nja. (Walpiri; Hale 1989,
water AUX-1SG PART-drink-IMP cited in Filip 1996)
'Drink some (not all) of my water.'

b. Q'i-utl John miai-xi. (Haisla; Bach 1995)
much-catch John fish-DEM.3
'John caught much fish.'

In fact, given the (presumed) quantity-telic interpretation of (1), it appears more than reasonable to assume that the structure in (1) is an instantiation of that schematized in (3) in Chapter 5. Specifically, $[_{Asp_Q}\langle e\rangle_\#]$ is assigned range by *puta*. In turn, that very same value is assigned to $[_{DP}\langle e\rangle_\#]$ through agreement with the value of # in Asp_Q, giving rise to the representation in (2), where α is the specific range assigned by *puta*, and where the arrow indicates range assignment through specifier–head agreement (see Schmitt 1996 for a similar claim):[2]

---

[1] Examples such as those in (1) are often analysed as involving incorporation of nominal determiners onto the verb. See Bach (1995) and Schmitt (1996) for compelling arguments against an incorporation analysis. For more discussion of this point, see Chapter 9, Section 9.5.1.

[2] Care must be taken here to construe *puta* as having scope over the water drinking event as a whole, so as to avoid the undesirable interpretation according to which the event involves partial drinking of part of the water. Likewise, in (3), *na*, 'a lot of', when affixed to the verb, does not give rise to a reading of a lot of baking of a lot of rolls. I assume, however, that as neither the verb nor any of its affixes is interpreted

(2) $[_{Asp_Q} [_{DP} \langle e^\alpha \rangle_\# [_{Asp_Q} \text{puta}^\alpha \langle e^\alpha \rangle_\#]]$

A particularly informative discussion of the relations between markers attached to the verb stem and the interpretation of DP objects is found in Filip (1996) for Czech (and see also Piñon 1995). Filip (1992, 1993, 1996) argues explicitly that one of the salient functions of Slavic verbal morphology and verbal forms is to provide certain nominal arguments with quantificational force. Thus consider the prefix *na-*, roughly 'a lot', in (3):

(3) Petr **na**-pekl housky.
 Petr **na**-baked rolls.PL.ACC
 'Peter baked a lot of rolls/a batch of rolls.'

Czech, like most Slavic languages, has neither definite nor indefinite articles. In the context of the bare noun in (3), the prefix *na* accomplishes a double role: first, it gives rise to a quantity-telic interpretation, and secondly, it binds a variable in the DP interpreted as the 'objective' argument (specifically, Filip assumes, an incremental theme, following Dowty 1991 and Krifka 1992). The binding of the direct object, in turn, results in the interpretation 'a lot', or 'a batch of'. It might be worthwhile to note that the role of *na* here goes beyond that which is derived from assigning quantity range to $[_{Asp_Q} \langle e \rangle_\#]$, deriving quantity–telicity in our terms, in that quantity assignment to Asp_Q in general need not be associated specifically with quantification over the object. Nor is an analysis which restricts the scope of *na* to the verb appropriate (or, for that matter, a correct interpretation of (3)). One can do a lot of baking, and the event could still be neither telic, nor give rise to a lot of rolls. Further, a telic event of prolonged baking need not give rise to multiple rolls. And finally, restricting the scope of *na* to the direct object would not do either. As already noted in Chapter 4, Section 4.1, quantity direct objects do not necessarily trigger telicity, and an atelic event of baking a lot of rolls is a perfectly coherent one, and would emerge with the direct object marked overtly as partitive in a language such as Finnish. We must then conclude with Filip (op. cit.) that the interpretation associated with (3) must involve the execution, by *na*, of the double duty of marking the event as quantity and assigning quantity to the DP.

Alongside *na* we find the prefix *u*, usually interpreted as 'all (the-)'. Not surprisingly, *u*, too, accomplishes the double role of giving rise to quantity–telicity within the event domain, and a quantity interpretation to the DP:

---

in isolation, *puta*, as well as *na*, will be construed with the resulting predication structure, rather than with each of its parts separately. See Filip (1996) for some discussion of this point.

(4) Petr u-pekl   housky
    Petr u-baked.3SG rolls.PL.ACC
    'Peter baked all the rolls'

Following traditional classifications, Filip refers to the verbal forms in both (3) and (4) as perfective. Morphologically, the forms in (3) and (4) consist of the bare verbal stem, otherwise interpreted as non-culminating, and the prefixes *na* and *u* respectively. The output is clearly quantity-telic. It is thus fair to say that for Filip (1996), perfectivity is a derived notion, brought about as a result of the presence of a quantity verbal prefix, which in turn binds the argument 'rolls', making it quantity as well.[3] Matters of syntactic execution notwithstanding, we will concur with this view of perfectivity as derived from the presence of quantity-telic structures. The incorporation of Filip's analysis into the syntactic structures proposed here is entirely straightforward, where ⟨na⟩ and ⟨u⟩ are the phonological realizations of the relevant head features assigning range to $[_{Asp_Q}\langle e \rangle_\#]$. Irrelevant details are glossed over in (5):[4]

(5) a. Petr [$_{TP}$ napekl [$_{Asp_Q}$ [$_{DP}$ ⟨e⟩$_d$ [$_{\#P}$ ⟨e^{na}⟩$_\#$ [housky]]] ⟨na⟩ ~~pekl~~ ⟨e⟩$_\#$ [$_{VP}$ ~~pekl~~]]]
    b. Petr [$_{TP}$ upekl [$_{Asp_Q}$ [$_{DP}$ ⟨e⟩$_d$ [$_{\#P}$ ⟨e^u⟩$_\#$ [housky]]] ⟨u⟩ ~~pekl~~ ⟨e⟩$_\#$ [$_{VP}$ ~~pekl~~]]]

Making things explicit, I assume that the quantificational nature of perfective head features, when coupled with specifier–head agreement, results in the copying, onto DP in [Spec, Asp$_Q$], of the open value [$_{DP}$ ⟨e⟩$_\#$], to which the quantificational head feature ('prefix') assigns range (and see Section 6.3 for a follow up discussion of this point). We remain silent, at this point, on the assignment of range to ⟨e⟩$_d$ in (5), only to return to this point in Section 6.3. For the time being, however, suppose we define perfectivity in Czech (and in the other Slavic languages which pattern with it) as the presence of a (set of) head features which can assign range to [$_{Asp_Q}$⟨e⟩$_\#$], and which, according to the specific range assignment properties of each particular head feature, are realized phonologically as *na, u,* or others.[5]

---

[3] But see Section 6.3 for a more complete review of the system proposed by Filip (1996, 2000).

[4] And see also Borer (1995a), Benua and Borer (1996), and Schmitt (1996), where the transfer of features to the DP in Slavic languages is assumed to be mediated through specifier–head relations.

[5] Formally, I opt to represent perfective marking as the phonological realization of a head feature, i.e. as devoid of morphemic structure. Alternatively, perfective markers could be viewed as bound, prefixal f-morphs, in the sense discussed in Volume I, Chapter 2, Section 2.2, (and see Chapter 1, Section 1.3, in this volume, for a summary), projecting independently. Here, again, two options are available—prefixes may merge directly with Asp$_Q$, triggering, in turn, the incorporation of the verb, or alternatively, they may be viewed as preposition-like elements, merging originally in the L-domain and incorporating into the verb, which then moves to Asp$_Q$, assigning range to it through that merged preposition. Ultimately, I believe, the choice between these different options is not a semantic or a syntactic matter, but a morphological one, and I return to this, and related issues, in Borer (forthcoming). Here, I favour the view of

Filip (op. cit.) extends her analysis of *na* and *u* to the perfective–imperfective distinction in general, even where there are no clear, overt markers with a perfective quantificational interpretation. Specifically, she suggests that perfectivity involves a (covert) totality operator. The totality operator functions exactly like the *na* and *u* operators, in binding the DP argument and giving it a totality interpretation. The totality interpretation of the DP is, in turn, realized in the obligatorily holistic (and by extension definite) interpretation associated with direct objects such as those in (6):[6]

perfectives as the phonological realization of a head feature largely because it is consistent with the presumed role of perfective marking as range assigner to an open value heading a functional category. Nor does such an execution face, I believe, the type of morpho-phonological problems discussed in Piñon (2001) and Filip (2000), a matter I return to in Chapter 7, Section 7.2. Should it turn out, however, that empirical considerations strongly favour a view of perfective marking as affixal in nature, it would not crucially affect issues of (a)telicity and the assignment of range to $[_{\text{Asp}_Q} \langle e \rangle_{\#}]$. For expository purposes, I continue to use the term 'perfective prefixes', although the reader should bear in mind that in actuality, 'perfective head feature' is intended.

[6] As Filip shows, the distribution of definite–indefinite is quite independent of aspect. This conclusion is directly compatible with the conclusion reached here, according to which indefinite quantity expressions may trigger telicity, and definite expressions, always quantity, may freely occur in atelic contexts. Filip further argues, following Jackendoff (1990), that definites may be non-quantity expressions, a claim which allows her to have them within imperfective structures, following her own analysis which requires *part-of* agreement in imperfective structures. However, if it is indeed the case that definites may be non-quantity expressions, the account developed here faces a problem. Specifically, we suggested that in a language such as English, in order for Asp_Q to become a quantity, the DP in [Spec,Asp_Q] must be a quantity. As definite expressions can give rise to telicity, if it turned out that definite expressions are non-quantity, we would have to assume that they are always quantities in telic structures, but not (necessarily) in atelic structures, clearly an unfortunate result, given that the system tries to derive the properties of Asp_Q from the properties of the DP, and not the other way around. Jackendoff (op. cit.), working within an approach which is not likewise constrained, actually makes the claim that definite expressions are quantities in telic contexts (as in (ia–b)), but non-quantities in atelic or progressive contexts (as in (iia–b)), a matter that we touched upon briefly in Volume I, Chapter 6, Section 6.1. Specifically, recapitulating the discussion there, consider the contrasts in (i)–(ii), where, Jackendoff assumes e.g. that *the water* is a quantity in (ia), but not in (iia):

(i) a. The water rushed out of the faucet.
    b. The people streamed into the room.

(ii) a. The water was rushing out of the faucet.
    b. The people were streaming into the room.

Analysing the definite article as having a deictic function, Jackendoff claims that it designates a previously known *medium*, rather than quantity. On the other hand, in Volume I, Chapter 6, Section 6.1, I explicitly suggested that the definite article, a discourse anaphor (=deixis), designates not only a previously known medium, but also previously known reference and, hence, previously known quantity, thereby making definite descriptions by definition quantity. I noted the grammaticality of (iiia–c) with an atelic interpretation rather akin to that in (ii), but clearly involving quantity expressions, and thereby refuting the claim that the uncertain amount interpretation associated with (ii) is perforce associated with the nature of definite descriptions as non-quantity expressions. (The reader is referred to Volume I, Chapter 6, Section 6.1, for some more relevant discussion.)

(iii) a. All the children/more than a hundred children were streaming into the room.
    b. All water/millions of drops of water flows/were flowing down the gutter.
    c. I was building many houses.

(6) Pavel snûdl^P jablko.
    Paul ate.3SG.PERF apple.SG.ACC
    'Paul ate (up) the whole apple.'
    'Paul finished eating the (whole) apple.'

In turn, in the presence of a bare stem, most typically classified as imperfective, the interpretation assigned to the DP is considerably freer:

(7) Pavel jedl^I jablko.
    Paul ate.3SG.IMPERF apple.SG.ACC
    'Paul ate an/the/some apple.'
    'Paul was eating an/the/some apple.'

In discussing the interpretational differences between 'apple' in (6) and 'apple' in (7), Filip says:

> The speaker of [6] commits himself to the proposition that the whole apple was consumed when the event was terminated. This does not necessarily hold for [7]. From the point of view of the direct object argument, 'apple', what is at issue in [6] contrasted with [7] is whether the whole apple was eaten [6] or just possibly part of it, but not necessarily the whole apple [7].   (Filip 1996)

Within the model presented here, we will assume that an abstract, covert totality operator, if indeed present, is only available, and indeed only needed, in those few cases in which a bare stem appears to give rise to a quantity-telic reading without overt marking. More concretely, such cases, idiosyncratic as they indeed are, should be compared with, for example, the absence of an overt past tense phonological realization for a verb such as *put*, or the absence of an overt plural inflection distinguishing between *fish*.SG and *fish*.PL, and represent an 'irregular' phonological realization of the stem+quantificational head feature conglomerate. The reading associated with (overtly marked) perfectives follows if we assume that perfective marking is, indeed, the phonological realization of a head feature which is the range assigner to $[_{Asp_Q}\langle e\rangle_\#]$, much on a par with the way that past tense marking is the phonological spell-out of a head feature which assigns range to $[_{TP}\langle e\rangle_T]$, and 'plural' marking a phonological spell-out of a head feature assigning range to $[_{CL^{max}}\langle e\rangle_{DIV}]$. The very same head feature, whether phonologically realized on the stem or not, triggers through specifier-head agreement the projection of $[_{DP}\langle e\rangle_\#]$, to which it assigns value, resulting in a quantity interpretation for that DP, as required (see Section 6.3 for additional discussion).

While in Filip (1996) the relations between the prefixes *na*, *u*, and others and the totality operator associated with the perfective are not pursued in detail, an explicit proposal addressing this issue is made in Filip (2000), where it is suggested that an explicit semantic distinction should be drawn between quantity prefixes and perfectivity. Specifically, Filip (2000) assumes that *na* and *u* are derivational prefixes which are best described as contributing to the meaning of the verb an extensive measure function, in the sense of Krifka (1998). While she does attribute to the prefixes a quantificational property of some sort, this quantificational property, she claims, is semantically distinct from the semantics of perfectivity, which consists of the presence of an abstract, morphologically unrealized, totality operator. There is no relationship, Filip (2000) claims, between the presence of prefixation and a perfective (i.e. total, telic) interpretation.

I believe, however, that Filip's (2000) conclusion, separating what she refers to as perfective aspect from the semantics of quantificational prefixes, is in error. I return to this matter in some detail in Chapter 7, when I consider the interaction, in Slavic, between perfective marking and Verkuyl's generalization. In the remainder of this chapter, I discuss Slavic imperfectives as well as the effects which quantificational perfectives have on the interpretation of DPs, as well as other aspects of the perfective–imperfective system in Slavic.

6.2 Against Atelic Agreement

Consider what would be the account given to sentences such as (7) under the analysis presented in this work. Recall that, crucially, under the analysis presented here atelicity is the absence of quantity structure. Although a direct object may be licensed in the absence of a well-formed Asp_Q, such a direct object is licensed in the context of a shell FP (F^sP), which assigns (partitive) case, but which is devoid of any semantic value. If indeed (7) is atelic, then in line with these assumptions, the relevant aspects of its derivation would be as in (8) (TP omitted for expository purposes):[7]

Significantly, the structure in (8) means that a quantificational interpretation of the DP in [Spec,F^sP] in (8) is entirely independent of the properties of either F^sP (which is by definition devoid of any semantic properties) or the VP and the verb which it dominates. Further, recall that the structure, as such, does not assign any argument role to the DP in [Spec,F^sP]. Rather, because *Pavel* is assigned the role of originator in [Spec,EP], *jablko* is assigned the default 'other participant' role, as consistent with the conceptual encyclopedic meaning for

---

[7] Filip (1996) briefly discusses and dismisses the claim that atelicity involves the absence of telic structure, making reference primarily to claims made by Tenny (1987, 1994). The criticism of Tenny's proposals, however, is crucially dependent on Tenny's assumption that verbs are either telic or atelic, and that those of the former class project more structure than those of the latter. Such criticism is clearly not valid for the analysis presented here.

(8)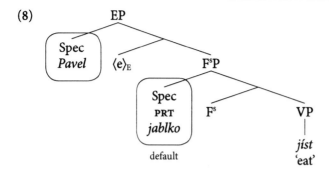

the listeme *jíst* 'eat', with the existence of an originator, and with the event being non-stative.

We turn now to the analyses proposed for imperfectives by Krifka (1992) and by Filip (1996, 2000). Before doing so, however, a terminological comment is in order. The reader should bear in mind that by (a)telic, we are referring here to the presence vs. absence of quantity, as instantiated syntactically through the presence or the absence of a well-formed Asp_Q. (A)telicity, as used here, is thus a semantic notion. By (im)perfectivity, we are referring here to a paradigmatic notion, as typically employed in the Slavic literature. In the case of the perfective paradigm, it includes cases in which an overt prefix is attached to the stem, typically a locative preposition historically, and often with quantificational interpretation—that is, 'perfective' is a morpho-phonological classification. In the case of imperfectives, on the other hand, and unless more is said, I will follow traditional classification in taking it to refer to *two* distinct morphological paradigms, at times labelled primary and secondary imperfective. While the former involves a bare stem, the latter involves suffixation, typically onto an already prefixed (i.e. perfective) form. This is an important terminological distinction to keep in mind, as we shall see shortly.

In the previous section, I equated quantity (= telicity) with perfective marking, taking perfective marking to be the phonological realization of quantity range assignment to $[_{Asp_Q} \langle e \rangle_{\#}]$ and at times to $[_{DP} \langle e \rangle_{\#}]$ as well, through specifier–head agreement. As we shall see, however, imperfectives are neither 'atelic' as such, nor are they a *part* structure in the sense of Filip (1996, 2000). Rather, 'imperfectivity' in Slavic, as traditionally referred to, is neither semantically nor morpho-phonologically (or syntactically) a well-defined notion. Primary imperfectives, I will suggest, are atelic (i.e. non-quantity) because they lack syntactic quantity structure. Secondary imperfectives, on the other hand, are in all likelihood a species of outer aspect, in the sense of Verkuyl (1972 and subsequent work).

Although the analyses proposed by Krifka (1992) and Filip (1996, 2000) differ in ways which I will review shortly, they do share one important property. Both assume that just as telic events require a quantized argument, an atelic event requires a non-quantized argument. Specifically, for Krifka (1992), this means that while (9a) is atelic—that is, non-quantized and cumulative—(9b–d) are not straightforwardly atelic, as the direct objects here are not cumulative:

(9) a. We drank wine (for three hours).
    b. We drank the wine (for three hours).
    c. We drank a bottle of wine (for three hours).
    d. We drank some wine (for three hours).

As the objects of (9b–d) are not cumulative, the failure of (9b–d) to have a straightforward telic interpretation (i.e. to have a set terminal point) must be otherwise accounted for; Krifka suggests that they are best characterized as involving *part-of* relations. Such part-of relations can hold within the verbal domain, where they (may) give rise to progressive of the English type, and within the nominal domain, where, Krifka argues, they give rise to partitive nominals, of the Finnish type (and recall that partitive case, indeed, does not impose non-quantity restrictions on the direct object, thus preventing Krifka, by definition, from analysing it as an atelic structure):

(10) a. $\text{PART} = \lambda P \lambda x' \exists x [P(x) \wedge x' \sqsubseteq x]$
     b. $\text{PROG} = \lambda P \lambda e' \exists e [P(e) \wedge e' \sqsubseteq e]$

When applied to verbal reference or to nominal reference, the result is that the PART relations impose a part-of relation either on the event (English progressive) or on the object, as expressed by (11), where α is a verbal predicate (e.g. *eat*), δ a nominal predicate (e.g. *a fish*), and θ a particular thematic role associated with the object (i.e. incremental or gradual theme):

(11) $\phi_n = \lambda e \exists x, x' [\alpha(e) \wedge \delta(x) \wedge \theta(e, x') \wedge x' \sqsubseteq x]$ (nominal progressive, part of the object)

$\phi_v = \lambda e' \exists e, x [\alpha(e) \wedge \delta(x) \wedge \theta(e, x) \wedge e' \sqsubseteq e]$ (verbal progressive, part of the event)

The verbal predicate α, furthermore, must be divisive, and the account in general is couched in terms of homomorphism between events and objects, as defined by the conditions in Chapter 5, Section 5.3.

Some problems for the analysis of Finnish partitive case faced by Krifka's system are pointed out by Kiparsky (1998), focusing on the fact that partitive case, in Finnish, is used in contexts in which the verb is not divisive (*buy, prove*), in which the uniqueness of objects, required by Krifka (1992), is not met (notably stative verbs, but not only), etc.[8] We note, in addition to the specific objections raised in Kiparsky (1998), that objects of stative verbs (such as *love Mary, see the birds*) do not receive a part-of interpretation in any sensible way, and yet they are marked with partitive case in Finnish, suggesting that at the very best, a part-of analysis of the Finnish partitive case accounts only for a subset of its occurrences.

The criticism of Krifka (1992) to be offered here, however, does not focus on the part-of analysis, but rather on another aspect of the system, namely, the assumption that atelic structures require the direct object itself to have cumulative reference, an assumption which is the motivating force behind the assignment of a non-aktionsart interpretation to Finnish partitive case, to begin with. Specifically, Krifka does assume that Slavic imperfectives are atelic, and that they do give rise to a cumulative interpretation of the direct object, citing, as evidence, the following examples:

(12) a. Ota pil^I víno.
 'Ota drank wine/?the wine.'
 b. Ota vypil^P víno.
 'Ota drank the wine/*wine.'

However, as the strength of the judgements in (12) indicates, and as Krifka himself notes, the object in perfective cases is always quantized, in the relevant sense (or, as we argued, quantity, with the modified definition in mind). Bare NPs, in the context of the perfective, are never interpreted as bare plurals (see Filip 1996; Piñon 2001), a point to which I return in Chapter 6, Section 6.3. On the other hand, bare NPs in the context of the imperfective may be interpreted as either bare or definite. Nor are quantized, or quantity DPs in general barred in imperfective paradigms, leading Krifka to state that 'in a similar way, the imperfective aspect may force a non-quantized interpretation on the verbal predicate, which consequently enforces a non-quantized interpretation on the object NP. However, this requirement seems to be much weaker' (p. 50).

It is precisely this 'weakness' which leads Filip (1996) to reject the assumption that imperfectives in Slavic are *ever* atelic. Concurring with Krifka's main claim—that atelic predicates require a cumulative direct object—she points out

---

[8] And note in this context that as verbs in the present model cannot have properties such as divisive or non-divisive (although events may), and as the uniqueness of object-event mapping has been directly challenged by the account of quantity, Kiparsky's observations do not present a problem in the present framework, under the assumption that partitive case is indeed a marker of the absence of quantity structure at the functional level.

that no such restriction holds for imperfectives, as was already illustrated by the interpretation(s) of (7), and is as well by the example in (13):

(13) Pil^I víno, co mu jeho neunavny hostitel stale doleval^I.
  drank.3SG wine that...
  'He drank (of) the wine that his tireless host kept pouring.'

As a further problem for the claim that imperfectives impose a cumulative reading on their objects, Filip (op. cit.) cites the example in (14).

(14) Psal^I dopis.
  wrote.3SG letter.SG.ACC
  'He wrote a/the letter.'

If indeed objects of imperfective verbs must be cumulative, we would be committed to the claim that in (14), *dopis* 'letter' is cumulative, that is, a mass noun, with (14) presumably having uniquely the interpretation whereby he was engaged in letter writing. However, (14) clearly does have an interpretation whereby he was writing a specific letter. One might mention that it is also perfectly grammatical in Czech to write five letters, imperfectively, although a cumulative interpretation for 'five letters' in this case is clearly unavailable:

(15) Psal^I pet dopisu.
  wrote.3SG five letters.PL.GEN

The internal argument in (15) is clearly not cumulative, making it necessary, at the very least, to assume that the cumulativity imposed on the direct internal argument (the incremental theme) by Krifka's system may be overridden or cancelled by an overt cardinal.

Before proceeding to a discussion of Filip's own analysis, note that given the structures proposed here, the failure of agreement between the properties of atelic events and their internal arguments is exactly what we would expect. Assuming that (14)–(15) are indeed atelic, we note that this would mean that there is no $[_{Asp_Q}\langle e\rangle_{\#}]$ open value, the event is a non-quantity event, and there simply exists no configuration in which the quantity properties of the internal argument, whatever they are, may translate through a specifier–head configuration to the functional head. Quite independently of what is the correct notion of quantity and what is the correct notion of homogeneity (non-quantity), the latter will never be instantiated through specifier–head relations, because by definition there is no homogeneous structure. There is only the failure of a quantity structure to be instantiated. Further, note, given the analysis of atelicity proposed here, there is no reason to assume that the structure of (9a) is different from that of (9b–d)—both having the structure in (8). In short, while we concur with Filip's objections to Krifka's analysis of Slavic imperfectives, unlike Filip, the failure of cumulative interpretation for the objects of imperfectives, just like the failure of cumulative interpretation for the objects in (9b–d), does not force us to the conclusion that imperfectives are not atelic, nor does it force us to the conclusion that there exist two distinct formal relations, atelicity and part-of, quite simply because under the analysis put forth here, there is no expectation that objects in atelic cases should be cumulative.[9]

Filip (op. cit.), having accepted that atelic structures must have cumulative objects, and faced with the fact that imperfectives in Slavic are not thus constrained, concludes that all imperfectives fall under the part-of analysis and do not indicate atelicity. We note before proceeding that this raises a very obvious question concerning the instantiation of atelicity in any language. If (9b–d) are part-of relations, as are Slavic imperfectives and Finish partitives, one wonders whether a notion such as atelicity, instantiated, according to both Krifka and Filip (op. cit) only in cases such as (9a), is indeed grammatically ever necessarily. In other words, do we have two relations here, atelicity and part-of, or just one relation, however defined? In the latter case, note, the debate basically reduces to the question of whether telicity, however defined, is in opposition to atelicity, however defined, as in the account outlined here (where the opposition is between quantity and non-quantity structures), or alternatively, all cases of 'atelicity' are in fact cases of part-of relations which are not in opposition with telicity (or more accurately, Krifka's quantization), as Filip (op. cit.) believes.

As it turns out, Filip's assumption that all imperfectives fall under the part-of analysis and are not in opposition with telicity (= quantization) faces some serious problems. Concretely, Filip (1996, 2000) proposes that paralleling the existence of a totality operator for perfectives, there is a part operator for imperfectives. Together with the lexical semantics of the verb root, and whether or not it selects an incremental theme, the following picture emerges:[10]

(16)   *Without quantificational prefixes*
   a. Perfective verb + incremental theme:
      [(affix) root]$_{TOT}$ [incremental theme]$_{TOT}$
   b. Imperfective verb + incremental theme:
      [root]$_{PART}$ [incremental theme]$_{PART}$

---

[9] A separate question concerns the source of the possible (but not obligatory) definite interpretation of the bare NP in imperfectives such as (14), an issue which I set aside here. For some brief relevant comments in the context of Chinese bare NPs, see Volume I, Chapter 6, Section 6.4.

[10] As already noted, Czech has two imperfective paradigms, one consisting in essence of the bare stem, the second a morphologically complex form derived from the perfective paradigm. Thus *psat* 'write.IMP'–*napsat, zapsat* 'write-up'–*zapisovat* 'writing up'.

(17) *With quantificational prefixes*
 a. Perfective verb + incremental theme:
  [affix$_Q$ root]$_{TOT}$ [incremental theme]$_{Q+TOT}$
 b. Secondary imperfective verb + incremental theme:
  [[affix$_Q$ + root]+ impf-suffix]$_{PART}$ [incremental theme]$_{Q+PART}$

Most crucially, from our perspective, Filip's system implies that just as within the perfective domain the TOT operator associated with the head stem binds the direct object, making it TOT, so within the domain of imperfectivity, a (covert) PART operator associated with the head stem binds the direct object, making it PART. I believe that this conclusion is not borne out by the facts.

Note first that when *na* or *u*, or any other quantificational prefix, attaches to the verb stem, and provided that no other marking is added, a quantity–telicity interpretation always emerges. Put differently, in the presence of quantificational prefixes, and without secondary imperfective morphological marking, PART interpretation is excluded and TOT interpretation forced, as schematized in (18).

(18) *[affixQ+root]$_{PART}$ [*incremental theme*]$_{Q+PART}$

The interpretation that would be associated with an imperfective, part-of event with the structure in (18), for example, that of '(being engaged in) baking (part of) many rolls' or '(being engaged in) eating (part of) many apples', is a perfectly sensible one, and is in fact available for the bare DP in (7), when no quantificational prefixes are associated with the verb. In turn, quantification could be expressed by directly marking the DP object of an imperfective V, as in (19):

(19) Petr pekl^I mnoho housek/dvů   housky.
 Peter baked.IMPERF many-of rolls.PL.GEN/two rolls.PL.ACC

As noted, this interpretation is not, however, available in the presence of quantificational prefixes, unless a secondary imperfective morphological marking is added. But if Filip is right, and imperfectivity, for both primary and secondary imperfectives consists of a covert PART operator, the absence of the PART reading with quantificational prefixes remains unexplained.[11] This is especial-

---

[11] We note a certain potential circularity here. The problem presented by the absence of the structure in (18) is based on the assumption implied in Filip (op. cit.) that the presence of a PART operator defines what is (semantically) imperfective, while the presence of a TOT operator defines what is (semantically) perfective, and that quantificational prefixes are specifically *not* semantically perfective. One could, of course, claim that the exclusion of the structure in (18) stems from the fact that a PART operator is only available in the morphological imperfective cases, but not the morphological perfective ones, i.e. that it is the presence of imperfective morphology that gives rise to PART, and the presence of quantificational prefixes that licenses TOT. This, however, would amount to claiming that semantic imperfectivity

ly so as Filip (1996, 2000) assumes that the telic effect, for perfectives, is obtained by the presence of a totality (TOT) operator, which is independent of the presence of quantificational affixes. As telicity within the perfective domain is not induced by the quantity nature of the perfective prefixation, there is little reason to exclude such quantity prefixation from co-occurring with the PART operators. And yet, the combination of quantity prefixation with a bare stem cannot give rise to an atelic or part-of reading of any sort. The problem is further exacerbated by the fact that quantification prefixation does not conflict with a part-of reading, and may co-occur with it, but only if additional *overt* imperfective morphology is added, giving rise to the secondary imperfective scheme in (17b).[12]

Even more surprising, given that Filip assumes the presence of a PART operator in the imperfective paradigm, is the complete absence of overt quantificational marking in the Slavic languages (prefixal or otherwise) associated specifically with the imperfective paradigm, on the one hand, and the grammaticality of (19) on the other hand. If indeed the TOT operator in the perfective paradigm is distinct from quantificational affixation, the latter being non-perfective by Filip's assumptions, why do we not find, within the imperfective domain, an array of quantificational prefixes which agree with the object DP? Further, within the perfective paradigm, any conflict between the quantificational properties of the DP and the quantificational properties of the marking on the verb results in ungrammaticality. On the other hand, no such ungrammaticality is associated with (19), where presumably the verb stem is marked as

does not reduce to the presence of a PART operator, but has some other defining characteristics, presumably morphological, which supersede the presence of such an operator, and which condition its distribution, although by assumption they are not, themselves, the PART operator. Likewise, one would have to claim that semantic perfectivity has some other defining characteristics, presumably morphological, which suprecede the presence of a TOT operator and condition its distribution, although by assumption they are not, themselves, the TOT operator. However, given the morphologically diverse nature of perfective affixation, and the existence of two entirely distinct morpho-phonological imperfective paradigms, a coherent classification is hard to find within the morphological domain. It therefore emerges that if there is a coherent perfective/imperfective semantic classification which determines the distribution of PART and TOT, it cannot be based on the morphological paradigm, and further, must be independent of the PART and TOT distinction, if (18) is to be excluded in a non-circular fashion. It is not obvious, however, what such a classification could be based on, or, that if and when postulated, it could derive in a non-arbitrary fashion the fact that 'morphological' perfectivity, with some presumed property *P*, should correlate with TOT, while 'morphological' imperfectivity, with some presumed property *not-P*, should correlate with PART.
[12] Filip's (2000) system is largely couched within lexicalist terms, assuming perfective affixation to be derivational and lexical, but imperfective affixation to be grammatical. We note that a lexicalist approach here is not, however, particularly helpful in resolving the problems noted in the text. An account for the impossibility of (18) together with the grammaticality of (17b) would require marking all prefixed verb combinations, lexically and arbitrarily, as having a TOT operator, which can then be overridden by the grammatical projection of imperfectives, associating it with a PART operator. In turn, as stems may emerge from the lexicon unmarked, and hence imperfective and with a PART operator, we must assume that imperfectives are both lexical and syntactic.

PART, but the direct object is not interpreted as PART (i.e. in (19), there is no baking of a part of two rolls, a point to which I return directly).

In turn, the absence of quantificational, prefixal marking in the primary imperfective paradigm follows directly if we are correct in assuming that there is no dedicated atelic structure, and if the primary imperfective, so-called, is the paradigm associated with atelicity. In the model presented here, the difference between a telic-quantity paradigm and an atelic paradigm consists of the presence in the former, vs. the absence in the latter, of a projected $[_{Asp_Q}\langle e \rangle_\#]$ in need of range. If *na*, *u*, and similar prefixes are the phonological instantiation of head features (with quantificational properties) which assign range to $[_{Asp_Q}\langle e \rangle_\#]$, their presence in the structure is only licit if they spell out a head feature which does assign range to $[_{Asp_Q}\langle e \rangle_\#]$. Otherwise, vacuous quantification results. It follows, then, that *na* and *u*, or any other quantificational marking on the V-head, can only be licit in a derivation that includes the merger of $[_{Asp_Q}\langle e \rangle_\#]$. The merger of $[_{Asp_Q}\langle e \rangle_\#]$, together with range assignment by quantificational markers such as *na* and *u*, however, immediately gives rise to a quantity structure—that is, telicity. We therefore predict directly the fact that the transmission of an $\langle e \rangle_\#$ value to a direct object from quantificational markers such as *na* and *u* is never possible in atelic contexts, as required, as by assumption, $[_{Asp_Q}\langle e \rangle_\#]$ does not merge in such structures. Not so within the Filip system. Here, the operator on V, be it TOT or PART, binds a variable introduced by the incremental theme. The structural relations that hold between PART, in the imperfective, and its incremental theme are identical to those which hold between the TOT operator, in the perfective, and its incremental theme. There is thus no reason in principle for the systematic absence in Czech of overt quantifier prefixes which bind an incremental theme without telicity emerging. Their absence (outside the secondary imperfective paradigm) must be independently stipulated.

We return shortly to the fact that overt quantificational prefixes do occur in the secondary imperfective paradigm. We turn first to the relation between an incremental theme and the primary imperfective, assumed to be regulated by the existence of a covert PART operator. According to Filip, in the context of imperfective stems, incremental themes must be interpreted as part of a whole, rather than a whole. As an illustration, consider the following contrast:

(20) a. Vypil^P víno.
      perf.drank.3SG wine.SG.ACC
      'He drank (up) all the wine.'

   b. Pil^I víno.
      drank.3SG wine.SG.ACC
      'He was drinking the/some wine.'/'He drank the/some wine.'

c. Rozbíjel^I šálky.
broke.3SG cups.PL.ACC
'He was breaking (some/the) cups.'/'He broke (some/the) cups.'

With respect to (20b), Filip (1996) notes, the interpretation crucially is 'something like "drink only some wine, not all of it".' Likewise, (20c) seems to imply that not all the cups were broken.

However, as Filip's text itself indicates, the PART relation is not always clearly instantiated on the direct object. Thus consider the examples in (21) ((21a) from Filip (2000); (21b) from Polish):[13]

(21) a. Plotła^I svetry.
knitted.3SG.F pullovers.PL.ACC
'She was knitting pullovers.'

b. Malowałem^I kubki.
painted.1SG (the) mugs

Sentence (21a), Filip suggests, is ambiguous between a reading in which part of the pullover set has been knitted and a reading in which possibly every pullover, rather than part of the pullover set, has been part of some sub-event of knitting. We note, in this context, that (21a) is in fact entirely vague as to how many pullovers have been completed and how many partially knitted, a reading that quite simply seems to involve a non-delimited knitting event, in which any PART interpretation of the pullover set appears irrelevant. If anything, it seems to correspond to Krifka's *part-of-event* reading—that is, the progressive—(and see (10)–(11)). Example (21b) displays a similar vagueness: it is certainly possible that some subset of the mugs has been completely painted (PART interpretation), but it is equally possible that any number of mugs have been manipulated (including all of them), some fully painted, others partially painted, while others remain untouched. In short, here as well, the reading is of a non-delimited event, in which a PART interpretation of the mug set appears only one of many possible scenarios.

Consider now the imperfective cases in (22), from Polish, which do not involve an incremental theme altogether.

(22) a. Prowadziłem^I samochody.
'I drove (the) cars.'

b. Prowadziłem^I Nissana.
'I drove the/a Nissan.'

---

[13] With thanks to A. Lazorczyk (pers. comm.) for the examples in (21b) and (22).

c. Kopałem^I piłkę.
'I kicked (the) ball.'

Unsurprisingly, in the absence of an incremental theme the internal arguments here have no PART interpretation. In (22), under a definite interpretation for *cars*, or the interpretation corresponding to *some cars*, both possible, it is clear that *Kim* drove all the relevant cars, and not some of them. While the sentences remain clearly atelic, that atelicity involves the fact that the motion was not delimited, and follows neither from the part interpretation of *cars*, nor, for that matter, from the part interpretation of the driving. As to (22b), the properties are clearly the same, except highlighted by the singularity of the specific car under consideration, the Nissan. Although in (22a) all relevant cars are driven under a definite interpretation, it is at least coherent to claim that the cars, as a collective, could have a partitive interpretation with respect to driving. A partitive interpretation of a single car in the context of *driving* is clearly absurd. Sentence (22c) could have a partitive interpretation in a very specific sense, in that the kicking could (but does not have to be) interpreted iteratively, with the imperfective signalling a subset of the kicking events (and see Krifka 1992 for some discussion of this point). This interpretation, however, would clearly fail to give the ball itself a PART interpretation. Of course, given the fact that the objects in (22) are not incremental themes, a part reading for them is not expected. We note, however, that the events themselves are not always interpreted as partial in any sensible way, and rather, they are interpreted as non-delimited and failing to have a well-defined culmination. And yet, here, too, we find the imperfective.

If one wishes to adopt the PART analysis, then, one might be driven to the unfortunate conclusion that the Slavic imperfective is ambiguous. In the presence of an incremental theme it may be interpreted as involving a PART operator which binds the object. However, when an incremental theme is not in presence, no PART operator is involved, and instead, a non-delimited interpretation is assigned to the event. To make matters worse, a non-delimited interpretation, in the presence of an imperfective, is possible for cases of incremental themes as well, making them ambiguous, under this analysis, between a PART reading and a non-delimited reading. And finally, we note that if atelicity (in the sense of non-quantized) continues to be a possible formal relations alongside the PART relations, there is no way to prevent (20a), for example, from being ambiguous between a PART reading (and the incremental theme interpreted as *some of the wine*), and a cumulative reading, short of stipulating the fact that bare stems *must* include a PART relations.

Suppose we consider another view, according to which (21a–b) are not ambiguous but rather just vague. According to this view, what unifies the occurrences of the imperfectives in (21)–(22) is the absence of a well-defined culmination point, otherwise known as atelicity. For the emergence of this atelicity, what is required is precisely the failure of any formal relations between the imperfective marking and the direct object, be it an incremental theme or otherwise. In turn, the failure of such a formal relations follows directly from the structure in (8). According to such an analysis, the internal DPs in imperfective–atelic structures only play a role in the interpretation of the event by entailment, if such entailment is relevant. To the extent that so-called incremental themes are perceived as having well-defined subparts, an event, delimited or otherwise, may be perceived as progressing incrementally along these subparts. Certainly, it is part of our world knowledge that pullovers, in the process of being knitted, are partial prior to completion, that books have discrete subparts and that reading normally involves progressing through these subparts (but not *burning*, for instance). On the other hand, to the extent that the integrity of cars does not seem to be dependent on the existence of a culmination to the driving, nor the integrity of a ball dependent on kicking (which may or may not culminate), no such part interpretation is applied to the object in the relevant events. Whatever lack of completion or presumed partitivity remains of the interpretation here is exclusively within the domain of the event, with its relationship to the interpretation of the object remaining entirely undetermined by the grammar and entirely determined by world knowledge.[14]

This conclusion is not a surprising one, of course, and is a direct parallel of the conclusion we reached concerning the distribution of partitive case in Finnish. As in Finnish, there is no evidence that atelicity involves any relations between the verb and an argument, or between aspectual morphology and an argument. The correlation, clearly, works the other way around: when there are such (well-formed) relations, telicity emerges. Atelicity is precisely the absence of such relations.

---

[14] H. Filip (pers. comm.) notes that while the subset of pullovers or mugs involves a proper-part interpretation, all other readings involve a part interpretation and not necessarily a proper part. Thus the non-delimited reading, under this interpretation, would emerge from the presence of a part interpretation which is not a proper-part one. While this is certainly true for pullovers and mugs, it is clearly not applicable to non-incremental themes, where part-of relations are often altogether incoherent, as we noted, but the event is nevertheless imperfectively marked and is non-delimited. In turn, viewing the events, regardless of the presence of an incremental theme, as non-delimited, extends to all cases. A unified approach to imperfectives thus suggests that the formal PART relations with the direct object is not needed, and that to the extent that a part-of interpretation does emerge for the direct object it is based on considerations of world knowledge, rather than grammatical structure.

We note, in summary, that while the structure in (8) and an atelic interpretation are highly plausible for the primary imperfective which is morphologically unmarked in any way, the structure in (8) is clearly not available for secondary imperfectives, which typically involve the suffixation of overt imperfective morphology to an overtly perfective form. As Filip (2000) notes, the co-occurrence of imperfective morphology and perfective prefixation clearly shows that morphological perfectives and (secondary) imperfective morphology are not in semantic opposition. Filip (2000) concludes from this that quantificational prefixes are not perfective. We adopt a different conclusion. Having concluded that quantificational prefixes are markers of quantity (= telicity), and that the absence of quantificational prefixes marks the absence of quantity (= atelicity), we must assume that overt imperfective morphology does not mark aktionsart, and that the primary and the secondary imperfectives are by necessity not a uniform semantic class. The conclusion, we note, is eminently plausible given their different morpho-phonological status, and we will assume it to be so without further discussion. Relying on Zucchi (1999) we suggest that secondary imperfective inflection has at least up to a point a progressive function, in turn a species of outer aspect, in the sense of Verkuyl (1972) and subsequent work. Should such a solution turn out to be workable, it would provide additional evidence for the distinction between outer aspect and inner aspect, in showing them to be associated with distinct morphological marking and with distinct morphological history. Being concerned here primarily with inner aspect, I leave this matter aside. See, however, Chapter 7, Section 7.2 for some additional comments on the interaction of prefixes and the secondary imperfective paradigm.[15]

---

[15] As already noted, Schmitt (1996) shares with the present account the assumption of symmetrical specifier–head relations, in telic structures. Specifically, within her system the argument in [Spec,AgrO] agrees with the functional head AgrO, thus giving rise to quantization, in the sense of Krifka (1992). In turn, the head, in Slavic, when quantificational, determines the quantificational properties of the object through specifier–head relations. Schmitt's account nevertheless differs from the account outlined here in a number of fundamental ways, not least of which is the adoption of Krifka's (1992) notion of quantization. First, Schmitt continues to assume that partitive case is assigned internal to the VP, contra our claims (and see Chapter 4, Section 4.2, for discussion). Secondly, Schmitt continues to assume that a predicate is homogeneous, i.e. atelic, or non-quantized, 'if the PATH built by the verb and the object is homogeneous, which *entails in other words that the DP complement is homogeneous (or can be interpreted as such)*' [p. 94, emphasis mine, HB]. Thus Schmitt fundamentally subscribes to the view that, at least semantically, there are such things as atelic structures, and to the view that imperfective morphology represents the existence of such structures, which in turn trigger agreement in cumulativity or homogeneity between the verb's lexical meaning and the DP complement. Thirdly, Schmitt continues to adhere to Verkuyl's generalization as a crucial building block for the emergence of a telic interpretation, attributing it, in essence, to the properties of measuring-out events, essentially following Tenny (1987, 1994) and Krifka (1992). Finally, as is clear from the above quote, Schmitt remains fundamentally committed to a crucial role, in the emergence of (a)telic interpretation, for the lexical semantics of the verb, an assumption that has been rejected here (see Chapter 5, Section 5.2, for the relevant discussion).

6.3 Licensing DP-internal Structure

We adopted Filip's analysis (op. cit), which involved the binding of, or range assignment to, in our terms, [$_{DP}$ ⟨e⟩$_\#$] through the quantification properties of a head feature which spells out as a quantificational prefix, *na* and *u* being two such cases. Specifically, we proposed that quantificational prefixes trigger, through specifier–head agreement, the projection of [$_{DP}$ ⟨e⟩$_\#$], therefore barring the occurrence of a non-quantity DP in [Spec, Asp$_Q$]. For bare N-stems, then, the following structure emerges for the DP in [Spec, Asp$_Q$] (with ±CL marking the difference between plural and mass readings; see Volume I, Chapter 4, Section 4.1 as well as Chapter 3, Section 3.2 of this volume):

(23) [$_{DP}$ ⟨e⟩$_d$ [$_{\#P}$ ⟨e⟩$_\#$ ([$_{CL}$ ⟨e⟩$_{div}$) [$_{NP}$ N]]] ( ])

We turn now to a more detailed investigation of how range is assigned, in (23), to ⟨e⟩$_d$ as well as to [$_{DP}$ ⟨e⟩$_\#$].

Consider first the interpretation of bare N stems in perfective contexts in Slavic. As both Filip (1992, 1996) and Piñon (2001) show, such bare N-stems may never receive a non-quantity interpretation (i.e. that of bare plurals or bare mass). Further, they must be interpreted as strong, even if not as definite (examples from Piñon 2001).[16]

(24) a. Basia czytała^I artykuły.   (Polish)
Basia read.IMPERF articles.ACC
'Basia read.IMPERF articles.'

b. Basia prze.czytała^P artykuły.
Basia read.PRF   articles.ACC
i. *'Basia read articles.'
ii. 'Basia read the articles.'

(25) a. Basia prze.czytała^P inny artykuły.   (Polish)
'Basia read another (i.e. different) article.'

b. Basia u.dowodniła^P podobne twierdzenie.
'Basia proved a similar theorem.'

Consider now the properties of DPs containing bare N-stems in Slavic from the perspective of our conclusions concerning the internal structure of DPs, argued for in Volume I, Chapters 3–6. Addressing specifically the strong–weak

---

[16] Although Piñon (op. cit.) does not highlight the fact that the interpretation must be strong (involving, according to his account an obligatory generalized quantifier), the choice of adjectives in (25), as well as Piñon's own statement that the adjectives which allow an indefinite reading must be 'judiciously' chosen, clearly suggests that reading must be strong.

distinction, I suggested in Chapter 5 in Volume I that these readings are syntactically distinguished. While the former involves DP-internal range assignment by the same f-morph (or head feature) to both $[_{DP}\langle e\rangle_{\#}]$ and $\langle e\rangle_d$, the latter involves an internal range assigner to $[_{DP}\langle e\rangle_{\#}]$ (if $[_{DP}\langle e\rangle_{\#}]$ projects) but the assignment of range to $\langle e\rangle_d$ by an external operator, specifically, an existential operator. In fact, I argued that a weak reading was the direct result of the presence, in D, of an open value $\langle e\rangle_d$ which is subject to existential closure from without. Viewed from the perspective of the output structure, rather than the properties of particular range assigners, the structure–interpretation correlation was argued to be as in (26):

(26) a. $\exists$ $[_{DP}\langle e^{\exists}\rangle_d$ $([_{CL}{}^{max}\ldots)[_{NP}\ldots]]$ ( ])
    b. $\exists$ $[_{DP}\langle e^{\exists}\rangle_d$ $[_{\#P}Q^i\langle e^i\rangle_{\#}$ $([_{CL}{}^{max}\ldots)[_{NP}\ldots]]]$ ( ])
    c. $[_{DP}Q^i\langle e^i\rangle_d$ $[_{\#P}Q^i\langle e^i\rangle_{\#}$ $([_{CL}{}^{max}\ldots)[_{NP}\ldots]]]$ ( ])
    d. GEN $[_{DP}\langle e^{GEN}\rangle_d$ $[_{\#P}\langle e^{GEN}\rangle_{\#}$ $([_{CL}{}^{max}\ldots)[_{NP}\ldots]]]$ ( ])

    a: non-quantity structure: bare mass and plurals
    b: weak NPs (Q = cardinals, weak quantifiers, *a*)
    c: strong NPs (Q = strong quantifiers, weak quantifiers and *a* with 'widest scope', *the*)
    d: generic operators, possibly other adverbs of quantification

Consider now the structure in (23), assumed to be that of the DP in [Spec, Asp$_Q$]. We assume that the specifier–head agreement with Asp$_Q$, and specifically with the perfective quantificational prefix which assigns range to it, results in the obligatory copying of #P onto the DP structure. Given this assumption, it is clear that we can now exclude, in principle, the occurrence of DPs of type (26a) in [Spec, Asp$_Q$]. Their exclusion follows from the fact that they are non-quantity structures, without a projected $[_{DP}\langle e\rangle_{\#}]$, as coupled with the specific assumption on the structural nature of specifier–head agreement with quantificational perfective prefixes.

What we must ask now is what assigns range to $[_{DP}\langle e\rangle_{\#}]$ and to $\langle e\rangle_d$ in licit structures and whether the output configuration is akin to any of the structures in (26b–d). We note before proceeding that given the specifier–head agreement between DP in [Spec, Asp$_Q$] and Asp$_Q$ combined with the quantificational nature of perfective prefixes, the relation between the quantificational marking on the verb and the DP in [Spec, Asp$_Q$] is by definition that of operator binding (indeed, explicitly assumed by Filip 1992, 1996). As a result, it renders the DP in [Spec, Asp$_Q$] opaque to binding relations with any operator other than the quantificational prefix. We can thus exclude, in principle, any instantiation of the structure in (23) in which a generic operator or an existential operator assigns range to $\langle e \rangle_d$, to $[_{DP}\langle e \rangle_\#]$, or to both. We note that this rules out not only a generic interpretation for (23), in which GEN assigns range to both $\langle e \rangle_d$ and $[_{DP}\langle e \rangle_\#]$, as in (26d), but also all three logically possible derivations in (27), as all involve a relation between the DP in [Spec, Asp$_Q$] and an operator distinct from the perfective prefix:[17]

(27) a. $\exists\,[_{DP}\langle e_\exists \rangle_d\,[_{\#P}\langle e \rangle_\#\quad ([_{CL}{}^{max}\ldots)\,[_{NP}\ldots]]]\,(\,]\,)$
    b. $\exists\,[_{DP}\langle e_\exists \rangle_d\,[_{\#P}\exists\langle e \rangle_\#\quad ([_{CL}{}^{max}\ldots)\,[_{NP}\ldots]]]\,(\,]\,).$
    c. $\exists\,[_{DP}\langle e_\exists \rangle_d\,[_{\#P}\langle perf \rangle\langle e \rangle_\#\quad ([_{CL}{}^{max}\ldots)\,[_{NP}\ldots]]]\,(\,]\,).$

Given that both $[_{DP}\langle e \rangle_\#]$ and $\langle e \rangle_d$ must be assigned range, and given that they may only be assigned range by the perfective, quantificational marking on the verb, the only licit structure is as in (28) (CL^{max} and head movement not represented; superscripts indicate range assignment):

(28)

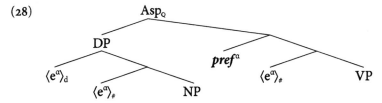

The representation in (28) is necessarily a strong one, as a weak representation would require a null $\langle e \rangle_d$ which would be assigned range by an existential operator, a possibility already excluded. We note, interestingly, that the configuration in (28) is precisely that of the template in (26c), in which the very same quantifier assigns range to both $\langle e \rangle_d$ and $[_{DP}\langle e \rangle_\#]$. The emerging reading, in such cases, is always strong as indeed it is in the cases under consideration here.

As it turns out, however, not all DPs which occur in [Spec, Asp$_Q$] are bare, and we must now turn our attention to the way in which range is assigned to $\langle e \rangle_d$ and $[_{DP}\langle e \rangle_\#]$ in such cases. Specifically, consider the paradigm in (29):[18]

(29) a. Petr **na**-pekl^P mnoho housek. (Czech)
    Petr **na**-baked many rolls.PL.GEN

b. Petr **u**-pekl^P dvû housky.
    Peter **u**-baked two rolls.PL.ACC

---

[17] Note in this context that (27a, b) are ruled out independently: (27a) due to the failure of range assignment to $[_{DP}\langle e \rangle_\#]$, and (27b) due to the assignment of range to $[_{DP}\langle e \rangle_\#]$ by $\exists$, a possibility which is explicitly excluded in Volume I, Chapter 5, Section 5.1.

[18] The realization of the complements of some cardinals and quantifiers as genitive, rather than accusative, is taken in this work to be orthogonal to the issue of telicity. Specifically, we assume that the DP as a whole receives structural accusative case in [Spec, Asp$_Q$] in the case of perfectives, and a structural partitive case in [Spec, F^{s}P], in the case of imperfectives.

c. Vypil^P   tri   kavy.
   drank-3SG three coffee.PL.GEN
   'He drank (up) three portions of coffee.'

Sentences (29a–c) present an interesting puzzle. As is the case for DPs containing bare N-stems, we assume that the perfective affixation gives rise obligatorily to the merger of [$_{DP}$ ⟨e⟩$_\#$], thereby forcing a quantity interpretation and excluding both bare mass and bare plurals. However, in (29a–c), and in contrast with (28), range is assigned to [$_{DP}$ ⟨e⟩$_\#$] by an f-morph (a cardinal, a quantifier) which merges internal to the DP itself, making range assignment to [$_{DP}$ ⟨e⟩$_\#$] by the perfective prefix unnecessary, and indeed impossible. Plausibly, then, the structure of the DP in [Spec, Asp$_Q$], for (29a–c) is as in (30):

(30)   [$_{DP}$ ⟨e⟩$_d$[$_{\#P}$ {mnoho, dvû, tri}$^\alpha$ ⟨e$^\alpha$⟩$_\#$ ([$_{CIP}$ ...)[$_{NP}$ ...]]] ( ])
        many, two, three

The structure in (30) gives rise to a host of questions. First, if in (29a–c) range is assigned to [$_{DP}$ ⟨e⟩$_\#$] by an f-morph internal to the DP, what of the quantificational properties of the perfective prefixes? Note that we must prevent the quantificational prefix from assigning range to [$_{DP}$ ⟨e⟩$_\#$] through specifier–head agreement in (30) or double marking of [$_{DP}$ ⟨e⟩$_\#$]—and ungrammaticality—are predicted to result. Secondly, the reverse question must be posed as well. If range is assigned in (29a–c) directly to [$_{DP}$ ⟨e⟩$_\#$], and assuming that DP and Asp$_Q$ are in specifier–head agreement, how can we prevent the quantity value of DP from binding [$_{Asp_Q}$⟨e⟩$_\#$], thereby giving rise to the double marking of [$_{Asp_Q}$⟨e⟩$_\#$]? Finally, what assigns range to ⟨e⟩$_d$ in (30)? Note that if we assume that the f-morph which assigns range to [$_{DP}$ ⟨e⟩$_\#$] is also the assigner of range to ⟨e⟩$_d$, we expect (29a–c) to have a strong reading. Is this prediction correct?

Addressing these questions in turn, consider first the ungrammaticality of (31), noted in Filip (1996):

(31)   Na-koupil^P   *jedno   jablko/   ??pet jablek/
       na-bought.3SG one.SG.ACC apple.SG.ACC/??five apples.PL.GEN/
       *nekolik jablek   (Czech)
       *several apples.PL.GEN

The ungrammaticality of (31), Filip suggests, is due to the incompatibility between 'one', 'several', and even 'five' with the meaning of 'a lot'. In turn, the grammaticality of (29a–c) would follow from the absence of such incompatibility. Supporting evidence for the assumption that the ungrammaticality of (31) stems from some incompatibility between *na* and the value of the quantifiers/cardinals comes from the grammaticality of (32) in Polish, from Schmitt (1996):

(32)   Irenka **na**-łuskała^P sto   orzechów.
        Irenka **na**-shelled hundred.ACC nuts.GEN

That such compatibility is indeed required is not particularly surprising, and we will assume, indeed, that in the absence of such compatibility interpretation fails. Considering the paradigm in greater detail, however, reveals that incompatibility alone cannot account for the ungrammaticality of the co-occurrence of *na* with **any** (unambiguous) strong quantifier, including *every, each,* and *all*:

(33) a. Na-trhala^P (*kazdou)   jahodu.   (Czech)
        picked.3SG.F each.SG.ACC strawberry.SG.ACC
     b. Na-delal^P (*všechny) dluhy.
        make.3SG all.PL.ACC debt.PL.ACC
     c. Na-ber^P (*všechny) vody   do dzbanu!
        pour   all.SG.GEN water.SG.GEN into jug

Extending the puzzle, it turns out that strong readings for cardinals and for measure phrases are blocked with perfective prefixes, even when no incompatibility emerges, as Filip points out, and as (34) illustrates:

(34)   Vypil^P tri   kavy.   (Czech)
        drink.3SG three coffee
        i. 'He drank up three portions of coffee.' (weak)
        ii. *'He drank up those three portions of coffee' (strong) (Filip 1996)

The restriction against a strong reading for cardinals and measure phrases appears to generalize to other languages which lack articles, as observed by Bittner and Hale (1995):[19]

(35) a. Znowu zobaczyłem^P jedno   dziecko.   (Polish)
        again see-PST-1SG.M one-ACC child-ACC
        i. 'I again saw a child.' (weak)
        ii. *'I saw the child again.' (strong)
     b. Miiraq   otaasiq   taku-qqip-p-a-ra.   (Eskimo)
        child-ABS$_5$ one-ABS$_5$ see-AGAIN-IND-[+tr]-1SG.3SG$_5$
        i. 'There was one child which I saw again.' (weak)
        ii. *'I saw the child again.' (strong)   (Bittner and Hale 1995)

---

[19] Note that the impossibility of a strong reading within this or any subset of the perfective paradigm is at least prima facie very surprising from the perspective of the analysis proposed in Krifka (1998), as it is precisely the perfective/telic paradigm which he argues to correlate with object shift, wide scope, and hence a strong reading for the quantity DP. It presents similar difficulties for the scoping-out analysis of Schein (2002) (see Chapter 5, Section 5.3, for discussion).

The picture in (34)–(35) clearly contrasts with the obligatoriness, in perfective contexts, of a strong reading for bare N-stems. In order to account for the paradigm in (35), together with the strong reading for bare N-stems, Bittner and Hale (1995) postulate, in languages without articles, a type-shifting operator (σ) whose semantic effect is equivalent to that of a definite article. The question, of course, is how to restrict the operation of the σ operator so as to bar it in (34)–(35), but allow it in the cases of bare N-stems, as in (24b) and (25). Appealing to a sort of structure preservation principle restricting semantic typeshifting, Bittner and Hale propose that the application of the σ operator can only take place if there are, in the grammar under consideration, constituents of the same category and the same basic meaning as the output type.[20] The σ operator could operate on bare nouns, turning N predicates to individuals, because there are in the Slavic languages and in Eskimo other constituents of the category N whose basic meaning is of the individual type, namely, proper names. However, cardinality expressions in Slavic and Eskimo, which are either determiners or adjectives, are not N, and hence are not a proper input to the typeshifting operator σ. A weak reading results. The situation in Eskimo and Slavic languages, in turn, contrasts with Walpiri, likewise a language without articles, in which both bare N-stems and cardinality expressions can be strong. This difference, Bittner and Hale claim, derives from the fact that in Walpiri cardinality expressions are of the N type, and hence an appropriate input to the σ operator.

Consider a different perspective on this issue, however, capitalizing on our discussion of the internal structure of DPs, and in particular the proposed range of DP structures in (26). We concluded that a strong reading for bare N-stems in Slavic is forced for structures such as those in (28) by the fact that the perfective prefix assigns range to both $\langle e \rangle_d$ and $[_{DP} \langle e \rangle_\#]$, and an existential operator is prevented from assigning range to $\langle e \rangle_d$. The resulting template, we noted, mimicked that which emerges with strong quantifiers, as in (26c), giving rise to the generalization that a strong reading always emerges when $\langle e \rangle_d$ and $[_{DP}\langle e \rangle_\#]$ are assigned range by the same element. By a similar rationale, note, a weak reading emerges whenever $\langle e \rangle_d$ and $[_{DP} \langle e \rangle_\#]$ are assigned range by distinct range assigners, and more specifically, whenever $\langle e \rangle_d$ (but not $[_{DP} \langle e \rangle_\#]$) is assigned range external to the DP.[21] Consider now again the structures in

---

[20] Specifically, following Link (1983), Bittner and Hale (op. cit.) assume a variable-binding operator σ, which, when applied to a predicate P, yields a term, σx.P(x), which denotes the maximal element in the extension of P if there is such an element, and otherwise is undefined. The 'structure preserving restriction' is in (i):

(i) 'A typeshifting operator of type $\langle a,b \rangle$ could apply to a constituent of type a and syntactic category κ only if there are constituents of category κ whose *basic meaning* is of type b.' (op. cit., p. 102)

[21] The system outlined in Volume I, Chapters 4–6 excludes, in principle, the assignment of range internally to $\langle e \rangle_d$ by an element distinct from that which assigns range to $[_{DP} \langle e \rangle_\#]$, by assuming that all DP-internal $\langle e \rangle_d$ range assigners must merge no higher than $\langle e \rangle_\#$, thereby collapsing the two require-

Direct range assignment: The Slavic Paradigm 179

(26), this time in reference to the structure in (30), which involves DP-internal range assignment to [$_{DP}$ ⟨e⟩$_{\#}$], but not to ⟨e⟩$_d$. Excluding as irrelevant (26a) and (26d), as before, the following possible representations emerge for (29a–c) (CL^{max} ignored).

(36) a. [$_{Asp_Q}$ [$_{DP}$ ⟨e⟩$_d$ [$_{\#P}$ {mnoho, dvû, tri}⟨e⟩$_{\#}$ [$_{NP}$]]] [$_{Asp_Q}$⟨*perfa*⟩⟨e^a⟩$_{\#}$]]

 b. [$_{Asp_Q}$ [$_{DP}$ {mnoho, dvû, tri} ⟨e⟩$_d$ [$_{\#P}$ {~~mnoho, dvû, tri~~}⟨e⟩$_{\#}$ [$_{NP}$]]] [$_{Asp_Q}$⟨*perfa*⟩⟨e^a⟩$_{\#}$]

Structure (36a), if possible, is predicted to have a weak interpretation if we assume that ⟨e⟩$_d$ is assigned range from without, but note that it is not obvious, prima facie, what assigns range to it. Recall specifically that given the agreement with Asp$_Q$, ⟨e⟩$_d$ cannot be assigned range by any external operator other than the perfective prefix, and specifically, it may not be assigned range by an existential operator. On the other hand, (36b), if possible, is predicted to have a strong interpretation, as range is assigned to ⟨e⟩$_d$ and [$_{DP}$ ⟨e⟩$_{\#}$] by the same quantifier.

Viewed differently, however, if structure (36b) is adopted, involving the assignment of range to ⟨e⟩$_d$ by the quantifier internal to the DP, we directly predict it to be ruled out as a case of vacuous quantification. Specifically, there are no open values in (36b). If we take seriously the claim that perfective prefixes are quantifiers, and if we take equally seriously the claim that they are coindexed, through specifier–head agreement, with the DP in [Spec, Asp$_Q$], such coindexation perforce marks a variable binding relation. As there are no free variables in the DP representation in (36b), we predict the structure to be ungrammatical. Put differently, we predict any quantificational DP in [Spec, Asp$_Q$] to have a free variable which can be bound by the quantificational prefix. Now, as ⟨e⟩$_{\#}$ is, by assumption, already bound by the cardinal or quantifier f-morph, the only possible open variable that may be bound by the quantificational prefix is ⟨e⟩$_d$. Weak reading now emerges, as required, because ⟨e⟩$_d$ is assigned value from without, by an operator which does not assign range to ⟨e⟩$_{\#}$, giving rise, in essence, to a template on a par with (26b). In effect, then, the perfective prefix here functions as an existential operator, giving rise to a weak DP, to the requirement for quantificational compatibility, and to the surprising, prima facie paradoxical state of affairs that a strong reading is imposed on bare NPs with perfective prefixes, but a weak reading on quantificational DPs. The resulting structure is as in (37), where range is assigned to ⟨e⟩$_d$ by the perfective prefix, range is assigned to [$_{DP}$⟨e⟩$_{\#}$] through the quantificational head, where the requirement that the perfective prefix bind some free variable within the DP is met, and

ments for weak interpretation. We nevertheless noted (see Volume I, Chapter 4, n. 23), that this result may be in need of weakening. Even insofar as such weakening might be necessary, we note that as long as weak interpretation requires range assignment to ⟨e⟩$_d$ from without, the results to be outlined below still follow.

where double marking is avoided, as the perfective prefix assigns range to $\langle e \rangle_d$, but not to $[\langle e \rangle_\#]$:

(37) $[_{Asp_Q} [_{DP} \langle e \rangle_d [_{\#P} \{mnoho, dvû, tri\} \langle e \rangle_\# [_{NP}]]] [_{Asp_Q} \langle \mathit{perf}\ \alpha \rangle \langle e^\alpha \rangle_\#]]$

We note that as quantificational prefixes by assumption assign range to, and hence bind, $[_{Asp_Q}\langle e \rangle_\#]$, the requirement that they bind a variable within the DP in [Spec, Asp$_Q$] as well cannot follow from vacuous quantification. As we will see shortly, quantificational prefixes can be well-formed when they do not bind a variable within such a DP, precisely in cases in which there is no DP in [Spec, Asp$_Q$], licensing quantity interpretation against Verkuyl's generalization. The need for the DP to be interpreted as a variable follows here from precisely the same restriction that would disallow a pronoun coindexed with a quantifier to be interpreted referentially. In other words, it is the specifier–head agreement which gives rise to a coindexation with a quantifier that forces a variable within the DP in [Spec, Asp$_Q$] and it is the absence of a syntactic variable representation in (36b) that renders it ungrammatical in the presence of coindexation with a perfective prefix.[22]

We now predict the range of DP interpretations in perfective/quantity structures in its fullest:

(38) a. Bare NPs must be strong (definite or strong indefinites)
     b. Cardinality expressions and weak quantifiers may not receive a strong interpretation.

---

[22] A detailed comparison of the system presented here and that developed in Bittner and Hale (1995) is not attempted. We do note, however, that the predictions made by the two systems overlap largely, but are not identical. Specifically, the system proposed here predicts the impossibility of strong quantifiers in perfectives, but the possibility of such strong quantifiers (i.e. *all, every*) for imperfectives. The Bittner and Hale system is neutral on the distribution of strong quantifiers altogether, as these can be interpreted without typeshifting. The system proposed by Bittner and Hale (op. cit.) predicts the impossibility of strong reading for cardinals and measure phrases in imperfective contexts as well as in perfective contexts. The system we adopt here, however, predicts their impossibility only in perfective contexts. At least in Czech, Filip reports that the picture in (35) does generalize to imperfective paradigms as well, as the example in (i) shows:

(i) Znovu vidĕl^I jedno auto.
    again saw.3SG one car.SG.ACC
    'He saw a car again.' (Weak)
    '*He saw that car again.' (Strong)

The issue here is clearly complicated by the fact that *again*, in and of itself, induces telicity. Nevertheless, should it turn out to be the case that the predictions made by Bittner and Hale (1995) are correct, it suggests that within the model proposed here, more would need to be said about the interpretation of cardinals in Slavic, barring, specifically, the structure in (26c) for cardinals and measure phrases. I leave this matter for future research.

c. Strong quantifiers are impossible.
d. Non-quantity interpretations are impossible.
e. Generic interpretation for bare NPs is impossible.

We return now to the sentences in (29), to their structure in (30), and to the host of questions that we posed regarding that structure. We asked first why, if in (29a–c) range is assigned to $[_{DP}\langle e\rangle_{\#}]$ by an f-morph internal to the DP, double marking does not emerge, given the presence of a quantificational perfective prefix which likewise assigns range to some open value within the very same DP. This question has already been answered. If we assume that the operator–variable relations between a perfective prefix and the DP in $[\text{Spec}, \text{Asp}_Q]$ need not be realized as range assignment to $[_{DP}\langle e\rangle_{\#}]$, but can be realized as range assignment to $\langle e\rangle_d$ as well, double marking does not emerge. Another question posed in the same context, that concerning the assignment of range to $\langle e\rangle_d$ in (30), has been fully answered: $\langle e\rangle_d$ is assigned range by the perfective prefix, a fact that gives rise to, indeed forces, a weak interpretation.

Finally, consider the last issue raised in conjunction with the structure in (30). We noted that in principle, as the DP in (30) is a quantity DP through internal range assignment, its coindexation with Asp_Q should make it a range assigner, indirectly, to $[_{\text{Asp}_Q}\langle e\rangle_{\#}]$. Such range assignment, however, is clearly undesirable, for two reasons. First, as a perfective prefix is in place, it would give rise to double marking of $[_{\text{Asp}_Q}\langle e\rangle_{\#}]$. More seriously, it would predict incorrectly that quantity DPs of the type in (30) can assign range to $[_{\text{Asp}_Q}\langle e\rangle_{\#}]$ in Slavic in the absence of perfective prefixation, clearly a wrong result. It is thus clear that indirect range assignment, as attested in English and similarly structured languages, in which a DP in $[\text{Spec}, \text{Asp}_Q]$ assigns range to $[_{\text{Asp}_Q}\langle e\rangle_{\#}]$, is simply not available for Slavic, or at any rate, is not available in the configuration in (30). We note that while restricting a DP-internal operator from assigning range to $[_{\text{Asp}_Q}\langle e\rangle_{\#}]$ in structures such as those in (30) might not be difficult to derive (for one, it would lead to a referential circularity, as the DP would be dependent on Asp_Q, and Asp_Q dependent on DP), the need to exclude, across the board, indirect range assignment by a quantity DP to $[_{\text{Asp}_Q}\langle e\rangle_{\#}]$ in the absence of perfective quantificational prefixes shows that something deeper is afoot, specifically, that the grammar of Slavic specifies a non-symmetrical, unidirectional relationship between Asp_Q and any DP specifier, such that the latter may be bound by the former, but not vice versa. One does suspect that the structure of the determiner system in Slavic is at the root of this non-symmetrical relationship, but at this point, we must leave this as speculation, pending future research.

7

Direct Range Assignment: Telicity without Verkuyl's Generalization

7.1 Slavic Intransitive Perfectives

Consider again the conclusions reached in Chapter 4 (1):

(1) a. Atelicity is lack of telicity. There is no atelic structure as such.
   b. Verkuyl's generalization is an instantiation of indirect range assignment to $[_{Asp_Q}\langle e \rangle_\#]$, one out of at least two possible modes of assigning range to $[_{Asp_Q}\langle e \rangle_\#]$. In the presence of direct range assignment, Asp_Q may be well formed without a (quantity) DP in its specifier.

We have now provided substantial evidence in favour of the claim that the best characterization for atelicity is as the absence of telicity, rather than as involving some specific (atelic) structure. We have further established the existence of structures in which range is assigned directly to $[_{Asp_Q}\langle e \rangle_\#]$, and specifier–head agreement is responsible for the copying of that range onto some open value in the DP in [Spec, Asp_Q] (indirect range assignment to the specifier by the head). This, alongside the indirect range assignment to $[_{Asp_Q}\langle e \rangle_\#]$ by its specifier, as is exhibited by languages such as English and Hebrew. Not surprisingly, the grammars we have studied so far show a substantial degree of complementary distribution between the existence of direct range assigners to $[_{Asp_Q}\langle e \rangle_\#]$ and the existence of direct range assigners to values within the DP, be it $[_{DP} \langle e \rangle_\#]$ or $\langle e \rangle_d$. While in English there are direct range assigners to $\langle e \rangle_d$, but no (inflectionally productive) direct range assigners to $[_{Asp_Q}\langle e \rangle_\#]$, the converse seems to hold in (most) Slavic languages, where there is direct range assignment to $[_{Asp_Q}\langle e \rangle_\#]$, but direct range assignment to $\langle e \rangle_d$ seems restricted to proper names, and where $[_{DP} \langle e \rangle_\#]$, in addition to being assigned range within the DP, can also be assigned range through specifier–head agreement. Such a correlation, once properly tuned, could and should follow from the interaction between direct and indirect range assignment, together with the role played by specifier–head agreement.

We are now in a position to tackle the assertion (1b), namely, the claim that Verkuyl's generalization is an instantiation of indirect range assignment for $[_{Asp_Q}\langle e\rangle_\#]$, and the prediction that in the presence of direct range assignment, a (quantity) DP is not necessary to give rise to telicity. A prime example of range assignment to $[_{Asp_Q}\langle e\rangle_\#]$ without Verkuyl's generalization, one would expect, is to be found in a grammar that actually has a phonologically realized head feature devoted specifically to the assignment of range to $[_{Asp_Q}\langle e\rangle_\#]$. We have argued that Slavic is precisely such a system, claiming, following Filip (1996), that the verbal perfective prefixes in Slavic languages are quantificational in nature, but more precisely that they assign range to $[_{Asp_Q}\langle e\rangle_\#]$. And indeed, as I will now argue, telicity without Verkuyl's generalization is found in Slavic. As I will show, this lends support to the specifier–head agreement mechanism suggested as an account for Verkuyl's generalization. It also constitutes strong support for the syntactic representation of telicity and event structure proposed here.

Before illustrating that there exists telicity without Verkuyl's generalization in Slavic, let us consider briefly the context in which such a prediction could be tested. Given the system presented here, a peculiar asymmetry emerges between the behaviour of dyadic and monadic predicates whenever $[_{Asp_Q}\langle e\rangle_\#]$ is assigned range directly and not through specifier–head agreement with a quantity DP. In order to see that this is so, we must consider the following logically possible configurations of direct arguments:

(2) a. Perfective dyadic predicate, nominative, accusative
  b. Perfective dyadic predicate, nominative, partitive
  c. Perfective monadic predicate, nominative

Structure (2a) is the one associated with standard transitive perfectives in the Slavic languages. Here, $[_{Asp_Q}\langle e\rangle_\#]$ is assigned range by a head feature phonologically realized as quantity affixation, and in turn, through specifier–head agreement, the value of Asp_Q is transmitted to some open value in the DP, resulting in the DP in [Spec, Asp_Q] receiving a subject-of-quantity interpretation, being quantity, and receiving accusative case.

Consider now (2b). To give rise to quantity/telicity in (2b), we must project Asp_Q. A quantity affix in turn assigns range to $[_{Asp_Q}\langle e\rangle_\#]$, as needed. No quantity DP is needed for this purpose, therefore. However, an object DP, provided that one exists, and regardless of its range assigning properties, does need structural case, and structural case is available either in [Spec, Asp_Q] (accusative) or in [Spec, F^sP] (partitive). In turn, the nodes Asp_Q and F^sP are mutually exclusive, the latter being the shell of the former. It therefore follows that in the presence of telic structures, partitive case can never occur. In turn, the agreement between Asp_Q and the DP in its specifier forces $[_{DP}\langle e\rangle_\#]$ to project and to be assigned range, as already discussed in Chapter 6, Section 6.3. Therefore, if a DP object exists, it must be quantity, it must have accusative (rather than partitive) case, and it receives a subject-of-quantity interpretation. We therefore derive the fact that in Slavic languages as well, in transitive perfective structures the internal argument must be quantity (i.e. it may not be interpreted as a weak bare plural or a weak bare mass noun), even though it need not be quantity for the sake of range assignment to $[_{Asp_Q}\langle e\rangle_\#]$.

Consider now perfective monadic predicates. Range is again assigned to $[_{Asp_Q}\langle e\rangle_\#]$ by a head feature realized as the 'perfective' marking, making indirect range assignment by a quantity DP unnecessary. But in these cases, note, a DP need not occur in [Spec, Asp_Q]. The obligatoriness of the quantity DP for transitive cases followed directly from the need for structural case distinct from nominative, which, due to the presence of Asp_Q in telic structure, forced merger in [Spec, Asp_Q] and subsequent accusative assignment. For intransitives, however, this necessity does not arise, quite simply because nominative case must be assigned to the single argument regardless of telicity. Should the single argument merge directly in [Spec, TP] and then move to [Spec, EP], thereby receiving nominative case as well as an *originator* interpretation in the presence of a quantity affix, we expect a converging derivation. We therefore derive the result that while transitive telic predicates will always have a quantity direct object in [Spec, Asp_Q] regardless of whether $[_{Asp_Q}\langle e\rangle_\#]$ is assigned range directly or through specifier–head agreement, for intransitive telic predicates a (quantity) argument in [Spec, Asp_Q] is possible, but not obligatory, and even in its absence a telic interpretation may arise. We note, however, that we are postulating here two possible derivations for telic intransitives, as (3) illustrates. There is only one DP in (3a), the predicate is a quantity predicate, the DP is interpreted as an *originator* of the quantity event, and there is no direct object which is otherwise interpreted as subject-of-quantity. This reading, however, is clearly rather difficult to tease apart from the classical unaccusative structure in (3b), in which the nominative subject is interpreted as the subject-of-quantity of a quantity event. Nevertheless we note that the existence of the structure in (3a), if established, is precisely what our account predicts as the case in which quantity may emerge without Verkuyl's generalization:

(3) a. $[_{EP} DP_{NOM} [_{TP} \text{DP}_{NOM} [_{Asp_Q}$ V.⟨*perf*⟩ ⟨e⟩$_\#$ $[_{VP}$ ...
         Originator

 b. $[_{EP} DP_{NOM} [_{TP} \text{DP}_{NOM} [_{Asp_Q} \text{DP}$ V.⟨*perf*⟩ ⟨e⟩$_\#$ $[_{VP}$ ...
                                Subject-of-quantity

Showing that both structures in (3) exist is not a trivial matter. Tests for internal arguments, or in our terms, a DP in [Spec, Asp_Q] in Slavic languages, such as those involving genitive of negation and the distribution of the distributive marker *po* (see Pesetsky 1982; Schoorlemmer 1995, to appear) can confirm the existence of a DP in [Spec, Asp$_Q$] for telic intransitives and thus confirm the existence of the structure in (3b), but they remain entirely silent on the possible presence of the structure in (3a)—that is, they do not show that it does not exist. It is thus not easy to establish that all telic intransitives in Slavic are structurally ambiguous between (3a) and (3b), as predicted by our account. Indeed, to show that the structure in (3a) does exist, we must demonstrate specifically the presence of an originator in quantity structures without a copy in [Spec, Asp$_Q$]. Such a demonstration need not be done theory-internally. If configurations such as (3a) do occur, we expect the single argument to never pass tests for internal arguments such as genitive-of-negation and *po* distribution, and to have an agentive or a causer interpretation. In turn, the predicate as a whole should behave as a telic, non-homogeneous one, given that there are indeed tests for telicity which are independent of the existence of the internal argument. Candidates for such tests are, for example, modification by *in x-time* and *gradually*. Thus we are looking, specifically, for configurations in which the subject is clearly 'external' in relatively agreed-upon ways, both structurally and interpretationally, but in which (inner) telicity nevertheless can be shown to exist, as triggered by perfective quantificational marking.

Consider from this perspective the paradigm which Schoorlemmer (to appear) refers to as the *semelfactive* paradigm, involving verbal marking that expresses one instance of a potentially repetitive action, as illustrated in Russian by (4)-(5):[1]

(4) a. Ja morgnula^P (*casami).
    I blinked   (*for hours)

  b. Ja kašljanula^P (*casami).
    I coughed   (*for hours)

  c. On kriknul^P za minutu (*casami).
    he shouted in minute (*for hours)

(5) a. Ja morgala^I casami.
    I blinked for hours

  b. Ja kašljala^I casami.
    I coughed for hours

  c. On krical^I za minutu.
    he shouted in minute

---

[1] The discussion of semelfactive verbs is based on Schoorlemmer (to appear). I am indebted to M. Schoorlemmer for making her work available to me, and for discussing it with me extensively. This statement by no means commits her to an agreement with my conclusions.

In (5), imperfective forms are used. In (4), on the other hand, the verb stem has a *-nu* suffix, roughly translatable as 'once'. The resulting interpretation is telic, as is clear from the ungrammaticality of modification with adverbials such as *for hours*.

Schoorlemmer (to appear), within an approach to telicity which requires an internal quantity argument (i.e. an approach which crucially assumes there is no telicity without Verkuyl's generalization), points out that there is little evidence that in (4) there is indeed such an internal argument. *Po*, a distributive marker argued by Pesetsky (1982) and Schoorlemmer (to appear) to be sensitive to the existence of a direct internal argument, is not possible with (5). Furthermore, to the extent that some semelfactives can take an (optional) object, that object is often instrumental rather than accusative, and certainly does not receive an interpretation compatible with establishing any sort of homomorphism between events and objects, which Schoorlemmer assumes to be a requisite for (grammatical) telicity. Furthermore, such objects cannot be passivized, indicating clearly that they are not direct arguments, and hence cannot be considered to be the quantity DP relevant to instantiating Verkuyl's generalization:

(6) a. Vasja tolknul dver.
    Vasja pushed door
    'Vasja gave a push into (the) door.'

  b. Sobaka maxnula xvostom.
    dog   wagged   tail.INSTR
    ('the dog wagged with the tail')

  c. Vasja pnul   (mašinu) nogoj.
    Vasja kicked (the car) leg.INSTR
    'Vasja kicked (the car) with his leg.'

(7) a. *Dver' byla tolknuta Vasej.
    door was pushed by-Vasja
  b. *Mašina byla pnuta nogoj.
    car   was kicked leg.INSTR

Schoorlemmer thus concludes that semelfactive verbs, in the specific sense of the paradigm in (4), are *lexically* marked as perfective, and that telicity, to the extent that it is derived with such verbs, is not compositional in these cases.[2] We

---

[2] For Schoorlemmer (1995, to appear), perfectivity is the result of agreement of the verb stem with an internal argument, making the latter crucial. Because the perfectivity involved in semelfactive verbs cannot be derived through agreement with an internal argument, it must be lexical, in the intended sense. We note that within the account suggested here, perfectivity is not agreement, but rather, a head feature independently projected. While agreement certainly plays a role in our account, it is the agreement of

note, nevertheless, that the suffix *nu*, found in (4) and (6) is entirely productive, and that its affixation to a particular verb stem gives rise to compositional rather than idiosyncratic information. Nor is the emerging telicity surprising, in view of the existence of telic paradigms such as those in (8), with roughly identical interpretation, which cannot be lexically derived, but which, we will argue in Section 7.3, are nevertheless cases of (inner) aspect:

(8) a. Pat laughed twice and cried twice.
    b. Robin danced once and sang once.
    c. Robin loved Kim three times.

The behaviour of -*nu* is not unique in Russian. Other verbal markers can give rise to perfectivity (and quantity/telicity) without a discernible internal argument (example (11) is from Filip 2000; see Section 7.2 for additional discussion):[3]

(9) a. **po**-spat'   'sleep for a while'
    b. **pro**-spat'   'sleep for a long time'
    c. **po**-igrat'   'play for a while'

(10) a. **ras**-smejat'sja   'burst out laughing'
     b. **ot**-smejat'sja   'stop laughing'
     c. **za**-revet'   'start to bawl'

(11) a. Ivan guljál^I.
        Ivan walk.PST
        'Ivan walked'/'Ivan was walking.'
     b. Ivan **na**-guljálsja^P po   górodu.
        Ivan na-walk.PST.REFL around town
        'Ivan walked a lot/enough/to his heart's content around the town.'
     c. Ivan **po**-guljál^P po   górodu.
        Ivan po-walk.PST. around town
        'Ivan took a (short) walk around the town.'

We note that all the events in (9)–(11) are non-homogeneous, although none involve a quantity object DP. While it is possible to assume that (9a–c), (10b), and (11) have a telos, the non-homogeneity of (10a, c) arises from there being a specified starting point, rather than specified end point.

---

the DP with the marking of the stem which is implicated here, rather than the other way around, which allows perfectivity without a direct argument, and avoids the need to postulate two distinct sources for perfectivity.

[3] Note, following Schoorlemmer (op. cit.), that *nu*, with the most predictable of output interpretations, is a suffix, while other telicity-inducing affixes are typically prefixes.

The distribution of the suffix *nu* and the prefixes in (9)–(11) is not restricted to intransitives or to agentive contexts. Thus the very same affixes occur in transitive contexts and in the context of non-agentive intransitives, as (12) illustrates, with or without -*nu*:

(12)   **po**-stroit 'build'

(13) a. **pro**-moknut   'get wet, soak'
      b. **pro**-niknut   'penetrate'.

(14) a. **za**-čerknut   'cross out'
      b. **za**-xvorat   'fall ill'
      c. **za**-cvesti   'flower, come into bloom'

However, this is exactly what one would expect, if perfective prefixes as well as the suffix -*nu* are direct range assigners to $[_{Asp_Q}\langle e\rangle_{\#}]$. No need, then, to have a subject of quantity or, for that matter, any quantity DP moving through [Spec, Asp$_Q$]. Quantity is otherwise achieved, and can thus co-occur with a single argument receiving an originator role in [Spec, EP], as in the structure in (3a).

We note, however, that at least in principle, one could argue that the sole argument in (9)–(11) could be moving through [Spec, Asp$_Q$], thereby triggering a quantity reading (but note that such an account is considerably less attractive for objects that are marked by an instrumental, or do not passivize, as in (7)). Can we show, then, that the arguments in (9)–(11) do not move through [Spec, Asp$_Q$]? As it turns out, there do exist important diagnostics which are sensitive to the presence of a quantity DP in [Spec, Asp$_Q$], rather than to the presence of a well-formed Asp$_Q$, as such. Specifically, Schoorlemmer (1995, to appear) argues that secondary imperfective suffixation applies only to perfectives with a quantity DP (i.e. transitives and unaccusatives, but not unergatives). As such, it is possible with the cases in (15), for instance.[4]

---

[4] A few morphological points are in order here. The co-occurrence, in perfective forms, of prefixes such as *na-* and *vs-* with prefixes such as *za-*, *pro-*, etc., is impossible, quite possibly due to a morphological conflict or double marking. We note, however, that *na-* and *vs-* may co-occur with -*nu*, although stems such as *krac* when prefixed with *vs-* alone, or when prefixed with *vs-* and suffixed with -*nu*, have an identical meaning. We can speculate here that the apparent perfective doubling for forms such as *vskriknu* may emerge precisely because -*nu* assigns range only to $[_{Asp_Q}\langle e\rangle_{\#}]$, whereas *vs-* always assigns range to some open value within the DP (either $[_{DP}\langle e\rangle_{\#}]$ or $\langle e\rangle_d$), and in the absence of another range assigner, to $[_{Asp_Q}\langle e\rangle_{\#}]$ as well. An additional morphological conflict bars the co-occurrence of the suffix -*nu* with secondary imperfective suffixes, although the occurrence of the secondary imperfective suffix with perfective prefixes is otherwise well-formed. We speculate that the conflict here is fundamentally morphological, as issues of double marking are largely irrelevant in this case. For additional relevant comments, see Section 7.2. Special thanks to Maaike Schoorlemmer, Agnieszka Lazorczyk, and Roumi Pancheva for walking me through the data in (15)–(16).

(15) a. **vy-prosit'**^{P} 'request'
 vy-prošivat'^{I}
 b. **pere-dvigat'sja**^{P} 'move'
 pere-dvižit'sja^I
 c. **na-pisat**^{P} 'write'
 na-pisyvat'^{I}
 d. **vz-bodrit**^{P} 'stimulate, cheer'
 vz-badrivat'^{I}
 e. **vy-rasti**^{P} 'grow, unaccusative'
 vy-rastat'^{I} 'grow, unaccusative'

It is, however, ruled out for (16), where telicity is induced with a perfective marker assigning range to Asp$_Q$, but there is no quantity DP in [Spec, Asp$_Q$]:

(16) a. *** po-sypat'**^{I} 'sleep for a while'
 b. *** pro-sypat'**^{I} 'sleep for a long time'
 c. *** ras-smeivat'sja**^{I} 'burst out laughing'
 b. *** ot-smejivat'sja**^{I} 'stop laughing'
 c. *** za-revyvat'**^{I} 'start to bawl'

Although we do not offer, at this point, an account for the impossibility of secondary imperfectives without a quantity DP in [Spec, Asp$_Q$] (and see Schoorlemmer 1995 and to appear, for some discussion), the correlation seems robust enough for us to conclude that there is, in Slavic, a construction which exhibits precisely the properties one would expect from the structure in (3b). Morphologically, it is marked as perfective; semantically, it is quantity (non-homogeneous). It does not, however, have an internal argument, and it violates Verkuyl's generalization. It is nonetheless a licit quantity structure, we submit, precisely because range can be assigned to $[_{\text{Asp}_Q}\langle e\rangle_{\#}]$ without a quantity DP in [Spec, Asp$_Q$], given the presence of quantificational prefixes which do precisely that—assign range to $[_{\text{Asp}_Q}\langle e\rangle_{\#}]$.[5]

Note now that while semelfactives (in the sense used by Schoorlemmer, op. cit.) are quantity, they are not systematically quantized, in the sense of Krifka (1982, 1998), a matter to which we now turn directly.

---

[5] A separate question concerns the impossibility of an unaccusative derivation for the semelfactive paradigm, as illustrated by the ungrammaticality of secondary imperfective in these contexts. This question, in turn, is of some generality, as already noted in the context of intransitive agentive manner verbs. The reader is referred to Chapter 8, Section 8.3, for some discussion.

7.2 Does the Perfective Mark Quantity?

Let us return now to the claim made in Filip (2000), according to which semantic perfectivity and imperfectivity are the presence, respectively, of a totality operator and a PART operator, and where quantity affixation, as such, is analysed as a verbal modification involving the existence of an extensive measure function. In Chapter 6, we equated the existence of quantity prefixation with the existence of a telic reading, which we take to be that of quantity predicates. We further suggested that the secondary imperfective is a species of grammatical (outer) aspect. We did claim, however, that the primary imperfective is atelic (and hence presents the logical opposition to perfective).

In order to make clear the conclusion reached in Filip (op. cit.), according to which quantificational prefixes are not, in and of themselves, markers of telicity or perfectivity, we must elaborate briefly on some assumptions underlying Filip's analysis. As noted earlier, Filip crucially assumes that imperfectives, primary and secondary, are a uniform semantic class. Secondly, Filip assumes that perfectivity and imperfectivity represent incompatible, conflicting values. If a verb is perfective, which is to say, it is associated with a covert totality operator, it cannot be imperfective, which is to say, it cannot be associated with a covert PART operator. As the two distinctions have exactly the same grammatical status, it follows, for Filip, that their marking should constitute a uniform morphological class. Finally, Filip (2000) assumes the notions quantization and incremental theme, essentially as used in Krifka (1992), already discussed extensively.

Now, from Filip's perspective, the classification of quantity affixes in Slavic as non-perfective (i.e. in Filip's terms, disassociated from telicity or quantization) is inevitable. Indeed, within her set of assumptions, postulating Slavic 'perfective' prefixes as markers of telicity is problematic in a number of semantic and morphological ways. First, Filip notes the paradigm in (17) from Russian (Filip's 2000: 47, example (9)):

(17) a. Ivan guljál^I.
Ivan walk.PST.
'Ivan walked'; 'Ivan was walking.'

b. Ivan **na**-guljálsja^P po górodu.
Ivan NA-walk.PST.REFL around town
'Ivan walked a lot/enough/to his heart's content around the town'

c. Ivan **po**-guljál^P po górodu.
Ivan po-walk.PST. around town
'Ivan took a (short) walk around the town.'

The prefixed verbs in (17) are associated with events which, Filip notes, are neither quantized nor cumulative, by Krifka's (1992, 1998) definition. Quoting, Filip says:

Take *poguljál*^{P} in the sense of 'to walk for a (short) time', where *po-* functions as a measure of time. Suppose that *e* is an event of walking for a short time, then there is a proper sub event of *e*, *e'*, which also counts as an event of walking for a short time. Hence both *e* and *e'* fall under the denotation of *poguljál*^{P}, and consequently, *poguljál*^{P} fails to be quantized.... At the same time *poguljál*^{P} fails to be cumulative... because two events of walking for a (short) time do not necessarily add up to one event of walking for a short time...
Now let us take *naguljálsja*^{P}, in the sense of 'to walk for a long time'. If six hours of walking is considered to be walking for a long time in a given context (event *e*), then in the same context walking for five hours (event *e'*) may be as well, but not walking for one hour (event *e"*). This means that there are events like *e* (walking six hours) in the denotation of *naguljálsja*^{P} 'to walk for a long time' that have a proper subpart like *e'* (walking for five hours) which is also an event in the denotation of this verb. Therefore *naguljálsja*^{P} fails to be quantized... and it qualifies as cumulative. (Filip 2000: 51)

From the failure of *na* and *po* verbs to return a quantized output, Filip concludes that the function of prefixes such as *na* and *po* cannot be equated with semantic perfectivity, where by semantic perfectivity she means, in essence, telicity.

We note in considering the paradigm in (17) that it parallels exactly cases within the nominal and the verbal domains which we have already discussed, in presenting a problem for the quantized/cumulative picture. Considering again the relevant cases, note that (18a) behaves exactly like *poguljál*^{P}, 'to walk for a (short) time' while (18b) behaves exactly like *naguljálsja*^{P} 'to walk for a long time'. Within the verbal domain, (19a) illustrates a case which is neither quantized nor cumulative (and hence like *poguljál*^{P}), while the examples in (19b) are both cumulative and non-quantized, although telic by other tests, on a par with *naguljálsja*^{P}.

(18) a. less than three apples
b. more than three apples

(19) a. run to the store
b. cook eggs; write a sequence of numbers; fill the room with smoke

The DPs in (18) may trigger a telic reading, although by Krifka's definition they are not quantized. The events in (19) may be telic, although again, by Krifka's definition they are not quantized. Even if we assume that (17a–c) are not telic because they are not quantized, Krifka's treatment of telicity, as dependent on the quantized/cumulative distinction, would still need to be fixed to account for the telic properties of (18)–(19). Rather than relegating quantificational affixes which are not quantized in Slavic to some other semantic domain, then, what is needed is a revised notion of quantity. Once the appropriate notion of quantity is in place, the anomaly of the paradigm in (17) vanishes, just as it vanished for (18)–(19). All the events under consideration are quantities, and hence telic, exactly as would be predicted if prefixation does indeed correlate with telicity-quantity (or, in Filip's terms, semantic perfectivity).[6] To see that this is so, consider again the properties of quantity, as proposed in Chapter 5, Section 5.3.

(20) a. *Quantity*
P is quantity iff P is not homogeneous
b. P is homogeneous iff P is cumulative and divisive.
i. P is divisive iff for all x with property P there is a y, proper subset of x, with property P, such that subtracting y from x yields a set with the property P.
ii. P is cumulative iff for all x with property P and all y with property P, a union of x and y has the property P.

Consider first *na-guljálsja*, 'walk a lot'. As Filip (2000) points out, it is, indeed, cumulative, as 'walk a lot' added to 'walk a lot' is clearly 'walk a lot'. However, by the definition in (20bi), it is clearly not divisive. Subtracting 'walk a lot' from 'walk a lot' need not give rise to 'walk a lot', and may result in 'walk a little'. *Na-guljálsja* is thus not homogeneous, and is quantity, as required. Similarly, *more than three apples* is not divisive, because subtracting more than three apples from more than three apples need not give rise to more than three apples. Consider now *poguljál*^{P} 'walk for a short time'. As Filip points out, it is neither cumulative nor quantized, by Krifka's definition. However, by the definition in (20), failing to be cumulative suffices to give rise to non-homogeneity, and hence quantity, and thus *poguljál*^{P}, too, is quantity by the definitions in (20). Similarly, *less than three apples* is not cumulative, and hence non-homogeneous and a quantity.

---

[6] Filip notes that with respect to (almost) all other tests, the forms in (17) pattern with 'verbs that are both clearly perfective and semantically quantized'. The one exception is attenuative *po*-verbs, as in (17c), which may not occur with temporal measure phrases such as *in-x-time*, but can occur with durative time spans, such as *for-x-time*. We note that the exclusion of measure phrases is to be expected, given the fact that time span is already built into the meaning of *po* (although H. Filip, in pers. comm., notes that measure phrases are possible for 'walk for a long time', thus suggesting that 'short' and 'long' have different semantic properties, a fact otherwise discussed in Hay, Kennedy, and Levin 1999). In turn, the possibility of durative temporal expressions could very well be licensed as a modifier on 'short' (i.e. how short? One hour).

Prefixed forms such as *poguljál*^{P} *naguljálsja*, then, behave exactly like other telic predicates which violate quantization, but which abide by the definition of quantity in (20). Thus there are no semantic arguments to reject perfectivity as a morphological realization of telicity/quantity range assignment.

Let us now consider Filip's morphological argument against viewing quantificational prefixes as marking telicity. The morphological argument is based on two claims, summarized in (21):

(21) a. Quantity prefixation is derivational while (secondary) imperfective marking is inflectional. If quantity prefixation were aspectual in nature, we would have expected it to be inflectional (and see Piñon 2001 for a similar point concerning the morphology of perfective prefixation).
   b. Quantity prefixation does co-occur with imperfectivity, notably in the secondary imperfective paradigm. If quantity prefixation were perfective, its occurrence with imperfective inflection would be ungrammatical.

We note that both of these objections are fundamentally based on the assumption that perfectivity, and whatever semantic class it may correspond to, is the logical opposite of imperfectivity, and more specifically, secondary imperfectivity and whatever semantic class it may correspond to. This claim has already been discussed at great length in Chapter 6, Section 6.2, where I argued explicitly that perfectivity corresponds to telicity/quantity, while secondary imperfectivity corresponds to grammatical aspect, possibly akin to the progressive. Perfectivity, as a realization of quantity, is not contrasted with secondary imperfectivity, but with primary imperfectivity, which, I suggested, is the true correlate of atelicity in Slavic. Within the domain of primary imperfectives, quantificational affixation is absolutely non-existent, a fact which remains entirely unexplained under Filip's (2000) analysis. In turn, if perfectivity is quantity, but secondary imperfectivity is grammatical aspect, we no longer expect them to be in complementary distribution, nor do we expect them to show any measure of morphological uniformity (i.e. in being both inflectional or both derivational).

Piñon (2000), arguing specifically against severing the perfective prefix from the verb, raises similar objections, arguing that any analysis in which the prefix is generated in some functional head, above the VP, and which involves some incorporation of the verb onto that prefix, would predict that the prefix should have inflectional properties rather than derivational properties. However, Piñon points out, the choice of particular prefixes associated with any particular verb is idiosyncratic, a hallmark of lexical-derivational morphology, rather than inflectional, he suggests. Finally, Piñon points out, any such derivation is in violation of the Lexical Integrity Hypothesis, in allowing words to be formed through syntactic operations.

Insofar as the analysis proposed here could be construed as involving the severing of the prefix from the verb, it must be defended against this criticism. Specifically, I proposed that perfective prefixes are the phonological spell-out of head features assigning range to $[_{Asp_Q}\langle e \rangle_{\#}]$, as represented roughly in (22):[7]

(22) $[_{Asp_Q}\langle quan^{\alpha}\rangle.V \langle e \rangle_{\#} [_{VP} V]]$

In (22), $\langle quan^{\alpha}\rangle$ is a head feature, where α is a specific quantificational value (e.g. that associated with *na-*). To give rise to a licit derivation, the verb moves to support the head feature $\langle quan^{\alpha}\rangle$. The combination $\langle quan^{\alpha}\rangle.V$ is in turn assigned phonological value, on the basis of the paradigmatic entry of the verb in question, by the phonological component.

It now turns out that the specific execution proposed here suffers from none of the problems pointed out by Piñon, quite simply because they all arise on the basis of distinctions which within the present framework are ill-defined, and quite possibly non-existent. I suggested explicitly that there are no computational processes which can be sorted out, as such, into inflectional morphology or derivational morphology. Rather, I assumed that the functional lexicon consists of two types of elements—free morphemes (f-morphs) and head features. F-morphs, I argued, come in two varieties—those which assign range to open functional values (*the, three,* possibly *up,* possibly also *-ing,* as a bound f-morph, etc.), and those which are categorial and project a category label ($[_N$ *-ation*], $[_A$ *-al*], etc.). A curious intermediate status seems to be associated with prefixes in languages like English, where they are sometimes indeed fully merged with the phonological properties of the listeme (e.g. *sub-* in *suggest*), at other times function as modifiers of a listeme (e.g. *trans-* as in *transatlantic*), and finally, at times can be possibly assumed to have a functional role, specifically if it turns out that they may assign range to some open functional value (see specifically the discussion of *out-* and *half-* in Section 7.3.3).

The functional lexicon also contains head features. Head features are abstract range assigners which are spelled out phonologically in conjunction with a host.

---

[7] The specific structure Piñon (2001) is arguing against is as in (i):

(i) $[_{Asp}$ PREFIX $[_{VP}$ NP$_{ext}$ V NP$_{int}$]]

Given that in the analysis proposed here, there is no internal structure to the VP, nor are there external arguments and internal arguments, as such, projected within the VP, at least some of Piñon's criticism is not valid. However, the analysis proposed here could be construed as involving, at least in some sense, the severing of the prefix from the verb, and aspects of Piñon's criticism which are applicable to this point must be addressed. We note as an aside that although checking, as such, is not assumed in this work, a checking account involving the base-generation of perfect-stem combinations together with movement to some presumed PERF aspectual head can trivially solve the morphological problems highlighted by Piñon.

The phonological spell-out of such forms is crucially dependent on the existence of a paradigm, and while some sub-regularities do occur, ultimately there is no correlation from function to form, nor is there a correlation from form to function (e.g. *-ed* need not be past, nor does past need to be *-ed*; see Chapter 1, Section 1.3 for discussion). It is thus within the area of so-called inflectional morphology—that is, the domain of head feature spell-out—that we find most morpho-phonological idiosyncrasy, as dependent on properties of a particular phonological index of the L-head under consideration. In contrast, within the area of functional f-morphs there is little, if any, divergence of form and function, and within the area of categorial f-morphs function is always predicted from form (although the converse is not the case). For example, [$_N$ *-ation*] always attaches to verbs to form nouns, etc. (The reader is referred to Borer 2003*a* and forthcoming, for some discussion.)

Consider now the properties of the perfective paradigm, as based on a review by Peter Svenonius (2003). Svenonius notes the existence of three distinct types of perfective prefixes, which he refers to as *lexical prefixes, superlexical prefixes,* and *purely perfectivizing prefixes,* as exemplified by (23)–(25).

(23) *Lexical prefixes* (Russian)
    a. pere-kinuti   a′. pere-kusitj   a″. pere-bitj
        across-throw   across-bite   across-beat
        'throw across'   'bite in half'   'interfere'

    b. is-tech   b′. is-koren-itj   b″. iz-datj
        out.of-leak   out.of-root   out.of-give
        'drain out (blood)'   'root out (evil)'   'publish'

    c. na-brosiltj   c′. na-bratj+sja   c″. na-kopatj
        on-throw   on-take.on+REFL   on-dig
        'drape (e.g. shoulders)'   'get drunk'   'dig up'

(24) *Superlexical prefixes*
    a. na-kapatj   (Russian)
        CUM-drip
        'drip a lot'

    b. za-kuriti
        INCEP-smoke
        'start smoking'

    c. po-gonjatj
        DELIM-chase
        'chase for a while'

(25) *Purely perfectivizing prefixes*
   a. is-kupatj+sja (Russian)
      PERF-bathe+REFL
   b. na-kormitj
      PERF-feed
      'feed'
   c. po-lomatj
      PERF-break
      'break'

As it turns out, all have in common the fact that they are associated with a quantity reading of some sort. They differ, however, along two dimensions. For the pure perfectivizers and the superlexical perfectivizers, the meaning of the output word is directly related to the meaning of the stem in isolation. For the lexical prefixes this is not the case—the meaning of the stem in isolation does not seem to play a role in the meaning of the derived prefixed form. On another dimension, the forms differ on the predictability of the choice of prefix. While for the superlexical prefixes the sound–meaning correspondence is fixed (i.e. *na* is always cumulative; *za* is always inceptive, etc.), for both lexical prefixation and pure prefixation the choice of prefix appears arbitrary. Table 7.1 summarizes these characteristics.

Let us now consider the behaviour of each of these morphophonological paradigms from the perspective of Slavic prefixes as head features associated with Asp_Q, which views the derived word as a spell-out of $[\langle quan\rangle.V_{stem}]$, as in (22). Clearly, the superlexical paradigm presents no particular problem here—we have a head feature which, in addition to the $\langle quan\rangle$ feature associated with all head features that spell out as prefixes, is also endowed with some particular value, say CUM. The combination $\langle quan\text{-}cum\rangle$ always spells out as *na*, thereby representing a 'regular' piece of morphology. Consider now the paradigm associated with the pure perfectivizers. Here the form–function correlation breaks down in a very particular sort of way—while the function is regular, and is always associated with $\langle quan\rangle$ and the assignment of range to $[_{Asp_Q}\langle e\rangle_\#]$, the form

TABLE 7.1

	Lexical prefixes	Superlexical prefixes	Pure perfectivizers
Bare stem is predictably related to stem in derived form	no	yes	yes
Function ↔ form for prefix	no	yes	no

is unpredictable and depends on the choice of stem. The picture that emerges here is curiously similar to the characterization of past-tense marking in English. While the common syntactic denominator for past tense is the assignment of range to [$_{TP}\langle e \rangle$], we find *-ed* suffixation, $\emptyset$-marking (e.g. *put–put*), stem alternations which represent sub-regularities (e.g. *sing–sang; ring–rang*), alongside others of an entirely unpredictable nature (*leave–left; see–saw*, etc.), as well as an altogether hectic paradigm involving the merger of two distinct phonological matrices (e.g. *go–went*). It is thus evident that morpho-phonological idiosyncrasy, or item-specific phonological realization in the context of a common syntactic denominator, cannot be considered the hallmark of derivation, rather than inflection, and certainly does not exclude the possibility that the pure perfectivizer prefixes in Slavic are head features which are spelled out in conjunction with a host when they assign range to a particular open value, in this case [$_{Asp_Q}\langle e \rangle_\#$]. More specifically, recall that we have assumed that inflectional morphology is paradigmatic. If that is indeed the case, and if it extends not only to English past tense but also to Slavic perfective prefixes, then the inflectional paradigm for a verb such as *catch* is as in (26a), the inflectional paradigm for, for example, *kormi(tj)* 'feed' is as in (26b), and *loma(tj)*, 'break' is in (26c):

(26) a. ⎡ Meaning: CATCH ⎤
        | Stem (category neutral)   *catch* |
        | (spell-out in environment V   *catch*)[8] |
        | spell-out in environment V.*pst*   *caught* |
        ⎣ (spell-out in environment N   *catch*) ⎦

    b. ⎡ Meaning: FEED ⎤
        | Stem (category neutral)   *kormi* |
        | spell-out in environment V   *kormitj* |
        ⎣ spell-out in environment V.*quan*   *na-kormitj* ⎦

    c. ⎡ Meaning: BREAK ⎤
        | Stem (category neutral)   *loma* |
        | spell-out in environment V   *lomatj* |
        ⎣ spell-out in environment V.*quan*   *po-lomatj* ⎦

Finally, let us turn to the lexical prefixes, where, it appears, the combination of

---

[8] The reader may note that the specification of the spellout in both N and V environments are redundant here, as they constitute simply the insertion of the stem. They are included, however, for two reasons. First, at least in principle, one of these pronunciations may be arbitrarily missing (and see below for discussion of *quoth* and lexical prefixation in Slavic). Secondly, the form may require an allomorph in a particular syntactic context, for example, *prógress$_N$* vs. *progréss$_N$* in English. For a detailed discussion of all these issues, see Borer (forthcoming).

prefix and stem changes the meaning of the stem. Clearly, one would imagine, a lexical process? Consider, however, a different perspective, which equates the behaviour of lexical prefixation with that of the morphology of missing stems of well-attested derived words. Within the realm of word formation, which is traditionally considered derivational in nature, this is the case of the paradigm *aggression, aggressor, aggressive*, where the stem, the verb *aggress*, is non-attested.[9] As it turns out, similar cases exist within the realm of 'traditional' inflectional morphology, where members of paradigms are often missing. The verb 'be' in Hebrew (*haya*) lacks a present-tense paradigm; the French verb *frire* 'fry' is missing past tense, plural of present indicative, the participle, the subjunctive, and the imperfective forms; the archaic English verb *quoth*, 'to quote' only exists in the past tense, etc. (and see Stump 1998 and Carstairs-McCarthy 1998 for some discussion). Suppose now that forms such as *iz-datj* 'publish' have, in effect, the structure of *trousers*. The stem from which they are derived is not attested; in the relevant meaning (singular for *trousers*, primary imperfective for 'publish'). However, the derived form is.

Consider the logic here in greater detail. Suppose there exists a stem for *quoth*, for instance, with the required meaning, to do with quotation, but, like *aggress*, is not phonologically attested. In effect, then, the phonological paradigm for *quoth* looks roughly as in (27), where forms marked with * represent missing paradigm members:

(27) $\begin{bmatrix} \text{Meaning:} & \text{QUOTATION} \\ \text{V.}pres & * \\ \text{V.}pst & \text{quoth} \\ \text{etc.} & \end{bmatrix}$

It is now clear what the natural course of action is for lexical prefixed verbs in Slavic. Consider as an example *iz-datj*, 'publish'. The form is perfective, and the prefix *iz* is a quantity prefix. However, the primary imperfective form, predicted to be *datj*, does not exist with the intended meaning. As traditional accounts would have it, the stem *datj* does exist, with the meaning 'give out', and upon prefixation of *iz-* its meaning is altered to give rise to 'publish'. While such an account may be historically plausible, however, we note that as an account for the synchronic morphological complexity of *iz-datj* it entails giving up on any attempt at compositional word formation, be it derivational or inflectional, lexical or syntactic. It might be worthwhile to note that once such compositionality is given up, the *form* ↔ *function* regularity of superlexical prefixes, as well as the *form* → *function* regular-

---

[9] Although *agress* does occur in present-day English as a result of back formation, there is no doubt that its existence post-dates the existence of the paradigm without it.

ity of perfectivizers become mysterious coincidences. The alternative is to bank on precisely that irregularity which is well-attested in inflectional paradigms—that of accidental paradigmatic gaps. In this case, the missing paradigm member is the 'bare' verb stem, the form which would have meant an atelic, unstructured 'publish'. The paradigm for 'publish' is thus as in (28):

(28) ⎡ Meaning: PUBLISH ⎤
     ⎢ Stem (category neutral)   da   ⎥
     ⎢ spell-out in environment V   *   ⎥
     ⎣ spell-out in environment V.*quan* iz-dat ⎦

In effect the paradigm of lexical perfectives now merges with that of pure perfectivizers—these are cases with an idiosyncratic, paradigmatically specified spell-out for a regular syntactic head feature, on a par with English past tense, or cases of English plural such as *children*. Insofar as they appear distinct, this is because the verb stem is phonologically missing, an accidental gap typical of inflectional paradigms.[10,11]

Finally, as an aside, we note that while a derivation such as that in (22) may violate some version of the Lexical Integrity Hypothesis, as this is a theory-internal objection, its validity is contingent on evidence that such a principle does, in fact, have explanatory value in further constraining a theory of paradigmatic inflection such as the one assumed here.

A more serious challenge, cited in Filip (2000), is presented by the possibility of more than one prefix occurring attached to the same stem, as illustrated by (29):[12]

(29) a. v-stat^P →   **pri**-v-stat^P
         v-stand   **pri**-v-stand
         to get up   'to rise', to stand up' (for a moment)

---

[10] We set aside here the distribution of secondary imperfective, only to note that the emergence of a secondary imperfective precisely for 'lexical perfectivizers' is natural—in the absence of an unstructured, atelic stem—and argues against an account that seeks to derive the missing 'atelic' form exclusively from the lexically specified (e.g. necessarily culminating) semantics of the verb.

[11] While the account given here to lexical perfectives in Slavic is based on a defective paradigm, the account could also be couched in terms of idiom-formation, on a par with the analysis given to *pluralia tantum* in Chapter 1, Section 1.4, or to the properties of verbs such as 'arrive' in Chapter 10, Section 10.3. We note in this context that the existence of a defective paradigm for idioms is necessary (and noted) in such cases—thus the singular noun *scissor* is not attested, nor is the non-locative version of *arrive*. The question of the division of labour between idioms, in the sense used in this work, and phonological paradigm would take us too far afield, however, and is set aside here, only to be returned to in Borer (forthcoming).

[12] We note that at least the example in (29b) is far from a straightforward case of double perfective, in that distributive *po* (not to be confused with attenuative *po*) is not clearly part of the perfective paradigm, as it is available in non-perfective contexts as well. For extensive discussion, see Schoorlemmer (1995, to appear). See also n. 4 on the co-occurrence of *nu* and perfective prefixes.

b. **na-tascit**^{P} →   **po-na-tascit**^{P}
na-drag   po-na-drag
'to accumulate gradually   'to accumulate gradually
by lugging'   by carrying one after the other'

From the perspective of the analysis we put forth here, the paradigm in (29a–b) and similar cases are problematic only if we assume that both prefixes attached to the stem are range assigners to $[_{Asp_Q} \langle e \rangle_\#]$ But as it turns out, a number of other possibilities present themselves as to the availability of two prefixes. One prefix may be an incorporated element, an adverb or a preposition, which is not associated with range assignment at all. Alternatively, functional structures may be considerably more expansive than proposed in this work, with the outer prefix indicating the existence of some additional open value, above Asp_Q, in need of range assigner. At least some prima facie evidence for this possibility is noted in Svenonius (2003), who cites the forms in (30), in which, he suggests, the presence of the secondary imperfective licenses a second perfective prefix which is interpreted semantically (although not morpho-phonologically) as having scope over the imperfective:

(30) na-so-biratj
      CUM-[from-take]

Although these possibilities are not pursued here in detail, we note that they are at least in principle perfectly executable within the approach suggested here.

Finally, Filip notes, verbal prefixes in Slavic behave very much like verbal prefixes in German and Hungarian, in having meanings derived historically from that of locative prepositions (and see Piñon, op. cit., for a similar observation). And yet, Filip complains, 'verbal prefixes in neither Hungarian nor German are taken to be grammatical markers of perfective aspect.' (p. 72). This author fully endorses Filip's complaint here. There is, indeed, no reason whatsoever why Hungarian and German verbal prefixes, to the extent that they induce quantity readings, should not be treated as grammatical markers of 'perfective' aspect. Although the accomplishment of this task remains outside the scope of this work, I remain confident that it is a manageable one.

7.3 Telicity Without Verkuyl's Generalization—English

7.3.1 *Range assignment to $[_{Asp_Q} \langle e \rangle_\#]$ through an adverb of quantification*

Cases of telicity in English which do not adhere to Verkuyl's generalization have been discussed in the literature, of course, and were already referred to, sporadically, in the preceding text. Consider specifically the paradigm in (31), already touched upon in Chapter 5, Section 5.2, following discussions of Mourelatos (1978) and Bach (1981):

(31) a. Robin danced *once* in five hours.
    b. Pat laughed *twice* in three days.

Examples (31a–b) have a telic interpretation, as illustrated not only by the availability of the *in x-time* phrase, but also by the fact that they are quantities (and non-homogeneous), in the required sense. For example, for the event described in (31b), there is at least one sub-event (i.e. a singular laughing) which does not fall under the predicate, which is therefore non-divisive. Further, (31a–b) are both non-cumulative (e.g. dancing once and then again is not to have danced once, etc.). Other tests of telicity confirm this result. Consider, for instance, the interpretation of (32a–b) when compared with the interpretation of (33a–b) and (34a–b):

(32) a. Pat laughed twice and cried twice.
    b. Robin danced once and sang once.

(33) a. Pat laughed and cried twice (in three years/*for three years).
    b. Robin danced and sang once (in three years/*for three years).

(34) a. Pat laughed and cried (for two hours/#in two hours).
    b. Robin danced and sang (for three hours/#in three hours).

Insofar as we take the expression *in x-time* to be a modifier of a well-formed quantity predicate, that is, a well-formed Asp_Q (and see Chapter 8, Section 8.2, for some more discussion), it is clear that we must claim that both (32a–b) and (33a–b) are quantity predicates—that is, telic. On the other hand, by the same logic, (34a–b) are atelic. However, the interpretations of (32a–b) and (33a–b), both telic, are not identical. Most specifically, we note that while in (32a) there are four events explicitly described, two of laughing and two of crying, in (33a–b) there are only two, each involving a potentially overlapping laugh-cry.

Viewed from the perspective of the system proposed here, however, this is exactly what we expect, if *twice* and similar adverbs of quantification assign range to $[_{Asp_Q}\langle e\rangle_\#]$, thereby giving rise to a quantity predicate and to telicity. In (32a–b), crucially, there are two occurrences of an adverb of quantification. It therefore must be the case that each occurrence is associated with a distinct event argument, and that each of the conjuncts projects its own $[_{Asp_Q}\langle e\rangle_\#]$, in turn assigned range by the adverb of quantification. The relevant representations are in (35a–b). On the other hand, in (33) only one type of event is implicated, that is, an overlapping laughing and crying. Range assignment to $[_{Asp_Q}\langle e\rangle_\#]$ is again by the adverb of quantification, giving rise to a quantity reading. However, as the adverb of quantification ranges over only one instance of Asp_Q, in this case, we have only two instances of the relevant event type, a laughing-crying, rather than a total of four. The relevant part of the representation is in (36).[13]

(35) ∃2e [quantity (e); subject of quantity (Pat,e) & laugh (e)]
and
∃2e [quantity (e); subject of quantity (Pat,e) & cry (e)]

(36) ∃2e [quantity (e); subject of quantity (Pat,e) & laugh (e) & cry (e)]

It might be worthwhile to note that in (32a–b) and (33a–b) telicity is not only induced without Verkuyl's generalization being instantiated, but also without the emergence of a state that is predicated of any object, or a *telos*, in the sense of Higginbotham (2000*a*, *b*), in any coherent sense. Certainly, the events under consideration are temporally bound, but not any more so than any event involving past running or laughing, which may give rise to a *resultant* state, in the sense of Parsons (1990), the post-running, non-running state, which is permanent, and which places an absolute boundary on the running event. And yet, such events (cf. (37)) continue to disallow modification with *in x-time*, and continue to be homogeneous, in the required sense:[14]

(37) Kim has run (*in two hours)

We note further that to the extent that the distribution of quantificational adverbs in paradigms such as those in (32) and (33) determines whether or not *in x-time* phrases may or may not occur, it suggests that these are instances of inner, rather than outer aspect, in the sense of Verkuyl (1989).

More interestingly, as we already noted in Chapter 5, Section 5.2, the presence of adverbs such as *once* or *twice* actually impacts the nature of the event under consideration, and specifically, it forces an eventive, rather than stative reading:

---

[13] The reader may note that *twice* performs here the double role of assigning quantity value to Asp_Q as well as ranging over the number of iterations of the relevant event. I leave aside execution issues concerning this double role. We note further that if it is indeed true that there are two events associated with cases such as those in (32), however many times they may be iterated, this would require the projection of two EP nodes, strongly suggesting that the coordination here is at the EP level, as is represented in (35), and is subsequently subject to conjunction reduction. This matter, as well, is left aside here.

[14] The distinction between the function of time measure adverbials, such as *in x-time*, which I propose to be a predicate modifier requiring the projection of an otherwise licensed Asp_Q, and the function of adverbials such as *once*, which, I propose, are range assigners to $[_{Asp_Q}\langle e\rangle_\#]$, is in need of some justification, a matter to which I return in Section 7.3.3. Note that for our purposes the most salient difference involves the fact that while *once* does have the power to convert an otherwise non-telic event to a telic one, as in (31), time measure adverbials cannot do so, as the ungrammaticality of the time measure adverbial in (37) indicates. If we assume this distinction to be a meaningful one, we must conclude that *once* may achieve what *in two hours* may not, i.e. the assignment of range to $[_{Asp_Q}\langle e\rangle_\#]$.

(38) a. Kim loved Robin twice last summer.
  b. The wall touched the fence (#twice today).
  c. Kim touched the fence (twice today).

If we assume that *twice* and similar adverbials in effect force the projection of Asp_Q, a quantity structure, *love* and *touch* in (38a–b) are 'coerced' and forced to be conceptually compatible with an eventive, rather than stative, interpretation. Such a simple account for the 'coercion' in (38a–b) is only available if we assume that Asp_Q indeed does project in such cases and is assigned range by the adverb, making this an instantiation of inner aspect.

7.3.2 Particles and prepositions as range assigners

Even if adverbs of quantification could for some cases be argued to be instances of outer aspect, in the sense of Verkuyl (1989), this would be a hard claim to make for the cases in (39), in which telicity is triggered by a (locative) preposition/particle complement:[15]

(39) a. Kim went out (in two seconds).
  b. Pat was off (in two seconds).
  c. Robin took off (in two seconds).
  d. Jake pulled up alongside us (in two minutes).
  e. When the crowd arrived he shoved off (in two minutes).
  f. We were ready to push off at ten o'clock.
  g. They paired up (in two minutes).

(40) a. The army took over (in two hours).
  b. The catcher wanted the pitcher to pitch out (in two seconds) and see if they could catch the runner stealing.

(41) a. While the boys were discussing the car accident, Ben put in that the road was icy.
  b. He moved in on my girl friend (in two seconds).
  c. He took up gardening (in two months).
  d. Frank took up with Lucy (in two weeks).
  e. Mary took to mathematics (in two minutes) like ducks take to water.

It is also worthwhile to note that, at least with respect to (40), the assumption that an elliptical object is implicated in bringing about a telic interpretation neither seems right, nor would be useful if right. Note first that *take over* does not in fact mean the same as *take something over*. More seriously, note that in principle reducing the telicity of (40a–b) to the presence of an elliptical object would only

---

[15] Examples (39d–g), (40b), and (41a–e) are based on Boatner and Gates (1975), *Dictionary of American idioms*. Example (39a) is from Mourelatos (1978).

serve to re-formulate the problem. As is well known, constructions with elliptical objects (with verbs such as *eat* and *drink*) are atelic. Intransitive alternates which involve a missing 'theme' rather than a missing 'agent', for instance, verbs such as *dance, shout, dream*, etc., which can take a cognate object, do not give rise to telicity either. Why, then, should (40a–b) be telic, when *eat, drink, smoke*, and *dance*, when they occur without an object, are not? Note further that elliptical objects for (40a–b) are as plausible as elliptical objects for other unergative intransitives, such as *dance, shout, dream*, etc.

One could, however, argue that at least in some of these cases the surface subject is in fact a deep object, or in other words, that some of these cases involve an unaccusative structure, with a subject-of-quantity DP in [Spec, Asp$_Q$], and as such, they obey Verkuyl's generalization. We note that at least prima facie, this approach appears very implausible for (40)–(41), given the fact that the surface subject in these cases clearly has an agentive flavour, and at any rate, does not seem in any way to undergo a change of state. The surface subjects in (39), however, do seem to undergo a change, raising the possibility that at least these constructions are unaccusative.

Consider in light of this the distribution of adjectival passives, which, we suggested, correlates largely with that of subject-of-quantity. We note in this respect that while adjectival passive formation is fully productive neither for unaccusative verbs nor for verb-particle and verb-preposition constructions, we nevertheless do find the relatively grammatical combinations in (42):

(42) a. ?the eaten-up cake
 b. ?the taken-over company
 c. the slept-in bed
 d. the broken-down car
 e. the burned-down house
 f. the caved-in roof
 g. the worn-in shoes

Although the examples in (42) may not all seem perfect, they contrast sharply with the verb+particle combinations in (39)–(41), where adjectival passives are clearly ungrammatical, as (43) illustrates. Not, we submit, because these combinations are not telic, but quite simply because they are telic without a subject-of-quantity, and hence there is no argument that can serve as the subject when an adjectival passive is formed.

(43) a. ??the gone-out person
 b. *the took-off person
 c. *the pulled-up person
 d. *the shoved-off man (with the intended reading)

An interesting conundrum is presented by the paradigm in (44), with the properties in (45):

(44) a. Pat climbed the mountain.
  b. Pat climbed down the mountain.
  c. Pat climbed down.

(45) a. the climbed mountain; *the climbed (down) woman
  b. There were three climbings {of the mountain/down the mountain/down}.

By standard accounts, *mountain* in (44a) is a *theme*. By standard accounts of telicity, including our own, it is *the mountain* in (44a) which is the DP that meets Verkuyl's generalization.

Consider now (44c). If this sentence is to meet Verkuyl's generalization, the only DP which can possibly be involved is *Pat*. If all telic structures were to obey Verkuyl's generalization, then it would follow that in (44c) *Pat* must be the incremental theme in the sense of Dowty (1991) (or measured theme in the sense of Krifka 1992), or, in terms of the account developed here, *Pat* would be interpreted as a subject-of-quantity. Now, however, consider (44b). From the perspective of any plausible view of events in the world, *Pat* participates in the event described in (44b) precisely in the same way that she participates in the events described in (44c) and (44a). Likewise, the role of *the mountain* in the event does not seem to change from (44a) to (44b). What DP, then, is responsible for Verkuyl's generalization being instantiated in (44)? If it is *the mountain* in (44a–b), but *Pat* in (44c), we must postulate a theory according to which the argument role of *Pat* in (44a–b) is completely different from the argument role of *Pat* in (44c), clearly a very arbitrary move. If, on the other hand, it is *Pat* which is the target of Verkuyl's generalization in (44b–c), but not in (44a), then we must postulate a theory according to which *Pat* receives the same interpretation in (44b) and in (44c), but an entirely distinct interpretation in (44a). And yet, our intuition tells us that *Pat* and *the mountain* have exactly the same interpretation in all their occurrences in (44), including the sense in which they might be considered to measure out the event, in the sense of Tenny (1987, 1994). *Pat* is always the one in motion, allowing the measuring out of the event by her progress on a delimited path. *The mountain*, whenever mentioned, constitutes some path to be traversed. When *the mountain* does not surface, as in (44c), there is simply no sense in which the event comes to be measured out in terms of the properties of *Pat* any more or less so than when the *mountain* does surface in the sentence. Rather, the path is measured here with respect to some delimiting point, *down*.

We note at this point that a small-clause type analysis, according to which *Pat* is an underlying subject of *down*, does not really improve matters. To be workable, such an account would have to assume that (44b–c) both involve a small clause structure, with *Pat* predicated of *down (mountain)*, as in (46a), but that (44a) involves the structure in (46b), where *Pat* is predicated of *climb (mountain)*, or alternatively, as in (46c), where *Pat* is predicated of *mountain*. *The mountain*, on the other hand, is at times a complement of down, and at other times, a complement of climb.

(46) a. climb [$_{SC}$ Pat, [down (mountain)]]
 b. Pat [$_{VP}$ climb mountain]
 c. Climb [$_{SC}$ Pat, mountain]

Either way, given the distinct predicates, we do not expect a uniform interpretation for *Pat* or for *the mountain*, contra intuition (and note that such a uniform interpretation could not be upheld either within theta-theoretic accounts or within accounts which assign event-participant roles). We note further that within a view that subscribes to UTAH, none of these variants maps into the other in a fully constrained fashion, unless we assume that *climb* is always associated with a silent preposition, which is deleted in (44a). The latter solution, which postulates *mountain* as an indirect object, even if tenable, we note, is independently incompatible with Verkuyl's generalization, and hence is of little help in our attempt to see whether Verkuyl's generalization could be rescued for the paradigm in (44).

None of these complications emerge if it is assumed that telicity may be induced without Verkuyl's generalization. The derivation of (44a) continues exactly as before, with *the mountain* being subject-of-quantity, the path reading here being a direct entailment from the existence of a quantity predicate. In turn, there is no subject-of-quantity in (44c), and possibly not in (44b) either (and see Section 7.3.3. for some follow-up discussion). In (44c), telicity is satisfied because the particle *down* assigns range to [$_{Asp_Q}\langle e \rangle_\#$], making the presence of a quantity DP in [Spec, Asp$_Q$] unnecessary. If an account is to be given in terms of measuring out, we simply restate the above as follows; while in (44a) the event entails progressing along the mountain, with the mountain top being the presumed culmination point, in (44c), the event entails progressing *down*, with some presumed culmination at a point which is *down* in a contextually defined sense. In all the derivations *Pat* continues to be an originator, and the fact that she herself is participating in the motion has no more status, here, than the fact that in simple unergative constructions such as *Pat danced* the subject undergoes a motion.

More specifically, and returning to the full paradigm in (39)–(41), we already suggested in Chapter 1, Section 1.4, that the best characterization for the relations which hold between verbs and obligatorily selected prepositions or particles is as idiomatized expressions, in which a partial functional structure is associated with a particular listeme, often giving rise to its categorization, as well as to a specific syntactic environment in which it may (or may not) occur. Specifically, we may assume that expressions such as *pair up* or *take over* have the representation in (47a–b), while *move in on* and *take up with* are represented as in (47c–d) (and see Chapter 10, Section 10.2-3, for some additional relevant discussion of idioms and idiom structure). We draw the reader's attention to the locative nature of all the particles which assign range to $[_{Asp_Q}\langle e\rangle_{\#}]$ in (47a–d), a point to which we return at great length in Chapters 9 and 10 (the structures in (47a–d) remain non-committed as to the presence in the L-Domain of a copy of the preposition; see footnote for some discussion).[16]

(47) a. $[_{Asp_Q}$ up $\langle e^{up}\rangle_{\#}$ $[_{L\text{-}D}$ pair $([\text{up}\ \langle e^{up}\rangle]$)]]
 b. $[_{Asp_Q}$ over $\langle e^{over}\rangle_{\#}$ $[_{L\text{-}D}$ take $([\text{over}\ \langle e^{over}\rangle]$)]]
 c. $[_{Asp_Q}$ in $\langle e^{in}\rangle_{\#}$ $[_{L\text{-}D}$ move$([\text{in}\ \langle e^{in}\rangle]$) $[_{P}\langle e^{on}\rangle$]]]
 d. $[_{Asp_Q}$ up $\langle e^{up}\rangle_{\#}$ $[_{L\text{-}D}$ take $([\text{up}\ \langle e^{up}\rangle_{\#}]$) $[_{P}\langle e^{with}\rangle$]]]

---

[16] Recall that prepositions and particles are assumed to be members of the functional lexicon. To recap some of the discussion in Chapter 1, Section 1.4, we suggested that idioms are listemes with partial subcategorization, consisting, specifically, of (adjacent) open values, at times with fixed range assigners, and that these open values force the projection of specific syntactic structure which is interpreted and realized in accordance with the independent interpretative formulas that otherwise apply to it. More specifically, we proposed that the listemes *depend on* and *trousers* are as in (i a–b) (in all cases π_n is the presumed phonological index of the non-functional part of the listeme, i.e. *depend* and *trouser* respectively).

(i) a. DEPEND ON ⇔ $\pi_9 + [\langle e^{on}\rangle]$
 b. TROUSERS ⇔ $[\pi_3 + \langle e^{\alpha}\rangle_{div}]$

By convention, the representation in (i a) is interpreted so as to force the insertion of the functional item *on* to assign range to $\langle e^{on}\rangle$, and the structure projects as a phrasal complement of the head phonologically indexed as π_9. In turn, by convention, the functional head feature $\langle div^{\alpha}\rangle$ in (i b), a non-singular range assigner to $\langle e\rangle_{div}$, projects as part of the extended projection of the head phonologically indexed as π_3 specifically in this case having the effect of producing 'plural' marking. The emerging syntactic structures are thus as in (ii) (possible verb movement in (ii a) set aside):

(ii) a. $[_{V}$ depend $[_{P}$ on $\langle e^{on}\rangle]]$
 b. $[_{DIV}$ trouser.$\langle div^{\alpha}\rangle$ $\langle e^{div\text{-}\alpha}\rangle$ $[_{N}$ trouser]] → /trauzerz/

Note now that unlike *depend* where the preposition *on* projects a full PP and remains within the L-domain, the particles in (40) are by assumption range assigners to an open value within the extended projection of the listeme. This is so quite independently of whether or not they merge, originally, within the L-Domain and then move to Asp_Q, or alternatively, merge directly with Asp_Q. This characteristic of e.g. *over*, in conjunction with *take*, is thus on a par with *trousers*, rather than *depend on*. It thus appears that the relevant representation for the listeme *take over* should be as in (iii a) (with π_5 the presumed phonological index of *take*), realized syntactically as (iii b):

(iii) TAKE OVER ⇔ $[\pi_7 + \langle e^{over}\rangle Asp_{Q-\#}]$
 $[_{Asp_Q}$ take $\langle$over$\rangle$ $\langle e^{over}\rangle_{\#}$ $[_{V}$ take]] ⇔ /teyk owvr/

Structure (iii) is neutral with respect to the original merging site of *over*, as long as eventually it merges with $[_{Asp_Q}\langle e\rangle_{\#}]$, and assigns range to it. Thus it might be that *over* always merges in the L-Domain, and that

In (47), range is assigned, by assumption, by the locative particle, a member of the functional lexicon, a range assigner to $[_{Asp_Q}\langle e\rangle_\#]$ which merges with $[_{Asp_Q}\langle e\rangle_\#]$. As an aside, we note that the presence of an Asp_Q above the listemes in (47) necessarily verbalizes them. Not surprisingly, locative particles here behave rather similarly to perfective prefixes in Slavic, themselves historically locative prepositions, in assigning range to $[_{Asp_Q}\langle e\rangle_\#]$. We may only speculate on the continuum of historical change, of which Slavic locatives, fully grammaticalized, may be an end point, free PPs which may assign range to $[_{Asp_Q}\langle e\rangle_\#]$ as adjuncts, to which we turn shortly, the beginning point, and the idiomatized particles in (47a–d) some intermediate point.

Turning now to range assignment to $[_{Asp_Q}\langle e\rangle_\#]$ by a PP adjunct, consider delimiters such as *to the store*, in the context of well-known cases such as those in (48). We assume that such PPs assign range to $[_{Asp_Q}\langle e\rangle_\#]$, as they do appear to 'create' telicity where it otherwise does not exist, as (48) shows. Like the cases in (39)–(41), and like (44b), then, such range assignment is accomplished, and a quantity reading emerges, although Verkuyl's generalization is not met. Just like adjuncts such as *twice* and *once*, so directional-locatives, such as *to, into, onto*, etc. can assign range to $[_{Asp_Q}\langle e\rangle_\#]$, indirectly, through the very same mechanism that allows adverbs of quantification to assign range to open values in general (and see Chapter 1, Section 1.2.3, for some discussion). We suggested, when discussing divided structures (range assigned to $\langle e\rangle_{div}$) within the nominal domain, that they create an infinite number of division matrices, or reticules, and the role of quantity expressions or adverbs of quantification is to select a specific (set of) reticule(s). Adapting the same intuition to the case of events, we suggest that the presence of an adverb of quantification ranging over an event (e.g. *twice*) or a PP delimitor (e.g. *to the store*) may function to select a specific (set of) event reticule(s) associated with a particular syntax:[17]

(48) a. John ran to the store.
 b. Jane swam into the room.
 c. Pat danced into the corridor.

it merges in Asp_Q as a result of movement, either independently, or through a prior incorporation with *take*. According to either one of these executions, the L-Domain contains not only a copy of *take*, but also a copy of *over* (note that if it turns out that all P elements must merge in the L-Domain, such an initial merger site need not be stipulated for (iii)). We note finally that an execution which involves incorporation into *take* requires a distinct structure for (transitive) cases of particle movement, as in *take the city over*, where such incorporation is at the very least not overt, but where range to Asp_Q could be assigned by the direct object, potentially not requiring *over* to merge in Asp_Q altogether. We leave these matters to future research, but see Section 7.3.3 for some more discussion.

[17] With thanks to N. Klinedinst for suggesting the applicability of reticule selection in this context.
The reader may note that we are assuming here that (51) and similar cases are in violation of Verkuyl's generalization, and hence that neither the subjects, originators, nor their copies are in [Spec,Asp_Q]. This, of course, immediately raises the question of how the well-known facts of *ne* cliticization, possible from

7.3.3 An open issue: predicate modifiers or range assigners?

One final point is worth considering concerning the assignment of range by adjuncts, such as we argued for adverbials such as *once*, as well as for *to the store* and similar expressions. We note that in contrast with direct range assignment by prefixes as in Slavic, and in contrast with direct range assignment by locative clitics, as will be discussed for Hebrew in Chapter 10, range assignment by adjuncts in English does not impose any restrictions on the direct object, in allowing it to remain quantity, indeed strong, at least prima facie in violation of double marking:

(49) a. Kim loved *her three times* last summer.
b. John hated *every doctor three times* in his life.

(50) a. Kim pushed *the cart to New York*.
b. Pat threw *the ball into the forest*.

Similarly, if we assume that particles are range assigners to $[_{\text{Asp}_\text{Q}}\langle e\rangle_\#]$ even when separate from the verb, note that they may co-occur with quantity DPs, as (51) illustrates (and see n. 12 for some relevant comments).

(51) a. I wrote *the letters up*.
b. I broke *the window down*.
c. I climbed *down the mountain*.
d. I took *over the company*.

(post-verbal) subjects in configurations such as those in (51), but not, typically, from post-verbal subjects of unergatives and transitives, are to be captured:

(i) a. *Ne   hanno corso/I due.
       of-them have   run   two
   b. Ne   sono corsi   due a casa.
       of-them are   run.AGR two to home

We return to this issue in greater detail in the context of the discussion of similar paradigms in Catalan in Chapter 9, Section 9.3. Essentially, we believe, the key to the *ne*-cliticization paradigm is not the unaccusative–unergative distinction (and the accompanying event-structure configurations), but rather the licensing of a post-verbal subject in a position that allows *ne*-cliticization without the empty category in effect c-commanding its antecedent, *ne*. If phrased this way, note, the post-verbal restriction on *ne*-cliticization follows immediately. If, in turn, subjects of unergatives occurring in the right periphery have been post-posed from [Spec,EP], they could not allow *ne*-cliticization any more than subjects overtly in [Spec,EP]. The grammaticality of (ib), then, is not about the unaccusative–unergative distinction, but about the licensing of the subject here, but not in (ia), in some position below [Spec,EP], say [Spec,TP]. In Chapter 9 I will argue that such positioning of the subject is a function accomplished, typically, by locative particles which may assign range to $\langle e\rangle_E$, the open value heading EP, in the absence of a filled [Spec,EP]. If that is on the right track, it suggests that *a casa* fulfils a double role here, assigning range not only to $[_{\text{Asp}_\text{Q}}\langle e\rangle_\#]$, but also to $\langle e\rangle_E$, on a par with the role which is performed, I will argue, by locative deictic pronouns in Hebrew.

The quantity nature of events such as those described in (50) can be demonstrated by the accusative case marking on the object in corresponding Finnish examples, as in (52):

(52) a. Tiina heitti keihasta.
Tiina threw javelin.PRT
'Tiina threw the javelin.'
b. Tiina heitti keihaan metsaan.
Tiina threw javelin.ACC into-the-forest
'Tiina threw the javelin into the forest.'

To make matters worse, it turns out that the paradigms in (49)–(51) do not actually behave uniformly with respect to the nature of the DP and its relations to the event structure. Thus for (49) a quantity reading can emerge in the presence of a non-quantity object (which, interestingly, can be interpreted existentially rather than generically in this case, further confirming the inner aspect nature of the modification here):

(53) a. Kim loved cats three times and feared cats three times.
b. Kim loved cats and feared cats three times (in three years/*for three years).
c. Kim loved and feared cats three times (in three years/*for three years).

In turn, for (50), and in spite of the presence of a delimiting expression, the quantity nature of the direct object continues to play a crucial role in determining the nature of the event. Thus while (50a–b) may be telic, (54a–b) may not:

(54) a. Kim pushed carts to New York (for several hours/*in several hours). (Single-event interpretation)
b. Pat threw balls into the forest (for several hours/*in several hours). (Single-event interpretation)

And finally, for (51), the DP must be quantity, but when it is not quantity, ungrammaticality rather than atelicity emerges:

(55) a. *Kim wrote letters up. (Single-event interpretation)
b. *Kim ate sandwiches up. (Single-event interpretation)

Interestingly, matters for particle-verb constructions improve considerably when the particle is adjacent to the verb, and the picture becomes akin to that in (50), (54):

(56) a. We ate up ?meat/sandwiches (for hours/all afternoon/*in three hours). (One-event reading)
 b. Pat wrote up letters (for hours/in three hours). (One-event reading)

The contrast between (55)–(56) replicates itself with the contrast in (57):

(57) a. Kim wrote up the letter (?for several hours/in several hours).
 b. Kim wrote the letter up (*for several hours/in several hours).

While native speakers are not entirely uniform in their judgements of (56) and (57), some assigning a question mark to (56a)/(57a) and a full star to (56b) and (57b), others assigning full grammaticality to (56a) and (57a) and a question mark to (56b) and (57b), they are uniform in maintaining that an atelic reading is considerably easier in [V+particle NP] configurations than it is in [V NP particle] configurations (see Chapter 8, Section 8.2.4, for discussion of these paradigms in derived nominals).

The degree of variability here is not trivial to explain. We note that the obligatoriness of a quantity DP for the verb-DP-particle constructions is easy to account for if we assume that the particles under consideration here, in contrast with the particles considered for intransitive cases such as those in (39)–(41), are not range assigners to $[_{Asp_Q}\langle e\rangle_{\#}]$, but rather, modifiers of Asp_Q. They force its projection, just like time measure modifiers such as *in-x-time*, but they do not themselves assign range. That task remains the role of the quantity DP. We must assume that such a modificational role may be suspended in the V-particle-DP configurations in (56) and (57a), possibly due to the merger of the verb and the particle at the level of the conceptual array, resulting in no requirement for the projection of Asp_Q. Delimiters such as *to New York* would have to be viewed as (optional) Asp_Q modifiers in such contexts, allowing, but not requiring, the projection of Asp_Q. The latter, note, is already rather problematic, in view of the fact that for intransitive cases, we assumed that the delimiter *is* a range assigner to $[_{Asp_Q}\langle e\rangle_{\#}]$, thereby allowing quantity interpretation without a quantity DP in [Spec, Asp_Q]. Finally, (49) and (53) present the trickiest paradox. To allow a quantity reading to emerge in the absence of a quantity DP, as in (53), we must assume that adverbials such as *once* and *three times* assign range to $[_{Asp_Q}\langle e\rangle_{\#}]$ in transitive cases as well as in the intransitive cases already discussed in (31), (33). However, to allow for a strong quantity DP alongside an adverbial such as *once* and *three times* in (49) without the emergence of double marking requires the assumption that even within the transitive class, such adverbials may sometimes act as range assigners for $[_{Asp_Q}\langle e\rangle_{\#}]$, while at other times they are predicate modifiers for $[_{Asp_Q}\langle e\rangle_{\#}]$.

As a particularly illuminating discussion in Schmitt (1996) reveals, the eclectic behaviour illustrated here by adjuncts is mirrored in the behaviour of some English prefixes assumed at times to impact event structure. Thus consider the prefixes *re-* (discussed in Wechsler 1989), *half-*, and *out-* (discussed in Schmitt 1996). First, note that in all these cases, a quantity direct object is obligatory (although cases with bare plurals are typically judged as better than bare mass nouns, which may be due to the availability of an iterative reading for the former, but not the latter), thereby seeming to pattern, surprisingly, with the separated particles in (55), and not with the incorporated ones in (57):

(58) a. *Kim re-read mail/??letters. (Single event, non-iterative reading)
 b. *Pat half-read junk mail/??letters.
 c. *Robin out-ran contestants.

However, *re-*, in contrast with verb–DP–particle constructions (but possibly not *half-* and *out-*) does occur with durative adverbs without ungrammaticality resulting:

(59) a. Kim re-read the mail for hours.
 b. ??Kim outran the contestants for hours.
 c. ??Kim half-ate the meat for hours.

And finally, note that (60) is grammatical under a simultaneous reading:

(60) Kim half-cried and half-laughed when she heard the news.

This situation, note, again suggests that the range of typological distinctions made here is rather broad. While Slavic prefixes as well as the particles in (39)–(41) are range assigners, separable particles, *out-*, and possibly *half-* (the grammaticality of (60) notwithstanding) seem to be predicate modifiers of Asp_Q, as are time-measure adverbs. Finally, *re-* appears to have altogether different properties, related, it would appear, to the interpretation of the direct object, barring the latter from being non-quantity, but unrelated to Asp_Q. As a result, bare DPs are impossible, but telicity, as such, remains optional. I leave these matters aside here, but the reader is referred back to Schmitt (1996) for an impressive range of relevant cases (and see n. 15 in Chapter 6 for some comments on the differences between the approach adopted by Schmitt and the one developed here).

We note, in conclusion, that while the descriptive tools differentiating between range assignment and predicate modifiers are available here, a principled explanation, predicting when a particular adjunct assigns range, and when it acts as a predicate modifier, remain wanting, and must await a future elaboration on the nature of adjuncts, their distinct semantics, and the way in which they interact with aspectual structure. We do note, nevertheless, that a close examination of the facts strongly suggests that adjuncts in English may be either range assigners to $[_{\text{Asp}_Q}\langle e\rangle_\#]$, making the occurrence of a quantity DP unnecessary, or alternatively, predicate modifiers which force the projection of $[_{\text{Asp}_Q}\langle e\rangle_\#]$, but which are incapable of assigning range to it, thereby necessitating the presence of some other range assigner, typically a quantity direct object. The final determination of the factors determining their specific role in specific contexts must, however, await future research.

8

How Fine-Grained?

8.1 Preliminaries

Ultimately, every event has a unique interpretation, as dependent on the unique context of its occurrence. The fully articulated interpretation, then, will of necessity be so specific and detailed as to make generalizations impossible. Pursuing such detailed interpretation assignment for events, however, has not typically been the goal of formal theories of interpretation and structure, nor is such a goal consistent with scientific pursuit in general, or formal linguistics in particular. Rather, it has been the task of the linguist to focus on what are, and what are not, legitimate and relevant grammatical generalizations. We must navigate here a rather treacherous path between the general and the particular. More concretely, and taking grammaticality judgements to be the primary source of linguistics evidence, as is well known grammaticality judgements do not come in black and white, but rather along a continuum, and do not wear the cause of their malaise on their sleeve. Barring the development of some means of better categorizing the shades of (in)felicity, it is, ultimately, the nature of the theoretical model employed that determines which shades of grey represent the violation of some formal principle of the grammatical computational system, and which are due to factors external to it.

The particular form of the investigation that I have undertaken in this study has been shaped by the assumption that whatever generalizations do apply within the grammar do not involve generalizations over the properties of concepts. While concepts certainly are amenable to generalization, I suggested that their properties do not interface with the grammar. Rather, the interface is between the interpretation returned by the grammar, and the meaning returned by the conceptual component as combined with world knowledge. Should these two outputs conflict, oddity emerges, at times so extreme that coercion of the relevant concepts is impossible, making it difficult to distinguish that oddity, a priori, from ungrammaticality as assigned by the formal grammatical system. In turn, it also follows that properties of particular concepts cannot play a role in determining grammatical structure.

Beyond that, however, we must also determine which of the many nuances of interpretation associated with grammatical objects are assigned by the structure, and which are artefacts of world knowledge, as combined with whatever principles may govern the formation of concepts. To illustrate, at one extreme, there are claims which most linguists would agree on, that is to say that the grammar need not represent formally the distinction between the role assigned to the (subject) argument of *eat* and the (subject) argument of *drink*, insofar as both occur in identical grammatical contexts, and have, for all intents and purposes, an identical grammatical representation. To take a less extreme example, common theories of argument projection from the lexicon postulate a specific set of grammatical properties for a given verb, assuming that some additional computation is required to license it in other grammatical contexts. In the domain of thematic structures, these are theories such as UTAH, which postulate grammatical operations to absorb and manipulate the assignment of thematic roles through incorporation and other devices. In the domain of telicity, there is the claim that some verbs are in some sense telic, while others are not, and that typeshifting is required to allow variable behaviour (see e.g. van Hout 1996, 2000). At the other extreme are claims that might give rise to considerably more controversy. To illustrate, Parsons (1990) suggests that as activities and accomplishments give rise to resultant states with identical properties, ultimately the distinctions between them may not be grammatically represented. As another illustration, Schein (2002) suggests that telicity is induced, in effect, by the presence of a DP which can take scope over time measure phrases (i.e. *in x-time*), and that in the absence of such time measure phrases, events are vague, rather than telic or atelic as such (see Chapter 5, Section 5.2, for some discussion). It is the task of this chapter to make explicit the degree to which the structures proposed here for events are fine-grained.

8.1.1 *Event structure or argument structure?*

As is already clear from the previous comments, the account proposed here occupies some intermediate spot between the extreme which postulates a unique structure for every instantiation of a particular lexical item, and the position put forth by Parsons (op. cit.) or by Schein (op. cit.). I already argued that contra Schein (2002), telicity is structurally represented regardless of the presence of a time measure phrase, as evidenced by accusative/partitive assignment in Finnish, marking (a)telicity in the absence of time measure phrases. Nor would it be coherent, within the approach advocated here, to argue otherwise. If indeed event structure determines the role and structure of arguments, and if there is more to the correspondence between roles and syntactic positions than evident in statements like those in (1), then it must follow that there is some event structure in every expression that involves arguments. We do note that to the extent that one opts for a representation such as that in (1), or for the type of model espoused by Parsons (1990, 1995) and Schein (2002), the grammar *must* be augmented with some other mechanism—structural, thematic, or otherwise—to ensure that in (1c–d), for example, the correct c-command relationship between the arguments comes to be (i.e. it is the understood *builder* that c-commands the *built* object and not the other way around).[1]

(1) a. ∃e [run (e) & argument (Kim, e)]
'Kim ran'

  b. ∃e [arrive (e) & argument (Kim, e)]
'Kim arrived'

  c. ∃e [build (e) & argument (Kim, e) & argument (the house, e)]
'Kim built the house'

  d. ∃e [push (e) & argument (Kim, e) & argument (the cart, e)]
'Kim push the cart'

I will assume, then, that the representations in (1) are too coarse. At the very least, they should be replaced with something like the representations in (2).

(2) a. *Telic intransitive (unaccusative)*
∃e [subject-of-quantity (Kim, e) & arrive (e)]

  b. *Atelic intransitive (unergative)*
∃e [originator (Kim, e) & run (e)]

  c. *Telic transitive*
∃e [originator (cat, e) & subject-of-quantity (the tree, e) & climb (e)]

  d. *Atelic transitive*
∃e [originator (cat, e) & default participant (the tree, e) & climb (e)]

Taking now the representations in (2) as our starting point, note that they are still quite coarse. Consider, specifically, some often discussed distinctions which (2a–d), as such, do not capture, as well as some assumptions implicit in the representations. First, note, to the extent that the distinction between telic

---

[1] And indeed, Parsons (1990, 1995) utilizes thematic roles alongside Neo-Davidsonian representations, tacitly assuming such roles to accomplish the hierarchical representation associated with argument structure. Schein (2002), on the other hand, discusses in great detail the workings of a generalized structural mechanism for such assignment, based on notions such as CAUSE and others, rather than on assignment by specific lexical entries.

eventives and atelic eventives is a grammatically real one, it is not directly represented in (2a–d), except through the interpretation of the arguments—that is, in (2a) the event argument is not an argument of quantity, in and of itself, but rather, the quantity interpretation is mediated through the existence of a subject-of-quantity relationship between the event argument and *Kim*. Telicity, then, is not directly represented as a property of the event argument in (2a, c). Only the presence of subject-of-quantity gives rise to such an interpretation. When no such subject-of-quantity projects, a telic reading fails to emerge.

As it turns out, we can exclude immediately the structures in (2), precisely by showing that reference to arguments does not suffice to draw the correct distinction. We already argued extensively, in Chapter 7, that quantity interpretation can emerge in the absence of subject-of-quantity, as for (3), for example.

(3) The army took over.   (Quantity)

Activity and stative interpretations, further, can emerge in the absence of an argument as well, as illustrated by (4), a point that will be discussed extensively in Chapter 9, Section 9.2.

(4) a. It rained.   (Activity)
    b. It was cold.   (Stative)

If indeed the event argument is never predicated of event types, the representations for (3)–(4) have to be as in (5), leaving out of the representation the fact that (3) is quantity, as well as the difference in event type between (4a) and (4b):

(5) a. ∃e [originator (the army, e) & take over (e)] (or, possibly, take (e) and over (e))
    b. ∃e [rain (e)]
    c. ∃e [cold (e)]

In a brief discussion in Chapter 3, Section 3.2.2, touching specifically on the distinction between statives and eventives, I assumed that stative interpretation emerges from the existence of some functional structure dedicated specifically to stative interpretation, and which can in turn preempt verbal categorization of its L-head complement. Suppose we continue to assume this. If it is on the right track, and given that event representations must distinguish between event types, and that quantities and statives (this latter one by assumption), but not activities, are associated with dedicated structure, two possibilities emerge for (3)–(4). One involves specifying that (3) and (4b) are quantity and stative, respectively, while leaving (4a) unspecified, as in (6). The other involves specifying (4b) as an activity, that is, assuming that activity interpretation emerges in the absence of any structure to the contrary. The emerging representation is in (7) (argument representation omitted for expository purposes):

(6) a. ∃e [quantity (e); take over (e)]
　　b. ∃e [rain (e)]
　　c. ∃e [state (e) & cold (e)]

(7)　　∃e [activity (e) & rain (e)]

Interestingly, note that the coarser representations in (2) force Verkuyl's generalization. Specifically, in the absence of an argument that is interpreted as subject-of-quantity, telicity quite simply could not emerge. In turn, to the extent that telicity *can* emerge without subject-of-quantity, this is not only an argument against the universality of Verkuyl's generalization, but against the representations in (2). Assuming the general veracity of the analyses proposed there, all event types—quantity, activity, and state—should be possible without an associated argument, and as such the representations in (2) are too coarse.

Suppose then that quantity and stativity, both syntactically represented, *must* be predicates of the event argument. Given the yet-to-be-determined status of activities, however, the following two revised versions of (2) are available, both involving the specification of quantity, but one specifying activity for atelic events (8), while the other (9) does not, but rather assumes, in effect, that an unspecified event argument defaults to activity:

(8) a. *Telic intransitive (unaccusative)*
　　　　∃e [quantity (e) & subject-of-quantity (Kim, e) & arrive (e)]
　　b. *Atelic intransitive (unergative)*
　　　　∃e [activity (e) & originator (Kim, e) & run (e)]
　　c. *Telic transitive*
　　　　∃e [quantity (e) & originator (cat, e) & subject-of-quantity (the tree, e) & climb (e)]
　　d. *Atelic transitive*
　　　　∃e [activity (e) & originator (cat, e) & default participant (the tree, e) & climb (e)]

(9) a. *Atelic intransitive (unergative)*
　　　　∃e [originator (Kim, e) & run (e)]
　　b. *Atelic transitive*
　　　　∃e [originator (cat, e) & default participant (the tree, e) & climb (e)]

The choice between the representations in (2) and those in (8) and (9) must ultimately be made empirically. If the representations in (2) were to be favoured, it would follow that event types could not be distinguished in the absence of arguments, a point we already disputed. It would further follow that quantity and activity could not be directly modified, and that any predicate modification would have to target either the originator or the subject-of-quantity. A similar rationale should dictate the choice between (8) and (9). If (8) is correct, we expect to find predicate modification of quantity, of activity, of originator, and of subject-of-quantity. On the other hand, if (9) is correct we expect predicate modification of quantity, originator, and subject-of-quantity, but not of activity. While in such a case activity might still be a well-defined interpretation, specifically, an event type that is neither stative nor quantity, it would not be a grammatical object, as such, and could not be specified to interact directly with grammatical operations.

I return in Sections 8.2–3 to empirical facts that may bear on the choice between (8) and (9). In advance of this discussion, note that to the extent that it is possible for the event argument to be predicated of at least some event types without any additional arguments, and to the extent that distinct event interpretation can emerge without arguments, we need not, indeed we cannot, assume that the main function of event nodes such as Asp_Q and EP (or for that matter, whatever functional structure is responsible for the emergence of a stative interpretation) is to license arguments in some form. Rather we must view argumental interpretation as orthogonal to the main function of event nodes. In short, neither originator nor subject-of-quantity, as such, contribute to the emergence of event classification. Event classification is achieved by direct predication of the event argument, and arguments, to the extent that they exist, receive their interpretation as an entailment from the event type. Most crucially, they do not determine what the event type is (see Davis and Demirdash 1995 for a similar view of argument interpretation).

It is worthwhile highlighting here a point which I will return to in Chapter 9, concerning the difference between the grammatical properties of the originator, as it may emerge in conjunction with an eventive EP, and the properties of external arguments assigned by a specialized node, often called little v, as articulated, for instance, in the work of Harley (1995, 1996, 2001) and Marantz (1999). Fundamentally, v is a verbal argumental scheme, and represents an attempt to generalize over types of thematic grids, as projected from verbal lexical entries. To consider Marantz (1999 and subsequent work), there are as many v-types as there are argument-structure configurations. That is, there is an external causation v, an internal causation v, a stative v, an inchoative v, etc., each associated with a template determining both the syntax and the interpretation of its arguments. A more parsimonious theory is suggested in Harley (op. cit.), in that v can only be specified as to whether it assigns an argument role or not (and see also VoiceP, which is either active, thereby assigning an external role, or passive, thereby not assigning an external role, as claimed in Kratzer 1994, 1996). Either way, each instantiation of v is clearly a way of forming a specific argumental configuration, much as traditional lexicalist accounts would associate, for example, verbs of emission with a particular argument structure (cf. Levin and Rappaport Hovav 1995 for the classical work within this domain). On the other hand, if the suggestions here are on the right track, Asp_Q and similar structures are first and foremost predicates of the event argument, and argument roles are by and large epiphenomena. If an originator or a subject-of-quantity emerges in the structure, it does so for reasons that are orthogonal to the semantics of activities or quantities. In the case of quantity, we argued, a quantity direct argument emerges because it is needed to assign range to $[_{Asp_Q}\langle e \rangle_\#]$. When range is assigned directly to $[_{Asp_Q}\langle e \rangle_\#]$, as illustrated in Chapter 7, a direct quantity argument need not project, but quantity, telic interpretation is licit nonetheless. Thus the role subject-of-quantity, as assigned to the argument in [Spec, Asp_Q], is but an artefact of the fact that a DP projects in [Spec, Asp_Q], together with the fact, specific to some grammatical configurations, that such a DP serves as the primary mode for assigning range to $[_{Asp_Q}\langle e \rangle_\#]$. If, however, such a DP does project, it bears, perforce, a predication relation with the syntactic projection of quantity, which results in its interpretation as a subject-of-quantity, by entailment. As such, then, Asp_Q, or quantity, is not a role assigner. Similarly, EP does not assign an originator role. A referential DP in [Spec, EP] which is not otherwise assigned a role is interpreted, by entailment, as the originator of an eventive (non-stative) event. However, EP, in and of itself, is devoted to the licensing of the event argument, and need not be associated with any other argument. Likewise, activities do not require an originator, as the paradigm in (4a) illustrates, a matter that we shall discuss at some length in Chapter 9.

8.1.2 *Against decomposition—resultatives and others*

It is frequently proposed (see McCawley 1968; Dowty 1979; Parsons 1990, 1995; Pustejovsky 1991, 1995; McClure 1995; Ramchand 1997; Higginbotham 2000*a*, *b*, among others) that telic events, most notably accomplishments, should be decomposed into two sub-events, roughly a development and a resulting state (alternatively, BECOME and CUL, as in Dowty, or process and *telos*, as in Higginbotham 2000*a*, *b*, etc.). The relationship between the development and the resulting state is taken to be causal in nature. Specifically, if Kim wrote a letter, the development part consists of the writing process, or the writing activity, while the resulting state consists of the letter being in a written state. An accompanying assumption (cf. Dowty 1979, and much subsequent literature) also assigns to the direct internal argument the role of the subject of the resulting state (subject of CUL). Note that to the extent that telicity requires such a resulting state, which in turn must be predicated of an argument, it is possible to thus derive Verkuyl's generalization.

Considering this view, specifically of accomplishments, we note that from the perspective of the account of telicity in this work, such event decomposition is uninformative at best. First, I suggested that culmination is a side effect of the existence of an event structured by quantifiable division, rather than an independent property that holds of quantity events. Secondly, I suggested that such a culmination, a specific instantiation of the lack of homogeneity in the intended sense, need not coincide with the end of the event, and hence there is no sense in which it can be coherently described as the starting point of a resulting state, or *telos*, as proposed by Higginbotham (2000a). I further argued that the (apparent) obligatoriness of a direct internal argument is to be derived not from the existence of some argument assignment properties of CUL, or from the existence of some interpretationally relevant resulting state which follows the event and which must share an argument with it (cf. Dowty 1979 and subsequent work), but rather, from the fact that in English-type languages, specifier–head relations is the primary mode of assigning range to $[_{\text{Asp}_Q}\langle e \rangle_{\#}]$. Finally, I suggested that atelic events, as such, are not associated with any structure, and that quantity is in a fundamental sense best viewed as a quantifiable predicate of the event argument. In its absence, the event argument is only predicated of the otherwise unstructured (eventive) verbal predicate. Decomposing an event into for instance, an atelic event and a telic event, the latter being quantity, thus makes little sense. The question then is whether or not, within the approach advanced here, analysing the interpretation of accomplishments, or quantity predicates in general, in terms of the conjunction of the properties of some development and some culmination contributes in any sense to our understanding of the phenomena under consideration.[2]

In Chapter 7 I discussed cases of quantity, or telicity, that do not conform to Verkuyl's generalization. To the extent that such cases do exist, they weaken

---

[2] It is interesting, from this perspective, to note that Higginbotham (2000b), in addressing the obligatoriness of quantity DPs, or what he refers to as 'singular-term internal arguments', suggests, contra Tenny (1987, 1992, 1994), that the measuring out effect is a consequence of the existence of a *telos*, rather than the basis for it, and that if, for example, the eating of the apple is to attain a telos, then it follows that there should be 'a systematic change in the apple, such that the attainment of the telos is brought closer and closer' (p. 66). While I certainly endorse the view here that the emergence of a measuring out effect with respect to an existing direct object is a consequence of, rather than the cause of telic interpretation, I also endorse Tenny's original insight that the best characterization of telic events is in terms of the nature of their development, and not in terms of the emerging result, and that it is the attainment of a telos which is the consequence of a 'measured' event, rather than the other way around (and see Rothstein 2000b, for a fundamentally similar view on the essential properties that distinguish accomplishments from activities).

considerably the empirical foundation for the decomposing of events into subevents of development and result, with the latter predicated of the direct (internal) argument of the former. This point aside, most of the arguments for the decomposition of accomplishments, specifically, into a development part and a resulting state of some sort, proceed by attempting to show that each of the implicated subevents may exist as a distinct syntactic constituent, and that when combined an accomplishment reading results, as a simple conjunction of their interpretations.[3] Consider, however, other types of evidence that have been brought to bear on the decomposing of events. An illustrative example is provided by the sentence in (10), as discussed by Higginbotham (2000*b*):

(10) a. The boat floated under the bridge for hours.
 b. The boat floated under the bridge in two hours.

While (10a) characterizes a non-directional floating under the bridge, taking place in the same location and lacking a telos, Higginbotham claims, (10b), telic, indicates a transition and a telos, the latter expressed through a locative preposition. In (10b), but not in (10a), the boat was once elsewhere, but has come to be under the bridge. In (10a), the boat is under the bridge throughout.

Viewing the paradigm from our perspective, we note that (10b) is non-homogeneous while (10a) is homogeneous in the required sense. We note further that to the extent that (10b) is non-homogeneous, precisely insofar as the boat is not under the bridge throughout the event, it does not actually imply that *under the bridge* is the telos, if we take *telos* here to be the starting point of some resulting state characterizing the location of the boat. If *under the bridge* did characterize the *telos*, and if we were to take the time adverbial *in two hours* to measure the time that passed between the origination of the event and its telos, as is specifically suggested in Higginbotham (2000*b*), we would expect the interpretation for (10b) to be that two hours passed from the time that the event originated to the time that the boat was actually under the bridge. Such an interpretation, while perhaps possible for (10b), is not in actuality the most salient one. The most salient interpretation is that at the time that two hours have elapsed, the boat is no longer under the bridge, and that it took two hours for the boat to pass from one side of the bridge to the other, with the strong suggestion that

---

[3] It is often assumed that event decomposition is the source of the difference between achievements, in the sense of Vendler (1967), and accomplishments. We note that even if the view that accomplishments are somehow achievements-*plus* could be supported, it certainly could not be sensibly supported by decomposing accomplishments into activities and resulting states. While both activities and resulting states may occur on their own, a resulting state is very clearly not an achievement. If, then, there is a sense in which accomplishments are complex events, but achievements, if indeed they exist as a distinct class, are simpletons, the decomposition under consideration could not be into development and resulting state, or process and telos. See Chapter 10, Section 10.3, for some relevant discussion.

the end point is, in fact, specifically *not* under the bridge. While time-measure adverbials do, we suggested, force a culmination and measure the duration of the event, we also note that the relevant culmination is not denoted by *under the bridge*, thereby strongly suggesting that the event implicated in (10b) cannot be decomposed, usefully, into a progression part, as denoted by the verb *float*, and a culmination point, as denoted by *under the bridge*.[4] Any floating from one side of the bridge to the other, note, suffices to give rise to a quantity reading in our sense. However, a decomposition of the event, so as to allow the expression *the boat (is) under the bridge* to act as characterizing the onset of some resulting state, clearly misses the most salient interpretation for (10b). *Float under the bridge*, then, is yet another instantiation of quantity defined not by the end point of the event, but by some intermediate point, specifically, by the change from not being under the bridge to being under the bridge, although being under the bridge does not coincide with the end of the event. *Float under the bridge* thus is a case of *fill the room with smoke* (see Chapter 5, Sections 5.2 and 5.3 for discussion), where quantity is defined on the basis of the existence of a particular point, a 'full' point or 'under the bridge' point, but where that point need not be at the end of the event.

If on the right track, then, this means that decomposing *float under the bridge*, either syntactically or semantically, so as to make *under the bridge* the basis of either a telos or resulting state, in some sense, is probably on the wrong track. Rather, it seems plausible to assume that *under the bridge* is simply a predicate modifier of the floating event, and we note in this respect that it is entirely neutral with respect to quantity, as it is perfectly comfortable giving rise to both quantity and non-quantity events, as the pair in (10a–b) indicates. Either way, not only is there no argument here for the existence of decomposition into a progression and a resulting state, such a decomposition actually gives rise to the wrong interpretation.

Another important construction which has been argued to give rise to an accomplishment reading through the conjunction of events denoted by distinct development and result constituents is the resultative, illustrated in (11) (transi-

---

[4] The problem here is distinct from that discussed in Higginbotham (2000a, b) in conjunction with English prepositions such as *to*, which have both an interpretation involving a directed motion and one involving an end point location. If one were to assume, for instance, that *to* has, roughly, a meaning akin to *to + in*, in *John ran to the store*, the culmination of the event does, in fact, involve *John* being *in the store*, thereby making such sentences amenable to a compositional analysis. Not so with *under*, which, under the interpretation intended in (10b), and regardless of the possibility of decomposing *under* into directed motion and location, involves in actuality the negation of *under* as the relevant end point for the motion. *Under* here does not appear to characterize any end point, but rather a significant landmark in measuring the progression of the motion under consideration.

tive resultative), (12) (intransitive resultative) and (13) (so-called ECM resultative).

(11) a. Kim hammered the metal flat.
b. Robin painted the barn red.
c. Pat wiped the table clean.

(12) a. The river froze solid.
b. The vase broke to pieces.
c. The ball fell down.

(13) a. Robin ran her shoes threadbare.
b. Pat sang the babies asleep.
c. The dog barked me awake.

The cases in (13) are typically taken to provide the strongest evidence for decomposition of telic events into a development part and a resulting state. Specifically, under such an analysis, in (13a), for example, *Robin* is the (lexically specified) subject of the verb *run*, typically a predicate of activity events, while *her shoes* is the subject of the stative predicate *threadbare*. The resulting interpretation, a presumed conjunction of the two, gives a clearly telic event, in which a process, otherwise atelic and as defined by *run*, gives rise to a resulting state, as defined by *threadbare*, which is in turn predicated of an object. If (13) could be viewed as a periphrastic representation of what is otherwise synthetic (e.g. *Robin wrote the letter*), it would provide strong evidence for the existence, for synthetic telic constructions, of a representation which is indeed decomposed into a development part (*Robin write*) and a culmination/result part (*letter written*), interpreted through a conjunction of some sort (for analyses of the 'result' part of resultative constructions in terms of a result-state, see Dowty 1979; Pustejovsky 1991; Levin and Rappaport Hovav 1999, 2000; Rapoport 1999; Higginbotham 2000a, among others). From a Neo-Davidsonian perspective, the representation for a resultative construction such as (11a) would be as in (14a); (13b) would be represented as in (14b):

(14) a. $\exists e$ [hammer (e) & originator (Kim, e) & participant (metal, e) & $\exists e'$ [flat (e') & subject-of- state (metal, e')] & cause (e, e')]
b. $\exists e$ [sing (e) & originator (Robin, e) & $\exists e'$ [asleep (e') & subject-of-state (the baby, e')] & cause (e, e')]

There are, however, a number of problems with this particular view of resultative constructions, and by extension, of accomplishments or telic events in general, as reducing to the analysis in (14). First, as noted by Rothstein (2000a), there is in fact no necessary causal relation between whatever development might be denoted in a resultative, and the emerging result:

(15) a. On May 5 1945, the people of Amsterdam danced the Canadians to Dam Square.
b. Reluctant to let him go, the audience clapped the singer off the stage.
c. At the opening of the new Parliament building, the crowd cheered the huge gates open.

In the absence of a causal relation between these sub-events, however, there is little to ensure any relation between them. The failure of causality suggests either that decomposing is the wrong move, or alternatively, that decomposing should be otherwise conceived.[5]

Consider next the following, based in part on Wechsler (2001):[6]

(16) a. John hammered metal/cans flat (for an hour/*in an hour).
b. Kim sang babies asleep (for an hour/*in an hour).

(17) a. You can paint these walls white for hours, and they won't become white (e.g. because something in the plaster oxidizes the paint) (and compare *You can paint these walls white in a week and they will not become white).
b. We yelled ourselves hoarse (for ten minutes).

The significance of (16)–(17) is that although they have the syntax of resultative constructions, they do not give rise to a telic interpretation, as indicated. Of course, we are already familiar with the optionality of telic interpretation with most so-called accomplishments. Thus *Kim wrote the letter, Robin read the book*, etc. are all ambiguous between a telic and an atelic interpretation. But the failure of telicity to emerge in such cases, is typically handled by assuming

---

[5] The latter is the direction pursued by Rothstein (2000b). Thus she proposes that accomplishments should be decomposed into an ACTIVITY event and a BECOME event, which are neither causally nor temporally ordered, but rather, '[t]he function of the incremental BECOME event is to "keep track" of the progress of the activity. This requires imposing a developmental structure, or ordered part structure, on the activity (this includes assigning it a culmination), and we do this by relating it to the developmental structure of the BECOME event via an incremental relation.' We already noted the similarity between Rothstein's notion of BECOME as the imposition of structure on an otherwise unstructured event, and the notion of quantity proposed here (see Chapter 3 at n. 10 for some discussion). We note, however, in disagreement with Rothstein, that an 'extended' BECOME event in her sense presupposes whatever properties are otherwise associated with ACTIVITY, and most specifically, it is entirely unclear what a BECOME event is without an ACTIVITY event. For some more discussion of this point in the context of the accomplishment/achievement division, see Chapter 10, Section 10.3.

[6] Wechsler (2001), noting these and some other problems, opts for the event-argument homomorphism model of Krifka and others. I return briefly to this point below. Wechsler further assumes that the availability of atelicity with quantity direct objects is restricted to ECM resultatives. As (17a) illustrates, this is not the case.

that for these verbs, and for the predicates that they head, the result state, or the culmination, is itself optional. Thus while for the telic instantiation of such verbs one would postulate, very schematically, something like the representation in (18a), for their atelic instantiation one would postulate the representation in (18b):

(18) a. Development (write (y, x)) + result state (written (x))
b. Development (write (y, x))

However, how are resultatives of the form in (16)–(17) to be analysed? Note that if the relationship between the adjectives and the direct objects in (16)–(17) is assumed to be predication or role assignment of any sort whatsoever, as in (14), then the emergence of a state is inevitable, as [*babies asleep*], or [*the walls white*], must denote a state, regardless of the overall interpretation of the entire resultative construction. And note that bare plurals are not independently barred as well-formed subjects of states, as (19) clearly illustrates:

(19) a. Babies are asleep in the bedroom.
b. There are babies asleep in the bedroom.
c. I consider walls white when they match my sheets.

Further, not much leeway is available here with respect to the interpretation of *paint the walls* or *sing* as involving development, or as causing whatever degree of whiteness or 'asleepedness' is associated with the walls or the babies, respectively. It thus emerges that if resultatives are indeed a syntactically transparent case of event decomposition, with the adjective describing the resulting state, then they must always be accomplishments, clearly a wrong prediction. It is of course possible to construct some kind of an account that would block an accomplishment reading in (16)–(17), as well as the state reading for [the walls white] for example, but one suspects that once such an account is fully articulated, it would render the putative evidence for event decomposition as based on resultative constructions inconclusive, at best.

Two conclusions emerge from the consideration of the examples in (16)–(17). First, it appears wise to reconsider the claim that, for example, *the walls* in (17a) is predicated of *white* in any way. If *the walls* is not predicated of *white*, serious doubt is cast not only on the analysis of resultatives as transparent cases of event decomposition, but also on the small clause analysis of the adjective phrase in resultative constructions. Secondly, it seems clear that resultative constructions are telic, or atelic, in exactly the same situations in which transitives in general are telic, or atelic; in the presence of a non-quantity DP they cannot be telic, while in the presence of a quantity DP they are ambiguous. This, it appears, is the case both for transitive resultatives and for ECM resultatives. The failure of the relationship between *the walls* and *white* to be correctly interpreted under a small clause analysis, along with the fact that the conditions on the emergence of telicity are the same in resultative and non-resultative transitives alike, provides strong motivation for an analysis of resultatives in terms of predicate composition, rather than event decomposition. Recall now that items such as *sing* and *asleep* do not have arguments, as such, in the XS-model. Rather, we suggested, items of the conceptual array, listemes, when embedded within syntactic event structure, function as predicates of these events, rather than role assigners or determiners of event type in any way. The composition of the relevant items would thus give rise to a representation such as that in (20):

(20) a. Hammer + flat → hammer-flat
    b. Sing + asleep → sing-asleep
    c. Clap + off → clap-off

The composed items in (20) are neither telic nor atelic. They are quite simply complex V-heads, of some sort, entered, I propose, into the semantic computation as such, giving rise to representation of the structures in (11)–(13) and (16)–(17) as in (21):

(21) a. ∃e [quantity (e) & originator (Kim, e) & subject-of-quantity (the metal, e) & hammer-flat (e)]
    b. ∃e [quantity (e) & originator (Robin, e) & subject-of-quantity (the baby, e) & sing-asleep (e)]
    c. ∃e [activity (e) & originator (Kim, e) & participant(the walls, e) & paint-white (e)]
    d. ∃e [activity (e) & originator (Robin, e) & participant(babies, e) & sing-asleep (e)]

The representations in (21) emerge precisely like their counterparts in (8c, d). To the extent that (21a–b), for instance, receive a quantity interpretation, it is because there is a quantity DP in [Spec, Asp_Q], capable of assigning range to [$_{Asp_Q}\langle e \rangle_{\#}$], indirectly, through specifier–head agreement. To the extent that there is no such reading for (21d) it is because *babies* is a non-quantity DP, and cannot assign range to [$_{Asp_Q}\langle e \rangle_{\#}$], barring its projection. Finally, to the extent that an atelic interpretation is associated with (17a), for instance, it is due to the option of merging, with VP, [$_{Asp_Q}\langle e \rangle_{\#}$] or F^s, the latter a head of a shell F^sP, in turn associated with partitive case in [Spec, F^sP] and no quantity reading.

To the extent that within the XS-model lexical items do not assign any roles to arguments, note now that the fact that in ECM resultatives the direct object is not an argument of the verb, or is not a *theme*, incremental or otherwise, is neither here nor there. In fact, none of the arguments in resultative constructions or otherwise are arguments of the verb, and to the extent that there is a privileged relationship between some arguments and the emergence of a telic interpretation, it stems from the structural position of those arguments—namely, [Spec, Asp$_Q$]—and not from any role that is otherwise assigned to them. In fact, we suggested that the role assigned to such an argument is an entailment from its position, and to the extent that this is the case, *the babies*, in (13b), is every bit as much subject-of-quantity as *the metal* is in (11a). There is no way to distinguish within an XS-model between these two types of structures, nor does such a distinction seem warranted. In turn, the felicity of expressions such as those in (13), as compared to the infelicity of (22), must be attributed to whatever conceptual difficulties are associated with assigning interpretation to an event of *singing* with *the babies* as a non-originator participant, or to an event of *running* with *her shoes* as a participant:

(22) a. #Kim sang the babies.
 b. #Robin ran her shoes.
 c. #Pat cried herself.

Of course, *sing*, *run*, or *cry* are not, strictly speaking intransitive, as (23) shows, and so the presence of the resultative adjective is clearly not *necessary* for the emergence of a direct argument:

(23) a. Kim sang Carmen.
 b. Robin ran a marathon.
 c. Pat ran three horses in yesterday's race.
 d. Cry me a river, I cried a river over you.

Nor is the presence of a resultative complement *sufficient* to give rise to well-formedness. Notice the contrast between (11)–(13), (16)–(17) and (24):

(24) a. #The king laughed himself healthy.
 b. #Kim sang the babies tired.
 c. #The crowd cheered the performer pale.
 d. #Pat cried herself awake.

The anomaly of (24) is most likely to be attributed to some conceptual restrictions on predicate composition, in the required sense. But if such conceptual restrictions are appealed to in order to rule out (24), it is hard to see how they can be excluded, in principle, as the reason for the ungrammaticality of (22). Finally, we note that a requirement that there be a direct object in resultative constructions follows, in our case, only for those resultatives that are telic, that is, for those that actually have a resultative interpretation of some sort. It is not a condition on predicate composition, nor is it a condition on the distribution of predicate modifiers. It remains a restriction on the emergence of telicity, quite simply because in English there are few other means of assigning range to $[_{Asp_Q}\langle e\rangle_{\#}]$. Thus (25a–d), we submit, are not ungrammatical. Rather, they are fully grammatical under the straightforward atelic interpretation according to which *asleep* is a modifier of *run*, assuming some predicate composition here between *run* and *asleep*. They are of course atelic, quite simply because there is nothing to assign range to $[_{Asp_Q}\langle e\rangle_{\#}]$, the sole present argument being an originator. In (26) range can be assigned to $[_{Asp_Q}\langle e\rangle_{\#}]$ by a quantity DP, which not only results in the appearance of a direct (internal) argument, but also in the emergence of quantity predicate with the requisite interpretation, and thus the implication of development towards a culmination:

(25) a. We sang off key.
 b. Robin ran asleep. (i.e. she ran while she was asleep)
 c. Kim danced wet with sweat.
 d. The king cried out of the palace.

(26) a. We sang Mary off key.
 b. Robin ran himself asleep.
 c. Kim danced herself wet with sweat.
 d. The king cried himself out of the palace.

It might be worthwhile to compare at this point our (admittedly sketchy) suggested treatment of resultatives with the recent account of resultative constructions in terms of predicate composition suggested by Wechsler (2001). Wechsler's and our account concur in rejecting an analysis of (at least transitive and intransitive) resultatives in terms of a result state. In its stead, Wechsler proposes that resultatives be analysed in terms of predicate composition, where the composition is between predicates and their arguments, as in

(27) hammer (x,y) + flat (y) → hammer-flat (x,y)

As Wechsler is not aiming at the characterization of a result state, the output of predicate composition need not be telic, thereby avoiding the problems for the result state model mentioned earlier. In turn, he proposes that predicate composition is restricted by the semantics of the emerging composed predicate, such that 'the resultative predicate must provide scale and bound at the point of predicate composition'. More specifically, the scale and bound are provided by the resultative secondary predicate, that is, the adjective, which must be gradable (in the sense of Kennedy 1999, among others) and closed-scale (in the sense of Hay, Kennedy, and Levin 1999; Kennedy and Levin 2000). Hay, Kennedy, and

Levin (1999) and Kennedy and Levin (2000) have argued independently that the lexical semantics of de-adjectival degree achievement verbs is dependent on the lexical semantics of the adjectives that they are derived from, and in particular that they give rise to telicity precisely when the source adjective is gradable and closed-scale (see Chapter 5, Section 5.4, for discussion). That a similar restriction should emerge in the presence of a predicate composed of a verb, with whatever properties, and an adjective which is gradable and closed-scale is thus to be expected. To support his point, Wechsler notes contrasts such as those in (28), with *dry* being (de facto) a closed-scale adjective, vs. *wet* (de facto) open scale:

(28) a. We wiped the table dry.
b. *We wiped the table wet.

In turn, Wechsler suggests, in ECM resultatives there is no predicate composition, because there are no shared arguments between the verb and the adjective secondary predicate. As a result, the adjective need not be gradable and closed-scale, and the result need not be (potentially) telic, thereby deriving (17b), for example. For such ECM resultatives, Wechsler notes, the original decomposition/result state analysis may very well be on the right track.

Although I share with Wechsler the assumption that resultatives involve predicate composition, and that there is little need to analyse (transitive or intransitive) resultatives in terms of result states, I also believe that the conditions on the emergence of predicate composition are considerably more erratic than one would hope for. Levin and Kennedy (2000) note themselves that the notions of gradable and closed-scale, as appealed to when attempting to derive the properties of degree achievement verbs, are massively subject to contextual factors. I already suggested in that very context (see Chapter 5, Section 5.4), that gradability and closed scale, in the intended sense, emerge from the structure, rather than from the lexical semantics of particular items, listemes, in this case as in general, giving rise to conceptual and contextual expectations, but not to grammatical structure. To make matters worse, within the transitive resultative domain, there is little evidence that open-scale adjectives are indeed barred, or that they cannot give rise to a telic interpretation, as (29) clearly shows:

(29) We sponged the table wet.

Not surprisingly, world knowledge dictates that *wiping-wet* should be odd, while *sponging-wet* should not be. It therefore emerges that here again the conditions are best stated in terms of extra-linguistic cognitive systems, and not as grammatical constraints. In other words, it is not obvious why resultative constructions should place a restriction on predicate composition such that the secondary predicate must be gradable and closed-scale, nor are such claims tenable in view of the grammaticality of (29) with a telic interpretation. It is of course possible to claim that only in the presence of a secondary predicate which is gradable and closed scale, will a telic interpretation emerge in such configurations, but if that is the case then we predict not the ungrammaticality of (28b), but the impossibility of a telic interpretation. And finally, if it is assumed that a resultative interpretation can emerge for ECM resultatives with the secondary predicate corresponding to a result state, one must ask what excludes this derivation for transitive resultatives, or put differently, why predicate composition is obligatory in transitive constructions, especially since at times (e.g. in (28b)) it gives rise to ungrammaticality which would be avoided if it did not take place.

We note, in conclusion, that while some appropriate notions of gradability and closed scale may be associated with telic resultatives, as they are indeed with degree achievements in general, the view promoted here is that such an interpretation is ultimately to be derived from the existence of a structured, quantity predicate, and from the fact that the existence of such a quantity predicate imposes gradability and some degree of boundedness on the event. Should the adjective under consideration be conceptually amenable to such an interpretation, felicity results. Should it be in conceptual discord with such an interpretation, (conceptual) coercion is required.

As a final comment on this topic, note that if indeed it is the case that the secondary predicate in a resultative is not in and of itself associated with a subevent of any sort, then its properties are fundamentally different in such constructions from the properties of stative predicates in contexts such as those in (30), or, for that matter, from the properties of stative predicates in causative constructions such as those in (31):

(30) a. Kim is sick.
     b. Robin is off the stage.
(31) a. I made Kim sick.
     b. I made the table dry/wet.
     c. I made babies sick.

Specifically, we assume that there is an event argument in (30) which is predicated of a state, and in (31), plausibly, two event arguments, the second predicated of a state, in contrast with resultative constructions, in which there is no event argument of any sort associated with the secondary predicate. Thus while the stative event in (30)–(31) is associated with functional event structure which may (or may not) license some event participants, arguments, the secondary predicate in resultatives is not associated with any functional event structure, and thus does not, in and of itself, license any event participants. It is then basically a bare modifier. As a final note, we observe that as predicted, and in contrast with (17a), for example, (31c), to be true, does require the existence of some sick babies.

8.2 What Gets Modified?

8.2.1 Preliminaries

Under consideration here is the extent to which our proposed building blocks of (non-stative) event interpretation, originator, subject-of-quantity, quantity, and possibly activity, are indeed grammatically real, insofar as predicate modifiers make reference to them. In what follows I will illustrate that modification is attested specifically for the predicates quantity, originator, and state, but that there appear to be no cases that target activity, as such. If on the right track, this suggests that although activity interpretation may emerge by default for some event representations, it is not otherwise associated with a well-formed grammatical object, insofar as grammatical operations may not refer to it directly.[7]

8.2.2 Referring to quantity, referring to non-quantity

I already suggested (see Chapter 5, Section 5.2, as well as Chapter 7, Section 7.3), that time measure phrases such as *in-x-time* are predicate modifiers of quantity, syntactically Asp_Q and as such, differ from adjunct phrases, which can assign range to $[_{Asp_Q}\langle e \rangle_\#]$. Thus consider again the following paradigm, from Chapter 5:

(32) a. Kim ran *once in two months*.
  b. Kim ran *to the store in two hours*.
  c. *Kim ran *in two months*.
  d. Kim loved Robin *twice in three months*.
  e. #Kim loved Robin *in three months*.

Specifically, we noted that while *once* and *twice* give rise to a quantity reading in contexts which otherwise bar one, or in which such a reading gives rise to strong coercion, time-measure phrases do not. The conclusion I reached was that while adverbials such as *once* do give rise to a quantity reading through range assignment to $[_{Asp_Q}\langle e \rangle_\#]$ (see Chapter 7, Section 7.3, for discussion), this is not the case for time measure phrases, which cannot change the fundamental

---

[7] Modification of subject-of-quantity is not investigated here. We note that as subject-of-quantity occurs in a proper subset of quantity constructions, illustrating the modification of subject-of-quantity, rather than quantity as such, is not a trivial matter. On the other hand, as subject-of-quantity is structurally constrained in obvious ways (i.e. it must be quantity when range assigner), its grammatical reality is not in question. Subject-of-state is likewise expected to allow direct modification, but an illustration is set aside, as we have not undertaken a detailed discussion of the properties of stative events.

properties of an event, but rather, require a well-formed $[_{\text{Asp}_Q}\langle e\rangle_\#]$, that is, quantity predicate, to be licit. Thus they are predicate modifiers of quantity and as such their well-formedness is a true diagnostic of at least some, if not all, quantity predicates.

Consider now the equally well-established test for the presence of atelic predicates, co-occurrence with *for x-time*. Strictly speaking, *for x-time* is not a predicate modifier, because unlike *in x-time*, which cannot affect a change in event structure, *for x-time* is in fact an operator of sorts, turning non-quantity predicates to quantity predicates, or at least, to bound ones, in the sense of Kiparsky (1998). Thus, note that an expression such as *Kim ran for three hours* is non-homogeneous (and in fact, also meets Krifka's stronger, quantization condition), in that no sub-event of it could be a running by Kim for three hours. Following in essence Verkuyl (1972 and subsequent work), I will assume that *for x-time* is an instantiation of outer aspect, in that the *Kim ran* portion of *Kim ran for three hours* is truly an activity and remains so, and that as an activity it is within the scope of *for-three-hours*. In fact, the need to define a domain for the licensing of *for-x-time* phrases which is aspectually distinct from the output of events thus modified provides independent evidence for the distinction between inner aspect and outer aspect. In turn, *for-x-time* phrases display what I shall refer to as 'anti-telicity' effects, being barred in the presence of an Asp_Q projection. It might be interesting to note that *for-x-time* phrases do differ from *once* or *twice*, for instance, insofar as they require atelicity—that is, they are antitelic—while *once* or *twice* may of course occur with both activity and quantity (cf. *John built the house twice*), and thus cannot serve as indicators for the aspectual nature of the predicates with which they occur.

Note now, with respect to the degree to which event structure must be fine-grained, that *for x-time* is not restricted to activities, but is licit with statives as well, as illustrated by (33). It thus emerges that the well-formedness of *for x-time*, just like the well-formedness of *in x-time*, makes reference to (non)-quantity, and not to activity as such. Most importantly, recall that a similar result emerged for partitive case, the presence of which was indicative of the absence of Asp_Q, and not the presence of any specific uniform atelic structure.

(33) a. Kim loved Robin for three years.
     b. Robin lived in my house for seven months.
     c. The bush was green for precisely three days.
     d. The baby was asleep during the entire raid.

The question, of course, is whether there are any cases in which activity, as such, is modified, as opposed to cases in which modification is sensitive to the absence of quantity structure. An equally important question concerns the difference between activity and state, both homogeneous. If no modification distinguishes between the two, and partitive case and *for x-time* certainly do not, then one wonders whether there is any motivation for postulating different structures for activities and statives.

As it turns out, establishing different modificational possibilities for states and non-states is a relatively straightforward matter. Thus manner adverbs such as *slowly* and *quickly* will modify any non-stative event, be it quantity or activity, but not statives:

(34) a. Kim arrived slowly.
     b. Robin ran quickly.
     c. Pat pushed the cart quickly.
     d. Jo build the house slowly.

(35) a. *Kim was sick slowly.
     b. #Robin loved Pat slowly.
     c. *Pat knew English quickly.
     d. *Jo owned the house slowly.

I submit here that modification that distinguishes between stative and non-stative predicates does exist, suggesting the grammatical reality of the event type stative. Likewise, modification that distinguishes between quantity and non-quantity predicates exists, suggesting the grammatical reality of the event type quantity. It appears, however, that there are no modifiers that make reference to homogeneous, non-stative events, as such, suggesting that while activity is certainly a well-defined notion, it does not have a direct grammatical reality, but rather, is the interpretation associated with events that are neither quantity nor stative.[8]

8.2.3 Anti-telicity effects 1: Hebrew reflexive datives

We saw that both *in x-time* and *for x-time* made reference to the notion quantity, *in x-time* being a modifier of quantity (or Asp_Q), and *for x-time* being excluded in the presence of quantity (or Asp_Q). Consider now an interesting aspect of the logic of elements such as *for x-time*, which we may refer to as 'anti-telic'. As

---

[8] We note in this context that there is no prediction here that stative (intransitive) structures should be unaccusative, in the sense that the sole argument merges at a point which is at least as low in the structure as Asp_Q (and see Chapter 9 at n. 10 for a brief comment). We further note that to the extent that e.g. (ia) is ambiguous between a stative and a non-stative reading, but (ib) is non-stative, there is further evidence for the fact that verbs, as such, are neither stative nor non-stative, and that the event structure which licenses manner adverbs likewise blocks a stative reading:

(i) a. The light shone on the parking lot.
    b. The light shone quickly on the parking lot.

they preclude the projection of Asp_Q, they of course preclude the projection of subject-of-quantity as well. When associated with transitive predicates, then, the direct object must be in [Spec, F^{s}P], receiving a default participant interpretation and (by assumption) partitive case. Consider, however, the projection of anti-telic elements in the context of intransitive predicates. Again, by assumption, Asp_Q may not project, and a subject-of-quantity interpretation is blocked. It thus follows that if there is an argument in need of licensing in the event, it must be interpreted as an originator, or alternatively, as subject-of-state. Importantly, if *for x-time* is anti-telic, rather than a modifier of, for example, activity or originator, we expect intransitive structures with anti-telic effects to allow both state and activity readings, as the impossibility of projecting Asp_Q is not sufficient to otherwise determine whether the output is stative or eventive, in the required sense.

Consider, from this perspective, Hebrew reflexive datives, already discussed as a test for the existence of an 'external' argument (cf. Chapter 2, Section 2.1). Reviewing, a reflexive dative may only enter into a coindexation relationship with the subject of a transitive sentence, and never with the object, and it may never be coindexed with the subject of a passive or with the (surface) subject of a clearly telic intransitive. It may, however, be coindexed with either the subject of an intransitive eventive predicate (activity) or of an intransitive non-eventive predicate (stative).

(36) a. ha.kla_bim$_2$ na_bxu la.hem$_2$.
       the.dogs$_2$ barked *to.them$_2$*

   b. rani$_2$ 'akal lo$_2$ 'et ha.tapuax be-hana'a.
      rani$_2$ ate *to.him$_2$* OM the.apple with-pleasure

   c. rani$_2$ šama lo$_2$ 'et ha.muziqa be-kep.
      Rani heard$_2$ *to.him$_2$* OM the.music in-fun

   d. ha.kadur$_2$ haya munax lo$_2$ ʿal ha.šulxan.
      the.ball$_2$ was [$_A$ laying] *to.it$_2$* on the.table

(37) a. ha.spina$_2$ šaqʿa la$_2$ (*tok šaloš šaʿot).
       the.boat sank *to.it* (*in three hours)

   b. ha.kadur$_2$ hunax   (*lo$_2$) ʿal ha.šulxan.
      the.ball [$_V$ placed.PASS] (*to.it) on the.table

   c. rani hizmin (*la.hem$_2$) 'et ha.yeladim$_2$.
      Rani invited (*to.them) OM the.children

We further noted that reflexive datives not only do not require culmination, they actually block culmination, even in the presence of an appropriate 'external' argument to be coindexed with, illustrated here by the examples in (38), verbs that strongly suggest culmination:

(38) a. rani harag lo 'et ha.yatušim   (le-ito/bemešex xaci ša ͨa/
Rani killed to.him the.mosquitoes (slowly/for half an hour/
*tok xaci ša ͨa).
*in half an hour)

b. #rani pocec lo   'et ha.balon.
Rani blew to.him ᴏᴍ the.balloon
(possible under changed presuppositions about balloons and what it takes to blow them)

The absence of culmination with reflexive datives could not, however, be taken as evidence for equating them with the English progressive. Specifically, the English progressive, as is well known, is oblivious to the role of arguments or to the position in which they are licensed. In particular, the progressive is equally felicitous with telics, atelics, and at least some statives, as well as with passives:[9]

(39) a. The wall is touching the fence.
b. The workers were being fired.
c. Bill is reaching the summit.
d. Kim is running.
e. The train is arriving.

Reflexive datives, on the other hand, cannot co-occur with passives or with telic intransitives, as already illustrated by (37). In view of the sensitivity of reflexive datives to the nature of the arguments with which they are associated, as opposed to the neutrality of the English progressive, it is plausible to assume that the English progressive is a case of outer aspect, in the sense of Verkuyl (1972 and subsequent literature). The progressive has the event in its entirety within its scope and its function, in essence, is to negate the event's culmination point (if there is one). Something else is going on in the case of reflexive datives, which are directly involved in the projection of the inner event structure.

---

[9] In Chapter 10, Section 10.3, I return to the fact, often observed, that the progressive with so-called achievement verbs is sometimes assumed to have a distinct interpretation from that associated with the progressive with activities or accomplishments. What is of significance here, however, is that regardless of whether or not this difference is theoretically important, (39c, e), and, likewise, (50), below, are assigned an interpretation. No interpretation, anticipatory or otherwise, is available for (38b). Thus, regardless of how one chooses to analyse the grammaticality of (39c, e), it is clearly not sensitive to the presence or absence of an external argument.

Note now that reflexive datives could not be considered modifiers of originators. Presumably, adverbs such as *carefully* could be considered as such, and likewise, in Hebrew, adverbs such as *bezehirut* 'carefully'. Such modifiers, however, are impossible in stative contexts, while reflexive datives are licit:

(40) a. rani$_2$ šama (lo$_2$) 'et ha.muziqa   (#be-zehirut).
     Rani$_2$ heard$_2$ *to.him$_2$* OM the.music in-fun (#carefully)
     (possible with an activity reading, essentially listen, rather than hear)

  b. rina$_2$ qarna (la$_2$) me-'ošer   (#be-zehirut).
     Rina$_2$ glowed *to.her$_2$* from happiness (#carefully)

  c. ha.kadur$_2$ haya munax (lo$_2$) ʿal ha.šulxan (*be-zehirut).
     the.ball$_2$ was [$_A$ laying] *to.it$_2$* on the table (*carefully)

Nor can we say, given the structural account developed here, that there is some atelic structure, ranging over statives and activities, such that reflexive datives must be associated with it.

We could, however, attribute to reflexive datives anti-telicity effects, in assuming that they bar the projection of Asp$_Q$. The result would be that they would straightforwardly prevent a subject-of-quantity reading from being assigned to any argument. With monadic predicates, that would translate directly to the obligatoriness of either a subject-of-state or originator reading.

More concretely, suppose now that reflexive datives are (inner aspect) operators on events, and that as such, they merge at E. Suppose further that as elements that merge at E, they exhibit a coindexation relation with [Spec,EP], a coindexation that is overtly marked, and is referential in nature, and which is realized, in the case of reflexive datives, as gender, number, and person agreement. The configuration for reflexive datives is thus as in (41):

(41)   [$_{EP}$ DP$_i$ E+RD$_i$ ⟨-*quantity*⟩$_i$]

We suggested that range is typically assigned to ⟨e⟩$_E$, the head of EP, through an overt element in its specifier position (but see Chapter 9 for much additional discussion). We further noted that the DP in [Spec,EP] need not be an originator, or, for that matter, a DP with any particular role. A referential DP in [Spec,DP] which is not otherwise assigned a role, however, would be interpreted in [Spec,EP] as an originator of a non-stative event. Consider, in view of this, what could be the interpretation of DP in (41). It could of course be an originator, as instantiated by (36a-b). It could, further, be a subject-of-state, in case it is assigned such a role in some position below [Spec,EP], as instantiated, for instance, by (40). It could not however be subject-of-quantity, quite simply because Asp$_Q$ is by assumption prevented from projecting. Finally, due to the referential nature of the coindexation in (41), the DP in [Spec,EP] could not be an expletive, a prediction confirmed by the ungrammaticality of (42):

(42)   ze hirgiz   (*lo)   'oti še-rani   šub   'exer.
       it annoyed *(to.it)* me that-Rani again late.PST.

In conclusion, the properties of the reflexive dative follow in full.

On a final note, we hinted already (see Chapter 2 at n. 28) that reflexive datives, while compatible with states, are nevertheless impossible in the context of individual level predicates, as the contrasts in (43)–(44) illustrate:

(43) a. ha.pesel   ʿamad lo   ba-pina.
         the.sculpture stood *to.it* in-the.corner
         'The sculpture was standing in the corner.'

   b. dani haya xole lo   be-kef kol ha.semester.
       Dani was sick *to.him* in-fun all the.semester
       'Dani was sick, and enjoyed it, all semester.'
       (deliberate reading possible, but not necessary)

   c. rina šamʿa la   'et ha.simfonia   be-kef.
       Rina heard *to.her* OM the.symphony in-fun
       'Rina heard the symphony with pleasure.'

(44) a. binyan ha.kneset ʿamad (#lo)   mul   ha.universita.
         building the.Knesset stood (#*to.it*) opposite the.university
         'The Knesset building stood/#was standing opposite the University.'

   b. ha.tinoq haya xole (#lo)   mi-leyda.
       the.baby was sick (#*to.him*) from-birth
       'The baby was congenitally sick.'

   c. ze'ebim šomʿim (*lahem)   qolot mimerxaqim gdolim.
       wolves hear   (**to.them*) voiced from distances large
       'Wolves hear voices from large distances.'[10]

If the analysis of reflexive datives proposed here, linking them crucially to E, is on the right track, their impossibility in individual-level and generic contexts would be entirely consistent with, and would indeed lend support to, the claim made in Kratzer (1989 and subsequent work) that there is no event argument for such predicates.

[10] To the extent that (44a–b) may be 'coerced', this follows from whatever conditions determine the possible transitional nature of the position of buildings or controlling congenital sickness. To the extent that (44c), in contrast, is ungrammatical, this follows from the fact that pre-verbal bare plurals in Hebrew must receive a generic interpretation for structural reasons.

8.2.4 Anti-telicity effects 2: nominalizer -ing

Evidence is directly available from the paradigm in (45) that the nominalizer -*ing*, just like Hebrew reflexive datives, is an anti-telic element (and compare with (46)). The examples in (47), with so-called achievement verbs, which, we shall claim in Chapter 10, Section 10.2, are idioms incorporating a range assigner to [$_{Asp_Q}\langle e\rangle_\#$] and are hence obligatorily quantity structures, give rise to a highly coercive, if not ungrammatical reading:

(45) a. Kim's formulating of government policy {for several weeks/*in two weeks/??twice}
   b. Pat's forming of a complex event {for three minutes/*in two minutes/ ??twice}
   c. Robin's dissolving of several chemicals {for three hours/*in two hours/??twice}
   d. Inny's writing of the letter {for three hours/*in two hours/??twice}

(46) a. Kim's formulation of government policy {twice/in two weeks}
   b. Pat's formation of a complex event {twice/in two minutes}
   c. Robin's dissolution of several chemicals {twice/in two hours}

(47) a. */#Kim's reaching of the summit
   b. */#Pat's ending of the flood
   c. */#Robin's finding of (the) oil
   d. */#The bulldozer's hitting of (the) bedrock

Interestingly, the anti-telic effects attested in (45), (47) are not present in gerunds, as indicated by the full grammaticality of the following, suggesting that the property in question is not related to the morpheme -*ing* as such, or alternatively, that there is more than one -*ing* morpheme—one anti-telic, the other neutral.[11]

(48) a. Kim formulating government policy {for several weeks/in two weeks/twice}
   b. Pat forming a complex event {for three minutes/in two minutes/ twice}

---

[11] Alexiadou (2001) attributes a similar observation to Graham Katz (pers. comm.), who also notes that verbal gerunds are grammatical with stative predicates, unlike -*ing* nominals, a point to which I return shortly. In assuming that -*ing* within gerunds has distinct properties from -*ing* as a nominalizer, I disagree with Pustejovsky (1995) and Siegel (1997), who argue that verbal gerund -*ing* and nominalizer -*ing* (in event contexts) are one and the same, and that both have a progressive interpretation (and see below on the comparison with the progressive).

c. Robin dissolving several chemicals {for three hours/in two hours/twice}.
d. Inny writing the letter {for three hours/in two hours/twice}.

(49) a. Kim reaching the summit.
b. Pat ending the flood.
c. Robin finding (the) oil.
d. The bulldozer hitting (the) bedrock.

In blocking culmination, nominal *-ing* does appear to directly share the properties of progressive *-ing*. And indeed, the claim that nominalizing *-ing* is a progressive marker inside a deverbal formation has been made by Pustejovsky (1995) and by Siegel (1997) (and see also Portner 1992; Zucchi 1989, 1993, among others). There are, however, some notable differences between the behaviour of progressive *-ing* and nominalizer *-ing*. Specifically, we noted already that progressive *-ing* does assign an interpretation to (50) (albeit a non-culminating one), but in the context of nominal *-ing* no such interpretation is available, as we already saw in (47), thereby showing that a straightforward unification of these two occurrences of *-ing* is not possible (and see n. 9 for some relevant discussion):

(50) a. Kim is reaching the summit.
b. Pat is ending the flood.
c. Robin is finding oil.
d. ?The bulldozer is hitting bedrock.

Recall now that a similar contrast was attested with reflexive datives, likewise impossible with unambiguous telic structures.

Consider now the following well-known contrasts, discussed originally in Chomsky (1970) (and see Harley and Noyer 1997 for a recent discussion):

(51) a. Kim wrote up the letter.
b. Kim wrote the letter up.

(52) a. Kim was writing up the letter.
b. ?Kim was writing the letter up.

(53) a. Kim writing up the letter.
b. Kim writing the letter up.

(54) a. Kim's writing up of the letter.
b. *Kim's writing of the letter up.

Here, again, we note a difference between the progressive, the verbal gerund, and nominalizer -*ing*. The progressive shows some marginality, though not extreme, when the particle and the verb are separated (52b). The verbal gerund exhibits precisely the same behaviour as the non -*ing* verbal paradigm in (51), with no ill-effects emerging. But in the presence of nominalizer -*ing*, ungrammaticality results when the verb is separated from the particle.

We touched briefly upon this paradigm in Chapter 7, Section 7.3.3, where we suggested that locative prepositions such as *up*, as in the case of *write DP up*, are predicate modifiers of Asp_Q. We noted specifically the contrasts in (55) (under a single event interpretation), as lending support to the obligatoriness of Asp_Q when *up* is separated from the verb:

(55) a. We ate up sandwiches (for hours/all afternoon/*in three hours).
    b. ??We ate sandwiches up (for hours/in three hours).

Note now that if this is at all on the right track, then it suggests that the status of nominalizer -*ing* as blocking culmination and the status of the progressive as blocking culmination are very different indeed. Although the progressive blocks a culmination reading in (52b), and although *up*, when separated from the verb, is by assumption a predicate modifier of Asp_Q, and hence requires its projection, no ungrammaticality results. In other words, the occurrence of the progressive here is compatible with the occurrence of Asp_Q, although culmination is negated. For nominalizer -*ing*, culmination is likewise blocked, but here the presence of *up*, an obligatory Asp_Q modifier when separated from the verb, does give rise to ungrammaticality.

This paradoxical situation lends itself to an immediate resolution, however, if we assume that the progressive is an instance of outer aspect, in the sense of Verkuyl (1972, 1993). That is, if we assume that it is an operator which takes scope over an event template constructed independently, much like negation (e.g. *the train did not arrive* means that there was no event of a train arriving, and not that there was an event of a train not-arriving), or alternatively, like *for-x-time* phrases, which take structures without Asp_Q as their input and return a bound event, but which nevertheless leave argument assignment intact within the inner aspectual domain. This, however, is not the case for nominalizer -*ing*, whose effect on the event structure we must view in terms of inner rather than outer aspect. Specifically, while the progressive has scope over a projected Asp_Q, acting to negate culmination if it exists, nominalizer -*ing*, just like Hebrew reflexive datives, blocks the projection of Asp_Q altogether. It does not negate culmination, in short, but prevents quantity predicates from ever emerging. Such an account, note, will immediately rule in (50) and (52b) and rule out (47) and (54b), the latter with a predicate modifier of Asp_Q, which, in the presence of an element that blocks the projection of Asp_Q cannot be licensed.[12]

That -*ing* nominals are always atelic is a conclusion also reached by Snyder (1998) and Alexiadou (2001). Suppose, however, we stretch the comparison with reflexive datives in Hebrew even further, and we assume that as an anti-telic element, nominalizer -*ing* must be associated with the event argument—that is, it must project in E—and that just like reflexive datives, it is coindexed, as a result, with an argument in [Spec,EP]. The emerging structure, omitting irrelevant details, is as in (56).

(56) [$_{DP}$ ... [$_{NP}$ V-*ing* [$_{EP}$ DP ~~V-ing~~ ⟨e⟩$_E$ ... [$_{VP}$ ~~V~~]]]

In (56), skipping some matters of execution, -*ing* further moves and merges with EP, thereby giving rise to an N projection (see also van Hout and Roeper 1998, for the assumption that nominalizing -*ing* is generated within the event structure). The structure in (56) gives rise to a post-V+*ing* argument in [Spec,EP], which may be realized directly, as in (57), all, note, non-culminating events:[13]

(57) a. the sinking of the ship   (Intransitive reading)
     b. the falling of stock prices
     c. the slipping of standards
     d. the laughing of the boys
     e. the jumping of the cows
     f. the dancing of the fairies

Alternatively, the DP in [Spec,EP] may raise to [Spec,DP], a raising forced in transitive contexts (and see Borer 1999*b* and forthcoming for a more detailed discussion of event structure within nominals). Note now that if we are correct and -*ing* is an anti-telicity marker, we expect the impossibility, in [Spec,EP] (or [Spec,DP]), of a subject-of-quantity argument. Therefore, just as we predict-

---

[12] A detailed study of the historical and semantic relations between progressive -*ing* and nominalizer -*ing* is clearly outside the scope of this enterprise. A full account must, of course, take note both of the ways in which they are the same (e.g. in blocking culmination) and the way in which they seem to operate at different levels, with differing scope properties.

[13] The existence, in English, of argument-structure nominals derived from atelic verbs (i.e. unergative verbs) is at times disputed (see Picallo 1992; Alexiadou 2001). That the nominals in (57d–f) are indeed argument-structure nominals is (Complex Event Nominals in the terminology of Grimshaw 1990) evident from the following:

(i) a. The frequent laughing of the boys from dawn till dusk.
    b. The deliberate jumping of the cows.
    c. The constant dancing of the fairies.

See Rozwadowska (2000) for detailed argumentation for the existence of such nominals, as well as for a review of the evidence for the existence of intransitive (unergative) argument-structure nominals in Slavic languages.

ed the ungrammaticality of the transitive achievements in (47), we predict the ungrammaticality of intransitive achievements as in (58), under the assumption, already touched upon, that achievements, so-called, are complex expressions including a range assigner to $[_{Asp_Q}\langle e\rangle_{\#}]$:

(58) a. */#the arriving of the train (at 5pm)
 b. */#the erupting of Vesuvius
 c. */#the exploding of the balloon

The ungrammaticality of (58) is particularly noteworthy, as it contrasts minimally with the grammaticality of (59):[14]

(59) a. the arrival of the train
 b. the eruption of Vesuvius
 c. the explosion of the balloon

We note that here, too, nominalizer *-ing* parts company with both progressives and gerunds:

(60) a. The train arriving at 5pm (is unlikely).
 b. Vesuvius erupting this morning was very unfortunate.
 c. ... as was the balloon exploding.

(61) a. The train is arriving.
 b. Vesuvius is erupting.
 c. The balloon is exploding.

Further, the DP in [Spec,EP] not only cannot be subject-of-quantity, it also cannot be an expletive, if we assume the indexation in question to be referential in nature. That expletives are indeed excluded, is well known (and see again Chomsky 1970); cf. the ungrammaticality of the much discussed examples in (62):[15]

(62) a. *Its constant seeming that John is late.
 b. *The constant seeming that John is late.

---

[14] We note in this context that given the well-formedness of pairs such as *formation–forming, formulation–formulating, survival–surviving,* and many others, which may co-occur in similar environments (precisely because none involve an achievement), indicates that the contrast between (58) and (59) cannot be reduced to some sort of a *blocking* effect.

[15] Example (62b) is ungrammatical under the assumption that either [Spec,EP] is unfilled, or, alternatively, that it is occupied by a PRO receiving an expletive interpretation, an impossibility. The text discussion does explain the impossibility of expletive or null subjects for *-ing* nominals, but remains silent on the impossibility of raising to subject, also observed in Chomsky (1970), as in (i). For additional discussion, see Borer (forthcoming):

(i) *John's constant seeming to run.

Again, no such restriction is attested for either gerunds or progressives.

It turns out, however, that the restrictions on the DP in [Spec,EP] go beyond those which hold for reflexive datives in Hebrew, in allowing only an originator in [Spec,EP], and specifically, in excluding a subject-of-state. That this is indeed the case, and that similar restrictions do not hold for gerund -*ing* (or, for that matter, nominals formed with affixes other than -*ing*) is illustrated by the following paradigm:

(63) a. Kim's loving of Pat
b. Kim's feeling of {#the cold/the coat on his shoulders}
c. #The wall's touching of the fence
d. #Kim's hearing of the symphony

(64) a. Kim loving Pat
b. Kim feeling the cold/the coat on his shoulders
c. The wall touching the fence

Under the most salient reading of *love*, it is a stative predicate. *Feel* and *touch* are compatible with both stative and non-stative readings; which one is applicable is often directly determined by context. Thus in combination with the weather, *feel* has a salient stative reading, and in combination with stationary objects, such as *wall* or *fence*, *touch* has a salient stative reading. In the context of gerunds, the salient readings are maintained. Examples (64a–c) may all receive a stative interpretation. This is not the case, however, for (63). Stative interpretation is not available at all, and the felicity of the nominals depends exclusively on the extent to which they can be interpreted as non-stative and their subject as an originator. Finally, it might be interesting to note here that the progressive does not treat these cases uniformly. While *feel* and *touch* do allow a stative reading with the progressive, such a reading is not available for *love*, for reasons that remain mysterious here. We do note that to the extent that progressive -*ing* is incompatible with at least some stative events, it shows, again, a subset of the properties of nominalizing -*ing*:

(65) a. #Kim is loving Pat.
b. Robin is feeling the cold.
c. The wall is touching the fence.

We must therefore conclude that nominalizer -*ing* has all the properties of Hebrew reflexive datives, but that in addition it is a modifier of originator, therefore forcing its projection, with the exclusion of stative readings following. Alternatively, but equivalently, we may say that in addition to being an anti-telic element, it is also an anti-stative element, potentially making impossible the projection of any event structure below EP.[16]

To conclude this section on a somewhat theory-internal note, the sceptical reader, having made it thus far, might now object that the behaviour of nominalizer -*ing* is in fact evidence for the existence of activities as grammatical objects which may be directly modified, that is, that -*ing* forces the projection of an activity structure, exclusive of both quantity and stative structures. However, postulating -*ing* as a modifier of activities cannot possibly be sufficient. Activities, as we already noted, do not force the projection of an originator, as is the case with activity weather predicates, for instance, which are in turn not possible as -*ing* nominals:

(66) a. It rained constantly for several hours yesterday.
 b. *The constant raining for several hours yesterday

At the very least, then, -*ing* the nominalizer must be specified as a modifier of activity and as an originator modifier, thereby forcing the projection of both, otherwise not forced in activities. Thus, postulating a grammatical object *activity*, which may be directly modified by -*ing*, does not in actuality simplify the statement of the latter's properties. In fact, it is otherwise costly, disallowing us to unify, at least up to a point, the properties of -*ing* and reflexive datives, and forcing us to make reference here to activity, which is otherwise never directly modified (and see Section 8.3 for some additional brief comments).

8.3 A Somewhat Speculative Note on the Conceptual Status of Some Predicate Modifiers

In a fundamental way, the view advocated in this book is a constructionist one. It is structure that assigns interpretation. Listemes are modifiers of that structure, rather than determinants of it. To return to the paradigm repeated in (67), the model allows us to say that in (67a), there is an event which is neither stative nor quantity, and an originator of it, and that the event is modified by a *siren* noise. In (67b), on the other hand, there is a quantity event, which is modified by a *siren* noise, etc.

---

[16] As raising to [Spec,DP] must be through [Spec,EP], and as subject-of-quantity is blocked in V-*ing* nominals, it emerges that any DP in the specifier of V-*ing* nominals must receive an originator interpretation, therefore deriving the well-known ungrammaticality of (ii):
(ii) *the city's bombing (by the army)
 For a detailed discussion of this, as well as a fuller analysis of event structure within -*ing* nominals and others, including the licensing of -*ing* in cases such as *the bombing of the city*, see Borer (1999b, forthcoming).

(67) a. The fire stations sirened throughout the raid.
  b. The factory sirened midday and everyone stopped for lunch.
  c. The police sirened the Porsche to a stop.
  d. The police car sirened up to the accident.
  e. The police car sirened the daylights out of me. (Clark and Clark 1979)

It is nevertheless a clear fact of natural language that many verbs do not actually occur in all the environments in (67a–e). While we have noted that many a verb typically assumed to be telic or atelic, unaccusative or unergative, respectively, do in fact occur in either context, there nevertheless remain verbs that do not exhibit such freedom.

As it turns out, the bulk of unyielding (non-stative) verbs belong to two categories. One is that of so-called achievements, and we return to those at some length in Chapter 10. The other is that of intransitive manner verbs which refuse quantity event structure, as illustrated by (68)–(69), contrasted with (70).

(68) a. *le-mi   ha.keleb rac?   (Hebrew)
       to-who the.dog ran?
       (Under the interpretation 'whose dog ran?')
  b. *le-mi   ha.xatula yilela?
       to-who the.cat   meowed?
       (Under the interpretation 'whose cat meowed?')
  c. *le-mi   ha.tuki   mepatpet?
       to-who the.parrot chats?
       (Under the interpretation 'whose parrot chats?')
  d. *le-mi   ha.kursa   hitnadneda?
       to-whom the.armchair rocked?

(69) a. ha.keleb rac lo.   (Hebrew)
       the.dog ran to.him
       'The dog ran/was running.'
  b. ha.xatula yilela   la.
       the.cat   meowed to.her
       'The cat meowed/was meowing.'
  c. ha.tuki   mepatpet lo.
       the.parrot chatters to.him
       'The parrot is chattering.'
  d. ha.kursa   hitnadneda la.
       the.armchair rocked   to.it
       'The armchair was rocking.'

(70) a. le-mi ha.perax na<u>b</u>al?/ha.perax na<u>b</u>al lo. (Hebrew)
to-who the.flower wilted?/the.flower wilted to.him
'Whose flower wilted?/The flower wilted/was wilting.'

b. le-mi ha.kursa zaza?/ha.kursa zaza la.
to-who the.armchair moved?/the.armchair moved to.her
'Whose armchair moved?/The armchair moved/was moving.'

c. le-mi ha.tiax hitporer?/ha.tiax hitporer lo.
to-who the.plaster crumbled/the.plaster crumbled to.him
'Whose plaster crumbled?/The plaster crumbled/was crumbling.'

Recall that possessor datives must c-command their possessed, and that reflexive datives, anti-telic elements, must be coindexed with an argument in [Spec,EP] which is distinct from subject-of-quantity. Note that given the system we have developed here, this in effect forces a single direct argument to be in [Spec,Asp$_Q$] in order to be bound by a possessor dative. Consider why this is so. In order to be within the c-command domain of the possessor dative, the single argument of an intransitive (or its lowest copy) cannot be in [Spec,EP] or [Spec,TP]. On the other hand, the only lower positions in which it may be instantiated (setting aside the precise structure for statives) are [Spec,Asp$_Q$] and [Spec,F^{s}P]. F^{s}P, in turn, is barred in principle in intransitive contexts, as it must assign partitive (objective) case. It thus emerges that in intransitive contexts, a direct argument that is bound by a possessor dative must, at the very least, have a copy in [Spec,Asp$_Q$], or differently put, it must be subject-of-quantity. The fact that manner intransitives cannot co-occur with possessor datives thus indicates that the subject of these intransitives (or its copy) cannot be in [Spec,Asp$_Q$], and cannot be interpreted as subject-of-quantity. We do expect them to co-occur with reflexive datives, of course, which is confirmed by the grammaticality of (69). In this respect, they contrast with the intransitives in (70) which can occur both with reflexive datives and with possessor datives, with distinct implications for telicity, as already discussed in Chapter 2, Section 2.1.

Now, why should this be so? Note that viewed from the perspective of conventional lexical semantics, verbs such as *move*—Hebrew *zaz*, and verbs such as *rock* and *swing*—Hebrew *hitnadned*, are not very different. Both denote motion, neither requires a volitional agent (none is +m in the terminology of Reinhart 2000), both are compatible with an external cause and with an internal cause interpretation, employing Levin and Rappaport Hovav's (1995) distinction. Why, then, should one be comfortable both as atelic/unergative and as telic/unaccusative, but the other be restricted to an atelic/unergative template?

The answer, I believe, resides ultimately in an understanding of the relations that hold between concepts in a properly formulated theory of concepts. In essence, note, whatever specifications are associated with the concept of moving are a proper subset of the specifications associated with the concept of rocking (differently put, *move* is less marked than *rock*). Those specifications of the concept *rock* which constitute added information with respect to the concept 'move' make reference to the manner in which movement was performed, and hence, perforce, to the existence of an origin for that movement—that is, an originator. As a listeme, then, '*rock*' is best viewed as a modifier of originator, but not so with *move*. If *rock* is a modifier of originator, then an originator must project, and if the event in question has only one argument, an activity, non-quantity interpretation emerges as a consequence of the failure of range assignment to $[_{Asp_Q}\langle e\rangle_\#]$. It might be worthwhile to recall here that the failure is precisely due to the failure of range assignment to $[_{Asp_Q}\langle e\rangle_\#]$, and not due to the fact that there is no subject-of-quantity. Thus, under the plausible assumption that *take-over* is likewise a modifier of originator, we note that in cases such as (71a), already discussed in Chapter 7, Section 7.3.2, the argument is an originator, but a quantity interpretation is available. Likewise, if we are correct in assuming that adverbs such as *twice* can assign range to $[_{Asp_Q}\langle e\rangle_\#]$, (71b) is a quantity event, although *run* is a modifier of originator (and *Kim* is indeed an originator):

(71) a. The army took over in two weeks.
      b. Kim ran twice (on Sunday and on Monday).

We discussed already the function of both reflexive datives and nominalizer *-ing* as anti-telic elements, as well as the function of nominalizer *-ing* as a modifier of originator. Note in this context that the verbs in (69) cannot be viewed as anti-telic in the required sense, as they are fully compatible with telicity, nor can they be viewed as modifiers of activity. Not only the grammaticality of (71), but also the grammaticality of the paradigm in (72)–(73), shows that they are fully compatible with a quantity interpretation and with a subject-of-quantity, when transitive:

(72) a. Mary ran the marathon.
      b. Bill laughed his way into the executive suite.
      c. Marcia whistled the thief away.
      d. Marcia whistled The Blue Danube (in five minutes).

(73) a. Mary ran a run.
      b. Bill laughed a big laugh.
      c. Marcia whistled a whistle.

In (72)–(73) quantity is licensed quite simply because there is an additional DP, which is in turn quantity and thus can assign range to $[_{Asp_Q}\langle e\rangle_\#]$ (and see

Mittwoch 1998, where the role of cognate objects as telicity inducers is spelled out in great detail).

We already admitted the existence of predicate modifiers of quantity (e.g. *in three hours*), non-quantity (i.e. structures in which Asp$_Q$ does not project), (*for three hours*, Hebrew reflexive dative and nominalizing *-ing*), as well as of originator, (i.e. nominalizer *-ing*). We argued independently that subject-of-quantity is a grammatical object, in that it is structurally constrained in well-defined ways and fulfils a well-defined grammatical function (see n. 7 for some relevant comments). We suggested, in contrast, that activities do not have a well-defined dedicated structure, that there are no modifiers which are restricted to activities, and that the range of interpretations associated with the listemes in (68)–(69) and (72)–(73) is entirely consistent with this conclusion. Nor are there, to the best of my knowledge, any adverbials that are restricted to activities, including those which may occur without an originator, but which exclude all other event types. If this is indeed so, it provides further evidence for the conclusion that activity is a derived notion and not in and of itself a well-formed grammatical object.

This point made, it is nevertheless the case that the predicate modifiers discussed until now were all fundamentally functional, and not listemes. As such, their existence is entirely consistent with the view that listemes, as such, do not determine syntactic structures. The role of listemes such as the verbs in (68)–(69) as originator modifiers, in effect forcing the projection of a particular syntactic structure, thus represents a clear way in which the conceptual array does, albeit indirectly, impact syntactic structure.

The role of non-functional modifiers in affecting argument structure is well known, as the following examples illustrate:

(74) a. Mary pleased the neighbours deliberately.
b. Pat died quickly.
c. The noise irritated the neighbours quickly.

(75) a. #The music pleased the neighbours deliberately.
b. #Pat died competently.
c. #Mary feared the storm deliberately/quickly/fast.

(76) a. Kim moved deliberately/competently (??in two hours/for two hours).
b. Robin moved quickly (in two hours/for two hours).

Deliberately and *competently* are typically classified as modifiers of an originator (agent-manner adverbs), thereby giving rise to the oddity of (75a–c), where an originator reading is inconsistent with world knowledge. *Quickly* and *fast*, on the other hand, are modifiers of non-stative predicates, (but not necessarily requiring an originator), and hence in the context of a stative event, such as that in (75c), oddity emerges. Consider finally (76). Because *deliberately* and *competently* are originator modifiers, and because the conceptual array allows only one argument, the event in (76a) cannot be a quantity event, as there is no range assigner to $[_{Asp_Q}\langle e\rangle_\#]$. A quantity reading is possible, however, in (76b), as *quickly* is not a modifier of an originator, but rather, a modifier of non-stative predicates, compatible with both quantity and non-quantity interpretation.

The interaction of predicate modifiers with argument structure is often viewed in terms of secondary predication (cf. Zubizarreta 1982, 1987, and much subsequent work). Within such a view, secondary predicates assign thematic roles to arguments, which are, in a sense, superimposed on, or composed with, the role assigned by verbs, to give rise to a complex role. Within the model developed here, note, the distinction between primary and secondary predication, as far as the distinction between verbs and adverbs goes, cannot be formulated. In a fundamental sense, all listemes are 'secondary' predicates, in that roles are assigned to arguments by functional structure, and listemes are always modifiers of structures, rather than determinants of it, be they verbs, adverbs, or adjectives. What then could be the role played by such members of the conceptual array in the system developed here? How is it best to characterize their interaction with the functional event templates created through the computational system?

The reader may recall that I suggested that the primary mode of interface between the grammar and the conceptual system is by means of comparing outputs. The interpretation assigned to a grammatical object by the computational system is matched against world knowledge, meaning of specific concepts, etc. Such matching returns a result ranging along a continuum from the completely felicitous to the highly abnormal, depending specifically on the degree to which the interpretation returned by the grammar deviates from world knowledge, on the one hand, and the salient value of specific concepts, on the other hand. The logic of the system thus dictates that the more specific—that is, marked—the concept, the larger the number of event templates that will clash with it. In turn, the more unmarked the concept, the smaller the number of event templates that will clash with it. Thus, to the extent that we are correct in assuming that *rock*, for example, is more marked, as a concept, than *move*, the fact that *rock* clashes with more event templates than *move* follows. To the extent that listemes do affect the interpretation, then, they do so by selecting among possible structures, rather than by creating them.

By way of lending some support to this picture, note that the radical freedom exhibited by *siren* with respect to the range of event templates that it allows (cf.

(67)) is a trait that is characteristic of tokens newly introduced, spontaneously coined, and otherwise the least standardized of listemes. The more standardized the use, the more conceptually marked it becomes, and the less likely it is to continue to allow, without coercive cost, a wide range of event templates. In this context, let us conduct a bit of a thought experiment, comparing the paradigm in (77) with the conventionalized verb *dog*, with the paradigm in (78), with the non-conventionalized verb *cat*, and assigning freely to (78a–e) whatever interpretation seems plausible in the context:

(77) a. I dogged during class.
b. I dogged midday and everyone stopped for lunch.
c. I dogged the Porsche to a stop.
d. I dogged up to the accident.
e. I dogged the daylights out of him.

(78) a. I catted during class.
b. I catted midday and everyone stopped for lunch.
c. I catted the Porsche to a stop.
d. I catted up to the accident.
e. I catted the daylights out of him.

The only difference between (77) and (78) is that the usage of *dog* as a verb has already picked up on a very specific subset of the conceptual properties of the animal *dog*, in effect creating a concept separate from, albeit linked to, that of domestic canines. As in (77a, b, d) the conventional interpretation is uncomfortable with the event structure, and oddity results. The homophony between the concept *dog*, as in following tenaciously, and the concept *dog*, as in a domestic canine, may give rise to a blocking effect for the insertion of the concept *dog* (domestic canine) fully productively in any event structure. Not so with *cat*, which has not been conventionalized in its verbal use with any specific properties of cats, and hence remains a uniform concept across all its occurrences. For that reason, embedding *cat* within all the event templates in (78) remains largely possible, subject to the use of any appropriate properties of *cat* as the modifier of the relevant event template (including, but not restricted to napping like a cat, plausible in (78a), emitting cat sounds, plausible in (78a–e), moving furtively like a cat, plausible in (78a, c–e), etc.). Broadly speaking, then, to acquire a conventional knowledge of a listeme is to have narrowed down the range of its associations with possible conceptual properties sufficiently so as to allow the conceptual exclusion of some computational outputs. This notion, note, is rather different from the conventional one, in which a lexical entry represents a particular insertion frame, and other insertion frame possibilities require an increase in computational complexity (through lexical mapping rules, syntactic operations, typeshifting, etc.). Here, the cost is in the narrowing down of the range of possible computational outputs, and not in their increase. As is argued in Borer (2003*b*), the 'narrowing down' effect is very much confirmed by errors made by young children, who freely assume that any verb stem can be inserted in just about any syntactic context. We leave this topic aside here, noting that although it is crucial to our understanding of the interface between the conceptual system and language, its resolution almost certainly resides in the understanding of the conceptual component, a task well beyond the scope of this work.

Part III
Locatives and Event Structure

9

The Existential Road: Unergatives and Transitives

9.1 Introduction: Post-verbal Nominatives

At the heart of Part III of this book is the following well-known paradigm from Italian and Hebrew:

(1) a. Sono arrivati (molti) studenti. (Italian)
   are arrived (many) students

(2) a. parca   mehuma (ha.boqer). (Hebrew)
   erupted.F.SG riot.F.SG (this.morning)

   b. hitxilu   hapganot   (ha.boqer).
   started.M.PL demonstrations (this.morning)

   c. hopiaᶜ   ᶜašan laban ba-šamayim (ha.boqer).
   appeared smoke white in-the.sky (this.morning)

(3) a. parcu šaloš mehumot.
   erupted three riots

   b. hitxilu harbe hapganot.
   started many demonstrations

   c. hopiaᶜ   harbe ᶜašan   laban ba-šamayim.
   appeared much smoke white in-the.sky

(4) a. *parac   ha.vikuax (ha.boqer).
   erupted.M.SG the.argument.M.SG

   b. *hitxilu   kol ha.hapganot   (ha.boqer).
   started.M.PL all the.demonstrations (this.morning)

   c. *hopiaᶜ   ha.ᶜašan   ha.laban ba-šamayim (ha.boqer).
   appeared the.smoke the.white in-the.sky (this.morning)

(5) a. *ᶜabad   ganan.
   worked.M.SG gardener.M.SG

    b. *caxaqa   yalda.
       laughed.F.SG girl
    c. *nazlu   mayim.
       dripped.M.PL water.M.PL

The facts illustrated by (1)–(5) are well known and extend beyond just Hebrew and Italian. For the languages under consideration, they have been discussed by Borer (1980, 1983, 1986) and Shlonsky (1987, 1997) (Hebrew), and Belletti (1988) (Italian). Both languages allow post-verbal nominative case assignment in V1 contexts (attested in these cases through subject–verb agreement). While in Italian post-verbal nominatives are possible for unergative constructions and in the presence of definiteness, Belletti (1988) shows that in these cases the post-verbal nominative is structurally higher, and certainly not within the traditional VP domain or in its 'original' argument position, be it the complement of V or the specifier of VP. Only in unaccusative and passive constructions are post-verbal nominatives 'closer to the verb', in what appears like the traditional position for internal arguments, and only in these constructions the post-verbal DPs exhibit a restriction against definites and strong quantifiers. As for Hebrew, post-verbal nominatives in V1 unergative constructions are highly restricted, typically possible only when the nominative is heavy and receives contrastive stress. Most typically, post-verbal nominatives in V1 contexts occur only as subjects of unaccusative and passive constructions, cannot be strong quantifiers, definite descriptions, or specific indefinites, and are, indeed, 'closer to the verb', in being inside the domain of adjuncts.

Historically, cases such as those in (1)–(3) have presented a problem for theories of nominative-case assignment and agreement, as well as for the Extended Projection Principle. Both nominative case assignment and agreement appear to occur here, at least prima facie, in complement position, and not in the highest specifier under CP (call it [Spec,IP]), otherwise also available in both Italian and Hebrew. On the other hand, [Spec,IP], at first sight at least, is empty. Accounts of the 'abnormality' of (1)–(3) have taken various routes. Some try to subsume (1)–(3) under analyses that have been proposed to account for aspects of the grammar of English, assuming a null expletive, on a par with *there*, which occupies [Spec,IP], assuming LF movement to nominative position, or both (e.g. through expletive replacement). Other analyses propose that the post-verbal nominals in (1)–(3) are not nominative (but inherent partitive, or objective; see especially Belletti 1988), and exist alongside a nominative expletive in [Spec,IP], the latter satisfying the EPP. Yet other analyses give up on the universality of the EPP and propose a mechanism for nominative case assignment that can be generalized to post-verbal arguments (Borer 1986; Chomsky 2000).

Some problems for the assumption that partitive case is inherent, or that it imposes indefiniteness, were already reviewed in Chapter 4, Section 4.2.[1] As to accounts which involve LF raising of the post-verbal subject, we note that they are semantically inadequate (see Runner 1993 for discussion). To illustrate, in a language such as Hebrew, (unfocused) bare pre-verbal subjects with an existential interpretation are ungrammatical (cf. (6) for unergatives, (7) for transitives, and (8) for unaccusatives), and bare plurals and mass nouns may only receive a generic interpretation in that position (cf. (9)). In turn, post-verbal bare DPs in Hebrew *must* be interpreted existentially; a generic interpretation is impossible (cf. (10) for unergatives, (11) for transitives, and (12) for unaccusatives). Similar facts hold in Italian and Spanish, the exception being the grammaticality in Hebrew, but not in Italian and Spanish, of generic bare plurals and mass nouns in pre-verbal position:

(6) a. *klabim nabxu 'etmol   kol ha.layla.   (Existential reading)
       dogs   barked yesterday all night

   b. *studentim ʿamdu ba-misdaron   ve-caxaqu.   (Existential reading)
       students stood in-the.corridor and-laughed

   c. *maim nazlu   min ha.tiqra   kol hayom.   (Existential reading)
       water trickled from the.ceiling all the.day

(7) a. *xatulim radpu 'axrey ʿakbarim.   (Existential reading)
       cats   chased after mice

   b. *xatul tapas   ʿakbar ba-gan.
       cat   caught mouse in-the.garden

(8) a. *'eben napla.
       stone fell

   b. *'abanim naplu.   (Existential reading)
       stones fell

---

[1] Interestingly, post-verbal indefinite subjects in contexts such as those in (1)–(3) can receive partitive case in Finnish, a fact clearly in need of an explanation. Note, however, that given the overall properties of partitive case, it is clear that the properties of the post-verbal argument in (1)–(3) cannot actually be derived from the presence of partitive case. First, (1)–(3) are telic, while partitive case correlates with absence of telicity. Secondly, if partitives were responsible for the imposition of the definiteness restriction in (1)–(3), one would have to postulate two distinct instantiations of partitive case, one which does impose a definiteness restriction, and one which does not. Finally, partitive subjects part company with the paradigm in (1)–(3) in an important respect—they do not exhibit agreement with the verb, indicating that to the extent that there is agreement in (1)–(3), it is independently untenable to explain the paradigm by positing partitive case for the post-verbal subjects, making them akin, incorrectly, to the non-agreeing partitive post-verbal subjects in Finnish.

c. *basar nirqab̲. (Existential reading)
   meat rotted
   (OK if generic, meaning 'meat had the property of rotting', e.g. before iceboxes were introduced)

(9) a. xatulim nop̲lim ʿal 'arba raglayim. (Generic only)
       cats   fall   on all   four
   b. basar nimkar be-qilogramim.
      meat sell.PASS in-kilograms
      'Meat is sold in kilograms.' (Generic only, meaning that kilograms is the normal measuring unit for meat.)
   c. dinozaurim 'ak̲lu ʿeseb̲. (Generic only)
      dinosaurs ate   grass
   d. klab̲im nob̲xim kol boqer. (Generic only)
      dogs   bark   every morning

(10) a. 'etmol   nab̲xu klab̲im kol ha.layla.
        yesterday barked dogs   all night
    b. 'etmol   ʿamdu studentim ba-misdaron ve-caxaqu.
       yesterday stood students in-the.corridor and-laughed
    c. kol ha.yom nazlu   maim min ha.tiqra.
       all day   trickled water from the.ceiling

(11) #be-derek̲ klal top̲sim xatulim ʿak̲barim be-qalut.
     usually   catch cats   mice   easily
     (Generic interpretation not available, existential odd)

(12) a. 'etmol   nap̲la 'eb̲en.
        yesterday fell   stone
    b. 'etmol   nap̲lu 'ab̲anim. (Existential only)
       yesterday fell   stones
    c. ha.šab̲ua nirqab̲ basar. (Existential only)
       this.week rotted meat

Any syntactic account for the paradigm in (1)–(3) which involves raising of the post-verbal (weak) subject into a pre-verbal LF position fails to predict this contrast, and is thus clearly missing an important generalization concerning the relation between the syntactic position of bare DPs and their interpretation.

Nor does the paradigm in (1)–(3) fare well from the perspective of the licensing of the EP node postulated in this work. Thus far, I have postulated the projection of an EP node, above TP, and I further made the assumption that just like $\langle e \rangle_d$, the head of DP, where range assignment amounts to establishing a mapping from predicates to objects (or quantifiers), so the head of EP, $\langle e \rangle_E$, is responsible for establishing a mapping from predicates to events. As to the assignment of range to $\langle e \rangle_E$, I assumed tentatively that any element in [Spec, EP] may, somehow, assign range to $\langle e \rangle_E$. However, what, specifically, could be the range assigner to $\langle e \rangle_E$ in (1)–(3), given that [Spec, EP] is unfilled? Suppose we assumed that the ungrammaticality of (5) is in fact due to the failure of $\langle e \rangle_E$ to be assigned range when [Spec, EP] is unfilled. Could a mechanism be developed such that it would allow for range assignment to $\langle e \rangle_E$ in (1)–(3), but not in the ungrammatical (unergative) cases in (5)?

Consider now another interesting property of the predicates in (1)–(3). In addition to presenting a problem for theories of nominative case, agreement, and the EPP, as well as for our own proposal concerning range assignment to $\langle e \rangle_E$, note that they present a problem for Verkuyl's generalization. We discussed in Chapter 7 counter-examples to Verkuyl's generalization, namely, cases of telicity which involved no DP-internal argument whatsoever. The problem for Verkuyl's generalization presented by predicates such as those in (1)–(3) is somewhat different. While there is an 'internal argument' here, and in fact, the presence of an 'internal' argument seems somehow crucial to delineating the difference between (1)–(3) and (5), the 'internal' argument does not need to have property α, under anybody's understanding of what α may amount to. As (2) illustrates, it can consist of bare DPs which are clearly not [+SQA] (cf. Verkuyl 1972 and subsequent literature), clearly not *quantized* (cf. Krifka 1992, 1998), clearly not *bound* (cf. Kiparsky 1998), and not *quantity*, under the definition suggested in this work. In fact, they are precisely the type of bare DPs which have been extensively argued to block telic interpretation. And yet, the predicates in (2) clearly receive a (single event) telic interpretation, as demonstrated by the series of tests proposed in Kamp (1979), Partee (1984), and Verkuyl (1989):

(13) a. parcu   mehumot ve-hitxilu   cᶜaqot.
         erupted.PL riots   and-started.PL screams
         'Riots erupted (first) and screams started (second).'

      b. hitxilu cᶜaqot ve-parcu   mehumot.
         started screams and-erupted riots
         'Screams started (first) and riots erupted (second).'

(14) a. hipocecu balonim ve-hopiaᶜ   ᶜašan.
         blew.PL   balloons and-appeared smoke
         'Balloons blew (first) and smoke appeared (second).'

b. hopiaᶜ ʕašan ve-hipocecu balonim.
appeared smoke and-blew balloons
'Smoke appeared (first) and balloons blew (second).'

(15) a. parcu mehumot be-yom rišon ve-be-yom šeni.
erupted riots on-Sunday and-on-Monday
(Two occasions of riot eruption)

b. hopiaᶜ ʕašan be-yom rišon ve-be-yom šeni.
appeared smoke on-Sunday and-on-Monday
(Two occasions of smoke appearance)

The existence of telicity with a non-quantity argument has already been noted by Mittwoch (1991), who takes this to be a diagnostic for achievements (rather than accomplishments). And indeed, the events in (13)–(15) clearly are achievements, in the sense of Vendler (1967). Nor is the phenomenon restricted to intransitive clauses with post-verbal subjects. Similar problems for Verkuyl's generalization are presented by the transitive achievements in (16) (examples based on Mittwoch 1991):

(16) a. The prospectors discovered gold and found rare coins.
b. The prospectors found rare coins and discovered gold.
c. Robin found oil on Monday and on Tuesday. (Requires two diggings)
d. The prospectors struck oil on Saturday and on Sunday.
e. The bulldozer hit bedrock on Saturday and on Sunday.
f. Mary noticed ink on her sleeve on Saturday and on Sunday.
g. John spotted wildfowl on Saturday and on Sunday.

Similar facts hold in Hebrew for at least some of these verbs.[2]

(17) rina gilta zahab ve-macʾa matbeʕot yeqarim.
Rina discovered gold and-found coins expensive

How, then, does telicity emerge specifically in (2) and (13)–(17)? Or, phrased in the terms of the account developed here for telicity, how is range assigned to $[_{Asp_Q}\langle e\rangle_\#]$ in these cases in the absence of a quantity DP?

The investigation of these cases requires a closer examination of a number of issues that were left aside in previous discussions. Specifically, it is clear that we

---

[2] In turn, the Hebrew correlate of 'notice/spot', *hibxin*, while clearly interpretationally telic, does not take a direct object altogether, and is thereby independently problematic for Verkuyl's generalization, but not for the account that we will propose here—see Chapter 10, Sections 10.2–3, for discussion.

(i) rina hibxina be-ketem (*be-mešek šaloš daqot)
Rina noticed in-stain (*for three minutes)

require a better understanding of the EP node and the nature of range assignment to $\langle e \rangle_E$, to resolve the grammaticality of (1)–(3) when contrasted with the ungrammaticality of (5). Further, if, indeed, it is true that achievements (but not accomplishments) somehow allow the telic interpretation in (2) and (13)–(17) without a quantity DP, then clearly the nature of the accomplishment-achievement distinction must be discussed. Finally, it may be that the clustering of properties in (1)–(3) is accidental—that is, the absence of an overt range assigner to both $\langle e \rangle_E$ and $[_{Asp_Q}\langle e \rangle_\#]$ is not correlated. But on the other hand, it is at least possible that these properties do cluster for a deeper reason, a possibility that must be explored. The remainder of Part III is devoted to exploring these issues. In Chapter 9, I investigate the properties of EP and range assignment to $\langle e \rangle_E$, especially in the context of unergative and transitive structures. Specifically, I will investigate the reasons for the ungrammaticality of (5), arguing that it is due to the failure of $\langle e \rangle_E$ to be assigned range in these cases. It turns out that locatives, in some configurations, do allow for post-verbal subjects in unergatives, and as we shall see, in some transitive structures as well. This fact will give rise to an analysis of some locatives as existential binders and as range assigners to $\langle e \rangle_E$, thereby shedding some important light on the nature of EP and $\langle e \rangle_E$. Following a general discussion of the event argument and its properties and licensing in Section 9.2, we turn in Sections 9.3–5 to the investigation of locatives. Cases of locative licensing of post-verbal subjects in transitives are discussed in Section 9.6.

In Chapter 10, I return to the paradigm in (1)–(3), and to the licensing of both $\langle e \rangle_E$ and $[_{Asp_Q}\langle e \rangle_\#]$ in unaccusatives—that is, in intransitive quantity structures—showing that here, again, locatives play an important role, with covert locatives potentially assigning range to both $\langle e \rangle_E$ and $[_{Asp_Q}\langle e \rangle_\#]$ in (1)–(3), but not, as we shall see, in all quantity intransitives. The resulting discussion will further shed light on the accomplishment/achievement distinction, showing the latter to be a non-uniform event type, and in general subsumable under quantity structures.

9.2 Projecting the Event Argument

In any attempt to represent syntactically at least some aspects of (Neo)-Davidsonian semantics, a central question is whether the event argument projects syntactically, and if so, under what conditions the projection is well-formed. Within this work, I have postulated the projection of an EP node, above TP. I further made the assumption that just like $\langle e \rangle_d$, the head of DP, where range assignment amounts to establishing a mapping from predicates to objects (or quantifiers), so the head of EP, $\langle e \rangle_E$, is responsible for establishing a mapping from predicates to events. When the predicate under consideration is Asp_Q, the event is interpreted as a quantity event. Finally, I assumed that any event participant that is not otherwise assigned interpretation, and which appears in [Spec, EP] is interpreted as *originator*. It is the purpose of this chapter to elaborate on the nature of EP, its interpretation, and the manner in which range is assigned to $\langle e \rangle_E$.

Consider from this perspective Higginbotham (1985), who proposes that the event argument is associated with the (lexical) head of the predicate and that it is syntactically licensed through being existentially bound by tense. We note that event arguments, for Higginbotham, are not actually syntactically projected, as such, in contrast with thematic arguments. An execution which does involve the syntactic projection of *e* in a phrasal position, on a par with other verbal arguments, is outlined in Kratzer (1994), assuming more specifically that the event argument projects in the syntax as 'the higher argument'.

We already noted that viewing the event argument as assigned by a lexical (open class) head of any sort is not a possibility within an XS-approach, as lexical items, as such, do not have arguments. Nevertheless, it would be compatible with an XS-approach to claim that an event argument is part of the properties of the syntactic node labels V or A, derived through either morphological or functional structure. However, the association of the event argument with V or A is clearly an empirically problematic claim. Consider this claim specifically in the context of the italicized words in (18)–(19), all derived from V:[3]

(18)   a. a *damaged* window
       b. a *drinkable* liquid
       c. a colossal (state of) *confusion*

(19)   a. The window is *damaged*.
       b. The water is *drinkable*.
       c. The *confusion* was complete.

Although a case presumably could be made that *drinkable* has an event argument, such a case would by no means be straightforward. We note further that if it assumed that there is no event interpretation in (18)–(19) due, for example, to the failure of the event argument to be bound by tense in such contexts, the question is, of course, why the utterances are not simply ruled out, given that the verb has an event argument that remains unbound. One could argue that the

---

[3] In Borer (2003a, forthcoming) it is argued that in cases such as (18)–(22), the derivational affixation serves to categorize the stem, e.g. *-ation* nominalizes *damage*. Insofar as *confuse*, when embedded within *confusion* is thus a V, a theory which associates the event argument with V labels would predict an event interpretation for *confusion*. We note that as within a Bare Phrase Structure system nodes are not specified inherently as maximal or minimal, a V embedded within N is by definition V^{max}, and not just V^{min}, and hence the exclusion of the event argument interpretation in this cases cannot follow, e.g. from the fact that V is a bare head. For a discussion of the applicability of BPS inside words, see Borer (forthcoming).

event argument for *damaged*, for instance, is saturated, somehow, internal to the word, thereby enriching the formal component in obvious ways. The direction taken in this work, however, has been to avoid such enrichment. Rather, we have tried to derive the possibility of projecting L-heads without any arguments, as is the case for the L-heads *damage* and *confuse* in (18), (19) and similar cases, from the fact that L-heads simply do not have any arguments, event or otherwise. Rather, arguments emerged as a result of the projection of some functional structure. If, indeed, the event argument is a true argument, then on a par with other arguments it must emerge in the context of some functional structure. And in fact, note that at least in (18c) and (19c), none of the (DP) arguments typically associated with the VP instantiation of *confuse* is realized. That the event argument is likewise missing suggests that it should indeed be treated exactly on a par with other arguments, in being licensed through functional structure, and not through lexical specification or categorical nodes such as V or A (and see Chapter 2, Section 2.4, for some discussion of the 'disappearance' of arguments in configurations such as (18)–(19)).

Consider now the licensing of an event argument, once it is projected. If, indeed, TP functions as the existential binder of such an event argument, it follows that in the absence of a TP, an event interpretation cannot emerge. And yet, an event interpretation does emerge in the absence of a TP, for example in event (derived) nominals, such as those in (20), as illustrated by the presence of event modifiers in (21):

(20) the examination of the students by the faculty

(21) a. the instructor's (intentional) examination of the student
      b. the frequent collection of mushrooms (by students)
      c. the monitoring of wild flowers to document their disappearance
      d. the destruction of Rome in a day

As is well known (see Grimshaw 1990 for extensive discussion), the event interpretation of (20) (a complex event nominal, in the terminology of Grimshaw 1990) contrasts with the absence of such an event interpretation in the so-called result nominal in (22), where no event modification is allowed (and see also (19c)). This is true even when the nominal, derived or underived, denotes an event, as is illustrated by (24) (and note in this context that *exam(ination)* in (22) denotes an event):

(22) The examinations were thorough/took seven hours.

(23) a. *Mary's frequent examination
      b. *the collection to document the disappearance of mushrooms
      c. *the destruction in a day

(24) a. The (*frequent) wedding lasted several hours.
    b. The lecture (*in a day) took three hours.
    c. The (*intentional) journey to the mountains took several days.

In (20)–(21) all the arguments, including the event argument, are retained, while in (22)–(23) none of the arguments, including the event argument, are. And yet, it is unlikely that derived nominals such as those in (20) are bound by tense, be it the matrix tense or otherwise, as their interpretation is clearly not dependent on that tense, or, for that matter, on any tense (i.e. the examination of the students may never come to be). We have no choice, then, but to assume that at least in (complex) event nominals, the event argument is licensed independently of tense. But in turn, if the event argument can be bound by some element distinct from T in (20), it is worth considering the possibility that it is never bound by T.

In Borer (1999b, forthcoming) the issue of event structure in derived nominals is discussed, and detailed arguments are presented showing that a linkage between an event argument in derived nominals and tense is untenable. Restricting our attention here to sentences, recall that we already postulated specifically a functional node responsible for the interpretation of the event argument, EP. Suppose, now, that we assume that an existential binder for the event argument is associated with in that same structural node, which is distinct from T. An EP node, specifically functioning as an existential binder for the event argument, is proposed in Travis (1994, 1997, 2000). For Travis, the EP node provides the means of existentially binding the event argument, but the event argument itself remains associated with the verb. The notion of EP as presented here does tally with that proposed by Travis, in disassociating the licensing of the event argument from the presence of tense. It differs from Travis's EP in two ways. First, the event argument is not associated with the verb. Secondly, I assume that EP projects above TP (or without TP altogether). T(P), then, becomes a predicate of the event argument (e.g. *past* (*e*)) and not, as the logic of the Higginbotham–Kratzer approach would have it, a head which selects *e* as its argument. The reader is asked for his/her continued patience in waiting for the rationale behind projecting EP above TP, and not below it.

We proposed in Chapter 3, Section 3.1, as well as in Chapter 8, Section 8.1.1, that in eventive (non-stative) contexts, EP is interpreted as atelic eventive—that is, activity—unless some additional structure, Asp_Q, projects to give it quantity. We set aside there, as we will continue to do here, the precise nature of the difference between eventive and stative event arguments, in the hope that future research will shed some light on how that difference is best to be characterized. We did note that within the model developed in this work, the best outcome would be a characterization of statives in terms of a dedicated structure projected below EP, which, in turn, would also have the property of preempting verbalization, thereby correctly deriving the fact that adjectives can be predicates of stative events. In the absence of such a structure, and in the absence of Asp_Q, EP emerges as an unstructured atelic event. Continuing to subscribe to the view that such an execution is ultimately possible, we will show below that the licensing of EP, which is to say, the need for the assignment of range to $\langle e \rangle_E$, will obey similar constraints for both eventives and statives. Even with the detailed structure for statives yet to be established, such an outcome does suggest that the differences between eventive and stative events should not be captured in terms of the properties of EP, but rather in terms of properties of some other structure, subordinate to it. As a first approximation, and assuming this to be on the right track, EPs come in the following flavours (irrelevant aspects of the structure omitted; SP* is some functional stative event structure, which preempts verbalization):

(25) a. Stative: $[_{EP} \langle e \rangle_E [_{TP} \quad [_{SP*} [_{VP/AP} \quad]]]]$
 b. Eventive, atelic (activity): $[_{EP} \langle e \rangle_E [_{TP} \quad \quad [_{VP} \quad]]]$
 c. Eventive, telic: $[_{EP} \langle e \rangle_E [_{TP} [_{Asp_Q} \quad [_{VP} \quad]]]]$

While Asp_Q and its interpretation have been discussed extensively up to this point, the configurations of range assignment to $[_{EP} \langle e \rangle_E]$ and the properties of the argument in [Spec, EP] have not enjoyed such attention. Thus far, we associated EP with exactly one property—that of assigning an originator role to a DP in its specifier, provided that it is not already assigned a role elsewhere. However, while it might be the case that a DP in [Spec, EP] can receive an originator interpretation, it is nevertheless clear that an eventive EP, whether telic or atelic, is possible without an originator. For telic events, this possibility is attested for unaccusatives; (26) attests that possibility for atelic eventives:

(26) It rained (for forty days).

If the representations in (25) are at all on the right track, it follows that (26) must have the structure in (27). However, one would be hard pressed to give *weather it*, whatever its other properties, the role of the originator of the raining activity. We are thus forced to assume that although *it* is in [Spec, EP], it is not associated with an originator role, noting that it moreover does not seem to play any other role as an event participant (the value of tense in (27) is set aside for expository purposes):[4]

---

[4] For concreteness, I assume that expletive *it* is a member of the functional lexicon which merges in some functional specifier (most likely, [Spec, TP]), and is associated both with case (here nominative) and with range assignment to $\langle e \rangle_E$ (see below). Specifically, it is not part of the conceptual array.

(27)   [$_{EP}$ it-NOM ⟨e⟩P [$_{TP}$ ~~it-NOM~~ [$_{VP}$ rain]]]

We must therefore conclude that it is possible for EP to project, and for a non-quantity process interpretation (i.e. activity) to emerge, without an originator role being assigned to the phrase in its specifier. As an aside, and quite independently of the structures proposed here, the assumption that *it* does not occupy the highest possible specifier in (26) (e.g. that it is in [Spec,TP] and not in [Spec,EP]), and for this reason does not receive an originator role, is clearly incompatible with well-established empirical observations about English, which suggest that the highest specifier under CP is barred from being null, and which place *it* to the left of modals (and in actuality, it is often argued that *weather it* is inserted in the highest specifier under CP precisely to prevent it from being null).

Note now that the role of EP as an originator assigner, at least in activities, cannot be rescued if it is assumed that TP projects above EP. To see this, consider the two alternative derivations in (28), involving TP projected above EP:

(28)   a. [$_{TP}$ it-NOM [$_{EP}$ ~~it~~ ⟨e⟩$_P$ [$_{VP}$ ...
       b. [$_{TP}$ it-NOM [$_{EP}$ ∅ ⟨e⟩$_P$ [$_{VP}$ ...

If one opts for the derivation in (28a), the problem remains exactly the same as it was in (27). A copy of *it* is in [Spec,EP], and if a DP in [Spec,EP], or its copy, must be assigned an originator role, the derivation in (28a) would be predicted illicit. On the other hand, if one opts for the derivation in (28b), it remains possible to subscribe to the view that a DP in [Spec,EP] is obligatorily interpreted as an originator. On the other hand, however, in the derivation in (28b) there is nothing in [Spec,EP], and no originator role is assigned altogether. Thus, at the very least, we have to assume that EP does not assign an originator role obligatorily, but only assigns it when there is a referential DP in its specifier position which is not already assigned a subject-of-quantity role, having moved from [Spec, Asp$_Q$]. It is not clear that this statement is in any way less or more problematic than the statement that EP quite simply need not assign an originator role, thereby ruling in the derivation in (27) as is.

We have now established that EP, even when atelic, need not be associated with an originator role. Rather, as we already suggested, a DP in [Spec,EP], if conceptually and contextually appropriate, and if EP is otherwise interpreted as eventive, is interpreted as the originator of the relevant event by entailment (and see Davis and Demirdash 1995 for such a view of argumental roles). There is then no role, as such, which must be *assigned* in [Spec,EP], just as there was no role which was obligatorily *assigned* in [Spec,Asp$_Q$]. A referential DP in [Spec, Asp$_Q$], if there is one, is interpreted as subject-of-quantity, as an entailment from the existence of a quantity predicate (and recall specifically that in some intransitive telic structures there was no DP in [Spec, Asp$_Q$] altogether). Likewise, a referential DP in [Spec, EP] is interpreted as originator, if the event in question is eventive rather than stative and if it does not carry any other role. In turn, the well-formedness conditions on EP, or $\langle e \rangle_E$, clearly should not depend on the presence of an originator role.[5]

So far, so good, but now a new puzzle emerges. If EP need not have an argumental specifier, and an (eventive) event need not have an originator, what is *it* doing in the sentence in (26)? What grammatical principle could possibly compel the presence of a semantically null element in a specifier that does not assign any interpretation to it, and which, in general, need not be associated with any interpretation? Another question must be posed, of course, with respect to the structure in (27) (or, for that matter, the structures in (28)): what assigns range to $\langle e \rangle_E$?

Suppose we combine these two questions, making the first an answer to the second. Expletive *it* is obligatory in (26) because it assigns range to $\langle e \rangle_E$, or in other words, the specifier of EP must be filled, because the only means of assigning range to $\langle e \rangle_E$ is indirect range assignment through specifier–head agreement with a DP in [Spec, EP]. We note now that this explanation harks back in nontrivial ways to Chomsky's 1981 Extended Projection Principle, the principle that requires the highest specifier to be overt. Specifically, as we are proposing that $\langle e \rangle_E$ (at least in English) can only be assigned range through the presence of a DP in its specifier, and as $\langle e \rangle_E$ is projected as the highest functional node in the structure, it directly emerges that the highest specifier must be filled. In turn, if on the right track, it also mandates the projection of EP above TP.

Returning to the structures in (25), it is clear that there is little reason to believe that such properties are associated only with the eventive, atelic EPs as in (25b). Rather, EPP effects are oblivious to aktionsart, with expletives licensed in statives, as well as in quantity EPs:[6]

(29) a. It is cold.
 b. It is possible that John will be late.
 c. It seems that Kim is early.

---

[5] In being associated with an originator role by entailment, and not as an assignment relation, EP differs from other functional nodes often proposed in the literature which are devoted to the assignment of 'external' arguments, such as *v* ('little *v*') and VoiceP. For a detailed discussion of this point see Chapter 8, Section 8.1.1.

[6] As is well known, expletive *it* does not occur, in English, in the context of monadic structures, but *there* does. The reason for this, I believe, involves some formulation of Burzio's generalization, requiring nominative to be assigned to a referential DP, if it can be thus assigned. Under the assumption that *it* is assigned an independent case, but *there* and its associate share case, according to some formulation or another, this contrast can be explained. See throughout this chapter for more discussion of English *there*.

(30) a. There arrived three trains at the station.
b. There walked into the room a man.

We may assume, then, that expletives such as *there* or *it* are obligatory in contexts such as those in (29)–(30), and EPP effects emerge in English, because $\langle e \rangle_E$ must be assigned range indirectly, and such range assignment requires the presence of some DP in its specifier.

But wrinkles emerge immediately. As is well known (cf. Borer 1986; Chomsky 2000, among others), the EPP does not generalize to other languages, which do in fact allow the highest functional structure below CP to project without a specifier, and in fact, the paradigm in (1)–(3), the starting point for our discussion here, illustrates precisely that. Further, what range could expletives *it* or *there* possibly be assigning to $\langle e \rangle_E$? Expletives are fundamentally non-referential, and do not have any thematic or event role. What, then, could be the value of $\langle e \rangle_E$, such that they can assign range to it in all event types?

Suppose the property expletives have is that they can existentially bind the event argument.[7] In Volume I, Chapter 5, Section 5.1 I motivated the binding of a variable in a head position (e.g. of DP) as a special case of range assignment. Suppose then that range assignment to $\langle e \rangle_E$ consists of existentially binding it. Note further that expletive *it* occurs in gerunds, where, arguably, there is no TP node (cf. (31)), thereby suggesting that *it* is, indeed, licensed in [Spec,EP], rather than in [Spec,TP], and insofar as it leaves a copy in [Spec,TP] in tensed clauses, it does so for reasons of case:

(31) It being so cold in California is atypical.

Finally, we must assume that the structural conditions that hold for EP and $\langle e \rangle_E$ are always the same, regardless of whether the event argument is interpreted as stative or as non-stative, as telic or as non-telic. The emerging structural possibilities are as in (32):[8]

---

[7] That English *there* does have an existential force is uncontroversial, although the attribution of this property to *it* may be less standard. We note that in the case of *there*, it is typically assumed that the existential force ranges not only over the event, but also over the associate of *there*, which, as a result, must be a weak DP. We further note that if it is assumed that *there* binds existentially not only its associate, but also the event argument, then we must also assume that in standard non-*there* sentences, such as *a man is in the yard*, *a man walked into the room*, something other than tense existentially binds the event. Finally, we note that as expletive *it* does not have an associate, the issue of existentially binding a nominal expression does not typically arise. An exception to this last statement—which we set aside—is presented by focus structures such as *it is John (who)* ...

[8] A particularly interesting issue concerns expletives in some Germanic languages, which occur in main clauses in the highest specifier, traditionally argued to be [Spec,CP], but which are not possible in embedded clauses (German, Icelandic). We note that if those expletives are likewise existential operators available in [Spec,CP], it would suggest that in at least some Germanic languages, $\langle e \rangle_E$ is in C. In turn, if it is correct, as is often assumed, that embedded [Spec,CP] in V2 languages may not be filled, it follows naturally that the relevant languages are forced to resort to means other than expletives to existential-

(32) a. Stative: [$_{EP}$ ex$^\exists$ ⟨e$^\exists$⟩$_E$ [$_{TP}$ **ex**$^\exists$ [$_{SP}$ [$_{VP/AP}$]]]]
      b. Eventive, atelic: [$_{EP}$ ex$^\exists$ ⟨e$^\exists$⟩$_E$ [$_{TP}$ **ex**$^\exists$ [$_{VP}$]]]
      c. Eventive, telic: [$_{EP}$ ex$^\exists$ ⟨e$^\exists$⟩$_E$ [$_{TP}$ **ex**$^\exists$ [$_{Asp_Q}$ [$_{VP}$]]]]

EP is licensed, of course, and the event argument existentially bound in the absence of expletives, in the presence of a standard subject, with any event role. With respect to the structures in (25), and continuing to assume that a referential DP in [Spec, EP] is interpreted as an originator if not otherwise assigned interpretation, we note the following possible structures:[9, 10]

(33) a. Stative: [$_{EP}$ DP ⟨e⟩$_E$ ...   [$_{SP}$ D̶P̶ ... ([$_{Asp_Q}$/$_{F^sP}$) [$_{VP/AP}$]]]
                               s-o-s   s-o-s

      b. Eventive, atelic: [$_{EP}$ DP ⟨e⟩$_E$ [$_{TP}$ D̶P̶   [$_{VP}$]]]
                               originator

      c. Telic, intransitive: [$_{EP}$ DP ⟨e⟩$_E$ [$_{TP}$ D̶P̶   [$_{Asp_Q}$ D̶P̶ [$_{VP}$]]]]
                                s-o-q   s-o-q

      d. Telic, transitive: [$_{EP}$ DP$_1$ ⟨e⟩$_E$ [$_{TP}$ D̶P̶$_1$ [$_{Asp_Q}$ DP$_2$ [$_{VP}$]]]]
                                originator   s-o-q

From the rationale employed thus far, it follows that in cases such as those in (33), it is the DP in [Spec, EP] which assigns range to ⟨e⟩$_E$, quite independently of the location of its role assignment. Thus in unaccusative structures, a DP with a subject-of-quantity role assigned in [Spec, Asp$_Q$] moves to [Spec, EP] through [Spec, TP], and we must assume it to be capable of assigning range to ⟨e⟩$_E$. The availability of range assignment to ⟨e⟩$_E$, by assumption existential binding, by such arguments is, however, hardly surprising. DPs in general are existentially closed, through their reference being otherwise established by a discourse antecedent, through a determiner or a quantifier in ⟨e⟩$_d$, through binding by an adverb of quantification or an existential operator, etc. Simple indirect range

---

ly bind embedded event arguments,. For considerations of space, this issue is not pursued any further. For extensive discussion of some of the relevant issues, see Vikner (1995) and Bobaljik and Jonas (1996), among others.

[9] An interesting question concerns range assignment, i.e. existential binding, of ⟨e⟩$_E$ by a null (definite) pronoun. It will emerge from the discussion below that such binding must be assumed possible, as the properties of (overt) V1 structures with an understood (possibly pre-verbal) pronominal subject are distinct in relevant ways from those of (overt) V1 structures without an understood (pre-verbal) pronominal subject. A natural account would involve an abstract DP in [Spec, EP] in the former, but no specifier whatsoever in the latter. For some discussion of range assignment by indefinite null pronouns, see Section 9.4.2.

[10] 's-o-s' stands for subject-of-state assigned by SP, dedicated stative structure. We remain noncommittal here as to the precise position of SP with respect to TP, noting only that constituency tests as well as the presence of transitive statives suggest that it must be higher than whatever functional structure licenses direct objects, be it Asp$_Q$ or F^{s}P.

assignment would thus suffice here to assign range to, indeed existentially bind, $\langle e \rangle_E$, as required.[11]

A comparison with the nominal domain may be useful here. To repeat the discussion in Chapter 1, Section 1.2.3 (and see also Volume I, Chapter 2, Section 2.1.3), in cases such as those in (34), range is assigned to $\langle e \rangle_d$, specifically as $\langle def \rangle$ (or its absence), indirectly through specifier–head relations with the possessor, presumably in [Spec,DP]:

(34) a. [$_{DP}$ [Kim]$^{+def}$ ['s $\langle e^{+def} \rangle_d$ [... hat]]]
    b. [$_{DP}$ [a boy]$^{-def}$ ['s $\langle e^{-def} \rangle_d$ [... hat]]]

By a similar rationale, as the DP in [Spec,EP] is existentially closed, by specifier–head agreement $\langle e \rangle_E$ becomes existentially closed as well.

Some interesting cases, in this respect, are those in (35), where the subjects are themselves bare DPs:

(35) a. Dogs barked last night.
    b. Students were standing laughing in the corridor.
    c. Water trickled through the ceiling all day.

We already touched at several points in this work upon the fact that, as is well-established, many grammars disallow weak bare DPs pre-verbally, thus ruling out the utterances in (35). The ungrammaticality of such cases in Hebrew, for example, was touched upon in Chapter 4, Section 4.3, and was already illustrated previously in this chapter by (6)–(8). No such restrictions are in evidence for post-verbal subjects, as already illustrated by (10) and (12). Standard accounts for (6)–(8) and similar cases attribute their ungrammaticality to the fact that the bare DPs are outside the domain of existential closure, typically taken to be the VP (following Diesing 1992), or alternatively, the c-command domain of the verb (cf. Benedicto 1997). In turn, (10), (12) are said to be grammatical precisely because the bare DPs are within the relevant domain of existential closure. Finally, the English cases in (35) are grammatical, it is typically argued, because the bare DP may be lowered, in Logical Form, so as to be within the domain of existential closure, a lowering not licit in Hebrew, for instance. It is tempting at this point to assume, in a fashion compatible with the standard account, that only DPs which are themselves existentially closed can assign range to $\langle e \rangle_E$—that is, existentially bind the event argument—thereby ruling out cases of existentially unbound DPs in [Spec,EP], and that an LF chain consisting of an existentially bound copy is responsible for the binding

---

[11] I return in Section 9.4 to the scope interaction between the DP in [Spec,EP] and the existentially bound $\langle e \rangle_E$ node.

of $\langle e \rangle_E$ in (35). Such a statement is certainly consistent with (35) and (6)–(8), as they are typically analysed, and we will tentatively subscribe to it as an account for the grammaticality of (35). As we shall see in Section 9.5, however, some improvement over the standard treatment, specifically in making lowering unnecessary in English, may be possible within the account to be developed in this chapter.

Some additional predictions, as well as some prima facie questions, are associated with the structures in (32)–(33). First, we note that if indeed EPP effects emerge from the need to assign range to $\langle e \rangle_E$, and if, indeed, any (existentially closed) constituent in [Spec,EP] may assign range to $\langle e \rangle_E$, we predict range assignment to $\langle e \rangle_E$ by elements which are neither expletives nor argument DPs, but which, in turn, do have in some sense existential force. Secondly, as in the case of range assignment to $[_{Asp_Q}\langle e \rangle_\#]$, there is no reason to exclude in principle direct range assignment to $\langle e \rangle_E$, either through an f-morph in E or through a head feature of some sort. In such cases, neither an expletive nor an argumental DP would be required, and a specifier would not need to project. We turn to a study of both of these cases in the following sections, showing that locative expressions, either in [Spec,EP] or merging directly with E can assign range to $\langle e \rangle_E$, although they are neither expletives nor argument DPs. Finally, we note that on the face of it, the structures in (32)–(33) predict the complementary distribution of expletives and originators (but not the complementary distribution of subject-of-quantity, or subject-of-state, and expletives). Yet, this prediction is incorrect. Transitive expletive constructions, as discussed extensively in the literature for languages such as Dutch and Icelandic, as well as cases of English presentational *there* insertion, as in (36), involve the co-occurrence of an expletive and an argument which is interpreted as an originator (examples based on Levin and Rappaport Hovav 1995).

(36) a. On the third floor, there worked two young women called Maryanne and Ava ...
      b. Above them, there pranced three horses on the Parthenon frieze.

The prediction, then, is too strong, and cases such as those in (36), as well as cases of transitive expletives, must be otherwise accounted for within this system. It is to the resolution of all these issues that we devote the rest of this chapter. In Section 9.3 I turn to a discussion of range assignment to $\langle e \rangle_E$ by locatives in Hebrew as well as in Spanish and Catalan, showing that such range assignment, whether direct or indirect, allows a post-verbal subject, albeit only a weak one, in configurations which otherwise would not allow it, and notably in unergative constructions. The interaction between locatives, specifically, and the licensing of $\langle e \rangle_E$—that is, the existential binding of the event argument—is discussed in Section 9.4, where it is shown the dual existential/locative role of locative markers is well established across languages. In Section 9.5 we turn to interaction between the licensing of $\langle e \rangle_E$ by a locative and the obligatoriness of a post-verbal weak subjects in that case. We conclude this chapter with an extension of the proposed system to post-verbal (weak) subjects in transitive constructions in Hebrew, in effect uncovering, precisely in these cases, the existence of a 'transitive expletive' construction in Hebrew. The ramifications of the interaction between locatives and range assignment for unaccusative structures are pursued in Chapter 10.

9.3 Assigning Range to $\langle e \rangle_E$—The Locative Paradigm

9.3.1 *Post-verbal nominatives in unergative structures*

Recall now that our starting point is the grammaticality of the paradigm in (1)–(4), repeated selectively here as (37)–(38):

(37) a. Sono arrivati (molti) studenti. (Italian)
   are arrived (many) students

(Hebrew)
   b. hitxilu hapganot/*ha.hapganot (ha.boqer).
      started.M.PL demonstrations/*the.demonstrations (this.morning)

   c. hopiaˤ harbe ˤašan laban ba-šamayim.
      appeared much smoke white in the sky

(38) a. *hitxila kol hapgana (ha.boqer).
      started.M.PL every demonstration (this.morning)

   b. *hopiaˤ ha.ˤašan ha.laban ba-šamayim (ha.boqer).
      appeared the.smoke the.white in-the.sky (this.morning)

In the context of the model presented in this work, we noted two problems associated with (37a–c) and similar cases. First, it is not clear what licenses $\langle e \rangle_E$ in these configurations, [Spec,EP] being null. Secondly, it is not clear what licenses $[_{Asp_Q}\langle e \rangle_\#]$ in (37b) and similar cases, in the absence of a quantity DP. In the remainder of this chapter, we consider the first of these questions—the assignment of range to $\langle e \rangle_E$ in the licit post-verbal cases in (37). The assignment of range to $[_{Asp_Q}\langle e \rangle_\#]$, together with a detailed discussion of the accomplishment/achievement distinction, will be taken up in Chapter 10.

Clearly, a closer investigation of post-verbal nominatives in V1 contexts is warranted at this point. Thus consider again the ungrammaticality of atelic structures with post-verbal subjects repeated here as (39), and specifically, the impossibility of a post-verbal subject in all the illustrated contexts (while illustrated with ʿa<u>b</u>ad 'work', the same facts hold, of course, for most verbs typically classified as (unambiguous) unergatives):[12]

(39) a. *('amarti še-) ʿa<u>b</u>ad   ganan   (ha.yom).
          (I said that)   worked gardener (today)

      b. *('amarti še-) ʿa<u>b</u>ad   ha.ganan   (ha.yom).
          (I said that)   worked the.gardener (today)

      c. *('amarti še-) ʿa<u>b</u>du   gananim   (ha.yom).
          (I said that)   worked gardeners (today) .

      d. *('amarti še-) ʿa<u>b</u>du   kol ha.gananim   (ha.yom).
          (I said that)   worked all the.gardeners (today)

(40)   ha.gananim ʿa<u>b</u>du (ha.yom).
        the.gardeners worked (today)

The explanation for the impossibility of V1 structures for intransitive atelic structures (i.e. unergatives), or, for that matter, transitives, is less than obvious within any account, especially in view of the grammaticality of (37) and similar structures. One might suggest that in (39) nominative case assignment fails. However, it is hard to imagine an account of post-verbal nominative case that would give rise to nominative case assignment in (37) but would fail in (39).[13] Nor would it be useful to suggest that the subject of an unergative or transitive verb is licensed in a higher position than the subject of unaccusative verbs, forcing the pre-verbal position of the former. While descriptively this may be something most accounts, including the present one, agree on, many accounts

---

[12] See Chapter 8, Section 8.3, for discussion of unambiguous unergative verbs.

[13] Bobaljik and Jonas (1996) propose a mechanism for post-verbal nominative assignment which crucially depends on the presence, in a language such as Icelandic, of two IP-type functional projections (AgrP, TP) vs. the presence in English of just one. In the presence of one functional specifier, the subject must occupy that specifier, which is perforce pre-verbal. If, however, two specifiers are available, a post-verbal position for the subject is possible in the lower specifier, as well as nominative case in that position. The account to be offered here will borrow from Bobaljik and Jonas the important intuition that post-verbal nominatives may exist in the presence of two functional IP-type nodes—within the architecture proposed here, two functional nodes above Asp_Q or F^sP, i.e. TP and EP. However, the mere presence of two functional IP-type nodes cannot explain the ungrammaticality of (39). Note first that in Hebrew, post-verbal nominative clearly is available for the unaccusatives in (37). Therefore, either Hebrew has both TP and AgrP (or some equivalents, thereof), or an additional mechanism must be postulated to account for nominative case assignment to unaccusative post-verbal subjects. Further, Bobaljik and Jonas correlate the existence of two functional nodes with the existence of a transitive expletive construction. As we will see below, Hebrew does actually allow transitive expletives, of a sort, with a post-verbal nominative 'external' argument, re-raising the question of why nominative is not available in (39). Note finally that if one postulates any specialized position for 'external' arguments, below or above TP, be it [Spec,v], [Spec,EP], [Spec,VoiceP], etc., which is not identical with TP, two nodes are always available in principle, and hence the contrast between (37) and (39) could not be reduced exclusively to the presence of two functional specifiers above the VP.

would also agree that the subjects of unergative and transitive verbs are not base-generated in their surface position, at the highest specifier under CP, but rather somewhere below T.[14] In turn, the generation of the subject of unergatives (or transitives) below T (whether in [Spec,VP], [Spec,v], [Spec,VoiceP], etc.), when combined with verb movement to T, would create a natural configuration for post-verbal nominative which could not be easily distinguished from unaccusative V1 contexts. Here, I proposed that the 'external' argument is licensed—that is, assigned interpretation—above TP. Nevertheless, I also assumed that it merges at [Spec,TP], where it is assigned nominative case, raising anew the question of why it may not stay there, in light of the fact that nominative is clearly available in the post-V position for subjects of unaccusatives.

It is worthwhile to make explicit the nature of the puzzle here, when considered from the perspective of the XS-system. EP, potentially consistent with originator entailment in its specifier position, projects above TP. I suggested that the event argument is existentially bound through the assignment of range to $\langle e \rangle_E$ by an element in [Spec,EP], provided that element itself is existentially closed. In turn, the constituent which merges with E to become its specifier need not be a referential DP, but can be an expletive, for example. If indeed this is on the right track, then the structure of (40) is as in (41a) (cf. (33b)) while the structure of the (ungrammatical) examples in (39) is as in (41b). Suppose now that (41b) is ruled out quite simply because $\langle e \rangle_E$ is not assigned range and hence the derivation does not converge (irrelevant details omitted):

(41) a. [$_{EP}$ ha.gananim$_{NOM}$$^\exists$ ʿabdu $\langle e^\exists \rangle_E$ [$_{TP}$ ~~ha.gananim~~$_{NOM}$ ~~ʿabdu~~ [$_{VP}$ ~~ʿabdu~~,]]]
 the gardeners worked

b. *[$_{EP}$ ʿabdu $\langle e \rangle_E$ [$_{TP}$ ha.gananim$_{NOM}$ ~~ʿabdu~~ [$_{VP}$ ~~ʿabdu~~,]]]
 worked gardeners

We note as an aside that at least from the perspective of what was said so far, it is not obvious how *gananim*, 'gardeners' is assigned a role in (41b) although I will argue that it not being assigned a role, in and of itself, would not rule out (41b). In turn, the ungrammaticality of (41b) is not very difficult to derive on the grounds that $\langle e \rangle_E$ is not assigned range. It is the grammaticality of (37) which presents a problem. Specifically, if $\langle e \rangle_E$ is not assigned range in (41b), why should a similar situation not hold for the unaccusatives in (37)? At a first approximation, the structure of V1 unaccusatives is as in (42), where, at least for (37b),

---

[14] But note that in this respect the account proposed here differs. The lowest instantiation of the DP which will eventually become the 'subject' of transitive and unergative constructions is in [Spec,TP], and its role, if it receives one, is assigned in [Spec,EP], above [Spec,TP].

range is assigned to neither $\langle e \rangle_E$, nor to $[_{Asp_Q}\langle e \rangle_{\#}]$. Why should it be a grammatical derivation, which furthermore has a quantity interpretation, in light of the ungrammaticality of (41b)? Note, incidentally, that the assignment of nominative case, in either (41) or (42), is not in and of itself problematic, nor would it be helpful in deriving the contrast in grammaticality between (37) and (39), if we assume that [Spec, TP] is the locus of nominative case assignment, and that EP dominates TP (see n. 13 for some discussion):

(42) [$_{EP}$ parcu $\langle e \rangle_E$ [$_{TP}$ mehumot$_{NOM}$ ~~parcu~~ [$_{Asp_Q}$ ~~mehumot parcu~~ [$_{Asp_Q}$$\langle e \rangle_{\#}$
 erupted riots [$_{VP}$ ~~parcu~~ ...

9.3.2 Locatives and unergative constructions

It turns out that some helpful light can be shed on the question of range assignment to $\langle e \rangle_E$ by contrasting (39) with (43):

(43) a. ('amarti še-) ʿab̠ad šam/kan/ecli ganan (ha.yom).
   (I said that) worked here/there/*chez*.me gardener (today)

b. *('amarti še-) ʿab̠ad šam/kan/ecli ran/ha.ganan (ha.yom).
   (I said that) worked here/there/*chez*.me Ran/the.gardener (today)

c. ('amarti še-) ʿab̠du šam/kan/ecli (kama, šloša) gananim
   (I said that) worked here/there/*chez*.me (several, three) gardeners
   (ha.yom).
   (today)

d. *('amarti še-) ʿab̠du šam/kan/ecli kol ha.gananim (ha.yom).
   (I said that) worked here/there/*chez*.me all the.gardeners (today)

Surprisingly, post-verbal subjects in V1 unergative contexts are possible in (43). In fact, the paradigm in (43) looks extraordinarily similar to the paradigm in (37)–(38): the post-verbal subjects occur inside the domain of adjuncts, which is to say 'close to the verb' in some relevant sense, and must be weak.

Torrego (1989) discusses a similar paradigm in Spanish and in Catalan, and a further discussion of the Catalan paradigm is found in Rigau (1997). In the normal course of events, a post-verbal subject is possible in unaccusative structures in Spanish, (44), but impossible in unergative structures, (45), as is true of Hebrew in non-contrastive contexts. However, in the presence of locatives, post-verbal subjects become possible in unergative structures, as (46) illustrates. The paradigm in Catalan is, on the other hand, extremely similar to Hebrew. Normally, (weak) post-verbal subjects are possible only in unaccusative contexts. However, in the presence of the locative clitic *hi*, weak post-verbal subjects are possible for unergative constructions. Furthermore, in these cases *en* cliticization is possible from the post-verbal subject. While strong, specific, post-verbal subjects *are* possible in V1 ergative contexts without a locative, such post-verbal subjects do not license *en* cliticization. Assuming *en* cliticization, like *ne* cliticization in Italian, to be sensitive to c-command considerations, its possibility with locatives vs. its impossibility without suggests that the position of the post-verbal subject in unergatives differs, depending on the presence of a locative: with locatives, it is somehow 'lower' or 'closer to the verb', like such subjects in both Hebrew and Spanish:[15]

(44) Crecen flores. (Spanish)
    grow   flowers
    'Flowers grow.'

(45) a. *Anidan cigueñas.
        shelter storks
        'Storks shelter.'

   b. *Han dormido animales.
       have slept   animals

   c. *Juegan niños.
       play   children

(46) a. Aquí han dormido animales.
        here have slept   animals

   b. En este parque juegan niños.
      in this park   play   children

   c. En este árbol anidan cigueña.
      in this tree   shelter storks

(47) a. Hi   canten molts nens. (Catalan)
        there sing   many boys

   b. Hi   dormen molts nens.
      there sleep many boys

   c. Canten molten nens.
      sang   many   boys
      'Many of the boys sang.' (Specific reading only)

[15] We note that the definition of 'lower', in the relevant context, is not trivial in any account which merges the surface subject, initially and in all cases, below the final landing site of the verb, be it in [Spec,VP], [Spec,VoiceP], [Spec,*v*] or, as in the present account, in [Spec,TP] below [Spec,EP]. The problem is a familiar one within theories that project the subject as [Spec,VP], and which must therefore devise a mechanism that prohibits, e.g. VP-adverbs from having scope over the subject, or the object in [Spec,AgrO] from c-commanding the trace of the subject in [Spec,VP]. We will assume here without further discussion that a solution is available in terms of an appropriate notion of reconstruction.

(48) a. N'hi   canten molts.
       of-them there sing   many
   b. N'hi   dormen molts.
       of-them there sleep   many

(49) a. *En   canten molts.
       of-them sing   many
   b. *En   dormen molts.
       of them sleep   many

Torrego (1989) further observes that the locative in question is configurationally restricted, and specifically, if it is phrasal it must be pre-verbal. If the locative occurs on the right periphery, post-verbal subjects in Spanish remain illicit, as (50) shows. Identical facts hold for Hebrew, as (51) illustrates:

(50) a. ??Han dormido animales aquí.
        have slept   animals here
   b. *Juegan niños   en este parque.
        played children in that park
   c. ??Han anidado cigüeñas en este árbol.
        have sheltered storks   in that tree

(51) a. *('amarti še-) ʿabad   ganan   ba-gan/'ecli/ecel ran.
        (I said that) worked gardener in-the garden/*chez*.me/*chez* Ran
   b. *('amarti še-) ʿabad   ha.ganan   ba-gan/ecli/ecel ran/šam.
        (I said that) worked the.gardener in-the garden/*chez*.me/*chez* Ran/
        there
   c. *('amarti še-) ʿabdu   gananim ba-gan/ecli/ecel ran/
        (I said that) worked gardeners in-the garden/*chez*.me/*chez* Ran/
        šam.
        there
   d. *('amarti še-) ʿabdu   kol ha.gananim   ba-gan/ecli/ecel ran/šam.
        (I said that) worked all the.gardeners in-the garden/*chez*.me/*chez*
        Ran/there

Hebrew *šam, kan, po*, and *ecel* + INFL; 'there', 'here', 'here', '*chez* + pronominal inflection', must all be phonological clitics for the effects in (43) to be realized. Their clitic status is rather phonologically transparent in cases such as (43), as their stress is much reduced. In turn, *šam, kan, po*, and *ecel* + INFL need not be cliticized to the verb or adjacent to it. When they are not, they carry main stress, and the effects illustrated in (43) do not hold. Non-cliticized, stressed versions of deictic locatives are in (52a–c), with (52b–c) showing that deictic locatives can be conjoined when stressed. When unstressed, deictic locatives cannot be separated from the verb (52d), or conjoined (52e). When unstressed and adjacent to the verb, on the other hand, they cannot be conjoined, as (52f) illustrates, with the only possible output being (52g), with an unstressed locative not conjoined and adjacent to the verb. The ungrammaticality of post-verbal subjects in V1 contexts without cliticized locative deictics is illustrated by (53) (judgements in the context of neutral intonation):

(52) a. kol ha.yeladim 'aklu 'aruxat ʿereḇ 'eclénu/kán.   (Stressed locatives,
       all the.boys ate supper *chez*.us/here   phrasal)

   b. ha.yeladim qiblu   mamtaqim kán ve-šám.
      the.boys   received candies here and-there

   c. ha.yeladim qiblu   kán ve-šám mamtaqim.
      the.boys   received here and-there candies

   d. *ha.yeladim qiblu   mamtaqim kan.   (Unstressed locatives,
      the.boys   received candies here   clitics)

   e. *ha.yeladim qiblu   mamtaqim kan ve-šam.
      the.boys   received candies here and-there

   f. *ha.yeladim qiblu   kan ve-šam mamtaqim.
      the.boys   received here and-there candies

   g. ha.yeladim qiblu   kan mamtaqim.
      the.boys   received here candies

(53) a. *ʿaḇad šam ve-kan ganan   (ha.yom).
        worked here and-there gardener (today)

   b. *ʿaḇad ganan   šam ve-kan (ha.yom).
      worked gardener here and-there (today)

   c. *ʿaḇdu (kama, šloša) gananim šam/kan/ecli   (ha.yom).
      worked (several, three) gardeners there/here/*chez*.me (today)

The effect illustrated here is further unique to locatives. In contrast with the grammaticality of (43a, c), we have the ungrammaticality of similar structures with temporal, rather than locative, deictic markers, although clearly these too are phonologically cliticized to the verb stem:

(54) a. ('amarti še-) *ʿaḇad 'az ganan   (ba-gan).
        (I said that) worked then gardener (in-thegarden)

b. ('amarti še-) *rac 'az yeled (ba-rexo<u>b</u>).
   (I said that) ran then boy (in-the street)

(55) a. ('amarti še-) *ᶜo<u>b</u>ed ᶜata/ᶜa<u>kš</u>av ganan (ba-gan).
   (I said that) works now/now gardener (in-the.garden)

b. ('amarti še-) *rac ᶜata/ᶜa<u>kš</u>av yeled (ba-rexo<u>b</u>).
   (I said that) run now/now boy (in-the street)

Thus in Spanish, Catalan, and Hebrew, a post-verbal unergative subject is licensed just in case a locative occurs either as a pre-verbal phrase (Spanish), or as a clitic on the verb (or the auxiliary), and specifically not when it appears as a right-periphery adjunct.[16]

Torrego (1989), in analysing these structures, suggests that the presence of the locative turns the verb (or the structure) under consideration from unergative to unaccusative. Crucial for her evidence is the possibility of *en* cliticization in Catalan from the post-verbal subject in the presence of a locative, illustrated by the contrast in (48)–(49) above. We note, however, that while analysing unergative verbs in the presence of locatives as unaccusatives will certainly derive the distribution of *en* cliticization, so will any analysis that places the subject within the scope of the verb, at some relevant stage of the derivation, in (48) but not in (49). Suppose, for instance, that not only must *en* c-command its extraction site within the relevant DP, but also, the (highest occurrence of) the DP cannot c-command *en*, a restriction which is independently plausible for Italian *ne* cliticization, possible only from post-verbal position (see Chapter 7, n. 13, for some discussion in the context of Italian *ne*). If this is indeed on the right track, note that a post-verbal subject within the c-command domain of the verb is

---

[16] As clitics in Semitic occur in the right periphery of their host, rather than on the left periphery, their status is rather easy to distinguish from both pre-verbal phrasal locatives and right-periphery phrasal locatives. It is further easy to see that these are, indeed, V1 structures. Similarly, for Catalan, the V1 status of constructions such as those in (47) and the clitic nature of *hi* can be shown by the placement of negation, which must precede the verb but follow an overt subject:

(i) a. No hi canten gaires nens.
   not there sing many boys
   b. No hi dormen gaires nens.
   not there sleep many boys

Whether or not pre-verbal phrasal locatives, certainly possible in Hebrew, license a post-verbal subject as in Spanish is, however, a tricky matter, as most pre-verbal constituents in Hebrew optionally license a post-verbal subject. However, locative licensing, as in (43), is accompanied with a restriction requiring a weak subject. No such restriction is attested when post-verbal subjects are licensed by a pre-verbal phrase, including locatives. As weak subjects are clearly a subset of those licensed by pre-verbal constituents, where no such restriction holds, pre-verbal locative licensing of post-verbal subjects would appear impossible to tease apart from other pre-verbal licensing by argument DPs, temporals, etc. As it turns out, however, some evidence suggests that pre-verbal phrasal locatives *do not* license post-verbal subjects in the same manner that locative clitics do, a matter to which we return, in a wider context, in n. 27.

predicted to allow *en* or *ne* cliticization, but not a subject in [Spec, EP], or a subject postposed from [Spec, EP].[17]

An analysis which assumes that the configurations in (43) and (46)–(48) are unaccusative is clearly not available within an approach to the unaccusativity/unergativity phenomena which seeks to reduce it to event structure. First, the interpretation of the sentences in (43a, c) clearly remains atelic, just like their standard SV word-order incarnations, as modification possibilities in (56) illustrate.

(56) a. ʿaḇad šam/kan/ecli   ganan   be-mešek kol ha.yom/
       worked here/there/*chez*.me gardener during   all-the day/
       *tok šaloš šaʿot.
       inside three hours

   b. ʿaḇdu šam/kan/ecli   (kama, šloša) gananim be-mešek
       worked here/there/*chez*.me (several, three) gardeners during
       kol ha.yom/*tok šaloš šaʿot.
       all-the day/inside three hours

   c. ʿaḇad šam/kan/ecli   ganan ve-šar.   (Simultaneous reading
       worked here/there/*chez*.me a gardener and sang   available)

Further, locative deictic clitics allow V1 word orders in statives with identical restrictions, thereby clearly indicating that there is no possible connection between their occurrence and quantity interpretation:

(57) a. ha.boʾeš gar ba-qayic   mitaxat la-bayit.
       the.skunk lives in-the.summer under to-the.house

   b. gar šam boʾeš ba-qayic   mitaxat la-bayit.
       lives there skunk in-the.summer under to-the.house

   c. *gar (ha.)boʾeš ba-qayic   mitaxat la-bayit.
       lives (the)skunk in-the.summer under to-the.house

   d. *gar šam ha.boʾeš ba-qayic   mitaxat la-bayit.
       lives there the.skunk in-the.summer under to-the.house

And finally, reflexive datives, which we took to be diagnostics for 'external' arguments, whether originators or subjects-of-state, and which, we argued are anti-telic elements (see Chapter 8, Section 8.2.3, for discussion), are possible

---

[17] This matter is largely orthogonal to our main purpose here, and an execution in terms of postposing (rather than remnant movement, for instance, in the sense of Kayne 1994) is not necessarily crucial in any way to deriving the relevant result. We note, nevertheless, that some re-formulation of Rizzi's (1986) chain condition would be plausibly violated by moving the DP over *ne* or *en*.

with the configurations in (43), as (58a) shows, while possessive datives, which, we argued, must be in possession relations with an argument no higher than Asp_Q or F^sP, are impossible, as (58b) shows. Similar facts hold for (57), as (59) illustrates:

(58) a. ʿabad lo   kan ('eyze) ganan   (kol ha.boqer).
         worked to-him₂ here (some) gardener₂ all morning

   b. *ʿabad šam {le-rani} ('eyze) ganan   {le-rani} (kol ha.boqer)
        worked here {to-rani} (some) gardener₂ {to-Rani} all morning
        '*A gardener of Rani's worked there all morning.'

(59) a. gar lo   šam bo'eš mitaxat la-bayit.
         lives to-him there skunk under to-the.house
         'there was a skunk living under the house.'

   b. *gar šam {le-rani} bo'eš {le-rani} mitaxat la-bayit
        lives there {to-rani} skunk {to-Rani} under to-the.house
        *Rani's skunk lived under the house.'

We therefore must conclude that the paradigm in (43) does not involve any fundamental change in event structure and that the post-verbal argument retains its originator role. It follows that the paradigm in (43) cannot be unaccusative, contra Torrego (1989).

Rigau (1997), considering the same paradigm primarily from the perspective of Catalan, proposes that in the relevant cases, a covert locative preposition is incorporated onto an unergative verb, and as a result, the verb loses its agentive meaning and becomes stative. In turn, the clitic *hi* functions as the subject of the (covert) preposition, giving rise to impersonal sentences. A sentence such as (60a), Rigau suggests, is synonymous with the one in (60b), due to the fact that in both *hi* is the subject of a covert preposition, while *nens* 'boys' is the object of that preposition. The resulting structure is essentially an existential one, as in (60c):

(60) a. En aquest coral, hi canten nens.
         in this   choir, CL sing   boys

   b. Hi ha(n) nens que canten en aquesta coral.
      CL have boys that sing in this   choir
      'There are boys who sing in this choir.'

   c. [$_{VP}$ {cantar, haver} [$_{PP}$ hi [$_{P'}$ e nens]]].

This account is extremely reminiscent of that proposed by Hoekstra and Mulder (1990), according to which variable-behaviour verbs (in the sense discussed in Chapter 2) may function either as main verbs, thereby selecting an agent, or as raising verbs, of sorts, selecting a small clause headed by a preposition and having the properties of unaccusatives quite simply because they lack an external argument (and see Moro 1990, 1997 for an extension of this structure to all unaccusatives). Hoekstra and Mulder's analysis does, however, differ from that of Rigau, in assuming that the post-verbal subject, 'boys', is the subject of the incorporated preposition, and not its object, as Rigau suggests. Under their analysis, the structure in (61) would presumably be postulated, with the arrow indicating movement, to account for (60a–b):

(61)   [$_{VP}$ cantar [$_{PP}$ nens [$_P$ locative -(hi)]]]

Although a small clause analysis, under any instantiation, does not in and off itself predict that (43) and (46)–(48) should be telic, and as such does not make the wrong predictions for the paradigms in (56)–(57), at least for Hebrew, Rigau's proposal, as well as Hoekstra and Mulder's (1990) original proposal, faces a number of problems when applied to the paradigm in (43). First, contra Rigau's observations concerning Catalan, (43) has no stative flavour. Originator-oriented adverbs, associated with manner, are clearly possible in (43), although they are barred in statives, as the contrast between (62) and (63) shows:

(62) a. hitpalelu šam ma'aminim be-hitkavnut   raba.
          prayed   there faithfuls   in-deliberation much
          'The faithful prayed there with much deliberation.'

      b. hištolelu   šam eyze yeladim be-toqpanut.
          made.noise there some children aggressively

(63) a. garu   šam ma'aminim (#be-hitkavnut   raba).
          resided there faithfuls   in-deliberation much
          'The faithful lived there with much deliberation.'

      b. xayu šam eyze studentim (#be-toqpanut).
          lived there some students aggressively

Secondly, we noted that possessor datives are barred in the structures in (43). This, too, remains unexplained under Rigau's analysis or a Hoekstra and Mulder-type approach, as it was under Torrego's analysis, as both postulate a base-generation position for the argument which would be within the scope of a possessor dative. Thirdly, and addressing specifically the hypothesized Hoekstra and Mulder-type structure in (61), we note that there is no forthcoming explanation here for the obligatory cliticization of the locative, and the impossibility, in V1 structures, of a locative in the right periphery. And yet, we saw that only when the deictic locative is adjacent to the verb can a V1 word order emerge. Finally, it turns out that locative deictic clitics do not just allow V1 word orders with unergatives, they also repair considerably the ungrammaticality of pre-verbal weak subjects, as (64) illustrates, a fact that cannot be accommodated under either Rigau's account (op. cit.), or by appealing to a small clause analysis of the type advanced in Hoekstra and Mulder (1990):[18]

(64) a. *ganan ᶜabad ba-gan/ha.boqer.
 gardener worked in-the.garden/this-morning

 b. *yeladim sixaqu ba-gan/ha.boqer.
 children played in-the.garden

 c. ?ganan ᶜabad kan ba-gan/ha.boqer.
 gardener worked here in-the.garden

 d. ?yeladim sixaqu šam ba-gan/ha.boqer.
 children played there in-the.garden

 (cf. the full grammaticality of
 ha.ganan ᶜabad ba-gan/ šloša yeladim sixaqu
 the.gardener worked in-the.garden/three children played

 ba-gan, etc.
 in-the.garden, etc.)

I will, however, concur with the important insights of Rigau's analysis that in some fundamental sense the structures carry existential force, and that the locative is responsible for the licensing of the V1 order (and see also Freeze 1992, to which we return shortly). No change in roles or in the interpretation of the event is involved, however, nor is there a small clause, of which the post-verbal subject is a subject or an object.

Continuing to assume that the ungrammaticality of (39) stems from the absence of existential binding for the event argument, as instantiated by the failure of $\langle e \rangle_E$ to be assigned range, we now must assume that the event argument *is* existentially bound in (43)—that is, that $\langle e \rangle_E$ is assigned range. As the difference between the paradigms is solely the presence vs. absence of a locative clitic, the obvious conclusion is that the locative clitic *is* the existential binder of the event argument—that is, the range assigner to $\langle e \rangle_E$—and that by extension, in Spanish and in Catalan existential binding of the event argument is accomplished by the pre-verbal locatives *aquí* and *hi*, respectively. In other words, locatives,

---

[18] For reasons that I can only speculate on, and which may be related to discourse structure (i.e. old vs. new information), (64c–d) are marginal rather than fully grammatical. The contrast with the full ungrammaticality of (64a–b) is however very clear.

deictic or prepositional, are f-morphs which can assign range to $\langle e \rangle_E$, an assignment which translates to existentially binding the event argument.[19] While in Spanish such range assignment is achieved through specifier–head agreement (i.e. indirectly), in Hebrew and in Catalan it can also be achieved directly, the locative being a clitic associated with the verbal head which moves to E, thereby assigning range to $\langle e \rangle_E$. Structurally, then, we have (65).

(65) a. [$_{EP}$ ʿa̠ba̠d-šam³ $\langle e^∃ \rangle_E$ [$_{TP}$ ganan$_{NOM}$ a̠ba̠d-šam [$_{VP}$]]]
        worked-there   gardener

     b. [$_{EP}$ aquí³ han $\langle e^∃ \rangle_E$ [$_{FP}$ dormito [$_{TP}$ animales$_{NOM}$ dormito [$_{VP}$]]]]
        here have   slept   animals

     c. [$_{EP}$ hi³-canten $\langle e^∃ \rangle_E$ [$_{TP}$ nens$_{NOM}$ hi-canten [$_{VP}$]]]
        here sing   boys

As to the assignment of an originator role to the post-verbal argument in (65), we note that if an originator role is associated with a DP as a result of the existence of an eventive EP with an argument which is not otherwise specified, then the assignment of an originator role to this DP in [Spec, TP] need not be problematic. Specifically, and looking to bar an originator role in [Spec, F^{s}P], the objective shell structure associated with partitive case (see Chapter 4 for discussion), suppose we follow a suggestion in Benua and Borer (1996), itself inspired by insights in Bobaljik (1993). According to this suggestion, in accusative languages the specifiers of EP and TP are identified, while in ergative languages the specifiers of Asp$_Q$ and TP are identified. From this, it follows that whatever case is assigned by T, and assuming this case to be the only one obligatorily assigned in tensed clauses, it will go to the originator in accusative languages, if there is one, but to subject-of-quantity in ergative languages, if there is one.[20] In turn, it follows from the identification in (65) of [Spec, TP] and [Spec, EP], together with the absence of Asp$_Q$, that the post-verbal subject must receive the originator role.[21]

---

[19] Crucially, we do not assume here an event decomposition. Locatives as well as other prepositions thus do not contain a separate event variable in need of range assignment.

[20] In Benua and Borer (1996), as well as in Borer (1998a), this idea is formulated in terms of the relationship between TP and AspP, a process node which is telicity-neutral, rather than EP. AspP, as proposed in Borer (1994, 1998a), does have, in many ways, the properties of EP. The change in labelling, in addition to involving a more detailed discussion of the syntactic properties of the event argument, was designed to highlight the fact that the grammar does not have a structure devoted specifically to process (or to activity), and that every event must have an EP, regardless of whatever additional structure might be associated with it.

[21] Clearly, something must be said about the possibility of identifying [Spec, TP] with [Spec, EP] in the case of passive, where an originator reading is available, but is associated with neither [Spec, TP] nor [Spec, EP]. If we assume that passive morphology, along lines suggested by Baker, Johnson, and Roberts (1989) or Kratzer (1994), is capable of licensing the role otherwise associated with [Spec, EP] away from

Returning now to (36), repeated here, we note that it shares, in essence, the structure of the Spanish examples in (46) given in (65b). In (36), range is assigned to $\langle e \rangle_E$ by the expletive *there*, just as in (46) it is assigned by the pre-verbal locative expression. The identification of [Spec, TP] and [Spec, EP] amounts in turn to the assignment of both nominative case and an originator role to the DP in [Spec, TP]. No conflict emerges, quite simply because the expression in [Spec, EP] is not itself an appropriate target for the assignment of an originator role, nor, plausibly, does it need Case (examples based on Levin and Rappaport Hovav 1995).

(36) a. On the third floor, there worked two young women called Maryanne and Ava ...
b. Above them, there pranced three horses on the Parthenon frieze.

The structures in (65) give rise to two new queries: Why is it specifically locatives which can have existential force? and, What is the source of the obligatorily weak reading of the post-verbal subject? We have now concluded that post-verbal subjects in unergative constructions are possible whenever $\langle e \rangle_E$ is otherwise assigned range, or differently put, whenever the event argument is otherwise existentially bound. However, at least the following puzzles concerning the properties of range assignment to $\langle e \rangle_E$ remain, a matter to which we turn in the following two sections:

(66) a. Supposing $\langle e \rangle_E$ is assigned range in (43) and similar configurations by the presence of a locative clitic in E, this still leaves unexplained the licensing of EP in the unaccusative cases in (1)–(3), where no such locative is in evidence.
b. Why locatives?
c. And why is the subject obligatorily weak in (43) and similar structures?

9.4 Why Locatives?

9.4.1 *The distribution of locatives and existentials*

We might as well say upfront here that the reason that locatives, as opposed to, for instance, temporal expressions, have existential force, remains rather mysterious. However, that they do indeed have existential force, and that this function

[Spec, EP] and [Spec, TP], then we derive the fact that in passive [Spec, TP] and [Spec, EP] are associated with a non-originator role, as well as capture the fact that passive may only emerge through the intervention of morphological marking. A detailed execution is left aside here, but see Borer (forthcoming) for some more discussion.

TABLE 9.1. Locatives, existentials, and the placement of the subject–Word order

Basic order	Example	Predicate locative	Existential
SVO	Russian	Th COP L	L COP Th
	Finnish	Th COP L	L COP Th
	Catalan	Th COP L	∅ P-COP Th
VOS	Chamorro	COP L Th	COP Th L
	Palauan	COP L Th	COP-P Th L
VSO	Tagalog	COP L Th	COP Th L
	Palestinian Arabic	Th COP L	COP-P Th L
SOV	Hindi	Th	L Th COP

Note: Th = theme subject; L = locative; COP = copula, p = locative prepositional clitic
Source: Freeze (1992: 564)

tends to go hand in hand with licensing post-verbal subjects, is well established. An extraordinarily detailed study of the correlation between locatives, existentials, and the placement of the subject is found in Freeze (1992). Freeze summarizes his empirical findings for numerous languages in a table, replicated here as Table 9.1 (with slight expository adjustments).

Specifically, Freeze concludes that locatives are systematically implicated in the derivation of existential meaning, and that such an existential meaning is available whenever the locative is either in the subject position, or, for languages such as Catalan, Palauan, and Palestinian Arabic, as well as for Italian (*ci*), when there is a proform of a locative nature attached to the verb or to the copula, in a position which, he argues, is I. In all these cases the subject is post-verbal, in the intended sense, in that it always occurs following the copula, and not immediately after the locative expression. Freeze concludes that full locative expressions in existentials must be in the canonical subject position, and that locative clitics in that context correspond to a null *pro* in the subject position (and see also Bresnan and Kanerva 1989). Further, predicate locatives and existentials are but two facets of the same coin, they must be derived from the same source, and for this reason are in complementary distribution. Our claim that the locatives in Hebrew, Spanish, and Catalan have an existential function, and that they are either in [Spec,EP] (Spanish) or in E (Hebrew, Catalan), with the (logical) subject in some specifier lower than E (and hence post-verbal) is clearly entirely consistent with this picture. Nevertheless, it is worthwhile noting several respects in which the picture presented by Freeze is, I believe, not general enough. First, Freeze claims that the phenomenon is restricted to structures with the thematic arguments locative and theme. However, while locatives are certainly required for the configuration in question to emerge, they can only be considered arguments in the most general sense and are certainly not arguments *of* any head, and could be adjuncts. More crucially, the existence of a theme is clearly not necessary. The constructions under consideration here specifically do not need to involve a theme, as traditionally understood, but may involve an agent. Secondly, as is clear from the relevant examples, the verbal element is not restricted to a copula. These expansions of Freeze's picture notwithstanding, it is clear that the paradigms discussed thus far for Hebrew, Spanish, and Catalan are but another instantiation of a broader phenomena, in which locatives, when occurring either as pre-verbal 'subjects', or, in effect, as subject clitics or clitics on I (where by I we refer to the highest functional head under C), have an existential force in configurations which involve the presence of an agreeing subject 'lower' in the structure, and specifically following the highest verbal element, be it a copula or the verb. While we must continue to ponder the issue of why this is so, that it is indeed so appears beyond dispute. Even in English, a language otherwise very particular about licensing post-verbal subjects, it is precisely locatives which can most freely do so, in the so-called locative inversion structure. Nor is locative inversion restricted to unaccusatives (or themes), as has been conclusively shown by Levin and Rappaport Hovav (1995), from which we note the following examples (discussion restricted to atelic cases):[22]

(67) a. Opposite the landing-place stood half-a-dozen donkeys with saddles on their backs, etc.
 b. On the third floor worked two young women called Maryanne Thomson and Ava Brent...
 c. ...rafts of styrofoam on which dozed naked oily bathers lying on their backs...
 d. Above them pranced the horses on the Parthenon frieze.
 e. Around here heaved and shuffled the jeaned and T-shirted... crowd.

From our perspective, of special interest is the example in (68). Note that here a weak post-verbal subject is licensed by a deictic marker (although not a clitic) which is not semantically vacuous, and yet has clear existential force in addition to whatever locative meaning it may convey (and see also Tortora 1997 for

---

[22] The few comments here on locative inversion are mostly intended to show that in principle, English does allow the event argument, argued to be in EP, to be assigned range by a locative phrase. It is not our purpose to propose a full analysis for locative inversion in English, which is restricted in ways which do not surface in the Hebrew construction (it creates island effects, it bars negation, etc.), and which are not clearly relevant to our discussion here. For a fuller discussion of locative inversion in English, see Bresnan (1994), as well as Levin and Rappaport Hovav (1995), among many others.

the claim that existentials derived from locatives retain their locative interpretation, and that it is the existential function which is derived from the locative one, rather than the other way around):

(68)   Here was a young girl who could out-strut anything on two legs. (From G. F. Edwards, *A toast before dying*, quoted in Levin 1999 in the context of the use of prefix *out*-)

We note, finally, the exclusively existential, i.e. non-locative, use of so-called 'existential' *there*, possible (contrary to what is commonly claimed) in a wide range of (intransitive) constructions, including stative and eventive atelic. Interestingly, however, the omission of the locative expressions in (70) causes a marked deterioration in their felicity:[23]

(69)   a.   There lived ??(in London) in the 19th century a famous author.
       b.   There danced ??(in the woods) this morning three elves.
       c.   There grazed ??(in my back yard) a brown moose this morning.

We consider the fact that English *there* (or, for that matter, Italian *ci*) has lost its locative meaning in the context of existential sentences to be neither necessary nor sufficient for the emergence of an existential meaning. In other words, *there* as well as, for example, Italian *ci* have lost their literal locative meaning and retained the existential one, but ultimately, I concur here with Freeze (1992) and with Tortora (1997) that the origin of the existential meaning resides with the locative function, still retained by *here*, as in (68), and by the entire deictic locative paradigm in Hebrew. The reason for the existential meaning of locatives, however, remains mysterious in Freeze's study, and is in fact largely unstudied, to the best of my knowledge.

---

[23] As is well known, *there*-insertion constructions with verbs other than *be* exhibit a (primarily weak) subject in the right periphery, following adjuncts. This is true for unaccusatives, statives, and unergatives alike. We speculate that while in *there-be* constructions the (logical) subject may be in some functional specifier above VP but below TP, that position, for reasons that are poorly understood, is not available in the absence of *be*, causing the subject to be adjoined to the right (note its position between adjuncts in (iib) below). As is further well known, the effects of *be* here are rather mechanical in nature, e.g. in allowing (ia), while (iia) is barred, thereby suggesting clearly that what is at stake here is not the semantics of the verb or event semantics of any other sort. For some discussion of the peculiarities of English *there*, as well as the conclusion that it is rather unique in its properties, see Freeze (1992):

(i)   a.   There was a cow jumping for an hour in the yard.
       b.   *There was jumping in the yard a cow (for an hour).
       c.   *There was jumping for an hour a cow in the yard.

(ii)   a.   ??There jumped a cow for an hour in the yard.
       b.   There jumped in the yard two cows for an hour.
       c.   There jumped for an hour in the yard two cows.

9.4.2 Existentially binding the event? Existentially binding the DP?

An independent proposal which briefly addresses the relations between location and existential binding, albeit not in the context of existential sentences, is found in Dobrovie-Sorin and Laca (1996), who reach the conclusion that 'localizing objects or eventualities in space entails asserting their existence'. Consider specifically their results as they hold for bare DP subjects. Dobrovie-Sorin and Laca note that an existential reading for bare DPs is possible if the clausal predicate containing them is compatible with what they call 'a Space Localizer'. Thus consider the following contrasts:

(70) a. Farmers were sleeping/dancing.
b. Butter was melting.
c. Linguistic books are available.
d. Blood was visible.

(71) a. *Children are dirty.   (With an existential reading for *children*)
b. *Cats are nasty.   (With an existential reading for *cats*)
c. *Butter was fresh.   (With an existential reading for *butter*)

The contrasts in (70)–(71) correlate, Dobrovie-Sorin and Laca argue, with the contrasts in (72)–(73):

(72) a. Where is John sleeping/dancing?
b. Where was the butter melting?
c. Where is Chomsky's book available?
d. Where was the blood visible?

(73) a. *Where was John dirty?
b. *Where was Jane nasty?
c. *Where was the butter fresh?   (Under the intended reading, with the locative ranging over *fresh*, but not over *fresh butter*)

These facts, Dobrovie-Sorin and Laca conclude, follow if we assume that bare DPs are licit precisely when they can be located in space. Their specific conclusion is that default existential closure applies only to formulas which contain a locative argument, possibly as a covert space variable, and that only those arguments of the predicate whose location in space is specified by the locative argument can be bound by existential closure (Dobrovie-Sorin and Laca 1996: 16). Before proceeding, note as an obvious advantage of the Dobrovie-Sorin and Laca account that it does not require lowering in English to bring about the existential binding of pre-verbal subjects, although it must retain, as a statement of language variation, the assumption that in English (covert) locatives can license existential bare DPs in pre-verbal position, but not in Hebrew, for instance.[24]

Independent confirmation for the proposal that the possibility of projecting existential pre-verbal subjects is linked to the occurrence of locative expressions, this time necessarily overt, is found in French. Roy (2001) notes the following contrasts:

(74) a. *Des enfants dansent/jouent.
       des children dance/play
       'Children are dancing/playing.'

   b. *Des enfants ont dormi.
       des children have slept
       'Children slept.'

(75) a. Des enfants dansent dans la classes/jouent sous ma fenêtre.
       des children dance in the classroom/play under my window
       'Children are dancing in the classroom/playing under my window.'

   b. Des enfants ont dormi sur la plage.
       des children have slept on the beach
       'Children slept on the beach.'

Striking a somewhat speculative note here, suppose we reformulate slightly Dobrovie-Sorin and Laca's (1996) account. Specifically, instead of focusing on the existential closure of pre-verbal subjects, suppose we suggest that the locative acts directly as a range assigner to $\langle e \rangle_E$—that is, it existentially binds the event argument. For concreteness, suppose that predicates such as those in (70), which in these cases are not associated with an overt locative but nevertheless allow a *where* question, are associated here with a covert locative (or a locative variable, in the terminology of Dobrovie-Sorin and Laca), and that this covert locative is assigned interpretation through the discourse. No such covert locative is available in (73). Rather than assume, as Dobrovie-Sorin and Laca (op.

---

[24] N. Klinedinst (pers. comm.) nevertheless notes that an existential reading for (i) is not available, in spite of the occurrence of an overt locative, raising the possibility that the relations between the locative and the DP is further restricted in ways which the Dobrovie-Sorin and Laca account remains silent on,

(i) Cats are nasty around here.

Presumably, *cats are nasty* cannot be relativized to the discourse in the way that *cats yawned* can. That is, *Cats are nasty* with a weak reading for *cats* is unfelicitous in a context in which it is clear that the speaker is only talking about cats in this town, or whatever. The reason for this, however, remains unclear. We may note as an aside that appealing to a distinction between stage and individual predicates is not necessarily helpful, as e.g. *dirty* is not necessarily an individual predicate (e.g. *my hands are dirty*), and yet *dirty*, as in (71a), does not appear to have a covert locative.

cit.) do, that existential closure applies to predicates localized in space, suppose we assume that localization in space is itself a type of existential binding of events, and possibly of DPs as well. We note that in the English cases in (70), an overt or a covert locative could assign range to $\langle e \rangle_E$ neither through direct range assignment, with a clitic or a head feature in E, nor through specifier–head relations. Rather, the range assigned to $\langle e \rangle_E$ by an overt or a covert locative adjunct is akin to range assignment to $[_{Asp_Q} \langle e \rangle_\#]$ by a locative adjunct or an adverb, already discussed in detail in Chapter 7, Section 7.3. In turn, the ungrammaticality of existentially bound pre-verbal subjects (illustrated in Hebrew by (6)–(8) and true for numerous other languages) indicates that such range assignment to $\langle e \rangle_E$ by a locative adjunct, whether covert or overt, is not available. Thus, in lieu of lowering we postulate for English the possibility of assigning range to $\langle e \rangle_E$ (i.e. binding the event argument) through an adjunct locative (overt or covert), a possibility which we must assume to be unavailable for languages such as Hebrew and Spanish.

We already argued that $\langle e \rangle_E$ can be assigned range through specifier–head agreement with a phrase which itself has existential force. A natural assumption is that a bare DP which is not otherwise existentially closed cannot provide existential closure over the event argument, or put differently, it cannot assign range to $\langle e \rangle_E$. Thus in the presence of a pre-verbal weak or bare subject, $\langle e \rangle_E$ can only be assigned range (and the event argument be existentially bound) through the mediation of a locative. When $\langle e \rangle_E$ is assigned range by a locative, however, the open value $\langle e \rangle_d$ associated with the pre-verbal bare DP in [Spec, EP] can likewise be assigned range, or in other words, the variable in D can be existentially bound through specifier–head agreement with $\langle e \rangle_E$, since the latter is assigned range by a locative with existential force. Following a similar rationale, *du/des* DPs in French involve the projection of an $\langle e \rangle_d$ which is not bound internal to the DP, and is hence in need of existential closure. As such, *du/des* DPs cannot themselves assign range to $\langle e \rangle_E$, and thus the event argument cannot be bound without an (overt) locative. The contrasts in (74)–(75) follow directly. We note now that the two possible configurations here mimic, formally, the two modes of licensing $[_{Asp_Q} \langle e \rangle_\#]$ already discussed, one involving indirect range assignment from the specifier to the head (discussed in Chapter 3), the other direct range assignment to the head which is copied onto the specifier, discussed in Chapter 6 (and see (80)–(82) below for the relevant structures). We note, crucially, that when range was assigned to a DP in [Spec, Asp_Q] through specifier–head agreement, it involved the obligatory copying of a $[_{DP} \langle e \rangle_\#]$ into the agreeing DP (see Chapter 6, Section 6.3, for extensive discussion). However, as E does not have any quantity properties, no such copying is expected, and the DP in [Spec, EP] is not expected to have a quantity interpretation in the absence of an

[$_{DP}\langle e\rangle_*$] which is independently licensed (e.g. through the projection of a quantity determiner).

Generalizing, and speculating some more, if Benedicto (1997) is on the right track, and the domain of existential closure is the c-command domain of the verb, rather than the VP, as originally argued by Diesing (1992), then we can now assume that the domain of existential closure is determined by the domain of the event argument, when itself existentially bound. Normally, such existential binding is accomplished by the presence of an overt subject with existential force. In the absence of such a subject, a locative is necessary (or some other operator, possibly), to assign range to $\langle e\rangle_E$. In the latter case, the domain of existential closure may actually be extended, in that an event argument that is existentially bound by a locative may, in turn, bring about the existential binding of its own subject, through specifier–head agreement and the subsequent existential closure of $\langle e\rangle_d$.

Supposing all this is correct, and range assignment by a locative adjunct is available in English, we derive precisely the fact that in English, in the presence of a (possibly covert) locative adjunct, but not otherwise, the subject may be a bare DP with an existential interpretation.[25]

It is worthwhile to digress briefly to consider the nature of the logical entailments here. Two executions are in principle possible (and possibly, both may be instantiated). According to both executions, the event argument must be existentially bound, and the bare DP must be existentially bound. According to both executions, the locative binds one of these elements, either the event argument or the bare DP, and the other becomes existentially bound through a process of specifier–head agreement. The question is, however, whether the locative directly existentially binds the bare DP or the event argument. According to the execution favoured here, the locative binds the event argument, and a bare DP, specifically in [Spec,EP], is existentially bound through specifier–head agreement with E. According to the other execution, more compatible with the spirit of Dobrovie-Sorin and Laca (1996), the locative binds the bare DP in [Spec,EP], and the bare DP, now having existential force, binds the event argument through specifier–head agreement. We note now that at least for the Hebrew locative clitic cases, the former execution must be preferred. Considering again the relevant structures, as in (65), note first that there are no specifier–head relations between the bare DP (singular and weak, in this case, and see (56) for a case of bare plural) and E, as the bare DP (or weak DP) is not in [Spec,EP]. In fact, we have suggested that it is precisely the absence of such

---

[25] The reader is referred to Dobrovie-Sorin and Laca (1996) for the extension of the account to existential bare DPs in object position.

specifier–head relations which made the presence of a locative direct range assigner to $\langle e \rangle_E$ necessary. Further, if one assumes, as appears plausible from the paradigm in (6)–(12), that the domain of existential closure is the c-command domain of E, thereby allowing only generic bare DP subjects pre-verbally and only existential bare DP subjects post-verbally, then the post-verbal DP in (65) is already existentially closed, and is in no need for any further help, so to speak, from the locative clitic. In turn, of course, it is possible that E in (65), in the absence of a locative, does not establish a domain of existential closure. But in that case, we must assume that the locative binds, first and foremost, the event argument, and not the DP. The distribution of locative clitics, then, could not be attributed solely to the need for existential closure for post-verbal DPs in V1 in Hebrew, and can only be compatible with the need of some other argument for existential closure—that is, the event argument. I return in Section 9.5.1 to more evidence which bears on this issue, showing specifically that the locative could not be construed with the post-verbal subject in cases with the structure in (65), quite simply because an overt locative within a post-verbal DP subject does not suffice to license these structures. Thus at least for the cases in Hebrew, the logic of Dobrovie-Sorin and Laca (1996) must be reversed.

Turning now to English, and applying a similar rationale, locatives, overt or covert, are obligatory in the presence of pre-verbal bare DP subjects with an existential interpretation not because the subjects could not otherwise be bound, but because the event argument could not be otherwise bound. The existential binding of pre-verbal subjects in English is thus the result of the existential binding of the event argument, and not the other way around. Of course, we cannot rule out in principle a derivation in which a locative existentially binds a pre-verbal bare or weak DP, and such binding, in turn, is transferred to the event argument through specifier–head relations, nor does it seem advantageous, at this point, to exclude such a possibility without further empirical support. We further note that at least one piece of evidence suggests that in English a direct closure of the DP by the locative, rather than the event, may give rise to desirable empirical results. Thus note that adjunct locatives in English do license pre-verbal bare DPs and possibly *there* as well, but nevertheless they do not permit EP to project without a specifier altogether, a situation which is allowed in Hebrew and in Catalan. We note in this context the ungrammaticality of (76), as well as the deteriorated status of (69) without locatives:

(76) a. *There were children dirty (this morning).
     b. *There were cats nasty (last night).
     c. *There was butter fresh (this week).

In addition to the fact that the ungrammaticality of (76) casts serious doubt on the generalization proposed in Diesing (1992), according to which *there* constructions are the hallmark of stage level predicates, we note that clearly English *there* is not sufficient to license a post-verbal subject, and just as a (covert) locative is necessary to assign range to $\langle e \rangle_E$ in the presence of bare DP subjects, so a locative appears necessary to augment, so to speak, *there* in the context of existential *there* insertion. This suggests that in English, adjunct locative range assignment to $\langle e \rangle_E$ is somehow mediated through [Spec, EP]. This would actually derive the presence of EPP effects in English, but not in Hebrew or Spanish. Leaving this matter open, and hoping that future empirical findings will bear on its resolution, we conclude that it can be shown conclusively that, at least in the case of locative clitics in Hebrew, existential closure applies to the event argument first, and then to the weak subject in [Spec, EP] by specifier–head agreement with range-assigned $\langle e \rangle_E$. Some prima facie evidence suggests that English may follow the other route, from the specifier to the event argument, but a full resolution of this issue is still pending.

Consider in this context the grammaticality of cases such as those in (77), already discussed extensively in Chapter 4, Section 4.3.

(77) a. dapqu ba-delet.
    knocked.PL in-the.door

  b. hipcicu 'et lebanon ha.boqer.
    bombed.PL OM Lebanon this.morning

  c. šamʿu 'ota šoberet 'et ha.delet.
    heard.PL her break OM the.door

The grammaticality of (77a–c), when viewed from the perspective of the paradigm discussed here thus far, appears at first sight rather puzzling. We already noted that the (missing) subjects in (77a–c) are interpreted very much on a par with weak bare plurals. And yet, in the presence of an overt bare plural DP with an existential interpretation in such constructions, whether pre-verbal or post-verbal, ungrammaticality results, as already noted (minimal contrasts in (78)). Why should such an asymmetry emerge?

(78) a. *'yeladim dapqu ba-delet.
    children knocked.PL in-the.door

  b. *metosim hipcicu 'et lebanon ha.boqer.
    planes bombed.PL OM Lebanon this-morning

  c. *škenim šamʿu 'ota šoberet 'et ha.delet.
    neighbours heard.PL her break OM the.door

The solution is obvious, however, when we recall, following the discussion in Chapter 4, that existential *pro* has inherent existential force, and as such, it need not be within the scope of existential closure. Note, however, that it follows that existential *pro* must be pre-verbal in (77). Only in that position can it assign range to ⟨e⟩$_E$ through specifier–head agreement. In turn, the behaviour of existential *pro* thus provides additional evidence for the fact that there is no restriction against pre-verbal weak subjects, as such, and that well-formedness emerges exactly when ⟨e⟩$_E$ can be assigned range either by a locative (directly), or by an existentially closed DP in its specifier (indirectly). It further provides evidence that existential closure, while defined with respect to the c-command domain of the verb, cannot be associated with the verb as such, but rather must be associated with the functional head which we labelled E, and which, we argued, corresponds with the licensing of the event argument.

Finally, note that the (relative) grammaticality in Hebrew of pre-verbal, weak subjects precisely in the presence of locatives, already noted in (64), now follows. If indeed the locative assigns range to ⟨e⟩$_E$ in (64), we expect a weak subject to be licit, due to specifier–head agreement (and see structure (81)).

There is substantial evidence, then, that the distribution of locatives does correlate with existential binding of the event argument. Opting for the simplest possible description, I will assume that anchoring in space, in and of itself, is sufficient to establish existence, thereby making locatives, potentially, existential binders. I will further assume that such an existential function exists independently of the specific information on location provided by the locative (i.e. *in the library, here, there*), and that in addition to serving as existential binders, locatives may quite simply be locatives, that is, pick out a location without existentially binding an event argument or a nominal expression altogether. As such, locatives fall within the domain of quasi-functional elements, on a par with heads of measure phrases (e.g. *box* and *cake* in *box of cigars* and *cake of soap*), in that they may or may not assign range to open values (and see Volume I, Chapter 1, n. 4 for some discussion). Thus cases such as (79) do not (need to) give rise to double range assignment to ⟨e⟩$_E$ (by the DP in [Spec,EP] and the locative adjunct) and are hence grammatical. Here, the locative adjunct remains, indeed, a locative adjunct, and it is the definite description in [Spec,EP] that assigns range to ⟨e⟩$_E$—that is, existentially binds the event argument:

(79) The cat meowed in the yard.

To summarize, the configurations in (80) are licensed in Hebrew, English, and Spanish, and quite possibly universally (but see n. 27 on Hebrew pre-verbal locatives), the configuration in (81) is licensed in English, but not, for example, in Hebrew or Spanish, and that in (82) occurs in Hebrew and Catalan, but not

English, quite possibly due to the fact that the former but not the latter have locative clitics (arrows indicate direction of range assignment):[26]

[26] As is often noted (Borer 1984, 1995b; Shlonsky 1987, 1997; Shlonsky and Doron 1992), Hebrew allows VS word orders quite freely in V2 or V3 contexts, as the paradigm (i)–(iv) shows (and see n. 16 for some brief comments):

(i) a. 'etmol ʿabad (ha.)ganan ba-gan.
yesterday worked (the-)gardener in-the-garden

b. ba-gan ʿabad (ha.)ganan ha.boqer.
in-the-garden worked (the-)gardener in-the-morning

c. be-derek klal ʿobed (ha.)ganan ba-gan ba-boqer.
usually works (the-)gardener in-the-garden in-the-morning

(ii) a. 'et ha.mekonit raxaca rina ha.boqer bemešek šaloš šaʿot.
OM the-car washed Rina this-morning for three hours

b. la-misrad higiʿu ha.miktabim ba-zman.
to-the-office arrived the-letters on-time

(iii) a. ba-qayic gar ha.boʾeš mitaxat la-bayit.
in-the-summer lives the-skunk under to-the-house

b. ba-xorep hayta ha.mora šelanu xola.
in-the-winter was the-teacher ours sick

(iv) a. lama ʿabad ha.ganan ba-gan?
why worked the-gardener in-the-garden

b. ʾeypo ʿabad ha.ganan?
where worked the-gardener?

It appears tempting to suggest that not just DPs and locatives, but any pre-verbal constituent may assign range to $\langle e \rangle_E$, thereby offering a unified account for the grammaticality of (i)–(iv) and that of post-verbal subjects in locative constructions. Such an extension, however, is not clearly on the right track. Most importantly, (i)–(iv) clearly allow a strong post-verbal subject, while post-verbal subjects which are licensed in the contexts of deictic clitics (in both Hebrew and Catalan), post-verbal subjects in *there* insertion in English, as well as post-verbal subjects in the context of sentence-initial locatives in Spanish all require that the post-verbal nominative arguments (specifically, we suggested, in [Spec, TP]) be weak when $\langle e \rangle_E$ is assigned range by a locative. For this reason, an extension of the account is not undertaken here. We note as an aside that like locative inversion in English, but unlike cases of locative deictic clitics or cases of *there* insertion, (i)–(iv) are islands:

(v) a. matay ha.ganan ʿabad ba-gan?
when the-gardener worked in-the-garden

b. matay ʿabad šam ganan?
when worked there gardener

(vi) a. *matay ba-gan ʿabad (ha.)ganan?
when in-the-garden worked (the-)gardener

b. *'eypo ba-qayic gar (ha.)boʾeš?
where in-the-summer lives (the-)skunk

c. *matay 'et ha.mekonit raxaca rina?
when OM the-car washed Rina

For proposals that the pre-verbal constituent in (i)–(iv) is in [Spec, CP] (and hence not in [Spec, EP]), see Shlonsky and Doron (1992) and Shlonsky (1997). For a proposal that it is in an A'-[Spec, IP], see Borer (1995b).

(80) Indirect range assignment to head by specifier

a.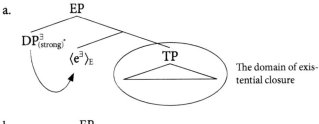

The domain of existential closure

b.

The domain of existential closure

(81) Range assignment to head by adjunct; indirect range assignment to specifier by head

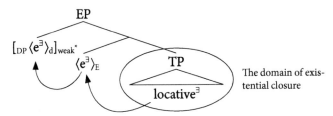

The domain of existential closure

(82) Direct range assignment to head

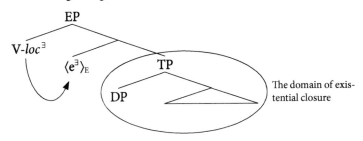

The domain of existential closure

*XP$^\exists$ is a constituent with existential force (strong, for DP), and [$_{DP}$ ⟨e⟩$_d$] is a DP with an open value for ⟨e⟩$_d$, an unbound variable, and hence weak.

9.5 Why a Weak Subject?

We have now explained why it is that a bare DP pre-verbal subject in English can receive an existential interpretation. However, in the cases under consideration here, locative V1 contexts, the post-verbal subject *must* receive an existential interpretation—that is, it must be weak. This is clearly a stronger restriction, and we must now ask what it follows from. Intuitively, the answer is obvious: the subject is weak because it must fall under the scope of the existential binder of the event argument. However, this solution is not straightforward. Specifically, why must a post-verbal subject, but no other argument, be weak whenever $\langle e \rangle_E$ is bound by a locative? Consider the example in (83); why is the DP *ha.xalon* 'the window' not within the obligatory scope of the existential binder? (See also (96) for a strong reading for direct objects in similar contexts).[27]

(83)   rac šam yeled mitaxat la-xalon.
       ran there boy   under   to-the.window

Now recall that we have already seen in Slavic a restriction forcing cardinals to be weak in the presence of verbal prefixes (see Chapter 6, Section 6.3). I suggested that this restriction is the direct result of the relevant prefixes being operators (realized on the verbal head) which assign range, indirectly, to $\langle e \rangle_d$. In turn, strong readings emerge either as a result of range assignment to $\langle e \rangle_d$ internal to the DP, or as the result of range assignment by one of these quantificational (perfective) prefixes to both $\langle e \rangle_d$ and $\langle e \rangle_\#$. I further suggested that in assigning range to $\langle e \rangle_d$ from without the DP, the function of such quantificational prefixes is akin to that of existential closure, in giving rise to a weak, variable reading whenever $\langle e \rangle_d$ is bound from without the DP phrase.

We noted already that locative clitics may assign range to $\langle e \rangle_E$ as well as to $\langle e \rangle_d$ in [Spec, EP]—through specifier–head agreement—if what occupies that position is a bare DP, for which this range assignment yields an existential interpret-

---

[27] Note that it is entirely possible that a similar restriction holds in pre-verbal positions for both Hebrew and English, i.e. that whenever the event argument is bound by a locative, a pre-verbal subject must be weak. Consider why this is so. We assumed explicitly that locative adjuncts may, but need not, function as existential binders. It thus follows that whenever the pre-verbal subject is itself strong, a locative need not, indeed may not, assign range to $\langle e \rangle_E$. The only cases in which locatives must assign range to $\langle e \rangle_E$ directly or through the assignment of range to the DP in [Spec, EP], thus by assumption forcing the subject to be weak, are precisely those in which the subject *is* an existentially-interpreted weak or bare DP, and those in which the subject is not in [Spec, EP] altogether, i.e. is post-verbal. It is thus possible that whenever Hebrew deictic clitics co-occur with a pre-verbal (strong) subject, they are just locatives, they do not existentially bind the subject, and range is assigned to $\langle e \rangle_E$ by the strong pre-verbal subject. In turn, when locatives do bind the event argument, the subject in [Spec, EP] must be weak. Of course, for pre-verbal subjects, the argument here is unfalsifiable. If one were to claim, however, that the correlation between the event argument being bound by a locative and the subject being weak in any position is mandated by UG principles, pre-verbal subjects in English and in general would not be a counter-example to such a claim.

ation. In a sense, then, Hebrew locative deictic markers, phonological clitics, are *slavified*. Specifically, these locative clitics function, at times, just like perfective prefixes in Slavic, in constituting material which attaches to a head, which assigns range directly to the open value associated with that head, and which may further assign range, indirectly, to certain open values within the head's DP specifier. Nevertheless, given the fact that locative deictic clitics are quasi-functional, in that they may also be pure locatives, they are not direct parallels of Slavic verbal prefixes, and as such we must fine-tune the description of their function here. Suppose, then, that locatives must realize their operator function only in those contexts in which ungrammaticality would otherwise result.[28] It is presumably for that reason that in (68) (cf. (84a)) we get existential force, as *here* is assigning range to an otherwise unlicensed $\langle e \rangle_E$. In contrast, no such existential interpretation occurs in (84b), as $\langle e \rangle_E$ is licensed through the presence of the subject:

(84) a. Here was a young girl who could out-strut anything on two legs.
 b. (Here), the girls (here) are capable of, etc.

In turn, the hallmarks of slavified structures are given in (86):

(85) a. A node licensed through slavification need not be otherwise licensed.
 b. If there is a DP in the specifier of a slavified head, at least one open value within that DP must be assigned range by the very same assigner which assigns range to the slavified head. As the salient property of direct range assignment to $\langle e \rangle_E$ is existential binding, it follows that a DP in [Spec, EP] must be weak (and see n. 27 for some relevant comments).

Suppose we return now to the paradigm of locatives in unergative contexts, considering, for the sake of completeness, both pre-verbal and post-verbal subjects, with locative clitics as well as without them. The cases under consideration are schematized in (86) and (87), with illustrations in (88) and (89), respectively:

(86) a. [$_{EP}$ DP$_{strong}$ V $\langle e \rangle_E$ [$_{TP}$ ~~DP~~   ~~V~~   [. . .]]]   (40), (88a)
 b. *[$_{EP}$ DP$_{weak}$ V $\langle e \rangle_E$ [$_{TP}$ ~~DP~~   ~~V~~   [. . .]]]   (6), (88b)
 c. [$_{EP}$ DP$_{strong}$ V-loc $\langle e \rangle_E$ [$_{TP}$ ~~DP~~ ~~V-loc~~ [. . .]]]   (52g), (88c)
 d. ?[$_{EP}$ DP$_{weak}$ V-loc $\langle e \rangle_E$ [$_{TP}$ ~~DP~~ ~~V-loc~~ [. . .]]]   (64c–d) (88d)

---

[28] Alternatively, within an overgenerating model—as opposed to an economy-driven one—locatives may optionally function as existentials in any context, with under-applications ruled out as cases of unbound variables, and over-applications ruled out as cases of double marking. The reader is referred to Chapter 2, n. 3 (Volume I) as well as to Chapter 1 in this volume (Section 1.3), for some brief comments on the morphological place of clitics as range assigners on the continuum from head features to f-morphs.

(87) a. *[$_{EP}$ V $\langle e \rangle_E$ [$_{TP}$ DP$_{strong-weak}$ ~~V~~   [...]]]   (39),(89a)
     b. [$_{EP}$ V-loc $\langle e \rangle_E$ [$_{TP}$ DP$_{weak}$ ~~V-loc~~   [...]]]   (43a,c),(89b)
     c. *[$_{EP}$ V-loc $\langle e \rangle_E$ [$_{TP}$ DP$_{strong}$ ~~V-loc~~   [...]]]   (43b,d),(89c)

(88) a. ha.gananim ʿabdu kol ha.boqer.
        the.gardener worked all the.morning
        'The gardeners worked all morning.'

   b. *gananim ʿabdu kol ha.boqer.
        gardeners worked all the.morning

   c. ha.gananim ʿabdu šam kol ha.boqer.
        the.gardeners worked there all the.morning

   d. ?Gananim ʿabdu šam kol ha.boqer.
        gardeners worked there all the.morning

(89) a. *ʿabdu (ha.)gananim kol ha.boqer.
        worked (the)gardeners all the.morning
        'The gardeners worked all morning.'

   b. ʿabdu šam gananim kol ha.boqer.
        worked there gardeners all thte.morning

   c. *ʿabdu šam ha.gananim kol ha.boqer.
        worked there the.gardeners all the.morning

The grammaticality of the structure in (86a), as attested by (89a), is straightforward: here range is assigned to $\langle e \rangle_E$ by the subject DP. Likewise, the structure in (86b) is straightforwardly ungrammatical: a weak subject, not itself existentially closed, cannot assign range to $\langle e \rangle_E$. In (86c), the locative must remain existentially inert, with range to $\langle e \rangle_E$ assigned by the existentially closed subject. Finally, in (86d), range cannot be assigned by the DP in [Spec, EP], as that DP is weak. Again, we must assume that range is assigned to $\langle e \rangle_E$ by the locative, and that the subject DP is existentially closed through indirect range assignment via specifier–head relations.

Turning now to post-verbal subjects, consider first (87a). Here too matters are straightforward. There is quite simply nothing to assign range to $\langle e \rangle_E$, and ungrammaticality results, regardless of the type of DP in the post-verbal subject position. Consider, however, (87b–c). Here, the locative must be an existential operator, as there is no other range assigner to $\langle e \rangle_E$. However, assuming T to be in the upward path of the movement of V+loc to E, the DP in [Spec, TP] now agrees, perforce, with (the copy of) ~~V + loc~~, where *loc* has existential force. Such agreement in turn gives rise precisely to the phenomenon we have seen in the Slavic languages, in which a range assigner to an open functional head value must also assign range to some open value within that functional projection's DP specifier, if one projects. As the range assigner under consideration is an existential binder, it must assign range to $\langle e \rangle_d$, resulting in an obligatorily weak DP. It might be helpful to remind the reader at this point that the requirement that the locative bind an open value within the DP in [Spec,TP] does not follow from the properties of the locative clitic itself as an existential binder, but rather, from the fact that because of specifier–head agreement, the clitic, an operator, perforce binds the DP, just as Slavic prefixes such as *na* perforce bind both the open value $[_{Asp_Q}\langle e \rangle_\#]$ and some value within the DP in [Spec, Asp$_Q$]. If all values within that DP are already assigned range—that is, bound—vacuous quantification results. Differently put, as (a copy of) an existential operator is in specifier–head relations with the DP in [Spec,TP], that DP must have an open value. As existential binders are not appropriate range assigners to $\langle e \rangle_\#$ (a point discussed in Volume I, Chapter 5, Section 5.1; see also Chapter 10), the only available open value is $\langle e \rangle_d$, and the DP in [Spec,TP] must be weak. The obligatory weakness of post-verbal subjects, as illustrated by the grammaticality of (87b) when contrasted with the ungrammaticality of (87c), now follows in full.[29]

9.5.1 A brief note on incorporation

It is often assumed that when an operator surfaces on the verb but has an effect for the nominal paradigm, such an operator has undergone incorporation from the nominal into the verbal domain. Baker (1988, 1996) proposes such an analysis for Mohawk, and Verkuyl (1993) assumes it to apply to the prefix *na* in Russian (and by extension, to the entire perfective paradigm), functioning roughly on a par with *na* in Czech, already discussed extensively in Chapter 6, Section 6.1. From Verkuyl's perspective, note, an incorporation analysis is essential if the requirement for a quantity argument in telic configurations is to be maintained (or, in Verkuyl's terms, [+SQA]). As we already saw, objects in the Slavic languages may be bare, and hence at least prima facie non-quantity ([−SQA]). Further, in such cases, their interpretation depends on the verbal affixation. An incorporation analysis would then allow, in principle, the projection of such DPs as non-bare and as quantity, and their bareness to emerge as a result of

---

[29] The reader is reminded here that for bare DPs in Slavic, Slavic quantificational perfective affixes assign range to both $[_{DP}\langle e \rangle_\#]$ and $\langle e \rangle_d$, thereby giving rise, by definition, to a strong reading. This is not the case for (87b), where a definite or specific reading is not available. The difference follows directly from the fact that the range assigner to $\langle e \rangle_E$ is not a range assigner to $\langle e \rangle_\#$, but rather an existential operator, which can assign range to $\langle e \rangle_E$ or, alternatively, to $\langle e \rangle_d$, but never to $[_{DP}\langle e \rangle_\#]$. Thus the DPs which agree with such an existential operator must be weak, and may receive a quantity interpretation only through an independent range assigner to $[_{DP}\langle e \rangle_\#]$ (e.g. a cardinal). For some more discussion of this point, see Chapter 10, where I discuss in detail the interaction between locative deictics and range assignment to $[_{Asp_Q}\langle e \rangle_\#]$.

syntactic incorporation (but see Bach 1995; Schmitt 1996 for compelling additional arguments against the incorporation analysis).

The overall plausibility of such accounts for Mohawk and the Slavic languages notwithstanding, we note that even if such an incorporation analysis is tenable for Hebrew, what is clear is that it strengthens, rather than undermines, our claim that the locative deictic expression is a range assigner to the event argument, and cannot be understood in terms of existentially closing a weak DP. Thus while locative deictic expressions may occur internal to the DP (on the right, as shown in (90)), they always occur with determiners in such contexts, and the DP involved is always strong as shown in (91), and thus in no need for existential closure. Proponents of an incorporation account would thus have to argue not only that incorporation is blocked out of strong DPs, which may be independently plausible, but also that locatives are incorporated determiners only in weak DPs, and that in such cases incorporation is obligatory, a considerably less plausible claim. Further, such an analysis would have to hold that the incorporation is somehow essential to existentially close the relevant DP:

(90) a. [ha.yeled kan] roce bananot.
 the.boy here wants bananas
 'The boy here wants bananas.'

b. *[kan ha.yeled] roce bananot.
 here the.boy wants bananas

(91) a. šalaxti ʾet [ha.yeled kan] la-qaytana.
 sent.I OM [the.boy here] to the summer camp

b. šalaxti [šloša yeladim kan] la-qaytana.
 sent.I [three boys here] to the summer camp
 (Strong reading only for *three children*)

c. *šalaxti [yeladim kan] la-qaytana.
 sent.I [boys here] to the summer camp

d. šalaxti [šloša yeladim] la-qaytana.
 sent.I [three boys] to the summer camp
 (Ambiguous—both weak and strong readings possible for *three children*)

Furthermore, DP-internal locatives do not license post-verbal (strong) unergative subjects in V1 contexts, as (92) indicates, suggesting that even if the locative may existentially bind the DP when it is internal to it, such existential binding does not suffice to license the relevant structures, strengthening our claim that the primary role of deictic locatives is to assign range to $\langle e \rangle_E$:

(92) a. *rac [yeled šam] ha.boqer.
        ran [boy there] this.morning
    b. *rac<u>u</u> [šloša yeladim šam] ha.boqer.
        ran [three boys there] this.morning
    c. *rac [ha-yeled šam] ha.boqer.
        ran [boy there] this.morning

Finally, deictic locatives clitics can occur together with locatives internal to the DP:

(93) [šloša yeladim kan] racu šam.
      three children here ran there
     'Three children here ran there.'

Of course, as the pre-verbal subject in (93) is obligatorily strong, and hence by assumption it assigns range to $\langle e \rangle_E$, the clitic *šam* may just be an adjunct. However, the existence of two locative expressions here, one interpreted in conjunction with the event, the other in conjunction with the subject without any apparent conflict, casts serious doubt on any attempt to collapse the function of DP-internal locatives with that of the deictic locatives discussed in this chapter.

9.6 Transitive Expletives? In Hebrew??

So far, the discussion of range assignment to $\langle e \rangle_E$, i.e. the existential binding of the event argument by a locative clitic or a locative specifier has been limited to intransitives, specifically unergatives. However, the logic of the analysis does not restrict it to intransitives; in principle, a locative existential can bind the event argument in EP in a transitive construction as well. In turn, if and when such licensing of the event argument takes place in Hebrew in transitive constructions, we expect a rather dramatic effect. Specifically, we predict that V1 word order will be attested in transitives, a configuration otherwise entirely absent from the language, under any intonation.[30] We further expect that the post-verbal subject will be obligatorily weak. Examples (94)–(96) illustrate that this prediction is borne out:

(94) a. kol matos hip̱cic 'et ha.ʕir ('az/'etmol/šam).
        every plane bombed OM the.town (then/yesterday/there)

---

[30] In fact, almost entirely absent. The exception is narrative inversion, as in (i), attested exclusively in matrix clauses, and allowed only in very restricted registers. The examples in the text clearly do not involve narrative inversion, and are licit in embedded clauses.

(i) patxa 'ima 'et piha ve-amra: paʕam 'axat hayta yalda
    opened mother OM mouth and-said once was girl

b. *metosim hipcicu 'et ha.ʿir   ('az/'etmol/šam).
   planes   bombed ᴏᴍ the.town (then/yesterday/there)

(95) a. *hipcic   (kol/ha.)matos 'et ha.ʿir.
       bombed (every/the.)plane ᴏᴍ the.town

   b. *hipcic 'az (kol/ha.)matos 'et ha.ʿir.
      bombed then (every/the.)plane ᴏᴍ the.town

   c. *hipcic 'etmol   (kol/ha.)matos 'et ha.ʿir.
      bombed yesterday (every/the.)plane ᴏᴍ the.town

(96) a. hipcic šam matos 'et ha.ʿir.
       bombed there plane ᴏᴍ the.town

   b. hipcicu šam metosim 'et ha.ʿir.
      bombed there planes   ᴏᴍ the town
      (Existential only; generic reading impossible)

   c. hipcicu šam šloša metosim 'et ha.ʿir.
      bombed there three planes   ᴏᴍ the.town

   d. *hipcicu šam šlošet ha.metosim 'et ha.ʿir.
      bombed there three the.planes ᴏᴍ the.town
      'The three planes bombed the town.'

   e. *hipcic šam ha.matos 'et ha.ʿir.
      bombed there the.plane ᴏᴍ the.town

   f. *hipcic šam kol matos 'et ha.ʿir.
      bombed there every plane ᴏᴍ the.city

The similarities between (96) and structures with transitive expletives, as discussed in languages in which expletives are overt pronominals (e.g. Icelandic and Dutch), are self-evident. We note that the system proposed here derives the similarities directly from the availability in Hebrew of a mechanism that can assign range directly to $\langle e \rangle_E$, thereby existentially binding the event argument, in the absence of a specifier for EP. Assuming that overt expletives, as attested in Icelandic and Dutch, are in [Spec,EP] rather than cliticized to the verbal head in E, the difference between Dutch and Icelandic, on the one hand, and Hebrew, on the other, reduces to the difference between direct range assignment to $\langle e \rangle_E$ (Hebrew), vs. indirect range assignment to $\langle e \rangle_E$ (Icelandic, Dutch), although a detailed analysis of Icelandic and Dutch transitive expletives along these lines is not attempted here.

The structures proposed for Hebrew 'transitive expletives', telic and atelic, are as in (97):

(97) a. Atelic: [$_{EP}$ V-loc$^\exists$ ⟨e$^\exists$⟩$_E$ [$_{TP}$ DP$^\exists_{weak}$ ~~V-loc~~$^\exists$ [$_F{^s}{_P}$ DP$_{PRT}$ ...]]]
                       originator   default

b. Telic: [$_{EP}$ V-loc$^\exists$ ⟨e$^\exists$⟩$_E$ [$_{TP}$ DP$^\exists_{weak}$ ~~V-loc~~$^\exists$ [$_{Asp_q}$ DP$_{ACC}$ ...]]]
                       originator   s-o-q

9.7 Conclusion

The main concern of this chapter has been to investigate the properties of the node EP, and the ways in which ⟨e⟩$_E$ is licensed. We did so by exploring the conditions that allow the occurrence of post-verbal subjects in V1 structures in Hebrew. We specifically stayed away here from unaccusative structures, in which the post-verbal subject in V1 contexts is often argued to be in its base-internal position, as well as from cases in which the post-verbal subject surfaces at the right periphery of the clause, arguably derived through phrasal movement (either of the subject to the right, or of some predicative constituent to the left). Instead, the investigation focused on the licensing of 'external' subjects immediately following the verb in V1 contexts, configurations which have been previously assumed to be ungrammatical in Hebrew (as well as in Italian, for instance). The investigation revealed that in both transitive and intransitive contexts, such 'external' subjects can surface post-verbally in V1 contexts, but only in the presence of a locative clitic. Based on this paradigm, and drawing parallelisms with similar phenomena in Catalan and Spanish, we suggested that the locative allows the occurrence of post-verbal subjects because it assigns range to the value ⟨e⟩$_E$, a role usually assumed by pre-verbal subjects in [Spec, EP]. Semantically, we suggested, such range assignment to ⟨e⟩$_E$ amounts to existentially binding the event argument, again, a role usually achieved through the presence, in [Spec, EP], of an existentially closed (i.e. strong) DP. The role which the locative fulfils in existentially binding the event argument in turn translates into clear ramifications for the DP (post-verbal) subject, allowing it a weak reading, exclusively.

This conclusion, if on the right track, sheds considerable light on the syntactic licensing of event arguments, and suggests strongly that locatives, rather than temporal expressions, are crucial for the licensing of events. In the next chapter, we return to the paradigm first introduced in the beginning of this chapter—that of post-verbal subjects in V1 *unaccusative* contexts. In that case as well, it will turn out that locatives play a crucial role, this time in the licensing of telicity/quantity reading, raising the additional possibility that locatives are one of the crucial building blocks of event structure in general.

10

Slavification and Unaccusatives

10.1 Re-Examining the Paradigm

We concluded in Chapter 9 that locative deictics in Hebrew can function in certain contexts as existential operators binding the event argument. This conclusion provided an answer to questions posed in (66b–c) of Chapter 9, repeated here as (1a–b), in that we now know why locatives, and why weak subjects in V1 contexts with locatives:

(1) a. Why locatives?
 b. And why is the subject obligatorily weak in (2) and similar structures?

(2) a. (ʾamarti še-) ʿabad šam/kan/ecli ganan (ha.yom).
 (I said that) worked here/there/*chez*.me gardener (today)
 b. *(ʾamarti še-) ʿabad šam/kan/ecli ran/ha.ganan (ha.yom).
 (I said that) worked here/there/*chez*.me Ran/the.gardener (today)
 c. (ʾamarti še-) ʿabdu šam/kan/ecli (kama, šloša) gananim
 (I said that) worked here/there/*chez*.me (several, three) gardeners
 (ha.yom).
 (today)
 d. *(ʾamarti še-) ʿabdu šam/kan/ecli kol ha.gananim (ha.yom).
 (I said that) worked here/there/*chez*.me all the.gardeners (today)

However, we must still provide an answer to the following questions (and see Chapter 9, Section 9.1, for a brief discussion of question (3a)):

(3) a. Supposing EP is licensed in (2) and similar configurations by the presence of a locative clitic in E, this still leaves unexplained the licensing of EP in the unaccusative constructions in (4)–(6) where no such locative is in evidence.
 b. How is $[_{Asp_0}\langle e\rangle_\#]$ assigned range in (4)–(5) and in (7)–(8), given the fact that the 'internal' DP is non-quantity but the interpretation is telic?

(4) Sono arrivati studenti. (Italian)
 are arrived students

(5) a. parca mehuma (ha.boqer). (Hebrew)
 erupted.F.SG riot.F.SG (this.morning)

 b. hitxilu hapganot (ha.boqer).
 started.M.PL demonstrations (this.morning)

 c. hopiʿa ʿašan laban ba-šamayim (ha.boqer).
 appeared smoke white in-the.sky (this.morning)

(6) a. parcu šaloš mehumot.
 erupted three riots

 b. hitxilu harbe hapganot.
 started many demonstrations

 c. hopiʿa harbe ʿašan laban ba-šamayim.
 appeared much smoke white in-the.sky

(7) a. The prospectors discovered gold.
 b. The prospectors found rare coins.
 c. Robin found oil.
 d. The prospectors struck oil.
 e. The bulldozer hit bedrock.
 f. Mary noticed ink on her sleeve.
 g. John spotted wildfowl on Saturday.

(8) a. rina gilta zahab. (Hebrew)
 Rina discovered gold

 b. rani maca matbeʿot yeqarim.
 Rina found coins expensive

A closer examination of the unaccusative paradigm reveals, however, that, at least for Hebrew, cases like (5)–(6) are scarce, and are restricted to a subset of mostly achievements. Other classical unaccusative contexts, whether intransitive or passive, pattern rather with unergatives and transitives, in barring V1 contexts, whether the post-verbal subject is bare, weak (but not bare), or strong:

(9) a. *hibšilu šlošet (ha.)tapuxim (ʿal ha.ʿec).
 ripened three (the.)apples (on the.tree)

 b. *hitmotetu (ha.)qirot (be-šabat).
 collapsed (the.)walls (on-Saturday)

c. *nirqab̲ (qcat)   basar (ba-meqarer).
   rotted (a little) meat (in-the.fridge)

d. *qap'u (kol ha.)mayim (ba-layla še-ʿab̲ar).
   froze (all the.)water (last night)

e. *putru   šloša ʿob̲dim (ha.boqer).
   fired.PASS three workers (this.morning)

f. *culma   ('eyze) zebra (ʿal yedey pil)   (ha.boqer).
   photographed.PASS (some) zebra (by an   elephant) (this.morning)

Nor are the achievements in (10) possible in V1 contexts:

(10) a. *nip̲sequ   gšamim (sop̲ sop̲).
        stopped.PL rains   (finally)

b. *nigmeru   (harbe) sukaryot (ba-bayit).
   finished.PL (many) candies   (at-home)

c. *neʿecru   (kama) diyunim   (ba-memšala).
   finished.PL (several) discussions (in-the.government)

d. *histaymu (šaloš) bxinot (ba-universita).
   ended.PL (three) tests   (in-the.university)

It should come as no surprise at this point to find out that at least the ungrammaticality of the examples in (9) is reversed in the presence of a locative deictic clitic, as (11) shows:

(11) a. hib̲šilu po šloša tapuxim (ha.qayic) (tok̲ xamiša šab̲uʿot).
        ripened here three apples   (this.week) (in five weeks)

b. nirqab̲ 'eclenu qcat   basar (ba-meqarer) (tok̲ yomayim).
   rotted *chez*.us a little meat   (in-the.fridge) (in two days)

c. putru šam   ʿasarot ʿob̲dim (ha.boqer)   (tok̲ ʿeser daqot).
   fired.PASS there tens (of) workers (this.morning) (in ten minutes)

d. culma   po zebra (ʿal yedey pil)   (ha.boqer)
   photographed.PASS here zebra (by an elephant) (this.morning)

   (tok̲ xameš daqot).
   (in five minutes)

(12) a. hib̲šilu po tapuxim (ha.qayic)   (tok̲ xamiša šab̲uʿot).
        ripened here apples   (this.summer) (in five weeks)

b. hitmotetu šam qirot (ha.boqer)   (tok̲ šaloš šaʿot).
   collapsed there walls (this.morning) (in three hours)

c. nirqab 'eclenu basar (ba-meqarer) (tok yomayim).
    rotted *chez*.us meat (in-the.fridge) (in two days)

d. qap'u šam mayim (ba-layla še-ʿabar) (tok xaci šaʿa).
    froze there water (last night) (in half an hour)

Emitting a partial sigh of relief, then, we note that at least for the events denoted by (11)–(12), the question in (3a) is no longer relevant. We can assume quite straightforwardly that the deictic locative in (11)–(12) assigns range to $\langle e \rangle_E$ in the now familiar manner, thereby accounting for their contrast in grammaticality with (9). For the resolution of (3a), there remains then only the clearly exceptional nature of range assignment to $\langle e \rangle_E$ in (4)–(6). However, as to (3b), the puzzle of how range is assigned to $[_{Asp_q}\langle e \rangle_\#]$ in (4)–(5) and in (7)–(8) is now augmented by the fact that in (12) telic interpretation is available, as in the case of (4)–(5) and in (7)–(8), without a quantity DP. Things, however, become considerably more complicated before they become simpler.

Locatives, as it turns out, do not improve matters for the achievements in (10). They continue to be ungrammatical, and thus part company not only with the paradigm in (4)–(6), but also with (11)–(12):

(13) a. *nipsequ šam gšamim.
         stopped.PL there rains

     b. *nigmeru kan (harbe) sukaryot.
         finished.PL here (many) candies

     c. *neʿecru 'eclenu (kama) diyunim.
         halted.PL *chez*.us (several) discussions

     d. *histaymu po (šaloš) bxinot.
         ended.PL here (three) tests

What is grammatical, in the context of these specific achievements, are postverbal strong DPs, as shown in (14), which are impossible both in the paradigm in (4)–(6), and in the paradigm in (9).[1]

(14) a. nipsequ ha.gšamim.
         stopped.PL the.rains

     b. nigmeru kol ha.sukaryot.
         finished.PL all the.candies

     c. neʿecru rob ha.diyunim.
         halted.PL most the.discussions

[1] With thanks to I. Landau (pers. comm.) for alerting me to the grammaticality of the examples in (14).

d. histaymu kol ha.bxinot.
ended.PL all the.tests

Achievements, then, as uniformly instantaneous as they might be, come in at least two varieties: the 'permissive' class, in (4)–(6), with which licensing of both $\langle e \rangle_E$ and $[_{Asp_Q}\langle e \rangle_\#]$ is accomplished through yet-to-be determined means, and the 'restrictive' variety in (14), with which a locative does not appear sufficient to assign range to $\langle e \rangle_E$, and instead, a strong subject is required in post-verbal contexts, which could, at least in principle, assign range to both $[_{Asp_Q}\langle e \rangle_\#]$ and $\langle e \rangle_E$ (a matter to which we return in Section 10.3).

But postponing, yet again, the persistently puzzling behaviour of achievements, and focusing on better-behaved events, suppose we stop to consider the assignment of range to $[_{Asp_Q}\langle e \rangle_\#]$ in (11)–(12). We note first that a problem really surfaces only in (12), as the post-verbal subject is non-quantity—that is, a bare plural or mass noun. In (11), a quantity DP is, presumably, available in [Spec, Asp_Q] to assign range to $[_{Asp_Q}\langle e \rangle_\#]$, in the usual way.

Recall now that we already assumed that locatives (specifically, locative adjuncts in English) can assign range to $[_{Asp_Q}\langle e \rangle_\#]$, in which case they are interpreted as delimiters of the event (see Chapter 7, Section 7.3, for discussion). We further assumed that locative particles (in verb-particle constructions) are range assigners to $[_{Asp_Q}\langle e \rangle_\#]$ in combinations such as *take over* and *pair up*. Suppose, then, that the locative clitic in Hebrew may do double duty, assigning range to $[_{Asp_Q}\langle e \rangle_\#]$, possibly as a delimiter, and to $\langle e \rangle_E$ as an existential operator.[2] Such an assumption would boil down to presuming the Slavification of locative clit-

[2] We reject here the possibility that the locative existentially binds both Asp_Q and E, as we have been assuming throughout that existential operators (unlike e.g. generic operators) are not quantity operators, and hence cannot assign range to $\langle e \rangle_\#$, regardless of whether it is dominated by DP or by Asp_Q (and see Volume I, Chapter 5, Section 5.1, as well as Chapter 6, Section 6.3 of this volume for a detailed discussion).

The question here is in fact a more general one, and concerns the possibility of unifying the existential function and the quantity function of locative deictic clitics. We note that it is not at all obvious that such a unification is possible, or even desirable. In English, locative existentials are not implicated in any way in the formation of telic predicates, and locative particles such as *up* and *down*, or adjuncts such as *to the store*, even when they force the projection of Asp_Q, do not have existential force. Likewise, in Slavic, perfective prefixes do not appear to have existential force over the event argument, their locative historical antecedents notwithstanding. Severing the functions, however, would result in attributing to coincidence the dual function of locatives as licensors of both telicity and existential binding, clearly an unfortunate conclusion. It is precisely because of this that one is tempted to assume that the unified function of locatives is as existential operators, with existential force over the event argument, $[_{Asp_Q}\langle e \rangle_\#]$, or both. However, an immediate drawback to this conclusion is the fact that what matters for range assignment to $[_{Asp_Q}\langle e \rangle_\#]$ is not existential closure but quantity, as demonstrated by the fact that *three apples*, even if weak, but not *apples*, can assign range to $[_{Asp_Q}\langle e \rangle_\#]$, the latter being homogeneous and lacking quantity. We leave these matters aside here, noting only that clearly there is much more to be said about the role of locatives and their function in event structure, and that the discussion here can only serve to reveal the tip of this iceberg.

ics not only as range assigners to $\langle e \rangle_E$, but also as range assigners to $[_{Asp_Q}\langle e \rangle_\#]$ (and recall now that historically, the Slavic perfective paradigm is related to locative prepositions). Specifically, let us assume that Hebrew locative clitics, in their role as quasi-functional items, are possible range assigners to both $[_{Asp_Q}\langle e \rangle_\#]$ and $\langle e \rangle_E$. More concretely, suppose a locative clitic may merge either with $[_{Asp_Q}\langle e \rangle_\#]$ or with T (or with some functional head below T but above Asp_Q). In the former case, it can function as a range assigner to $[_{Asp_Q}\langle e \rangle_\#]$, and subsequently, as it is carried to E through verb movement, it may assign range to $\langle e \rangle_E$ as well. When the locative merges above Asp_Q, however, it is of course prevented from assigning range to $[_{Asp_Q}\langle e \rangle_\#]$, but may still assign range to $\langle e \rangle_E$. Setting aside, for a moment, the position of the post-verbal subject, the former derivation is represented in (15a), the latter in (15b):

(15) a. [$_{EP}$ hibšilu.⟨*loc*⟩⟨e⟩$_E$ [$_{TP}$ ~~hibšilu~~.⟨*loc*⟩ [$_{Asp_Q}$ ~~hibšilu~~.⟨*loc*⟩ [$_{Asp_Q}$⟨e⟩$_\#$] [$_{VP}$ ...

b. [$_{EP}$ hibšilu.⟨*loc*⟩⟨e⟩$_E$ [$_{TP}$ ~~hibšilu~~.⟨*loc*⟩ [$_{Asp_Q}$ ~~hibšilu~~   [$_{Asp_Q}$⟨e⟩$_\#$] [$_{VP}$ ...
ripen

In view of this, let us consider first the paradigm in (11). As it turns out, both structures in (15a–b) are, at least in principle, available for derivations with a quantity, post-verbal DP, as depicted in (16a–b):

(16) a. [$_{EP}$ hibšilu.⟨*loc*⟩⟨e⟩$_E$ [$_{TP}$ šloša tapuxim ~~hibšilu~~.⟨*loc*⟩

[$_{Asp_Q}$ ~~šloša tapuxim hibšilu~~.⟨*loc*⟩[$_{Asp_Q}$⟨e⟩$_\#$] [$_{VP}$ ....

b. [$_{EP}$ hibšilu.⟨*loc*⟩⟨e⟩$_E$ [$_{TP}$ šloša tapuxim ~~hibšilu~~.⟨*loc*⟩
ripen   three apples

[$_{Asp_Q}$ ~~šloša tapuxim hibšilu~~ [$_{Asp_Q}$⟨e⟩$_\#$] [$_{VP}$ ....

Suppose we consider these derivations in turn. Range assignment in (16a) for both $[_{Asp_Q}\langle e \rangle_\#]$ and $\langle e \rangle_E$ is by assumption accomplished through the locative. *Three apples* moves to [Spec,TP] to be assigned nominative case, where it also comes under the jurisdiction of the locative, as an existential binder, through specifier–head agreement, requiring it to be weak. There is, then, nothing unusual about the derivation in (16a), although one point is worth noting. Recall that we argued in Chapter 6, Section 6.3 that Slavic quantificational prefixes, assigning range to Asp_Q, obligatorily give rise to the copying of #P onto the DP in [Spec, Asp_Q], thereby blocking a bare mass or plural DPs in that position. In turn, we also suggested that some value within the DP in [Spec, Asp$_Q$] in Slavic must remain open, so as to allow the agreement between that specifier and the quantificational prefix in Asp$_Q$ to be instantiated, in this case though indirect range assignment by the quantificational prefix to some open value within the DP specifier. Consider, however, Hebrew locatives in their function as Slavified affixes. Although by assumption they can assign range to [$_{Asp_Q}$ ⟨e⟩$_\#$], they are clearly not quantificational in nature. We will thus assume that range assignment to [$_{DP}$ ⟨e⟩$_\#$], imposed by the quantificational nature of Slavic quantificational prefixes, does not take place in the case of locative clitics. It nevertheless remains the case that the locative clitic, a range assigner to [$_{Asp_Q}$ ⟨e⟩$_\#$], by assumption must assign range to some value of the DP in [Spec, Asp$_Q$] by specifier–head agreement. It follows that for the structure in (16a), the DP in [Spec, Asp$_Q$] may not be strong, or no such open value would be available. It thus emerges that the post-verbal subject in derivations such as those in (1 6a) is weak not only because of specifier–head agreement with a locative existential binder, but also because it has a copy in [Spec, Asp$_Q$], and is therefore required to be weak by the presence of a direct quantificational range assigner to [$_{Asp_Q}$ ⟨e⟩$_\#$]. The reader may recall that a similar restriction was attested in Slavic, where quantified DPs in perfective contexts received, obligatorily, a weak interpretation (and see Chapter 6, section 6.3 for discussion).[3]

Little beyond that needs to be said about the derivation in (16b). We note that here range is assigned to [$_{Asp_Q}$ ⟨e⟩$_\#$] by the DP itself, and hence the DP is not required to be weak (but is required to be quantity, of course). However, given the post-verbal status of this DP in the presence of a locative existential range assigner to ⟨e⟩$_E$, and given the specifier–head agreement between such a DP and the locative existential range assigner in TP, the DP is independently required to be weak. The sentences returned by the derivations in (16a–b) are thus predicted, for the paradigm in (11), to have effectively indistinguishable properties.

Consider, however, a third possibility. Suppose the locative deictic clitic merges with the verb above Asp$_Q$, as in (15b), leaving the quantity DP in [Spec, Asp$_Q$] to assign range to [$_{Asp_Q}$ ⟨e⟩$_\#$]. Suppose now that the DP in [Spec, Asp$_Q$] does not move to [Spec, TP], but rather, stays in [Spec, Asp$_Q$]. No special assumptions are needed concerning the assignment of nominative case, as a mechanism such as I-Subject (cf. Borer, 1986) or *Agree* (cf. Chomsky 2000) could assign nominative

---

[3] As within the unergative paradigm, in the presence of a pre-verbal strong subject we must assume that at least the existential range assignment properties to ⟨e⟩$_E$ of the locative are inert. If the construction is telic and intransitive, then when the subject is strong (or even just quantity), the locative, quite possibly, does not assign range to [$_{Asp_Q}$ ⟨e⟩$_\#$] either. Thus it is only in the presence of post-verbal subjects or in the presence of a non-quantity DP subject which cannot, by assumption, assign range to [$_{Asp_Q}$ ⟨e⟩$_\#$], that the existential function of the locative deictic clitic must be instantiated.

case to a DP in [Spec, Asp$_Q$], within intransitive configurations such as those in (11), in an entirely straightforward way; see (17).

(17) [$_{EP}$ hib̠šilu.⟨*loc*⟩⟨e⟩$_E$ [$_{TP}$ ~~hib̠šilu.⟨*loc*⟩~~ [$_{Asp_Q}$ šloša tapuxim ~~hib̠šilu~~ [$_{Asp_Q}$⟨e⟩$_{\#}$] [$_{VP}$ ...
      ripened   three apples
                                      NOM by *Agree*

When compared to the derivations in (16a–b), however, the derivation in (17) does have one important distinct property. In (16a), recall, the post-verbal subject had to be weak, both by restrictions on [Spec, Asp$_Q$] in the presence of direct range assignment to [$_{Asp_Q}$⟨e⟩$_{\#}$], and restrictions on [Spec, TP] in the presence of an existential direct range assigner to ⟨e⟩$_E$. In (16b), on the other hand, the post-verbal subject had to be weak only due to the presence of existential direct range assignment to ⟨e⟩$_E$. However, in (17), neither set of restrictions is expected to hold. At no point of the derivation is the DP in [Spec, Asp$_Q$] in agreement relations with any direct range assigner, existential, quantificational, or otherwise, and the prediction is that it should be able to be strong. Put differently, we predict that the paradigm in (11), involving a post-verbal subject in an unaccusative context with a deictic clitic, should have a correlate which involves a strong DP in post-verbal position. This prediction is correct, as the grammaticality of (18) clearly shows:

(18) a. hib̠šilu kan/šam/eclenu ha.tapuxim (tok̠ šloša šabuʿot)/
     ripened here/there/*chez*.us the.apple (in three weeks)/
     (ha.qayic).
     (this.summer)
  b. qap'u eclenu kol ha.mayim (bin layla).
     froze *chez*.us all the.water (in one-night)
  c. nišxat šam kol ha.yebul (tok̠ šloša šabuʿot)/
     destroyed.INTRANS there all the.harvest (in three weeks)/
     (ha.šana).
     (this.year)

What is worth noting is that in contrast with the telic intransitives in (18), the derivation in (17) is excluded for intransitive atelic structures, barring absolutely strong DPs in post-verbal positions in unergative contexts regardless of the occurrence of a locative clitic, a fact already discussed at length in Chapter 9, and illustrated by the paradigm in (2). In unergative structures, note, there is no functional specifier that can host the post-verbal subject without giving rise to agreement with the existential locative, and hence requiring the subject to be weak. Specifically, recall that F^{s}P, the node we postulated to assign partitive structural case to objects of atelic transitive constructions, is only licensed in the presence of partitive case assignment, and hence does not come under the jurisdiction of *Agree*, and a DP in its specifier cannot receive nominative case (see Chapter 4, Section 4.2, for discussion). Not so for Asp$_Q$, which is semantically licensed, and which may occur without the assignment of accusative case to its specifier, and in fact routinely does in unaccusative constructions.

Returning now to the original puzzles associated with the properties of post-verbal subjects, we have now reached conclusions which at first sight contradict much of what has been assumed about the properties of these cases. If the discussion here is on the right track, then it is in unergative (and transitive) contexts that the post-verbal subject in V1 configurations must be weak, while in unaccusatives, as (18) illustrates, it may be strong! We further note that the derivation in (17) presents no problems whatsoever for the list of questions in (3), as it involves the assignment of range to Asp$_Q$ by a quantity DP (whether weak or strong) and the assignment of range to $\langle e \rangle_E$ by the locative deictic clitic. It further emerges that while the paradigms in (4)–(6), as well as the paradigm in (14) must still be explained, they do not represent the generalization concerning the distribution of post-verbal subjects in V1 contexts, but rather, the exception. In the majority of cases, be they unergative, transitive or unaccusative, post-verbal subjects in V1 contexts are licensed by an overt locative. There is, then, something special about (4)–(6) and (14), which is in need of a special explanation.

Consider now the paradigm in (12). By assumption, as the DP under consideration here is non-quantity, it cannot assign range to $[_{Asp_Q}\langle e \rangle_\#]$. It therefore follows that neither derivation (16b) nor derivation (17) are available, as in such cases there is no range assignment to $[_{Asp_Q}\langle e \rangle_\#]$. The only derivation available for non-quantity DPs, then, is that in (16a). Here, range is assigned as required to both $[_{Asp_Q}\langle e \rangle_\#]$ and to $\langle e \rangle_E$ by the locative. In turn, the DP in [Spec, Asp$_Q$] need not be quantity. Quantity DP is not required to assign range to $[_{Asp_Q}\langle e \rangle_\#]$, nor is a quantity interpretation imposed by the locative clitic assigning range to $[_{Asp_Q}\langle e \rangle_\#]$, as the locative clitic is not quantificational in nature. It therefore follows that precisely in these cases, we have a particular kind of violation of Verkuyl's generalization: there is, indeed, a direct object, but it does not have any quantity properties (nor is it +SQA, in the sense of Verkuyl 1972 and subsequent work, or *quantized*, in the sense of Krifka 1992).

It is worth recalling, in this context, that in Slavic, bare DPs in [Spec, Asp$_Q$] always receive a strong interpretation, a matter discussed at some length in Chapter 6, Section 6.3. We derived this effect by assuming that perfective prefixes copy #P onto the DP in [Spec, Asp$_Q$], and then proceed to assign range both to $\langle e \rangle_d$ and to $[_{DP}\langle e \rangle_\#]$, thereby giving rise to a strong interpretation. In contrast, we already suggested that there is no reason to assume such copying of ⟨e⟩# in the case of non-quantificational, albeit Slavified Hebrew locative clitics. As a result, the structures remain non-quantity, and the requirement that the locative clitic assign range to some open value within the DP in [Spec, Asp_Q] is met through the assignment of range to ⟨e⟩_d, thereby existentially binding it and giving rise to a weak, non-quantity DP. The emerging (relevant) structure for the Asp_Q node is in (19) (and see Volume I, Chapter 5, Section 5.1, for the relevant discussion of the internal structure of non-quantity DPs):

(19) [_Asp_Q [_DP ⟨e⟩_d [_CL tapuxim [_N ...]]] hib̲šilu ⟨*loc*⟩ ⟨e⟩#]
              apples   ripen

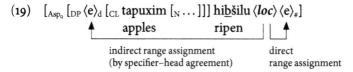

indirect range assignment   direct
(by specifier–head agreement)   range assignment

The differences between Slavic and Hebrew crystallize, we assume, around the distinct functional properties of quantity prefixes in Slavic, on the one hand, and the locative/existential properties of locative deictic clitics in Hebrew, on the other hand. Quantity prefixes require the DP in their specifier to have a #P, but not so locative deictic clitics, which are not quantificational in nature. In turn, this difference makes clear predictions concerning transitive derivations. If indeed the derivation in (19) is a licit one, with direct range assignment by a deictic clitic to [_Asp_Q ⟨e⟩#], alongside a non-quantity DP in [Spec, Asp_Q], there is little reason to assume that the effects of (12) should not replicate themselves for direct objects which are non-quantity, in this very context of [_Asp_Q ⟨e⟩#] being licensed through a locative clitic. We thus predict that while (20) should denote atelic, non-quantity events, (21) should allow a telic interpretation, in spite of the non-quantity nature of the direct object. The judgements, while subtle, confirm these predictions (all grammaticality judgements associated with a single event reading):

(20) a. michal katb̲a širim   (bemešek̲ šloša šab̲uot/*tok̲ šloša šab̲uʿot).
          Michal wrote poems   (for three weeks/*in three weeks)
      b. rina šatla   vradim (bemešek̲ šloša šab̲uot/*tok̲ šloša šab̲uʿot).
          Rina planted roses   (for three weeks/*in three weeks)
      c. ran limed šira   ʿib̲rit (bemešek̲ šloša yamim/*tok̲ šloša yamim).
          Ran taught poetry Hebrew (for three days/*in three days)

(21) a. michal katb̲a šam širim (bemešek̲ šloša šab̲uʿot/tok̲ šloša šab̲uot).
          Michal wrote there poems (for three weeks/in three weeks)
      b. rina šatla   eclenu vradim (bemešek̲ šaloš šaʿot/tok̲ šaloš šaʿot).
          Rina planted *chez*.us roses (for three hours/in three hours)

c. ran limed kan šira ʕibrit (bemešek šloša yamim/
   Ran taught here poetry Hebrew (for three days/
   tok šloša yamim).
   in three days

Other tests confirm the telicity of (21) when contrasted with (20). Suppose we assume, following the discussion in Piñon (2000), that an adverb such as *gradually*, or its Hebrew correlate, *be-hadraga*, is an indicator of a predicate being scalar, and that this property is necessary (but not sufficient) for quantity predicates to emerge, as discussed in Chapter 5, Section 5.4. We now note that the presence of a locative clitic is crucial for the licensing of *gradually*, as (22)–(23) show:

(22) a. michal katba širim (*be-hadraga).
        Michal wrote poems (*gradually)

   b. ran limed šira ʕibrit (*be-hadraga).
      Ran taught poetry Hebrew (*gradually)

(23) a. michal katba šam širim (be-hadraga).
        Michal wrote there poems (gradually)

   b. ran limed kan šira ʕibrit (be-hadraga).
      Ran taught here poetry Hebrew (gradually)

Likewise, the construal of the coordinated events in (24) as non-simultaneous is difficult, while such construal is straightforward in (25):

(24) a. rina šatla vradim ve-diqlema širim.
        Rina planted roses and-recited poems

   b. ran limed šira ʕibrit ve-katab proza gruʕa.
      Ran taught poetry Hebrew and-wrote prose bad
      'Ran taught Hebrew poetry and wrote bad prose.'

(25) a. rina šatla šam vradim ve-diqlema šam širim (tok šaloš šaʕot).
        Rina planted there roses and-recited there poems (in three hours)

   b. ran limed po šira ʕibrit ve-katab po proza gruʕa
      Ran taught here poetry Hebrew and-wrote here prose bad
      (tok šbuʕayim).
      (in two weeks)
      'Ran taught here Hebrew poetry and wrote here bad prose in two weeks.'

Note that in (21), (23), and (25) the locative *must* be a range assigner to $[_{Asp_o} \langle e \rangle_{\#}]$, as the DP is non-quantity. In turn, the subject-of-quantity, for instance, *vradim* 'roses', must be weak, as the deictic clitic must assign range to $\langle e \rangle_d$. The emerging structure for (21), (23), and (25) is thus as in (26) (TP structure omitted for expository reasons; arrows indicate range assignment):

(26)

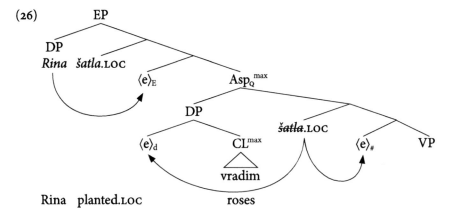

While the locative in (26) assigns range to $[_{Asp_Q}\langle e\rangle_\#]$, note, we cannot assume that it assigns range to $\langle e\rangle_E$, as in these cases we have a pre-verbal strong subject. It therefore follows that the locative assigns range to $[_{Asp_Q}\langle e\rangle_\#]$ and existentially binds the argument in [Spec, Asp_Q], but must remain existentially inert when it comes to range assignment to $\langle e\rangle_E$.

It now turns out that (12), on the one hand, and (21), (23), and (25), on the other, exhibit precisely the property attributed by Mittwoch (1991) to achievements, as exemplified by English (7) and Hebrew (8), in that they allow a quantity interpretation in the presence of a non-quantity object. But at least according to commonly used criteria, (12), (21), (23) and (25) are accomplishments, rather than achievements, and their interpretation in the presence of a locative carries no implication of instantaneity. I will argue directly below, in Sections 10.2 and 10.3, that the type of achievements discussed by Mittwoch (1991) are complex expressions which include an existential operator. Insofar as such an account is workable, it extends directly to the properties of (12), (21), (23), and (25). It does leave open, however, one interesting question: assuming that Slavic perfective prefixes require the copying of #P onto the DP in their specifier, but Hebrew Slavified locatives do not, and noting the fact that perfective prefixes, historically, are derived from locative prepositions, we must wonder at what point locatives lose their existential/delimiting function, and become quantificational in nature. And finally, does such a transition depend on the nature of the determiner system in the grammar under consideration, sensitive, specifically, to the presence vs. absence of articles (Slavic and Hebrew, respectively)? These questions, however, must await future research. Before we turn to the renewed discussion of remaining issues, Table 10.1 (p. 318) summarizes the event types discussed thus far with their properties.

TABLE 10.1. Event types and their properties

		Intransitive-atelic (unergative)	Transitive, telic	Intransitive, telic (unaccusative)		
				hibšil class 'ripen'	*parac* class 'erupt'	*nigmar* class 'finish'
Without locative		*V-SUBJ (cf. (2))	*V-SUBJ (cf. Chapter 9, (95))	*V-SUBJ (cf. (9))	V-SUBJ	V-SUBJ
	Post-verbal subject	*Strong (cf. (2b)) weak/bare (cf. (2a))	*Strong (cf. Chapter 9 (96d–e)) weak/bare (cf. Chapter 9, (96a–c))		*Strong (cf. Chapter 9, (4)) weak/bare (cf. (4)–(6))	Strong (cf. (14)) *weak/bare (cf. (13))
	Direct object	n/a	Quantity *non-quantity (bare) (cf. (20))	n/a	n/a	n/a
With locative		V-SUBJ	V-SUBJ	V-SUBJ	V-SUBJ	V-SUBJ
	Post-verbal subject	*Strong (cf. (2b)) weak/bare (cf. (2a))	*Strong (cf. Chapter 9 (96d–e)) weak/bare (cf. Chapter 9, (96a–c))	Strong (cf. (18)) weak/bare (cf. (11)–(12))	*Strong weak/bare (cf. (29))	Strong (cf. (52)) *weak/bare
	Direct object	n/a	Quantity/non-quantity (cf. (21))	n/a	n/a	n/a

Note: Shaded boxes indicate paradigms that are still in need of explanation.

10.2 And Returning to Erupting Riots

It is time to return to the original paradigm in (4)–(6), repeated here:

(4)   Sono arrivati studenti.   (Italian)
      are   arrived   students

(5) a. parca   mehuma (ha.boqer).   (Hebrew)
        erupted.F.SG riot.F.SG (this.morning)
    b. hitxilu   hapganot   (ha.boqer).
        started.M.PL   demonstrations (this.morning)
    c. hopiʿa   ʿašan laban ba-šamayim (ha.boqer).
        appeared smoke white in-the.sky   (this.morning)

(6) a. parcu   šaloš mehumot.
        erupted   three riots
    b. hitxilu   harbe hapganot.
        started   many   demonstrations
    c. hopiʿa   harbe ʿašan laban ba-šamayim.
        appeared much smoke white in-the.sky

The relevant, puzzling properties of the paradigm are summarized in (27):

(27) a. There is no apparent range assigner to $\langle e \rangle_E$ in (4)–(6).
     b. There is no apparent range assigner to $[_{Asp_Q}\langle e \rangle_\#]$ in (4)–(5).

More specifically, I suggested that when the subject is post-verbal (in unergative, transitive, and unaccusative structures), a locative is required to assign range to $\langle e \rangle_E$, as in (18), for example. In (4)–(6), however, the subject is post-verbal, but a locative is not available. Further, I suggested that when the DP in [Spec, Asp_Q] is non-quantity, range to $[_{Asp_Q}\langle e \rangle_\#]$ could still be assigned by a Slavified locative, as in (12a) and (25a), giving rise to a quantity interpretation without a quantity DP. However, in (4)–(5) a quantity reading emerges without a quantity DP and without a Slavified locative.

To the puzzling properties in (27) we may add one more. Recall that for V1 quantity intransitive structures, the configuration in (28) was licit, giving rise to a strong post-verbal subject in V1, telic contexts (cf. (18) and related discussion):

(28) $[_{EP} V.\langle loc \rangle \langle e \rangle_E [_{TP} V.\langle loc \rangle [_{Asp_Q} DP_{strong} V [_{Asp_Q}\langle e \rangle_\#] [_{VP} \ldots$

But in contrast with the paradigm in (18), the addition of a locative to (5)–(6) has no effect whatsoever on the obligatory weakness of the post-verbal subject; see (29).

(29) a. parca   kan/šam/eclenu   (*ha.)mehuma (ha.boqer).
       erupted here/there/*chez*.us (*the.)riot   (this.morning)

   b. hitxilu kan/šam/eclenu   (*kol ha.)hapganot   (ha.boqer).
      started here/there/*chez*.us (*all the.)demonstrations (this.morning)

   c. hopiʿa   kan/šam/eclenu   (*ha.)ʿašan (*ha.)laban ba-šamayim
      appeared here/there/*chez*.us (*the.)smoke (*the.)white in-the.sky
      (ha.boqer).
      (this.morning)

When viewed from a different angle, however, note that in all relevant respects, short of the overt occurrence of a locative, the paradigm (4)–(6) behaves exactly on a par with (12):

(12) a. hibšilu po   tapuxim (ha.qayic)   (tok xamiša šabuʿot).
       ripened here apples (this.summer) (in five weeks)

   b. hitmotetu šam qirot (ha.boqer)   (tok šaloš šaʿot).
      collapsed there walls (this.morning) (in three hours)

   c. nirqab ʾeclenu basar (ba-meqarer) (tok yomayim.
      rotted *chez*.us meat (in-the.fridge) (in two days)

   d. qapʾu šam mayim (ba-layla še-ʿabar) (tok xaci šaʿa).
      froze there water (last night)   (in half an hour)

Suppose we review the structure for (12) (and cf. (15a) and (16a)):

(30)

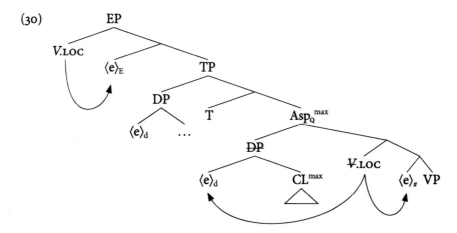

The relevant properties of the structure in (30) are summarized in (31).

(31) a. V1 structure.
   b. The DP in [Spec, Asp$_Q$] must be weak.
   c. The DP in [Spec, TP] must be weak.
   d. Quantity interpretation is available without a quantity DP.

But these are precisely the properties of the paradigm in (4)–(6). It thus emerges that (4)–(6) behave as if they have a locative assigning range to both $\langle e \rangle_E$ and [$_{Asp_Q}\langle e \rangle_\#$], although no such overt locative is in evidence.

A similar correlation holds between the transitive cases discussed by Mittwoch (1991), as in (7)–(8) (repeated here together with telicity tests) and cases of transitives with overt locatives, as in (21) repeated here. In both cases, we find a quantity reading without a quantity DP (cf. structure (26)):

(32) a. The prospectors discovered gold and found rare coins.
   b. The prospectors found rare coins and discovered gold.
   c. Robin found oil on Monday and on Tuesday (requires two events).
   d. The prospectors struck oil on Saturday and on Sunday (two events).
   e. The bulldozer hit bedrock on Saturday and on Sunday (two events).
   f. Mary noticed ink on her sleeve on Saturday and on Sunday (two events).
   g. John spotted wildfowl on Saturday and on Sunday (two events).

(33)   rina gilta   zahab ve-mac'a matbeʿot yeqarim.
       Rina discovered gold and-found coins   expensive

(21) a. michal katba šam širim (bemešek šloša šabuʿot/tok šloša šabuot).
       Michal wrote there poems (for three weeks/in three weeks)
   b. rina šatla   eclenu vradim (bemešek šaloš šaʿot/tok šaloš šaʿot).
       Rina planted *chez*.us roses (for three hours/in three hours)
   c. ran limed kan šira   ʿibrit   (bemešek šloša yamim/tok šloša
      Ran taught here poetry Hebrew (for three days/in three

      yamim).
      days

In view of the clear similar properties of (4)–(6) and (12), on the one hand, and (7)–(8), (32)–(33) and (21) on the other hand, it appears extremely promising to assume that they all contain a covert locative, which functions exactly on a par with its overt counterpart in (12) and (21), assigning range to $\langle e \rangle_E$ in (4)–(6), and to [$_{Asp_Q}\langle e \rangle_\#$] in (4)–(8), (32)–(33).

Note now that all the (internal) DPs in (4)–(8), (32)–(33) emerge in the discourse as a direct result of the event involved. Thus, in some important sense, they are all presentational. It is worthwhile noting that this is clearly *not* the case for the achievements in (14), which are not presentational, but rather, tend to have a presupposed argument. We note further that the events in (4)–(8), (32)–(33) have a strong locative interpretation, in assigning a particular location to the emerging DP. The presence of a covert locative/existential, on a par with overt deictic locatives is thus independently plausible. In terms of execution, suppose we assume that the verbs occurring in (4)–(8), (32)–(33) are all idioms, in the technical sense discussed in Chapter 1, Section 1.4. Specifically, I suggested that idioms are listemes with partial subcategorization, consisting of (adjacent) functional open values, at times with fixed range assigners, and that these open values force the projection of a specific syntactic structure which is interpreted and realized in accordance with the independent interpretative formulas that otherwise apply to it. Thus, for instance, a *pluralia tantum* expression such as *trousers* is the phonological realization of an idiom which consists of the phonological index of *trouser*, together with the functional range assignment $\langle e^\alpha \rangle$, with $\langle e \rangle$ an open value that can only be assigned range by a (non-singular) $\langle div \rangle$, as in (34a). The representation in (34a) (where π_3 is the phonological index, *trouser*) gives rise to the structure in (34b), where the merger of the head feature $\langle div \rangle$ is necessary to assign range to $\langle e \rangle$, thus giving rise to a 'plural' marked form:

(34) a. TROUSERS ⇔ $[\pi_3 + \langle e^{div} \rangle]$
 b. $[_{\text{DIV}}$ trouser.$\langle div \rangle \langle e^{div} \rangle [_N \text{~~trouser~~}]] \rightarrow$ /trauzerz/

Suppose now that likewise, Hebrew *parac*, 'erupt' as well as its English correlate project as $[_{\text{Asp}_Q} \langle e^{loc/\exists} \rangle_{\#} [_{\text{L-D}} erupt]]$, that is, accompanied by the open value $\langle e^{loc/\exists} \rangle_{\#}$. An abstract head feature, $\langle loc/\exists \rangle$, now assigns range directly to $\langle e^{loc/\exists} \rangle_{\#}$, rather on a par with its Hebrew overt, possibly prepositional counterpart. In turn, the phonology returns, for V.$\langle loc/\exists \rangle$, in these cases, a representation which is indistinct from that of the original phonological index—that is, the instantiation of the head feature $\langle loc/\exists \rangle$ is phonologically covert, and the instantiation of the phonological index as a bare verb is paradigmatically missing. The relevant representation for Hebrew *parac*, 'erupt' and for English *notice*, for example, are in (35):[4]

---

[4] Note that we are assuming that the locative–existential which assigns range to $[_{\text{Asp}_Q} \langle e^{loc/\exists} \rangle_{\#}]$ is a head feature, rather than an f-morph, and that, as such, it is distinct from the overt deictic locative in Hebrew, or from particles in verb-particle constructions which likewise merge to assign range to a 'named' open value, as in (i) (see Chapter 7, Section 7.3.2. for discussion):

(i) a. $[_{\text{Asp}_Q}$ up $\langle e^{up} \rangle [_{\text{L-D}}$ pair $\langle e^{up} \rangle]]$
 b. $[_{\text{Asp}_Q}$ over $\langle e^{over} \rangle [_{\text{L-D}}$ take $\langle e^{over} \rangle]]$

(35) a. PARAC ⇔ $[\pi_5 + \langle e^{loc/\exists}\rangle_\#]$
     b. NOTICE ⇔ $[\pi_2 + \langle e^{loc/\exists}\rangle_\#]$
     c. $[_{Asp_Q} \text{parac.}\langle loc/\exists\rangle\ \langle e^{loc/\exists}\rangle_\# [_V \text{ parac}]]$ → parac
     c. $[_{Asp_Q} \text{notice.}\langle loc/\exists\rangle\ \langle e^{loc/\exists}\rangle_\# [_V \text{ notice}]]$ → notice

We now note that as the combination *parac.⟨loc/∃⟩* moves to E (cf. structure (30)) for the derivation for an overt locative, it also is in a position to assign range to ⟨e⟩_E, making the derivation of (4)–(6) an exact parallel to that of (12).

The proposal that some verbs include a 'lexicalization' of a preposition is not new—it was made by Talmy (1985, 2000). That some of these lexicalizations have an aspectual impact is not new either, having been discussed by Higginbotham (2000*b*), who proposes that the possibility of incorporating a prepositional, delimiting meaning into a lexical verb constitutes a semantic parameter distinguishing languages. The proposal that a locative preposition may incorporate into a verb resulting in an existential interpretation is specifically argued for in Mateu and Rigau (2000), to characterize the Catalan locative *hi* already discussed in Chapter 9, Section 9.3.2, (see (47)–(49) and related discussion). Adopting the spirit of these proposals, although not their execution, we will assume that the 'incorporation' in question is the association of an empty functional value with a listeme, giving rise to the obligatory merger of a head feature which assigns range to that empty value, much on a par with other idioms. In turn, whatever language variation we may find will depend on the nature of the range assigner to the empty value, which may be an abstract head feature which is not phonologically realized, an abstract head feature which is phonologically realized, or alternatively, an f-morph, as in the case of English verb-particle constructions. As such, it is intra-language variation, rather than inter-language variation (contra Higginbotham 2000*b*, and see also Mateu and Rigau, op. cit. for a similar claim).

Consider now, in this context, the grammaticality of (36)–(38):

(36) a. Kim discovered the gold.
     b. The prospectors found the oil.
     c. Mary noticed the ink on her sleeve.
     c. John spotted the wildfowl on the tree.

The failure of the abstract head feature ⟨*loc/∃*⟩ to be phonologically realized in the context of *parac* or *notice* is now exactly on a par with the failure of other abstract head features to be phonologically realized, e.g. the past tense of forms such as English *put* or the plurality of *fish* and *sheep*.

For some general discussion of the status of specifications such as those in (35) in a model that attributes no formal grammatical features to listemes, see the discussion in Chapter 11, Section 11.2. For a discussion of the relationship between idioms, in the sense used here, and paradigm gaps, see Borer (forthcoming).

(37) a. ran gila 'et ha.zahab.
Ran discovered OM the.gold

b. dina mac'a 'et ha.nept.
Dina discovered OM the.oil

(38) a. ha.mehumot parcu ba-boqer.
the.riots erupted in-the.morning

b. ha.ʿašan ha.laban hopiʿa be-šaʿa 'arba.
the.smoke the.white appeared at 4pm

c. ha.hapganot hitxilu sop sop.
the.demonstrations started finally

If indeed verbs such as English *notice* and *find*, and Hebrew *parac* 'erupt' and *hitxil* 'start' are idioms containing a phonologically unrealized locative always assigning range to $[_{Asp_Q}\langle e\rangle_{\#}]$, and at times possibly also to $\langle e\rangle_E$, how can the direct object in (36)–(37) and the subject in (38) be strong? The answer here, I suggest, is actually different for each case. Specifically, suppose that for the cases in (36)–(38), the incorporation of ⟨*loc*/∃⟩ is optional, and that the phonological indices *discover, find, spot*, etc. exist as bare verb stems as well. If this is correct, we predict the idiomatized uses to differ in meaning from the non-idiomatized ones precisely along the ⟨*loc*/∃⟩ lines, and indeed, it is entirely clear that the events implicated in (36)–(37) are rather different from those implicated in (7)–(8), in that they do not bring about the creation, or the emergence into the discourse, of the relevant object DP denotation, nor is the DP in [Spec, Asp$_Q$] existentially bound (perforce). To illustrate, if the prospectors found the oil, that oil has already been found before, in the sense of emergence, but was hidden and re-revealed by the prospector's search. The contrast is particularly clear for (7d, e), where the presence of a strong DP object radically changes the nature of the event, and is incongruous under either emergence or re-emergence reading:

(39) a. The prospectors struck the oil on Saturday.
b. The bulldozer hit the bedrock on Saturday.

Consider now (38). Here, the denotations of the DPs under consideration, although brought into existence by the event in some sense, are nevertheless presupposed to the extent that the events are clearly anticipated in some sense. Nevertheless, we must assume that the verbs under consideration do involve the obligatory projection of ⟨*loc*/∃⟩. If such a projection were optional here, we would predict that when ⟨*loc*/∃⟩ does not project, such verbs would behave exactly on a par with the paradigm (11)–(12), (17)–(18), ruling in, specifically, the paradigm in (29) with the derivation in (28) with a strong direct object, contrary to fact. We must then assume that for (38), range to [$_{Asp_Q}$⟨e⟩$_#$] continues to be assigned by ⟨*loc*/∃⟩. But the subject in (38) is strong. If we were to assume that it merged a copy in [Spec,Asp$_Q$], the derivation would be predicted ungrammatical, contrary to fact, either because [$_{Asp_Q}$⟨e⟩$_#$] is doubly marked (directly by a locative existential, indirectly through specifier–head agreement), or, alternatively, because the existential locative has clearly failed to assign range to any value within the DP in [Spec, Asp$_Q$]. Any merger of a copy of a strong DP in [Spec, Asp$_Q$], then, is predicted ungrammatical here.

As it turns out, however, there is no particular need for the subject in (38) to merge a copy in [Spec, Asp$_Q$]. Rather, it could merge its lowest copy, and thus be categorized, in [Spec,TP], a configuration already argued to be licit for telic intransitives in Slavic, where a quantity interpretation is available without a DP in [Spec, Asp$_Q$], in violation of Verkuyl's generalization (see Chapter 7 for discussion). That the subject in (38) need not be weak thus follows both from the fact that ⟨*loc*/∃⟩ need not assign range to the event argument in the presence of a strong subject, as well as from the fact that none of the copies of the subject in (38) were ever in specifier–head relations with an active ⟨*loc*/∃⟩ or within its c-command domain. The derivation of (38) is thus as in (40):[5]

(40) [$_{EP}$ DP$_{strong}$ V.⟨*loc*⟩⟨e⟩$_E$ [$_{TP}$ V̶.⟨*loc*⟩ [$_{Asp_Q}$ V̶ [$_{Asp_Q}$⟨e⟩$_#$] [$_{VP}$ ...

It should come as no surprise at this point, then, that precisely the strong preverbal subjects in (38) should bar possessive dative, as illustrated by the contrast in (41)–(42):

(41) a. ??ha.ᶜašan hop̱ica   le-dani.
          the.smoke appeared to-Dani
          'The smoke appeared, affecting Dani/at Dani's.'

      b. ??ha-mehuma parca   le-rina.
          the riot   erupted   to-Rina
          'The riot erupted, affecting Rina/at Rina's.'

---

[5] Although the optionality vs. obligatoriness of the covert locative seems to cluster here around the transitive/intransitive paradigm, at least one verb in Hebrew appears to be intransitive, but have an optional, rather than obligatory covert locative, namely *nap̱al* 'fall'. Thus, like *parac* 'erupt' or *hopiᶜa*, 'appear' it allows a post-verbal weak subject without an overt locative, as in (ia), but unlike *parac* and *hopiᶜa*, and like e.g. *hiḇšil*, 'ripen', it allows a strong post-verbal subject in the presence of an overt locative, as in (ib):

(i)   a. nap̱lu (*ha.)'aḇanim.
          fell   (*the.)stones

      b. nap̱lu šam (ha.)'aḇanim.
          fell there (the.)stones

(42) a. hopica   le-dani ʿašan.
       appeared to-Dani smoke
       'Smoke appeared at Dani's/smoke appeared affecting Dani.'
    b. parca   le-rina mehuma.
       erupted to-Rina riot
       'A riot erupted affecting Rina/a riot erupted at Rina's.'

10.3 Achievements?

Following original insights in Dowty (1979), it is often proposed that the relationship between accomplishments and achievements should be defined in terms of compositionality. Dowty (1979) specifically proposes that accomplishments are essentially a CAUSE predicate added to an achievement, the latter being a BECOME predicate. Under other proposals, challenging specifically the need for accomplishments to have a CAUSE, accomplishments are a development plus a culmination, but achievements are culminations without a development, hence accounting for their perceived instantaneity. A recent proposal put forth (but not executed in detail) in Rothstein (2000b) is that accomplishments consist of an ACTIVITY event, fundamentally homogeneous in the familiar sense, and an extended BECOME event which imposes structure, so to speak, on the homogeneous ACTIVITY. Crucially, these events are not linearly or causally ordered. Possibly, Rothstein suggests, achievements should be viewed as the BECOME event without an ACTIVITY component.

Note now that from the perspective of the account proposed here, quantity events, whether they fall under Vendler's accomplishment or achievement class, are not compositional. They are not segmented into a development part and a resulting state, or a culmination, nor are they segmented into CAUSE event and CAUSED event, however described. Rather, quantity events are distinguished from non-quantity events by having internally quantifiable divisions. It is thus clear that any account which distinguishes between accomplishments and achievements, both quantity events, based on the latter being a complex event including the former cannot be defined within such an approach. In what follows, I will argue that achievements are not a distinct event type, nor are they subparts in any sense of accomplishment events. Rather, they are quantity events. What does single out achievements, so called, is the fact that the V-head typically found in so-called achievements is more specified than listemes typically are, in being part of an idiom which forces the projection, and hence the assignment of range to $[_{Asp_Q}\langle e\rangle_\#]$, thereby making their insertion in non-quantity structures impossible. In contrast, accomplishments, so called, are associated with V-heads that can be inserted in either quantity structures or non-quantity, activity structures. It is in this way that we seek to capture, indeed capitalize on, the generalization proposed by Mittwoch (1991), who points out that all accomplishment 'verbs' in English are in fact ambiguous between accomplishment and activity.

Before turning to the argument that this is indeed so, and to an elaboration of the properties of the relevant V-heads in achievement contexts, we note that attempts to account for the accomplishment–achievement distinction in terms of decomposition are independently problematic. Dowty's (1979) original suggestion, that accomplishments must include a CAUSE component, is quite problematic, as has been often pointed out. Thus the events implicated in (43), for instance, have none of the characteristics of achievements, and yet they do not have a CAUSE component (or at least, it is difficult to see how they have such a component any more than *Vesuvius erupted* or *Bill arrived*, for instance).[6] In turn, the events described in (44) do, plausibly, have a CAUSE component, but are typically considered to be achievements (and see Kennedy and Levin 2000, for a similar point recently made):

(43) a. The ship sank in two hours.
 b. The apple reddened in three weeks.
 c. The line straightened in four minutes.

(44) a. The government ended the project.
 b. The prospectors discovered gold.
 c. Kim reached the summit.
 d. Pat won the race.

The assumption that achievements are culmination points without a development part is likewise problematic. Typically, a culmination is taken to be a *telos*, in the sense of Higginbotham (2000a, b)—that is, a point which is the beginning of a resulting state which prevails at the end of the development part of the telic event. However, if culminations really are the beginning of a resulting state, it is not clear how achievements can be thus described, given the fact that achievements most certainly denote a transition, albeit a 'short' one, and not a state. In turn, the segmentation of accomplishments into a development part and a culmination point which is distinct from a resulting state, and which has, built into it, the notion of transition, amounts to claiming that accomplishments

---

[6] The reader is referred here specifically to the suggestion in Levin and Rappaport Hovav (1995) according to which the unaccusative instantiation of *sink* must be accompanied by an understood external causer, while the unergative instantiation involves an internal causer, a distinction which is clearly hard to maintain for the examples in (43). For some additional brief comments on this issue, see Chapter 2 at n. 20.

consist of a homogeneous activity part which ends in an instantaneous transition, an analysis which seems difficult to maintain in view of the clear interpretation of progressive change associated with many accomplishments. Finally, when Rothstein's (2000a, b) view is considered, we note that its merits can only be considered with respect to an account which fundamentally subscribes to the view that verbs, as such, are specified as either accomplishments or achievements. Consider why this is so. According to Rothstein's suggestion, the BECOME event, which is built into accomplishments and achievements alike, is an extended one. One must ask, then, why both ACTIVITY and BECOME (sub-)events are necessary to describe accomplishments, as opposed to BECOME events alone. The answer, speculating somewhat, would be that, assuming accomplishments to consist of both ACTIVITY and BECOME (sub-)events, one could capture the often observed fact that accomplishments do lend themselves to the negation of their culmination, thereby giving rise to ACTIVITY, while achievements do not. However, as achievements do not have an ACTIVITY part but only a BECOME part, an achievement minus the BECOME event is no longer an event at all.

Note, however, that the generalization thus captured is, by definition, only statable if it is assumed that there are accomplishment verbs or achievement verbs as such, a view which we rejected here (and which has likewise been rejected by lexicalist accounts such as Levin and Rappaport Hovav 1995 as well as Reinhart 2000). Specifically, such an account could capture very easily the fact that achievement verbs are obligatorily telic (i.e. they must involve only a BECOME event), while accomplishment verbs are typically ambiguous between a telic reading and an atelic reading, a fact that can be captured, by assumption, if it is assumed that the BECOME sub-event can be negated or omitted. Events, however, are never ambiguous (i.e. an accomplishment event is never ambiguous between being an ACTIVITY + BECOME as opposed to just an ACTIVITY), thereby restricting any claims about ambiguity to the lexical domain. Instead, when a view is considered according to which event types are *not* typically properties of lexical items, so-called 'accomplishment verbs' become the standard case (listemes which can be inserted in any event frame, be it activity or quantity), while something special needs to be said about 'achievement verbs', specifically, what makes it impossible for them to be inserted in activity contexts. The empirical advantages of assuming that accomplishments are both ACTIVITY and BECOME thus disappear.

In turn, the existence of achievements as a distinct event type, originally proposed in Vendler (1967), has come under considerable criticism. It has been often noted that while many achievements seem to give rise to a culmination instantaneously without a lead-up development or a perceptible transition of any sort, instantaneity, in and of itself is neither necessary nor sufficient to give rise to a telic reading. Thus Smith (1991) notes that the class of instantaneous events includes both telic events (*notice a problem, reach the summit, erupt*) and atelic events (*jump, cough*), the latter labeled *semelfactives* by Smith. Focusing on culminating instantaneous events, it turns out that tests which in effect distinguish achievements from accomplishments are rather difficult to come by. Parsons (1990) and Verkuyl (1989) both note that the progressive, typically assumed to tease apart achievements from accomplishments, is actually fully grammatical in utterances such as those in (45):

(45) a. She is winning the race.
 b. Pat is reaching the summit.
 c. The king is dying.
 d. The train is arriving.
 e. He is starting to leave.

While it might be true that in all these cases the actual event being referred to cannot be said to have a duration (the transition between life and death is a dichotomy rather than a process, as is reaching a summit, etc.), it is nevertheless the case that the progressive is well-formed, and that whatever process it does refer to is understood as being preparatory, or relevant, to the subsequent culmination point. We already noted in a different context that accomplishments denoted by events such as *build a house* and similar cases, may include not only the actual progression of the construction of an object, but also numerous relevant preparatory steps, such as making a blueprint, purchasing lumber, digging ground for a foundation, etc. To the extent that *Kim is building a house* may describe an event that involves not only the gradual construction of a structure but also relevant preparatory steps intended to further the eventual existence of a structure, such preparatory steps are rather difficult to distinguish from whatever relevant preparatory steps are undertaken by *Pat* in (45b) to further her eventual presence on the summit, such as her climbing. What is at stake here, then, are ontological and conceptual differences, tied in with our understanding of what may and what may not count as a relevant intermediate step towards a particular culmination. The grammar, however, seems rather oblivious to such ontological considerations, a point explicitly made by Verkuyl (1989, 1993). We note in addition that as in most other cases, the verb in and of itself seems to have little to do with the instantaneous effect in (45). Thus consider the sentences in (46):

(46) a. Kim is (gradually) winning my affection.
 b. They are reaching an understanding on the contract.
 c. The Amazon forest is dying.

d. The winter is arriving.

Assuming the common-sensical interpretations of (46a–d), in (46a) Kim has already won quite a bit of my affection, and has certainly brought about already some change in my attitude, when (46b) is true, although, of course, she has not won my affection fully yet. There is little to differentiate the situation here from the painting of a picture. Likewise, reaching an understanding involves having already agreed on some items but not all, and the death of the Amazon forest is definitely a development, not an instantaneous achievement. Finally, the arrival of the winter is typically marked by the gradual increase of cold days and is, likewise, a development.

Nor are other tests more useful. Mittwoch (1991), following Mourelatos (1978), notes that the 'it took x time' test has properties identical to those of the progressive when used with achievements, in that the time passage is understood as preparatory and relevant, as illustrated by (47). Specifically, note that after three hours Kim is not yet (partially) at the summit. On the other hand, while it stands to reason that after three weeks the house was partially constructed, it is equally plausible that after three weeks the foundation was dug, the lumber was bought and all the permits were in place, but there was no structure in evidence:

(47) a. It took Kim seven hours to reach the summit.
b. It took them seven hours to win the race.
c. It will take the king two more years to die.
d. It will take seven hours for the train to arrive.

(48) a. It took Kim seven weeks to build the house.
b. It took Jake three minutes to drink that beer.

Further, as in the case of the progressive, the 'anticipatory' reading of 'it took x time' can be overridden:

(49) a. It took Kim a long time to win my affection.
b. It will take them many months to reach an understanding.
c. It will take the Amazon forest ten years to die.
d. It will take winter at least two more weeks to finally arrive here.

Other proposed tests, including *start to* and *in x time* adverbials, at times claimed to exclude achievements, do not fare any better:

(50) a. Kim started to reach the summit.
b. They started to reach an understanding on the contract.
c. They reached the summit in 10 hours.
d. They reached an understanding in 10 hours.

(51) a. The king started to die sometime last night.
b. The Amazon forest started to die about 25 years ago.
c. The king died in 10 minutes.
d. The Amazon forest died in 10 years.

Mindful of the failure of most of these tests, Mittwoch (1991) nevertheless suggests that achievements do exist, and that their hallmark is precisely the property we have already discussed in this chapter—the existence of a telic reading in the absence of a quantity DP. Telicity in the absence of a quantity DP in transitive achievements is amply illustrated, as already noted, by the paradigm in (32), repeated here:

(32) a. The prospectors discovered gold and found rare coins.
b. The prospectors found rare coins and discovered gold.
c. Robin found oil on Monday and on Tuesday (requires two diggings).
d. The prospectors struck oil on Saturday and on Sunday.
e. The bulldozer hit bedrock on Saturday and on Sunday.
f. Mary noticed ink on her sleeve on Saturday and on Sunday.
g. John spotted wildfowl on Saturday and on Sunday.

Although Mittwoch (1991) suggests that various factors conspire to make the phenomenon more difficult to illustrate for intransitives, the examples in (52) seem straightforwardly illustrative:

(52) a. Lava erupted (from Vesuvius) on Sunday and on Monday.
b. Ghosts materialized in the living room on midnight and at 2am.
c. Poisonous gas exploded on Fairfax on Sunday and on Monday.

As it turns out, however, Mittwoch's diagnostic does not capture all events typically classified as achievements. Thus the events in (53) are typically interpreted as involving an instantaneous obligatory culmination, and are hence achievements, by Vendler's (1967) diagnostics. However, unlike the situations with the events in (4)–(6) or in (7)–(8), bare DPs are impossible (and cf. (10) above):

(53) a. nipsequ   *(kol ha.)gšamim (ha.boqer).
       stopped.PL *(all the.)rains   (this.morning)

b. nigmeru   *('eyze) diyunim   (ha.boqer).
   finished.PL *(some) discussions (this.morning)

c. neᶜecru   *(rob ha.)siksukim (sop sop).
   halted.PL *(most the.)disputes (finally)

d. histaymu *(kama)   bxinot (ha.šabuᶜa).
   ended.PL *(several) tests (this.week)

Further, we noted that the presence of a locative allows post-verbal subjects to be bare for some unaccusatives (e.g. (12)), and we suggested that when bare post-verbal subjects co-exist with a quantity reading, a covert locative is responsible for range assignment to $[_{Asp_o}\langle e \rangle_\#]$. However, for the events denoted by (53), the presence of a locative does not result in a similar effect, and the subject must remain non-bare:

(54) a. nipsequ šam *(kol ha.)gšamim (ha.boqer).
  stopped.PL there *(all the.)rains (this.morning)
 b. nigmeru šam *('eyze) diyunim (ha.boqer).
  finished.PL there *(some) discussions (this.morning)
 c. neˁecru šam *(rob ha.)siksukim (sop sop).
  halted.PL there *(most the.)disputes (finally)
 d. histaymu šam *(kama) bxinot (ha.šabuˁa).
  ended.PL there *(several) tests (this.week)

The ungrammaticality of the examples in (53)–(54) with bare DPs, in turn, is directly mirrored by the ungrammaticality of the English transitives in (55) and the Hebrew transitives in (56) (and see Sybesma 1992 for the observation that (55) and similar cases in English are ungrammatical).[7]

(55) a. *The government ended negotiations.
 b. *The plumber stopped water.
 c. *The court halted discussions.
 d. *The baby finished milk.

(56) a. asap gamar *('et ha.)xalab (ha.boqer).
  Asaf finished *(OM the.)milk (this.morning)
 b. hagai siyem *(kama) bxinot (ha.šabuˁa).
  Hagai finished *(several) tests (this.week)
 c. *ha.memšala hipsiqa *('et ha.)siyua (be-pitˀomiyut).
  the.government stopped *(OM the.)support (suddenly)
 d. *ha.vaˁada ˁacra *('et ha.)yisumim (sop sop).
  the.committee halted *(OM the.)applications (finally)

And yet, the predicates in (53)–(56) denote instantaneous culminations just as much as those in (32), (52) and in (4)–(6). If we adopt Mittwoch's claim (op. cit.), according to which a telic interpretation being possible in the presence of

---

[7] Unsurprisingly, (54a–d) are grammatical in the 'Abbreviated English' dialect, which allows article omission. See Stowell (1996) for some relevant discussion of the dialect under consideration.

a bare NP is the hallmark of achievements, should we then conclude that (53)–(56) are not achievements?

Intuitively, the ungrammaticality of (53)–(56) is easy to explain. Suppose, specifically, that the events here have an uncancellable culmination, which is to say that Asp_Q must project, and as such, must be assigned range. Suppose, further, that there are no independent means for assigning range directly to $[_{Asp_Q}\langle e \rangle_\#]$ in such structures, and crucially, that in these cases there is no covert $\langle loc/\exists \rangle$. The result is that the only way to assign range to $[_{Asp_Q}\langle e \rangle_\#]$ is through the projection of a quantity DP in $[Spec, Asp_Q]$, thereby deriving the obligatoriness of a quantity DP in (53)–(56), or in other words, the conformity to Verkuyl's generalization.

But if we conclude this concerning (53)–(56), then we must conclude that at least some 'achievements' have exactly the same event structure as other, non-instantaneous, quantity events, and that at least for these cases, positing a distinct event type, achievement, is not warranted. In turn, this considerably weakens whatever claim may remain for postulating a distinct event type for (32) and (52), or, for that matter, for (4)–(6). Rather, a plausible account would be that achievements, so-called, are precisely those cases in which the projection of a quantity structure is obligatory, and that what singles out (32), (52), and (4)–(6) from other obligatory quantity structures, as in (53)–(56), is the fact that range is can be assigned here to $[_{Asp_Q}\langle e \rangle_\#]$ without a quantity DP in $[Spec, Asp_Q]$, thereby giving rise to a violation of Verkuyl's generalization. We already argued that the existence of quantity events where Verkuyl's generalization fails is not evidence for the existence of a distinct event type, nor does it provide justification for postulating a distinction between lexical aktionsart and grammatical aktionsart. Rather, the assignment of range to $[_{Asp_Q}\langle e \rangle_\#]$ by a quantity DP in $[Spec, Asp_Q]$ is but one mode of giving rise to a quantity predicate. Another mode involves the assignment of range to $[_{Asp_Q}\langle e \rangle_\#]$ directly. In Slavic languages, such direct range assignment may be accomplished through prefixation, at least sometimes giving rise to quantity events without an argument DP (and see Chapter 7, Section 7.1, for discussion). In Hebrew, such direct range assignment may be accomplished by a locative deictic element. And finally, for verbs such as those in (32), (52), and (4)–(6), we suggested that they are idiomatic expressions and specifically that a (phonologically unrealized) $\langle loc/\exists \rangle$ must assign range to an idiomatically specified $[_{Asp_Q}\langle e^{loc/\exists} \rangle_\#]$, thereby forcing the DP in $[Spec, Asp_Q]$, if present, to be weak. We note again that this conclusion is eminently plausible, given the presentational nature of the events in (32), (52) and (4)–(6), vs. the absence of such a presentational interpretation for (53)–(56).

If we are on the right track here, the implication is that there is no independent achievement event type any more than there is an independent DP structure to accommodate *pluralia tantum*. Rather, what we have here is a complex expression, an idiom, which in effect forces the projection of a particular event type, otherwise already attested, to the exclusion of all other event types. Specifically, whatever event type is already associated with quantity interpretation must project here. In turn, we submit, the obligatory culmination which emerges in the context of such idiomatic expressions (but not in the context of other listemes) may give rise to the outstanding salience of the culmination of these events which may be translated into a pragmatically favoured instantaneous interpretation (and see, in this context, Pustejovski 1991, as well as the account put forth by Erteschik-Shir and Rapoport 2000, attributing the achievement/accomplishment distinction to the effects of focus).

Having concluded that there is no evidence for positing achievement as a distinct event type on the basis of the occurrence of bare DPs in (32) and (4)–(6), let us conclude by elaborating on the nature of the events in (53)–(56), and on the means by which the obligatory projection of Asp_Q is achieved here.

Note that at first sight, at least the paradigm in (53) is puzzling. If indeed the quantity DP in (53) is in [Spec, Asp_Q], thereby assigning range to $[_{Asp_Q}\langle e \rangle_{\#}]$, why are such derivations blocked for other intransitive unaccusative verbs, or specifically, what excludes the paradigm in (9), under a similar derivation? Recall, specifically, that we excluded (9) by arguing that such derivations leave $\langle e \rangle_E$ without range assignment, in the absence of either a DP in [Spec, EP], or alternatively, a locative which can existentially bind the event. But if range is not assigned to $\langle e \rangle_E$ in (9), how is it assigned in (53)?

A careful examination, however, reveals that the problem is not as substantial as it first appears. Specifically, consider in the context of (53) the following contrasts:

(57) a. nipsequ   ha.boqer   kol ha.gšamim.
        stopped.PL this-morning all the.rains

   b. nigmar   ha.boqer   ha.diyun.
        finished.PL this-morning the.discussion

   c. neˁecru   sop sop rob   ha.siksukim.
        halted.PL finally most the.disputes

   d. histaymu ha.šabuˁa kama   bxinot.
        ended.PL this-week several tests

(58) a. ??nipsequ   kol ha.gšamim ha.boqer.
         stopped.PL all the.rains   this-morning

   b. ??nigmar   ha.diyun   ha.boqer.
         finished.PL the.discussion this-morning

c. ??ne⁽c⁾ecru rob   ha.siksukim sop sop.
   halted.PL most the.disputes finally

d. ??histaymu kama   bxinot ha.šabu⁽c⁾a.
   ended.PL several tests   this-week

While the sentences in (58) could be improved with strong emphasis on the DP, on neutral intonation the word order in (57) is clearly favoured. In turn, the right-periphery, post-adjunct position of such DPs suggests that they have been postposed, or that at any rate, that they are not in [Spec, Asp$_Q$] (and note in this context that the definite post-verbal subjects in (18), repeated below, are not subject to a similar constraint). Thus although the quantity DPs in (57a–d) are responsible for the assignment of range to $[_{Asp_Q}\langle e \rangle_{\#}]$, it is also entirely clear that they cannot remain in [Spec, Asp$_Q$]. Rather, we must assume that they move to [Spec, TP] and then to [Spec, EP], receiving nominative in the former position and assigning range to $\langle e \rangle_E$ in the latter. In turn, they may be postposed, thereby ending up in the right periphery, due to some other mechanism, plausibly connected to discourse structure. Range assignment for $[_{Asp_Q}\langle e \rangle_{\#}]$ and for $\langle e \rangle_E$ is thus not problematic, and asymmetry with the ungrammaticality of (9) (repeated here) only apparent. That this is indeed on the right track is further indicated by the fact that in the presence of a locative, the constraints on the word order are much relaxed, again, as was the case in (18), precisely because in these cases range is assigned to $\langle e \rangle_E$ by the locative, allowing the quantity DP to remain in situ, as already discussed, and as is illustrated by (59) (and see, specifically, the derivation in (28)).[8]

---

[8] An issue does remain, however, when the complete grammaticality of (57) under any intonation is compared with the variable judgements for (i) and the ungrammaticality of (ii), without a very strong emphasis on the post-verbal subject:

(i) a. hibšilu ha.qayic   ?kol ha.tapuxim/*ha.tapuxim.
       ripened this-summer ?all the.apples/*the.apples

   b. hitmotetu ha.boqer   šloša qirot/??ha.qirot.
      collapsed this-morning three walls/??the.walls

   c. nirqab ha.xodeš   ?qcat basar/*ha.basar.
      rotted this-month a little meat/the.meat

   d. qap'u ba-layla še-⁽°⁾abar *kol ha.mayim.
      froze last night   *all the.water

(ii) a. *⁽c⁾abdu ha.boqer   kol ha.gananim/ha.gananim.
        worked this-morning all the.gardener/the.gardeners

    b. rakdu ha.xodeš   ??šloša talmidim/*ha.talmidim.
       danced this.month ??three students/*the.students

    c. *šaru ba-xacer   kol ha.yeladim/ha.yeladim.
       sang in-the.yard all the.children/the.children

(18) a. hibšilu kan/šam/eclenu ha.tapuxim (tok šloša šabuʿot)/
ripened here/there/*chez*.us the.apple (in three weeks)/
(ha.qayic).
(this.summer)

b. qap'u eclenu kol ha.mayim (bin layla).
froze *chez*.us all the.water (in one-night)

c. nišxat šam kol ha.yebul (tok šloša šabuʿot)/
destroyed.INTRANS there all the.harvest (in three weeks)/
(ha.šana).
(this.year)

(9) a. *hibšilu šlošet (ha.)tapuxim (ʿal ha.ʿec).
ripened three (the.)apples (on the.tree)

b. *hitmotetu (ha.)qirot (be-šabat).
collapsed (the.)walls (on-Saturday)

c. *nirqab (qcat) basar (ba-meqarer).
rotted (a little) meat (in-the.fridge)

d. *qap'u (kol ha.)mayim (ba-layla še-ʿabar).
froze (all the.)water (last night)

(59) a. nipsequ kan kol ha.gšamim ha.boqer.
stopped.PL here all the.rains this-morning

b. nigmeru šam 'eyze diyunim ha.boqer.
finished.PL there some discussions this-morning

c. neʿecru 'eclenu rob ha.siksukim sop sop.
halted.PL *chez*.us most the.disputes finally

d. histaymu po kama bxinot ha.šabuʿa.
ended.PL here several tests this-week

We suggested that idioms come in several varieties, differing as to the degree of specification of the particular functional structure associated with a phono-

d. navxu ba-xacer ??šloša klavim/*ha.klavim.
barked in-the.yard ??three dogs/*the.dogs

At least two factors seem to be involved in determining the relative grammaticality of (i)–(ii), one involving the nature of the event (activity vs. quantity), the other involving the nature of the DP. Thus definite descriptions seem to be the most deteriorated, and strong quantifiers are excluded in (ii), but not necessarily in (i). We note, in view of this, that clearly more is going on here, and that a system which regulates the postposability of the subject is in need of further articulation. While there is little prima facie reason to believe that the model developed in this work would be inconsistent with such an articulation, it does not in itself provide an account for this paradigm.

logical index. Thus an idiom may involve the specification of a unique range assigner, of a specific type of range assignment to a functional head, in principle compatible with more than one assigner, and finally, it may specify a particular open value, leaving entirely open the means of range assignment. The possibilities are schematized in (60a–c):

(60) a. $[\pi_i + \langle e \rangle_F]$ where F is a label of some functional node
   b. $[\pi_j + \langle e^\alpha \rangle]$ where α is a specific type of range assigned to the open value (e.g. +def)
   c. $[\pi_k + \langle e^{\pi_3} \rangle]$ where π_3 is a fixed phonological representation for a fixed terminal range assigner (e.g. *the*)

Instantiations of (60b) are cases of *pluralia tantum*, already discussed. As an illustration of (60c), consider not only verb-particle constructions, such as *take over* and *pair up* (cf. n. 6), but also cases such as *kick the bucket*, where the f-morphs associated with the DP *the bucket* are fixed, as already noted in Chapter 1, Section 1.4. Thus *the bucket*, rather than *this bucket, the buckets, every bucket, some bucket*, etc. are required for an idiomatic reading to emerge. However, the choice of f-morphs in the DP dominating *bridge*, in the idiom *cross that bridge when (x) come to it*, is considerably less fixed, with *the bridge, every bridge, those bridges*, as well as *bridges*, all possible. As such, we have an idiomatic expression here which consists of the phonological index for *bridge* (alongside some additional phonological indices), together with one or more open values ($\langle e \rangle_{div}$, possibly $\langle e \rangle_d$), but not with a specified range which must be assigned to them, and certainly not with a fixed range-assigning terminal. Thus *bucket* in its idiomatic context is best represented as in (60c), and *bridge*, in its idiomatic context, as in (60a).

In view of this, consider the distinction between *notice*, which can license quantity interpretation with a bare DP, contra Verkuyl's generalization, and *finish* which can only occur in quantity contexts, but which nevertheless cannot violate Verkuyl's generalization. *Notice*, clearly, is like *bucket*. *Finish*, however, is like *bridge*. The emerging idiomatic representations are as in (61):

(61) a. $[_{Asp_Q} \langle e^{loc/\exists} \rangle_\# [_{L\text{-}D} \text{notice}]]$
   b. $[_{Asp_Q} \langle e \rangle_\# [_{L\text{-}D} \text{finish}]]$

Some element now must be provided by the grammar to assign range to $[_{Asp_Q} \langle e^{loc/\exists} \rangle]$ and $[_{Asp_Q} \langle e \rangle_\#]$ in (61a) and (61b) respectively, or ungrammaticality results. Aside from the head feature $\langle loc/\exists \rangle$ available, by assumption, to assign range to $[_{Asp_Q} \langle e^{loc/\exists} \rangle]$ in idioms such as *notice, spot, erupt*, etc., with their consequent presentational function, and not counting the particles associated with idioms such as *pair up* or *take over*, all fully idiomatically specified, the grammar of English does not have head features or f-morphs which may assign range to $[_{Asp_Q}\langle e\rangle_\#]$. The standard, fully grammaticalized mode of assigning such a range is through the presence of a quantity DP in [Spec, Asp$_Q$]. It therefore follows that when an idiom's specification is for a functional open value, but not for a specified range assigner to such an open value, the grammar will make use of whatever mechanisms are otherwise available. The result is a strict adherence to Verkuyl's generalization together with the impossibility of a non-quantity event structure for idioms specified as (61b), namely the class of achievements that are not presentational in nature. The properties of the paradigm in (53) result.

10.4 Summary

Fundamentally, all structures proposed in Part III of this work are based on the licensing possibilities for the structure in (62):

(62)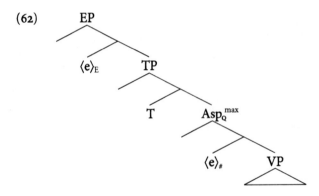

In the most standard cases, a strong DP in [Spec, EP] will assign range to $\langle e\rangle_E$ (as discussed in Chapter 9, Section 9.2), and in languages such as Hebrew and English, a quantity DP in [Spec, Asp$_Q$] will assign range to $[_{Asp_Q}\langle e\rangle_\#]$, as discussed extensively in Chapters 3 and 5. The subject matter of Chapters 9 and 10 was the licensing of the structure in (62), in Hebrew, without such DPs, and rather, through the presence of a locative/existential element, overt and covert, which could assign range to $\langle e\rangle_E$, to $[_{Asp_Q}\langle e\rangle_\#]$, or to both. In the domain of range assignment by a locative to $[_{Asp_Q}\langle e\rangle_\#]$ there was a direct parallelism with the ability of the perfective paradigm in Slavic, historically related to locative prepositions, to assign such range.

The ability of locative/existential deictic expressions to assign range to open values greatly increases the range of word orders available in Hebrew, resulting in a complex and at times entirely surprising paradigm. The range of possible configurations are given below, together with the sentences which exemplify them (all arrows indicate range assignment):

(63) *Quantity cases*

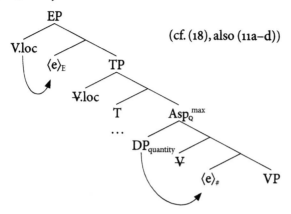

(cf. (18), also (11a–d))

(18) a. hib̲šilu kan/šam/eclenu ha.tapuxim (tok̲ šloša šab̲uʿot)/
ripened here/there/*chez*.us the.apple (in three weeks)/
(ha.qayic).
(this.summer)

b. qap̲'u eclenu kol ha.mayim (bin layla).
froze *chez*.us all the.water (in one-night)

c. nišxat šam kol ha.yeb̲ul (tok̲ šloša šab̲uʿot)/
destroyed.INTRANS there all the.harvest (in three weeks) /
(ha.šana).
(this.year)

(64)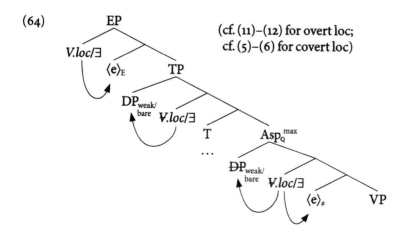

(cf. (11)–(12) for overt loc;
cf. (5)–(6) for covert loc)

(11) a. hibšilu po šloša tapuxim (ha.qayic) (tok xamiša šabuʿot).
ripened here three apples (this.week) (in five weeks)

b. nirqab ʾeclenu qcat basar (ba-meqarer) (tok yomayim).
rotted *chez*.us a little meat (in-the.fridge) (in two days)

c. putru šam ʿasarot ʿobdim (ha.boqer) (tok ʿeser daqot).
fired.PASS there tens (of) workers (this.morning) (in ten minutes)

d. culma po zebra (ʿal yedey pil) (ha.boqer)
photographed.PASS here zebra (by an elephant) (this morning)

(tok xameš daqot).
(in five minutes)

(12) a. hibšilu po tapuxim (ha.qayic) (tok xamiša šabuʿot).
ripened here apples (this.summer) (in five weeks)

b. hitmotetu šam qirot (ha.boqer) (tok šaloš šaʿot).
collapsed there walls (this.morning) (in three hours)

c. nirqab ʾeclenu basar (ba-meqarer) (tok yomayim.
rotted *chez*.us meat (in-the.fridge) (in two days)

d. qap'u šam mayim (ba-layla še-ʿabar) (tok xaci šaʿa).
froze there water (last night) (in half an hour)

(5) a. parca mehuma (ha.boqer).
erupted.F.SG riot.F.SG (this.morning)

b. hitxilu hapganot (ha.boqer).
started.M.PL demonstrations (this.morning)

c. hopiʿa ʿašan laban ba-šamayim (ha.boqer).
appeared smoke white in-the.sky (this.morning)

(6) a. parcu šaloš mehumot.
erupted three riots

b. hitxilu harbe hapganot.
started many demonstrations

c. hopiʿa harbe ʿašan laban ba-šamayim.
appeared much smoke white in the sky

(38) a. ha.mehumot parcu ba-boqer.
the.riots erupted in-the.morning

b. ha.ʿašan ha.laban hopiʿa be-šaʿa 'arba.
the.smoke the.white appeared at 4pm

c. ha.hapganot hitxilu sop sop.
   the.demonstrations started finally

(65) 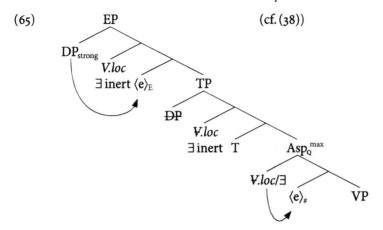 (cf. (38))

(66) 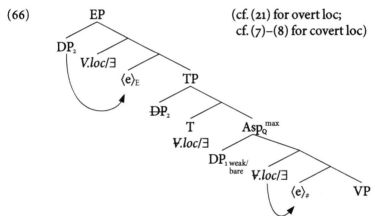 (cf. (21) for overt loc; cf. (7)–(8) for covert loc)

(21) a. michal katba šam širim (bemešek šloša šabuˁot/tok šloša šabuot).
       Michal wrote there poems (for three weeks/in three weeks)

   b. rina šatla eclenu vradim (bemešek šaloš šaˁot/tok šaloš šaˁot).
       Rina planted *chez*.us roses (for three hours/in three hours)

   c. ran limed kan šira ˁibrit (bemešek šloša yamim/tok šloša
       Ran taught here poetry Hebrew (for three days/in three

       yamim).
       days

(7) a. The prospectors discovered gold.
    b. The prospectors found rare coins.

c. Robin found oil.
d. The prospectors struck oil.
e. The bulldozer hit bedrock.
f. Mary noticed ink on her sleeve.
g. John spotted wildfowl on Saturday.

(8) a. rina gilta zaha<u>b</u>.
Rina discovered gold

b. rani maca matbeʿot yeqarim.
Rina found coins expensive

(67) Non-quantity, intransitive; transitive expletives

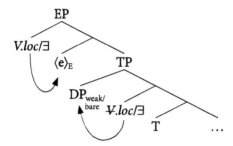

(2) a. (ʾamarti še-) ʿa<u>b</u>ad šam/kan/ecli ganan (ha.yom).
(I said that) worked here/there/*chez*.me gardener (today)

b. *(ʾamarti še-) ʿa<u>b</u>ad šam/kan/ecli ran/ha.ganan (ha.yom).
(I said that) worked here/there/*chez*.me Ran/the.gardener (today)

c. (ʾamarti še-) ʿa<u>b</u>du šam/kan/ecli (kama, šloša) gananim
(I said that) worked here/there/*chez*.me (several, three) gardeners
(ha.yom).
(today)

d. *(ʾamarti še-) ʿa<u>b</u>du šam/kan/ecli kol ha.gananim (ha.yom).
(I said that) worked here/there/*chez*.me all the.gardeners (today)

(68) ((96) of Chapter 9)
a. hip̄cic šam matos ʾet ha.ʿir.
bombed there plane OM the.town

b. hip̄cicu šam metosim ʾet ha.ʿir.
bombed there planes OM the.town
(existential only; generic reading impossible)

c. hip̄cicu šam šloša metosim ʾet ha.ʿir.
bombed there three planes OM the.town

11

Forward Oh!
Some Concluding Notes

11.1 Inter-Language and Intra-Language Variation

Within any generative approach to the study of the language faculty, what is common to all languages may, in principle, come for free. While it might still be in need of description, the null hypothesis is that it is fundamentally part of the human biological structure, however described. The true challenge is to account, within a biological approach to language, for precisely those facets of linguistic behaviour which differ from one language to the other, and hence, by assumption, are sensitive to facets of the input. Within the Principles-and-Parameters approach, the task, then, is to describe and delimit variation, while bearing in mind that its acquisition must be sensitive to the linguistic environment. It has now become quite accepted (cf. Borer 1984; Chomsky 1995a) that variation is to be attributed to formal properties of grammatical formatives. Thus, rather than looking at a picture of language variation which includes 'big parameters' (the selection of bounding nodes for subjacency, the determination of a domain for binding, etc.), we are looking at the properties of any single E-language as they emerge from the collection of specific computational properties associated with members of its functional lexicon. As such, the set of constructions instantiated in any given language is not determined by some disjunction, within UG, with respect to some formal principle, but rather from the collection of UG-specified features which are associated with the inventory of the specific of formatives available in any given language.

I have suggested that the actual functional hierarchy associated with grammars is uniform. Thus, the selection of grammatical categories within a particular language cannot be responsible for the emergence of distinct architecture. Functional category labels, associated as they are here with functional open values such as $\langle e \rangle_d$, $\langle e \rangle_{\#}$, $[_{Asp_Q}\langle e \rangle_{\#}]$, $\langle e \rangle_T$, $\langle e \rangle_E$, etc., must be uniform across languages, being responsible, in turn, for the projection of DP, #P, TP, etc. Variation within the functional domain, then, can only be attributed to the mode in which such open values are assigned range. I further suggested that such range assignment can be accomplished in a number of well-specified ways, specifically, via direct range assignment by an abstract head feature or by an f-morph (free or bound), and via indirect range assignment, either by an adverb of sorts (including discourse operators and covert generic operators) or via specifier–head agreement. The mode of range assignment had structural ramifications, within both the syntactic and the morphological domain. For instance, range assignment by an abstract head feature or by a bound f-morph resulted in obligatory head movement, while head movement was altogether blocked for cases in which range assignment is accomplished by a free f-morph. In turn, the morphological output of head movement in the case of abstract head features was argued to be mono-morphemic, while the output of head movement in the case of bound f-morphs, if needed, is morphologically complex. Finally, indirect range assignment competes with direct range assignment, giving rise, likewise, to syntactic effects. Thus, for instance, in the presence of range assignment by an adverb of quantification, an f-morph assigning range to the same value is blocked (thereby accounting for the fact that in (1a) *mostly* must range over events, and cannot range over the interpretation of the DP). Similarly, in the presence of specifier–head range assignment to $\langle e \rangle_d$, a strong interpretation is blocked, for example in Slavic, as illustrated by (1b) (see Chapter 6, Section 6.3, for extensive discussion):

(1) a. Most water in the pond is mostly lost through evaporation.
 b. Znowu zobaczyłem^P jedno dziecko.   (Polish)
    again see-PST-1SG.M one-ACC child-ACC
    i. 'I again saw a child.' (weak)
    ii. *'I saw the child again.' (strong)

The picture of language variation which emerges, if indeed generalizable to all other domains of variation, is thus a very specific one. It is reducible to phonological properties of (direct) range assigners, on the one hand, and to the availability, in specific languages, of phonological instantiations for particular range assignment combinations. To wit, if in a language such as English the combination of the verb with some abstract head feature which may assign range to $[_{Asp_Q}\langle e \rangle_{\#}]$ (say $\langle asp^\# \rangle$) does not give rise to a well-formed phonological output (i.e. there is no phonological representation for V.$\langle asp^\# \rangle$), and given the fact that English does not have an f-morph which can assign range to $[_{Asp_Q}\langle e \rangle_{\#}]$, specifier–head relations remains as the primary available option for range assignment to $[_{Asp_Q}\langle e \rangle_{\#}]$. It thus emerges that in English, Verkuyl's generalization must hold (but see the exceptions noted in Chapter 7, Section 7.3, precisely in the presence of other range assigners to $[_{Asp_Q}\langle e \rangle_{\#}]$). On the other hand, in Slavic languages, $[_{Asp_Q}\langle e \rangle_{\#}]$ can be assigned range directly, by an abstract head feature, giving rise not only to obligatory verb movement in such contexts, but also to the violability of Verkuyl's generalization, to the obligatorily strong reading associated with bare DPs in [Spec, Asp$_Q$] and to the obligatorily weak interpretation of cardinal expressions in [Spec, Asp$_Q$]. The extension of such a reduction to phonological properties of grammatical formatives of all attested variation, whether inter-linguistic or intra-linguistic, is clearly a formidable task, outside the scope of any one project. We nevertheless note that if indeed possible, such a reduction represents a huge simplification of the task of language acquisition. Fundamentally, it consolidates syntactic acquisition with the acquisition of the phonological properties of grammatical formatives. That the particular phonological representation of any given formative is language specific is beyond dispute, as is the fact that phonological representations must be learned on the basis of exposure. If the applicability of grammatical principles, otherwise universal, is constrained only by the (morpho-)phonology of grammatical formatives, much of the acquisition of syntax becomes, in principle, the task of matching the properties of phonological forms with the set of otherwise available and unchanged grammatical computational operations. To the extent that the variations discussed in this work, both inter-linguistic and intra-linguistic, do, indeed, conform to such a characterization, they potentially point to towards a research agenda in which all variation is thus accounted for.

It is worthwhile noting that if indeed we are on the right track, the expectation that emerges is that there should not be any 'grammatical' variations between languages which are substantially different from variations which may be found in language internally (although, of course, some such generalizations may emerge from phonological, rather than syntactic, generalizations). Thus, we suggested, N-to-D movement is always instantiated in Hebrew, for both proper names and for definite expressions, due to the fact that $\langle e \rangle_d$ is always assigned range by an abstract head feature, be it $\langle \textbf{\textit{def-u}} \rangle$ in proper names, or $\langle \textbf{\textit{def}} \rangle$. In Italian, in contrast, $\langle \textbf{\textit{def-u}} \rangle$ is an abstract head feature, triggering N-to-D movement, while for definite expressions, range to $\langle e \rangle_d$ is assigned by the article, which is a free f-morph. No N-movement is attested in such cases. Finally, we noted that the system as such imposes its own constraints on the inventory of range assignments in any given language. Thus, if a 'high' functional value is assigned range by an abstract head feature, thereby requiring head movement, 'lower' functional values cannot be assigned range directly by free f-morphs. As by assumption f-morphs block head movement, the 'higher' head feature could not be supported, and ungrammaticality would result. It is precisely this configuration which gave rise to the ungrammaticality in Romanian of (2b–d), and to the need in Hebrew for the formation of a construct nominal to allow the configuration in (3) (see Volume I, Chapter 7, Section 7.2.1. for a detailed discussion).

(2) a. pisici.le
    cat.F.PL.DEF
  b. *trei.le   pisici
    three.F.PL.DEF cats
  c. *pisici.le   trei
    cat.F.PL.DEF three
  d. *trei pisici.le
    three cat.F.PL.DEF

(3)   šlošet ha.xatulim
      three the.cats

We do note, in closing, that the claim here is distinct from the one made in Chomsky (1999 and subsequent literature) that head movement is phonological. While phonological considerations could in effect rule out derivations in which head movement does not take place, head movement, as proposed in this work, clearly does change meaning, insofar as cardinals, for example, when they move to D and assign range to $\langle e \rangle_d$ give rise to the interpretation associated with strong indefinites, while cardinals which do not move to $\langle e \rangle_d$ give rise to the interpretation associated with existential, weak indefinites. The claim is consistent, however, with the possibility that the movement of L-heads, in and of itself, does not give rise to interpretational distinctions.

11.2 Some Final Notes on the Nature of Listemes

11.2.1 Introductory comments

In a perfect XS system, all listemes would constitute a unique phonological index associated with a unique conceptual package. Such listemes would be devoid of any grammatical marking, be it morphological or syntactic in nature, and would thus be devoid of any formal properties, short of those associated with their sound structure. It would be up to formal structural configurations, be they morphological or syntactic, to give rise to syntactic category, to argument structure configurations, to inflectional marking, and to morphological derivatives. In principle, then, any such listeme could occur in any architectural configuration, with the resulting interpretation to be computed solely on the basis of the structure, with the listeme in question acting as a pure modifier. It is precisely these cases which served as the primary case studies in this work, with illustrations both within the domain of DP structure and event structure. To the extent that considerable mileage can be gotten from pursuing a research agenda in which listemes are indeed thus characterized, the obvious simplicity and parsimonious nature of the system recommends itself.

As the reader has no doubt observed by now, however, it is not the case that all of English vocabulary, including vocabulary items which are not morphologically or inflectionally marked in any obvious way, exhibit the sort of flexibility attested with *siren*, for example, illustrated by the paradigm in (1) of Chapter 3 and repeated here:

(4) a. The factory horns sirened throughout the raid.
 b. The factory horns sirened midday and everyone broke for lunch.
 c. The police car sirened the Porsche to a stop.
 d. The police car sirened up to the accident site.
 e. The police car sirened the daylight out of me.
 (from Clark and Clark 1979)

Nor is it the case that languages in general exhibit even the degree of freedom attested in English. Thus in Hebrew, and in Semitic languages in general, argument structure alternations are almost without exception reflected in the morphology of the verbal form, and there is no noun-verb homophony of the type so common in English. Likewise, when the Romance languages are considered, transitivity alternations are typically marked, and specific verbal instantiations cannot occur with varying argument structure configurations, or as nouns. The XS system, then, overgenerates. These final comments point to some ways in which this overgeneration can be curtailed.

11.2.2 *More on phonological indices*

Note now that much of the vocabulary of English has a phonological index which is, in and of itself, a well-formed phonological word. *Form*, for example, a phonological index of a listeme which is in principle unspecified for any syntactic properties, may emerge from at least some verbalizing and nominalizing contexts unchanged, phonologically, as illustrated by (5):

(5) a. the [$_N$ form]
 b. to [$_V$ form] a word

Further, even if the listeme *form* occurs in the context of inflectional marking of derivational affixation, it will retain, by and large, its phonological discreteness, as illustrated by (6):

(6) a. form*s*
 b. form*ed*
 c. form*ing*
 d. form*ation*

The properties of *form* are shared by many (although probably not all) underived vocabulary items in English, giving rise to the well-known malleability of categorization in English, as well as to the possibility of such vocabulary, in verbal contexts, occurring in multiple argument structure configurations. There is, however, nothing inherent to the XS approach that requires such homophony between phonological indices and well-formed phonological units. It is thus conceivable, and eminently plausible, that other vocabulary systems exist in which phonological indices do not correspond to a well-formed phonological word. Possibly at the other extreme from English, we find the Semitic morpho-phonological system, where, plausibly, (non-borrowed) phonological indices are never well-formed phonological words. Specifically, suppose we assume that the relevant notion of a phonological index within the Semitic languages corresponds to a consonantal root, consisting of two, three, or four consonants (see Marantz 2000 and Arad 2003 for the same assumption). Such a phonological index is appropriately related to some conceptual package, to be sure, but in and of itself can never surface as a well-formed phonological output. As an illustration, consider the consonantal root *KTB*, clearly associated with some conceptual feature bundle related to writing. As such, it may occur as part of both a verbal and a nominal paradigm, as illustrated by (7)–(9):

(7) Verbal forms

Morpho-phon. template	Past tense (3SG.M)	Interpretation
I	kata<u>b</u>	'wrote' (dyadic/monadic)
II	ni<u>k</u>tab	'was-written (monadic)
III	kite<u>b</u>	'copy-edit' (dyadic)
IV	(kuta<u>b</u>)	(not attested)
V	hi<u>k</u>tib	'dictate' (triadic)
VI	hu<u>k</u>tab	'was-dictated' (monadic)
VII	hitkate<u>b</u>	'correspond' (monadic, symmetrical)

(8) Nominal and Adjectival forms derived from verbs

Template	Nominal	Interpretation	Adjective	
I	kti<u>b</u>a	'writing'	katu<u>b</u>	'written'
III	kitu<u>b</u>	'copy-editing'		
V	ha<u>k</u>taba	'dictation'		
VII	hitkat<u>b</u>ut	'correspondence'	me<u>k</u>uta<u>b</u>	'correspondent'

(9) Nominal forms not derived from verbs
   a. mi<u>k</u>ta<u>b</u>   'letter'
   b. ma<u>k</u>te<u>b</u>a 'desk'
   c. kat<u>b</u>an   'typist'
   d. kto<u>b</u>et   'address'
   e. ktuba   'marriage contract'
   f. kta<u>b</u>   'hand-writing'
   g. kata<u>b</u>   'correspondent'

Further, inflection as well corresponds to templates, in which consonantal roots are supplied with a vocalic melody, and at times with affixal material, to give rise to different tenses for example, as well as different moods. In fact, templates IV and VI are typically considered inflectional, passive variants of templates III and V, respectively, rather than independent templates:[1]

(10) Root: XŠB ('consider')

Template	Imperfective/future (3SG.M)	Passive (3SG.M)	
I	yaxšo<u>b</u>		'consider.FUT' ('consider something', 'think')
II	yexaše<u>b</u>		'be considered.FUT' ('be considered as')
III	ye<u>x</u>aše<u>b</u>	yexuša<u>b</u> (IV)	'calculate.FUT'
V	ya<u>k</u>ši<u>b</u>	(yuxša<u>b</u> (VI) not attested)	'consider.FUT', ('consider as')
VII	yitxaše<u>b</u>		'be considerate.FUT'

Within an XS system, it must be assumed that the vowels and whatever affixal material occurs in well-formed phonological words based on roots such as *KTB* and *XŠB* are the realization of some formal structure, be it syntactic or morphological. We note that the morpho-phonology here cuts across the inflection/derivation line, in that similar morpho-phonological principles appear to govern both the formation of well-formed inflection paradigms and the formation of words which have, at times, unpredictable meaning (albeit always related to the meaning of the root), as in (9), for instance. Setting aside, however, the specific execution involved in word formation, and whether it is best characterized

---

[1] Within the nominal domain, Hebrew inflection is by and large non-vocalic (plural and definiteness, both, by assumption, abstract head features, are not intervocalic). In Arabic, on the other hand, plurals are at least at times vocalic, giving rise to broken plurals.

(across the board) as the phonological realization of abstract head features or as based on actual morphemes, we note that the type of homophony attested in English between nominal stems and verbal stems with multiple argument structure realizations is neither expected nor attested, but that the system is exoskeletal, nevertheless, in that listemes (e.g. *KTB*), once properly characterized, need not have grammatical properties, as such. Indeed, any attempt to specify grammatical features on such listemes is doomed to fail, given their occurrence in such a wide array of formally diverse outputs (the reader is referred to Arad 2003, for a specific execution within a constructionist approach, as well as to Borer, forthcoming, for an alternative constructionist view).

Non-trivially, it emerges that all phonologically well-formed words in Semitic languages are derived and categorized. Thus the absence of an English type polysemy follows not only from the fact that tri-consonantal roots are not in and of themselves phonologically well-formed words, but also from the fact that any morpho-phonological word by definition represents a complex grammatical structure and is hence no longer category neutral. Its occurrence in any other categorial context, without added affixation, is expected to be impossible. Put differently, any verb or (unborrowed) noun in a Semitic language is the formal equivalent of *formed* or *formation*, and never the equivalent of *form*. Just as *formed* cannot be embedded under D, so Semitic verbs and nouns cannot be embedded under functional structure which conflicts with their categorial specification.

The impossibility under the set of assumptions made here of embedding a derived word under functional structure which cannot 'categorize' it properly (albeit vacuously; see Volume I, Chapter 1, Section 1.2.3, for some comments) suggests an obvious way to deal with the fact that even in English some vocabulary items allow only a rigid insertion frame, as well as the fact that in some languages (the Romance languages, for instance) much of the vocabulary is similarly rigid. Thus note that Romance verbs are rarely simpletons (inflection excluded). First, Romance verbs contain a theme vowel which is attested only in verbal contexts (and forms derived from verbs), and appear to mimic the Semitic system, on a small scale, in having a vocalic (sub-)melody which is assigned by some formal structure. Further, few Romance verbs are morphological simpletons, but rather involve prefixation of some sort. If we assume that the prefixation here reflects the presence of some functional structure, whether morphological or syntactic, which in turn has verbalizing properties, it would emerge that little of the Romance verbal stock is underived, and as such is akin to Semitic words or overt derived forms in English. If there is, then, a listeme embedded within such derived forms in Romance, one must look for it after stripping the prefix. It is with respect to that listeme, which may never give rise to a phonological word on its own, that one must examine the applicability of the XS model to such languages.

Turning to Latinate verbs in English, we note that an extension of the Romance picture would require the assumption that, for example, *mit* is a listeme, and that for the forms in (11), the presence of a prefix constitutes a verbalizing environment, either syntactic, or more plausibly, purely morphological:

(11) remit, commit, submit, permit, emit

Positing the existence of a listeme *mit* in English (and likewise, *struct/stroy*, *duce, gest*, and others) is, however, not without problems. For one thing, if a listeme consists of a sound–meaning pair, the presence of sound representation here is clear enough, but the assignment of meaning to *mit* or *duce* is at best an a posteriori matter, based on a conscious attempt to find a common denominator among all its occurrences. Suppose, however, we assume that *mit* is not a complete listeme as such, but rather, is a pure phonological index. Consider the ramifications of such a move. Here is a phonological index without any structural properties, by assumption, and without any meaning. As it is not a grammatical formative, it is not part of the functional lexicon, and it cannot merge within the functional domain or categorize any listeme. In short, it can only be inserted in a syntactic or morphological structure which by assumption categorizes it. We proposed that the main function of listemes is as modifiers of structure. Under the plausible assumption that meaningless phonological indices cannot meaningfully modify a structure, the embedding of *mit*, for instance, in a syntactic structure will, at best, give rise to an incomplete interpretation. The following (possible) Neo-Davidsonian representation involving the verb *mit* illustrates this point:

(12) a. The cat *mitted* the tree.
      b. ∃e [quantity (e) & originator (cat, e) & subject-of-quantity (the tree, e) & **mit** (e)].

While some partial interpretation can be assigned to (12b), it is incomplete precisely insofar as *mit* does not correspond to any bundle of conceptual features.

There remains one option for the embedding of *mit* within a meaningful structure, as there is exactly one structure in which phonological indices, rather than full listemes, play a crucial role—idioms. Idioms, recall, are cases in which some grammatical formative is specified to occur with a phonological index, and meaning is assigned to the complex constituent as a whole. Within the domain of syntax, I suggested that idioms consist of the association of a phonological index with some functional structure, with varying degrees of specificity for the properties of the open value ⟨e⟩ heading that structure, as in (13) (see Chapter 1, Section 1.4):

(13) a. MEANING ⇔ [π$_i$ + ⟨e⟩]
     b. MEANING ⇔ π$_k$ + [⟨e⟩]

If we assume that morphology may put forth hierarchical structures which are independent from those produced by the syntax, note, the idiomatic templates in (13) must be augmented by the representations in (14), with M standing for a bound f-morph:

(14) a. [π$_i$ + M]
     b. π$_i$ + [M]

Meaning, in (13)–(14), is not necessarily linked with the interpretation of the associated phonological index. To wit, in *kick the bucket*, there is no commitment to the conceptual bundle associated with *bucket*. Rather, it is associated with the configuration as a whole. Furthermore, some words (rather than morphemes) may only occur in idiomatic contexts, having no independent interpretation, otherwise, in the language. Thus consider the word *ixpat*, in Hebrew, as it occurs in the contexts in (15):

(15) a. lo 'ixpat li.
        no IXPAT to.me
        'I don't care'

     b. 'ixpat lo.
        IXPAT to.him
        'He cares.'

     c. *ha.'ixpat, *le.'ixpat.
        the IXPAT, to IXPAT

Not only is it the case that *'ixpat* never occurs in any other context in the language, its categorial membership is extremely difficult to determine. While it clearly is not a verb (past tense requires a copula), on the whole its properties are a combination of properties of nouns and properties of adjectives.[2]

---

[2] While modifiers such as *me'od* 'very' are possible with *ixpat*, suggesting that it might be an adjective, we also note that to derive the noun *ixpatiut*, colloquially 'caring', with the nominalizer *-ut*, typically attached to adjectives, the suffix *-i* must be added, otherwise in the language typically a derivational suffix attached to nouns to turn them to adjectives:

(i) *Israel* → *Israel-i* → *Israeli-ut*
    Israel → Israeli → Israeliness

    bayit → *beyt-i* → *beyti-ut*
    house → domestic → domesticity

It thus emerges that within an idiomatic structure, and only within such structures, pure phonological indices can receive an interpretation. We may now propose that *mit* is associated with the idiomatic structure in (16a), with α standing for the relevant range of categorial V morphemes such as *re, e, con*, etc. The emerging structure is as in (16b).[3]

(16) a. $[\pi_{mit} + M^\alpha]$
b. $[_V \{re\text{-}, con\text{-}, e\text{-}\} [\pi_{mit}]]$

Under such an analysis *remit* in English will be a verb, and will not occur under DP or in the context of plural inflection. The remaining need for narrowing down the overgenerating capacity of the XS model can thus be considerably reduced.

Clearly, this is but an outline for future research. One must investigate, specifically, the nature of prefixed expressions in Romance, determining, specifically, whether they are idiomatic, in the sense of (16), or more plausibly, whether they represent cases in which the prefixes are range assigners to some functional structure (e.g. aspectual structure) or are potentially derivationally complex forms with combinatorial interpretations, and where *mit* is a true listeme which contributes its own interpretation albeit one that is possibly not an

---

(ii) kar → *kar-i
cold (and cf.kar li, 'I am cold', ostensibly on a par with (15))

ra'eḇ ⇔ *re'eḇ-i
hungry

[3] Note that a 'complementation' idiom (as e.g. *depend on*), within the morphological domain, would involve the hierarchical structure in (i), which is in need of categorization, on a par with its syntactic counterpart in (14b). Outside the domain of idioms, such structures may be the correct ones for category-neutral prefixes, which may then adjoin to the head, itself a full listeme, rather than a pure phonological index. As we are assuming here that idioms involving *mit* are by definition categorized as V by the idiomatic structure, these are clearly not the correct structures for them. We leave the matter of whether complementation idioms such as (i) actually exist as an open issue.

(i)   mit
         ╱   ╲
      mit   M (re-, per-, e-, con-, etc.)

Of some interest in this context is the existence, in English, of nominal forms such as *import* and *export*, as well as *permit*, all with a penultimate stress. Two avenues are available here, as to their account. It might be the case that exactly for such cases, but not e.g. for *emit* and *commit*, the structure is as in (i), leaving these forms category-neutral, to be categorized by the structure. In turn, it is possible that the stress shift is indicative of some derivational process (albeit probably not affixal in nature) which derives nouns from verbs. We note, in this context, the existence in English of the verb *to pérmit*, alongside the verb *to permít*, with a final stress. If the noun *pérmit* is derived from the verb *permít*, the existence of *to pérmit* becomes a puzzle. If, on the other hand, *pérmit* and *permít* are but stem allomorphs instantiated in distinct categorial contexts, the emergence of a verbal form with the erstwhile nominal allomorph (albeit with a slightly different meaning) is less puzzling. We leave these matters aside here, but see Borer (2003a, forthcoming) for more discussion.

attested phonological word and hence must be subject to further prefixation (see Chapter 7, Section 7.2 for discussion). If that is the case, then the structure of Romance prefixed verbs is as in (17a) (if the prefixes are range assigners to functional open values), or alternatively, as in (17b) (if the prefixes are morphological categorizers), and the importation of Romance forms into English involves preserving the morpho-phonological complexity, but not the functional value of the relevant prefix, a rather plausible assumption:

(17) a. $[\,\langle e^{\alpha}\rangle\,[_{L\text{-}D}\,\pi_{mit}\,]\,]\Leftrightarrow[\,\{\text{re-; con-; e-}\}.\pi_{mit}\,\langle e\rangle\,[_{V}\,\pi_{mit}]\,]$
b. $[_{V}\,\{\text{re-; con-; e-}\}[_{L\text{-}D}\,\pi_{mit}\,]\,]$

A more detailed investigation is not attempted here. The reader is referred, however, to Arad (2003) and to Borer (forthcoming) for some relevant discussion.

11.2.3 *A last note on idioms*

Although by assumption a listeme cannot be associated with any grammatical properties, one device used in this work has allowed us to get around the formidable restrictions placed on the grammar by such a constraint—the formation of idioms. We have analysed as idioms not only *kick the bucket, trousers, take over*, and *remit*—cases where there is an obvious tension between the existence of a complex hierarchy alongside non-compositional meaning—but also cases such as *depend on*, and, possibly most controversially, *arrive* (cf. Chapter 10, Sections 10.2–3), for which we assumed a hidden existential/locative to be in place. Potentially, then, within the system developed here, any syntactic or morphological property which does not reduce directly to some formal computational principle is to be captured by classifying the relevant item as an idiom—a partial representation of a phonological index with some functional value. It is the functional value which in turn determines the categorial environment for the insertion of a phonological index, and by extension, its interpretation. Such idiomatic specification could be utilized, potentially, not just for *arrive* and *depend on*, but also for obligatorily transitive verbs (e.g. as requiring an objective $\langle e\rangle$ correlating with either Asp_Q or F^s), for verbs such as *put*, with their obligatory locative, and for verbs which require a sentential complement.[4]

---

[4] And see in this context Ramchand (2003), where the claim that interpretation follows from listed categorial features associated with L-syntax is explicitly made. See also Marantz (2000, 2001) and Arad (2003), where the claim is made that in effect, all 'words' are interpretations associated with fully articulated structures, and hence are all idioms which, by definition, are categorially specified. The claims made here are considerably narrower.

In Borer (1994) it is suggested that listemes do specify the number of arguments, although not their role or their insertion frame. As such, that system can state directly that some verbs are obligatorily transitive, while others are not. Although a system in which the number of arguments is specified over-

The reader may object that subcategorization, of sorts, is introduced here through the back door, with the introduction, in lieu of lexical syntactic annotation, of an articulated listed structure, called an *idiom*, which accomplishes, de facto, the same task. The objection has of course some validity, and at the present state of the art, the introduction of idioms may represent somewhat of a concession, an attempt to integrate the richness of syntactic environments conditioned, as they at times appear to be, by listemes. On the positive side, we note that to the extent that the existence of idioms is costly, we have attempted to put in place here a system which at least potentially extricates from the costly component of language all properties of listemes which are otherwise derivable from the structure. Formally unmarked listemes become the norm. The listing of fixed associations between functional values and listemes, sometimes associated with phonological indices—that is, creating idioms—handles the residue of cases which cannot be otherwise derived. Fundamentally, then, the research agenda outlined here must now branch into the study of idioms, in the technical sense defined here. Can the class of idioms be narrowed down? Is it the case that a more articulated functional structure along with a better understanding of its semantic function could do away with at least some of the cases which are here handled via listing as idioms? Are there conditions on the well-formedness of idioms from which the existence of some, but not others, would emerge? These are all issues which must be investigated in detail before an exo-skeletal approach can be completely successful, and it is to be hoped that future research will indeed shed some light on them.

generates less, we note that it gives rise to problems precisely where those arguments do not surface, for example, in the context of (result) derived nominals (to wit, where are the arguments of *destroy* in *destruction*? See Chapter 2, Section 2.4, for some discussion). This, among other factors, is the reason why I opted here for the most limited statement possible with respect to the grammatical properties of listemes. As noted before, it is only under such a strong version that the full explanatory power of such a system can be investigated, and it is only when its full explanatory power has been researched that it is appropriate to consider the ways in which this aspect of its statement is to be relaxed.

References

ABUSCH, DORIT. (1993). 'The scope of indefinites', *Natural Language Semantics* 2: 83–135.

ADGER, DAVID and GILLIAN RAMCHAND. (2001). 'Avoiding symmetry: the syntax and semantics of equation in Scottish Gaelic', MS., York University and Oxford University.

ALEXIADOU, ARTEMIS. (1997). *Adverb Placement: A Case Study in Antisymmetric Syntax*. Amsterdam: John Benjamins.

——(2001). *Functional Structure in Nominals: Nominalization and Ergativity*. Amsterdam: John Benjamins.

——ELENA ANAGNOSTOPOULOU and MARTIN EVERAERT (eds.). (2003). *The Unaccusativity Puzzle*. Oxford: Oxford University Press.

ALLAN, KEITH. (1980). 'Nouns and countability', *Language* 56: 541–67.

ANDERSON, STEPHEN. (1982). 'Where's morphology?', *Linguistic Inquiry* 13: 571–612.

——(1992). *Amorphous Morphology*. Cambridge: Cambridge University Press.

ARAD, MAYA. (1998). 'VP structure and the syntax-lexicon interface', Ph.D. dissertation, University College London.

——(1999). 'Psychological verbs and the syntax/lexicon interface', MS., Harvard University.

——(2003). 'Locality constraints on the interpretation of roots: the case of Hebrew denominal verbs', *Natural Language and Linguistic Theory* 21: 737–78.

BACH, EMMON. (1981). 'On time, tense, and aspect: an essay in English metaphysics', in *Radical Pragmatics*, (ed.) Peter Cole. New York: Academic Press, 63–81.

——(1986). 'The algebra of events', *Linguistic and Philosophy* 9: 5–16.

——(1995). 'A note on quantification and blankets in Haisla', in Bach et al. (1995), 13–20.

——ELOISE JELINEK, ANGELIKA KRATZER, and BARBARA PARTEE (eds.). (1995). *Quantification in Natural Languages*. Dordrecht: Kluwer.

BAKER, MARK. (1985). 'The Mirror Principle and morphosyntactic explanation', *Linguistic Inquiry* 16: 373–416.

——(1988). *Incorporation*. Chicago: University of Chicago Press.

——(1996). *The Polysynthetic Parameter*. Oxford: Oxford University Press.

——(2003). *Lexical Categories: Verbs, Nouns and Adjectives*, Cambridge: Cambridge University Press.

——KYLE JOHNSON and IAN ROBERTS. (1989). 'Passive arguments raised', *Linguistic Inquiry* 20: 219–52.

BAT-EL, OUTI. (1989). 'Phonology and word structure in Modern Hebrew', Ph.D. dissertation, University of California, Los Angeles.

BEARD, ROBERT. (1981). *The Indo-European Lexicon*. Amsterdam: North-Holland.

——(1995). *Lexeme-Morpheme Based Morphology*. Albany, NY: State University of New York Press.

BEGHELLI, FILIPPO and TIM STOWELL. (1997). 'Distributivity and negation: the syntax of *each* and *every*', in Szabolcsi (1997), 71–107.

BELLETTI, ADRIANNA. (1988). 'The case of unaccusatives', *Linguistic Inquiry* 19: 1–34.
—— and LUIGI RIZZI. (1981). 'The syntax of *ne*: some theoretical implications', *The Linguistic Review* 1: 117–54.
BENEDICTO, ELENA. (1997). 'The syntax and semantics of non-canonical NP positions'. Ph.D. dissertation, University of Massachusetts.
BENMAMOUN, ELABBAS. (1998). 'Arabic morphology: the central role of the imperfective', *Lingua* 108: 175–201.
BENNET, MICHAEL and BARBARA PARTEE. (1972). *Toward the logic of tense and aspect in English*, Distributed by Indiana University Linguistics Club.
BENUA, LAURA and HAGIT BORER. (1996). 'The passive/anti-passive alternation', paper presented at GLOW, Athens, April 1996.
BITTNER, MARIA. (1995). 'Quantification in Eskimo: a challenge for compositional semantics', in Bach et al. (1995), 59–80.
—— and KEN HALE. (1995). 'Remarks on definiteness in Walpiri', in Bach et al. (1995), 81–106.
————(1996). 'Ergativity: towards a theory of heterogeneous class', *Linguistics Inquiry* 27: 531–604.
BOATNER, MAXINE TULL and JOHN EDWARD GATES. (1975). *A Dictionary of American Idioms*. New York: Barron's Educational Series.
BOBALJIK, JONATHAN. (1993). 'On ergativity and ergative unergatives', *MIT Working Papers in Linguistics* 19, Cambridge, MA: MIT Press.
——(2002). 'A-chains at the PF interface: copies and "covert" movement', *Natural Language and Linguistic Theory* 20: 197–267.
—— and DIANNE JONAS. (1996). 'Subject positions and the roles of TP', *Linguistic Inquiry* 27: 195–236.
BORER, HAGIT. (1980). 'Empty subjects in Modern Hebrew and constraints on thematic relations', *Proceedings of the North Eastern Linguistic Society* 10, Ottawa.
——(1983). *Parametric Syntax*. Dordrecht: Foris.
——(1984). 'Restrictive relatives in Modern Hebrew', *Natural Language and Linguistic Theory*, 2: 219–60.
——(1986). 'I-Subjects', *Linguistic Inquiry* 17: 375–416.
——(1989). 'Anaphoric AGR', *The Null Subject Parameter*, (eds.) Osvaldo Jaeggli and Ken Safir. Dordrecht: Kluwer, 69–109.
——(1994). 'The projection of arguments', *University of Massachusetts Occasional Papers in Linguistics* 17, (eds.) Elena Benedicto and Jeff Runner. Amherst: GLSA, University of Massachusetts.
——(1995a). 'Passive without thematic roles', paper presented at the Morphosyntax-Morphophonology workshop, University of California, Davis, May, 1995.
——(1995b). 'The ups and downs of Hebrew verb movement', *Natural Language and Linguistic Theory* 13: 527–606.
——(1998a). 'Passive without theta grids'. *Morphology and its Relations to Phonology and Syntax*, (eds.) Steven Lapointe, Patrick Farrell, and Diane Brentari. Stanford, CA: Center for the Study of Language and Information, 60–99.

BORER, HAGIT. (1998b). 'Morphology and syntax', *Handbook of Morphology*, (eds.) Andrew Spencer and Arnold Zwicky. Oxford: Blackwell, 151–90.

—— (1999a). 'Deconstructing the construct', *Beyond Principles and Parameters*, (eds.) Kyle Johnson and Ian Roberts. Dordrecht: Kluwer, 43–90.

—— (1999b). 'The form, the forming and the formation of nominals,' paper presented at the 2nd Mediterranean Morphology Meeting, September 1999.

—— (2003a). 'Exo-skeletal vs. endo-skeletal explanations: syntactic projections and the lexicon', *The Nature of Explanation in Linguistic Theory*, (eds.) John Moore and Maria Polinsky. Stanford, CA: Center for the Study of Language and Information.

—— (2003b). 'The grammar machine', in Alexiadou et al. (2003), 288–331.

—— (2004). *Structuring Sense*: Vol. II. Oxford: Oxford University Press.

—— (forthcoming). *Structuring Sense*: Vol. III. Oxford: Oxford University Press.

—— and BERNHARD ROHRBACHER. (2003). 'Minding the absent: Arguments for the full competence hypothesis', *Language Acquisition* 10: 123–75.

—— and YOSEF GRODZINSKY. (1986). 'Syntactic cliticization and lexical cliticization: the case of Hebrew dative clitics', *The Syntax of Pronominal Clitics*, (ed.) Hagit Borer. (Syntax and Semantics 19). New York: Academic Press, 175–215.

BOWERS, JOHN. (1975). 'Adjectives and adverbs in English', *Foundations of Language* 13: 529–62.

BRESNAN, JOAN. (1970). 'On complementizers: towards a syntactic theory of complement types', *Foundation of Language* 6: 297–321.

—— (1994). 'Locative inversion and the architecture of universal grammar', *Language* 70: 72–131.

—— and JONI M. KANERVA. (1989). 'Locative inversion in Chichewa: a case study of factorization in grammar', *Linguistic Inquiry* 20: 1–50.

—— and LIOBA MOSHI. (1990). 'Object asymmetries in comparative Bantu syntax', *Linguistic Inquiry* 21: 147–86.

BRODY, MICHAEL. (2001). 'Syntactic complement series as morphological units', paper given at the Workshop on Head Movement, UCLA, October 2001.

BRUGGER, GERHARD. (1993). 'Generic interpretation and expletive determiners', *University of Venice Working Papers in Lingusitics* 3: 1–30.

BURZIO, LUIGI. (1986). *Italian Syntax: A Government-Binding Approach*. Dordrecht: Reidel, (originally Ph.D. dissertation, MIT, 1981).

CARLSON, GREGORY N. (1977a). 'A unified analysis of English bare plural', *Linguistics and Philosophy* 1: 413–57.

—— (1977b). 'Reference to kinds in English', Ph.D. dissertation, University of Massachusetts.

CARSTAIRS-MCCARTHY, ANDREW. (1998). 'Pragmatic structure: inflectional paradigms and morphological classes', *Handbook of Morphology*, (eds.) Andrew Spencer and Arnold Zwicky. Oxford: Blackwell.

CHENG, LISA L.-S. and RINT SYBESMA. (1998). '*Yi-wan tang, yi-ge tang*: classifiers and massifiers', *Tsing Hua Journal of Chinese Studies* 28: 385–412.

—— —— (1999). 'Bare and not-so-bare nouns and the structure of NP', *Linguistic Inquiry* 30: 509–42.

——— (2000). 'Classifiers in four varieties of Chinese', MS., HIL/Leiden University.
CHIERCHIA, GENNARO. (1989). 'A semantics for unaccusatives and its syntactic consequences', MS., Cornell University.
——— (1998a). 'Reference to kinds across languages', *Natural Language Semantics* 6: 339–405.
——— (1998b). 'Plurality of mass nouns and the notion of "semantic parameter"', in Rothstein (1998), 53–103.
——— (2003). 'A semantics for unaccusatives and its syntactic consequences', in Alexiadou et al. (2003), 22–59. (Originally MS., Cornell University, 1989).
CHOMSKY, NOAM. (1965). *Aspects of the Theory of Syntax*, Cambridge, MA: MIT Press.
——— (1970). 'Remarks on nominalization', *Readings in English Transformational Grammar*, (eds.) Roderick Jacobs and Peter Rosenbaum. Waltham, MA: Ginn, 184–221.
——— (1981). *Lectures on Government and Binding*. Dordrecht: Foris.
——— (1986). *Knowledge of Language: Its Nature, Origin and Use*. New York: Praeger.
——— (1991). 'Some notes on the economy of derivation and representation', *Principles and Parameters in Comparative Grammar*, (ed.) Robert Freidin. Cambridge, MA: MIT Press, 117–54.
——— (1993). 'A minimalist program for linguistic theory', in Hale and Keyser (1993), 41–85.
——— (1995a). *The Minimalist Program*. Cambridge, MA: MIT Press.
——— (1995b). 'Bare phrase structure', *Government and Binding Theory and the Minimalist Program*, (ed.) Gert Webelhuth. Cambridge, MA: Basil Blackwell, 383–440.
——— (1999). 'Derivation by phase', *MIT Occasional Papers in Linguistics* 17.
——— (2000). 'Minimalist inquiries: the framework', *Step by Step: Essays on Minimalist Syntax in Honor of Howard Lasnik*, (eds.) Roger Martin, David Michaels, and Juan Uriagereka, Cambridge, MA: MIT Press, 89–155.
CINQUE, GUGLIELMO. (1988). 'On *si* constructions and the theory of ARB', *Linguistic Inquiry* 19: 521–82.
——— (1997). *Adverbs and Functional Heads: A Cross-Linguistic Perspective*. New York: Oxford University Press.
——— (2000). 'On Greenberg's Universal 20 and the Semitic DP', paper presented at the Antisymmetry Conference, Cortona.
CLAHSEN, HARALD, SONJA EISENBEISS, and MARTINA PENKE. (1996). 'Lexical learning in early syntactic development', *Generative Perspectives on Language Acquisition*, (ed.) Harald Clahsen. Amsterdam: John Benjamins, 129–59.
CLARK, EVE and HERBERT CLARK. (1979). 'When nouns surface as verbs', *Language* 55: 767–811.
CONTRERAS, HELES. (1986). 'Spanish bare nouns and the ECP', *Generative Studies in Spanish Syntax*, (eds.) Ivonne Bordelois, Heles Contreras, and Karen Zagona. Dordrecht: Foris, 25–50.
CORVER, NORBERT. (1997). 'The internal structure of Dutch extended adjectival projections', *Natural Language and Linguistic Theory* 15: 289–368.
CROFT, WILLIAM. (2001). *Radical Construction Grammar*. Oxford: Oxford University Press.

DALRYMPLE, MARY, SAMUAL E. MCHOMBO, and STANLEY PETERS. (1994). 'Semantic similarities and syntactic contrasts between Chichewa and English Reciprocals', *Linguistic Inquiry* 25: 145–63.

DAVIDSON, DONALD. (1967). 'The logical form of action sentences', *The Logic of Decision and Action*, (ed.) Nicholas Rescher. Pittsburgh: University of Pittsburgh Press, 81–95.

——(1980). *Essays on Actions and Events*. Oxford: Clarendon Press.

DAVIS, HENRI and HAMIDA DEMIRDASH. (1995). 'Agents and events', paper presented at GLOW, 1995.

——— (2000). 'On lexical verb meanings: evidence from Salish', in Tenny and Pustejovsky (2000), 97–142.

DE HOOP, HELEN. (1992). *Case Configuration and Noun Phrase Interpretation*, (Groningen Dissertations in Linguistics). Groningen: University of Groningen. (Published by Garland, New York, 1997.)

DE SOUZA, SUELI MARIA. (1990). 'The system of personal reference of the Kraho language', MA thesis, University of Goias, Goiania.

DE SWART, HENRIETTA. (1998). 'Introduction to natural language semantics', *CSLI Lecture Notes* 80. Stanford, CA: Center for the Study of Language and Information.

DI SCIULLO, A.-M. and EDWIN WILLIAMS. (1987). *On the Definition of Word*. Cambridge, MA: MIT Press.

DECHAINE, ROSE-MARIE. (1993). 'Predicates across categories', Ph.D. thesis, University of Massachusetts.

DELFITTO, DENIS. (2001). 'Genericity in language: issues of syntax, logical form, and interpretation', MS., University of Utrecht.

DIESING, MOLLY. (1992). *Indefinites*. Cambridge, MA: MIT Press.

DOBROVIE-SORIN, CARMEN. (1999). 'Spec DP and (in)definiteness spreading: from Romanian genitives to Hebrew construct state nominals', in the Chomsky Celebration Project, mitpress.mit.edu/chomskydysc.

——and BRENDA LACA (1996). 'Generic bare NPs', MS., University Paris 7 and University of Strasburg.

DOETJES, JENNY. (1996). 'Mass and count: syntax or semantics?', *Proceedings of Meaning on the HIL*. 34–52.

——(1997). 'Quantifiers and selection: on the distribution of quantifying expressions in French, Dutch and English', Ph.D. dissertation, Leiden University.

——and MARTIN HONCOOP. (1997). 'The semantics of event-related readings: a case for pair quantification', in Anna Szabolcsi (1997), 263–310.

DORON, EDIT. (1992). 'Haceruf Hašemani' [The Nominal Phrase], *Balšanut xišuvit ivrit* [*Hebrew Computational Linguistics*], (eds.) Uzi Ornan, Gidon Arieli, and Edit Doron. Jerusalem: Ministry of Science and Technology, 116–22. (In Hebrew).

DOWNING, PAMELA. (1984). 'Japanese numeral classifiers: a syntactic, semantic and functional profile', Ph.D. dissertation, University of California, Berkeley.

DOWTY, DAVID R. (1979). *Word Meaning and Montague Grammar*. Dordrecht: Reidel.

——(1991). 'Thematic proto-roles and argument selection', *Language* 67: 547–619.

EMONDS, JOSEPH. (1978). 'The verbal complex V'-V in French. *Linguistic Inquiry* 9: 151–75.

ERTESCHIK-SHIR, NOMI and TOVA R. RAPOPORT. (1995). 'A theory of verbal projection', MS., Ben Gurion University of the Negev.
——(2000). 'Aspectual focus', paper presented at GLOW, Bilbao.
——(2001). 'The CDP model: aspectual projection', paper presented at the workshop The Syntax of Aspect. Ben Gurion University of the Negev, June 2001.
EVERAERT, MARTIN. (1992). 'Auxiliary selection in idiomatic constructions', MS., Research Institute for Language and Speech, University of Utrecht.
FANSLOW, GISBERT. (to appear). 'Münchhausen-style head movement and the analysis of verb second', *Journal of Comparative Germanic Syntax: Proceedings of the workshop on Head Movement, UCLA, 2001*, (ed.) Anoop Mahajan.
FASSI FEHRI, ABDELKADER. (1989). 'Generalized IP structure, case and VS word order', *MIT Working Papers in Linguistics* 10, (eds.) Iziar Laka and Anoop Mahajan, 75–113.
——(1999). 'Arabic modifying adjectives and DP structure', *Studia Linguistica* 53: 105–54.
——(2003). 'Mass, count, bare'. Paper presesented at the Sixth National Meeting of the Linguistic Society of Morocco, Mohammed V University, Rabat, May 2003.
FILIP, HANA. (1992). 'Aspect and interpretation of nominal arguments', *Papers from the Twenty-eighth Regional Meeting of the Chicago Linguistic Society*. Chicago, 139–58.
——(1993). 'Aspect, situation types and nominal reference', Ph.D. dissertation, University of California, Berkeley. (Publ. in 1999 by Garland, New York.).
——(1996). 'Domain restrictions on lexical quantifiers'. MS., University of Illinois at Urbana-Champaign.
——(2000). 'The quantization puzzle', in Tenny and Pustejovsky (2000), 39–96.
FILLMORE, CHARLES and PAUL KAY. (1997). 'The formal architecture of Construction Grammar'. MS., University of California, Berkeley.
FODOR, JANET and IVAN SAG. (1982). 'Referential and quantificational indefinites', *Linguistic and Philosophy* 5: 355–98.
FODOR, JERRY and ERNEST LEPORE. (1998). 'The emptiness of the lexicon: critical reflections on J. Pustejovsky's "The Generative Lexicon"', *Linguistic Inquiry* 29: 269–88.
FOX, DANI. (2002). 'Antecedent contained deletion and the copy theory of movement', *Linguistic Inquiry* 33: 63–96.
FREEZE, RAY. (1992). 'Existentials and other locatives', *Language* 68: 553–95.
FREGE, GOTTLOB. (1950). *The Foundation of Arithmetic*. Oxford: Blackwell. (Originally published as *Die Grundlagen der Arithmetik, Eine Logisch mathematische Untersuchung Über den Begriff der Zahl*. Breslau: Wilhelm Köbner, 1884.).
FUKUI, NAOKI. (1986). A theory of category projection and its applications', Ph.D. dissertation, MIT.
GIL, DAVID. (1994). 'Summary: numeral classifiers', *Linguist List*, Vol. 5: 466.
——(1995). 'Universal quantifiers and distributivity', in Bach (1995), 321–62.
GIORGI, ALESSANDRA and FABIO PIANESI. (1997). *Tense and Aspect: From Semantics to Morphosyntax*. New York: Oxford University Press.
GIVÓN, TALMY. (1981). 'On the development of the numeral *one* as an indefinite marker', *MIT Working Papers in Lingusitics* 3: *Issues in the grammar of Semitic Languages*, (eds.) Hagit Borer and Joseph Aoun. Cambridge, MA: MIT Press, 233–55. (Also appeared in *Folia Linguistica Historica* 2: 35–53.)

GLEITMAN, LILA. (1995). 'When prophesy fails: how do we discard our theories of learning?' Keynote address at the Twentieth Annual Boston University Conference on Language Development. Boston, November 1995.

GOLDBERG, ADELE. (1995). *Constructions: A Construction Grammar Approach to Argument Structure*. Chicago: University of Chicago Press.

GREENBERG, JOSEPH. (1975). 'Dynamic aspects of word order in the numeral classifier', *Word Order and Word Order Change*, (ed.) Charles Li. Austin: Univeresity of Texas Press, 27–46.

GREUDER, WILLIAM and MIRIAM BUTT (eds). (1998). *The Projection of Arguments*. Stanford, CA: Center for the Study of Language and Information.

GRIMSHAW, JANE. (1979). 'Complement selection and the lexicon', *Linguistic Inquiry* 10: 279–326.

—— (1990). *Argument Structure*. Cambridge, MA: MIT Press.

—— (1991). 'Extended projections', MS., Brandeis University.

HALE, KENNETH. (1989). 'Walpiri categories', handout, MIT.

—— and SAMUEL JAY KEYSER. (1993). 'On argument structure and the lexical expression of syntactic relations', in Hale and Keyser (1993), 53–110.

—— —— (eds.) (1993). *The View from Building 20*. Cambridge, MA: MIT Press.

HALLE, MORRIS. (1973). 'Prolegomena to a theory of word formation', *Linguistic Inquiry* 4: 3–16.

—— and ALEC MARANTZ. (1993). 'Distributed Morphology and the pieces of inflection', in Hale and Keyser (1993), 111–76.

HARLEY, HEIDI. (1995). 'Subject, events and licensing', Ph.D. dissertation, MIT.

—— (1997). 'Events, agents and the interpretation of VP-shells', MS., University of Pennsylvania.

—— (2001). 'Restrictions on measuring out and the ontology of verb roots in English', paper presented in the workshop The Syntax of Aspect, Ben Gurion University of the Negav, June, 2001.

—— and ROLF NOYER. (1997). 'Mixed nominalizations, object shift and short verb movement in English', *Proceedings of the North Eastern Linguistic Society* 28. University of Massachusetts at Amherst: GLSA.

—— —— (1998). 'Formal vs. encyclopedic properties of vocabulary: evidence from nominalizations', MS., University of Pennsylvania.

—— —— (1999). 'State-of-the-Article: Distributed Morphology', *Glot International* 4.4: 3–9.

HAY, JENNIFER. (1998). 'The non-uniformity of degree achievements', paper presented at the Seventy Second Annual Meeting of the Linguistic Society of America, New York.

—— CHRISTOPHER KENNEDY and BETH LEVIN. (1999). 'Scalar structure underlies telicity in Degree Achievements', in Mathews and Strolovitch (1999), 127–44.

HAZOUT, ILAN. (1991). 'Verbal nouns: theta theoretic studies in Hebrew and Arabic', Ph.D. dissertation, University of Massachusetts.

—— (1995). 'Action nominalization and the Lexicalist Hypothesis', *Natural Language and Linguistic Theory* 13: 355–404.

HEIM, IRENE. (1982). 'The semantics of definite and indefinite noun phrases', Ph.D. dissertation, University of Massachusetts.
HIGGINBOTHAM, JAMES. (1985). 'On semantics', *Linguistic Inquiry* 16: 547–93.
——(1987). 'Indefinites and predication', *The Representation of (In)definites*, (eds.) Eric Reuland and Alice ter Meulen. Cambridge, MA: MIT Press, 43–70.
——(1994). 'Mass and count quantifiers', *Linguistics and Philosophy* 17: 447–80.
——(2000a). 'On events in linguistic semantics', Higginbotham et al. (2000), 49–80.
——(2000b). 'On the representation of telicity'. MS., Oxford University.
——FABIO PIANESI and ACHILLE C. VARZI (eds.). (2000). *Speaking of Events*. New York: Oxford University Press.
HOEKSTRA, TEUN A. and RENÉ MULDER. (1990). 'Unergatives and copular verbs; locational and existential predication', *The Linguistic Review* 7: 1–79.
HOLMBERG, ANDERS. (1991). 'Head scrambling', paper presented at the GLOW conference, Leiden University, 1991.
——(2000). 'Scandinavian stylistic fronting: How any category can become an expletive', *Linguistics Inquiry* 31: 445–83.
HORNSTEIN, NORBERT. (1999). 'Movement and Control', *Linguistic Inquiry*, 30, 69–96.
HUDSON, WESLEY. (1989). 'Functional categories and the saturation of noun phrases', *Proceedings of the North Eastern Linguistic Society* 19: 207–22.
HUNDIUS, HARALD and ULRIKE KÖLVER. (1983). 'Syntax and semantics of numeral classifiers in Thai', *Studies in Language* 7: 165–214.
HYAMS, NINA. (1996). 'The underspecification of functional categories in early grammar', *Generative Perspectives on Language Acquisition. Empirical Findings, Theoretical Considerations and Crosslinguistic Comparisons*, (ed.) Harald Clahsen. Amsterdam: John Benjamins, 91–127.
IATRIDOU, SABINE. (1990). 'About Agr(P)', *Linguistic Inquiry* 21: 551–76.
JACKENDOFF, RAY. (1977). *X-bar Syntax: A Study of Phrase Structure*. Cambridge, MA: MIT Press.
JACKENDOFF, RAY. (1990). *Semantic Structure*. Cambridge, MA: MIT Press.
——(1996). 'The proper treatment of measuring out, telicity and perhaps even quantification in English', *Natural Language and Linguistic Theory* 14: 305–54.
JAEGGLI, OSVALDO. (1986a). 'Passive', *Linguistic Inquiry* 17: 587–622.
——(1986b). 'Arbitrary pro and pronominals', *Natural Language and Linguistic Theory* 4: 43–76.
JOHNSON, KYLE. (1991). 'Object positions', *Natural Language and Linguistic Theory* 9: 577–636.
KAMP, HANS. (1979). 'Events, instances and temporal reference', *Semantics from Different Points of View*, (eds.) Rainer Bauerle, Uwe Egli, and Armin von Stechow. Berlin: Springer, 376–417.
——(1981). 'A theory of truth and semantic interpretation', *Formal Methods in the Study of Language*, (eds.) Jeroen Groenendijk, Theo Janssen, and Martin Stokhof. (Mathematical Centre Tracts 136). Amsterdam: Mathematisch Centrum, 277–322.
KAYNE, RICHARD. (1984). *Connectedness and Binary Branching*. Dordrecht: Foris.

KAYNE, RICHARD. (1993). 'Toward a modular theory of auxiliary selection', *Studia Linguistica* 47: 3–31.

——(1994). *The Antisymmetry of Syntax*. Cambridge, MA: MIT Press.

KENNEDY, CHRISTOPHER. (1999). *Projecting the Adjective: The Syntax and Semantics of Gradability and Comparison*. New York: Garland.

——and BETH LEVIN. (2000). 'Telicity corresponds to degree of change', paper presented at Michigan State University, 30 Nov. 2000.

——and LOUISE MCNALLY. (1999). 'From event structure to scale structure: degree modification in deverbal adjectives', in Matthews and Strolovitch (1999),163–80.

KIPARSKY, PAUL. (1996). 'Partitive case and aspect.' MS., Stanford University.

——(1998). 'Partitive case and aspect', in Greuder and Butt (1998), 265–307.

——(2001). 'The partitive revisited', paper presented at the workshop The Syntax of Aspect. Ben Gurion University of the Negev, June 2001.

KLOOSTER, WILLEM G. (1972). *The Structure Underlying Measure Phrase Sentences*. Dordrecht: Kluwer.

KOOPMAN, HILDA and ANNA SZABOLCSI. (2000). *Verbal Complexes*. Cambridge, MA: MIT Press.

KRATZER, ANGELIKA. (1994). 'The Event Argument', MS., University of Massachusetts.

——(1996). 'Severing the external argument from the verb', *Phrase structure and the Lexicon*, (eds.) Johan Rooryck and Laurie Zaring. Dordrecht: Kluwer, 109–37.

——(1998). 'Scope or pseudoscope? Are there wide-scope indefinites?', in Rothstein (1998), 163–196.

——(1999). 'The relations between verb meaning and argument structure', paper presented in the conference on Explanation in Linguistics, University of California, San Diego, December 1999.

KRIFKA, MANFRED. (1989). 'Nominal reference, temporal constitution and quantification in event semantics', *Semantics and Contextual Expressions*, (eds.) Renate Bartsch, John van Benthem, and Peter van Emde Boas. Dordrecht: Foris, 75–115.

——(1990). '4000 ships passed through the lock', *Linguistics and Philosophy* 13: 487–520.

——(1992). 'Thematic relations as links between nominal reference and temporal constitution,' *Lexical Matters*, (eds.) Ivan A. Sag and Anna Szablocsi. Stanford, CA: Center for the Study of Language and Information, 29–53.

——(1998). 'The origins of telicity', in Rothstein (1998), 197–235.

LANDAU, IDAN. (1997). 'Possessive raising', MS., MIT.

——(2001). 'Control and extraposition: the case of Super-Equi', *Natural Language and Linguistic Theory* 19: 109–52.

LARSON, RICHARD. (1988). 'On the double object construction.' *Linguistic Inquiry* 19: 335–91.

LEINONEN, MARJA. (1984). 'Narrative implications of aspect in Russian and Finnish', *Aspect Bound*, (eds.) Casper de Groot and Hannu Tommola. Dordrecht: Foris, 239–55.

LEVIN, BETH. (1993). *English Verb Classes and Alternations*. Chicago: University of Chicago Press.

——(1999).'Objecthood: An event structure perspective', *Proceedings of the Chicago Linguistic Society* 35, Vol. 1: The Main Session. Chicago: University of Chicago, 223–47.

——and MALKA RAPPAPORT HOVAV. (1986). 'The formation of adjectival passive', *Linguistic Inquiry* 17: 623–61.

————(1989). 'An approach to unaccusative mismatches', *Proceedings of the North Eastern Linguistic Society* 19. GSLA, University of Massachusetts, Amherst, 314–28.

————(1992a). 'The lexicon semantics of verbs of motion: the perspective from unaccusativity', *Thematic Structure: Its Role in Grammar*, (ed.) Iggy Roca. Berlin: Mouton de Gruyter, 247–69.

————(1992b). 'Unaccusativity: at the syntax-semantics interface', MS., Northwestern University and Bar Ilan University. (A revised version of this manuscript was published as Levin and Rappaport Hovav 1995.).

————(1995). *Unaccusativity: At the Syntax-Lexical Semantics Interface.* Cambridge, MA: MIT Press.

————(1999). 'Two structures for compositionally derived events', in Matthews and Strolovitch (1999), 199–233.

————(2000). 'An event structure account of English resultatives', MS., Stanford University and The Hebrew University of Jerusalem.

LEWIS, DAVID. (1975). 'Adverbs of quantification', *Formal Semantics of Natural Language*, (ed.) Edward L. Keenan. Cambridge: Cambridge University Press, 3–15.

LI, CHARLES N. and SANDRA A. THOMPSON. (1981). *Mandarin Chinese: A Functional Reference Grammar.* Berkeley: University of California Press.

LI, Y.-H. AUDREY. (1997). 'Structures and interpretation of nominal expressions.' MS., University of Southern California.

——(1998). 'Argument determiner phrases and number phrases', *Linguistic Inquiry* 29: 693–702.

LIEBER, ROCHELLE. (1980). 'On the organization of the lexicon', Ph.D. dissertation, MIT.

LIN, Y. W. (1993). 'Object expletives, definiteness effect and scope interpretation,' MS., University of Massachusetts.

LINK, GODEHARD. (1983). 'The logical analysis of plurals and mass terms: a lattice-theoretic approach', *Meaning, Use and Interpretation of Language,* (eds.) Rainer Bäuerle, Christophe Schwarze, and Arnim von Stechow. Berlin: de Gruyter, 303–23.

——(1987). 'Algebraic semantics for event structures', *Proceedings of the Amsterdam Colloquium 6,* (eds.) Jeroen Groenendijk, Martin Stokhof, and Frank Veltman. University of Amsterdam, Institute for Language, Logic, and Information, 243–62.

LONGOBARDI, GIUSEPPE. (1994). 'Reference and proper names', *Linguistic Inquiry* 25: 609–66.

MCCAWLEY, JAMES. (1968). 'Lexical insertion in a transformational grammar without deep structure', *Papers from the Fourth Regional Meeting of the Chicago Linguistics Society,* (eds.) Bill J. Darden, Charles-James N. Bailey, and Alice Davidson. University of Chicago, 71–80.

MCCLURE, WILLIAM. (1995). 'Syntactic projections of the semantics of aspect', Ph.D. dissertation, Cornell University.

MANZINI, M. RITA and ANNA ROUSSOU. (1999). 'A minimalist theory of A-movement and control', *University College Working Papers in Linguistics* 11. London: University College London.

MARANTZ, ALEC. (1984). *On the Nature of Grammatical Relations*. Cambridge, MA: MIT Press.

—— (1996). 'Cat as a phrasal category', MS., MIT.

—— (1997). 'No escape from syntax: don't try morphological analysis in the privacy of your own lexicon', *University of Pennsylvania Working Papers in Linguistics* 4.2, (eds.) Alexis Dimitriadis, Laura Siegel, Clarissa Surek-Clark, and Alexander Williams (1997), 201–25.

—— (1999). 'Creating words above and below little v', MS., MIT.

—— (2000). 'Roots: the universality of root and pattern morphology', paper presented at the Conference on Afro-Asiatic Languages, University of Paris VII, June 2000.

—— (2001). 'Words', keynote address to the West Coast Conference on Formal Linguistics, University of Southern California, February 2001.

MATEU, JAUME and GEMMA RIGAU. (2000). 'A minimalist account of conflation processes: parametric variation at the lexicon-syntax interface'. Research Report GGT-00-1, Group de Gramática Teórica, Universitat Autonoma de Barcelona.

MATHEWS, TANYA and DEVON STROLOVITCH (ed.) (1999). *Proceedings of Semantics and Linguistic Theory* 9, Ithaca: CLC Publications.

MATTHEWS, PETER H. (1972). *Inflectional Morphology: A Theoretial Study Based on Aspects of Latin Verb Conjugations*. Cambridge: Cambridge University Press.

MAY, ROBERT. (1985). *Logical Form*. Cambridge, MA: MIT Press.

MILSARK, GARY. (1974). 'Existential sentences in English'. Ph.D. dissertation, MIT.

MITTWOCH, ANITA. (1991). 'In defense of Vendler's achievements', *Belgian Journal of Linguistics* 6, 71–84.

—— (1998). 'Cognate objects as reflections of Davidsonian event arguments', in Rothstein (1998), 309–32.

MOHAMMAD, MOHAMMAD. (1988). 'On the parallelism between IP and DP', *Proceedings of West Coast Conference on Formal Linguistics* 7, 241–54.

MORO, ANDREA. (1990). 'The raising of predicates: copula, expletives and existence'. *MIT Working Papers in Linguistics* 13. Cambridge, MA: MIT.

—— (1997). *The Raising of Predicates*. Cambridge: Cambridge University Press.

MOURELATOS, ALEX P. D. (1978). 'Events, processes and states', *Linguistic and Philosophy* 2: 415–34.

MUROMATSU, KEIKO. (1998). 'On the syntax of classifiers', Ph.D. dissertation, University of Maryland.

NOYER, ROLF. (1997). *Feature Positions and Affixes in Autonomous Morphological Structures*. New York: Garland Press.

ORTMAN, ALBERT. (2000). 'Where plural refuses to agree: feature unification and morphological economy', *Acta Linguistica Hungarica* 47: 249–88.

OUHALLA, JAMAL. (1991a). *Functional Categories and Parametric Variations*. London: Routledge.

——(1991b). 'Functional categories and the head parameter', paper presented at the GLOW conference, Leiden, April 1991.
PARSONS, TERENCE. (1990). *Events in the Semantics of English. A Study in Subatomic Semantics*. Cambridge, MA: MIT Press.
——(1995). 'Thematic relations and arguments', *Linguistic Inquiry* 26: 635–62.
PARTEE, BARBARA. (1984). 'Nominal and temporal anaphora', *Linguistics and Philosophy* 7: 243–86.
PERELTSVAIG, ASYA. (2000). 'On accusative adverbials in Russian and Finnish', in *Adverbs and Adjunction*, (eds.) Artemis Alexiadou and Peter Svenonius. Potsdam: Universität Potsdam, 155–76.
PERLMUTTER, DAVID. (1978). 'Impersonal passives and the unaccusative hypothesis', *Proceedings of the Fourth Annual Meeting of the Berkeley Linguistic Society*. Berkeley: University of California, 157–89.
——and PAUL POSTAL. (1984). 'Impersonal passives and some relational laws', *Studies in Relational Grammar*, (eds.) David Perlmutter and Carol Rosen. Chicago: University of Chicago Press, 126–70.
PESETSKY, DAVID. (1982). 'Paths and categories', Ph.D. dissertation, MIT.
——(1989). 'Language particular processes and the Earliness Principle', MS., MIT.
——(1995). *Zero Syntax*. Cambridge, MA: MIT Press.
PETROVA, MILENA. (2000). 'Some indefinites in Bulgarian', MS., University of Southern California.
PIÑÓN, CHRISTOPHER. (1995). 'A mereology for aspectuality', Ph.D. dissertation, Stanford University.
——(2000). 'Happening gradually', *Proceedings of the Twenty Sixth Meeting of the Berkeley Linguistic Society*. Berkeley: University of California.
——(2001). 'A problem of aspectual composition in Polish', MS., University of Düssseldorf.
PLATZACK, CHRISTER. (1979). *The Semantic Interpretation of Aspect and Aktionsarten*. Dordrecht: Foris.
POLLOCK, JEAN-YVES. (1989). 'Verb movement, Universal Grammar and the structure of IP', *Linguistic Inquiry* 20: 365–424.
PORTNER, PAUL. (1992). 'Situation theory and the semantics of propositional expressions', Ph.D. dissertation, University of Massachusetts.
POSTAL, PAUL. (1974). *On Raising*. Cambridge, MA: MIT Press.
PRINCE, ALAN. (1973). 'The phonology and morphology of Tiberian Hebrew', Ph.D. dissertation, MIT.
PRINCE, ELLEN. (1981). 'On the inferencing of indefinite-*this* NPs', *Elements of Discourse Understanding*, (eds.) Aravind K. Joshi, Bonnie L. Webber, and Ivan A. Sag. Cambridge: Cambridge University Press, 231–50.
PUSTEJOVSKY, JAMES. (1991). 'The syntax of event structure', *Cognition* 41: 47–81.
——(1998). 'Generativity and explanation in semantics: a reply to Fodor and Lepore', *Linguistic Inquiry* 29: 289–311.

RAMCHAND, GILLIAN C. (1997). *Aspect and Predication*. Oxford: Oxford University Press.
—— (2003). 'First phase syntax', MS., Oxford University.
RAPOPORT, TOVA. (1999). 'The English middle and agentivity', *Linguistic Inquiry* 30: 147–55.
RAPPAPORT HOVAV, MALKA and BETH LEVIN. (1989). 'Is there evidence for deep unaccusativity in English? An analysis of resultative constructions', MS., Bar Ilan University and Northwestern University.
—— —— (1998). 'Building verb meaning', in Greuder and Butt (1998), 97–134.
REINHART, TANYA. (1991). 'Lexical properties of ergativity', paper presented at the Workshop on Lexical Specification and Lexical Insertion, Research Institute for Language and Speech, University of Utrecht.
—— (1995). *Interface Strategies*. Utrecht: UiL OTS Working papers.
—— (1996). 'Syntactic effects on lexical operations: reflexives and unaccusatives'. Utrecht: UiL OTS Working papers.
—— (2000). 'The theta system: syntactic realization of verbal concepts', Utrecht: UiL OTS Working papers.
—— and TAL SILONI. (2003). 'Against the unaccusative analysis of reflexives', in Alexiadou et al. (2003), 159–80.
RIGAU, GEMMA. (1997). 'Locative sentences and related constructions in Catalan: *ésser/haver* alternations', *Theoretical Issues at the Morphology-Syntax Interface*, (eds.) Amaya Mendikoetxea and Myriam Uribe-Etxebarria. (Supplement of the *International Journal of Basque Linguistics and Philology*.) Bilbao and Donostia: UPV, 395–421.
RITTER, ELIZABETH. (1988). 'A head movement approach to construct-state noun phrases', *Linguistics* 26: 909–29.
—— (1991). 'Two functional categories in Noun Phrases: evidence from Modern Hebrew', *Perspectives on Phrase Structure*, (ed.) Susan Rothstein (Syntax and Semantics 25). New York: Academic Press, 37–62.
—— (1995). 'On the syntactic category of pronouns and agreement', *Natural Language and Linguistic Theory* 13: 355–404.
—— (1997). 'Agreement in the Arabic prefix conjugation—evidence from a non-linear approach to person, number and gender features', *Proceedings of the Canadian Linguistic Society*, (eds.) Leslie Blair, Christine Burns and Lorna Rowsell. Calgary: University of Calgary, 191–202.
—— and SARAH ROSEN. (1998). 'Delimiting events in syntax'. In Greuder and Butt (1998), 97–134.
—— —— (2000). 'Event structure and ergativity', in Tenny and Pustejovsky (2000), 187–238.
RIZZI, LUIGI. (1986). 'On chain formation', *The Syntax of Pronominal Clitics*, (ed.) Hagit Borer. (Syntax and Semantics 19). New York: Academic Press, 65–95.
ROBERTS, IAN. (1987). *The Representation of Implicit and Dethematized Subjects*. Dordrecht: Foris.
ROSEN, SARA THOMAS. (1999). 'The syntactic representation of linguistic events', *GLOT International* 4: 3–11.

ROTHSTEIN, SUSAN (ed.). (1998). *Events and Grammar*. Dordrecht: Kluwer.
——(2000a). 'Secondary predication and aspectual structure', MS., Bar Ilan University.
——(2000b). 'What are incremental themes?' MS., Bar-Ilan University.
ROY, ISABELLE. (2001). '*Des-du* NPs in French', MS., University of Southern California.
ROZWADOWSKA, BOŻENA. (2000). 'Derived nominals', MS., Case 134, *Syncom*.
RUNNER, JEFF. (1993). 'Quantificational objects and Agr-O', *MIT Working Papers in Linguistics* 20: *Papers from the Fifth Students Conference in Linguistics*, (eds.) Vern Lindblad and Michael Gamon. Cambridge, MA: MIT, 209–24.
——(1995). 'Noun phrase licensing and interpretation', Ph.D. dissertation, University of Massachusetts.
RUSSELL, BERTRAND. (1905). 'On denoting', *Mind* 14: 479–93.
——(1919). *Introduction to Mathematical Philosophy*. London: Allen and Unwin.
RUYS, EDDY G. (1992). 'The scope of indefinites', Ph.D. dissertation, OTS, University of Utrecht.
SAFIR, KEN and TIM STOWELL. (1989). 'Binominal *each*', *Proceedings of the North Eastern Linguistic Society* 18: 426–50. Amherst, MA: GLSA Publications, University of Massachusetts.
SANCHES, MARY and LINDA SLOBIN. (1973). 'Numeral classifiers and plural marking: an implicational universal. *Working Papers in Language Universals* 11: 1–22. Stanford, Calif.: Stanford University.
SCHEIN, BARRY. (2002). 'Events and the semantic content of thematic relations,' *Logical Form and Language*, (eds.) Gerhard Preyer and Georg Peter. Oxford: Clarendon Press, 263–344.
SCHMITT, CRISTINA, J. (1996). 'Aspect and the syntax of noun phrases', Ph.D. dissertation, University of Maryland.
——and ALAN MUNN. (1999). 'Against the nominal mapping parameter: bare nouns in Brazilian Portuguese', *Proceedings of the North Eastern Linguistic Society* 29, (eds.) Pius Tamanji, Masako Hirotani, and Nancy Hall. University of Massachusetts at Amherst: GLSA. 339–53.
SCHOORLEMMER, MAAIKE. (1995). 'Participial passive and aspect in Russian', Ph.D. dissertation, Utrecht University.
——(2003). 'Syntactic unaccusativity in Russian', in Alexiadou et al. (2003), 207–42.
SCHWARZSCHILD, ROGER. (2001). 'How we talk about amount', paper presented at the University of Southern California Linguistic Colloquium.
——and KARINA WILKINSON. (2002). 'Quantifiers in comparatives: a semantics of degree based on intervals', *Natural Language Semantics* 10: 1–41.
SELKIRK, ELIZABETH. (1977). 'Some remarks on noun phrase structure', *Formal Syntax*, (eds.) Peter Culicover, Thomas Wasow and Adrian Akmajian. New York: Academic Press, 285–316.
SHARVY, RICHARD. (1978). 'Maybe English has no count nouns: notes on Chinese semantics', *Studies in Language* 2: 345–65.
SHLONSKY, UR. (1987). 'Null and displaced subjects', Ph.D. dissertation, MIT.

SHLONSKY, UR. (1997). *Clause Structure and Word Order in Hebrew and Arabic.* New York and Oxford: Oxford University Press.
—— (2000). 'The form of Semitic noun phrases: an antisymmetric, non-N-movement account', MS., University of Geneva.
—— and EDIT DORON. (1992). 'Verb second in Hebrew', *Proceedings of the West Coast Conference on Formal Linguistics* 10, (ed.) D. Bates. Stanford, CA: Center for the Study of Language and Information, 431–46.
SICHEL, IVY. (in press). 'Phrasal movement in Hebrew adjectives and possessives', *Dimensions of Movement*, (eds.) Artemis Alexiadou, H. Gaertner, Elena Anagnostopoulou and Stef Barbiers. Amsterdam: John Benjamins.
SIEGEL, LAURA. (1997). 'Gerundive nominals and the role of aspect', *Proceedings of the East Coast Conference on Linguistics (ESCOL '97)*, (eds.) Jennifer Austin and Aaron Lawson. CLCP Publications.
SILONI, TAL. (1996). 'Hebrew noun phrases: generalized noun raising', *Parameters and Functional Heads*, (eds.) Adrianna Belletti and Luigi Rizzi. New York: Oxford University Press, 239–267.
—— (1997). *Noun Phrases and Nominalizations: The Syntax of DPs.* Dordrecht: Kluwer.
—— (2000). 'Prosodic case checking domain: the case of constructs', MS., Tel Aviv University.
—— (2001). 'Reciprocal verbs', paper presented at the third Conference on the Syntax and Semantics of Semitic Languages, University of Southern California, Los Angeles, May 2001.
SIMPSON, ANDREW. (to appear). 'Classifiers and DP structure in Southeast Asia', *Parametric Variation in Syntax*, (eds.) Guglielmo Cinque and Richard Kayne. New York: Oxford University Press.
SMITH, CARLOTA. (1999). 'Activities: states or events?' *Linguistics and Philosophy* 22: 479–508.
—— (1991). *The Parameter of Aspect.* Dordrecht: Kluwer.
SNYDER, WILLIAM. (1998). 'On the aspectual properties of English derived nominals', *MIT Working Papers in Linguistics* 25: 125–39.
SPEAS, MARGARET. (1994). 'Null argument in a theory of economy of projections', *University of Massachusetts Occasional Papers in Linguistics* 17, (eds.) Elena Benedicto and Jeffrey Runner. Amherst: GLSA, University of Massachusetts, 179–208.
STOWELL, TIM. (1981). 'Origins of phrase structure', Ph.D. dissertation, MIT.
—— (1989). 'Subjects, specifiers and X-bar theory', *Alternative Conceptions of Phrase Structure*, (eds.) Mark Baltin and Anthony Kroch. Chicago: University of Chicago Press, 232–62.
—— (1991). 'Determiners in NP and DP', *Views on Phrase Structure*, (eds.) Karen Leffel and Denis Bouchard. Dordrecht: Kluwer, 37–56.
—— (1996). 'The hidden structure of abbreviated English: headlines, recipes, diaries', MS., University of California at Los Angeles.
STUMP, GREGORY. (1998). 'Inflection', *The Handbook of Morphology*, (eds.) Andrew Spencer and Arnold M. Zwicky. Oxford: Blackwell, 13–43.

SVENONIUS, PETER. (2003). 'The morphosyntax of Slavic prefixes', paper presented at the East European Generative Summer School, Lublin, Poland.

SYBESMA, RINT. (1992). 'Causatives and accomplishments: the case of Chinese *ba*', Ph.D. dissertation, HIL/Leiden University.

SZABOLCSI, ANNA. (1987). 'Functional categories in the noun phrase', *Approaches to Hungarian*, Vol. 2., (ed.) István Kenesei. Szeged: JATE, 167–89.

——(ed.) (1997). *Ways of Scope Taking*. Dordrecht: Kluwer.

TALMY, LEN. (1985). 'Lexicalization patterns: semantic structure in lexical forms', *Language Typology and Syntactic Description*, Vol. 3: *Grammatical Categories and the Lexicon*, (ed.) Timothy Shopen. Cambridge: Cambridge University Press, 57–149.

——(2000). *Toward a Cognitive Semantics*. Cambridge, MA: MIT Press.

TENNY, CAROL. (1987). 'Grammaticalizing aspect and affectedness', Ph.D. dissertation, MIT.

——(1992). 'The Aspectual Interface Hypothesis', *Lexical Matters*, (eds.) Ivan A. Sag and Anna Szabolcsi. Stanford, CA: Center for the Study of Language and Information, 1–27.

——(1994). *Aspectual Roles and the Syntax-Semantics Interface*. Dordrecht: Kluwer.

——and James Pustejovsky (eds.). (2000). *Events as Grammatical Objects*. Stanford, CA: Center for the Study of Language and Information.

TORREGO, ESTER. (1989). 'Unergative-unaccusative alternations in Spanish', *Functional Heads and Clause Structure*, (eds.) Itziar Laka and Anoop Mahajan (*MIT Working Papers in Linguistics* 10). 253–72. Cambridge, MA: MIT.

TORTORA, CHRISTINA M. (1997). 'The syntax and semantics of the weak locative', Ph.D. dissertation, University of Delaware.

TRAVIS, LISA. (1994). 'Event phrase and a theory of functional categories', *Proceedings of the 1994 Anuual Conference of the Canadian Linguistic Association*, (Toronto Working Papers in Linguistics), (ed.) P. Koskinen. Toronto, 559–70.

——(1997). 'The syntax of achievements', MS., McGill University.

——(2000). 'The L-syntax/S-syntax boundary: evidence from Austronesian', *Formal Issues in Austronesian Syntax*, (eds.) Ileana Paul, Vivianne Phillips, and Lisa deMena Travis. (Studies in Natural Language and Linguistic Theory 49.) Dordrecht: Kluwer: 167–94.

T'SOU, BENJAMIN K. (1976). 'The structure of nominal classifier systems', *Austoasiatic Studies*, vol 2, (eds.) Philip N. Jenner, Stanley Starosta, and Laurence C. Thompson. Honolulu: University Press of Hawaii, 1215–47.

T'UNG, PING-CHENG and DAVID E. POLLARD. (1982). *Colloquial Chinese*. London: Routledge.

VAN GEENHOVEN, VEERLE. (1998). *Semantic Incorporation and Indefinite Descriptions: Semantic and Syntactic Aspects of West Greenlandic Noun Incorporation*. Stanford, CA: Center for the Study of Language and Information.

VAN HOUT, ANGELIEK. (1992). 'Linking and projection based on event structure', MS., Tilburg University.

VAN HOUT, ANGELIEK. (1996). *Event Semantics of Verb Frame Alternations* (TILDIL dissertation Series, 1996-1). Tilburg: Tilburg University.
—— (2000). 'Event semantics in the lexicon-syntax interface'. In Tenny and Pustejovsky (2000), 239-282.
—— (2001). Paper presented at the workshop The Syntax of Aspect, Ben Gurion University of the Negev, June, 2001.
—— and THOMAS ROEPER. (1998). 'Events and aspectual structure in derivational morphology', *Papers from the University of Pennsylvania/MIT Roundtable on Argument Structure and Aspect*, (ed.) Heidi Harley. (MIT Working Papers in Linguistics 32). Cambridge, MA: MIT, 175-200.
VAN RIEMSDIJK, HENK. (1990). 'Functional prepositions', *Unity in Diversity: Papers Presented to Simon C. Dik on his 50th birthday*, (eds.) Harm Pinkster and Inge Genee. Dordrecht: Foris, 231-41.
—— (1995). 'Hjelmslev meets minimalism: prolegomena to the study of the expression of spatial notions in the functional domain of DP and PP', paper presented at the Vienna Workhop on Transcendental Syntax, July 1995.
—— (1998). 'Categorial feature magnetism: the endocentricity and distribution of projections', *Journal of Comparative Germanic Linguistics* 2: 1-48.
—— (2000). 'Location and locality', paper presented at the Sixteenth Annual Meeting of the Israeli Society of Theoretical Linguistics, June 2000.
VAN VALIN, ROBERT D. JR. (1991). 'Semantic parameters of split intransitivity', *Language* 66: 221-60.
VAN VOORST, JAN G. (1988). *Event Structure*. Amsterdam: John Benjamins.
—— (1993). 'The semantic structure of causative constructions', MS., University of Quebec at Montreal.
VAINIKKA, ANNE. (1993). 'The three structural cases in Finnish', *Case and Other Functional Categories in Finnish Syntax*, (eds.) Anders Holmberg and Urpo Nikanne. Berlin: Mouton de Gruyter, 129-59.
—— and JOAN MALING. (1993). 'Is partitive case inherent or structural?', MS., University of Massachusetts, Amherst and Brandeis University.
VALOIS, DANIEL. (1991). 'The internal structure of DP', Ph.D. dissertation, University of California, Los Angeles.
VENDLER, ZENO. (1967). *Linguistics in Philosophy*. Ithaca: Cornell University Press.
VERGNAUD, JEAN-ROGER and MARIA LUISA ZUBIZARRETA. (1992). 'The definite determiner and the inalienable constructions in French and English', *Linguistic Inquiry* 23: 595-652.
VERKUYL, HENK J. (1972). *On the Compositional Nature of the Aspect*. Dordrecht: Reidel.
—— (1989). 'Aspectual classes and aspectual composition', *Linguistic and Philosophy* 12: 39-94.
—— (1993). *A Theory of Aspectuality. The interaction between Temporal and Atemporal Structure*. Cambridge: Cambridge University Press.

——(2000). 'Events as dividuals: aspectual composition and event semantics', in Higginbotham et al. (2000), 169–205.
VIKNER, STEN. (1995). *Verb Movement and Expletive Subjects in the Germanic Languages.* Oxford: Oxford University Press.
WARE, ROBERT X. (1975). 'Some bits and pieces', *Mass Terms: Some Philosophical Problems*, (ed.) Francis J. Pelletier. Dordrecht: Reidel, 15–29.
WECHSLER, STEPHEN. (1989). 'Accomplishments and the prefix *re-*', *Proceedings of the North Eastern Linguistic Society* 19: 419–34.
——(2001). 'Resultatives under the "event-argument homomorphism" model of telicity', paper presented at the workshop The Syntax of Aspect, Ben Gurion University of the Negev, June 2001.
WILLIAMS, EDWIN. (1981). 'Argument structure and morphology', *The Linguistic Review* 1: 81–114.
——(1994). *Thematic Structure in Syntax.* Cambridge, MA: MIT Press.
WU, ZOE. (2000). 'The development of functional categories in Mandarin Chinese', Ph.D. dissertation, University of Southern California.
ZUBIZARRETA, MARIA LUISA. (1982). 'On the relationship of the lexicon to syntax', Ph.D. dissertation, MIT.
——(1987). *Levels of Representation in the Lexicon and in the Syntax.* Dordrecht: Foris.
ZUCCHI, ALESSANDRO. (1989). 'The language of propositions and events: issues in the syntax and semantics of nominalization', Ph.D. dissertation, University of Massachusetts.
——(1993). *The Language of Propositions and Events.* Dordrecht: Kluwer.
——(1999). 'Incomplete events, intensionality and imperfective aspect', *Natural Language Semantics* 7: 179–215.
——and MICHAEL WHITE. (2001). 'Twigs, sequences and the temporal constitution of predicates', *Linguistics and Philosophy* 24: 187–222.

Index of languages

Arabic (Palestinian)
  Vol II 349 n.
Arabic (Standard)
  Vol I 83, 132 n., 204
  Vol II 286
Armenian
  Vol I 94–6, 114, 117–18, 178–9, 182

Bulgarian
  Vol I 155 n.
  Vol II 126 n.

Cantonese
  Vol I 90, 96 n., 179–82, 184–7
Catalan
  Vol II 209, 271, 275–6, 279–84, 286, 287, 293, 295, 296 n., 305, 323
Chamorro
  Vol II 286
Chichewa
  Vol II 156
Chinese
  Vol I 38, 59, 68 n., 86–94, 96–100, 107–9, 114 n., 141, 141 n., 178–84, 187, 187 n., 189, 246
  Vol II 165 n.
Czech
  Vol II 126 n., 156–7, 164, 165 n., 168, 180 n., 301

Dutch
  Vol I 92 n., 190
  Vol II 32–3, 38, 40, 103–4, 106–7, 171, 304

English
  Vol I 3, 9, 12–13, 23, 26 n., 27, 27 n., 29, 31–3, 32 n., 33 n., 36, 38–40, 42, 51–5, 58–60, 62, 65–7, 69–74, 79–85, 90–4, 96, 99–101, 103, 103 n., 108–12, 115–17, 119, 128, 131–2, 137 n., 139, 141, 144 n., 145, 149–51, 154–5, 157–8, 163, 163 n., 171, 173, 177–9, 184–6, 188, 194, 197, 199, 199 n., 202, 204–11, 214 n., 215 n., 227, 233, 238–40, 242, 246–7, 249, 255
  Vol II 12, 14–17, 22, 24, 26, –27, 30 n., 41–3, 46 n., 53, 58 n., 65, 70, 74–6, 80 n., 81 n., 87–8, 91, 97, 99, 99 n., 102, 122–3, 126, 129–130, 143 n., 144, 147, 158 n., 162, 181–2, 194, 197–200, 209, 212–13, 221, 223 n., 229, 234, 236, 242 n., 256, 266–68, 270–1, 273 n., 287–9, 291–6, 298, 298 n., 310, 310 n., 317, 322–4, 327, 332, 338, 344, 347–8, 350–1, 353–4
English, Abbreviated ~
  Vol II 332 n.
Eskimo, West Greenlandic ~
  Vol II 156, 177–8
Estonian
  Vol II 99 n.
Finnish
  Vol II 48, 99, 99 n., 101, 101 n., 103–7, 108 n., 109, 129, 135 n., 137–9, 156, 162–3, 171, 215, 257 n., 286
French
  Vol I 89
  Vol II 198, 290–1
German
  Vol I 79, 85 n., 92 n., 144 n., 150
  Vol II 103–4, 106–7, 200, 268 n.
Germanic Languages
  Vol II 268 n.
Greek
  Vol I 85

Haisla
  Vol II 155
Haitian
  Vol I 38
Hebrew
  Vol I xvi, 12–13, 36–7, 39, 41–2, 47 n., 54, 56–7, 60, 71 n., 75, 79, 81–3, 91, 100 n., 103 n., 111 n., 114 n., 116 n., 118 n., 132 n., 137 n., 144 n., 150–2, 154–5, 158, 171, 174, 178–9, 186, 187 n., 189, 193–5, 197–202, 204–16, 219–25, 232–5, 237–42, 244, 246–7, 249, 253 n., 255, 257, 259–60, 263, 265
  Vol II xvi, 15, 32–3, 36, 39, 42 n., 43, 53, 62–3, 65, 76, 88, 91–2, 111–15, 117–19, 126, 141, 182, 198, 209, 234–5, 237–9, 241–2, 244, 247, 249, 255–7, 260, 260 n., 270–3, 275–7, 279, 279 n., 282, 284, 279, 279 n., 282, 284, 286–7, 288, 290–6, 298–9, 302–7, 310–12, 315–17, 319, 321–2, 324–5, 332–3, 338–41, 345, 347, 349 n., 352.
Hindi
  Vol II 268
Hmong
  Vol I 180

Hungarian
   Vol I 94 n., 97 n., 114, 116–19, 140, 167 n., 178–9, 187, 193, 250, 258
   Vol II 126, 200

Icelandic
   Vol II 268 n., 271, 273 n., 304
Italian
   Vol I 64–7, 70–2, 80–1, 87, 89–91, 93, 104, 150, 235 n., 245 n.
   Vol II 256–7, 272, 276, 279, 286, 288, 305, 307, 319, 345

Japanese
   Vol I 98 n., 100 n.

Kraho
   Vol I 33, 42, 265

Mandarin (*see also* Chinese)
   Vol I 90, 96 n., 179, 180–2, 184, 184 n., 185 n., 186, 186 n., 187 n.
Min
   Vol I 180, 186–7
Min, Southern ~
   Vol I 184

Nung
   Vol I 180

Palauan
   Vol II 286
Polish
   Vol II 126 n., 169, 176–7, 344
Portuguese (Brazilian)
   Vol I 63 n., 138 n.

Romance Languages
   Vol I 72 n., 909, 123, 139, 165
   Vol II 347, 350–1, 353–4

Romanian
   Vol I 212–14, 263–4
   Vol II 345
Russian
   Vol II 62, 108 n., 126 n., 138, 185, 187, 190, 286, 301

Semitic Languages
   Vol I 39, 71 n., 198, 215 n., 228, 228 n., 265
   Vol II 279 n., 347–8, 350
Serbo–Croatian
   Vol II 126
Slavic Languages
   Vol II 34 n., 65, 126, 126 n., 137–8, 141 n., 155–9, 161, 163–5, 167, 170, 172–3, 178, 180–5, 189–90, 192–3, 196–200, 208–9, 212, 242 n., 298–302, 310–12, 314–15, 317, 325, 333, 335, 344
Spanish
   Vol I 65–6, 70, 89, 132 n.
   Vol II 283–7, 291, 294–5, 296 n., 305

Tagalog
   Vol II 286
Thai
   Vol I 186, 259
Turkish
   Vol I 94 n., 97, 114, 166, 178–9, 187

Vietnamese
   Vol I 180, 186, 256

Walpiri
   Vol II 155, 178

West Greenlandic *see* Eskimo, West Greenlandic
Wu
   Vol I 179–81, 184–7

Index of names

Abusch, Dorit
   Vol I 146, 149
Ackema Peter
   Vol I 84
Adger, David
   Vol I 67 n.
Alexiadou, Artemis
   Vol I 25 n.
   Vol II 239 n., 242, 242 n.
Allan, Keith
   Vol I 88 n.
Anderson, Stephen
   Vol I 32 n., 51, 53, 56
   Vol II 22–3
Arad, Maya
   Vol I 265
   Vol II 83, 348, 350, 354 n.

Bach, Emmon
   Vol II 74, 129, 155, 155 n.
Beard, Robert
   Vol I 51, 53, 56
   Vol II 22–4
Beghelli, Filippo
   Vol I 6, 7 n., 8 n. 113 n.
Belletti, Adriana
   Vol II 101, 103, 105 n., 256
Benedicto, Elena
   Vol I 137, 137 n.
   Vol II 270, 292
Benmamoun, Elabbas
   Vol I 57 n.
Bennet, Michael
   Vol II 82
Benua, Laura
   Vol II 73 n., 157 n., 284, 284 n.
Bittner, Maria
   Vol II 155, 157, 177–8, 180 n.
Boatner, Maxine Tull
   Vol II 203
Bobaljik, Jonathan
   Vol I 72 n.
   Vol II 269, 273 n., 284 n.
Bowers, John
   Vol I 140, 141 n.
Bresnan, Joan
   Vol I 4, 23
   Vol II 4, 286, 287 n.
Brody, Michael
   Vol I 24 n.

Brugger, Gerhard
   Vol I 114 n.
Burzio, Luigi
   Vol II 80, 120, 267 n.

Carlson, Gregory N.
   Vol I 138 n.
   Vol II 144
Carstairs-McCarthy, Andrew
   Vol II 198
Cheng, Lisa L.-S.
   Vol I 88 n., 90, 94 n., 96 n., 97–9, 179–82,
      185 n., 186 n., 187 n., 259
Chierchia, Gennaro
   Vol I 66 n., 68 n., 87 n., 87–94, 97–9, 99 n.,
      101–2, 104–7, 121 n., 122 n., 235 n., 246
   Vol II 43 n.
Chomsky, Noam
   Vol I 4, 11, 18, 19 n., 20, 22, 27, 37 n., 45, 46 n.,
      48 n., 52, 71, 262, 265 n.
   Vol II 11, 20, 20 n., 71 n., 72 n., 81, 81 n., 86, 87,
      240, 243, 243 n., 256, 258, 312, 343, 346
Cinque, Guglielmo
   Vol I 18 n., 25 n., 26, 48 n., 198 n., 228 n., 229
   Vol II 112–13, 113 n., 118–19, 118 n.,
Clahsen, Harald
   Vol I 26
Clark, Eve
   Vol I 8
   Vol II 70, 240, 347
Clark, Herbert
   Vol I 8
   Vol II 70, 240, 347
Contreras, Helas
   Vol I 65, 69, 139
Corver, Norvin
   Vol I 48
Croft, William
   Vol I 14–15

Dalrymple, Mary
   Vol II 156
Davidson, Donald
   Vol I 19
   Vol II 59, 82
Davis, Henri
   Vol I 15 n.
   Vol II 50 n., 83, 219, 266
Dechaine, Rose-Marie
   Vol I 36–8

Index of names

Delfitto, Denis
  Vol I 66, 120 n., 235 n.
Demirdash, Hamida
  Vol II 50 n., 83, 219, 266
Diesing, Molly
  Vol I 69, 137, 137 n.
  Vol II 105, 202, 292, 294
Dobrovie-Sorin, Carmen
  Vol I 138, 212
  Vol II 289–90, 292–3
Doetjes, Jenny
  Vol I 93–4, 103–4, 232
  Vol II 15
Doron, Edit
  Vol I 250–1
  Vol II 39, 296
Downing, Pamela
  Vol I 100 n.
Dowty, David R.
  Vol II 130, 134, 156, 205, 220–1, 224, 326–7

Emonds, Joseph
  Vol I 71
Erteschik-Shir, Nomi
  Vol II 56 n., 334
Everaert, Martin
  Vol II 38–9

Fanslow, Gisbert
  Vol I 46, 46 n.
Fassi Fehri, Abdelkader
  Vol I 39, 132 n., 198 n., 228 n., 229
Filip, Hana
  Vol I 129 n., 167
  Vol II 124 n., 125, 155–69, 171 n., 172–4, 176–7, 180 n., 183, 190–3, 199–200
Fillmore, Charles
  Vol I 14
Fodor, Janet
  Vol I 144–7, 149
Fodor, Jerry
  Vol I 14
Fox, Dani
  Vol I 72
Freeze, Ray
  Vol II 286–8
Frege, Gottlob
  Vol I 128 n.
Fukui, Naoki
  Vol I 24 n.

Gates, John Edward
  Vol II 203 n.
Geenhoven, V. van
  Vol II 103
Gil, David
  Vol I 43, 144, 182, 259

Giorgi, Alessandra
  Vol I 24 n., 68 n., 68, 107 n., 113–14 n., 183
Givón, Talmy
  Vol I 150
Gleitman, Lila
  Vol I 8
Goldberg, Adele
  Vol I 14–15
Greenberg, Joseph
  Vol I 182
Grimshaw, Jane
  Vol I 3–4, 20, 22
  Vol II 4, 78 n., 263
Grodzinsky, Yosef
  Vol II 33 n., 39, 41

Hale, Kenneth
  Vol I 5
  Vol II 33, 48, 50, 50 n., 86, 156, 177–8, 180 n.
Halle, Morris
  Vol I 13 n., 53, 55
  Vol II 23
Harley, Heidi
  Vol I 9, 14, 58 n.
  Vol II 61, 219
Hay, Jennifer
  Vol II 130, 149, 151, 154, 192 n., 229
Hazout, Ilan
  Vol I 39
Heim, Irene
  Vol I 34, 137–8, 161
  Vol II 15
Higginbotham, James
  Vol I 66–7, 107, 246
  Vol II 77, 86, 202, 220–4, 262, 264, 323, 327
Hoekstra, Teun A.
  Vol II 32–3, 281–3
Holmberg, Anders
  Vol I 46, 46 n.
Honcoop, Martin
  Vol I 232
Hoop, Helen de
  Vol II 99, 102–4
Hornstein, Norbert
  Vol I 6 n., 208 n.
Hout, Angeliek van
  Vol I 14
  Vol II 31 n., 49, 50 n., 72 n., 102–5, 103 n., 130, 215, 242
Hudson, Wesley
  Vol I 140 n.
Hundius, Harald
  Vol I 88 n.
Hyams, Nina
  Vol I 37

Iatridou, Sabine
  Vol II 72 n.

Jackendoff, Ray
   Vol I 5, 140 n., 167-8
   Vol II 92 n., 128, 158 n.
Jaeggli, Osvaldo
   Vol II 96 n., 112-13, 118, 118 n.
Johnson, Kyle
   Vol I 27 n.
   Vol II 80 n., 96 n., 284 n.
Jonas, Dianne
   Vol II 269, 273 n.

Kamp, Hans
   Vol I 137, 161
   Vol II 50, 259
Kanerva Joni M.
   Vol I 4
   Vol II 4, 286
Kay, Paul
   Vol I 14
Kayne, Richard
   Vol I 22, 50
   Vol II 6 n., 57 n., 88, 280 n.,
Kennedy, Christopher
   Vol I 48
   Vol II 78, 98 n., 130 n., 149, 151-2, 154, 192, 229-30, 327
Keyser, S. Jay
   Vol I 5
   Vol II 50, 50 n., 86 n.
Kiparsky, Paul
   Vol I 125-7
   Vol II 33, 99 n., 100 n., 104, 105 n., 107, 130, 135-8, 142 n., 144, 146, 148, 162-3, 233, 259
Klinedinst, Nathan
   Vol I 170 n.
   Vol II 209 n., 290 n.
Klooster, W. G.
   Vol I 246
Kölver, Ulrike
   Vol I 88
Koopman, Hilda
   Vol I 46 n.
Kratzer, Angelika
   Vol I 14, 147-8
   Vol II 59-60, 63-4, 134, 220, 238, 262, 264, 284 n.
Krifka, Manfred
   Vol I 115 n., 124 n., 125-7, 130 n., 232
   Vol II 42 n., 46 n., 47, 73-4, 77-8, 93, 124-5, 130-5, 131 n., 133 n., 134 n., 142, 144-8, 156, 160-3, 165, 170, 172 n., 177 n., 189-90, 205, 225 n., 259, 314

Laca, Brenda
   Vol I 138, 212
   Vol II 289-90, 292-3

Larson, Richard
   Vol I 25
Landau, Idan
   Vol I 162 n.
   Vol II 33 n., 39 n., 309 n.
Lazorczyk, Agnieszka
   Vol II 168 n., 188 n.
Leinonen, Marja
   Vol II 138
Lepore, Ernest
   Vol I 14
Levin, Beth
   Vol I 4-5, 5 n.
   Vol II 4-5, 36-8, 42-5, 53 n., 54, 61, 69, 78, 78 n., 98 n., 130, 140, 149, 151-2, 154, 192 n., 220, 224, 229-30, 247, 271, 285, 287-8, 327-8
Lewis, Carroll
   Vol I vi
   Vol II vi
Lewis, David
   Vol I 34, 102
   Vol II 15
Li, Charles N.
   Vol I 88 n., 96
Li, Y.-H. Audrey
   Vol I 88 n., 96, 141 n., 186-7 n., 247
Lieber, Rochelle
   Vol I 51
   Vol II 22
Lin, Y. W.
   Vol I 141
Link, Godehard
   Vol II 74, 178 n.
Longobardi, Giuseppe
   Vol I 64-5, 69-73, 71 n., 72 n., 80-1, 81 n., 138 n., 139, 144 n., 174, 235 n.
   Vol II

McCawley, James
   Vol II 86, 220
McClure, William
   Vol II 50 n., 220
McNally, Louise
   Vol II 151
Maling, Joan
   Vol II 99, 104, 106
Manzini, M. Rita
   Vol I 6
Marantz, Alec
   Vol I 13 n., 14, 20 n., 55, 58 n.
   Vol II 10 n., 38 n., 57 n., 61 n., 63 n., 110 n., 219, 348, 354 n.
Mateu, Jaume
   Vol II 323
Matthews, P. H.
   Vol I 51
   Vol II 22

May, Robert
  Vol I 137 n.
Mchombo, Samual E.
  Vol II 156
Milsark, Gary
  Vol I 34
Mittwoch, Anita
  Vol II 43, 249, 260, 317, 321, 327, 330–1
Mohammad, Mohammad
  Vol I 39
Moro, Andrea
  Vol II 282
Moshi Lioba
  Vol I 4
  Vol II 4
Mourelatos, A. P. D.
  Vol II 78, 129, 201, 203 n., 330
Mulder, René
  Vol II 32–3, 281–3
Munn, Alan
  Vol I 63, 138
Muromatsu, Keiko
  Vol I 87, 94 n., 98 n., 100 n., 103–4 n., 128 n., 140 n., 180 n.

Noyer, Rolf
  Vol I 9, 56, 58 n.
  Vol II 240

Ortman, Albert
  Vol I 116
Ouhalla, Jamal
  Vol I 24 n., 27, 39
  Vol II 12

Pancheva, Roumyana
  Vol II 188 n.
Parsons, Terence
  Vol II 59, 82, 86, 98, 202, 215–16, 220, 328
Partee, Barbara
  Vol I 134 n.
  Vol II 50, 82, 259
Penke, Martina
  Vol I 26
Pereltsvaig, Asya
  Vol II 108 n
Perlmutter, David
  Vol II 31 n., 32, 34, 58 n.
Pesetsky, David
  Vol I 3, 22, 27 n.
  Vol II 4, 62, 80 n., 88–9, 118 n., 185–6
Peters, Stanley
  Vol II 156
Petrova, Milena
  Vol I 155 n.
Pianesi, Fabio
  Vol I 24 n., 68, 68 n., 107 n., 113–14 n., 183

Piñon, Christopher
  Vol II 156, 148 n., 163, 173, 173 n., 193–4, 200, 316
Platzack, Christer
  Vol II 73
Pollard, D. E.
  Vol I 183
Pollock, Jean-Yves
  Vol I 71
Portner, Paul
  Vol II 240
Postal Paul
  Vol II 58 n., 106
Prince, Alan
  Vol I 215 n.
Prince, Ellen
  Vol I 150
Pustejovsky, James
  Vol I 14 n.
  Vol II 86, 220, 224, 239 n., 240

Ramchand, Gillian C.
  Vol I 67 n.
  Vol II 50 n., 102, 103 n., 105, 130, 220, 354 n.
Rapoport, Tova R.
  Vol II 50 n., 224, 334,
Rappaport Hovav, Malka
  Vol I 4–5, 5 n.
  Vol II 4–5, 36–8, 42 n., 42–5, 53–4, 61, 69, 78 n., 130, 149, 220, 224, 247, 271, 285, 287, 287 n., 327 n., 328
Reinhart, Tanya
  Vol I 4–5, 146, 148–9
  Vol II 4, 33, 38 n., 43 n., 44–5, 50–4, 57 n., 82, 247, 328
Riemsdijk, Henk van
  Vol I 10 n., 20, 24, 49, 92 n., 247
Rigau, Gemma
  Vol II 275, 281–2, 323
Ritter, Elizabeth
  Vol I 14, 18 n., 39, 41 n., 56, 112 n., 140, 140 n., 142, 177 n., 207 n., 209 n., 247, 247 n.
  Vol II 50 n., 114, 115 n.
Rizzi, Luigi
  Vol II 37, 63
Roberts, Ian
  Vol II 92 n., 96 n., 284
Roeper, Thomas
  Vol II 242
Rohrbacher, Bernhard
  Vol I 26, 37 n., 165
  Vol II 11 n.
Rosen, Sara Thomas
  Vol I 14
  Vol II 47–8, 50 n.
Rothstein, Susan
  Vol II 76–8, 125, 132, 140 n., 221 n., 224–5, 326

Index of names

Roussou, Anna
  Vol I 6 n.
Roy, Isabelle
  Vol II 290
Rozwadowska, Bożena
  Vol II 63 n., 242 n.
Runner, Jeff
  Vol I 27
  Vol II 72 n., 80 n., 106, 257
Russell, Bertrand
  Vol I 787 n., 181 n.
Ruys, Eddy G.
  Vol I 146, 149

Safir, Ken
  Vol I 149
Sag, Ivan
  Vol I 144–7, 149
Schein, Barry
  Vol I 112 n., 123, 124 n., 232 n.
  Vol II 128, 134, 142, 142 n., 144 n., 177, 215–16, 216 n.
Schlenker, Philippe
  Vol I 127 n.
Schmitt, Christina J.
  Vol I 63 n., 138 n., 171 n.
  Vol II 50 n., 72 n., 73 n., 124 n., 130, 156, 156 n., 172 n., 176 n., 212, 302
Schoorlemmer, Maaike
  Vol II 185–9, 199 n.
Schwarzschild, Roger
  Vol I 246–7
Sciullo, Anna-Maria di
  Vol I 4
Selkirk, Elizabeth
  Vol I 246
Sharvy, Richard
  Vol I 88 n., 94 n.
Shlonsky, Ur
  Vol I 18, 36, 39, 57 n., 140 n., 195–8, 213 n., 214 n., 215 n., 228
  Vol II 256, 296 n.
Sichel, Ivy
  Vol I 18 n., 198 n., 228 n., 229
Siegel, Laura
  Vol II 239 n., 240
Siegler, Michele
  Vol I 94
Siloni, Tal
  Vol I 39, 41 n., 71, 211, 216, 218 n.
  Vol II 38 n., 57 n.
Simpson, Andrew
  Vol I 183–7
Slobin, Linda
  Vol I 87
Smith, Carlota
  Vol II 82, 97, 329

Snyder, William
  Vol II 242
Souza, S. M. De
  Vol I 33
Speas, Margaret
  Vol II 108–9
Stowell, Tim
  Vol I 6, 7–8 n., 19, 22, 65, 113 n.
  Vol II 332 n.
Stump, Gregory
  Vol I 51, 56
  Vol II 22, 24, 198
Svenonious, Peter
  Vol II 195, 200
Swart, Henrietta de
  Vol I 246
Sybesma, Rint
  Vol I 88 n., 90, 94 n., 96 n., 97–9, 179–82, 185 n., 186 n., 187 n., 130, 259
  Vol II 332
Szabolcsi, Anna
  Vol I 19, 46, 65

Talmy, Len
  Vol I 10
  Vol II 323
Tenny, Carol
  Vol II 47, 49, 73, 75, 75 n., 78, 124, 124 n., 130, 134, 160 n., 172 n., 205, 221 n.
Thompson, Sandra A.
  Vol I 88 n., 96
Torrego, Ester
  Vol II 275, 277, 279, 281
Tortora, Christina M.
  Vol II 287, 288
Travis, Lisa
  Vol II 50 n., 83 n., 264
T'sou, Benjamin K.
  Vol I 92
T'ung, P. C.
  Vol I 183

Vainikka, Anne
  Vol II 99, 104, 106
Valois, Daniel
  Vol I 18 n., 72 n., 81 n., 197
Van Valin, Robert, D
  Vol II 34–8, 45, 98 n.
Vendler, Zeno
  Vol II 54, 139, 222 n., 260, 328
Vergnaud, Jean-Roger
  Vol I 81 n.
Verkuyl, Henk
  Vol I 124, 130
  Vol II 34 n., 41 n., 46 n., 47, 73, 98, 99 n., 128–30, 134–7, 152 n., 161, 172, 202–3, 233, 236, 241, 259, 301, 314, 329

Vikner, Sten
   Vol II 104, 106–7, 269
Voorst, J. G. van
   Vol II 49, 83
Ware, Robert X.
   Vol I 88 n., 182–3
Wechsler, Stephen
   Vol II 212, 225, 225 n., 229–30

White, Michael
   Vol I 129–30 n.
   Vol II 145
Wilkinson, Karina
   Vol I 246, 246 n.

Williams, Gwyn
   Vol I 259
Williams, Edwin
   Vol I 4–5, 51, 67
   Vol II 4, 22, 28, 85 n.
Wu, Zoe
   Vol I 184 n.

Zubizarreta, Maria Luisa
   Vol I 81 n.
   Vol II 250
Zucchi, Alessandro
   Vol I 129–30 n.
   Vol II 145 n., 172, 240

Index of subjects

⟨e⟩ *see* Functional Structure: ⟨e⟩

a (English indefinite determiner)
   Vol I 61, 67 n., 110–14, 116, 119, 142–3, 149 n., 160, 163–4, 169, 178

Accomplishment (events, predicates) (*see also* Quantity events; Telicity)
   Vol II 34 n., 43–4, 52–3, 76 n., 97–8, 215, 220–6, 260–1, 317, 326–9, 334

Accomplishment verbs *see* Verbs, Accomplishment ~

Accusative languages
   Vol II 284

Achievement
   Vol II 34 n., 52–4, 97–8, 139–40, 222 n., 243, 246, 260–1, 307–10, 317, 322, 326–31, 333–4, 338

Achievements as instantaneous events
   Vol II 328–9, 332, 334

Active (voice)
   Vol II 220

Activity (*see also* Atelicity; Quantity, Non-~ events)
   Vol II 82, 76 n., 78 n., 217–20, 222 n., 224–5, 232–5, 237, 245, 248–9, 264, 266, 327–8

Activity as a grammatical object
   Vol II 245, 249

Activity interpretation *see* Homogeneous and Homogeneity

Activity verbs *see* Verbs, Activity ~

Adjective
   Vol I 48, 71, 72 n., 83, 98–101, 110 n., 141 n., 176–7, 183, 193, 195–8, 210, 216, 228–9, 234–7, 249, 252
   Vol II 30 n., 58 n., 63 n., 151–2, 178, 226, 229–30, 250, 265

Adjectival agreement
   Vol I 197, 216

Adjectival modification
   Vol I 176, 249, 252

Adjectival passives *see* Passive, Adjectival ~

Adjectives, closed-scale (*see also* Scalar predicates and structures)
   Vol II 151, 229–31

Adjectives, gradable ~ (*see also* Scalar predicates and structures)
   Vol II 230–13

Adjectives, open-scale (*see also* Scalar predicates and structures)
   Vol II 151

Adjunction
   Vol I 45–7, 198
   Vol II 20–1

Adjunction, Head ~
   Vol I 46–7, 219 n.

Adjuncts
   Vol I 25, 71
   Vol II 209, 212–13, 232

Adverb of Quantification
   Vol I 34–5, 38, 42, 130, 139, 164–6, 262–3
   Vol II 15–19, 123, 129, 142, 174, 201–3, 208, 269, 344

Adverb
   Vol I 48–9, 138, 262–3
   Vol II 211, 232, 237, 248–9, 250, 316, 344

Adverbs, covert ~
   Vol I 138

Adverbs, durative ~ (*see* Aspectual Predicate Modifier)

Adverbs, Manner ~
   Vol II 234, 282

Adverbs, Originator modifiers ~ (agent–oriented ~) ~ *see* Originator, Modifiers of ~

Affectedness
   Vol II 92 n.

Affixation *see* Morphology: Affixation

Agent/agentivity/agentive interpretation (*see also* Originator)
   Vol II 5, 34–5, 39, 46, 97 n., 98 n., 185

Agentive, Non-~ (interpretation)
   Vol II 34–5, 46

AGR, infinitival
   Vol I 162 n., 163 n.

Agree (mechanism)
   Vol II 81 n., 101, 115, 312, 314

Agreement
   Vol I 6–7, 20, 24, 103, 198 n., 222, 226–7
   Vol II 72 n., 186 n., 237, 256–7, 259

Agreement features
   Vol I 68
   Vol I 115 n.

Agreement, Adjectival ~ *see* Adjectival ~

Agreement, Anaphoric ~ *see* Anaphoric ~

Agreement, Cardinal ~ *see* Cardinal ~

Agreement, Definiteness ~ *see* Definiteness spreading

Agreement, Gender ~
   Vol I 195, 197–8, 222, 239, 244, 257–8

Agreement, Plural ~ *see* Plural ~

Agreement (cont.)
  Agreement, Specifier–head ~ see Specifier–head ~
  Agreement, Subject–verb ~
    Vol II 117, 256
AgrO
  Vol II 72 n., 103, 172 n.
Aktionsart (see also Event structure)
  Vol II 10, 34 n., 45–9, 65, 73, 100, 130, 149, 172, 267, 333
  Aktionsart, Coordinated verbs ~ test
    Vol II 50–2
all (see also kol (Hebrew 'all', 'every', 'each'))
  Vol I 116, 172–4, 199 n., 200 n., 223
Amorphous morphology
  Vol I 56
  Vol II 23–4
Anaphor
  Vol I 161
Anaphoric Agreement
  Vol I 162
Animacy
  Vol II 118 n.
Antipassive
  Vol II 48
Antisymmetry
  Vol I 197 n.
Anti–telicity see Telicity: Anti ~
AP (Adjective Projection, A, A^{max})
  Vol I 72 n., 131 n.
Argument projection
  Vol II 5, 32, 57, 69, 215, 262–3
Argument structure (see also Event structure)
  Vol I 7 n., 13, 24
  Vol II 4, 6, 8 n., 11, 30, 43–5, 47, 55–8, 61, 69–70, 112, 121–2, 215–16, 219–20, 249–50, 346–8
Arguments
  Vol I 17, 27, 64–6, 86–7, 89–90, 166 n.
  Vol II 5–6, 12, 31–46, 49, 57, 69–70, 73, 76, 85–6, 91, 136, 215–16, 219, 227–9, 250, 262–4, 354 n., 355 n.
  Arguments as theta–role recepients
    Vol II 64, 75, 87, 122, 160, 205, 215–16, 220, 227–8
  Argument, Default participant ~
    Vol II 110–12, 160, 216, 235
  Argument, Direct ~ (see also Quantity direct object)
    Vol II 12, 31, 46–50, 60, 73, 85, 92, 102, 121–3, 130–2, 134, 136, 156, 160, 162–6, 183, 186, 204, 210, 226, 235, 228–9, 247, 269 n., 318, 324
  Argument, External ~
    Vol I 22, 25
    Vol II 5, 31, 33, 35–7, 53, 59–61, 63, 85 n., 185, 194 n., 219–20, 235–6, 267 n., 273–4,
    280, 282, 305
  Argument, Goal ~
    Vol II 78 n., 88 n.
  Argument, Indirect ~
    Vol II 50
  Argument, Internal
    Vol I 22, 25
    Vol II 5, 31, 33, 35–8, 53, 59–61, 63, 85 n., 170, 185–7, 189, 194 n., 256, 259
  Argument, Nominal ~
    Vol I 66, 72 n., 87, 89–90
Article see Determiner
Aspect
  Vol II 34 n., 39, 41, 43 n., 46, 65, 72, 74, 135, 137, 139, 158 n., 172, 323
  Aspect, Grammatical ~
    Vol II 193
  Aspect, Inner ~
    Vol II 172, 187, 202–3, 210, 233, 237, 241
  Aspect, Morphological ~
    Vol II 138, 171
  Aspect, Outer ~
    Vol II 161, 172, 190, 202–3, 233, 236, 241
  Aspect, Quantity ~ Phrase (Asp$_Q$P, telicity inducing) see Quantity (events)
Aspectual decomposition see Decomposition, Event ~
Aspectual predicate modifiers
  Vol II 142–5, 192 n., 201–2, 211–13, 215, 223, 232–5, 241–2, 330
Atelicity/atelic (see also Activity; Quantity events: Quantity, Non–~ events)
  Vol I 124, 168, 206
  Vol II 34–6, 43–4, 46, 48, 52–3, 64, 74–5, 82, 99, 103 n., 105, 107, 109, 111, 124–5, 127–8, 132–3, 135, 137, 139–42, 146, 149, 151, 153, 158 n., 160–5, 168, 170–2, 182, 190, 201, 204, 211, 215–18, 224–7, 229, 233, 236–7, 242, 246–7, 264–7, 269, 272–3, 280, 304–5, 313–15, 318
Auxiliaries and auxiliary selection
  Vol I 33 n., 118 n.
  Vol II 33, 36, 38

Bare mass nouns see Mass, Bare ~
Bare nominal see Nominal, Bare ~. see also:
  Bare plural see Plurals, Bare ~
  Bare singulars see Singulars, Bare ~
  Bare stem see Stems, Bare ~
Bare Phrase Structure
  Vol I 18–20, 44, 169, 189 n.
  Vol II 19, 25, 262 n.
BECOME predicate
  Vol II 76 n., 78 n., 225 n., 326, 328
Binary Branching
  Vol I 22
Bounded and Boundedness (see also DP, Bound

Index of subjects   385

~; f–morph, Bound ~; Event, Bound ~;
    Unbounded and unboundedness)
  Vol II 34 n., 122, 135–9, 144, 146, 148, 231
Burzio's generalization
  Vol II 80–1, 120, 267 n.
by-phrases (*see also* Passive)
  Vol II 95 n., 96 n.

Cardinal, cardinality expressions (*see also*
    Number)
  Vol I 109, 111–19, 124, 148–9, 154–7, 185–6, 193–
    9, 238, 242–50, 254–8, 260 n., 265 n.
  Vol II 175 n., 176–80, 298, 301 n., 345–6
Cardinal, divider–counters ~ *see* Division:
    Dividing-Counters
Cardinal agreement
  Vol I 257–8
Cardinal one *see* one
Cardinal zero *see* zero
Cascade structure
  Vol II 89–90
Case and Case assignment
  Vol I 18, 27–8, 33 n., 40, 44, 49. 52, 131 n.
  Vol II 71, 81, 85, 99, 101, 108–9, 285
  Case, Accusative ~
    Vol II 23, 48, 72, 79–81, 85, 99, 101–6, 108–
    9, 127–8, 135–9, 141–2, 175 n., 183–4,
    210, 215, 314
  Case, Genitive ~ (*see also* Genitive)
    Vol II 102–3
  Case, Inherent ~
    Vol I 49
    Vol II 71, 87, 101, 103, 106–7
  Case, Nominative ~
    Vol II 80–1, 101, 183–4, 256, 259, 265 n.,
    167 n., 272–5, 285, 311–14, 335
  Case, Partitive ~ (object)
    Vol II 48, 99–110, 120, 125, 127–8, 135–42,
    156, 160, 162–3, 165, 171–2, 175 n., 183–
    4, 215, 227, 233–5, 247, 256–7, 284, 314
  Case, Partitive ~ (subject) *see* Subjects, Par-
    titive ~
  Case, Structural ~
    Vol II 92, 101, 103–4, 106–7, 175 n., 183–
    4, 314
Categorial features
  Vol I 20, 20 n.
Category and categorizing
  Vol I 13, 17, 20–1, 28–31, 35, 42, 44–5
  Vol II 5, 8 n., 16, 20, 25, 28, 30 n., 71, 194, 207,
    262 n., 346, 348, 350–1, 353–4
Causality
  Vol II 225
Causative constructions
  Vol II 231
CAUSE predicate
  Vol II 326–7

Causer interpretation
  Vol II 185
Chains and Chain Condition
  Vol II 83 n., 280 n.
Checking system
  Vol I 6, 17, 20, 48 n.
  Vol II 5, 86, 194 n.
Choice functions
  Vol I 146–7, 149
CL head feature *see* Division: ⟨*div*⟩ (dividing
    head feature)
Classifier Projection (CL^{max}) (*see also* Division)
  Vol I 59, 72 n., 91, 95–6, 100 n., 108–11, 119, 162,
    166–8, 175–6, 183 n., 188, 204, 208–9,
    242, 248
  Vol II 75, 114, 173
  CL head (CL°, ⟨e⟩$_{DIV}$)
    Vol I 95, 108, 163, 201, 209, 247 n.
    Vol II 159
  CL head feature *see* Division: ⟨*div*⟩ (dividing
    head feature)
  CL structure, Bare ~
    Vol I 166 n., 179–83, 185–7, 259

Classifiers (*see also* CL^{max}; Division)
  Classifier function
    Vol I 94, 108–9, 111, 128, 178–86, 188
  Classifier languages
    Vol I 86–94, 259
  Classifier marking (inflection)
    Vol I 86, 91–5, 97–101, 109, 117–18, 182–3,
    259–60
  Classifier system
    Vol I 86–7, 93, 109, 178
  Classifier, Non-plural ~
    Vol I 184–5
  Classifier, Plural ~
    Vol I 96 n., 97 n., 184–5
  Classifier, Covert ~
    Vol I 94 n., 104–5
Clausal complements *see* Complements, Claus-
    al ~
Clitic and Cliticization (*see also en* cliticization;
    Locative clitics, *ne* cliticization; Sub-
    ject clitics)
  Vol I 32 n., 47 n., 111 n., 150, 169, 264 n.
CL^{max} *see* Classifier Projection
Coercion
  Vol I 8–10, 79, 105–6
  Vol II 7, 129, 138–9, 153, 203, 214, 231–2, 251
Co-finality (*see also* Telicity: telos; Culmination)
  Vol II 148–9
Cognate object *see* Object, Cognate ~
Co–initiality
  Vol II 148
Common name
  Vol I 10, 59, 73–7, 79–81, 84–5, 175–6

Complement
  Vol I 22, 24–7, 50, 139
  Vol II 11–12
  Complement, Clausal ~
    Vol II 12, 88 n.
Complementizer *see* CP
Compositionality
  Vol I 52–3
  Vol II 22–3, 198, 326
Compound and compounding *see* Morphology, Compounding
Computational system
  Vol I 11–13, 15, 106
  Vol II 8, 345
Conative alternation and conatives
  Vol II 48, 91, 103 n., 125
Concepts and the Conceptual component
  Vol I 11–13, 15, 106, 128–9, 133
  Vol II 6–9, 129, 139, 152–3, 214–15, 228, 230, 329, 247–8, 250–2, 346, 351–2
Conceptual array
  Vol I 27
  Vol II 227, 249–50, 265 n.
Construct State nominals and Construct formation (Hebrew)
  Vol I 47 n., 71, 196, 199, 214–21, 226–7, 251–2
  Vol II 345
Construction grammar
  Vol I 14
Constructionist and Neo–Constructionist approaches
  Vol I 14–15
  Vol II 42, 45, 245, 350
Container Phrases
  Vol I 250–7
Copula
  Vol II 286–7
Count (as opposed to Mass)
  Vol I 9–10, 59, 88, 91, 93–4, 97–9, 101–9, 115, 120 n., 132–5, 162, 167, 203–4, 245–6
  Vol II 27
Count structure
  Vol I 106–8, 130, 188,
Counter
  Vol I 111–19, 122–3, 128–9, 140 n., 210, 240, 242
Counter–divider– *see* Division: Dividing–Counters
Count–mass distinction *see* Mass–count distinction
CP (C, C^{max}, Complementizer Phrase)
  Vol I 22–4
  CP, Specifier of ~ ([Spec, CP])
    Vol II 268 n.
Creole (languages)
  Vol I 33
C–selection (*see also* Subcategorization)
  Vol I 4, 22, 38
  Vol II 25

Culmination (*see also* Telicity: Telos)
  Vol II 74–5, 76–8, 86, 133–4, 143, 148–9, 170–1, 223–4, 226, 229, 235–6, 240–2, 326–9, 331–4
  Culmination, Non–~
    Vol II 157, 242
Cumulative reference
  Vol I 124–7
  Vol II 74, 131, 135, 144–8, 162–5, 170, 172 n., 191–2

D *see* DP
Dative alternation
  Vol II 88 n.
Dative, Possessor ~ (Hebrew)
  Vol II 33–4, 39–42, 53, 62–3, 247, 281–2, 325
Dative, Reflexive ~ (Hebrew)
  Vol II 33–4, 41 n., 42 n., 53, 62–3, 235–8, 240–2, 244–5, 247–9, 280
Davidsonian approaches to event structure
  Vol II 82–3
  Davidsonian, Neo ~ 59, 77, 84, 86, 216 n., 224, 261, 351
  Davidsonian, Neo ~ formulas
    Vol II 60, 77, 84–5, 94, 109, 202, 216–18, 224, 227, 351
  Davidsonian, Semi ~ 59
Decomposition, Event ~
  Vol II 220–7, 230, 284 n., 327
Default participant *see* Argument, Default participant ~
Definite and Definiteness (*see also* Determiner; DP)
  Vol I 38–41, 59, 68, 79, 82–4, 97, 158, 161, 165–6, 167–8, 175, 181–2, 189, 212–18, 223–5, 246, 263–4
  Vol II 17, 104–5, 158, 158 n., 163, 165 n., 173, 180, 256–7, 295, 336 n., 345
  Definite determiner (*see also* the)
    Vol I 60, 63, 72, 78, 81–5, 90, 109, 118–19, 140–1, 158, 160–74, 177–8, 187, 189, 197, 199–200, 211–12, 214 n., 215 n., 226–7, 246, 265
    Vol II 17, 28, 114, 158 n., 178
Definite head feature *see* Determiner Projection, ⟨***def***⟩
Definiteness agreement *see* Definiteness spreading
Definiteness spreading
  Vol I 39, 197–8, 216–17, 222, 227
DegP
  Vol I 48–9
  Vol II 153
Degree Achievement (de–adjectival) (*see also* Scalar predicates and structures)
  Vol II 230–1, 239
Degree–of–change predicate
  Vol II 149–53

Index of subjects 387

Deixes
  Vol I 140, 168
Delimiting and delimitors
  Vol II 142, 208, 210–11, 310, 323
  Delimited, Non–~ (interpretation)
    Vol II 170–1
Demonstrative
  Vol I xv, 38, 82, 140–1, 150, 163, 166 n., 170, 182–3, 212–14, 246
Derivational morphology *see* Morphology, Derivational ~
Determiner
  Vol I xv, 59–60, 63–6, 70, 74, 78, 80–1, 87, 90, 101, 104, 110–13, 119–20, 123–4, 131, 138 n., 140–3, 163, 169, 173, 188–9, 203, 213 n., 234, 240–3
  Vol II 120, 122, 126, 136–7, 147, 156, 177–8, 317, 345
Determiner, # ~ *see* Determiner, Weak ~
Determiner, Count ~ *see* Count determiner
Determiner, Definite ~ *see* Definite determiner (*see also the*)
Determiner, Indefinite ~ *see* Indefinite determiner, (*see also a*)
Determiner, Mass ~ *see* Mass determiner
Determiner, Null ~ *see* DP: Null D
Determiner, Overt ~
  Vol I 65, 131, 141, 144 n.
Determiner, Plural ~ *see* Plural determiner
Determiner, Singular ~ *see* Indefinite determiner; *a*
Determiner, Strong ~ (*see also* Scope, Wide ~)
  Vol I 38, 43, 59, 139–46, 150–4, 157–8, 172, 177, 185–9, 200–2, 220, 230–7, 246–7
  Vol II 120, 178, 180 n., 181, 256, 336 n.
Determiner, Unrestricted ~
  Vol I 119, 161, 203, 240
Determiner, Weak ~ (*see also* Scope, Narrow ~)
  Vol I 137–40, 140–5, 149–50, 152, 157, 163, 169–70, 177, 186–9, 230–3, 246–7, 269
  Vol II 120, 180
Determiners and proper names *see* Proper names
Determinerless nominals *see* Nouns and Nominals, Bare ~ (*see also* Mass, Bare ~; Plural, Bare ~, DP, Null D)
Determinerless proper names *see* Proper Names, Determinerless ~ (*see also* DP: Null D)
Detransitivization, (lexical) ~
  Vol II 43 n.
Development subevent
  Vol II 76 n., 220–2, 326–7
Diminutives
  Vol I 92 n.
Directional locatives
  Vol II 208

Discourse anaphor, discourse antecedent
  Vol I 69, 78, 78 n., 82, 119, 161–3, 166, 170–2, 176–8
  Vol II 114–15, 158 n.
Discourse operator (D–operator)
  Vol I 38, 42, 138
  Vol II 17–18, 344
Distributed Morphology
  Vol I 30 n., 58 n.
Distributivity
  Vol I 6
  Distributive marker *po*- (Slavic) *see po*, Distributive marker ~
  Distributive universals quantifiers (*see also each; every; kol*)
    Vol I 7, 81 n., 113–14, 129 n., 179, 182, 187,
  Distributor, abstract ~
    Vol I 129 n.
Diverse (reference)
  Vol I 125
  Vol II 135
Division and dividers (*see also* CL^{max})
  Vol I 59, 88, 93–7, 99, 101, 104 n. 108–23, 125 n., 127–9, 133, 167 n., 173, 178–80, 188, 193, 197, 209–11, 238, 240, 240 n., 242, 250, 260 n.
  Vol II 208
⟨*div*⟩ (Dividing head feature)
  Vol I 95–7, 109–10, 119, 167, 173, 187, 210–11, 242
  Vol II 26, 29, 322
⟨*div-2*⟩ (Dual division head feature) *see* Dual
⟨*e*⟩$_{DIV}$ (Division open value)
  Vol I 43, 59, 67 n., 95–6, 101, 109–19, 123, 129–32, 136–7, 143, 157–8, 161–4, 167, 173, 175–84, 186–9, 197, 199, 201–2, 204–5, 207, 209–11, 220, 224–5, 238, 242, 250,
  Vol II 26–9, 208
Dividing counters and the identified division–quantity head feature (⟨*div-#*⟩)
  Vol I 97 n., 114–15, 117–18, 140 n., 157–8, 176–85, 193, 197, 200–2, 204–5, 220, 224–5, 254, 256, 258, 260 n.
Division, Creating individual ~ s
  Vol I 120–9, 132 n., 134, 178
Divisive and Divisive reference
  Vol I 125–7
  Vol II 74, 77, 135, 144, 146–8, 162–3, 192
Divisive, Non–~ (reference)
  Vol II 147, 163 n., 201
D-linking
  Vol I 37–8
Double marking, double range assignment *see* Range Assignment, Double ~
Dowty's correlations
  Vol II 35, 50, 54

DP (Determiner Projection, D, D^{max})
  Vol I xv, 19–20, 45, 59–60, 63–9, 71–3, 77–81, 83–4, 87–90, 96–100, 108, 124, 133, 140 n., 141 n., 166 n. 170–2, 214–16, 221–2, 233–4, 246, 261–2, 265 n.,
  ⟨*def*⟩ (definite head feature)
    Vol I 39, 47–8, 72, 79, 197, 199, 211–19, 221–5, 227, 238, 263–5
    Vol II 270, 345
  ⟨*def-u*⟩ (definite–unique head feature, proper names) *see* Proper Names: ⟨*def-u*⟩
  ⟨e⟩$_d$ (DP open value)
    Vol I 38–9, 41, 45, 59–60, 68–9, 72–4, 77–81, 83–4, 137–40, 142–3, 145, 150, 166 n., 170, 177–8, 185–6, 188–9, 200–2, 211–12, 222, 227, 233–4, 261–2, 265
    Vol II 17, 20, 28–9, 114–16, 120, 126, 157, 173–6, 178–9, 181–2, 259, 261, 269–70, 291, 297–8, 301, 314–16, 343–6
  D, Indefinite ~ *see* Indefinite determiner
  D, Null ~
    Vol I 59, 65–6, 69–70, 74, 81 n., 89–90, 94 n., 131, 136–9, 143–4, 158, 188–9
  D-determiner *see* Determiner, Strong ~
  DP, Bare ~ *see* NP, Bare ~ (*see also* Mass, Bare ~; Plural, Bare ~)
  D-pronoun *see* Pronoun, D- ~
  D-structure
    Vol I 4–5
  Dual (marking; ⟨*div-2*⟩)
    Vol I 36, 207–10

each (*see also* *kol* (Hebrew 'all/every/each'))
  Vol I 7, 38 n., 113–19, 129 n., 140–1, 167 n., 176–9
Empty Category Principle (ECP)
  Vol I 65–6, 69
en cliticization (*see also* *ne* cliticization)
  Vol II 276, 279–80
Encyclopedia and encyclopedic entries
  Vol I 30, 77, 79–80, 85, 107 n.
  Vol II 14
Endo-skeletal approaches
  Vol I 5, 15, 19–20, 77, 103
  Vol II 5–7, 31, 42–3, 55
Equidistance Principle
  Vol II 86
Ergative languages
  Vol II 284
Event
  Vol I 17, 19, 34–5, 127 n., 129 n., 130 n., 137 n., 139, 168, 168 n., 232–3, 262
  Event argument
    Vol II 49, 59, 63 n., 65, 81–5, 217–21, 231, 238, 242, 261–4, 268–71, 274, 283–5, 287 n., 290–5, 302–6, 310 n., 325
  Event decomposition *see* Decomposition,

Event ~
Event participant
  Vol II 121–2, 231
Event type
  Vol II 47, 217–19, 234, 317, 326, 328, 333–4
Event, Bound ~ (bound predicate)
  Vol II 233, 241
Event, Complex ~
  Vol II 222 n., 326
Event Phrase (EP, E, E^{max})
  Vol II 64–5, 82–5, 111–12, 160, 209 n., 219–20, 237–8, 242, 258–9, 261, 264, 267, 269, 271, 273–5, 284, 291–3, 295, 303–6, 323
EP, Specifier of ~ [Spec, EP]
  Vol II 83, 85, 112, 120, 123, 184, 209 n., 220, 237–8, 237, 242–4, 247, 259, 262, 265–72, 274, 280, 285–6, 291–2, 294, 299, 304–5, 334–5, 338
⟨e⟩$_E$ (EP open value)
  Vol II 2, 82–3, 85, 209 n., 259, 261, 265, 267–72, 274–5, 283–5, 290–6, 298–300, 301–5, 309–11, 313–14, 317, 319, 321, 323–4, 334–5, 338, 343
Event structure
  Vol II 9–10, 12, 30–1, 47, 49–50, 60, 64, 69–70, 75, 82, 95, 107, 112, 120, 121, 123–4, 126, 129, 215–16, 227, 231, 233, 241, 245, 280–1, 305
Event templates
  Vol II 250–1
Eventives (non-stative events) (*see also* Activity; Quantity events)
  Vol I 53
  Vol II 2, 34 n., 82, 202–3, 217, 220, 235, 264–5, 267, 269, 284
every (*see also* *kol* (Hebrew 'all', 'every', 'each'))
  Vol I 7, 8 n., 38 n., 43, 45 n., 87, 89–90, 102, 113–15, 117, 119, 128, 128 n., 137, 140–1, 143, 145–8, 164, 172 n., 182–3, 185 n., 199 n., 232
Exceptional Case Marking (ECM)
  Vol II 48–9, 106
Existential binding/closure
  Vol I 63–6, 69–70, 74–5, 87 n., 129 n., 130 n., 137–42, 144–7, 151, 157–8, 165–6, 179, 186–7, 189, 200–1, 220, 234, 262
  Vol II 65, 83 n., 105 n., 118, 261–4, 120, 174, 268–71, 274, 283–5, 289–95, 297–9, 301–6, 310–13, 315, 317, 324, 334
Existential force
  Vol II 283, 285, 287, 291–2, 295, 297, 299–300, 310 n.
Existential operator
  Vol II 115, 174–5, 178–9, 268–9, 300–1, 306, 310, 317
Existential reading/meaning (*see also* Scope, Narrow ~)

Index of subjects 389

Vol II 114–18, 120, 210, 257–8, 286, 288–90, 292–4, 298–9, 323, 346
Existentially–bound bare nouns *see* Mass, Bare ~, Plurals, Bare ~
Existential locative
    Vol II 303, 313, 315, 322, 325, 338, 354
⟨$e^{loc/\exists}$⟩ (Existential locative open value)
    Vol II 322–5, 333, 337
Existential *there* constructions
    Vol II 281, 286, 288, 293–4
Exo-skeletal (XS-) (approach)
    Vol I 15, 17, 20, 29, 51, 60
    Vol II 6, 45, 151–3, 227–8, 262, 274, 346–51, 353, 355
Expletives
    Vol II 112, 243, 256, 265, 268 n., 271, 274, 304
Expletive determiner
    Vol I 71, 81 n.
Expletive it
    Vol II 265–7
Expletive replacement
    Vol I 71, 73, 81
    Vol II 256
Expletive *there*
    Vol II 267 n., 285
Expletives, Transitive ~
    Vol II 271, 273 n., 304
Extended Projection Principle (EPP)
    Vol II 65, 256, 259, 267–8, 271, 294
Extended Standard Theory (EST)
    Vol I 16
Extension Condition
    Vol I 28 n., 45–6
    Vol II 20
External argument *see* Arguments, ~

Features
    Features, Agreement ~ *see* Agreement features
    Features, Agreement in ~
        Vol I 20, 226
    Features, Categorial ~ *see* Categories and categorizing: Categorial features
    Features, Conceptual ~ *see* Concepts and the conceptual component
    Features, Functional ~ *see* Functional features
    Features, Head ~ *see* Head features
    Features, Lexical ~ *see* Lexical features
F-morph
    Vol I 31–4, 36–9, 42 n., 43 n., 58, 72, 78–9, 84, 95–6, 110–11, 118, 118 n., 157–8, 166 n., 176, 178, 193, 205 n., 212, 214 n., 238, 262–5
    Vol II 14–15, 16–17, 18, 24, 25, 29, 122–4, 126, 176, 194–5, 271, 284, 323, 337, 344–5
F-morph, bound ~
    Vol I 32 n., 58, 264 n.
    Vol II 24, 25, 157 n., 344, 352

Focus
    Vol I 153 n.
    Vol II 334
Fractions
    Vol I 115
Functional lexicon (functional items, functional vocabulary)
    Vol I 6, 10–11, 20–1, 29, 31, 31 n., 37–8, 42, 45, 49, 51, 68, 78, 80 n., 100, 107 n., 131, 239, 261
    Vol II 8–11, 14, 17–18, 25, 122, 126, 194–5, 207 n., 208, 265 n., 343, 345, 351
Functional Structure and functional categories
    Vol I 7, 7 n., 14–35, 38–9, 41–3, 46–8, 50, 59, 68, 71, 88–9, 103–4, 107, 114 n., 182–3 n., 185 n., 198 n., 199, 211, 247, 261–2, 265
    Vol II 3, 6, 9–11, 13–15, 18, 20, 30–1, 46, 50, 57–60, 64, 70–1, 108, 121, 207, 250, 263, 351
⟨e⟩ (Functional open value)
    Vol I 35–7, 42–5, 47, 78, 113–14, 118 n., 140, 143, 166, 178, 188, 193, 201, 219, 225 n., 233–4, 238, 261–2, 264–5
    Vol II 16–17, 18, 20, 25, 28, 108, 126, 194, 207 n., 322, 337, 343
Functional features
    Vol I 21, 24 n., 68, 103
Functional heads
    Vol I 25, 27–8, 33–7, 68, 72 n., 198 n., 213 n.
    Vol II 16, 18, 71
Functional hierarchy
    Vol I 261
Functional label
    Vol I 42, 45
Functional range assignment *see* Range assignment
Functional shells (F*P) *see* Shell Phrase
Functional specifiers *see* Specifier, ~
Functional structure acquisition *see* Language Acquisition
Functional, Quasi ~ L-heads *see* L-head, Quasi ~
    Vol I 101, 256
Fusion
    Vol I 68, 113 n., 114 n., 183

Gender agreement *see* Agreement, Gender ~
Generative semantics
    Vol I 16
Generics and Genericity
    Vol I 16 n., 40 n., 63–4, 66, 66 n., 74–6, 106, 120, 130, 137–9, 142, 144 n., 164–6, 179–80, 183, 185 n., 186 n., 189, 234–5, 262
    Vol II 113–17, 119–20, 174–5, 181, 210, 238, 238 n., 257–8, 293, 310 n., 344
Genitive construct formation *see* Construct nominals

Genitive (*see also* Case, Genitive ~)
  Vol I 41 n., 251–2
  Genitive marking
    Vol I 18, 40
  Genitive of negation
    Vol II 62–3, 185
  Genitive of quantification
    Vol II 175 n.
Gerunds (*see also* -*ing*)
  Vol II 239–40, 243–4, 268
Government and Binding model (GB)
  Vol I 22
  Vol II 5, 31
Government, Lexical ~
  Vol I 65–6, 69–71, 139
Grammatical formatives (*see also* Functional
    lexicon)
  Vol I 10, 10 n., 21, 31–2, 37 n., 42, 45–6, 47 n.,
    80, 80 n., 261, 264;
Grammatical variation (inter–language and
    intra–language) (*see also* Phonologic-
    al source of grammatical variation)
  Vol I 32, 33 n., 60, 79, 96, 107 n., 131, 136, 187,
    289, 193, 205 n., 238, 261–6
  Vol II 15, 126, 323, 343–5

half
  Vol I 116 n., 207–8
  Vol II 212
Head adjunction *see* Adjunction, Head ~
Head features (abstract) ~
  Vol I 31–9, 42–3, 47–8, 57–8, 68 n., 78–81, 83,
    95–6, 109–11, 118 n., 188–9, 204, 212,
    214, 225, 234, 238, 262–5
  Vol II 14–18, 21–25, 122–4, 126, 157–9, 168,
    183–4, 194–7, 271, 323, 344–5
  Head feature, Definiteness ~ (⟨*def*⟩)) *see*
    Determiner Projection: ⟨*def*⟩
  Head feature, Division ~ (⟨*div*⟩) *see* Division
    and Dividers: ⟨*div*⟩
  Head feature, Dual ~ (⟨*div-2*⟩) *see* Dual
  Head feature, identified division–quantity ~
    (⟨*div-#*⟩) *see* Division and Dividers:
    Dividers and counters
  Head feature, Proper names ~ (⟨*def-u*⟩) *see*
    Proper names: ⟨*def-u*⟩
Head Movement Constraint
  Vol I 143, 176, 198–9, 205, 212, 262
Head movement *see* Movement, Head ~
Head
  Vol I 24, 32, 42–5, 47, 169–74, 183 n., 188–9, 193,
    197, 205, 212–13, 216, 219 n., 224–7, 234,
    238, 247 n., 258
  Vol II 11–12, 19–20, 166, 172, 207, 291, 227,
    299, 337
  Head pair
    Vol I 45–7, 73, 80, 264
    Vol II 20

Head, Null ~
  Vol I 89
Head-Driven Phrase Structure Grammar
    (HPSG)
  Vol II 5
Homogenous and Homogeneity (*see also* Atelic-
    ity; Activity; Quantity events: Quan-
    tity, Non-~)
  Vol I 96, 125 n., 127–30, 168
  Vol II 74, 77, 82, 104–5, 115, 146–7, 164, 172 n.,
    192, 202, 217, 222, 234–5, 266, 326, 328
  Homogeneity, Non-~ (*see also* Quantity)
    Vol I 130–1
    Vol II 147, 187, 189, 192, 201, 222, 233

Idiom
  Vol I 84
  Vol II 25–9, 54, 63 n., 64 n., 87 n., 98, 199 n.,
    207–8, 239, 322–4, 326, 333–4, 336–8,
    351–5
Imperfective and imperfectivity (*see also*
    Atelicity)
  Vol II 34 n., 65, 158–61, 163–7, 169–72, 175 n.,
    180 n., 186, 189–90, 193, 199–200
  Imperfective marking/affixation
    Vol II 137–9, 165, 167, 172, 193
  Imperfective, Primary ~
    Vol II 161, 166, 168, 172, 190, 193, 198
  Imperfective, Secondary ~
    Vol II 161, 166–7, 172, 189–90,
Impersonal constructions
  Vol II 112
Inalienable possession construction
  Vol I 81 n.
Incorporation
  Vol I 216–19, 120 n.
  Vol II 55, 71 n., 127, 155 n., 157 n., 193, 200,
    208 n., 215, 239, 281–2, 301–2, 323–4
Incremental theme *see* Theme, Incremental ~
Indefinite and indefiniteness (*see also* plurals,
    Bare ~; Mass, Bare ~; Scope, Wide;
    Scope, Narrow)
  Vol I 16, 40–1, 59–60, 66–7, 75, 75 n., 109–11,
    123, 131, 136–8, 140 n., 142, 144–60, 163,
    180, 184, 188–9, 193, 201–2, 205 n., 214–
    15, 219–21, 224–5, 244 n.
  Vol II 4, 104–5, 158 n., 180, 257
  Indefinite determiner (*see also a*)
    Vol I 40–1, 59–60, 63–4, 67 n., 90, 93–4, 101,
      109–16, 123, 138 n., 163, 178, 184 n.188–9,
      205 n., 208 n.
  Indefinite, Strong ~ *see* Determiner, Strong ~
  Indefinite, Weak ~ *see* Determiner, Weak ~
Individual (divisions) *see* Division, Creating
    individual ~ s
Individual-level predicate
  Vol II 238
Inflection *see* Morphology, Inflectional ~

Index of subjects 391

-*ing*
-*ing*, Gerundive ~ (*see also* Gerunds)
  Vol II 239–40, 243–4
-*ing*, Nominalizer ~ (*see also* Nominals, Derived ~)
  Vol II 239–40, 242–5, 248–9
-*ing*, Progressive ~
  Vol II 34 n., 142 n., 158 n., 162, 169, 172, 193, 236, 240–4, 329–30
Instantaneity and instantaneous events *see* Achievements: Instantaneous events
Intermediate scope *see* Scope, Intermediate ~
Internal argument *see* Arguments, Internal ~
Intransitivity (*see also* Unaccusative; Unergative)
  Intransitive (monadic) predicates
    Vol II 183–5, 235–6, 243
  Intransitive structures/derivations
    Vol II 216, 218, 260, 267, 269, 273, 303, 307, 318, 325, 342
  Intransitive verbs *see* Verbs, Intransitive ~
Island
  Vol I 145–7, 157
I-Subject (mechanism)
  Vol II 81 n., 101, 115, 312
Iterative (interpretation)
  Vol II 170

Join semi-lattice approach
  Vol I 121–2

Kind
  Vol I 87–90, 105 n., 108, 129 n., 138 n., 144 n.
Kol (Hebrew 'all', 'every' 'each')
  Vol I 194, 198–200, 203–4, 209 n., 223, 223 n., 230–1, 233, 240–2, 246

Language acquisition
  Vol I 264–6
  Vol II 345
  Language Acquisition, Functional ~
    Vol I 265
Language variation *see* Grammatical Variation
L-Domain (L–D)
  Vol I 19, 27–9, 31–4, 42, 48–51, 177 n., 198 n., 217–18, 248, 258
  Vol II 12, 14, 30, 207 n., 208 n.
Lexical /lexicalist approach(es)
  Vol II 42, 44–5, 140, 167 n., 220, 328
Lexical ~
  Lexical domain (L–domain, L–D) *see* L–Domain
  Lexical entry (item) (*see also* Listeme)
    Vol I 3–5, 14, 22, 44, 55, 77, 104 n., 142, 209
    Vol II 4–7, 31, 43–5, 49, 55, 69–70, 133, 136, 227, 251, 262
  Lexical features
    Vol I 77

Lexical government *see* Government, Lexical ~
Lexical head *see* L-head
Lexical listing (encoding, specification, properties)
  Vol I i, 3–8, 10, 10 n., 12, 14–15, 17, 22, 24–6, 48, 55, 58–9, 73, 77, 88, 88 n., 91, 93, 93 n., 97–9, 103–7, 120 n., 132, 135, 188–9
  Vol II 122, 130, 141, 186, 263
Lexical plurals *see* Plurals, Lexical ~
Lexical Projection (*see also* L–Domain)
  Vol I 19–21, 24–5, 27
  Vol II 12
Lexical rules (mapping, derivation)
  Vol I 8, 52, 103
  Vol II 4, 45, 70, 252
Lexical selection
  Vol I 24, 51
Lexical categories *see* L–Domain, L-heads; Lexical Projection
Lexical Integrity Hypothesis (LIH)
  Vol II 194, 199
Lexical semantics
  Vol I 3–6, 14 n., 25, 59, 88, 93 n., 99, 104 n., 106–7, 135
  Vol II 5, 32, 69, 121, 130, 133, 137–9, 151–4, 165, 172 n., 230, 247
Lexical–Functional Grammar (LFG)
  Vol I 4
  Vol II 5
Lexicalist approach(es)
  Vol I 103, 103 n., 132, 135
Lexicon (*see also* Encyclopedia)
  Vol I 3, 10–15, 52, 77, 104 n., 106–7, 132, 135, 210
  Vol II 4, 10, 45–6, 69
Lexicon, Functional ~ *see* Functional lexicon
LF movement *see* Movement, LF ~
L-head
  Vol I 20, 25, 27, 33, 33 n., 37 n., 44, 47, 51, 57–9, 72–3, 78–81, 105 n., 118 n., 206 n., 211–12, 250, 256, 258–9, 263–5
  Vol II 10, 24, 20, 263 10
L-head movement *see* Movement, L-head ~
L-head, Null ~
  Vol I 256–8
L-head, Quasi–functional ~
  Vol I 10 n., 49 n., 100 n., 213 n., 247, 254, 258
  Vol II 295, 299, 311
Linearization *see* Word order
Linearization Correspondence Axiom (LCA)
  Vol I 50
  Vol II 88
Listeme
  Vol I 3, 10–15, 27, 30, 77, 79, 84, 88, 100 n., 103–8, 135, 178, 188, 206, 265
  Vol II 2–3, 8, 11–12, 14, 25–6, 29, 30, 69–71, 139, 151, 153–4, 207, 227, 230, 245, 248–51, 322– 323, 346, 350–1, 354–5

Little *v*
  Vol II 219–20, 267 n.
Locative–Directionals *see* Directional–locatives
Locative–existential *see* Existential Locatives
Locatives
  Vol II 100 n., 261, 271, 275–303, 305–6, 308–23, 325 n., 332, 334–5, 338
  Locative adjunct
    Vol II 291–5, 298 n., 310
  Locative argument
    Vol II 289
  Locative clitics
    Vol II 209, 272, 275, 277–86, 292–4, 296, 298–9, 301, 303, 305–6, 308, 310–16
  Locative inversion
    Vol II 287, 296 n.
  Locative preposition/particles
    Vol II 203, 207–9, 222, 241, 284, 310, 323, 338
  Locatives, Covert ~
    Vol II 281, 289–94, 321–5, 332
  Locatives, Deictic ~
    Vol II 278, 283–4, 296 n., 298–9, 302–3, 306, 308–9, 312–16, 322, 333, 338

Mass
  Vol I 9–10, 59, 63, 65, 75, 87–94, 96, 99–123, 129–33, 129 n., 131 n., 132 n., 135 n., 137, 139, 147–8, 161–2, 164, 166 n., 173, 175–8, 187–8, 198, 202–4, 206–8, 210–11, 222, 234, 238, 240, 243, 245–6, 249–50, 253, 260,
  Vol II 27, 48, 119, 173
  Mass determiner
    Vol I 105, 203
  Mass noun, Bare ~
    Vol I 59, 88, 90, 96–7, 120–1, 124–5, 130, 137, 152, 161, 166, 189, 238
    Vol II 74–5, 173–4, 176, 184, 212, 257, 310–11
  Mass structure *see* Structures, Mass ~
  Mass, Collective ~ noun
    Vol I 103
  Mass–count distinction
    Vol I 59, 88, 94 n., 97–9, 102, 104–8, 119, 132, 135, 161, 166, 181, 188, 242
    Vol II 27, 74
Massifier
  Vol I 97–101, 108, 242–59
Measure constructions (*see also* Container Phrases)
  Vol I 60, 80 n., 91, 93, 99–101, 104 n., 108, 116 n., 174 n., 203, 206–8, 246–51, 254–6, 258
  Vol II 160, 177, 180 n., 190
Merge
  Vol I 31, 33
  Vol II 25
Middle construction
  Vol II 4, 6, 92 n.

Minimalist Program (MP)
  Vol I 5–6, 29 n., 37 n., 103
  Vol II 5, 86
Mirror Theory 24 n.
Morphology and Word Formation
  Vol I 46–7, 51–3, 60, 132–3, 135, 216, 219–20, 261–2
  Vol II 23, 58, 198, 349
  Morphological conversion (Ø-affixation)
    Vol II 30 n.
  Morphological template
    Vol II 348–9
  Morphology, Agreement ~ *see* Agreement
  Morphology, Derivational ~
    Vol I 51, 53, 92 n., 133
    Vol II 22–4, 193–4, 197–8, 262 n., 346, 349, 353 n.
  Morphology, Inflectional ~ (*see also* Aspectual marking; Classifier marking; Dual; Genitive marking; Plural marking; Singular marking; Tense marking)
    Vol I 26, 48 n., 51–8, 92 n., 105, 114 n., 261
    Vol II 22–4, 193–5, 197–8, 346, 349
  Morphology: Affixation (*see also* Prefixes and prefixation; Perfective prefixes; Perfective marking)
    Vol I 21
  Morphology: Compound and compounding
    Vol I 52, 82, 84, 133
  Morphology, Amorphous ~ *see* Amorphous Morphology
  Morphology, Distributed ~ *see* Distributed Morphology (DM)
  Morphology–syntax interface
    Vol II 58
Move (operation) (*see also* Merge; Movement)
  Vol II 25
Movement (*see also* Merge; Move)
  Vol I 262, 265–6
  Movement, Head ~
    Vol I 32 n., 42–6, 51, 114 n., 197, 262–5
    Vol II 12, 15, 18, 20–1, 24, 344–6
  Movement, L-head ~
    Vol I 36–7, 58, 110, 167, 176, 217
  Movement, LF ~ ,
    Vol I 71, 158
    Vol II 7 n. 256–8
  Movement, lowering ~
    Vol II 270–1
  Movement, N(oun) ~
    Vol I 71, 110 n., 143, 174, 177, 197–9, 211, 201, 205, 209, 213–14, 234, 235–7, 263, 265
    Vol II 17, 345
  Movement, V(erb) ~
    Vol I 265
    Vol II 79 n., 80 n., 87, 345
ne cliticization (*see also en* cliticization)
  Vol II 33, 35–40, 63, 209 n., 276, 279–80

no
 Vol I 114–15
Nominals, Derived ~ (*see also* -*ing*, Nominal-
   izer ~)
 Vol II 61, 63 n., 78, 263–4, 355
Nominals, Argument structure~ (Complex
   Event Nominals)
 Vol II 78 n., 242 n., 263–4
Nominals, Result
 Vol II 263
Non-agentive interpretation *see* Agentive, Non-
   ~ interpretation
Non-culmination *see* Culmination, Non-~
Non-delimited *see* Delimited, Non-~
Non-divisive *see* Divisive, Non-~
Non-homogeneous *see* Homogeneous, Non-~
Non-quantity events *see* Quantity events: Quan-
   tity, Non-~ events
Noun and Nominal (N, NP, N^{max}) (*see also*
   Count, Mass, Plural, DP)
 Vol I 65–6, 86–7, 89–90, 108–10, 140 n., 166 n.,
   186 n., 197–8, 205, 233, 254
N-stem *see* Stems, N– ~
Nominal functional structure *see* DP; Quanti-
   ty Phrase; Classifier Phrase
Nominal, Argumental ~ *see* Arguments,
   Nominal ~
Nominal, Bare ~ (*see also* Mass, Bare ~; Plural,
   Bare ~)
 Vol I 63–6, 69, 75, 87, 90, 96–7, 110, 120, 133,
   135, 143–4, 152–3, 165–6, 175, 177, 180–1,
   184, 187, 233
 **Vol II 163, 178, 180–1, 258–9, 270, 298, 314,
   318, 332– 334, 337, 345**
Nominal, Non-argumental ~
 Vol I 71
Nominal, Null D ~ *see* DP: Null D
Nominal, Predicate ~ *see* Predicate nominals
Nominal, Argument structure ~ *see* Nominals,
   Derived ~ : Argument Structure ~
Nominal, Complex Event ~ *see* Nominals,
   Derived: Argument structure ~
Nominal, Determinerless ~ *see* Nominals,
   Bare ~
Nominal, De-verbal ~ (*see also* Nominals,
   Derived ~)
 Vol II 60
NP predicates
 Vol I 87, 89–90, 108
Nu– (Semelfactive marker, Russian)
 Vol II 185–6, 188
Null
Null $\langle e \rangle_\#$ *see* Quantity, Null ~
Null $\langle e \rangle_d$ *see* D, Null ~
Null determiner *see* D, Null ~
Null NumP *see* NumP, Null ~
Null pronominal/pronoun *see* Pronoun,
   Null ~

Null quantity (Null #P) *see* Quantity, Null ~
Number (grammatical) (*see also* Cardinal, Frac-
   tions, *One, Zero*)
 Vol I 94 n., 110, 123, 182, 193, 199 n., 213 n.,
   214 n., 215 n., 243, 246, 257
Number agreement *see* Cardinal agreement
Number function
 Vol I 185, 219
Number marking
 Vol I 93 n. 94 n., 170, 184, 255, 264
Number pronoun *see* Pronoun, Num ~
NumP (Number Phrase, Num^{max}, Num) (*see also*
   Quantity Phrase)
 Vol I 59–60, 78 n., 109, 183, 185 n., 247 n.
NumP, Null ~
 Vol I 185 n., 187 n.
NumPs, Bare ~
 Vol I 247

Object shift
 Vol II 104, 106–7, 177 n.
Object, Direct ~ *see* Argument, Direct ~
Object, Cognate ~ 47, 203–4, 249
Object, Elliptical ~ 204
One (including in Hebrew)
 Vol I 111–15, 119, 142–3, 148–52, 158, 163, 167,
   169, 178, 183–5, 187–8, 193–8, 201, 219,
   221, 224–6, 228–9, 233–4, 236–8, 243–4,
   249, 250, 258–65
Open value fusion *see* Fusion
Open value *see* Functional Structure: $\langle e \rangle$
Operator–variable pair
 Vol I 35
 Vol II 16
Originator
 **Vol II 64, 83, 85, 92, 95–6, 111–12, 123, 160,
   184, 206, 209 n., 216, 219–20, 229, 232,
   235, 237, 244–5, 248–9, 262, 265–7, 269,
   271, 280–1, 284–5, 305**
Originator, Modifiers of ~
 Vol II 54, 219, 244–5, 248–50, 282
Overgeneration
 Vol II 86, 347, 353

Partitive Construction
 Vol I 100 n., 116 n., 196, 199 n., 206–8, 215 n.,
   221, 224, 244 n.
Partitivity
 Vol II 162–3, 165, 168–71
PART-OF Operator,
 Vol I 104–5
 Vol II 162, 165–8, 170–1 190
Passive
 **Vol II 60–3, 95 n., 186, 220, 235–6, 256, 284 n.
   285 n., 307**
Passive, Adjectival ~
 Vol II 56, 60–3, 78, 204

Path
  Vol II 151
Perfect
  Vol II 34 n.
Perfective aspect
  Vol II 160, 200
Perfective prefixation/affixation (*see also* Perfectivity marking; Quantity affixation)
  Vol II 157–61, 167, 172, 174–81, 183, 188, 190, 193–4, 197, 200, 208, 298–9, 301, 310 n., 314, 317
Perfective (prefix) doubling
  Vol II 188 n.
Perfective prefixes, Lexical ~
  Vol II 195–6, 198–9
Perfective prefixes, Purely perfectivizing ~
  Vol II 195–7, 199
Perfective prefixes, Superlexical ~
  Vol II 195–6, 198
Perfectivity
  Vol II 34 n., 65, 157–61, 163, 165–8, 173, 175 n., 178, 180 n., 183–4, 186–7, 189–93, 195, 198
Perfective head features
  Vol II 157, 158 n.
Perfectivity marking
  Vol II 138–9, 157–9, 161, 184–5
Perfective paradigm
  Vol II 161, 338
Phonological index
  Vol I 12, 15, 30 n., 42, 56, 83–4
  Vol II 14, 18, 22, 24–6, 29, 87 n., 207, 207 n., 322, 336–7, 346–55
Phonological (PF) licensing
  Vol I 130 n., 131 n.
  Vol II 108–10, 120–2
Phonological paradigms (*see also* Morphology, Inflectional ~)
  Vol I 56–7
  Vol II 23–4, 194–5, 197–8
Paradigmatic gaps (Defective paradigms)
  Vol II 199, 323 n.
Paradigmatic morphology
  Vol II 197, 199
Phonological source of grammatical variation
  Vol I 32–3, 79, 261–6
  Vol II 2, 15, 323, 345
Phonological representations, phonological realization
  Vol I 3, 12–13, 26 n. 30–3, 36–7, 39, 42, 51, 55–7, 68, 72 n., 78–9, 85, 110–11, 151, 157, 183, 187 n., 202, 234 n., 237–8, 262
  Vol II 12, 18, 22, 24, 26, 58, 75 n., 122, 126, 157–61, 168, 183, 194–5, 197–200, 227, 322–4, 222, 244, 250
Phonological word
  Vol I 58, 199
  Vol II 56, 347–50, 354

Pluralia tantum
  Vol I 54, 105–6
  Vol II 29 n., 199 n., 322, 334, 337
Plurals and plurality
  Vol I 36, 59, 74–5, 88, 92–6, 100–1, 103–6, 109–23, 126–9, 131–5, 161, 165–6, 175–7, 180, 188–9, 204, 207–11, 220, 222, 234–5, 240, 244, 250, 253–4
  Vol II 173
Plural agreement
  Vol I 115 n.
  Vol II 113
Plural classifiers *see* Classifier, Plural ~
Plural determiner
  Vol I 112, 123, 203
Plural marking (inflection)
  Vol I 86–8, 91–6, 101, 104–5, 109, 111–13, 115–19, 122, 125 n., 127, 132–3, 143, 167, 173, 175, 177–88, 199, 202, 209 n., 211, 238–40, 242, 244, 247 n., 249, 250, 255–6
  Vol II 146, 159
Plural proper names *see* Proper names
Plural, Bare ~
  Vol I 59, 63, 74–5, 90, 94, 96–7, 120–5, 127, 129–30, 137, 139, 147, 148–9, 152, 160–1, 179, 181, 188, 234–5, 238, 247, 249–50
  Vol II 48, 74–5, 113–14, 116–19, 127, 146, 163, 173–4, 176, 184, 212, 226, 238 n., 257, 294, 310–11
Plural, Lexical ~
  Vol I 105–6, 121, 135
Pluralizing
  Vol I 91–3
po- (Attenuative marker, Russian)
  Vol II 192 n., 199 n.
po- (Distributive marker, Slavic)
  Vol II 185–6, 199 n.
Polysemy
  Vol I 3, 188
  Vol II 30–1, 54
Portmanteau morph
  Vol I 33 n., 43, 68, 113–14, 178, 182, 204, 204, 213 n.
Possession construct nominal *see* Construct nominal
Postposing
  Vol II 335–6
PP delimitors *see* Delimitors
Predicate–argument structure (PAS)
  Vol I 5
  Vol II 5, 9
Predicates
  Vol I 87–90, 133, 138, 141 n.
  Predicate modifiers *see* Aspectual predicate modifiers; Originator, modifiers of ~
  Predicate composition
    Vol II 227–31

Predicate modifiers
  Vol II 212–13, 229, 232–4, 241–2, 249, 250
Predicate nominal
  Vol I 66–7, 81 n., 87, 89, 108
Predicate, Bare ~
  Vol I 65, 81, 82
Predication, Secondary
  Vol II 250
Prefixes and Prefixation *see* Quantity aspectual (verbal) affixation; Perfective prefixation
Prepositional Phrases and prepositions (PP, P, P^{max})
  Vol I 49–51
  Vol II 12, 29, 33, 35, 45, 50, 71, 75 n., 83, 87–92, 95, 105 n., 108, 127, 203–4, 207–8, 284 n., 223
Presentational constructions
  Vol II 99 n., 100 n., 271, 333, 337
Presuppositional interpretation/reading *see* Specificity
Principles and Parameters model
  Vol I 261
  Vol II 343
pro see Pronoun, Null~
Process *see* Activity; Atelicity; Quantity events: Quantity, Non-~ events
Progressive *see* -*ing*, Progressive ~
Projectionist approach(es) *see* Endo-skeletal approaches
Pronoun
  Vol I 142, 161, 175, 177 n.
  Vol II 115 n.
Pronoun, Bound ~
  Vol I 147
Pronoun, D-~
  Vol I 142
Pronoun, Null (*pro*)
  Vol I 83, 162 n., 165 n., 177 n.
  Vol II 113–20, 268 n., 269 n.
Pronoun, Null indefinite ~
  Vol II 113–14, 116–19, 269 n., 295
Pronoun, Num ~
  Vol I 142
Proper name
  Vol I 10, 59, 70–85, 100 n., 113 n., 138–9, 143–5, 157, 174–6, 186 n., 188–9, 233–4, 265
  Vol II 178, 182, 345
⟨*def-u*⟩ (definite–unique head feature, proper names)
  Vol I 72–3, 78–80, 85, 174–7, 189, 233–4, 265
  Vol II 345
Proper name, Determinerless ~
  Vol I 80–2
Proper names with determiners
  Vol I 70, 72, 74, 82–5
Proper names, Plural ~
  Vol I 74 n.

Proper names: uniqueness
  Vol I 83–4, 134, 175–7
Pseudopartitive
  Vol I 246–9
Psychological predicates
  Vol II 103 n.

QR *see* Movement, LF ~
Quantification and quantificational expression
  Vol I 6, 88–90, 92, 97 n., 109, 111–16, 118–19, 122, 124 n., 125 n., 138, 140–1, 144–7, 170–3, 175–7, 187, 193–9, 205 n., 209–10, 212, 214–15, 220, 222–3, 225–7, 232–4, 240, 246–7, 249, 260 n.
  Vol II 146, 175–6, 179
Quantification, Distributive ~ *see* Distributivity
Quantification, Universal ~
  Vol I 78 n., 116, 161 n., 166–8, 199 n.
Quantification, Vacuous ~
  Vol I 37 n., 41, 43, 47 n., 205 n., 227
  Vol II 18, 168, 179, 301
Quantificational reading *see* Variable reading
Quantifier, Complex ~
  Vol I 170
Quantifier, Strong ~ *see* Determiner, Strong ~
Quantifier, Weak ~ *see* Determiner, Weak ~
Quantificational affixes and affixation (quantificational marking) (*see also* Perfective affixation; Perfectivity: perfective marking; Quantity aspectual (verbal) affixation)
  Vol II 157, 160, 166–8, 172–5, 179–81, 183–5, 189–90, 192–3, 198, 298, 301 n., 311–12, 315
Quantifier, Negative ~ *see no*
Quantity and Quantity Projection (within DP) (#, #P, $#^{max}$)
  Vol I 16, 59–60, 72 n., 78 n., 94–7, 99, 109–11, 113, 119–20, 125, 127–31, 133, 141 n., 143–4, 151, 158, 160–70, 172, 174–80, 182, 185–9, 197–9, 204–7, 211–12, 215 n., 217, 220–2, 224–5, 233, 246–52, 254–5, 258, 264
  Vol II 27–8, 42, 64, 73–5, 79–80, 85, 85 n., 93, 102, 104, 108, 119–28, 133, 136, 163, 174, 181, 209, 211, 220–1, 225–7, 229, 259, 301, 310–11, 314–15, 317, 333–5, 338
⟨e⟩_# (Quantity open value)
  Vol I 36, 60, 109, 111–19, 122–4, 128–32, 136–9, 141 n., 143, 150–1, 157–8, 160–2, 164–73, 175–89, 193, 197, 199, 201–2, 204–7, 209–11, 220, 224–6, 238, 240, 242, 250, 258–61, 263
  Vol II 16, 28–9, 75, 114–15, 120, 124, 126–7, 157, 159, 161, 168, 173–6, 178–9, 181–3, 291–2, 298, 301, 301 n., 314, 343
Quantity, Non-~ *see* Quantity, Null ~

Quantity and Quantity Projection (*cont.*)
  Quantity (#) determiner (*see also* Determiner, Weak ~)
    Vol I 145, 165, 253
  Quantity Phrase, Bare ~
    Vol I 166 n., 247
  Quantity, Null ~ (Null #, Null ⟨e⟩$_\#$)
    Vol I 96–7, 131, 136, 143–4, 160–1, 167–8, 177, 189, 207
    Vol II 74, 115, 119–20, 127, 158 n., 173, 226–7, 301, 310, 314–15, 317, 319
  Quantity, Predicate modifier of ~ *see* **Aspectual predicate modifiers**
Quantity aspectual (verbal) affixation
  Vol II 157, 159–60, 194, 200 209, 212, 298–9, 333, 350, 353–4
Quantity (direct) object/argument 107, 102, 132, 148, 158 n., 163, 184, 210, 212–13, 220, 225 n., 259, 301
Quantity Events and Quantity Event Projection (Asp$_Q$, Asp$_Q$P, Asp$_Q$^{max}) (*see also* Telicity)
  Vol II 64–5, 72–7, 79–82, 85, 93, 97–8, 104, 107–11, 115, 119–27, 129, 133, 136, 139, 147–61, 153–61, 164–6, 168, 172–4, 180–4, 187, 190, 192–3, 203, 206–11, 217–21, 223, 227, 229, 239–40, 245–48, 261–2, 264–5, 267, 269 n., 275, 291, 301 n., 316–17, 319, 321, 325–7, 332–4, 337, 339
[$_{Asp_Q}$ ⟨e⟩$_\#$] (Quantity event open value)
  Vol II 75–7, 80, 85, 97–8, 108, 110, 119, 122–7, 147, 151, 153, 155–7, 159, 161, 164, 168, 176, 180–4, 188–9, 194, 197, 200–2, , 211–13, 220–1, 227, 229, 232–3, 239, 243, 248, 250, 260–1, 271–2, 291, 301, 306, 309–17, 319, 321, 324–6, 332–4, 337–8, 343–4
Quantity, Non-~ events (activity, process) (*see also* Activity; Atelicity, Homogeneity)
  Vol II 164, 223, 249, 266, 315, 326
Quantity Phrase, Specifier of ~ ([Spec,AspQ])
  Vol II 72–3, 76, 81, 85, 91–2, 101–2, 119, 123, 158 n., 173–5, 183–5, 188–9, 204, 220, 228, 247, 266–7, 269, 284, 291, 311–15, 317, 319, 321, 325, 333–5, 338, 345
Quantity, Interpretation of ~
  Vol I 125, 166, 168, 182, 251
  Vol II 64–5, 72–7, 80–2, 85, 93, 97–8, 104–5 n., 110, 115, 121–2, 124, 133, 136, 141–59, 161, 166, 168, 172, 176, 180, 183–4, 187, 189, 217, 221, 227, 232, 248, 275, 291, 301 n., 305, 310 n., 317, 319, 321, 325, 332–4, 337
Quantity, Interpretation of Non-~ *see* Homogeneity
Quantity expressions (*see also*
  Vol I 111, 130, 139, 164–6, 177 n., 179, 181, 185, 189, 198 n., 254
  Vol II 208

Quantization
  Vol I 124–7, 130 n.
  Vol II 77, 122, 131–4, 143, 145–8, 165, 172 n., 190, 192–3, 233
  Quantized object/argument
    Vol II 131–2, 143, 145, 147, 149–51, 162–3, 259
  Quantized predicate/verb
    Vol II 189, 191
Quasi-functional L-head *see* L-head, Quasi functional ~

Range Assignment
  Vol I 35–8, 42–3, 45, 60, 72–3, 78, 107 n., 109, 111–14, 119, 122–3, 129–31, 138, 140–1, 143, 145, 150–1, 158, 160–2, 165–7, 172–3, 176–80, 186, 188–9, 193, 197–206, 209–12, 220, 222, 224 n. 225 n., 227, 233–4, 238, 240, 250, 258–60, 262–6
  Vol II 16–18, 20–1, 25–6, 108, 121–3, 126, 173–4, 176, 178–81, 195, 208–9, 211–13, 221, 232, 243, 259, 261, 267–71, 283–4, 290–2, 295, 298–302, 310–12, 319, 322–3, 337–8, 343, 345 353–4
Range assignment, Direct ~
  Vol I 38, 78, 96, 262
  Vol II 17, 122–6, 182–4, 188, 209, 271, 284, 291, 293, 295, 297, 304, 313, 315, 333, 344
Range assignment, Double ~ (double marking)
  Vol I 37 n., 41, 43, 45–7, 60, 73, 113, 138, 162. 170–1, 177, 205, 205 n., 225–7, 262–3
  Vol II 18, 176, 180–1, 188 n., 209, 211
Range assignment, Indirect ~
  Vol I 38, 41–2, 44–5, 262
  Vol II 17–20, 123–6, 181–4, 227, 267–70, 284, 291, 295, 297, 300, 304, 312, 315, 344
Reference
  Vol I 38, 67–9, 78, 84, 135, 146, 161, 166 n., 170, 172, 176, 247, 261
Reflexive dative (in Hebrew) *see* Dative, Reflexive ~
Relative clause and relativization
  Vol I 141 n., 148–9, 170 n. 171 n.
Result nominals *see* Nominals, Derived ~ : Nominals, Result
Resultant/resulting state/result (sub–event)
  Vol II 202, 220–4, 226, 229–31, 326–7
Resultatives
  Vol I 50 n.
  Vol II 48, 132, 138 n., 223–31
Root (in the sense of Distributed Morphology)
  Vol I 20 n., 21 n., 30 n.
Root, Tri–consonantal ~ (Semitic Languages)
  Vol I 37, 132 n., 265
  Vol II 348–9

Index of subjects   397

Scalar predicates and structures (*see also* Adjectives, Open scale ~; Adjectives, Closed scale ~; Degree achievements)
    Vol II 149–51, 153, 316
Scope
    Vol I 6, 7 n., 8 n.
    Scope, Intermediate ~
        Vol I 137 n., 145–9, 154–5, 157–8, 189
    Scope, Narrow ~
        Vol I 146, 149, 154–5, 157, 189, 202
        Vol II 4, 37
    Scope, Wide ~
        Vol I 153
        Vol II 4, 102–7, 144, 173–5, 177–81, 209, 211, 297–303, 305, 309, 311–14, 318, 324–5, 338, 344–6
    Scope, Widest ~
        Vol I 137 n., 144–7, 149–50, 152, 154–5, 157–8, 202
Selectional restrictions
    Vol II 6, 7 n.
Semantic selection *see* S-selection
    Vol I 22, 24
Semi-lexical L-head *see* L-head, quasi–functional ~
several
    Vol I 148–9, 167, 184–5, 240
Shell FP (F^{s}P)
    Vol I 130 n.
    Vol II 109–11, 120, 127, 160, 175 n., 183, 227, 247, 269 n., 273 n., 284, 314
    Shell FP specifier ([Spec, F^{s}P]) (*see also* Case, Partitive ~)
        Vol II 28 n., 85 n., 110–11, 160, 175 n., 183, 227, 235, 247, 284
Singulars
    Vol I 59–60, 74–5, 88, 94, 100 n., 103–5, 110–16, 119–20, 122, 125–9, 131–6, 150, 152–8, 161–4, 167, 173, 175–80, 184, 186–8, 197, 200–2, 204–11, 223–6, 234, 236–9, 242–3, 247, 249–50, 253–4, 259
    Singular determiner *see* Indefinite determiner; *a*)
    Singular marking (inflection)
        Vol I 131, 136, 160, 163, 175, 197, 207
    Singular structure
        Vol I 110, 207, 208, 249
    Singular, Bare ~
        Vol I 63 n., 74–5, 151–2, 154–5, 157–8, 186, 200–2, 204–5, 210, 220, 234, 249
Small clauses
    Vol I 50
    Vol II 106, 206, 226–7, 282–3
some
    Vol I 147–9, 154–5, 158, 169–70, 184–5, 188
    Vol II 144–5
Specificity (presuppositionality) (*see also* Scope, Wide ~; Determiners, Strong ~)

Vol I 134, 137 n., 144–5, 147 n., 234
Specificity marker
    Vol I 150–9
Specifier (for specifiers of particular projections *see* entry of particular projection)
    Vol I 6, 18, 22, 24–7, 47, 131 n., 169, 170–2, 174, 177–8, 183 n., 185, 189, 197 n., 198 n., 205–6, 212, 214 n., 220, 222–3, 225–9, 234, 236, 238, 247 n., 255, 264
    Vol II 11–12, 21, 50, 71–2, 85, 267–8, 271, 273 n., 284, 293
Specifier–head agreement (configurations)
    Vol I 38, 41–2, 47, 170, 172, 185, 193, 205–6, 212, 222, 226–7, 262–3
    Vol II 17–18, 21, 27, 72–3, 76, 97, 110, 115 n., 121, 123–4, 126, 155, 157, 159, 161, 164, 172–4, 176, 179–84, 221, 227, 267, 270, 284, 291–3, 294–5, 297–301, 312, 315, 344
Specifiers, Functional ~
    Vol I 6, 18–19, 21–2, 27, 72
Spray-load alternation
    Vol II 92, 132
S-selection
    Vol I 22, 24
Stage-level predicates
    Vol II 294
State, stative
    Vol II 34 n., 82–3, 99 n., 103 n., 125, 129, 135 n., 139, 142 n., 163, 202–3, 217–19, 222 n., 224, 226, 231–8, 244–5, 250, 265, 267–9, 280–2
Stative Phrase (SP)
    Vol II 265, 269 n.
Stative verbs *see* Verbs, Stative ~
Stative, Anti- ~ elements
    Vol II 245
Stems
    Stems, Bare ~
        Vol I 110–13, 115, 133, 167, 201–2, 204–10, 239, 243, 246
        Vol II 159, 161, 173, 176, 178, 324
    Stems, N- ~
        Vol I 199 n., 201, 204, 215–16, 240, 245
Stress shift
    Vol II 353 n.
Strong quantifier *see* Determiner, Strong ~
Strong reading *see* Scope, Wide ~
Structures
    Adverb of Quantification (individual reading)
        Vol I 139, 165
    Bare CL–N combinations (Chinese)
        Vol I 183
    Cardinals (Chinese)
        Vol I 186
    Construct Nominals
        Vol I 217–19

Structures (cont.)
  Count (English, Chinese)
    Vol I 97, 110, 130
  Definite descriptions
    English
      Vol I 131, 137, 160-1, 163-4, 167
      Vol II 74
    Hebrew
      Vol I 211, 212, 225
  Demonstratives (Chinese)
    Vol I 183
  Dividing cardinals (Hungarian, Armenian)
    Vol I 117
  Dual
    Vol I 209
  Eventive atelic events
    Vol II 269
  Existential locatives: Event structure licensing
    Vol II 297, 299-300, 320, 339-41, 342
  Existential structures (DP)
    Vol I 138, 164
    Vol II 174
  Expletive, Transitive ~ (Hebrew)
    Vol II 305
  Generic structures
    Chinese
      Vol I 183
    English
      Vol I 138, 164, 165
      Vol II 174
    Hebrew
      Vol I 204, 240, 241
  Mass (English, Chinese)
    Vol I 97, 110, 130
    Vol II 74
  Measure phrases
    English
      Vol I 208
    Hebrew
      Vol I 208
  Multiple determiner structures
    (*all+the+three*)
    English
      Vol I 174
    Hebrew
      Vol I 223
  Non-Quantity structures *see* Quantity, Non-~ structures
  Plural
    Vol I 114, 117, 137
    Vol II 74
  PP Cascade structure
    Vol II 90
  pro, Indefinite ~ and event structure
    Vol II 115
  Proper names
    Vol I 80, 176, 177
  Quantity structures (English)
    Vol I 97, 137, 161
    Vol II 74
  Quantity structures, Post-nominal ~ (Hebrew)
    Vol I 226-7
  Quantity, Non-~ structures
    Vol I 97
    Vol II 74
  Singular
    English
      Vol I 114, 137
      Vol II 74
    Hebrew
      Vol I 200, 201, 204
  Spray-load-type Alternations
    Vol II 93-4
  Stative events
    Vol II 269
  Strong reading (wide scope)
    Chinese
      Vol I 185
    English
      Vol I 143, 145, 157, 158, 164
    Hebrew
      Vol I 222
  Transitive, Atelic event structure (Homogeneous, non-quantity transitives)
    Vol II 109
  Transitive, Telic event structure (Quantity transitives)
    Vol II 85, 269
  Unaccusative event structure (Quantity intransitive)
    Vol II 84, 269
  Unergative predicates (Homogeneous, non-quantity intransitive)
    Vol II 84
  Weak reading (narrow scope)
    Chinese
      Vol I 186
    English
      Vol I 143, 145, 158, 164
    Hebrew
      Vol I 222
Subcategorization
  Vol II 4-5, 251, 322, 350, 355
Subjects
  Subjects, Bare DP ~ (*see also* Generics and genericity; Scope)
    Vol II 289-94, 298, 314, 318
  Subjects, Bare pre-verbal ~ (*see also* Scope, Wide ~; Generics and genericity)
    Vol II 257, 270
  Subject, External *see* Arguments, External ~
  Subjects, Null ~ (*see also* Pronouns, Null ~)
    Vol II 113-16

Subjects, Partitive
  Vol II 105 n., 257 n.
Subjects, Post-verbal ~ (*see also* Scope, Narrow)
  Vol II 37, 105 n., 111, 209 n., 256, 258, 260–1, 270–4, 257 n., 272, 275–9, 281–7, 293–4, 296 n., 298, 300–3, 305, 307, 309–10, 312–14, 318–20, 325 n., 332, 335–6
Subject, Strong ~ (*see also* Scope, Wide ~, Determiners, Strong ~)
  Vol II 303, 309–10, 312 n., 314, 317–18, 319, 324–5
Subjects, Weak ~ (*see also* Scope, Narrow ~; Determiners, Weak ~)
  Vol II 283, 294–5, 298, 300–1, 303, 305–6, 312–14, 318, 320, 325 n.
Subject-of-change
  Vol II 57
Subject-of-process
  Vol II 57
Subject-of-quantity
  Vol II 64, 72, 76–8, 80, 83, 85, 92–5, 119, 123, 183–4, 204–6, 216–20, 228, 232, 235, 237, 242–3, 245 n., 247–9, 266, 269, 271, 284, 316
Subject-of-state
  Vol II 57, 232 n., 235, 237, 244, 269, 271, 280

Subject–verb agreement *see* Agreement, Subject–verb ~
Substantive items *see* Listemes
Syntactic insertion frame *see* Subcategorization
Syntax–semantics interface
  Vol I 14–17, 22, 68
  Vol II 122

Telic structure *see* Quantity events
Telicity
  Vol I 121–5, 129, 130 n., 132 n., 165–6, 168, 168 n., 175, 177 n., 179, 206–7, 238
  Vol II 34–6, 39, 43–4, 46–8, 50–3, 64–5, 72–8, 80–1, 91–3, 97–108, 121–62, 165–8, 171–2, 180 n., 182–3, 185–7, 189–93, 200–6, 208, 212, 215–18, 220–1, 224–6, 228–31, 235–6, 246–9, 257 n., 259–61, 265, 267–269, 301, 304–6, 309–10, 313, 315–16, 318, 321, 325, 327–9, 331–2
Telic–atelic distinction
  Vol II 36, 64, 74
Telicity, Anti- ~
  Vol II 233–5, 237, 239, 242, 244–5, 247–8, 280
Telos
  Vol II 77, 143 n., 187, 202, 220–3, 327
Tense *see* TP and Tense
the (*see also* Definite determiner)
  Vol I 63, 67–9, 118–19, 158, 160–74, 176, 178, 211, 222–3, 226–7, 238

Vol II 17, 28, 114
Thematic structure, thematic roles (θ-roles), thematic hierarchy
  Vol I 6, 6 n.
  Vol II 4, 5, 48–9, 56–7, 122, 132, 215, 227, 250
Theme
  Vol II 42 n., 57, 75, 93, 122, 131–2, 205
Theme, Incremental ~, quantized ~
  Vol II 124, 131–2, 140 n., 164–6, 168–71, 190, 205
Time-measure phrase/adverbials *see* Aspectual predicate modifiers
Totality operator (TOT) and totality interpretation
  Vol II 158–60, 165, 166–8, 190
TP (T, T^{max}) and tense
  Vol I 16–17, 20–4, 26, 26 n., 28–9, 34, 36–8, 40, 137 n.
  Vol II 259, 261, 263–4, 266–8, 273–5, 284
$\langle e \rangle_T$ (Tense open value)
  Vol I 31–2, 36–8, 42–3, 261–2
  Vol II 159, 197, 343
T, Null ~
  Vol I 37–8, 55
Temporal expressions
  Vol II 278, 285, 305
Tense
  Vol II 262, 264
Tense features
  Vol I 118, 213 n.
Tense marking (inflection)
  Vol I xv, 10, 21 n., 26 n., 29, 31–2, 34, 37, 37 n., 40, 53, 55, 58 n.
  Vol II 159, 197
TP, Specifier of ~ ([Spec, TP])
  Vol II 80–1, 85, 101, 111, 120, 184, 247, 268–9, 274–5, 284–5, 301, 311, 313, 321, 335
Transitive expletive constructions *see* Expletive, Transitive expletive ~
Transitivity (dyadicity)
  Vol II 94 n., 108–9, 111, 127, 139, 183–4, 212, 218, 226–7, 235, 242–3, 260–1, 269, 273, 303, 314–15, 318, 347
Transitive verbs *see* Verbs, Transitive ~
Transitivization, De- ~ (lexical) *see* Detransitivization
Type-shifting
  Vol I 8, 16, 59–60, 89–90, 94 n., 104–8
  Vol II 122, 132, 178, 215, 252

Unaccusativity
  Vol II 79–80, 84, 108, 118–20, 184, 216, 218, 247, 256, 261, 269, 275, 280–1, 305–7, 313–14, 318, 332
Unaccusative subjects
  Vol II 62–3
Unaccusative verbs *see* Verbs, Unaccusative ~

Unaccusativity (*cont.*)
  Unaccusative–unergative distinction/alternation/diagnostics
    Vol II 31–2, 34–9, 42, 44, 61, 63 n., 209 n.
Unbounded and Unboundedness
  Vol II 135–9, 144, 146–7
Unergativity
  Vol II 79, 84, 120, 125, 216, 218, 247, 256, 259, 261, 271, 273, 275–6, 279–80, 285, 299, 303, 307, 313–14, 318
  Unergative subjects
    Vol II 62–3, 179, 302
  Unergative verbs *see* Verbs, Unergative ~

Uniformity Condition
  Vol I 45–7
  Vol II 20
Uniqueness *see* Proper Names: uniqueness
Universal Alignment Hypothesis
  Vol II 58 n.
Universal Grammar (UG)
  Vol I 14, 16, 26, 28, 68, 118 n., 214 n., 261, 265
  Vol II 11–12, 343
Universal Theta Assignment Hypothesis (UTAH)
  Vol I 5, 104 n.
  Vol II 46, 55–6, 58, 60–1, 206, 215
Unrestricted determiner *see* Determiner, Unrestricted ~

v (Little *v*) *see* Little *v*
V1 structures/contexts
  Vol II 256, 269 n., 272–6, 278–80, 282–3, 293, 298, 302–3, 305–8, 314, 318–19, 321
V2 languages
  Vol II 268 n.
Vacuous quantification *see* Quantification, Vacuous ~
Variable reading and variable binding
  Vol I 38 n., 43, 67, 67 n., 69, 81 n., 137–9, 142, 144–7, 149–50, 152, 154, 157, 170–2, 176, 189, 200, 202, 202 n., 233–4
  Vol II 16, 114–15, 156, 179–80, 268
Verb movement *see* Movement, Verb ~
Verb particles and verb–particle constructions
  Vol II 48, 75 n., 141, 203–4, 207, 211–12, 241, 310, 322–3, 337
Verbs
  Verbs, Accomplishment ~ 43, 53, 327–8
  Verbs, Activity ~
    Vol II 34 n., 43–4, 52–3, 215, 217, 221
  Verbs, De-adjectival ~
    Vol II 151–2
  Verbs, Intransitive ~
    Vol II 6, 31–3, 35, 39–41, 44–6, 53–4, 56, 242 n., 247
  Verbs, Intransitive manner ~ 246–7
  Verbs, Manner of motion ~
    Vol II 32–3, 54, 140
  Verbs, Raising ~
    Vol II 31 n., 282
  Verbs, Semelfactive ~
    Vol II 185–6, 189, 329
  Verbs, Stative ~
    Vol I 139, 165 n.
  verbs, Transitive
    Vol II 6, 31, 41, 56, 58, 85, 99, 140, 188, 248, 257, 273–4, 354
  Verbs, Unaccusative ~
    Vol II 31–8, 41–5, 50–1, 53–4, 56–8, 61, 188, 204, 246, 257, 265, 273, 279–80, 282, 334
  Verbs, Unergative ~
    Vol II 31–8, 40–5, 53–4, 56–8, 61, 125, 188, 204, 242 n., 246, 257, 273–4, 281, 283
  Verbs, Variable–behavior ~
    Vol II 31–4, 42–3, 45–6, 52, 56–7, 61, 79, 100–1, 215, 281
Verkuyl's Generalization
  Vol II 73, 76, 97, 102–3, 122–6, 130, 143, 172 n., 180, 182–3, 189, 200, 202, 204–6, 208–9, 218, 221, 259–60, 314, 325, 333, 337–8, 344–5
V–head
  Vol II 168, 227, 284, 298, 326–7
Vocabulary, Functional ~ *see* Functional lexicon
Vocabulary, Substantive ~ *see* Lexicon, Listeme
VoiceP
  Vol II 59–60, 63 n., 220, 267 n.

Weak reading *see* Scope, Narrow ~
WH-in-situ
  Vol I 148–9
Wide scope *see* Scope, Wide ~
Widest scope *see* Scope, Widest ~
Word and Paradigm
  Vol I 51, 56
  Vol II 22
Word formation *see* Morphology
Word order (*see also* V1 structures)
  Vol I 7 n., 19, 24 n., 39, 50, 70–2, 171, 177, 198–9, 215 n., 222, 228–9, 233, 236, 266
  Vol II 87–8, 111, 280–3, 286, 296 n., 335

X' theory
  Vol I 22, 44
  Vol II 19
Xit (Hebrew specificity marker) 150–9

zero
  Vol I 114–16, 122–3, 239